Principles of Organizational Behavior

Principles of Organizational Behavior

The Handbook of Evidence-Based Management

Third Edition

Craig L. Pearce
Edwin A. Locke

Wiley

This edition first published 2023

Registered Offices
John Wiley & Sons, Inc., 111 River Street, Hoboken, NJ 07030, USA
John Wiley & Sons Ltd., The Atrium, Southern Gate, Chichester, West Sussex, PO19 8SQ, UK

Editorial Office
The Atrium, Southern Gate, Chichester, West Sussex, PO19 8SQ, UK

For details of our global editorial offices, customer services, and more information about Wiley products, visit us at www.wiley.com.

Wiley also publishes its books in a variety of electronic formats and by print-on-demand. Some content that appears in standard print versions of this book may not be available in other formats.

Library of Congress Cataloging-in-Publication Data

Names: Locke, Edwin A., editor. | Pearce, Craig L., editor. | John Wiley & Sons, publisher.
Title: Principles of organizational behavior : the handbook of evidence-based management / Edwin A. Locke, Craig L. Pearce.
Description: 3rd edition. | Hoboken, NJ : Wiley, 2023. | Includes index.
Identifiers: LCCN 2022056231 (print) | LCCN 2022056232 (ebook) | ISBN 9781119828549 (paperback) | ISBN 9781119828617 (adobe pdf) | ISBN 9781119828600 (epub)
Subjects: LCSH: Organizational behavior.
Classification: LCC HD58.7 .P7423 2023 (print) | LCC HD58.7 (ebook) | DDC 658—dc23/eng/20230221
LC record available at https://lccn.loc.gov/2022056231
LC ebook record available at https://lccn.loc.gov/2022056232

Cover Design: Wiley
Cover Image: © Peopleimages/Getty Images

SKY10043893_031123

Contents

Preface

Our goal with this book was to bring together comprehensive, science-based, actionable advice, from the world's leading experts, for managing organizations. We deliver on this goal.

There are 29 chapters in this book, each dedicated to a specific management challenge. The chapters are written by the foremost thinkers on the topics. The authors hone in on the key principle for their respective topics – the key piece of advice – for turning knowledge into action. All of their advice is solidly based upon science. In other words, you can have confidence in their advice.

Our book is in stark contrast to "normal" textbooks, which provide endless lists of factoids to memorize about topics. Such books are of little value if the reader desires to apply the information to real-world situations. It is difficult to glean from such lists exactly what one should implement – in this book, we prioritize knowledge into overarching principles, which facilitates the implementation of concrete actions in real-world situations.

Books in the "popular press," on the other hand, generally offer pithy advice from self-declared experts, but these books generally have little to no basis in science. These types of books are typically easy to read and do attempt to provide ideas to put into action. Nonetheless, the advice provided is largely overly specific to the author's experience and thus lacks transferability to the circumstances of the reader. As such, while these types of books are generally engaging, they are best regarded as nonfiction stories, with limited practical value.

Our book is different. It combines science and action. The range of subjects is expansive, encompassing 29 areas – ranging from selection, to motivation, to leadership, and all topics in between. In the section on selection, for instance, there are chapters on how to select based on intelligence (In-Sue Oh and Frank Schmidt), how to select based on personality (Murray Barrick and Michael Mount), and the proper use of interviews (Cynthia Stevens). In the section on motivation, there are chapters on how to manage emotions (Edwin Locke), how to implement goal setting (Gary Latham), how to cultivate self-efficacy (Albert Bandura), how to pay for performance (Kathryn Bartol), and how to enhance satisfaction (Timothy Judge, Ryan Klinger, and Meng Li).

In the section on the development of employees, there are chapters on the science of training and development (Eduardo Salas and Kevin Stagl), how to use performance appraisals (Maria Rotundo and Kelly Murumets), how to use employee participation (John Wagner), how to use recognition (Jean Phillips, Kameron Carter, Kathryn Dlugos, Hee Man Park, and Dorothea Roumpi), and how to foster continuous learning (Michael Beer). In the section on leadership, there are chapters on how to empower effectively (Jay Conger and Craig Pearce), the proper use of power and influence (Gary Yukl), how to create unifying vision (David Waldman), and how to foster trust (Jason Colquitt and Michael Baer).

In the section on teams, there are chapters on diagnosing and understanding team processes (Allison Traylor, Scott Tannenbaum, Eric Thomas, and Eduardo Salas), how to manage the boundaries of teams (Deborah Ancona, Henrik Bresman, and David Caldwell), and how to manage intrateam conflict (Laurie Weingart, Karen Jehn, and Kori Krueger). In the section on micro-organizational processes, there are chapters on how to communicate effectively (Jean Phillips), how to stimulate creativity (Colin Fisher and Teresa Amabile), how to manage stress (Ralf Schwarzer and Tabea Reuter), and how to negotiate effectively (Kevin Tasa and Ena Chadha).

In the section on macro-organizational processes, there are chapters on how to foster entrepreneurship (Jaume Villanueva, Harry Sapienza, and J. Robert Baum), how to integrate work and family (Malissa Clark, Katelyn Sanders, and Boris Baltes), how to use information technology effectively (Dongyeob Kim, Maryam Alavi, and Youngjin Yoo), how to navigate organizational and international culture (Miriam Erez), and how to align organizational strategy and structure (John Joseph and Metin Sengul).

Something that both teachers and students will appreciate about this book is that the chapters contain cases and exercises to help to illustrate the material. For example, the chapters have cases that demonstrate both the positive and negative applications of the primary principle of the chapter. The cases exhibit the concrete application of the chapter principle to the real world, which enables deeper understanding, as well as a degree of practice for the implementation of the principle in future situations.

The chapters also contain skill sharpening exercises to reinforce the knowledge of the topic at hand. The types of exercises vary by chapter. Some exercises, for instance, involve a degree of role playing, to facilitate the understanding of how the principles play out in action. Other exercises involve, in part, completing questionnaires, helping the readers understand where they fall on a particular dimension. Additional exercises are focused on watching and diagnosing videos pertaining to the principles. Together, all of the exercises complement the core reading of the chapters, buttressing the development of knowledge about the principles.

On a more somber note, since the passing of Sabrina Salam, the rising star who wrote a chapter for the first edition of this book (which is now updated by Jason Colquitt and Michael Baer), two of the contributors to the current edition, Frank Schmidt and Albert Bandura, passed away during the process of writing their chapters. Both were giants in the field of organizational science.

Frank Schmidt was known for many advances in organizational science, but most notably for his cutting-edge work on employee selection and for his definitive contributions on research methods. His chapter in this book is focused on the importance of intelligence in employee selection. He and his coauthor, In-Sue Oh, distilled the knowledge on this topic, which will leave a lasting mark well into the future.

Albert Bandura was the giant among giants. At the time of his passing, he was, by far, the most widely cited organizational scientist. His contributions were deep and broad. Nonetheless, he was best known for his work on social cognitive theory and on the concept of self-efficacy. His work provides the foundation for most other organizational science. His chapter in this book provides a stake in the ground for transferring his knowledge to the practice of management.

In sum, our book provides comprehensive advice, based on science, written by the foremost experts, for practicing and aspiring managers. Each chapter focuses on a core principle that can be applied, with confidence, in real-world organizations. In many ways, one can think of this book as a roadmap to organizational success. We hope you enjoy reading it. More importantly, we hope you find success in applying the principles in action.

Acknowledgments

The editors are grateful to many people, not the least of whom are the contributors to this book. It could not have happened without their ability to distill the principles of organizational behavior from science-based evidence. The editors would also like to specifically acknowledge the exceptional work of Jeremy Sanville, Craig Pearce's research assistant, in bringing this book to fruition – he worked tirelessly in keeping everything coordinated and on track, from beginning to end.

Introduction[1]

This handbook is about management principles; each chapter is written by an expert in the field – but why do we need principles?

To quote Ayn Rand (1982, p. 5):

> . . . abstract ideas are conceptual integrations which subsume an incalculable number of concretes – and without abstract ideas you would not be able to deal with concrete, particular, real-life problems. You would be in the position of a newborn infant, to whom every object is a unique, unprecedented phenomenon. The difference between his mental state and yours lies in the number of conceptual integrations your mind has performed.
>
> You have no choice about the necessity to integrate your observations, your experiences, your knowledge into abstract principles.

What, then, is a principle? A "principle" is a general truth on which other truths depend. Every science and every field of thought involves the discovery and application of principles. A principle may be described as a fundamental reached by induction (Peikoff, 1982, p. 218).

Everyday examples of principles that we use (or should use) in everyday life are:

"Be honest" (a moral principle)
"Eat plenty of fruits and vegetables" (a nutrition principle)
"Exercise regularly" (a health principle)
"Save for the future" (a personal finance principle)
"Do a conscientious job" (a work or career principle)
"Do not drive under the influence of alcohol or text while driving" (personal safety principles)

It would be literally impossible to survive for long if one did not think in terms of principles, at least implicitly. In terms of concrete details, every situation is dif-

[1]This introduction is adapted from Locke (2002). I thank Jean Binswanger, Paul Tesluk, Cathy Durham, and James Bailey for their helpful comments on the original article.

ferent from every other. Suppose, for example, that a child were told, "Do not run across that part of this street today." What is the child to do on other days? On other streets? On other parts of the same street? Such a dictum would be useless to the child after the day had passed or if they were in another location. Properly, the child (at the right age) would be taught a principle such as "Never cross any street without first looking twice in each direction." This could guide the child's actions for life and in every location in the world.

How are principles formulated? They are formulated by integrating conceptual knowledge (for more on concept formation, see Locke, 2002 and Peikoff, 1991). Principles, in turn, are integrated into theories, again by induction (Locke, 2007).

Teaching

The use of principles is critical to both the teaching and practice of management. Let us begin with teaching. Most instructors would agree that management is a difficult subject to teach. First, it is very broad in scope. It entails scores if not hundreds of different aspects. The more one studies the field, the more complex and bewildering it seems to become. Second, there are no concrete rules or formulas to teach as in the case of accounting, finance, or management science. Management is as much an art as a science. Third, although there are theories pertaining to different aspects of management (e.g. leadership), many find these theories to be less than satisfactory (to put it tactfully), because they are too narrow, trivial, or esoteric and/or lack firm evidential support. Often, they are based on deduction rather than induction (Locke, 2006). The potentially useful theories are mixed in with those that are not.

Traditionally, teaching has been done with either textbooks and/or the case method. Both methods contain the same epistemological limitation. Textbooks, because they try to be comprehensive, pile up detail after detail and theory after theory, but the details, even of subtopics, are very difficult to integrate. As noted, any theories that are presented often have severe limitations because they come and go like snowflakes. The result is that students routinely suffer from massive cognitive overload and a sense of mental chaos; thus, little of the material is retained once the final exam is over. This makes it unlikely that what was memorized will be applied to the students' jobs and career.

With regard to case studies, these allow for the possibility of induction, but shockingly, it has been reported that some business schools openly *prohibit* connecting the cases to each other. This is very unfortunate. Each case is a unique, concrete instance. Suppose, for example, a business student concluded from the analysis of a particular case study that a certain high technology firm in New Hampshire should replace the CEO, develop a top management team, and change to a matrix structure. What could students take away from such an analysis that would help them be better managers? Nothing at all if the analysis were left in this form. The case would only be useful if the student could formulate some general principles from studying a variety of cases. The best way to do this is by induction from a series of cases (see Locke, 2002 for a detailed example) though even this could be limited depending on the choice of cases. Faculty whom I knew who used cases have admitted to me that they have to use theoretical materials (e.g. principles) for the students to be able to even analyze the cases in the first place.

The value of this book for teaching, therefore, is twofold. *First, it is an alternative to a traditional textbook.* The material in this book is *essentialized.* Only what the expert chapter writers consider important is included; thus, there is far less to remember than in a text. This means the material can be more easily retained and more readily applied to the real world of work. *Second, the principles are evidence-based and thus tied firmly to reality.* This teaching procedure would be mainly deductive, because the inductively based principles would be provided in advance (by this book) and students would have practice applying them to the exercises at the end of each chapter, and/or to their current (and later their future) jobs. Of course, students could be asked to search out other examples of principles and how they were used or not used.

Second, this book can be used as an adjunct to a course which uses cases. Here, both deduction and induction can be used. The book's principles can help students to analyze the cases, yet new principles (or qualifications to principles) could be developed through induction from the cases used.

(There are other problems with the case method that we can only note briefly here, e.g. the emphasis on verbal glibness; the fact that all the information needed is already in the case; the fact that the case is taken out of a wider organizational context; the fact that real action is not possible; and the lack of face-to-face contact with actual employees. Primarily, these problems are inherent in the attempt to teach a practical skill in a classroom and so have no perfect solution, though student mini projects within real businesses help).

Management

This book can also help managers and executives be more effective. However, reading a book of evidence-based principles does not magically turn one into a good manager. Principles cannot be mastered overnight and cannot be applied mechanically. Regardless of the level of abstraction at which they are formulated, they are still abstractions, not concrete rules such as "turn off the lights when you leave the room." Principles, however, are used to guide specific actions in specific contexts.

Consider the principle: "Motivate performance through goal setting" (Chapter 5 of this book). This principle does not tell one what to set goals for (a very critical issue); who is to set them; what the time span will be; what strategy to use to reach them; how performance will be measured; how flexible the goals will be; or how performance will be rewarded. (The latter involves another principle; see Chapter 7).

To some extent, formulating subprinciples can be a help because these would give some idea of how to implement the principles. For example, subprinciples for goals (given in Chapter 5) would include (i) make the goals clear and challenging; (ii) give feedback showing progress in relation to the goals; (iii) get commitment through building confidence and showing why the goals are important; (iv) develop action plans or strategies; (v) use priming; and (vi) find and remove organizational blocks to goal attainment. But these subprinciples do not tell one everything. There will always be judgment calls to be made, because one cannot teach every possible context factor that a future manager might face.

Furthermore, principles cannot be applied in a vacuum, or one at a time in some arbitrary order. Many – maybe dozens or possibly hundreds – of principles must be used to run a successful business. (The problem of cognitive overload is mitigated over time by gradually automatizing the principles in the subconscious.) Furthermore, the principles must be orchestrated so that they function in concert rather than working at cross-purposes. It is not known how effectively one can teach such orchestration, although one can make the student aware of the issue and give some examples. For example, the goal system must be integrated with the performance appraisal system and the reward system.

It is worth observing here how principles are used in the real world of management. We will use Jack Welch as an example in that he is considered among the greatest CEOs in history, the creator of $300–400 billion in stockholder wealth at General Electric (e.g. see Slater, 1999; Tichy and Sherman, 1993). Some principles that Welch used as his personal guides to action are as follows:

- Reality. Face reality as it really is, not as you want it to be. (We believe that the failure to practice this principle is a major cause of business failures, e.g. Enron. Such failures may involve flagrant dishonesty, but they also may involve simple evasion – the refusal to look at pertinent facts – or putting emotions ahead of facts.)
- Change before you have to (view change as an opportunity, not as a threat).
- Possess energy and energize others.

Welch also helped develop a code of values or guiding principles for GE as a whole. These included integrity (backed up by control systems).

Obviously, Welch was able not only to formulate but also to apply and orchestrate principles in a way that no one else had. It helped that he had ambition and energy, a brilliant business mind, an insatiable curiosity, the capacity to judge talent, and an uncanny ability to figure out what businesses GE should and should not be in.

It is interesting that Jacques Nasser was a great admirer of Welch and tried to emulate his principles at Ford but was unable to do so and ultimately lost his job. It is clear that there is a long road between knowing good principles and being able to implement them successfully in the context of a given organization.

Management principles need to be organized and integrated hierarchically so that the leader will know what to do first, second, and so forth. Except for facing reality as it is (not evading), which should be the primary axiom of every manager, the hierarchy may not be the same from business to business or in the same business at different times. Nor will they all be organizational behavior principles. For example, in one context, the most critical factor may be to decide, as Welch did, what business or businesses a corporation should be in. This is an aspect of vision and strategic management. There is no point in trying to manage the wrong business or working hard to do the wrong thing. But in another context, the critical issue may be cash flow, for example, how to avoid bankruptcy in the next six months (a finance issue). In a different context, the core problem might be getting the right people in the right jobs or revamping the incentive system (HR issues).

What factors would determine the hierarchy? Three are critical: (i) *Context.* What are the most important facts regarding the present situation of this company? Context means seeing the whole and the relationship of the parts to the whole. (ii) *Urgency.* What has to be fixed right away if the company is to survive? (iii) *Fundamentality.* What is the cause of most of the different problems the organization is faced with or what must be fixed before any other fixes will work (e.g. get good people in key jobs)?

The hierarchy can change over time. For example, when Welch took over at GE, he focused first on changing the business mix (selling and buying businesses) and cutting costs (increasing productivity) and layers of management. Later, he focused on better utilizing people (empowerment) and still later on improving quality (quality goals). Reversing the sequence would not have worked, because empowerment and quality would not help businesses that were not viable and would not "take" in a ponderous bureaucracy.

The foregoing is to make an important point for the second time: *Business is an art as much as a science.* Having correct principles will not work unless the leader knows how and when to use them. Great leaders are rare because not many of them can effectively perform all the tasks that leadership requires (Locke, 2003).

The way to manage complexity is not to complexify it, as academics love to do. After reading some six books about and one book by Jack Welch, we were struck by how frequently he stressed the importance of simplicity. He said:

> Simplicity is a quality sneered at today in cultures that like their business concepts the way they like their wine, full of nuance, subtlety, complexity, hints of this and that . . . cultures like that will produce sophisticated decisions loaded with nuance and complexity that arrive at the station long after the train has gone . . . you can't believe how hard it is for people to be simple, how much they fear being simple. They worry that if they're simple, people will think they are simpleminded. In reality, of course, it's just the reverse. Clear, tough-minded people are the most simple (quoted in Lowe, 1998, p. 155).

Consider a recent conversation with a consultant who works as a coach to top executives. He told one of us that one question he always asks in the first meeting is "By the way, how do you make money?" The ones who answered by wallowing in complexity usually did not make any. The ones who gave succinct, clear answers usually did.

For a business leader, achieving simplicity, as opposed to simplemindedness, is much harder than achieving complexity. To achieve simplicity, one must look through the morass of complexity one is seemingly faced with, integrate the key observations, and come up with the *essential* ideas that will make one's business succeed. That is, one must bring order out of chaos. This includes knowing what to ignore. The way to do this is to think inductively and integrate one's observations into principles.

Notes Regarding the Third Edition

The third edition of this book includes the following changes: (i) there are new chapters with new authors and some new authors for some of the original chapters; (ii) all the chapters have been updated with respect to the latest research, and nearly all present new cases examples; typically, however, the original principles have remained the same (or been slightly reformulated); (iii) all the chapters now have exercises at the end to help students better understand the principles. Although authors were asked to title their chapters in terms of a single principle, a few have two or three related principles, and all have subprinciples.

This last relates to the issue of what the appropriate level of abstraction should be for management principles. If they are formulated too broadly (e.g. "be rational"), it can be hard to connect them to specific actions without very extensive elaboration. On the other hand, if they are too narrow ("turn out the light when leaving every room"), they are not broadly applicable, and one would need thousands of them – too many to retain – to cover the waterfront. Thus, I encouraged mid-range principles and the authors thankfully complied.

In closing, we should note that the principles in this book do not include all possible management principles (e.g. none of the chapters discussed strategic management principles – that would be another book). Also, we do not include the race issue because that is much too complex an issue to be dealt with in one chapter. That topic would require a whole book. We chose topics from I/O psychology, human resource management, and organizational behavior (fields that all overlap) that I thought would be of most interest and use to present and future managers. I hope these hopefully timeless principles will contribute to your success at work.

References

Locke, E. A. (2002). The epistemological side of teaching management: Teaching through principles. *Academy of Management Learning and Education,* 1, 195–205.

Locke, E. A. (2003). Foundations for a theory of leadership. In S. Murphy and R. Riggio (eds), *The Future of Leadership Development.* Mahwah, NJ: L. Erlbaum.

Locke, E. A. (2006). Business ethics: A way out of the morass. *Academy of Management Learning & Education,* 5(3), 324–332.

Locke, E. A. (2007). The case for inductive theory building. *Journal of Management,* 33, 867–890.

Lowe, J. (1998). *Jack Welch Speaks.* New York: Wiley.

Peikoff, L. (1982). *The Philosophy of Objectivism: A Brief Summary.* Santa Ana, CA: Ayn Rand Institute.

Peikoff, L. (1991). *Objectivism: The Philosophy of Ayn Rand.* New York: Dutton.

Rand, A. (1982). *Philosophy: Who Needs It.* New York: Bobbs-Merrill.

Slater, R. (1999). *Jack Welch and the GE Way.* New York: McGraw Hill.

Tichy, N. and Sherman, S. (1993). *Control Your Own Destiny or Someone Else Will.* New York: Currency Doubleday.

1

Select on Intelligence

Frank L. Schmidt[1] and In-Sue Oh[2]

[1] University of Iowa
[2] Temple University

Co-author's Note

Frank Schmidt died on 21 August, 2021 in Iowa City, IA. I am greatly indebted to him for his legacy in intelligence testing and meta-analysis, intellectual honesty and courage, and endless support and mentoring over the years. He will be forever remembered and forever missed.

The principle that we wish to convey in this chapter is quite simple: Ceteris paribus, higher intelligence leads to better job performance. Intelligence is the best determinant of job performance, and hiring people based on intelligence leads to marked improvements in job performance. These performance improvements have great economic value for organizations, giving organizations that hire people based on intelligence a leg-up over other organizations. This principle is incredibly broad and generalizable as it has been empirically validated across numerous jobs, occupations, and industries.

But before elaborating further on this principle, we would like to emphasize that, surprisingly, most human resource (HR) managers do not hire based on intelligence. In fact, most HR managers do not make decisions based on research-informed best practices at all (Rynes, Colbert, and Brown, 2002). This gap between practice and research findings is especially large in the area of staffing, where many HR managers are unaware of this most fundamental staffing principle based on extensive research findings and, as a result, fail to use scientifically established valid employment selection procedures. You may think that this is true only for a small portion of HR managers, but this is not the case.

In a survey of 5000 Society for Human Resource Management members whose title was at the manager level and above, Rynes and her research team (2002) asked two questions relevant to this chapter:

(a) Is conscientiousness, a personality trait, a better predictor of employee performance than intelligence?
(b) Do companies that screen job applicants for values have higher performance than those that screen for intelligence?

The answer to both the questions is (definitely) no![1] But shockingly, 72% of respondents answered yes to the first question and 57% answered yes to the second question. That is, on average, two-thirds of the respondents did not know the most basic principle established by extensive research findings; namely, that intelligence is the single best predictor of employee job performance. And worse, these were largely HR managers and directors with an average 14 years of work experiences in HR. Of the 959 respondents, 53% were HR managers, directors, and vice presidents, occupying an important role in designing and implementing HR practices. Given the respondents' high-level HR positions and considerable experience, we speculate that the percentage of wrong answers would be even higher among less experienced HR staff. This problem is not limited to the United States but is also widely observed in other countries (e.g. Tenhiälä, Giluk, Kepes, Simon, Oh, and Kim, 2016). Thus, we believe that many would benefit by reading this chapter.

What Is Intelligence?

The concept of intelligence is often misunderstood. Intelligence is not the ability to adapt to one's environment: Insects, mosses, and bacteria are well adapted to their environments, but they are not intelligent. There are many ways in which organisms can adapt well to their environments, of which intelligence is only one. Instead, intelligence encompasses the ability to understand and process abstract concepts to solve problems. Gottfredson (1997, p. 13), in an editorial originally published in the *Wall Street Journal* and later reprinted in *Intelligence,* defined *intelligence* as "a very general mental capability that, among other things, involves the ability to reason, plan, solve problems, think abstractly, comprehend complex ideas, and learn quickly and learn from experience." This traditional definition captures well *what* intelligent people can do, but this definition is still insufficient in capturing *why* smart people can do it. For the purposes of this chapter, we define intelligence as *the capacity to learn and retain complex information.* Higher levels of intelligence lead to more rapid learning, and the more complex the material to be learned, the more this is true. Intelligence is often referred to as general mental ability (GMA), and we use the terms "intelligence" and "GMA" interchangeably throughout the remainder of this chapter.[2]

---

[1]With regard to the first question, the validity of conscientiousness measured via self-reports is 0.22, whereas that of General Mental Ability is 0.65 in predicting supervisory ratings of job performance (Schmidt, Shaffer, and Oh, 2008). With regard to the second question, the answer exists only at the individual level, not at the company level. Arthur, Bell, Villado, and Doverspike's (2006) meta-analysis has shown that the validity of person-organization fit (or value congruence) is 0.13, even less than that of conscientiousness measured via self-reports.

[2]In the applied psychology and HR/OB literatures, another term, "cognitive ability" is widely used.

Another important nature of intelligence is that it is the broadest of all human mental abilities. Narrower abilities include verbal ability, quantitative ability, and spatial ability. These narrower abilities are often referred to as special aptitudes. These special aptitudes also predict job performance (although not as well as GMA), but only because special aptitude tests measure general intelligence as well as specific aptitudes (Brown, Le, and Schmidt, 2006). In other words, it is the GMA component in these specific aptitude tests that predicts job performance. For example, when a test of verbal ability predicts job or training performance, it is the GMA part of that test – not specifically the verbal part – that primarily does the predicting, thus "not much more than *g* (GMA)" (Brown et al., 2006; Ree and Earles, 1991, 1992; Ree, Earles, and Teachout, 1994).

Finally, although behavioral geneticists have concluded that GMA is highly influenced by heredity, it does not necessarily mean that nothing can improve GMA (Gottfredson, 1997). A recent meta-analysis by Ritchie and Tucker-Drob (2018) has reported that an additional year of education improves GMA by approximately one to five IQ points across the life span: "Education appears to be the most consistent, robust, and durable method yet to be identified for raising intelligence" (p. 1358).

Higher Intelligence Leads to Better Job Performance

Intelligence plays a central role in virtually all of our daily activities and lifelong pursuits. It predicts many important life outcomes such as performance in school, amount of education obtained, rate of promotion on the job, ultimate job level attained, and salary (Gottfredson, 1997, 2002; Judge, Klinger, and Simon, 2010; Schmidt and Hunter, 2004). More relevant to this chapter is that it predicts job and training performance (Schmidt et al., 2008). No other trait predicts so many important real-world outcomes so well.

However, until several decades ago, most people believed that general principles of this sort were impossible in personnel selection and other social science areas. It was believed that it was not possible to know which selection methods would be most effective for a given organization unless a local validation study was conducted for each job in that organization. This belief, called "situational specificity," was based on the fact that validity studies of the same selection procedures in different jobs in the same organization and across different organizations appeared to give different and often conflicting results. The differences were attributed to the assumption that each job situation includes subtle yet significantly different (i.e. situation-specific) characteristics related to the nature of job performance. Therefore, practitioners at that time (to the delight of consulting firms) were advised to conduct time-consuming and costly local validation tests for virtually all jobs in all organizations to determine if a selection procedure was valid (Ghiselli, 1966).

We now know that these "conflicting results" were caused mostly by statistical and measurement artifacts (e.g. sampling error[3]), and that some selection procedures (e.g. intelligence) have higher validity for predicting performance than others (e.g. age, graphology) across all jobs (Schmidt and Hunter, 1981, 1998). This discovery was made possible by a new method, called meta-analysis or validity generalization, that allows practitioners and researchers to statistically synthesize the results from individual studies.[4] Many meta-analyses synthesizing numerous individual studies based on data collected from various jobs, occupations, organizations, industries, business sectors, and countries all point to the same conclusion that intelligence is the single best predictor of job performance (Schmidt et al., 2008). Thus, there is little to no need to conduct a local validation study to see whether intelligence is predictive of job performance.

Below, we will briefly review some notable studies among the vast body of literature documenting the strong link between intelligence and job performance. Ree and colleagues have shown this for jobs in the Air Force (Olea and Ree, 1994; Ree and Earles, 1991, 1992; Ree et al., 1994), as have McHenry, Hough, Toquam, Hanson, and Ashworth (1990) for the US Army in the famous Project *A* study. (With a budget of 24 million dollars, Project *A* is the largest test validity study ever conducted.) Hunter and Hunter (1984) showed this link for a wide variety of civilian jobs, using the US Employment Service database of studies. Schmidt, Hunter, and Pearlman (1980) have documented the link in both civilian and military jobs. Other large meta-analytic studies are described in Hunter and Schmidt (1996), Schmidt (2002), and Schmidt and Hunter (2004). Salgado and his colleagues (Salgado, Anderson, Moscoso, Bertua, and de Fruyt, 2003a; Salgado, Anderson, Moscoso, Bertua, de Fruyt, and Rolland, 2003b) demonstrated the link between GMA and job performance across a variety of settings in European countries. Further, the strong link between GMA and job performance was found whether performance was measured objectively – via work samples or productivity records – or subjectively – using rankings of performance ratings (Nathan and Alexander, 1988). Finally, the validity of

[3]The sampling error is the error caused by using a (non-representative, small) sample instead of the entire population of interest. Because of this error, sample-based statistics (validity coefficients) can be smaller or greater than their population parameters, thus causing "conflicting results" (i.e. artifactual variance) across local validation studies (Schmidt, 1992).

[4]Meta-analysis has also made possible the development of general principles in many other areas beyond personnel selection (Schmidt and Hunter, 2015). For example, it has been used to calibrate the relationships between job satisfaction and job performance with precision (Judge, Thorensen, Bono, and Patton, 2001), between organizational commitment and work-related outcomes including job performance (Cooper-Hakim and Viswesvaran, 2005), and between transformational leadership and employee, team, and firm performance (Wang, Oh, Courtright, and Colbert, 2011).

GMA for predicting job performance does not differ across major ethnic groups and gender groups (e.g. Roth, Le, Oh, Van Iddekinge, Buster, Robbins, and Campion, 2014; Schmidt, 1988).

On a more technical note, there has recently been an important development in the method of estimating the validity of a selection procedure by correcting for range restriction more accurately.[5] Applying this procedure to a group of existing meta-analytic data sets shows that previous figures for the validity of GMA (0.51 for job performance and 0.56 for training performance as noted in Schmidt and Hunter, 1998) underestimated its real value by around 30%. Specifically, when performance is measured using ratings of job performance by supervisors, the average of eight meta-analytic correlations with intelligence measures is 0.65–65% as large as the maximum possible value of 1.00, which represents perfect prediction (Schmidt et al., 2008, table 1). Another performance measure that is important is the amount learned in job training programs. For training performance (either based on exam scores or instructor ratings), the average of eight meta-analytic correlations with intelligence measures is 0.67 (Schmidt et al., 2008, table 2). Thus, the more accurate estimate of validity of intelligence is even higher than we previously thought.

Why Does Higher Intelligence Lead to Better Job Performance?

It is one thing to have overwhelming empirical evidence showing a principle is true and quite another to explain *why* the principle is true. Although part of the answer to this question of why higher intelligence leads to better performance in the definition of intelligence was discussed earlier (i.e. learning ability), a more convincing answer can be found by examining the causal mechanism through which intelligence influences job performance. According to Schmidt and Hunter (1998), people who are more intelligent are able to hold greater amounts of job knowledge because they can learn more and more quickly than others. Hence, the more "direct" determinant of job performance is job knowledge, not GMA.[6] Said another way, the biggest influence on job performance is job knowledge, and the biggest influence on job knowledge is GMA. People who do not know how to do a job cannot perform that job well. Research has shown that considerable job knowledge is required to perform even jobs most people would think of as simple, such as data entry.

---

[5]A new and more accurate method for correcting the biases created by range restriction has been developed and applied (see Hunter, Schmidt, and Le, 2006; Oh, Schmidt, Shaffer, and Le, 2008; Schmidt, Oh, and Le, 2006; Schmidt et al., 2008). (Range restriction is the condition in which the variance of the predictor [here intelligence] in one's sample of people [job incumbents] is lower than that in the population of people [job applicants] for which one wants estimates.)

[6]The traditional psychological theory of human learning (Hunter, 1986; Hunter and Schmidt, 1996; Schmidt and Hunter, 2004) posits that the effect of GMA on job performance would be mostly explained by the learning of job knowledge.

More complex jobs require much more job knowledge. The simplest model of job performance is this: GMA causes job knowledge, which in turn causes job performance.

But even this model is too simple, because GMA also *directly* influences job performance. That is, GMA does not have to be converted to job knowledge before it can influence job performance. In all professions, unforeseen problems arise that are not covered by one's prior education or a body of job knowledge (i.e. manuals), and GMA is used directly to solve these problems. Based on two large samples (in total, over 4500 managers), Dilchert and Ones (2009) found that problem-solving across various assessment center dimensions is most highly correlated with GMA. That is, GMA is not only an ability to learn facts and structured procedures but also an ability to tackle unstructured, real-life problems and solve them. This means that even when workers of varying levels of intelligence have equal job knowledge, the more intelligent workers still have higher job performance given their advantage in problem-solving skills.

Many studies have tested and supported this causal model (Borman, White, Pulakos, and Oppler, 1991; Hunter, 1986; Ree et al., 1994; Schmidt, Hunter, and Outerbridge, 1986). Using an extremely large data set from the US Army Selection and Classification Project (Project *A*), McCloy, Campbell, and Cudeck (1994) differentiated two types of job knowledge – declarative knowledge and procedural knowledge – and showed that GMA was related to each of the two types of job knowledge, which was, in turn, related to job performance. This research is reviewed by Hunter and Schmidt (1996) and Schmidt and Hunter (2004).

What Is Required to Make This Principle Work?

Based on research on selection procedure utility (Le, Oh, Shaffer, and Schmidt, 2007; Schmidt and Hunter, 1998), there are three conditions that are required for companies to improve job performance levels by using GMA tests in hiring and to reap the resulting economic benefits.

First, the company must be able to be selective in who it hires. If the labor market is so tight that all who apply for jobs must be hired, then there can be no selection and hence no gain. The gain in job performance per person hired is greatest with low selection ratios. For example, if one company can afford to hire only the top 10%, while another must hire the bottom 10% of all applicants, then with other things equal the first company will have a much larger gain in job performance. There is another way to look at this: Companies must provide conditions of employment that are good enough to attract more applicants than they need to fill the vacant jobs. It is even better when they can go beyond that and attract not only a lot of applicants, but the higher-ability ones that are in that applicant pool. In addition, to realize maximum value from GMA-based selection, organizations must be able to retain high-performing hires. As discussed later in this chapter, one excellent way to retain high-intelligence employees is to place them in jobs consistent with their levels of intelligence. Otherwise, high-intelligence employees who are ill-placed (and thus not satisfied with their job) may look for alternatives outside the organization; if they leave, then the organization will incur enormous direct and indirect costs (e.g. unpaid-off selection and training costs, performance loss, low morale among existing coworkers).

Second, the company must have some effective way of measuring GMA. The most common and most effective method is a standardized employment test of general intelligence, such as the Wonderlic Personnel Test, the Wesman Personnel Classification Test, or the Watson-Glaser Critical Thinking Appraisal Form. Such tests are readily available at modest cost. This method of measuring GMA is highly cost-effective given its excellent validity and reliability, low cost, and ease of administration and scoring. However, there are alternative methods of measuring intelligence as listed as follows. We advise the reader that part of the reason that these alternative methods can be somewhat successful is often due to their high correlation with GMA. For example, meta-analytic evidence has shown that grade point average (Roth, Bevier, Switzer, and Schippmann, 1996), work sample tests (Roth, Bobko, and McFarland, 2005), assessment center scores (Collins, Schmidt, Sanchez-Ku, Thomas, McDaniel, and Le, 2003), employment interviews (Huffcutt, Roth, and McDaniel, 1996), and situational judgment tests (particularly, knowledge-based ones; McDaniel, Hartman, Whetzel, and Grubb, 2007) are moderately to strongly correlated with GMA. That is, as Schmidt (2002) pointed out, performance on these selection procedures is moderately to strongly a consequence of GMA and, hence, reflects GMA. These findings further attest to the fact that what is more important is the constructs (i.e. the traits themselves) measured during the selection process, not the formats/methods (how the traits are measured). These alternative selection procedures are generally less valid and more costly (especially assessment centers and employment interviews) than standardized tests of GMA. Therefore, we recommend that hiring managers simply use GMA tests whenever possible to maximize cost-effectiveness. However, many organizations that rarely use written GMA tests build oral GMA tests into the interview process. For example, high-tech companies such as Microsoft and Google use multiple job interviews to measure GMA (and other important characteristics) among their highly intelligent applicants perhaps because standardized GMA tests are too easy for many of their highly intelligent applicants and, thus, cannot differentiate their applicants in terms of GMA. Moreover, these highly profitable organizations may not care about selection costs.

Third, the variability in job performance among employees must be greater than zero. That is, if all applicants after being hired have the same level of job performance anyway, then nothing is gained by hiring "the best." However, this is never the case. Across all jobs studied, there have been large differences between different workers in both quality and quantity of output. Hunter, Schmidt, and Judiesch (1990) meta-analyzed all the available studies on this topic and found large difference between employees. In unskilled and semi-skilled jobs, they found that workers in the top 1% of performance produced over three times as much output as those in the bottom 1%. In skilled jobs, top workers produced 15 times as much as bottom workers. In professional and managerial jobs, the differences were even larger. At the CEO level, we can easily find many examples supporting huge performance variability (e.g. Steve Jobs, Bill Gates). These are precisely the reasons why it pays so handsomely to hire the best workers, managers, and CEOs.

But there is another advantage to hiring the best workers: the pool of talent available for future promotion is greatly increased. This is of great value to organizations, because it helps ensure high performance all the way up through the ranks of managers. When the right people are promoted, their value to the organization in their new jobs is even greater than it was in their original jobs. Thus, the selection of high ability people has implications not only for the job they are hired onto, but also for other jobs in the organization.

Are There Moderators or Exceptions to This Principle?

Is Intelligence More Valid for More Complex Jobs?

For many predictors of job performance (motivational techniques, personality, etc.), their relationship with job performance depends on some moderators or boundary conditions (e.g. situational constraints). In addition, some predictors can replace other predictors. Many relationships in personnel psychology are bounded by situational constraints, which can be frustrating to managers who are looking for broad, overarching principles that are applicable across their organization. There is no relationship in the field of personnel psychology for which there are as few situational constraints as there are for the relationship between GMA and job performance.

The only major moderator to the relationship between GMA and job performance is job complexity level. That is, the validity of GMA for predicting job performance increases as the difficulty or complexity of the job in question increases. Schmidt et al. (2008) also reported validities for GMA ranging from 0.55 for low-complexity jobs to 0.61 for medium-complexity jobs to 0.78 for high-complexity jobs based on two meta-analyses that tested job complexity level as a moderator for the validity of GMA (Hunter, 1986; Salgado et al., 2003b). Similarly, Schmidt et al. (2008) also reported that the validity of GMA for training performance varies by job complexity level: 0.56, 0.69, and 0.81 for low-, medium-, and high-complexity jobs, respectively (Hunter, 1986; Salgado et al., 2003b). That is, while intelligence is predictive of performance on jobs of all the complexity levels, it is more predictive for jobs of high complexity.

Contrary to many lay people's intuition that applicants for high-complexity jobs do not differ much from each other in intelligence and thus intelligence may not work as a selection tool for them, the research findings mentioned here have clearly shown that there is still considerable variability in intelligence among applicants for high-complexity jobs and intelligence is still an excellent selection tool in these situations (Sackett and Ostgaard, 1994). We believe that the straightforward nature of the link between GMA and job performance comes as good news for many practitioners who are under time and competitive pressures to allocate resources as efficiently as possible, because it means that they do not have to consider many situational peculiarities when designing and implementing an intelligence-based staffing system. Given the massive amount of evidence available, there can be no doubt that intelligence is the best, most useful predictor of job performance across most situations (Schmidt, 2002).

Can Job Experience Replace the Role of Intelligence?

As long as the three conditions described earlier are met, there are no known cases or situations in which it is inadvisable to select employees for general intelligence. Nevertheless, some believe there is one exception (as we illustrate later in the example of *US Steel*): That companies should not select on GMA if they can select on job experience. That is, they believe that job experience is a better predictor of job performance than is GMA or job experience may replace GMA.

But what does available research show? For applicants with job experience between zero and five years, experience is a good predictor of job performance. But in the range of higher levels of experience, say 5–30 years of job experience, job experience does not predict performance very well (Hunter and Schmidt, 1996; Schmidt, Hunter, Outerbridge, and Goff, 1988). On most jobs, once people have about five years of experience, further experience does not translate into higher performance. This is likely because experience beyond five years does not lead to further increases in job knowledge. In other words, after five years of on-the-job learning, people in the typical job are forgetting old job knowledge about as fast as they are learning new job knowledge.

Even for new hires in the one-to-five-year range of job experience, where experience is a valid predictor of job performance, the validity of experience as a predictor declines over time. Specifically, experience predicts performance quite well for the first three years or so on the job and then starts to decline. By 12 years on the job, experience has low validity. In contrast, GMA continues to predict job performance quite well even after people have been on the job 12 years or longer (Schmidt et al., 1988). What this means is that job experience is not a substitute for GMA. In the long run, hiring on intelligence pays off much more than does hiring on job experience (Hunter and Schmidt, 1996). Hence, if you must choose, you should choose GMA. However, typically you do not have to choose; more than one procedure can be used. It may be desirable to use both experience and GMA in hiring; as discussed later, it is usually best to use multiple hiring methods whenever possible. But in this case, the weight given to GMA should be higher than the weight given to job experience.

Can Intelligence Predict Nontask Performance?

When supervisors assess overall job performance for each employee, they incorporate into their final ratings both nontask performance (i.e. organizational citizenship behaviors [OCBs] and counterproductive work behavior [CWB]) and core job performance (i.e. task performance) (Orr, Sackett, and Mercer, 1989; Rotundo and Sackett, 2002). One may ask, given the expanded criterion domain of job performance beyond task performance (e.g. bookkeeping tasks as an accountant): Is the validity of GMA for nontask performance, an important aspect of overall job performance, also strong?

As noted earlier, many people find it hard to believe that GMA is the dominant determinant of overall job performance (Rynes et al., 2002). Often, they say they have known people who were very intelligent but who were not a good citizen. This is related to a facet of job performance called "contextual performance" or "organizational citizenship behaviors." Broadly speaking, there are three types of OCBs (Chiaburu, Oh, Berry, Li, and Gardner, 2011: (i) cooperation (e.g. willingness to help other employee such as new employees and employees with work-related problems), (ii) compliance/loyalty (e.g. willingness to work late in an emergency or on a holiday, supporting the community relations and reputation of the company), and (iii) change (e.g. willingness to communicate concerns and suggestions organizational and work-related problems and play the role of a change agent). The Project *A* research showed that GMA is the predictive of contextual performance such as extra effort and taking initiative, although the validity of GMA was a bit lower than that of conscientiousness-related personality traits. However, a comprehensive meta-analysis by Gonzalez-Mulé, Mount, and Oh (2014) revealed that the validity of GMA for OCB (0.16 for cooperation, 0.18 for compliance/loyalty, and 0.24 for change) is moderate and generally similar to that of some of the most valid Big Five personality traits, such as conscientiousness and emotional stability (Chiaburu et al., 2011). Note that these meta-analytic findings contradict and thus inform the previous notion that "the major source of variation in contextual performance, however, is not proficiency, but volition and predisposition . . . predispositional variables represented by personality characteristics" (Borman and Motowidlo, 1993, p. 74).

Lay people may also say they have known people who were very intelligent but dismal failures on the job because of "bad behaviors" such as repeated absences, carelessness, hostility toward the supervisor, unwillingness to work overtime to meet a deadline, or stealing from the company. These are examples of the so-called counterproductive work behaviors. These behaviors reflect another facet of overall job performance that is also not directly related to core job performance (i.e. task performance) but is still considered when assessing overall job performance. Some individual studies have suggested that people who are more intelligent are likely to engage in fewer CWBs – self-reported or other-rated or objectively recorded – because they are more aware of the potential negative consequences of engaging in CWBs and better able to control their impulses and behaviors. However, a comprehensive meta-analysis by Gonzalez-Mulé et al. (2014) showed that while the relationship between GMA and self-rated CWB is almost zero or slightly positive (0.05), the relationship between GMA and non-self-rated CWB (supervisor-rated or objectively recorded) is moderately negative (–0.11). Although there may be other interpretations, these results seem to suggest that intelligent people do not necessarily engage in fewer CWBs, *but* they are better able to avoid getting caught by others, thus reminding us of the famous phrase, "catch me if you can." Moreover, the validity of GMA for CWB is lower than that of the Big Five personality traits.

In summary, the validity of GMA when predicting nontask performance (OCB and CWB) is at best moderate (similar to or lower than that of self-rated conscientiousness). However, as Ones, Viswesvaran, and Dilchert (2005, p. 400) emphasized, there is one important caveat that practitioners and researchers should not forget: "Even if this were true, no organization is likely to forgo hiring on task performance (Gottfredson, 2002); also, equal validity does not mean that the same kinds of individuals would be hired using different predictors." That is, most selection decisions are and should be generally based on who will show higher task or overall performance, the best predictor of which is undeniably GMA. Thus, there is no exception to the principle that GMA is the best predictor of job performance.

Five Common Questions About Implementing an Intelligence-Based Hiring System

Can an Applicant Be Too Intelligent for a Job?

An applicant was rejected for a job as a police officer in a New Jersey city on the grounds that his intelligence test score was too high! Officials in this city believed something that many people believe: Intelligence leads to better job performance but only up to a point, and, after that point, more intelligence actually leads to lower job performance. Of course, this statement is false, and assumes a nonlinear relationship between intelligence and job performance. Can job performance suffer from having "too much of a good thing" (GMA)? Hundreds of studies have shown that this is not the case: There is a straight line (linear) relationship between intelligence and job performance, and higher intelligence has been shown to lead to better job performance even up to the highest levels of intelligence (Coward and Sackett, 1990).

Why then do so many people believe the false assumption? Perhaps it is because it makes intuitive sense. When imagining a university professor or a medical doctor working as a janitor, it is easy to think, "This person would be so bored with this job that he or she would do a poor job." But such a conclusion ignores the fact that the university professor or doctor would be highly unlikely to apply for the janitor's job to begin with. Among people who actually apply to get real jobs, there is a linear relationship between intelligence and performance; the higher the intelligence, the better the job performance.

Moreover, some lay people tend to think that applicants for high-complexity jobs are so similar in terms of intelligence that an intelligence test may not differentiate them from one another. If this were true, intelligence tests would not be a valid selection tool for high-complexity jobs. However, as discussed previously, there is substantial variability in intelligence even among the most educated people with the most advanced degrees. Furthermore, intelligence is a more valid selection procedure than educational level among applicants with varied levels of education applying for the same job (Berry, Gruys, and Sackett, 2006). The validity of intelligence remains substantial even in a group of the most talented individuals even at

1-in-10000 scarcity (Lubinski, Webb, Morelock, and Benbow, 2001). In general, there should be no concern about hiring someone who is too intelligent for a job, ceteris paribus. Relatedly, recent research by Brown, Wai, and Chabris (2021) has shown that "there is little evidence for any robust detrimental effects of or risk associated with having high cognitive ability" in predicting various "beneficial outcomes in work, education, health, and social contexts" (p. 18). That is, a saying such as "the relationship between success and IQ works only up to a point" is only a misconception, which should be discredited given the continued positive linear relationships between GMA and important life outcomes even at the very high end of GMA.

Interestingly, it has also been shown that over their careers people gradually move into jobs, either within a single organization or by moving to another organization, that are consistent with their levels of GMA. This "sorting" process occurs over time and has been called the gravitation process (Wilk, Desmariais, and Sackett, 1995; Wilk and Sackett, 1996). People whose GMA exceeds their job level tend to move toward more complex jobs (internal or external upward movement) and people whose GMA is below their job level tend to move toward less complex jobs.

Is Intelligence All That Matters?

If some hypothetical sets of constraints allowed that only a single assessment would be used in the hiring process, and if the goal of the hiring process were to maximize future job performance, then we would strongly recommend the use of an intelligence assessment. However, in reality, no such constraints exist. Although GMA is the best predictor of job performance, it does not follow that the use of intelligence alone in hiring is the best way to select people. In fact, it is well known that other predictors can be used along with GMA to produce better predictions of job performance than can be produced by GMA alone. For example, according to the authors' recent work, for most jobs, the use of a structured employment interview in addition to a GMA test increases validity by 18%. And, the use of self-reported measures of conscientiousness in addition to a GMA test increases validity by 8%. It is almost always possible to add some supplemental selection procedure(s) that can further increase the validity offered by a GMA test. The best supplementary selection procedure is one that has high validity in and of itself and a low correlation with scores on a GMA test (in order to minimize measurement redundancy), and a low cost. It follows that practitioners should use well-established measures of personality traits such as conscientiousness (as shown in the next chapter) and structured employee interviews (Schmidt and Hunter, 1998).

Does the Use of GMA Tests Have Any Adverse Impact?

This is an important question, and one that requires a thorough response. In terms of gender differences, it has been found that there is no difference in mean levels of GMA test scores between males and females (Ployhart and Holtz, 2008), although there are some well-known gender differences in specific aptitudes (i.e. higher mean scores for females in speech production and higher mean scores for males in spatial perception). Though we mention differences in specific aptitudes, we do not recommend the use of specific abilities in staffing contexts, given that the validity of GMA tests is almost always higher than that of specific aptitudes ("not much more than GMA") – even when specific aptitudes are chosen to match the most important aspects of job performance (i.e. spatial perception for the pilot job). Further, research generally does not support differential validity of GMA tests for males and females (Hartigan and Wigdor, 1989; Rothstein and McDaniel, 1992), particularly for jobs that are gender-neutral (i.e. jobs that tend to have a largely even distribution of men and women). Rothstein and McDaniel's meta-analysis (1992) found slightly higher validity of GMA tests for job performance in female-dominated jobs (e.g. nursing) for females, and the opposite was found in male-dominated jobs. Today, most jobs are gender-neutral or are becoming more so. Overall, one can conclude that intelligence test scores predict equally accurately for females and males in most, if not all, cases.

Perhaps, more controversial is the adverse impact that GMA tests seem to produce in terms of ethnic group differences. Research shows that members of some minority groups have lower average scores on GMA tests. If applicants are selected based solely on their GMA test scores, this can lead to lower hiring rates on average for lower scoring groups.[7] These lower hiring rates for minority applicants raise two potential problems: Legal risks and decreased workplace diversity.

From a legal standpoint, GMA tests are quite defensible in court given that the tests are valid predictors of job performance and their validity does not differ across major ethnic groups (e.g. Roth et al., 2014; Schmidt, 1988). In other words, "greater cognitive ability [GMA] is likely advantageous in many aspects of life [including job performance, practically to the same degree], no matter one's race or ethnicity" (Brown et al., 2021, p. 18). Such demonstrations rely increasingly on summaries of the kinds of research findings discussed in this chapter, rather than on studies conducted by organizations (this is part of the move away from the false notion of situational specificity, as discussed earlier). Since the mid-1980s, organizations have been winning more and more such suits, and today, they prevail in 80% or more of such suits. Moreover, today, there are simply far fewer such suits. In recent years, less

[7]The research surrounding the issue of ethnic group differences in test scores is quite extensive (see Roth, Van Iddekinge, DeOrtentiis, Hackney, Zhang, and Buster, 2017 for updated estimates of Hispanic-White and Asian-White differences for 12 widely used selection procedures including GMA tests). For readers who are interested in a more technical, detailed treatment of this issue, we recommend Roth, Bevier, Bobko, Switzer, and Tyler (2001); Sackett, Schmitt, Ellingson, and Kabin (2001); Sackett, Borneman, and Connelly (2008); Schmidt (1988); and Wigdor and Garner (1982).

than 1% of employment-related lawsuits are challenges to selection tests or other hiring procedures, and from a purely economic standpoint, research shows that the value of the increases in job performance from good selection practices overshadows any potential costs stemming from defending against such suits. Thus, there is little legal risk stemming from the use of GMA tests.

However, solving the problem of legal defensibility still leaves the problem of decreased workplace diversity. Given the fact that many hiring managers are under constant pressure to increase the diversity of their workforce, this can be a serious issue. Sackett and colleagues (2001) explain that emphasizing GMA tests in selection with the purpose of maximizing performance typically results in a lower ratio of minority hires, while eschewing the use of GMA tests with the purpose of increasing workplace diversity typically results in a decrease in job performance. The authors go on to ask, "What are the prospects for achieving diversity . . . without sacrificing the predictive accuracy and content relevancy present in knowledge, skill, ability, and achievement tests?" (p. 303). Over the years, some organizations tried to reduce this adverse impact by introducing various forms of minority preferences in hiring, and others used adjusted test scores (e.g. score banding[8]) or other test scoring methods with the goal of equalizing minority and nonminority hiring rates. However, the 1991 Civil Rights Act made such score adjustments illegal, leaving hiring managers with more questions than answers. Fortunately, a good and legally appropriate solution to the so-called validity-diversity dilemma lies well within the realm of currently accepted best hiring practices. Specifically, the use of GMA tests can be supplemented with the use of valid noncognitive predictors – such as self-reported measures of conscientiousness – that show little, if any, adverse impact. In this way, a battery of predictors can be assembled that not only will predict future job performance, but also will help reduce the adverse impact associated with GMA tests. In recent years, some organizations have also attempted to address this dilemma by balancing the biobjectives of validity (performance) and diversity using co-optimization (Pareto-optimal weighting) methods (De Corte, Lievens, and Sackett, 2011; Rupp et al., 2020).[9]

How Do Job Applicants React to the Use of GMA Tests?

Some have argued that the administration of GMA tests during the hiring process can be a detriment to an organization's recruitment efforts because applicants do not like to take ability tests. On the contrary, meta-analytic research on this subject

---

[8]Score banding is a method associated with "using standard errors to create score bands where applicants within a band are considered equal and then making diversity-related hires within a band" (Rupp, Song, and Strah, 2020, p. 247).

[9]According to Rupp et al. (2020), "Pareto-optimal weighting is similar to regression weighting in that it also seeks "optimized" composite scores. However, it differs from regression weighting in that it aims to optimize two (or more) outcomes simultaneously" (p. 249).

reveals that applicants perceive mental ability and GMA tests to be relevant to job performance, and that applicants generally react more favorably to GMA tests than they do to personality assessments, bio-data, and integrity tests, which they view as irrelevant to job performance (Hausknecht, Day, and Thomas, 2004). At the same time, applicants react less favorably to GMA tests than they do to the most widely used selection tools – employment interviews and résumés (Hausknecht et al., 2004). Interestingly, it appears to be the case that when GMA or other ability tests are used, applicants tend to perceive the selection requirements as being more stringent, thus increasing their perceptions of the status and attractiveness of the job in question. The conclusion is this: Job applicants generally respond relatively well to a GMA test because they believe it is relevant to job performance.

Economically, Is a GMA-Based Hiring System Really Worth the Effort?

One argument against using GMA assessments is that if an organization hires more intelligent people, then the organization will have to pay them a higher salary, and this will cancel out any economic gains associated with increases in job performance. This claim is utterly false. In fact, the potential economic gains that can be realized by hiring a more intelligent workforce are quite substantial. Several key research findings are particularly relevant to this issue. First, research has shown that job performance can be measured in actual dollar value. Second, there is considerable variance in job performance among employees. Third, the dollar value of the standard deviation of job performance is at least 40% of a given employee's salary. These findings have been synthesized into a single equation that allows hiring managers to compute the actual dollar value of a particular hiring method. After reviewing all of the available data and computing the value of various hiring methods, it is clear that the value gained from the use of GMA assessments far outstrips the cost of hiring intelligent people. For readers who are interested in a more detailed explanation of how to compute the dollar value of job performance, we recommend articles by Le et al. (2007) and Schmidt and Hunter (1998).

As top-performing employees are promoted to higher levels in the organization, they are rewarded with higher pay, but the value of those employees' performance to the organization increases much more than the employees' salaries do. This creates large net benefits to organizations that are careful to use the most effective selection procedures available. In some cases, offering top performers a salary increase might be necessary to retain them. In any event, the payoff to the organization in terms of enhanced job performance is much greater than any increase in the compensation costs. On the other hand, organizations that hire less intelligent people for entry-level positions find that their higher-level jobs also become filled with mediocre or poor performers. Thus, selection based on GMA improves performance not only in the job in question, but also later in higher-level jobs in the organization.

Last but not least, a recent meta-analysis (Van Iddekinge, Aguinis, Mackey, and DeOrtentiis, 2018) has shown that intelligence predicts job performance practically to the same degree regardless of the level of motivation (e.g. effort level), thus providing little to no support to the interaction of intelligence and motivation. That is, this meta-analysis shows that the effects of ability and motivation on performance are additive rather than multiplicative. We believe many would find this finding – i.e. performance = *f*(Ability + Motivation) – counterintuitive given the prevalent belief that performance = *f*(Ability × Motivation). However, it is noteworthy that intelligence is a "trait" variable and motivating is a "state" variable in the meta-analytic finding mentioned here. A growing number of studies on goal difficulty have shown that ability (e.g. task-specific strategies, knowledge, or expertise) and motivation (e.g. goal specificity and difficulty) both at the "state" level "interact" to predict task performance. In other words, specific challenging goals usually have a more positive effect on task performance when individuals use smart rather than poor task strategies (see Wood, Whelan, Sojo, and Wong, 2013 for a review). In addition, as an "all-purpose" tool, intelligence is even involved in everyday activities such as shopping, driving, and paying bills (Gottfredson, 1997). On a fun note, a recent meta-analysis has shown that intelligence is also positively related to "reading the mind in the eyes," telling others' mental/emotional states just by seeing their eyes (Baker, Peterson, Pulos, and Kirkland, 2014).

Case Examples

We will first look at one positive example of real-world applications of GMA-based hiring followed by one negative example.

The Philip Morris Plant in Cabarrus County, North Carolina

The US Employment Service began a new nationwide program of employment testing, operated through state employment offices, in the early 1980s. Like its earlier program, it was based on the General Aptitude Test Battery. One of the three abilities measured in that program was GMA (the other two were general perceptual ability and general psychomotor ability). This new program was based on the methods of meta-analysis or validity generalization that were mentioned at the beginning of this chapter.

The large Philip Morris plant in Cabarrus County, North Carolina, was one of the first organizations to subscribe to the new testing program. They signed an agreement under which the state employment service tested and referred the higher scoring applicants to Philip Morris for possible hires. For the jobs at Philip Morris, most of the weight was placed on GMA in determining who was hired.

The human resources department at Philip Morris conducted a study to compare the performance of the workers who had been selected using the GMA assessments and those who had been hired without use of the test. They found that the

GMA-selected workers were superior across a variety of performance measures, including a 35% gain in performance output. The GMA-selected workers learned 8% more skills during job training and had 25% fewer operator failures and 58% fewer disciplinary actions. In addition, the incidence of unsafe job behaviors decreased by 35% and the reduction in work days lost to accidents decreased by 82%.

These are large differences. The Philip Morris personnel researchers, Dennis Warmke and William Van Arnam, noted that the employment interview that the company was using might have contributed somewhat to the performance superiority of these workers. However, they stated that because the GMA test was the method used to screen out most of the applicants who were not hired, the GMA test was the dominant influence producing the performance improvements. This research is described in McKinney (1984).

US Steel Plant at Fairless Hill, PA

Up until 1978, the US Steel plant at Fairless Hills, PA, selected applicants into their skilled trades apprentice programs based on the applicants' total scores on a battery of ability tests. These total scores were a good measure of GMA, and selection was from the top down. The plant maintained apprentice programs in the wide variety of skilled trades needed to run a steel mill: machinists, tool and die makers, electricians, sheet metal workers, etc. The local unit of the United Steel workers union, however, did not like this selection method. In negotiations with the union, the company agreed to modify the selection system. In the new system, all applicants who scored above a low cut-off on each test, set at about the seventh-grade level, were considered equally qualified and eligible for hire. Only a few applicants were screened out by this procedure. Applicants in the passing group were selected based on plant seniority only. Hence, this plant went from a GMA-based hiring system to one in which GMA played only a very minor role.

The apprentice training center at Fairless Hills was a well-run facility that kept excellent records of apprentice performance. However, after the new selection system was introduced, performance plummeted. Scores on the mastery tests of amount learned in training declined markedly. The flunk-out and drop-out rates increased dramatically. The training time and training costs of those who did make it through the program increased substantially – because many apprentices had to re-take multiple units in the training. And finally, the ratings of later performance on the job out in the plant declined.

This was a well-controlled, natural quasi-experiment. The only change made was the lowering of mental ability standards in selection. The training program and the tests given in the program remained the same. The decline in performance was clearly due to the lower intelligence of the new apprentices.

Conclusion

Higher intelligence leads to better job performance on all jobs, and the increases in job performance resulting from hiring on intelligence have high economic value for organizations. Higher intelligence causes higher job performance primarily because it causes people to learn more job knowledge and to learn it more quickly. However, intelligence is also used directly on the job to solve performance-related problems, independent of prior job knowledge. The primary requirement that an organization must meet to make intelligence-based hiring work well is the ability to attract job applicants and to retain them once they are hired. Although intelligence is the most important determinant of job performance, it is not the only determinant. Therefore, organizations should use other valid noncognitive procedures such as a self-reported measure of conscientiousness along with an intelligence test whenever possible. This composite use of predictors will also help reduce the adverse impact associated with an intelligence test while maintaining its high validity quite well.

References

Arthur, W. Jr., Bell, S. T., Villado, A. J., and Doverspike, D. (2006). The use of person-organization fit in employment decision making: An assessment of its criterion-related validity. *Journal of Applied Psychology,* 91(4), 786–801. https://doi.org/10.1037/0021-9010.91.4.786

Baker, C. A., Peterson, E., Pulos, S., and Kirkland, R. A. (2014). Eyes and IQ: A meta-analysis of the relationship between intelligence and "Reading the Mind in the Eyes". *Intelligence,* 44, 78–92. https://doi.org/10.1016/j.intell.2014.03.001

Berry, C. M., Gruys, M. L., and Sackett, P. R. (2006). Educational attainment as a proxy for cognitive ability in selection: Effects on levels of cognitive ability and adverse impact. *Journal of Applied Psychology,* 91(3), 696–705. https://doi.org/10.1037/0021-9010.91.3.696

Borman, W. C., and Motowidlo, S. J. (1993). Expanding the criterion domain to include elements of contextual performance. In N. Schmitt and W. C. Borman (eds), *Personnel Selection in Organizations* (pp. 71–98). San Francisco: Jossey-Bass.

Borman, W. C., White, L. A., Pulakos, E. D., and Oppler, S. H. (1991). Models of supervisory job performance ratings. *Journal of Applied Psychology,* 76(6), 863–872. https://doi.org/10.1037/0021-9010.76.6.863

Brown, K., Le, H., and Schmidt, F. L. (2006). Specific aptitude theory revisited: Is there incremental validity for training performance? *International Journal of Selection and Assessment,* 14(2), 87–100. https://doi.org/10.1111/j.1468-2389.2006.00336.x

Brown, M. I., Wai, J., and Chabris, C. F. (2021). Can you ever be too smart for your own good? Comparing linear and nonlinear effects of cognitive ability on life outcomes. *Perspectives on Psychological Science.* Advance online publication. https://doi.org/10.1177/1745691620964122

Chiaburu, D. S., Oh, I.-S., Berry, C. M., Li, N., and Gardner, R. G. (2011). The five-factor model of personality traits and organizational citizenship behaviors: A meta-analysis. *Journal of Applied Psychology,* 96(6), 1140–1166. https://doi.org/10.1037/a0024004

Collins, J. M., Schmidt, F. L., Sanchez-Ku, M., Thomas, L., McDaniel, M. A., and Le, H. (2003). Can basic individual differences shed light on the construct meaning of assessment center evaluations? *International Journal of Selection and Assessment,* 11(1), 17–29. https://doi.org/10.1111/1468-2389.00223

Cooper-Hakim, A., and Viswesvaran, C. (2005). The construct of work commitment: Testing an Integrative framework. *Psychological Bulletin,* 131(2), 241–259. https://doi.org/10.1037/0033-2909.131.2.241

Coward, W. M., and Sackett, P. R. (1990). Linearity of ability-performance relationships: A re-confirmation. *Journal of Applied Psychology,* 75(3), 295–300. https://doi.org/10.1037/0021-9010.75.3.297

De Corte, W., Lievens, F., and Sackett, P. R. (2021). A comprehensive examination of the cross-validity of pareto-optimal versus fixed-weight selection systems in the biobjective selection context. *Journal of Applied Psychology.* Advance online publication. https://doi.org/10.1037/apl0000927

Dilchert, S., and Ones, D. S. (2009). Assessment center dimensions: Individual differences correlates and meta-analytic incremental validity. *International Journal of Selection and Assessment,* 17(3), 254–270. https://doi.org/10.1111/j.1468-2389.2009.00468.x

Ghiselli, E. E. (1966). *The Validity of Occupational Aptitude Tests.* New York, NY: Wiley.

Gottfredson, L. S. (1997). Why *g* matters: The complexity of everyday life. *Intelligence,* 24(1), 79–132. https://doi.org/10.1016/S0160-2896(97)90014-3

Gottfredson, L. S. (2002). Where and why *g* matters: Not a mystery. *Human Performance,* 15(1–2), 25–46. https://doi.org/10.1080/08959285.2002.9668082

Gonzalez-Mulé, E., Mount, M. K., and Oh, I.-S. (2014). A meta-analysis of the relationship between general mental ability and nontask performance. *Journal of Applied Psychology,* 99(6), 1222–1243. https://doi.org/10.1037/a0037547

Hartigan, J. A., and Wigdor, A. K. (eds) (1989). *Fairness in Employment Testing: Validity Generalization, Minority Issues and the General Aptitude Test Battery.* Washington, DC: National Academy of Sciences Press.

Hausknecht, J. P., Day, D. V., and Thomas, S. C. (2004). Applicant reactions to selection procedures: An updated model and meta-analysis. *Personnel Psychology,* 57(3), 639–683. https://doi.org/10.1111/j.1744-6570.2004.00003.x

Huffcutt, A. I., Roth, P. L., and McDaniel, M. A. (1996). A meta-analytic investigation of cognitive ability in employment interview evaluations: Moderating characteristics and implications for incremental validity. *Journal of Applied Psychology,* 81(5), 459–473. https://doi.org/10.1037/0021-9010.81.5.459

Hunter, J. E. (1986). Cognitive ability, cognitive aptitudes, job knowledge, and job performance. *Journal of Vocational Behavior,* 29(3), 340–362. https://doi.org/10.1016/0001-8791(86)90013-8

Hunter, J. E., and Hunter, R. F. (1984). Validity and utility of alternate predictors of job performance. *Psychological Bulletin,* 96(1), 72–98. https://doi.org/10.1037/0033-2909.96.1.72

Hunter, J. E., and Schmidt, F. L. (1996). Intelligence and job performance: Economic and social implications. *Psychology, Public Policy, and Law,* 2(3–4), 447–472. https://doi.org/10.1037/1076-8971.2.3-4.447

Hunter, J. E., Schmidt, F. L., and Judiesch, M. K. (1990). Individual differences in output variability as a function of job complexity. *Journal of Applied Psychology,* 75(1), 28–42. https://doi.org/10.1037/0021-9010.75.1.28

Hunter, J. E., Schmidt, F. L., and Le, H. (2006). Implications of direct and indirect range restriction for meta-analysis methods and findings. *Journal of Applied Psychology,* 91(3), 594–612. https://doi.org/10.1037/0021-9010.91.3.594

Judge, T. A., Klinger, R. L., and Simon, L. S. (2010). Time is on my side: Time, general mental ability, human capital, and extrinsic career success. *Journal of Applied Psychology,* 95(1), 92–107. https://doi.org/10.1037/a0017594

Judge, T. A., Thoresen, C. J., Bono, J. E., and Patton, G. K. (2001). Another look at the relationship between job satisfaction and job performance. *Psychological Bulletin,* 127(3), 376–407. https://doi.org/10.1037/0033-2909.127.3.376

Le, H., Oh, I.-S., Shaffer, J. A., and Schmidt, F. L. (2007). Implications of methodological advances for the practice of personnel selection: How practitioners benefit from recent developments in meta-analysis. *Academy of Management Perspectives,* 21(3), 6–15. https://doi.org/10.5465/amp.2007.26421233

Lubinski, D., Webb, R. M., Morelock, M. J., and Benbow, C. P. (2001). Top 1 in 10,000: A 10-year follow-up of the profoundly gifted. *Journal of Applied Psychology,* 86(4), 718–729. https://doi.org/10.1037/0021-9010.86.4.718

McCloy, R. A., Campbell, J. P., and Cudeck, R. (1994). A confirmatory test of a model of performance determinants. *Journal of Applied Psychology,* 79(4), 493–505. https://doi.org/10.1037/0021-9010.79.4.493

McDaniel, M. A., Hartman, N. S., Whetzel, D. L., and Grubb, W. (2007). Situational judgment tests, response instructions, and validity: A meta-analysis. *Personnel Psychology,* 60(1), 63–91. https://doi.org/10.1111/j.1744-6570.2007.00065.x

McHenry, J. J., Hough, L. M., Toquam, J. L., Hanson, M. L., and Ashworth, S. (1990). Project A validity results: The relationship between predictor and criterion domains. *Personnel Psychology,* 43(2), 335–354. https://doi.org/10.1111/j.1744-6570.1990.tb01562.x

McKinney, M. W. (1984). *Final Report: Validity Generalization Pilot Study.* U.S. Employment Service, Southern Test Development Field Center.

Nathan, B. R., and Alexander, R. A. (1988). A comparison of criteria for test validation: A meta-analytic investigation. *Personnel Psychology,* 41(2), 517–535. https://doi.org/10.1111/j.1744-6570.1988.tb00642.x

Oh, I.-S., Schmidt, F. L., Shaffer, J. A., and Le, H. (2008). The Graduate Management Admission Test (GMAT) is even more valid than we thought: A new development in meta-analysis and its implications for the validity of the GMAT. *Academy of Management Learning & Education,* 7(4), 563–570. https://doi.org/10.5465/amle.2008.35882196

Olea, M. M., and Ree, M. J. (1994). Predicting pilot and navigator criteria: Not much more than g. *Journal of Applied Psychology,* 79(6), 845–851. https://doi.org/10.1037/0021-9010.79.6.845

Ones, D. S., Viswesvaran, C., and Dilchert, S. (2005). Personality at work: Raising awareness and correcting misconceptions. *Human Performance,* 18(4), 389–404. https://doi.org/10.1207/s15327043hup1804_5

Orr, J. M., Sackett, P. R., and Mercer, M. (1989). The role of prescribed and nonprescribed behaviors in estimating the dollar value of performance. *Journal of Applied Psychology,* 74(1), 34–40. https://doi.org/10.1037/0021-9010.74.1.34

Ployhart, R. E., and Holtz, B. C. (2008). The diversity-validity dilemma: Strategies for reducing racioethnic and sex subgroup differences and adverse impact in selection. *Personnel Psychology,* 61(1), 153–172. https://doi.org/10.1111/j.1744-6570.2008.00109.x

Ree, M. J., and Earles, J. A. (1991). Predicting training success: Not much more than *g. Personnel Psychology,* 44(2), 321–332. https://doi.org/10.1111/j.1744-6570.1991.tb00961.x

Ree, M. J., and Earles, J. A. (1992). Intelligence is the best predictor of job performance. *Current Directions in Psychological Science,* 1(3), 86–89. https://doi.org/10.1111/1467-8721.ep10768746

Ree, M. J., Earles, J. A., and Teachout, M. (1994). Predicting job performance: Not much more than *g. Journal of Applied Psychology,* 79(4), 518–524. https://doi.org/10.1037/0021-9010.79.4.518

Ritchie, S. J., and Tucker-Drob, E. M. (2018). How much does education improve intelligence? A meta-analysis. *Psychological Science,* 29(8), 1358–1369. https://doi.org/10.1177/0956797618774253

Roth, P. L., Bevier, C. A., Bobko, P., Switzer, III, F. S., and Tyler, P. (2001). Ethnic group differences in cognitive ability in employment and educational settings: A meta-analysis. *Personnel Psychology,* 54(2), 297–330. https://doi.org/10.1111/j.1744-6570.2001.tb00094.x

Roth, P. L., Bevier, C. A., Switzer, F. S., and Schippmann, J. (1996). Meta-analyzing the relationship between grades and job performance. *Journal of Applied Psychology,* 81(5), 548–556. https://doi.org/10.1037/0021-9010.81.5.548

Roth, P. L., Bobko, P., and McFarland, L. (2005). A meta-analysis of work sample test validity: Updating and integrating some classic literature. *Personnel Psychology,* 58(4), 1009–1037. https://doi.org/10.1111/j.1744-6570.2005.00714.x

Roth, P. L., Le, H., Oh, I.-S., Van Iddekinge, C. H., Buster, M. A., Robbins, S. B., and Campion, M. A. (2014). Differential validity for cognitive ability tests in employment and educational settings: Not much more than range restriction? *Journal of Applied Psychology,* 99(1), 1–20. https://doi.org/10.1037/a0034377

Roth, P. L., Van Iddekinge, C. H., DeOrtentiis, P. S., Hackney, K. J., Zhang, L., and Buster, M. A. (2017). Hispanic and Asian performance on selection procedures: A narrative and meta-analytic review of 12 common predictors. *Journal of Applied Psychology,* 102(8), 1178–1202. https://doi.org/10.1037/apl0000195

Rothstein, H. R., and McDaniel, M. A. (1992). Differential validity by sex in employment settings. *Journal of Business and Psychology,* 7, 45–62. https://doi.org/10.1007/BF01014342

Rotundo, M., and Sackett, P. R. (2002). The relative importance of task, citizenship, and counterproductive performance to global ratings of job performance: A policy-capturing approach. *Journal of Applied Psychology,* 87(1), 66–80. https://doi.org/10.1037/0021-9010.87.1.66

Rupp, D. E., Song, Q. C., and Strah, N. (2020). Addressing the so-called validity-diversity trade-off: Exploring the practicalities and legal defensibility of Pareto-optimization for reducing adverse impact within personnel selection. *Industrial and Organizational Psychology: Perspectives on Science and Practice,* 13(2), 246–271. https://doi.org/10.1017/iop.2020.19

Rynes, S. L., Colbert, A. E., and Brown, K. G. (2002). HR professionals' beliefs about effective human resource practices: Correspondence between research and practices. *Human Resource Management,* 41(2), 149–174. https://doi.org/10.1002/hrm.10029

Sackett, P. R., Borneman, M. J., and Connelly, B. S. (2008). High stakes testing in higher education and employment: Appraising the evidence for validity and fairness. *American Psychologist,* 63(4), 215–227. https://doi.org/10.1037/0003-066X.63.4.215

Sackett, P. R., and Ostgaard, D. J. (1994). Job-specific applicant pools and national norms for cognitive ability tests: Implications for range restrictions corrections in validation research. *Journal of Applied Psychology,* 79(5), 680–684. https://doi.org/10.1037/0021-9010.79.5.680

Sackett, P. R., Schmitt, N., Ellingson, J. E., and Kabin, M. B. (2001). High-stakes testing in employment, credentialing, and higher education: Prospects in a post-affirmative action world. *American Psychologist,* 56(4), 302–318. https://doi.org/10.1037/0003-066X.56.4.302

Salgado, J. F., Anderson, N., Moscoso, S., Bertua, C., and de Fruyt, F. (2003a). International validity generalization of GMA and cognitive abilities: A European community meta-analysis. *Personnel Psychology,* 56(3), 573–605. https://doi.org/10.1111/j.1744-6570.2003.tb00751.x

Salgado, J. F., Anderson, N., Moscoso, S., Bertua, C., de Fruyt, F., and Rolland, J.P. (2003b). A meta-analytic study of general mental ability validity for different occupations in the European community. *Journal of Applied Psychology,* 88(6), 1068–1081. https://doi.org/10.1037/0021-9010.88.6.1068

Schmidt, F. L. (1988). The problem of group differences in ability scores in employment selection. *Journal of Vocational Behavior,* 33(3), 272–292. https://doi.org/10.1016/0001-8791(88)90040-1

Schmidt, F. L. (1992). What do data really mean? Research findings, meta-analysis, and cumulative knowledge in psychology. *American Psychologist,* 47(10), 1173–1181. https://doi.org/10.1037/0003-066X.47.10.1173

Schmidt, F. L. (2002). The role of general cognitive ability in job performance: Why there cannot be a debate. *Human Performance,* 15(1–2), 187–210. https://doi.org/10.1080/08959285.2002.9668091

Schmidt, F. L., and Hunter, J. E. (1981). Employment testing: Old theories and new research findings. *American Psychologist,* 36(10), 1128–1137. https://doi.org/10.1037/0003-066X.36.10.1128

Schmidt, F. L., and Hunter, J. E. (1998). The validity and utility of selection methods in personnel psychology: Practical and theoretical implications of 85 years of research findings. *Psychological Bulletin,* 124(2), 262–274. https://doi.org/10.1037/0033-2909.124.2.262

Schmidt, F. L., and Hunter, J. E. (2004). General mental ability in the world of work: Occupational attainment and job performance. *Journal of Personality and Social Psychology,* 86(1), 162–174. https://doi.org/10.1037/0022-3514.86.1.162

Schmidt, F. L., and Hunter, J. E. (2015). *Methods of Meta-Analysis: Correcting Error and Bias in Research Findings* (3rd edition). Sage. https://doi.org/10.4135/9781483398105

Schmidt, F. L., Hunter, J. E., and Outerbridge, A. N. (1986). Impact of job experience and ability on job knowledge, work sample performance, and supervisory ratings of job performance. *Journal of Applied Psychology,* 71(3), 432–439. https://doi.org/10.1037/0021-9010.71.3.432

Schmidt, F. L., Hunter, J. E., Outerbridge, A. N., and Goff, S. (1988). The joint relation of experience and ability with job performance: A test of three hypotheses. *Journal of Applied Psychology,* 73(1), 46–57. https://doi.org/10.1037/0021-9010.73.1.46

Schmidt, F. L., Hunter, J. E., and Pearlman, K. (1980). Task difference and validity of aptitude tests in selection: A red herring. *Journal of Applied Psychology,* 66(2), 166–185. https://doi.org/10.1037/0021-9010.66.2.166

Schmidt, F. L., Oh, I.-S., and Le, H. (2006). Increasing the accuracy of corrections for range restriction: Implications for selection procedure validity and other research findings. *Personnel Psychology,* 59(2), 281–305. https://doi.org/10.1111/j.1744-6570.2006.00065.x

Schmidt, F. L., Shaffer, J. A., and Oh, I.-S. (2008). Increased accuracy of range restriction corrections: Implications for the role of personality and general mental ability in job and training performance. *Personnel Psychology,* 61(4), 827–868. https://doi.org/10.1111/j.1744-6570.2008.00132.x

Tenhiälä, A., Giluk, T. L., Kepes, S., Simon, C., Oh, I.-S., and Kim, S. (2016). The research-practice gap in human resource management: A cross-cultural study. *Human Resource Management,* 55(2), 179–200. https://doi.org/10.1002/hrm.21656

Van Iddekinge, C. H., Aguinis, H., Mackey, J. D., and DeOrtentiis, P. S. (2018). A meta-analysis of the interactive, additive, and relative effects of cognitive ability and motivation on performance. *Journal of Management,* 44(1), 249–279. https://doi.org/10.1177/0149206317702220

Wang, G., Oh, I.-S., Courtright, S., and Colbert, A. (2011). Transformational leadership and performance across criteria and levels: A meta-analytic review of 25 years of research. *Group & Organization Management,* 36(2), 223–270. https://doi.org/10.1177/1059601111401017

Wigdor, A. K., and Garner W. R. (eds) (1982). *Ability testing: Uses, consequences, and controversies* (Report of the National Research Council Committee on Ability Testing). Washington, DC: National Academy of Sciences Press.

Wilk, S. L., and Sackett, P. R. (1996). Longitudinal analysis of ability-job complexity fit and job change. *Personnel Psychology,* 49(4), 937–967. https://doi.org/10.1111/j.1744-6570.1996.tb02455.x

Wilk, S. L., Desmarais, L. B., and Sackett, P. R. (1995). Gravitation to jobs commensurate with ability: Longitudinal and cross-sectional tests. *Journal of Applied Psychology,* 80(1), 79–85. https://doi.org/10.1037/0021-9010.80.1.79

Wood, R. E., Whelan, J., Sojo, V., and Wong, M. (2013). Goals, goal orientations, strategies and performance. In E. A. Locke and G. P. Latham (eds), *New Developments in Goal Setting and Task Performance* (pp. 90–114). New York, NY: Routledge.

Exercises

Hiring Office Workers

You are the human resources director at a large organization and you are faced with designing a system for hiring office workers. An office manager comes to you and says the organization should not use written GMA tests because of the danger of law suits. He says he knows GMA is important to job performance but maintains that you can use "GMA-loaded" interviews to measure GMA and thus get the benefit of using GMA without leaving a "paper trail" of test scores that could stimulate a law suit. Respond to this manager based on what you learned from this chapter. What would you tell him? What is the foundation for your response?

Educating the CEO

You are the human resources director in your organization. The CEO calls you to her office for a meeting and tells you that she knows from 35 years of experience in dealing with people that the key determinant of high job performance is personal values and sense of responsibility. She says she would like to have all hiring in the company done using measures of values and sense of responsibility. Based on what you learned in this chapter, what would you tell her? What is the basis for the position you are taking?

Video Analysis and Discussion

Please watch the following video(s):

- Mark Zuckerberg: Hiring the Right People (https://www.youtube.com/watch?v=JPHVeQ7-ynA&list=WL&index=11)
- Laszlo Bock on how Google's hiring process works (https://www.youtube.com/watch?v=wBRJ01NNKj8)

- The Best Recruiter at Google | Talent Connect San Francisco 2014 (https://www.youtube.com/watch?v=hvebAGerh88) 16:42 – 17:36
- Jack Ma's hiring tip: "If you think s/he will be your boss in five years, hire her/him" (https://www.youtube.com/watch?v=SWjN3sVNwMQ) 00:15 – 00:45

Now form small groups to discuss the video(s) and answer the following questions:

1. What are the major points of the video?
2. How can you use information from the video in your career?
3. Based on the video, what advice do you have for leaders in organizations?

Be prepared to present the ideas from your small group discussion with the class as a whole.

Discussion Questions

- Why do you think many high-tech companies such as Facebook, Google, and Samsung rely more heavily on GMA – i.e. raw intelligence (per Mark Zuckerberg) and capability or general cognitive ability (per Lazlo Bock) – than on specific skills, expertise, and experiences in hiring new employees? It is noted that these companies do not use written GMA tests but assess GMA using multiple job interviews. Also think about the benefits of hiring highly intelligent people in terms of subsequent HR practices.
- Why do you think many HR managers believe that a GMA test is less predictive of employee performance than conscientiousness and value-based fit measures despite the extensive evidence that tells the opposite? Is their ignorance of research findings the real problem? Or something else?

2

SELECT ON CONSCIENTIOUSNESS AND EMOTIONAL STABILITY

MICHAEL K. MOUNT[1] AND MURRAY R. BARRICK[2]

[1] University of IOWA
[2] Texas A & M

SELECT ON CONSCIENTIOUSNESS AND EMOTIONAL STABILITY

The previous chapter clearly demonstrated that intelligence is a strong predictor of job performance. But hiring smart people is not enough. Many important work behaviors that are critical for organizational success are influenced by employees' work motivation rather than their intelligence. For example, motivated employees persist in the pursuit of goals, complete work thoroughly and accurately, work well under stress, display positive work attitudes, demonstrate honesty and integrity, are more likely to remain with the firm, and are helpful organizational citizens. A major determinant of motivated work behaviors is the underlying personality traits of individuals. The general principle that we advocate in this chapter is that organizations should select employees based on the personality traits of conscientiousness and emotional stability. A subprinciple is that organizations should select employees based on other personality traits (agreeableness, extraversion, and openness to experience) depending on the specific requirements of the job. We discuss the broad and diverse outcomes predicted by conscientiousness and emotional stability, how conscientiousness and emotional stability predict work outcomes, exceptions to the general principle, legal issues, and best practices for implementation, along with real-world examples.

Conscientiousness and Emotional Stability Predict Broad and Diverse Outcomes

We define personality as an individual's relatively stable and enduring pattern of thoughts, feelings, and actions. Although there are more than 15000 trait terms in the English language that can be used to describe personality, most researchers agree that there are five broad dimensions, often called the Big Five or the Five-Factor Model (FFM) of personality: conscientiousness, emotional stability, extraversion, agreeableness, and openness to experience. When measures of the FFM traits are developed according to professional guidelines, they can predict numerous work outcomes that are important to organizations. Research has shown that two FFM traits, conscientiousness and emotional stability, are the best personality predictors across jobs and work outcomes vital to organizational success. This chapter focuses on the importance of selecting individuals on these two personality traits. We discuss the breadth and diversity of work outcomes that conscientiousness and emotional stability affect, including overall performance, counterproductive work behaviors, organizational citizenship behaviors (OCBs), teamwork and collective effort, work attitudes, and withdrawal behaviors.

Overall Job Performance

Conscientious individuals are goal-directed, hardworking, dependable, persistent, responsible, organized, rule-abiding, careful, and reliable. One way these traits influence performance is through self-regulatory processes associated with achievement striving. Conscientious traits lead to increased effort, direct effort toward the attainment of specific goals, and facilitate sustained effort over time. Conscientiousness also leads to fewer undesirable work behaviors (e.g. tardiness, safety violations, theft, and slacking) through motivational processes associated with behavioral restraint. There is strong research evidence that, other things being equal, individuals higher on conscientiousness perform better on the job. This principle is very broad, and like intelligence, it applies to all job types.

Emotionally stable people are calm, resilient, confident, and secure. Conversely, viewed in terms of low emotional stability, neurotic individuals are nervous, high-strung, stress prone, emotionally unsteady, impulsive, have poor self-esteem, and fear failure. One reason neurotic individuals perform poorly is because they have dysfunctional thought processes. They spend more personal resources trying to avoid failure than they do formulating strategies to attain success. All else equal, individuals higher on emotional stability perform better on the job. This principle is also quite broad and applies to all jobs.

The general principle that organizations should select and retain employees based on conscientiousness and emotional stability is derived from the results of hundreds of individual studies and numerous meta-analytic studies. The first meta-analysis of the relationship between the FFM traits and job performance was conducted by Barrick and Mount (1991). Their study discovered that conscientiousness was a valid predictor of overall job performance for all jobs. These findings are significant because they showed that there are two characteristics of individuals, intelligence and conscientiousness, whose validity in predicting performance generalized across jobs. Numerous other meta-analytic studies (e.g. Barrick, Mount, and Judge, 1999; Hough, 1992; Hurtz and Donovan, 1998; Salgado, 1997, 1998; Wilmot and Ones, 2019) have been conducted since the Barrick and Mount (1991) study and all confirm the robustness of conscientiousness in predicting performance. The Wilmot and Ones (2019) study is noteworthy because it reviewed the validity of conscientiousness spanning 100 years of research based on 92 previous meta-analyses and included 175 distinct variables and over 1.1 million participants. Additionally, there is evidence of the cross-cultural validity of conscientiousness, as positive findings have been reported in Europe (Salgado, 1997, 2002), South Africa (van Aarde, Meiring and Wiernik, 2017), and East Asia (Oh, 2009). In sum, the evidence in support of conscientiousness as a moderately strong predictor of job performance is clear, consistent, and compelling. Simply stated, selecting employees based on conscientiousness will lead to more productive employees who are more likely to remain with the firm.

Results of meta-analytic studies also support the usefulness of emotional stability as a predictor of overall performance. For example, Barrick et al. (1999) reviewed eight previous meta-analyses and found that emotional stability moderately correlated with overall job performance across a wide variety of jobs. Similarly, Salgado (1997) conducted a meta-analysis with studies conducted in the European Community and found that emotional stability was a valid predictor across job criteria and occupational groups. In a subsequent meta-analysis using a large database consisting of both American and European validity studies, Salgado (2002) found that emotional stability was a valid predictor across jobs. Collectively, these results show that emotional stability is a valid predictor of job performance in a wide variety of jobs, although we note that the effects are not quite as robust as for conscientiousness.

A practical question of interest is whether conscientiousness and emotional stability should be used together to select employees. The answer is yes, as research has shown that conscientiousness and emotional stability have only moderate correlations with each other, which means that each adds unique information to the other when predicting job performance. Another practical question is whether it makes sense to use conscientiousness and emotional stability together with intelligence to select employees. Again, the answer is yes as research has shown that conscientiousness and emotional stability have only small correlations with intelligence, which means both traits can predict work behaviors over and above that explained by intelligence.

Counterproductive Work Behavior

Unfortunately, a harsh reality is that some, perhaps many, employees engage in dishonest behaviors at work. These intentional negative behaviors are called counterproductive work behaviors and negatively impact the quality of work life of employees and are detrimental to the success of the organization. Such behaviors can take many forms such as belligerence with customers or fellow coworkers, social loafing, bullying and sexual harassment, sabotage of equipment or products, falsifying expense reports, use of alcohol and drugs at work, and theft of goods or money. The US Chamber of Commerce reports that employee dishonesty costs US businesses about $50 billion annually. Further, the Chamber reports that 75% of employees have stolen from their employer at least once, and half of these employees steal repeatedly (FORTUNE, 2018). Moreover, up to 30% of business failures, especially among small businesses, are due to employee fraud and embezzlement (e.g. check tampering, payroll and billing schemes, and expense padding). Research demonstrates that people who are high on conscientiousness and emotional stability (and agreeableness) are much less likely to engage in dishonest behaviors at work. In fact, there are professionally developed, commercially available integrity tests based on the personality traits of conscientiousness and emotional stability (and agreeableness) that help identify people who are likely to engage in counterproductive work behaviors. (See the Wonderlic productivity index available from the Wonderlic Corporation Inc. for an example.)

Organizational Citizenship

Most employees understand the formal role requirements of their jobs and try to perform the expected behaviors in a satisfactory way or at least to meet supervisor expectations. But some employees go above and beyond formal requirements of their jobs by engaging in positive behaviors that are not directly or formally compensated by the organization. These helpful, voluntary behaviors are called *organizational citizenship behaviors* and play a key role in organizational success. Examples include relatively minor but helpful behaviors such as refilling the copy machine with paper rather than waiting for someone else to do it, as well as more significant behaviors such as helping a new employee who has fallen behind on assigned tasks or volunteering for extra work during peak times. An important point is that employees engage in OCBs because they choose to, not because they have to or because they will be formally rewarded for doing so. Research has shown that employees who are high on conscientiousness and emotional stability (along with other FFM traits, particularly agreeableness) are more likely to engage in these helpful, discretionary behaviors. A likely explanation for these findings is similar to that discussed earlier for overall performance. Conscientious and emotionally stable individuals have a strong desire to achieve. When they engage in citizenship behaviors like helping a new employee or working longer hours to complete a job, they likely fulfill (at least partially) their desire to demonstrate competence and to get things done.

Teamwork and Collective Effort

Organizations are increasingly organizing work through teams to achieve business goals. This places a premium on employees who can work effectively in teams and who are able to work collaboratively with others. Teamwork includes working with a group or even a dyad (e.g. a client) to attain a goal. It involves cooperating, providing constructive feedback, and avoiding personal conflict with others. Research reveals that employees who are high in conscientiousness, agreeableness, and emotional stability (in that order) are higher performers in jobs that involve interpersonal interactions. Not surprisingly, employees who are more effective interpersonally are better team members and collaborators, which leads to greater success in attaining collective goals. This research provides further support for the general principle we advocate. One way organizations can improve teamwork and collaboration is by selecting employees who are high on conscientiousness and emotional stability (as well as agreeableness).

Attitudes – Job Satisfaction and Organizational Commitment

Another reason to select on conscientiousness and emotional stability is that both traits are related to positive work attitudes such as job satisfaction and organizational commitment. This is noteworthy because work attitudes have been shown to be positively related to job performance and negatively related to undesirable withdrawal behaviors such as absenteeism and turnover. For example, Judge, Higgins, Thoresen, and Barrick (1999) found that conscientiousness and emotional stability assessed at an early age (12–14) were strong predictors of overall job satisfaction in late adulthood, even after controlling for other personality traits. Judge, Heller, and Mount (2002) conducted a meta-analysis of the relationship of the FFM traits and job satisfaction and found that neuroticism (low emotional stability) and conscientiousness (along with extraversion) displayed moderate correlations with job satisfaction, with neuroticism showing the strongest and most consistent (negative) relationship. Interestingly, neuroticism and conscientiousness are also among the strongest personality-based predictors of life satisfaction. Neurotic individuals likely have reduced job and life satisfaction because they experience more adverse events and react negatively and more strongly when such problems occur. On the other hand, emotionally stable people experience greater satisfaction because they have a more positive view of the world around them, including their views of themselves and others. They experience fewer negative emotions and dysfunctional thought processes and, therefore, have more positive experiences. Conscientious people have greater job and life satisfaction because their hard work and responsible behavior lead to a heightened sense of control and competence, which in turn leads to more positive work outcomes. Overall, these results illustrate that an additional benefit of hiring based on conscientiousness and emotional stability is that employees will be more satisfied at work and with their lives in general. One implication of these findings is that a meaningful part of job and life satisfaction can be explained by one's personality traits and has nothing to do with the conditions of the job or one's life. The important takeaway for employers is that one way to build a more satisfied workforce is by selecting employees on conscientiousness and emotional stability.

Organizational commitment, defined as an individual's psychological bond with an organization, has been shown to be linked to important work outcomes such as job performance and turnover. Like job satisfaction, we would expect organizational commitment to have a basis in personality because there are idiosyncratic differences in the way individuals view the same work environment. Conscientiousness, more than any other trait, naturally leads people to be committed and loyal to their organizations. Conscientious people are hardworking, persistent, and goal-directed, which leads them to become more immersed and involved in their organizations. Emotionally stable individuals are also more likely to be committed to their organization. Their calm, resilient, and stable demeanor enables them to build more positive relationships with supervisors and coworkers. This leads to increased commitment because more positive interpersonal relationships and social support creates more positive connections within and to the organization. Emotionally stable people also tend to experience fewer negative organizational events and better cope with such events if they occur. They are more likely to take personal responsibility and are less likely to attribute the cause of the negative events to the organization itself, which leads to greater commitment. As discussed earlier, both conscientious and emotionally stable employees perform better on the job, and as a result, they receive more rewards from the organization, which leads them to reciprocate these positive outcomes and support by becoming more attached and committed to the organization. The interested reader can see the meta-analytic study by Choi, Oh, and Colbert (2015) for more information about the relationship of conscientiousness and emotional stability to overall organizational commitment. Essentially, research has shown that selecting on these two traits is an important way to obtain committed employees.

Withdrawal Behaviors

People can withdraw from their jobs psychologically and physically. Psychological withdrawal includes passive compliance, minimal effort on the job, and thoughts and intentions about leaving the organization. Physical withdrawal includes behaviors such as lateness, absenteeism, and turnover. Withdrawal behaviors are disruptive to the operation of the organization and are very costly. It has been estimated that companies in the United States incur costs of more than 100 billion dollars each year because of withdrawal behaviors (Ghadi, Fernando, and Caputi, 2013) such as absenteeism, tardiness, and turnover and consume approximately 15% of an organization's payroll (Faulk and Hicks, 2015). When total costs associated with turnover are considered, the cost of replacing an employee is between 50% and 200% of the first-year salary (Bryant and Allen, 2013). Selecting on conscientiousness and emotional stability can reduce withdrawal behaviors. Conscientious people exhibit fewer withdrawal behaviors for several reasons. They are more likely to feel more contractually obligated to the organization, feel morally and ethically obligated to remain, and are less impulsive so will not make sudden decisions to quit. People high on emotional stability are also less likely to withdraw. Viewed from the perspective of low emotional stability, neurotic people experience more stress because they feel less secure and confident of their ability to do the job. They also experience more interpersonal conflict and have more negative perceptions of the work environment, which make it difficult to become socialized in the organization. One way neurotic people cope with negativity and conflict is to withdraw from the situation. A meta-analysis by Zimmerman (2008) found that both conscientiousness and emotional stability were moderately correlated with fewer quit intentions and less turnover. A meta-analysis by Rubenstein, Eberly, Lee, and Mitchell (2018) found similar results. In summary, withdrawal behaviors are disruptive to organizations, take a personal toll on employees, and represent a major business expense. Selecting employees based on conscientiousness and emotional stability can have a positive economic impact on organizations by reducing withdrawal behaviors thereby increasing workforce stability.

How Do Conscientiousness and Emotional Stability Affect Job Performance?

Behavior in organizations is largely a function of individuals' levels of ability and motivation (as well as situational cues and influences). Measures of ability (intelligence or physical) are often referred to as "can-do" predictors because they assess the extent to which a person has the capability to accomplish tasks. In contrast, personality traits are often referred to as "will-do" predictors because they assess the strength of an individual's willingness or desire to accomplish tasks. Barrick, Mount, and Li (2013) suggest that personality traits influence work outcomes through four pathways: communion, status, autonomy, and achievement. Communion striving is the motivation to achieve meaningful contact and to get along with others. Status striving is the strong desire to exert power and influence over others within the organizational hierarchy. Autonomy striving is the desire to gain control and understanding of important aspects of the work environment and to pursue personal growth opportunities. Finally, achievement striving is the motivation to demonstrate personal competence and accomplishment. The importance or value attached to each pathway differs depending on the strength of the individual's personality traits.

Of the four motivational strivings, achievement striving is most directly related to accomplishing work tasks. The two personality traits that are most strongly associated with achievement striving are conscientiousness and emotional stability. Conscientious people have a strong willingness and desire to achieve through their tendencies to be organized, reliable, hardworking, determined, persistent, self-disciplined, and rule-abiding. People high on emotional stability have a strong desire to achieve through their positive self-concept, high self-confidence, calm and steady demeanor (even in stressful situations), resilience, and the ability to avoid distractions associated with worrying and fear of failure.

There is empirical support for the idea that conscientiousness and emotional stability are important sources of achievement motivation. Judge and Ilies (2002) conducted a meta-analysis of the relationship of the FFM personality traits to three categories of performance motivation: goal setting (e.g. sales goals for salespersons), expectancy (e.g. perceptions of whether working on an activity would result in attaining a specific outcome), and self-efficacy (e.g. confidence in one's ability to complete an activity and successfully attain a specific outcome). These three sources of performance motivation are closely associated with achievement striving motivation discussed earlier. Judge and Ilies (2002) found that neuroticism and conscientiousness were the strongest and most consistent correlates of all three types of performance motivation. These results support the idea that conscientiousness and emotional stability are important "will-do" predictors that influence performance through motivational processes (goal setting, expectancy, and self-efficacy) associated with achievement motivation. Consequently, the primary reason to select on conscientiousness and emotional stability is that these individuals naturally strive to get things done and persistently exert effort to pursue deadlines, attain goals, and act responsibly. These individuals do not have to be prodded by the supervisor nor require extra rewards to achieve high job performance because they are internally driven and naturally self-motivated to strive for achievement.

Are There Exceptions to the General Principle?

Although the research surrounding our general principle that organizations should select based on conscientiousness and emotional stability is quite robust, there are some exceptions that can moderate its applicability. The first pertains to situational influences. Personality traits predict behavior best when the situation is relevant to the expression of the particular trait and when the situation enables the person to choose how to behave. When situations allow people to naturally express their personality traits in the pursuit of their chosen motivational goals, they invest more personal resources such as mental attention, emotional connections, and energetic activity, which in turn leads to greater intensity and persistence of motivated work behaviors. For example, employees working in a convenience store who are low on conscientiousness and emotional stability would have a predisposition to engage in counterproductive work behaviors such as theft, abusing break times, and tardiness. But if the organization installs a 24-hour surveillance camera, the employees know that their behavior is constantly being monitored. If they steal, take extra beak time, or are argumentative with coworkers or customers, their inappropriate behaviors will be detected, and they likely will be punished. The existence of the camera constitutes a "strong" situation that constrains the natural expression of the motivational tendencies (negative in this case) associated with conscientiousness and emotional stability. Obviously, by changing the situation (installing the camera), the individual's personality traits will not predict work behaviors in the expected ways.

Another possible limitation is that conscientiousness may be a stronger predictor of job performance in jobs that are low to moderate in occupational complexity (e.g. skilled/semiskilled, customer service jobs) compared to occupations that are high in complexity (e.g. professional jobs). One explanation is that conscientious traits are more naturally expressed in low-complexity jobs, where the motivation to engage in persistent, goal-directed behavior in structured, predictable environments is particularly important. Conscientiousness may work less well in high-complexity jobs where the work situation requires problem-solving ability in novel, unstructured situations rather than persistence in doing the task the same way, over and over. Although the general principle that we advocate is that conscientiousness predicts performance in all jobs remains true, one caveat to the principle is that the job environment or complexity of the job can influence how well conscientiousness predicts performance. (See Wilmot and Ones (2019) for a more detailed discussion.)

Another possible exception to our general principle is that the relationship of conscientiousness and emotional stability to performance may not be the same throughout all levels of the trait. Le, Oh, Robbins, Illies, Holland, and Westrick, (2011) reported that beyond a certain point, further increases in the potency of conscientiousness and emotional stability will not result in higher levels of job performance and may even lead to reduced performance. In other words, it is possible that there is "too much of a good thing" whereby very high levels of the motivational and emotional resources associated with conscientiousness and emotional stability may be disruptive or maladaptive. One implication for measures of conscientiousness and emotional stability is that it may be appropriate to set both lower and upper limits when screening out applicants. Clearly, more research is needed before this strategy is widely adopted, but the findings may provide useful guidance for the way measures of conscientiousness and emotional stability are used in selection systems.

Subprinciple: Other Traits Predict Performance in Particular Jobs

The general principle in this chapter is that organizations should select individuals based on conscientiousness and emotional stability. However, this does not mean these are the only personality traits that predict performance. A subprinciple is that other traits in addition to conscientiousness and emotional stability should be used to select employees depending on the specific requirements of the job and/or the nature of the criterion. Research has shown that the other three personality dimensions in the FFM model (agreeableness, extraversion, and openness to experience) are critical for some jobs and/or for some aspects of performance. A job analysis should be conducted to clearly identify the job requirements, cues, demands, and competencies that are essential to achieve successful job performance. For example, if the job requires teamwork or strong customer service orientation, the trait of agreeableness would be relevant because it is a good predictor of collaboration. Research has shown that agreeableness is a useful predictor of teamwork and is also related to service orientation (Mount, Barrick, and Stewart, 1998). On the other hand, if the nature of the interpersonal interaction is competitive (rather than cooperative) or requires persuasion or negotiating, then extraversion would be a relevant predictor. Indeed, extraversion has been found to be a valid predictor of success in sales and management jobs (Barrick and Mount, 1991). Finally, when companies are seeking employees who are motivated to increase their job knowledge or to improve their job-related skills, the trait of openness to experience would be especially relevant. Barrick and Mount (1991) found that employees higher on openness to experience perform better in training programs. Further, trainees who score high on extraversion tend to be more successful in training programs most likely because extraverts are more active participants, asking clarification questions, for example, during the training program, which leads to deeper immersion in the learning activity resulting in greater knowledge acquisition. In summary, the subprinciple that we advocate is that in addition to conscientiousness and emotional stability, the personality traits of agreeableness, extraversion, and openness to experience can be highly relevant predictors contingent upon the specific requirements of the job and the component of job performance of interest to the employer. Thus, while selecting applicants on conscientiousness and emotional stability is advocated in all jobs, other personality traits will likely be valid predictors when the occupation requires or the criterion used to define success draws on that trait's intrinsic motivational force (e.g. agreeable people, who naturally exhibit more teamwork and collaboration, will be more successful when work is organized using teams).

Are There Legal Issues in Implementing These Principles?

Any selection device should be scrutinized to ensure that it is consistent with laws and legal guidelines pertaining to the selection of employees. Personality testing is a means to learn about applicants' traditional ways of thinking, feeling, and performing. A concern in the use of personality inventories is that some of the items may be seen as an invasion of privacy and confidentiality. For example, items such as "I see myself as someone who is depressed or blue" or "I see myself as someone who is moody" may be perceived as invasive. Nonetheless, employers who focus on assessing only job-relevant personality traits should be on solid ground. When the information obtained bears a demonstrable relationship to some legitimate employer goal, such as higher job performance, it is generally considered acceptable. In addition to being able to justify the selection method legally, employers are less likely to have legal challenges due to negative reactions by applicants about objectionable test questions. Nevertheless, practitioners should always examine the personality test to determine whether there are potentially invasive or offensive test items.

A key question is whether a selection method disproportionately screens out protected subgroups such as minorities and women. If it does, it adversely impacts the selection of individuals in these subgroups, which may result in legal action. For example, research on intelligence tests has shown that there are large mean score differences of approximately one standard deviation between African Americans and Whites and, thus, is likely to show adverse impact based on race. In contrast, research shows that there are relatively small differences on conscientiousness and emotional stability scores between ethnic groups or between men and women. Foldes, Duehr, and Ones (2008) conducted a meta-analysis to examine the extent to which five racial groups (White, Black, Asian, Hispanic, and Native Indian) differ across the FFM personality factors. They reported that most group comparisons and personality scales yielded small differences and are unlikely to cause adverse impact in selection. However, the authors caution that it would be incorrect to conclude that the use of personality measures in selection would never result in adverse impact. Regarding gender differences, a meta-analysis by Feingold (1994) reported only small gender differences on measures like conscientiousness and emotional stability (men score slightly lower and higher than women, respectively). These findings are noteworthy because they demonstrate that when organizations select on conscientiousness and emotional stability, they are unlikely to adversely impact applicants based on race or gender.

One area that employers need to monitor is how personality tests affect people with mental or emotional disabilities. The key question is whether personality tests screen out people who suffer from mental illnesses such as depression or bipolar disorder, even though they may be otherwise qualified for the job. This concern is especially relevant for measures of emotional stability. If a person's responses are affected by the fact that they have a mental or emotional disability, and the results are used to exclude the person from a job, the employer would need to defend the use of the test.

Best Practices for Implementation

Personality traits like conscientiousness and emotional stability are usually assessed through professionally developed personality tests. According to a survey conducted by the Society of Human Resource Management (Meinert, 2015), approximately 20% of large organizations use personality tests as part of the employee selection process. Most contemporary personality tests are designed to measure the Big Five traits and consist of approximately 75–150 items. Respondents indicate the extent to which they agree or disagree with statements such as "I see myself as someone who does a thorough job" or "I see myself as someone who remains calm in tense situations." The tests are frequently administered online but may be administered via a paper and pencil format and typically take 20–30 minutes to complete.

The first implementation decision facing organizations is whether to use personality tests at all. Critics contend that correlations between personality traits such as conscientiousness and emotional stability and work outcomes are too small to be practically useful. Although it is true that the correlations are small to moderate in magnitude (approximately $r = 0.10$ to 0.20 in most cases), we believe it is erroneous to conclude that effects of this size are not practically useful. First, as discussed earlier in this chapter, selecting on conscientiousness and emotional stability impacts a wide and diverse set of work outcomes that are vital to organizational success and that are largely unmatched by other selection predictors. Second, the positive effects of conscientiousness and emotional stability can accrue to employers for years because employees will exhibit those positive behaviors every day they remain on the job. Third, the magnitude of the correlations for conscientiousness and emotional stability is typical of those reported in other subfields of psychology. Moreover, the effect sizes found in personnel selection and the broader psychology field are often higher than those found in medicine. For example, Meyer et al. (2001) report that the correlations between consuming aspirin to treat heart disease or using chemotherapy to treat breast cancer are 0.02 or 0.03, which are substantially smaller than correlations for conscientiousness and emotional stability with job performance. Finally, accounting for both traits results in stronger predictions of job success, as each adds unique information to the prediction of several criteria valued by the firm. For these reasons, we believe the concern that the correlations between conscientiousness and emotional stability and work outcomes are too small to be practically useful is unwarranted.

The implementation of the broad principle we advocate in this chapter requires that organizations accurately identify and measure applicant qualifications relative to job requirements. Even though there is evidence that conscientiousness and emotional stability predict performance in nearly all jobs, it is recommended that a work analysis be conducted to identify critical competencies and job requirements that are relevant. There is a trend whereby organizations are moving away from job-specific knowledge, ability, and skill requirements when describing work to focus on broader competency-based requirements. This implies that there will be greater emphasis on those traits and qualities that are valid for all jobs (intelligence, conscientiousness, and emotional stability). Nevertheless, a work analysis can identify when other personality traits (extraversion, agreeableness, and openness to experience) are essential to success on a job.

Once it is known which specific traits will be assessed, consideration must also be given to the best means for assessing personality. There are several commercially available, professionally developed measures that assess the Big Five traits. For example, the *Personal Characteristic Inventory* is a 150-item self-report measure of the Big Five. It has a sixth-grade reading level and typically takes 20–30 minutes to complete. In addition to scores on the Big Five, the PCI provides scores on subscales of the Big Five such as Leadership Orientation and Creative Thinking, as well as Teamwork, Commitment to Work, Learning Orientation, and Integrity. The PCI can be administered and scored online, and scoring results can be available soon after the test is completed. Another professionally developed, commercially available personality test is the Hogan Personality Inventory (HPI). The HPI is a self-report inventory based on the five-factor personality model that takes approximately 15–20 minutes to complete and is available in multiple languages (Hogan and Hogan, 2007). For those interested in a free, Internet-based measure of the Big Five, one example is the Big Five Inventory (BFI, John and Srivastava, 1999), which consists of 44 items and is self-administered and self-scoring. One cautionary note is that the BFI is not recommended for selection purposes as it has not been validated in selection settings and normative data are not available.

One implementation issue pertaining to the use of personality inventories is the pressures inherent in applicant settings that may affect how people respond. Understandably, when applying for a job, applicants are motivated to present themselves in a favorable way. This also happens in the traditional employment interview where people intentionally emphasize their qualifications and accomplishments and minimize their shortcomings. With personality tests, this concern arises because of the transparent nature of some items. For example, few applicants would agree with the statement that "Others would describe me as lazy or irresponsible at work." Given that it is virtually impossible to verify responses to questions such as these, the possibility that applicants actively engage in positive impression management is quite real. In fact, research shows that scores of applicants are about one-half standard deviation higher than scores of job incumbents on many personality traits, which is what would be expected if applicants engage in intentional impression management. Nevertheless, research shows that these tendencies by applicants to engage in impression management do not significantly reduce the predictive validity of the tests (Barrick and Mount, 1996). One important implication for the implementation of personality measures is that practitioners should use appropriate norms to interpret a test score (a percentile ranking for the score must be compared to other candidates). Norms based on responses made by applicants may be substantially different from those based on job incumbents.

A related implementation concern is that in selection contexts, measures of conscientiousness and emotional stability are almost always assessed using individuals' self-ratings. As noted, when people are applying for a job, they are likely to rate themselves in a way that makes them appear more suitable for the job. An interesting question is how well the two traits predict performance when they are assessed by other people (observers) such as coworkers, customers, and supervisors, who are less motivated to provide overly favorable ratings. A meta-analysis by Oh, Wang, and Mount (2011) addressed this question and found that compared to self-ratings, observer ratings of personality were much stronger predictors of performance. The use of a single observer rating yielded correlations that were approximately 60% higher than for self-ratings of conscientiousness and approximately 40% higher than for self-ratings of emotional stability. The correlations were even higher when multiple observer ratings were used. Overall, these findings strengthen the conclusion that conscientiousness and emotional stability predict overall job performance.

The higher predictive correlations for observer ratings of personality raise the question: Why not use observer ratings rather than self-ratings of conscientiousness and emotional stability to select people? Unfortunately, from an implementation perspective, there are a host of potential reasons that make this problematic. One issue is ensuring that the procedures for gathering observer ratings are standardized across applicants. For example, how are raters identified? If the applicants choose the raters, does this lead to a positive bias in the ratings? How many raters should be obtained for each applicant, and should the same number of raters be used for each applicant? Is it acceptable to have ratings from different perspectives (e.g. peers, subordinates, and customers) for applicants or should the procedures be standardized so that all applicants are rated by the same number of raters from the same perspective? This is an important issue because Oh et al. (2011) found that the validity of observer ratings is higher for ratings from some perspectives (superiors and peers compared to subordinate) and when there are more raters. Further, will colleagues from previous jobs be reluctant to make realistic, but perhaps negative ratings for fear of personal or legal repercussions? Once collected, an issue is how the information is combined to decide whom to hire. Is it a simple average of ratings or should more weight be given to ratings from certain perspectives (e.g. a previous supervisor) than others? We note that many of these same issues apply to the use of letters of recommendation as a selection tool, and despite these limitations, letters of recommendation continue to be a widely used selection method (even though the validity is relatively low). In sum, the use of observer ratings of personality is intriguing because it could increase the validity of conscientiousness and emotional stability (perhaps significantly) in predicting work outcomes. Nonetheless, there are logistical, psychometric, and ethical issues that need to be addressed before we advocate the use observer ratings of personality for the selection of candidates.

Another issue related to implementation is whether personality traits such as conscientiousness and emotional stability can be permanently changed through training and developmental activities. If so, instead of implementing personality tests to select people, organizations could train people to become more conscientious or emotionally stable. At present, there is little evidence that training programs can lead to changes in an individual's personality traits that transfer across situations and are sustained over time. Further, such training programs may be impractical as they would require intense and frequent activities conducted for a long time. Interestingly, there is evidence from longitudinal studies that individuals' personalities gradually and naturally change over time. The good news is that individuals appear to change for the better as they become more conscientious, emotionally stable, and agreeable as they grow older (Damian, Spengler, Sutu, and Roberts, 2019).

Finally, one cautionary note is in order regarding the implementation of personality tests. Selection procedures such as personality tests should not be adopted casually by managers who know little about them. A personality test can be an effective management tool, but it should be implemented with an understanding of its appropriateness for specific jobs or work outcomes and knowledge of how the test should be administered, scored, and interpreted. To successfully implement the general principle that we advocate in this chapter, it is essential that the measures of personality are developed according to scientific and professional guidelines to ensure high reliability and validity. (See Principles for the Validation and Use of Personnel Selection Procedures, 5th edition, developed by the Society for Industrial and Organizational Psychology for an authoritative document for employee selection testing.)

Case Examples

1. Relationship of Conscientiousness and Emotional Stability to Career Success

Judge and associates (1999) investigated the relationship between traits from the Big Five model of personality to success in careers spanning over 50 years. The ability to predict success 50 years after assessing personality provides a rigorous test of the utility of selecting applicants using conscientiousness and emotional stability. The data for this study were obtained from the Intergenerational Studies, administered by the Institute of Human Development, University of California at Berkeley. The sample (average $N = 194$) was derived from children born in Berkeley, CA, USA in 1928 and 1929. Many measurements were collected from participants over the 60-year course of the study. For example, there were two studies during later childhood (11–13 and again 16–18), as well as three major follow-up studies conducted when participants were in early adulthood (30–38), middle age (41–50), and in late adulthood (53–62). In addition to collecting personality and intelligence test data, the subject's job satisfaction, income, and occupational status were collected during each of these studies. Thus, the records were rich with evidence for personality and career outcomes, and comparisons were made across data collected at five different points in time (ranging from childhood to late adulthood).

Both childhood and early adulthood assessments of personality revealed enduring relationships between personality traits and later career success. For example, childhood assessments of conscientiousness and emotional stability were moderately strong predictors of job satisfaction, income, and occupational status, even in late adulthood. These results are remarkable as they show that measures of conscientiousness and emotional stability are effective predictors of satisfaction and career success over a 50-year time span. Another noteworthy finding is that these two personality traits explained measures of career success, even after controlling for the influence of intelligence. Taken together, these results show that highly conscientious and emotionally stable children earned higher salaries years later, were more satisfied with their work, and attained higher positions in the social hierarchy later in life. This real-world example forcefully illustrates the staying power of these personality traits to influence retention and productivity on the job. Obviously, organizations will be better off selecting individuals who, at hire, are more conscientious and emotionally adjusted, as they will be rewarded by those decisions with higher performance and more committed employees for years to come.

2. Conscientiousness and Emotional Stability and Astronauts Going to Mars

NASA is planning to send the first humans to Mars in the 2030s. People who apply to be astronauts will go through a rigorous selection process, as was demonstrated in the 1983 movie *The Right Stuff*, which focused on the seven military pilots who were selected to be the astronauts for Project Mercury, the first human spaceflight by the United States. Historically, "the right stuff" meant the astronauts possessed toughness and courage, had advanced degrees in science or math, were experienced test pilots, and were in excellent physical condition. But a recent study finds that these qualities may not be enough. In a study published in the journal *Astrobiology*, McMenamin, Allen, and Battler (2020) investigated the qualities of astronauts that were essential to survive in the Martian environment with a small team working in very close quarters. The authors simulated crew dynamics and exercises analogous to a Mars mission in the Dhofar region of Oman, which is a good representation of the Martian environment in terms of isolation and extreme conditions. The five astronauts, four men and one woman between the ages of 28 and 38, lived for four weeks in a simulated Mars environment. Before, during, and after the mission, the astronauts rated the performance of their team, severity of team conflicts, and their stress levels. At the end of the mission, the astronauts rated their own and teammates' personality traits. They also answered questions about their behavior in their respective roles and identified any counterproductive behaviors. Results showed that the most important trait among crew members was conscientiousness. The authors viewed conscientiousness collectively among the astronauts as a pooled team resource whereby the more conscientiousness a team has, the better it was at accomplishing tasks. The behavior among crew members that was most undesirable and considered completely unacceptable was social loafing, which refers to the tendency of people to exert less effort when working collectively as part of a group compared to performing a task alone. Obviously, a successful mission to Mars, and the very survival of the astronauts, depends on everyone doing their fair share of the work. Not surprisingly, there is zero tolerance for social loafing in astronaut crews. Moreover, the normatively low emotionality score of the team (a measure of the average member's neuroticism or low emotional stability) also likely contributed to the team's high functioning. Being higher on emotional stability allowed the team's members to deal with the stressful conditions, to avoid disruptions to the workflow and reduced the severity of interpersonal conflicts, which was viewed as reducing the stress experienced by the team. These findings with astronauts in a simulated setting affirm the general principle we have discussed in this chapter. People who are high on conscientiousness not only get more done, but also engage in less social loafing and other counterproductive behaviors. Similarly, people who are high on emotional stability will display reduced stress and anxiety as well as enhanced interpersonal relations.

Conclusion

Selecting employees based on conscientiousness and emotional stability positively impacts a broad and diverse set of work outcomes that are essential to organizational functioning. Conscientious and emotionally stable employees are more motivated to get things done; they exert greater effort, are more persistent in pursuing goals, and cope more effectively under stressful conditions. They also exhibit more positive work attitudes, are more committed to their work, and stay on the job longer. Additionally, they are better organizational citizens and team members and engage in fewer counterproductive work behaviors such as theft, bullying, and social loafing. In conclusion, hiring people based on higher levels of conscientiousness and emotional stability will lead to increased individual productivity and greater retention, which in turn will lead to increased organizational effectiveness.

References

Barrick, M. R., and Mount, M. K. (1991). The Big Five personality dimensions and job performance: A meta-analysis. *Personnel Psychology*, 44, 1–26.

Barrick, M. R., and Mount, M. K. (1996). Effects of impression management and self-deception on the predictive validity of personality constructs. *Journal of Applied Psychology*, 81, 261–272.

Barrick, M. R., Mount, M. K., and Judge, T. A. (1999). The FFM personality dimensions and Job Performance: Meta-Analysis of Meta-Analyses. Paper presented at the 15th Annual Conference of the Society of Industrial and Organizational Psychology, Atlanta, GA.

Barrick, M. R., Mount, M. K., and Li, N. (2013). The theory of purposeful work behavior: The role of personality, higher-order goals, and job characteristics. *The Academy of Management Review*, 38, 132–153.

Bryant, P., and Allen, D. (2013). Compensation, benefits and employee turnover: HR strategies for retaining top talent. *Compensation & Benefits Review*, 45, 171–175.

Choi, D., Oh, I. -S., and Colbert, A. E. (2015). Understanding organizational commitment: A meta-analytic examination of the roles of the five-factor model of personality and culture. *Journal of Applied Psychology*, 100, 1542–1567.

Damian, R. I., Spengler, M., Sutu, A., and Roberts, B. W. (2019). Sixteen going on sixty-six: A longitudinal study of personality stability and change across 50 years. *Journal of Personality and Social Psychology*, 117, 674–695.

Faulk, D., and Hicks, M. J. (2015). The impact of bus transit on employee turnover: Evidence from quasi-experimental samples. *Urban Studies*, 53.

Feingold, A. (1994). Gender differences in personality – A meta-analysis. *Psychological Bulletin*, 116, 42.

Foldes, H. J., Duehr, E. E., and Ones, D. S. (2008). Group differences in personality: Meta-analyses comparing five U.S. racial groups. *Personnel Psychology*, 61, 579–616.

Ghadi, M. Y., Fernando, M., and Caputi, P. (2013). Leadership and work engagement: The mediating effect of meaning in work. *Leadership & Organization Development Journal*, 34, 532–550.

Hogan, R. T., and Hogan, J. (2007). *Hogan Personality Inventory Manual (3e.)*. Tulsa, OK.: Hogan Assessment Systems.

Hough, L. M. (1992). The "Big-Five" personality variables – Construct confusion: Description versus prediction. *Human Performance*, 5, 139–155.

Hurtz, G. M., and Donovan, J. J. (1998). Personality and job performance: Will the real "Big Five" please stand up? Paper presented at the 13th Annual Conference of the Society for Industrial and Organizational Psychology, Dallas.

John, O. P., and Srivastava, S. (1999). The Big-Five trait taxonomy: History, measurement, and theoretical perspectives. In L. A. Pervin and O. P. John (eds), *Handbook of Personality: Theory and research* (Vol. 2, pp. 102–138). New York: Guilford Press.

Judge, T. A., and Ilies, R. (2002). Relationship of personality to performance motivation: A meta-analytic review. *Journal of Applied Psychology*, 87, 797–807.

Judge, T. A., Heller, D., and Mount, M. K. (2002). Five-factor model of personality and job satisfaction: A meta-analysis. *Journal of Applied Psychology*, 87, 530–541.

Judge, T. J., Higgins, C. A., Thoresen, C. J., and Barrick, M. R. (1999). The Big Five personality traits, general mental ability, and career success across the life span. *Personnel Psychology*, 621–652.

Le, H., Oh, I. -S., Robbins, S. B., Ilies, R., Holland, E., and Westrick, P. (2011). Too much of a good thing: Curvilinear relationships between personality traits and job performance. *Journal of Applied Psychology*, 96, 113–133.

McMenamin, J., Allen, N. J., and Battler, M. (2020). Team Processes and Outcomes During the AMADEE-18 Mars Analog Mission. *Astrobiology*, Nov, 1287–1294.

Meinert, D. (2015). What do personality tests really reveal? *HR Magazine*, Society of Human Resource Management.

Meyer, G. J., Finn, S. E., Eyde, L. D., Kay, G. G., Moreland, K. L., Dies, R. R., Eisman, E. J., Kubiszyn, T. W., and Reed, G. M. (2001). Psychological testing and psychological assessment: A review of evidence and issues. *American Psychologist,* 56, 128–165.

Mount, M. K., Barrick, M. R., and Stewart, G. L. (1998). Five-factor model of personality and performance in jobs involving interpersonal interactions. *Human Performance,* 11, 145–165.

Oh, I. -S. (2009). The five-factor model of personality and job performance in East Asia: A cross-cultural validity generalization study (Doctoral dissertation). Retrieved from ProQuest Dissertations and Theses database (3374065).

Oh, I. -S., Wang, G., and Mount, M. K. (2011). Validity of observer ratings of the five-factor model of personality traits: A meta-analysis. *Journal of Applied Psychology,* 96, 762–773.

Principles for the Validation and Use of Personnel Selection Procedures (2018). *Industrial and Organizational Psychology: Perspectives on Science and Practice,* 11, 2–97.

Rubenstein, A. L., Eberly, M. B., Lee, T. W., and Mitchell, T. R. (2018). Surveying the forest: A meta-analysis, moderator investigation, and future-oriented discussion of the antecedents of voluntary employee turnover. *Personnel Psychology,* 71, 23–65.

Salgado, J. F. (1997). The five-factor model of personality and job performance in the European Community. *Journal of Applied Psychology,* 82, 30–43.

Salgado, J. F. (1998). Criterion validity of personality measures based and non-based on the five-factor model. Paper Presented at the 106th Annual Convention of the American Psychological Association, San Francisco.

Salgado, J. F. (2002). The Big Five personality dimensions and counterproductive behaviors. *International Journal of Selection and Assessment,* 10(1–2), 117–125.

van Aarde, N., Meiring, D., and Wiernik, B. M. (2017). The validity of the Big Five personality traits for job performance: Meta-analyses of South African studies. *International Journal of Selection and Assessment,* 25(3), 223–239.

Wilmot, M. P., and Ones, D. S. (2019). A century of research on conscientiousness at work. *Proceedings of the National Academy of Sciences of the United States of America,* 116(46), 23004–23010. https://doi.org/10.1073/pnas.1908430116.

Zimmerman, R. D. (2008). Understanding the impact of personality traits on individuals' turnover decisions: A meta-analytic path model. *Personnel Psychology,* 61, 309–348.

Exercises

1. Consider the different strategies pursued by four food trucks located in a college community. The first food truck decides to compete on providing superior customer service through friendly, cordial, and welcoming interactions with customers. The second competes on innovation and adaptability by continually offering new, different, and trendy foods. The third food truck wants to compete by cutting costs associated with inventory shrinkage and cashier theft and will shut down trucks immediately once an employee is caught engaging in theft or other wrongdoing associated with counterproductive behavior.

The fourth seeks to compete based on speed and efficiency, because most customers are on their lunch break and have only limited time to receive and consume their food. When selecting employees, what personality traits should each food truck identify in applicants to help attain its stated goals? Explain why.
2. A large national retail organization specializing in upscale, trend-forward merchandise that appeals to a younger clientele is experiencing considerable difficulty managing its employees. Morale is very low, and there have been numerous incidences of bullying and incivility among employees. Theft among employees has increased and is much higher than the national retail average. Absenteeism and turnover rates are also much higher than the national average. The retailer is considering several interventions to address these problems including the use of personality tests but is very skeptical that personality tests could be of any help. Explain why the use of a professionally developed personality test based on the FFM of personality to select employees could be a viable way to help address the problems facing this employer.
3. This exercise pertains to your personal experience in the workplace or in school settings. Think about someone (coworker, boss, direct report, and teammate) you interacted with frequently who was low on conscientiousness or emotional stability (or both). What behaviors or attitudes did this person exhibit that are representative of low conscientiousness or low emotional stability? Did the behaviors and attitudes exhibited by this person hinder their ability to get things done? If so, how? Did these behaviors and attitudes impact you or your team's ability to accomplish work goals? Please explain.
4. Please watch the following video(s):
   a. Who are you, really?: https://www.youtube.com/watch?v=qYvXk_bqlBk
   b. How can different personality types work together effectively: https://www.youtube.com/watch?v=yzAxu1nBMfE

Now form small groups to discuss the video(s) and answer the following questions:

1. What are the major points of the video?
2. How can you use information from the video in your career?
3. Based on the video, what advice do you have for leaders in organizations?

Be prepared to present the ideas from your small group discussion with the class as a whole.

Discussion Questions

1. What is conscientiousness?
2. What is emotional stability?
3. Under what circumstances are conscientiousness and emotional stability important?
4. What would you advise employers regarding conscientiousness and emotional stability?

3

Structure Interviews to Recruit and Hire the Best People

CYNTHIA KAY STEVENS

Robert H. Smith School of Business, University of Maryland, College Park,
College Park, Maryland 20742
Tel: 301-405-2233
cstevens@rhsmith.umd.edu

Organizations use employment interviews as a primary means for applicants and hiring managers to meet and gather information from each other for the purpose of making selection and job choice decisions. When applicants or employers have limited time and many alternatives, interviews offer a flexible, efficient format in which to exchange information. Unlike other selection devices (e.g. tests and biodata inventories), interviews do not require expert advice and large samples for development and implementation. They typically do not raise the legal challenges and equal employment opportunity concerns that standardized tests do. Moreover, interviews can be easily adapted to accomplish different goals: introducing applicants and employers, attracting applicant interest, screening out unsuitable candidates, and clarifying the rank order of finalists. Such efficiency and flexibility may account for its popularity; interviews, along with reference checks, are the most common selection procedure used across a wide range of jobs and industries (Bureau of National Affairs, 1988; see Dipboye, 1992).

Paradoxically, their flexibility also makes it difficult to use interviews effectively. Interviews can vary widely in terms of how many applicants and interviewers are present, question types and sequences, topics covered, how much training and information interviewers and applicants have beforehand, consistency of practices across applicants, and how interviewers' evaluations are used. Some interview formats are better than others at achieving selection and recruitment goals; mismatches between the format and interview goals can impair the quality of managers' and applicants' decisions.

Empirical research has focused on how well interview ratings predict actual job performance, as measured by the correlation coefficient between interviewers' ratings and hired applicants' job performances. Although this research has offered useful insight into the interview formats needed to make good hiring decisions, the use of interviews to achieve other organizational goals (such as attracting top applicants) suggests the need for a broader perspective on how to design effective interviews.

An issue is the need to make good *joint* decisions – that is, to exchange accurate information that enables both applicants and organizations to make the best decisions given the alternatives available to each. To do this, managers can *structure* interviews so that they both provide and collect valid information for use in making decisions.

The purpose of this chapter is to review and summarize what we know about improving decision-making in employment interviews. A key theme of this chapter is that, by understanding the factors that impair information quality or exchanges, managers can structure interviews to improve both decision quality and hiring and recruitment outcomes. I begin by describing decision-making research and the factors that affect applicants' and interviewers' judgments and decisions. Then, I discuss nine subprinciples for designing interviews to improve decision-making. Finally, I conclude with examples of how poorly designed interviews might be restructured to enable both applicants and interviewers to make better decisions.

Decision-Making Research

Decision theorists have converged on the idea that people use one of two processes for making decisions: a rapid, largely unconscious, implicit approach in which choices are made with minimal effort, or a slower, deliberative, controlled approach in which alternatives are consciously weighed and compared (Evans, 2008). Particularly when facing numerous alternatives, decision-makers will use these processes sequentially – first automatically screening out candidates that fail to meet some possibly arbitrary criteria, then concentrating their efforts on a closer, more conscious, evaluation of those that remain (e.g. Payne, Bettman, and Johnson, 1988; Svenson, 1992). This two-stage approach is common in both hiring and application decisions, in which "unsuitable" choices are eliminated quickly and without much conscious thought, and conscious effort is focused on a smaller subset. For example, both applicants and hiring managers often make early decisions about whether to interview on the basis of limited information (e.g. presence of grammatical errors in résumés; company reputation or familiarity) and then use later information (including that gained from interviews) to evaluate each other more thoroughly.

Within this dual-process approach, researchers have identified many cognitive, motivational, and contextual factors that affect decisions. The *cognitive factors* include how decisions are framed (e.g. as the potential gain or possible loss of good employees; see Tversky and Kahneman, 1981), a number of heuristics or mental shortcuts used to evaluate alternatives (e.g. comparing the similarity of candidates to current employees to judge suitability – see Tversky and Kahneman, 1974; or considering résumé length to judge applicant quality – see Chinander and Schweitzer, 2003), and a tendency to look for information that confirms, rather than tests, one's expectations (e.g. seeking answers that "screen in" rather than rigorously evaluate a favored candidate; see Snyder and Swann, 1978). *Motivational factors* include decision-makers' goals, such as the desire to grow and develop versus to maintain a steady state (e.g. to hire someone with potential versus an established performer; see Brockner and Higgins, 2001), a desire to experience happiness or avoid disappointment with the decision's outcome (see Mellers, 2000), or the desire to justify a preferred conclusion (see Boiney, Kennedy, and Nye, 1997). Finally, *contextual factors* include the conditions or circumstances under which people make decisions, such as how many alternatives are available, what their characteristics are relative to each other, and the timing of the decision (see Hsee, Blount, Loewenstein, and Bazerman, 1999). For example, evaluations shift depending on the set of alternatives available: an applicant with average qualifications will be evaluated quite differently depending on whether they are the only candidate available or one of several candidates all of whom have either strong or weak qualifications.

In summary, applicants and hiring managers will use a combination of rapid/low effort and slower/deliberative decision processes when evaluating their choices. An examination of how the interview context and both individuals' cognitive processes and motivations influence these types of decision-making enables us to identify strategies for improving the quality of their decisions.

Decision-Making in Interviews

Interviews enable applicants and employers to meet – either face-to-face or via technology – to exchange information that will allow them to make decisions about each other. As such, it is useful to explore what we know about the context, cognitive demands, and motivations of each party and how these factors affect their evaluations.

Interviewers' Decisions

Available studies show that interviewers' judgments can be swayed by many of the cognitive, motivational, and contextual factors that affect other types of decisions. For example, interviewers often judge applicants' suitability using implicitly held stereotypes about race, gender, age or disability status (e.g. Hitt and Barr, 1989; Reilly, Bockettie, Maser, and Wenet, 2005; Segrest Purkiss, Perrewé, Gillespie, Mayes, and Ferris, 2006), although the impact of some factors such as applicants' race may be less than that found for standardized tests (Huffcutt and Roth, 1998). Some evidence suggests that interviewers weigh negative information about applicants more heavily than they do positive information (Macan and Dipboye, 1988), but the role that negative versus positive information plays depends on what sorts of judgments must be made and how involved interviewers are in the decision process (see Posthuma, Morgeson, and Campion, 2002).

Several features of the interview context and its goals can also shift interviewers' motivation and thus their evaluations. Research shows that when determining applicant suitability, interviewers often unconsciously consider personal qualities (e.g. interpersonal skills or appearance; see Huffcutt, Conway, Roth, and Stone, 2001;

Pingitore, Dugoni, Tindale, and Spring, 1994), how similar they are to applicants (e.g. Kristof-Brown, Barrick, and Franke, 2002), and how well they think applicants would fit with their organization's culture (Cable and Judge, 1997), regardless of whether others in their organization would agree with their assessments or whether those qualities are important for successful job performance. This subjectivity leaves room for applicants to present themselves as likable or similar to interviewers as a strategy to obtain higher interviewer evaluations (Levashina and Campion, 2007). Further, some studies have suggested that interviewers may use résumé and background information about applicants to form preliminary impressions about their suitability and then elicit information during interviews that confirms these early impressions (Dougherty, Turban and Callender, 1994), although additional careful studies of this issue are needed. Contextual factors such as whether applicants are evaluated sequentially (versus compared to one another at the same time) and the number of openings (few versus many) also affect interviewers' judgments, such that applicants are held to higher standards when evaluated as part of larger pool or when there are fewer openings available (Huber, Northcraft, and Neale, 1990).

Because interviewers' evaluations can be affected by so many extraneous factors, an important question is whether interviewers, in general, can do a reasonably accurate job of predicting which applicants will perform well if hired. One possibility is to use at least three or four interviewers to *independently* interview each applicant; averaging these ratings yields good predictions regarding likely job performance (Schmidt and Zimmerman, 2004). If it is not possible to arrange for multiple interviews for each applicant, other studies have suggested that there are individual differences in interviewer accuracy – that is, some interviewers consistently make better predictions than others (Dougherty, Ebert, and Callender, 1986; but see Pulakos, Schmitt, Whitney, and Smith, 1996).

Applicant's Decisions

Although less research has examined applicants' decisions, the existing studies do suggest that many cognitive, motivational, and contextual factors can sway applicants' judgments. For example, applicants are concerned with finding jobs and organizations whose attributes provide a good fit with their interests and needs (Judge and Cable, 1997). Given that they often have little information to determine whether a given job opportunity provides a good fit, applicants may rely on signals to infer these attributes, such as whether the organization has a good reputation (Highhouse, Zickar, Thorsteinson, Stierwalt, and Slaughter, 1999), their beliefs about the organization's personality (Slaughter et al., 2004), and whether the interviewer was warm and personable during the interview (Chapman, Uggerslev, Carroll, Piasentin, and Jones, 2005). Some data suggest that applicants dislike structured interviews and report being less likely to accept job offers from organizations that use them (Chapman and Rowe, 2002), although the data are mixed on the latter point. Applicants also show evidence of biased judgments depending on how difficult they think it will be to obtain a job: they evaluate the opportunity more favorably following interviews if they think they may receive fewer job offers than if they expect to have many offers (Stevens, 1997).

Researchers have not examined whether applicants' decisions following interviews predict their subsequent job satisfaction or tenure with organizations. Nonetheless, some data indicate that interviews providing structured, realistic job information may help applicants self-select out of jobs in which they might be unhappy, and among those who do accept jobs, exposure to realistic job information leads to longer tenure on the job (see Buckley, Mobbs, Mendoza, Novicevic, Carraher, and Beu, 2002). This effect may be limited to situations in which applicants have other job offers from which to choose, however (Saks, Wiesner, and Summers, 1994).

Structured Interviews

Several modifications have shown promise for improving interviewers' accuracy, including training interviewers (Dougherty et al., 1986), having them set goals to form accurate impressions (Neuberg, 1989), and holding them accountable for their decisions and recommendations (Motowidlo, Mero, and DeGroot, 1995). However, the largest and most consistent gains in predicting which applicants will perform well on the job seem to come from *structuring* interviews – that is, standardizing some aspects of the questions asked, delivery, and evaluation process. Across interviewers, the use of structured interview formats leads to a better prediction of job performance (correlations range from 0.35 to 0.62) than does the use of unstructured interviews (correlations range from 0.14 to 0.33; see Huffcutt and Arthur, 1994; McDaniel, Whetzel, Schmidt, and Maurer, 1994).

Although interview structure is an important means for improving joint decision-making, some managers are unclear regarding what it means to structure an interview, and many fail to see the value of increasing interview structure (Van der Zee, Bakker, and Bakker, 2002). Campion, Palmer, and Campion (1997) identified 15 possible content and process dimensions on which interviews could be structured (e.g. using job analysis to determine question content, standardizing interview lengths, and using statistical procedures to combine interviewers' ratings). To reduce this list, Chapman and Zweig (2005) surveyed applicants and interviewers and found three primary areas that increase structure and one that reduces it. Features that increase interview structure include *question sophistication*, or using question formats known to yield valid information (such as past behavior description or situational questions); *question consistency*, or asking the same questions in the same order to all applicants; and *evaluation standardization*, or using the same numeric scoring procedures for rating all answers. *Rapport-building*, or asking non-content-related questions and making light conversation, is thought to put applicants at ease and improve their attraction to the organization, although it may reduce interview structure and any information obtained from applicants may be unrelated to their job performance. Their study found that interviewer training increased interviewers' use of standardized evaluations and sophisticated question formats, but had no effect on increasing consistency in questions asked. Importantly, applicants found highly structured interviews to be more difficult, but this did not reduce their intent to accept job offers.

Structuring interviews has many benefits for organizations and applicants, particularly in terms of increasing the exchange of valid information to make decisions. Clearly, there may be some trade-offs with interviewer and applicant discretion (Van der Zee et al., 2002), although the loss of control may not be as great as managers assume it will be. The next section describes how to improve interview structure.

Improving Decision-Making by Increasing Interview Structure

Effectively structuring interviews to improve decision-making is not difficult, but it does require advance preparation and critical analysis. Involving interviewers in the process of developing an interview structure can improve their job challenge and satisfaction (see Chapter 8). Moreover, it can communicate a greater sense of professionalism to applicants. To assist managers in improving the quality of decisions following interviews, I offer the following nine subprinciples.

Subprinciple 1: Identify the primary goals for the interview: recruitment, selection, or a combined focus.

Goals enable people to channel their efforts in appropriate directions and gauge their progress (see Chapter 5). They also affect interview decision-making by orienting interviewers to accomplish important tasks. Thus, interviewers need to have clear guidance regarding the purpose of their interviews: recruiting and attracting a larger applicant pool, screening out unsuitable applicants, or a combined focus on recruitment and selection. Such knowledge helps them determine the appropriate structure for their interviews – in particular, how much time should be devoted to collecting or providing information.

Subprinciple 2: Develop a set of questions – based on job analysis – that ask about applicants' capacity to perform the job.

All interviewers ask questions, and having a prepared set of questions with clear links to job performance can only help applicants and interviewers by signaling what attributes are important. To ensure that questions are relevant to the job, begin by reviewing available job descriptions or specifications, which should state the knowledge, skills, abilities, and other characteristics (KSAOCs) needed for success, the tasks performed, and essential work conditions. (O*Net online is a good generic source of job analysis information if job descriptions or specifications are lacking.) Identify the KSAOCs, tasks, and work condition requirements that are best assessed in an interview (e.g. intelligence is most effectively and reliably measured through cognitive ability tests; see Chapter 1), and write questions that ask – in a nontransparent manner – whether applicants have or can demonstrate those capabilities.

Formats

Two question formats have proven to be most effective for interviews: past behavior description and situational questions. *Past behavior description questions* ask for examples of past performance (e.g. "Tell me about a time when . . ."), *whereas situational questions* ask what applicants would do in a given situation (e.g. "How would you deal with a situation in which . . ."). As an example assessing customer service orientation, a past behavior description question might be, "Tell me about a time when you had to deal with the concerns of an upset customer – what was the situation and how did you respond?" A corresponding situational question would be, "Imagine you had to deal with an upset customer who did not receive their order when it was promised. What specifically would you do to deal with their concerns?" Some research suggests that all other factors equal, past behavior description questions may yield more useful information than situational questions (Taylor and Small, 2002), although both formats are superior to other types of questions that may be asked (e.g. applicants' opinions).

Subprinciple 3: Develop a set of scoring criteria for evaluating applicants' answers.

Once a set of interview questions has been written, it is extremely useful to create a set of criteria for evaluating applicants' answers. Having a scoring guide ensures that, no matter who conducts the interview, all applicants will be held to the same standards. Managers can identify which responses are optimal and which are problematic by talking to job incumbents, reviewing the work behavior of current good and poor performers, and in some organizations, examining the performance evaluations themselves to identify important indicators. Research shows that having and using scoring criteria provides a significant and independent contribution to accuracy when predicting applicants' job performance (Taylor and Small, 2002). To the extent that interviewers are inexperienced, providing scoring guidelines can also help to make the task of conducting interviews easier.

Subprinciple 4: When interviewing, ask all applicants the same questions in the same order.

Asking all applicants the same questions in the same order helps to provide comparable information about each applicant. It is inherently fairer, in that all applicants are given the same opportunity to explain what they can do and why they are qualified for the position. Some managers may resist such consistency, in that it limits their spontaneity and can make the interviews seem more rote. However, to the extent that interviewers spend a portion of each interview answering applicants' questions about their organizations, this concern may be less problematic.

Subprinciple 5: Ask interviewers to take brief notes on each applicant and to review their notes before rating applicants.

Data concerning this recommendation are mixed: interviewers who take detailed notes show better recall of information about applicants, but their judgments about applicants' performance potential are not necessarily more accurate than those of interviewers who do not take notes (Middendorf and Macan, 2002). However, asking interviewers to take some notes accomplishes several objectives: (i) it aids in holding interviewers accountable for their recommendations, which has been shown to improve the quality of their recommendations (Motowidlo et al., 1995), (ii) it communicates an interest in what applicants have to say, which can help when recruiting applicants, and (iii) it enables interviewers to recall applicants' answers when comparing or discussing job candidates.

Middendorf and Macan (2002) found that interviewers who wrote down key points were better able to differentiate between applicants, possibly because their attention was less divided between listening to applicants and writing. Moreover, they found that asking interviewers to review their notes *prior* to making ratings of applicants helped them to make more accurate ratings. Such an approach should help interviewers to focus on what applicants have to say, and to make ratings without the added pressure of responding to or shielding their evaluations from applicants who are seated nearby.

Subprinciple 6: Select or train interviewers to build rapport with applicants.

Research indicates that most applicants have determined which organizations they prefer well before their interviews (Collins and Stevens, 2002), but it also consistently shows that exposure to warm, personable interviewers improves their intentions to pursue or accept job offers (see Chapman et al., 2005). Interviewers who are high in extraversion and agreeableness are likely to be more successful in establishing rapport than are introverts or those low in agreeableness. If it is not possible to select interviewers who are naturally skilled at putting others at ease, interviewers can also be trained to improve their rapport-building behavior. For example, open nonverbal behavior (e.g. eye contact, smiling, and open body posture), welcoming statements, and a willingness to fully answer questions can improve applicants' perceptions of interviewers' personableness.

Subprinciple 7: If interviews receive preinterview information about applicants, make sure that it is valid.

Research shows that, when interviewers have access to preliminary information about applicants (e.g. from résumés or test scores), it may prompt them to form impressions about applicant suitability, which then affects how they conduct the interview (Dougherty et al., 1994). This problem has led some experts to recommend that *all* preinterview information be withheld from interviewers (e.g. Dipboye, 1989). Although this recommendation may ensure that interviews are not biased, it may not always be practical. For example, this procedure would not enable interviewers to clarify incomplete or ambiguous résumé or application information, and it may make it more difficult for interviewers to understand fully the context for applicants' answers.

Thus, it is important to be aware of the problems associated with preinterview information and to take steps to ensure that it is accurate, valid, and used appropriately. For example, if interviews will be used for screening purposes, ensure that any preinterview information is valid – that is, it has a reliable, statistical relationship with job performance. It is also valuable to independently verify basic information from the résumé, such as degrees earned, prior employers and dates of employment, as a single phone call can quickly eliminate unscrupulous applicants. If interviews are being used to *recruit* applicants, access to preinterview information may help determine how best to describe the job and organization. If interviewers' preinterview expectations are based on valid, accurate information, behavioral confirmation tendencies during the interview should pose less of a problem and may enable interviewers to shift their emphasis to recruiting promising applicants (Posthuma et al., 2002).

Subprinciple 8: Ask applicants about their decision process and criteria, and share realistic information tailored to those processes and criteria.

Just as managers are interested in applicants who fit with their organizations, applicants typically seek organizations that provide a good fit with their interests and needs (Rynes, Bretz, and Gerhart, 1991). Most applicants share similar concerns such as job type, location, pay level, and training opportunities. However, the specific type of information they want and how it will affect their decision process can vary across applicants as well as within applicants over time. Thus, interviewers can structure interviews to help applicants make good decisions by asking about the criteria that will be important in their decisions and the context in which their decisions will be made.

There are several benefits to this form of interview structure. First, interviewers can offer realistic information tailored to applicants' interests, rather than giving a standard "speech" about their organizations' positive attributes. To the extent that other firms do not provide such individualized approaches, this practice may help firms gain an advantage in attracting applicants' interest. A second benefit is that such information can help interviewers estimate the probability that an offer would be accepted if extended. Applicants for whom one's organization does not meet important criteria are less likely to accept offers, and firms that identify such mismatches early may focus their effort toward pursuing other attractive applicants who are likely to accept offers.

Interviewers may also find it helpful to inquire about applicants' decision process, particularly the number of offers they expect to or have received. This contextual factor has dramatic effects on decision-making in other contexts – decision-makers may reverse their preference for the same option when it is presented by itself versus as one of multiple options from which to choose (Hsee et al., 1999). Consistent with this, recruitment research has shown that applicants who expect to receive fewer offers evaluate a given firm more favorably after their interviews than do applicants who expect to receive multiple job offers (Stevens, 1997). Interviewers, thus, may gain insight into how their recruitment information will be received by asking about applicants' expectations for success in their job searches.

Subprinciple 9: If it is not possible to structure interviews, then arrange for three to four independent interviewers to meet with each applicant.

As suggested earlier, structured interviews consistently provide valid, predictive information about which applicants are likely to perform well on the job (e.g. Huffcutt and Arthur, 1994). Yet, Schmidt and Zimmerman (2004) found that averaging the ratings of three to four *independent* interviewers who used unstructured interviews also yielded good predictions about applicants' likely job performance. Thus, if it is not possible to structure interviews, hiring managers can approximate their accuracy by obtaining and averaging the ratings from a set of unstructured interviewers. Of course, the best situation would be to conduct structured interviews with three or four independent interviewers – organizations would obtain high-quality information about applicants' capabilities, and applicants would be able to hear multiple perspectives on what they could expect from the job and organization if hired.

CASE EXAMPLES

Structure helps interviewers gather and disseminate information useful for making decisions. To illustrate this process, I provide several examples from my research (Stevens, 1998). The first comes from the transcript of an untrained interviewer who was screening applicants for a large public accounting firm. Untrained interviewers ask fewer open-ended, follow-up, and performance-differentiating questions, and they tend to ask such questions in ways that are transparent – that is, phrased to indicate the desired response. This interviewer's questions are typical of this (the numbers represent turns at talk).

Untrained Interview Case

INTERVIEWER: What else have you done that ah, you feel would be helpful to you in public accounting?

APPLICANT: Oh, gee, as far as extracurricular? Well, I was in a lot of service clubs and, you know, I've worked with people, done March of Dimes, things like that. Just dealing with people.

INTERVIEWER: How would you say your communication skills are?

APPLICANT: I think they're pretty good. I think I have pretty good communication skills. Listening is part of it, yeah, so –

INTERVIEWER: Okay.

To screen applicants effectively, this interviewer could improve the information obtained by rephrasing and following up on these questions. For example, the question about what the applicant has done that would be helpful in a career in public accounting would yield more helpful data if the interviewer asked follow-up questions about what roles the applicant had held in various service clubs, and what specific things she had done for the March of Dimes. Asking about specific instances in which the applicant had worked with other people in these roles would provide important indications about how the applicant would interact with clients and coworkers. Likewise, the question about communication skills would prompt most applicants to answer that they had good communication skills – the "correct" answer is transparent. Rather than asking applicants for an evaluation of their own skills and taking that information at face value, the interviewer might instead ask past behavior description questions about instances in which the applicant had misunderstandings with other students or coworkers, and what she did to address those problems. Answers to this type of question would provide more concrete data about the applicant's communication skills and would allow fewer opportunities for the applicant to manage the interviewer's impression.

Past Behavior Description-Based Interview Case

In contrast, the following (edited) segment shows how interviewers using past behavior description questions can gather high-quality information.

INTERVIEWER: . . . Now I'd like to spend a little bit of time talking about decision-making and problem solving. Tell me about a particular difficult decision you had to make.

APPLICANT: Um, well . . . that ah, decision on the design approach, it was very difficult for me. 'Cause I didn't want to – I had the authority to overrule the design team. But I didn't want to use that um, unless I was absolutely sure they were wrong. I didn't want to alienate either the architect-engineer or the design team. And that resulted in a lot of squabbles and a lot of running back and forth negotiating between people to find out what – what is the best way . . .

INTERVIEWER: Mmm. So what were the things, some things you just considered in your decision?

APPLICANT: Um, I had to consider the qualifications of the person. Ah, whether they really knew what they were talking about. Um, another factor was, there was a definite bias between the design team and the architect-engineer. They all took many years of, of infighting. And I had to try to consider how much of this is just due to the fact that "This person's designing it, so I know it's no good," as opposed to, "It's just . . . not going to work in our best interests."

INTERVIEWER: Okay. And so what do you . . . see then you decide where you ended up going with . . . ?

APPLICANT: Design team's modifications, even though it was more expensive. In the long run, it proved to be ah, a better, um more cost-effective way of operating.

Untrained Recruitments Interview Case

Recruitment goals can also be met by structuring interviews through training and use of standardized questions. Recruitment-oriented interviewers are less likely than screening-oriented interviewers to receive training; given that untrained interviewers are seen by applicants as less organized and less professional, this trend is unfortunate. Untrained interviewers tended to talk more, jumping between asking and answering questions, providing unrequested information, and digressing into non-job-related topics. This problem is illustrated in the next example, in which an untrained interviewer sought to recruit an applicant for an insurance sales position. Although this segment is edited, the dialogue between this interviewer and applicant followed the same pattern in which he did most of the talking.

INTERVIEWER: Here are some reasons why you would want to choose a career with [name of firm]. We guarantee your income while you start, develop your own image on being your own boss, getting, ah, getting into management career status, extra benefits, ah, and on the back here, 12 good reasons . . . why you would want to be an insurance agent. And, um, here is, ah, a brochure that explains ah, the training program in general . . . terms. It's a lifelong training program. Um, we have, we feel, the finest training, uh, in the industry, ahh, as a company . . . And I believe, in my district, we have ah, the finest training in America simply because we use the company training in the first six–twelve months or so, and after that we go into material, we make available to you material from the Insurance Institute of America. Now when I say make available to you, ah, we recruit and train people from all walks of life. Some people can't handle the material from the

Insurance Institute of America because it's college level and/or they don't have the math background or they don't have the interest, study skills . . . to do it. I put on six people in 19[. . .] and to date, ah, none of them have taken advantage of all the material that I could give them. Because, well, it's not all bad either. Some of them, three of them are college students and they're doing so well that they don't have the time, they won't take the time to, to attend the course. Ah, one of 'em has gone through a couple of 'em or attempted to go through a couple of 'em, but ah, nevertheless I've kept my end of the bargain and I would make it available to her and now in their second or third year, ah, they would take it a little more serious, ah the more advanced learning of insurance. Okay?

APPLICANT: Um-hmm.

INTERVIEWER: So we say we'll make it available to you, if you're good enough to take advantage of it, that's fine.

APPLICANT: Um-hmm.

This interviewer clearly had a lot of positive information about his company to convey to applicants. Yet, his approach – doing all the talking, without finding out the applicant's unique interests or criteria for making decisions – does not allow him to tailor his "pitch" to her as an individual. He may or may not cover information about his company that would be of interest to her. A smarter strategy would be to ask her questions about why she was exploring a career in insurance sales, what she is looking for in a job or company, and what other jobs and organizations she has considered. Not only would this approach be more efficient in assessing her interest and communicating the information of greatest value to her, it would also convey interest in and concern for her as an individual. This interviewer might also spend some time talking about the less attractive aspects of being in insurance sales as a way to make the rest of the information he provides appear more balanced and credible.

A good way to approach this issue is provided in a final example, which is too lengthy to reprint fully here. The opening was for a human resource internship rotation program in a large conglomerate, and the interviewer determined through the résumé and some preliminary questions that the applicant had excellent qualifications. She then shifted the focus of their discussion to the factors that would be important in the applicant's decision and discovered that his wife was applying to medical schools across the country. This enabled the interviewer to pinpoint several divisions to which he could be assigned that were located near his wife's preferred medical schools. Note that had she relied on a prepared speech about the company's programs and benefits, she would have neglected to provide this critical information about how her company could meet this applicant's needs.

Conclusion

Interviews are typically used as one in a set of selection/recruitment tools to make decisions about whom to hire and which job offers to accept. Because they are flexible, interviews can be used to accomplish multiple purposes, such as introductions, recruitment, screening out unsuitable candidates, and so on. However, this flexibility can also be a stumbling block, as research shows that decision processes are susceptible to many cognitive, motivational, and contextual influences that may degrade the quality of the final decision.

Increasing interview structure can help managers achieve their recruitment or selection goals by helping to minimize the impact of irrelevant factors on interviewers' and applicants' decision processes. Structuring interviews introduces some standardization in procedures to make the judgments that follow less idiosyncratic. Wisely structuring interviews to balance the need for standardization with the need for interviewer and applicant discretion can ensure that both organizations and applicants get the most out of the process.

References

Boiney, L.G., Kennedy, J., and Nye, P. (1997). Instrumental bias in motivated reasoning: More when more is needed. *Organizational Behavior and Human Decision Processes,* 72, 1–24.

Brockner, J., and Higgins, E. T. (2001). Regulatory focus theory: Implications for the study of emotions at work. *Organizational Behavior and Human Decision Processes,* 86, 35–66.

Buckley, M. R., Mobbs, T. A., Mendoza, J. L., Novicevic, M. M., Carraher, S. M., and Beu, D. S. (2002). Implementing realistic job previews and expectation-lowering procedures: A field experiment. *Journal of Vocational Behavior,* 61, 263–278.

Bureau of National Affairs. (1988, May). Recruiting and selection procedures. PPF Survey No. 146.

Cable, D. M., and Judge, T. A. (1997). Interviewers' perceptions of person-organization fit and organizational selection decisions. *Journal of Applied Psychology,* 82, 546–561.

Campion, M. A., Palmer, D. K., and Campion, J. E. (1997). A review of structure in the selection interview. *Personnel Psychology,* 50, 655–702.

Chapman, D. S., and Rowe, P. M. (2002). The influence of videoconference technology and interview structure on the recruiting function of the employment interview: A field experiment. *International Journal of Selection and Assessment,* 10, 185–197.

Chapman, D. S., Uggerslev, K. L., Carroll, S. A., Piasentin, K. A., and Jones, D. A. (2005). Applicant attraction to organizations and job choice: A meta-analytic review of the correlates of recruiting outcomes. *Journal of Applied Psychology,* 90, 928–944.

Chapman, D. S., and Zweig, D. I. (2005). Developing a nomological network for interview structure: Antecedents and consequences of the structured selection interview. *Personnel Psychology*, 58, 673–702.

Chinander, K. R., and Schweitzer, M. E. (2003). The input bias: The misuse of input information in judgments of outcomes. *Organizational Behavior and Human Decision Processes*, 91, 243–253.

Collins, C. J., and Stevens, C. K. (2002). The relationship between early recruitment-related activities and the application decisions of new labor-market entrants: A brand equity approach to recruitment. *Journal of Applied Psychology*, 87, 1121–1133.

Dipboye, R. L. (1989). Threats to the incremental validity of interviewer judgments. In R. W. Eder and G. R. Ferris (eds), *The Employment Interview: Theory, Research, and Practice* (pp. 45–60). Newbury Park, CA: Sage.

Dipboye, R. L. (1992). *Selection Interviews: Process Perspectives.* Cincinnati, OH: South-Western Publishing Co.

Dougherty, T. W., Ebert, R. J., and Callender, J. C. (1986). Policy capturing in the employment interview. *Journal of Applied Psychology*, 71, 9–15.

Dougherty, T. W., Turban, D. B., and Callender, J. C. (1994). Confirming first impressions in the employment interview: A field study of interviewer behavior. *Journal of Applied Psychology*, 79, 659–665.

Evans, J. St. B. T. (2008). Dual-processing accounts of reasoning, judgment, and social cognition. *Annual Review of Psychology*, 59, 255–278.

Highhouse, S., Zickar, M. J., Thorsteinson, T. J., Stierwalt, S. L., and Slaughter, J. (1999). Assessing company employment image: An example in the fast food industry. *Personnel Psychology*, 52, 151–172.

Hitt, M. A., and Barr, S. H. (1989). Managerial selection decision models: Examination of configural cue processing. *Journal of Applied Psychology*, 74, 53–61.

Hsee, C. K., Blount, S., Loewenstein, G. F., and Bazerman, M. H. (1999). Preference reversals between joint and separate evaluations of options: A review and theoretical analysis. *Psychological Bulletin*, 125, 576–590.

Huber, V. L., Northcraft, G. B., and Neale, M. A. (1990). Effects of decision strategy and number of openings on employment selection decisions. *Organizational Behavior and Human Decision Processes*, 45, 276–284.

Huffcutt, A. I., and Arthur, W., Jr. (1994). Hunter and Hunter (1984) revisited: Interview validity for entry-level jobs. *Journal of Applied Psychology*, 79, 184–190.

Huffcutt, A. I., and Roth, P. L. (1998). Racial group differences in employment interview evaluations. *Journal of Applied Psychology*, 83, 179–189.

Huffcutt, A. I., Conway, J. M., Roth, P. L., and Stone, N. J. (2001). Identification and meta-analytic assessment of psychological constructs measured in employment interviews. *Journal of Applied Psychology*, 86, 897–913.

Judge, T. A., and Cable, D. M. (1997). Applicant personality, organizational culture, and organization attraction. *Personnel Psychology*, 50, 359–395.

Kristof-Brown, A., Barrick, M. R., and Franke, M. (2002). Applicant impression management: Dispositional influences and consequences for recruiter perceptions of fit and similarity. *Journal of Management*, 28, 27–46.

Levashina, J., and Campion, M. A. (2007). Measuring faking in the employment interview: Development and validation of an interview faking behavior scale. *Journal of Applied Psychology*, 92, 1638–1656.

Macan, T. H., and Dipboye, R. L. (1988). The effects of interviewers' initial impressions on information gathering. *Organizational Behavior and Human Decision Processes*, 42, 364–387.

McDaniel, M. A., Whetzel, D. L., Schmidt, F. L., and Maurer, S. D. (1994). The validity of employment interviews: A comprehensive review and meta-analysis. *Journal of Applied Psychology*, 79, 599–616.

Mellers, B. A. (2000). Choice and the relative pleasure of consequences. *Psychological Bulletin*, 126, 910–924.

Middendorf, C. H., and Macan, T. H. (2002). Note-taking in the employment interview: Effects on recall and judgments. *Journal of Applied Psychology*, 87, 293–303.

Motowidlo, S. J., Mero, N. P., and DeGroot, T. (1995). Effects of interviewer accountability on interview validity. Paper presented at the Annual Conference of the Society for Industrial and Organizational Psychology, Orlando, FL.

Neuberg, S. L. (1989). The goal of forming accurate impressions during social interaction: Attenuating the impact of negative expectancies. *Journal of Personality and Social Psychology*, 56, 374–386.

Payne, J. W., Bettman, J. R., and Johnson, E. J. (1988). Adaptive strategy selection in decision making. *Journal of Experimental Psychology: Learning, Memory and Cognition*, 14, 534–552.

Pingitore, R., Dugoni, B. L., Tindale, R. S., and Spring, B. (1994). Bias against overweight job applicants in a simulated employment interview. *Journal of Applied Psychology*, 79, 909–917.

Posthuma, R. A., Morgeson, F. P., and Campion, M. A. (2002). Beyond employment interview validity: A comprehensive narrative review of recent research and trends over time. *Personnel Psychology*, 55, 1–81.

Pulakos, E. D., Schmitt, N., Whitney, D., and Smith, M. (1996). Individual differences in interviewer ratings: The impact of standardization, consensus discussion, and sampling error on the validity of a structured interview. *Personnel Psychology*, 49, 85–102.

Reilly, N. P., Bockettie, S. P., Maser, S. A., and Wenet, C. L. (2005). Benchmarks affect perceptions of prior disability in a structured interview. *Journal of Business and Psychology*, 20, 489–500.

Rynes, S. L., Bretz, R. D., and Gerhart, B. (1991). The importance of recruitment in job choice: A different way of looking. *Personnel Psychology*, 44, 487–521.

Saks, A. M., Wiesner, W. H., and Summers, R. J. (1994). Effects of job previews on self-selection and job choice. *Journal of Vocational Behavior*, 44, 297–316.

Schmidt, F. L., and Zimmerman, R. D. (2004). A counterintuitive hypothesis about employment interview validity and some supporting evidence. *Journal of Applied Psychology*, 89, 553–561.

Segrest Purkiss, L. S., Perrewé, P. L., Gillespie, T. L., Mayes, B. T., and Ferris, G. R. (2006). Implicit sources of bias in employment interview judgments and decisions. *Organizational Behavior and Human Decision Processes*, 101, 152–167.

Slaughter, J. E., Zickar. M. J., Highhouse, S., and Mohr, D. C. (2004). Personality trait inferences about organizations: Development of a measure and assessment of construct validity. *Journal of Applied Psychology*, 89, 85–103.
Snyder, M., and Swann, W. B. (1978). Hypothesis-testing processes in social interaction. *Journal of Personality and Social Psychology*, 36, 1202–1212.
Stevens, C. K. (1997). Effects of preinterview beliefs on applicants' reactions to campus interviews. *Academy of Management Journal*, 40, 947–966.
Stevens, C. K. (1998). Antecedents of interview interactions, interviewers' ratings, and applicants' reactions. *Personnel Psychology*, 51, 55–85.
Svenson, O. (1992). Differentiation and consolidation theory of human decision making: A frame of reference for the study of pre- and post-decision processes. *Acta Psychologica*, 80, 143–168.
Taylor, P. J., and Small, B. (2002). Asking applicants what they would do versus what they did do: A meta-analytic comparison of situation and past behaviour employment interview questions. *Journal of Occupational and Organizational Psychology*, 75, 277–294.
Tversky, A., and Kahneman, D. (1974). Judgment under uncertainty: Heuristics and biases. *Science*, 185, 1124–1130.
Tversky, A., and Kahneman, D. (1981). The framing of decisions and the psychology of choice. *Science*, 211, 453–458.
Van der Zee, K. I., Bakker, A. B., and Bakker, P. (2002). Why are structured interviews so rarely used in personnel selection? *Journal of Applied Psychology*, 87, 176–184.

Exercises

Interviewing Applicants Exercise

Imagine that you are preparing to interview applicants for a junior management consultant – a position in which incumbents conduct organizational studies and evaluations, design systems and procedures, conduct work simplifications and measurement studies, and prepare operations and procedures manuals to assist management in operating more efficiently and effectively. First, look up the necessary KSAOCs, required tasks, and common work environment conditions. You can find a wealth of information on O*Net (http://online.onetcenter.org). Using the information you find, choose three important requirements for the job and generate SIX structured interview questions (three using the behavior description format and three using the situational format).

Evaluating Applicant Answers Exercise

For each of the questions you listed earlier, come up with scoring criteria to evaluate applicants' answers. Using a scale that spans from 1 to 5, generate criteria that would help you differentiate very poor (1), low effectiveness (2), average (3), above average (4), and extremely effective (5) answers to your questions.

Video Analysis and Discussion

Please watch the following video(s):

1. Looking for a job? Highlight your ability, not your experience: https://www.youtube.com/watch?v=guXxy8LH2QM
2. Mastering the Art of the Interview: https://www.youtube.com/watch?v=ppf9j8x0LA8
3. Top Interview Tips: https://www.youtube.com/watch?v=HG68Ymazo18

Now form small groups to discuss the video(s) and answer the following questions:

1. What are the major points of the video?
2. How can you use information from the video in your career?
3. Based on the video, what advice do you have for leaders in organizations?

Be prepared to present the ideas from your small group discussion with the class as a whole.

Discussion Questions

1. Should companies use interviews to recruit and select employees? Why?
2. What advice do you have for managers regarding the use of interviews?
3. How can the interviewing process be improved?
4. What advice do you have for applicants regarding the interview process?

4

Attain Emotional Control by Understanding What Emotions Are[1,2]

EDWIN A. LOCKE

University of Maryland, Emeritus

"*Know thyself*"

— Inscription above the Temple of Apollo at Delphi, Greece

The theme of this chapter is that emotional control can only be attained by understanding what emotions are and that emotions can only be understood through introspection. There has been considerable interest in emotions in the workplace over the last decades, but most discussions of emotion (even those outside the fields of organizational behavior and industrial/organizational psychology) have lacked one thing: a definition of emotion!

Why? Because, as noted, one can only grasp the nature of emotions by introspection – by looking inwards at one's mental contents and processes – and introspection has been unofficially – and wrongly – banned (for reasons I need not go into here) from the field of psychology for close to 100 years (Locke, 2009).

[1] The author is indebted to Jean Maroney for helpful suggestions on this chapter.

[2] Note: Because my examples in this chapter refer to people's internal states, usable reports from businesspeople about their emotions are hard to come by. Thus, some of the cases I use in this chapter are fictional (the real ones will be noted). Nevertheless, I believe they are realistic, that is, representative of real experiences. Further, because introspection is the key to understanding emotions, there are substantial gaps in what quantitative studies of emotions reveal.

What Emotions Are

The causal sequence

I will begin by defining what I am talking about: *emotions are the form in which one experiences automatic, subconscious value judgments (value appraisals).* The appraisal theory was first identified in psychology, to the author's knowledge, by Arnold (1960), but see Peikoff (1991) for a more complete statement. Every emotion involves a specific type of value appraisal. For example:

- *Fear* is the form in which one experiences a perceived threat to one's life or well-being (or that of a loved one).
- *Anxiety* is similar to fear, but the nature of the threat is more uncertain and may involve one's self-esteem.
- *Sadness* is the form in which one experiences the loss of a value. (Depression is a more intense form of sadness involving self-deprecation and a sense of hopelessness.)
- *Anger* is the form in which one experiences a perceived injustice or goal frustration.
- *Guilt* is the form in which one experiences the perception of violating one's moral values.
- *Satisfaction* is the form in which one experiences having gained or possessed a value.
- *Love* is the response to something appraised as a positive value. (It is a stronger emotion than satisfaction and does not necessarily have to be possessed.)
- *Pride* is the form in which one experiences an achievement, including the achievement of one's moral character, due to one's own efforts.
- *Happiness* is the state of noncontradictory joy (stronger and more all-encompassing than satisfaction).
- *Admiration* is the form in which one appraises the achievement(s) of another person.

The universal pattern of every emotion (excepting those caused by abnormal brain states or hormone imbalances) is: object → cognitive identification → value appraisal → emotion. The *object* can be a thing, a person, an action, an event, an idea, a memory, or a previous emotion. (In some cases, people may not be aware of, or only peripherally aware of, what the precipitating object is.) *Cognitive identification* refers to observing the present context plus all the stored knowledge which the subconscious automatically associates with the object. The *value appraisal* stage involves "measuring" the object with respect to whether some value is perceived as being threatened or fulfilled in some form and to some degree. All *emotions* have either a positive or negative valence but to varying degrees – for example, loving is stronger than liking; hating is stronger than disliking.

Emotions are accompanied by various physiological reactions. However, there is not always a fixed, universal pattern of physiological sensations, that is, a unique indicator of one specific emotion for all people, though for certain basic emotions, such as fear, there may be broad similarities (e.g. increased heart rate). Basic emotions often have characteristic facial expressions.

The crucial point here is that the two middle stages, stored cognitive connections and value appraisals, are immediate and automatic (lightning fast and not chosen) rather than volitional, and they are subconscious rather than conscious. So, what one consciously experiences is: object → emotion. In a waking state, one is continually experiencing emotions because the subconscious is always at work, although many emotions are mild and fleeting and thus not significant enough to notice or analyze.

A mood is an enduring emotional state

A mood is enduring because the object (such as an unpleasant boss) is omnipresent or because the subconscious causes endurance based on memory (such as following the loss of a person or a job one loved) or due to rumination (replaying the triggering event or one's thoughts about it). Some have argued that moods are defined by their having no known causes. The cause of a mood is sometimes not known by the person experiencing it, but that does not mean it cannot be identified. A good strategy is to identify exactly when the mood began and what was happening at the time, with respect to events or thoughts. For example, a spat with one's romantic partner could cause one to feel depressed all day (or longer). The emotional remnants of an unpleasant work experience could linger for days or weeks or longer. (Admittedly, some moods, including ruminations, may be caused by hormone imbalances.)

It must be noted in passing that people can and have to make judgments consciously every day. Many decisions in life are made, and need to be made, by hard thinking (e.g. how to solve a problem at work, investment decisions, and conflicts with loved ones). But insofar as there is emotion involved, automatic judgments will always be in play.

What is the proof that the causal, subconscious processes noted earlier really exist and cause the emotion? One validates the process by introspecting backward in time. Consider the following example: Pat comes to a business meeting and is severely criticized by her boss for certain "mistakes" that caused the company to lose an important account. In reality, she was not to blame. It was the project leader who messed up the account, including by acting against her advice in several important respects, and then telling the boss that the outcome was Pat's fault.

The immediate, automatic emotion Pat will feel will be anger, because a grave injustice was committed toward her. The object was the attack. If asked what was upsetting after the fact, Pat could cognitively identify one key fact: the attack was based on false information. If asked what value was violated, Pat would say: the desire for just treatment (and/or honesty).

One can further validate the model by mental experiments in which the "script" is revised. "How," you ask Pat, "would you have felt if the boss had, instead of attacking you, blamed the project leader, after having gathered relevant information from reliable sources?" Pat's answer would probably be something like, "I would not feel anger. If the boss spoke factually without becoming enraged, I would have felt it was just but also a bit sad, because I wanted the project to succeed. If he had exploded with rage, I would have felt some anxiety, because it would mean the boss lacked self-control and could attack me next."

Next one could ask, "What would you feel if you deep down considered justice to be an unobtainable value in this world and never expected to see it." Pat would probably reply that what she would have experienced is a kind of hopeless, cynical resignation or sadness rather than anger.

One can validate the model by introspection, but one can also do it with a real-life pseudo-experiment. To show introductory psychology students the effect of ideas on emotions, I used to suddenly state, in the middle of a class, that we were going to have an unannounced quiz right then on the assigned reading which would count toward their final grade. The value standards involved are obvious. The two emotions that automatically emerged every time were: anxiety ("This could hurt my grade.") and anger ("This is unfair."). The emotions disappeared immediately when I said that I was just kidding in order to illustrate a point.

The important point here is that emotion is the result of three inputs: the object (event), the cognitive associations to the object and context, and the value appraisal(s). One input is conscious and two are subconscious, but change any of these, and the emotion is changed. (I will have more to say about changing emotional responses later.)

The findings of neuropsychology do not invalidate the previous model. Obviously, everything is stored in the brain, and physical processes occur somewhere (e.g. the limbic system and in several different places). But the brain is only the hardware. The ideas stored in the mind can be viewed as the software – they give the brain cognitive content. The concept of emotion would have no relevance or meaning to a totally unconscious being, nor would the concept of emotion have any meaning if all one talked about was the motions of neurons. You cannot introspect neurons. Consciousness is an emergent (and nonmystical) property of a certain type of nervous system and brain (Locke, 2018).

It is because people hold different ideas and values that the same object can cause different emotions in different people and different emotions at different times in the same person if the inputs change. An energized boss can be seen by one employee, who is very goal-directed and businesslike, as focused, whereas another employee who is very concerned with approval might see the same boss as cold and unfeeling. Even if the different emotions were processed in different parts of the brain, brain scans cannot identify the content of the person's ideas.

Multiple emotions

It is possible to experience more than one emotion toward an object, especially a person, at the same time. Pat could be not only angry but also anxious due to worry that she might be fired. Imagine an employee who cannot be located for three days. Then, he comes into the office with a brilliant marketing plan that could save the company. The manager might experience three different emotions: anger because of being frustrated by the employee's mysterious disappearance, relief that the employee showed up, and elation about the marketing plan. One can also hold emotions at different levels. At one level, an employee might admire a smart boss and at a deeper level feel jealous or inadequate. The human mind is an amazingly complex entity. (In romantic relationships, things can get even more complicated – but that is another book; see Locke and Kenner, 2011.)

Secondary appraisal

This term has caused some confusion. It can simply mean an appraisal of one's emotions or physical symptoms as noted earlier. But it is also used in another way to mean that there can be multiple appraisals of a situation. With more thinking and information gathering, there can always be more appraisals. After being fired, one might initiate many trains of though and information seeking, and each one could change one's appraisal and then one's emotions.

Emotions and action

Every emotion has a built-in action tendency (Arnold, 1960), that is, a felt impulse to action. (Again, such tendencies can be identified by introspection.) The survival value of, for example, lion → fear → run, etc. is obvious. The cave man who engaged in long, cognitive deliberation when confronted by a wild beast would not have many future opportunities to reproduce.

The action impulses for positive appraisals include wanting to keep, hold, or protect the valued objects. The impulses for negative emotions include wanting to avoid or harm (verbally or physically) the disvalued object.

It must be stressed that, although emotions automatically contain action impulses, everyone (this side of mental illness) has volitional choice as to what action to take in response to emotions. This too is validated by introspection.

Consider this example: Joe is called into the vice president's office and informed that he is being fired after 15 years with the company. Joe has long believed that he was unfairly treated and had all along been set up for failure by organizational politics. Joe is very angry at this perceived injustice. Joe's action impulse is to get justice. Many possible actions might occur to him immediately. (Others might occur to him later.) One is to punch the boss in the nose. Another is to give the vice president a tongue-lashing. Another is a blog attack on the company. Another is a lawsuit. Another is to pressure the company for a generous termination bonus. Another is to go home and get drunk. Another is to seek counseling, and so on.

Observe that Joe may consider many action alternatives, which might or might not be similar to those of a different fired employee, but no overt actions are forced on Joe by his subconscious. Joe will need to let go of the anger and think rationally. Joe has the power, despite whatever impulses he might have, to consider different responses and to choose among them. Here is where, although wanting to act, unlike the case of the lion menacing the cave man, he has time for deliberation, including the power to consider the pros and cons of various alternatives and to choose an appropriate course of action, including the choice of no action. Action choices can be delayed.

Which action Joe chooses will depend, in part, on his moral code. If he considers initiating physical force to be immoral, this will rule out all overtly aggressive acts. Of the remaining possibilities, the choice will depend on any number of personal factors such as knowledge, personality, thinking, and advice from others.

If Joe has spent his entire life acting impulsively, in which case he probably would never have held any job for very long and might even have a criminal record, self-control could be much more difficult because of the bad habits he had acquired.

Emotions and reason

It has been treated as a virtual axiom from ancient Greek philosophers to the present day that emotions and reason are inherently at odds, i.e. in conflict. This is known in philosophy as the mind-body dichotomy. (There are other versions of the mind-body dichotomy but reason versus emotion is the most common version.) The belief is considered even more rock-solid today because the center for emotions is partly located in a different part of the brain than the center for thinking. However, this does not prove the case, because different parts of the brain are widely interconnected. The evidence from cognitive therapy is that you can change emotions by changing the thoughts underlying them (Butler, Chapman, Forman, and Beck, 2006; Clark and Beck, 1999). And, as noted, one can see that emotions are the product of subconscious ideas by introspection.

I believe the concept of a mind-body dichotomy to be profoundly mistaken (see Peikoff, 1991, especially Chapters 5 and 7, for a more detailed discussion). The cause of this error is, most fundamentally, the inability or failure to introspect.

What people experience as clashes between reason and emotion are actually clashes between a consciously held and a subconsciously held idea. For example, a businessperson might feel conscious pride at making an honest profit but feel guilty because subconsciously they believe making a profit is immoral. A resolution would have to justify rational self-interest (see Peikoff, 1991, Chapter 11).

Consider Sandra, a unit manager. When things go wrong, she gets angry and has the automatic urge to lash out at her subordinates. She asks herself: "Why do I feel angry?" and realizes that her subconscious premise was, "All my employees should do everything right all the time." Or "I shouldn't have to be bothered by crises; I have other things I need to spend my time on." Or "This will make me look bad and hurt my career." Sandra may also experience disappointment, sadness, and anxiety.

Observe that the first two subconscious premises are mistaken; people do make mistakes and things just do not go perfectly all the time in any business. The third premise may be mistaken unless things go wrong constantly, but more relevant is what she learns from her mistakes, so that they are not repeated. If Sandra identifies her wrong premises through introspection, she has the power to correct them. Further, she can go deeper. She can ask herself why problems like this bother her in the first place. There may be self-doubt. "Am I hiring capable, conscientious employees? Are they getting proper direction and? Are crises occurring because there are issues that I did not make an effort to foresee? Do I need to take new actions?"

Although emotions contain action impulses, they are, in a fundamental respect, the passive part of one's psychology. Given the perceived objects and one's premises at a given time, emotions are not chosen or willed; they just happen. This is why one should never condemn oneself for an emotion as such. Reason is the locus of volition and the proper guide to action (Binswanger, 1991; Locke, 2018; Peikoff, 1991). This too is validated by introspection. One can choose whether to think or not to think. Reason is the active, self-caused part of one's psychology. Through reason, we have the power to understand our emotions, to choose what action we will take in response to them, and to reprogram them if needed. We can seek new knowledge or adapt our values based on what is possible. (Reprogramming can be very difficult in some cases – for example, childhood abuse and post-traumatic stress disorder.)

Consequences of emotion at work

It is interesting that studies of the consequences of subordinates' and leaders' emotions (or moods) at work – for example, decision-making, helping behaviors, absenteeism, and subordinate performance in response to leader emotions – often lead to inconsistent or contradictory findings (Grandey, 2008; Humphrey, 2008). This would be expected if there was no deterministic relationship between emotions and specific actions (as contrasted with felt action tendencies). One of the most consistent findings in the literature is that low job satisfaction is more likely to lead to turnover (quitting) than high satisfaction, but even here there are important exceptions (see Chapter 8). Since emotions in everyday life are not separate from cognitions (e.g. stored knowledge and interpretation of the current situation), one would need to know not only how a person feels but also how and what they think and their subconscious appraisals in order to predict and explain how they will act in the face of emotions.

Changing an emotion

Because emotions are automatic, one cannot change them directly; one can only change them indirectly by modifying their causes. Consider Joan who fails to get a much-wanted promotion at XYZ Corp. She feels great disappointment, sadness, some anger, and considerable anxiety because she "failed." What can Joan do? Check out the facts and her interpretations. Was there discrimination? Is her boss honest? What is the evidence? Did she lack some key skills? Can she get honest feedback about what she needs to do to improve her skills if necessary? Could they be acquired with more experience? Can she raise her self-efficacy? Is this the wrong company to work for? Could she do better at another company? Does she really like the work? Should she consider a career change? She can question her own value standards; is getting ahead here right now as important? Her choices have the power to affect how she feels. The point is that one is not helpless in the face of emotions, because, as I noted, *they are not psychological primaries, that is, unanalyzable* (chemical imbalances aside).

Emotions and life

The psychological role of emotions is not simply survival for the cave man. The issue goes deeper. *The role of emotions is to make your values psychologically real* – as opposed to flat, cognitive abstractions. There is an enormous difference between saying "X is logically a good thing" and feeling an actual (and sometimes burning) desire for it. You need to know WHY it is good for you. Without any desires, a person is just an unmotivated robot. Emotions are not tools of actual knowledge (knowing requires reason), but they are important aspects of motivation. They allow you to experience *wanting* and thus be motivated to act.

Tragic errors are made by those who reverse these roles of reason and emotion. Acting only on emotions without reason substitutes feelings for knowledge and thereby puts one's life out of control. An "emotionalist" will swing wildly from one impulse to the next with no sense of purpose or long-range goal and will make endless poor decisions. On the other side of the coin, using reason but repressing or denying emotions destroys one's capacity for joy and undermines one's motivation to pursue values. *The issue is not reason or emotion but both together, in harmony.* Harmony between reason and emotion is impossible without introspection. For example, a troublesome emotion can be caused by wanting the irrational – for example, wanting a promotion one does not deserve.

To summarize the key points made so far:

1. *Emotions are not unanalyzable primaries, but the consequences of ideas stored in the subconscious.*
2. *Emotions are automatic but can be changed indirectly by changing the inputs (their causes).*
3. *There is no innate or inherent conflict between reason and emotion; such clashes are actually clashes between consciously held and subconsciously held ideas.*
4. *Emotions do not compel action; everyone (who is not suffering from severe mental illness) has the power to make choices in the face of emotional responses (including the choice of taking no action).*
5. *Both emotions and reason are critical to a successful and happy life, but it is critical to understand the proper function of each and to keep them in harmony.*

Moderators

The key moderating factors in understanding emotion and in harmonizing reason and emotion are skill at introspection and the willingness to do it. People who will not or cannot introspect will feel afraid of their emotions, because they will seem causeless, incomprehensible, and uncontrollable. Change requires checking one's cognitions (beliefs), one's value standards, and one's implicit conclusions and trying to make rational changes and then acting accordingly.

Why do not people introspect? There are many reasons. One is that, in a way, it is not "natural." Extrospection is natural and necessary. Every child starts life by looking outward. Further, one gets immediate feedback if one fails to extrospect, like running into doors, or tripping over clothes, or touching something hot on the stove. There is no such immediate, unequivocal feedback for not introspecting, though one may come to believe that their feelings are mysterious and unchangeable.

Second, most people do not know how to introspect. No one teaches it, and psychologists have pretty much banned it from the literature for the past 100 years.

Third, most people do not see its value. The benefits are not immediately self-evident; it takes time to understand oneself and to see the payoff.

Fourth, introspection is hard work. Unlike extrospection (at the perceptual level), there is no special sense organ for looking inward. It is a volitional process requiring the use of one's conceptual faculty. Many people do not want to expend the effort of actually thinking (reasoning) about either their own consciousness or the outside world.

Fifth, many people fear introspection. They fear what they might find or what they might have to face. ("My God, I dislike my mother. I am a monster. Everyone is supposed to love their mother.") They fear that their emotions are primaries and are out of their control. They fear that understanding themselves might threaten their self-image or self-esteem, which is built on various defenses (e.g. denial, evasion) that they do not want to acknowledge. This can become a vicious circle, because the more they rely on defenses, the more vulnerable they become and the more defenses they have to erect. Defenses are designed subconsciously to escape from reality, but, in the end, reality cannot be escaped. The more "well-defended" an individual is, the more detached they are from reality. Of course, as implied earlier, people have the power to act against their fears.

Because most people are not very good at introspection, first self-reports of emotion should be at least partly suspect (i.e. acknowledged as subject to error) unless the individual has some skill at introspection.

Achieving Emotional Control

What does it mean to achieve emotional control? It does not mean to repress all emotion, that is, to give a standing order to one's subconscious not to allow any awareness of emotion to enter conscious awareness. This would be disastrous psychologically, as noted earlier.

Emotional control, as I view it, involves five elements:

1. Identifying, that is, *naming* your emotions – not every single one because that would occupy all your time but those which are most intense and/or enduring. This alone can enhance some feeling of control because naming emotions makes them less mysterious.
2. Identifying their causes. This includes positive emotions. If you know what brings you pleasure or happiness, you can take steps to expose yourself to the same object (assuming it is not harmful like smoking). For example, if you know what parts of your job you like the most, you can try to build more of those tasks into your job. This helps regulate your moods in a positive way. But usually when people talk of emotional control, they refer only to negative emotions. They mean things like not losing your temper or not being overwhelmed by panic or anxiety. This is too narrow.
3. Changing the causes when necessary. If the emotion is negative, you have three possible ways to intervene (object, cognition, values). You can change or avoid the objects, correct mistaken beliefs, and modify inappropriate values. The more strongly automatized they are and the more subconscious layers are involved, the more difficult the change process.
4. Consciously and rationally choosing what action(s), if any, to take based on your judgment and regardless of your emotions. *If you fail to act, your subconscious will file: This dweeb does not mean anything he or she says so I am not changing anything.*
5. Suppressing emotions temporarily, or actions based on them, *when necessary* in order to function in an emergency. Suppression is different from repression. Repression is subconscious and based on an implicit standing order to the subconscious ("Don't let me feel X."). Suppression is conscious. It involves deliberately and temporarily inhibiting an emotion (or an action based on it) because experiencing it or acting on it is not appropriate in a given context (e.g. it may be distracting or there may be conduct norms that it is important to honor).

When analyzing emotions, it can be very helpful to *write down* one's observations – for example, what emotion(s) one is feeling, the causal elements, the action tendencies and action choices, the errors one's subconscious may have made, etc. This makes the emotion more objective and helps one to slow down one's mental processes so that one can understand what has happened.

Case Examples

1. Mark

Let us begin with a negative example. Mark is a unit manager for a *Fortune* 1000 company. Since receiving his MBA from a high prestige school, Mark has received two promotions. Given his background, he wants and believes that he will surely become CEO of his company, or if not, of another *Fortune* 1000 company. However, he is having a hard time mastering his present job that is highly technical – nothing like the cases he studied in his MBA classes. He is feeling self-doubt, a threat to his self-esteem, and he cannot stand the feelings of anxiety that are the result of this doubt. Further, not being able to master something easily threatens his self-image as a brilliant person. He could study the technical aspects of his job more thoroughly, but this would imply that he cannot master things in a flash which his self-image requires. So, he tries desperately to work "around" his ignorance. He delegates some of the work but to people who know less than he does. He tries to bluff his way through meetings. When glitches occur, he angrily blames others, even though at some subconscious level which he will not make conscious, he knows that he is the one to blame. When his boss inquires about problems, he evades giving straight answers and assures his boss that things will be taken care of. Eventually things get more and more out of control and Mark has to reply increasingly on outright lies and then more lies to cover up those lies. Gradually, his projects fall apart, and he gets caught lying, because he can no longer recall which lies he told to which person. In the end, he is fired. His career, for now, is in tatters.

Imagine the difference in the outcome if Mark had honestly and openly identified his initial self-doubt and its cause: "I don't know how to do this job, and I feel inadequate and scared. I am trying to live up to a self-image which maybe is not a rational one." Then, he could have chosen what to do – for example, seek therapy, consult experts, study on his own, get more training, ask his boss for advice, change jobs, etc. The outcome could have been quite different if he had not evaded and let his unidentified emotions control him.

2. *Sandra*

Now, let us consider a real case sent to me by an acquaintance (with details changed to preserve anonymity). Sandra works as a manager in the software industry. She finds that introspection "is indispensable for running effective meetings. For instance, I have often been in meetings where people 'admit to a certain deception' such as being much farther behind in a project than they have been letting on." Her immediate reaction in this situation is anger and she knows the source: "It is unjust that this person misled me. At this point it is necessary to first let go of the anger [suppression] and be able to have enough concentration to determine what is the correct response" [consciously choosing what action to take]. She goes on, "I might even need to take into account future needs such as, 'I need to set an example'" so that others do not explode in anger when things go wrong. "Then I must decide how much emotion I want to express. How will each person at the meeting react to my reaction? For a while I thought that this whole process was itself a deception, but I realized that a good manager needs to be in control of their emotions and needs to be cognizant of the emotional responses of the people who work for them."

A manager must show self-control, or the employees will think they are living in an unpredictable, irrational universe. Sandra had to do two things in a situation like this in addition to understanding her emotions: (i) make clear that dishonesty was unacceptable, and (ii) make it safe for people who have a problem to admit them (but insist that it be done sooner).

Observe how many smart things Sandra ultimately did. First, she identified her emotional response (anger). Second, she identified its cause (injustice). Third, she thought about the proper response and realized that wrathful anger would be unwise and suppressed that impulse. Fourth, observe that her ability to introspect allowed her to empathize with others: she could foresee how others might react to her anger if it were extreme. That is why she suppressed it. Fifth, she used reason to decide exactly what she needed to communicate and how. (Incidentally, a precondition of empathy is understanding one's own emotions.)

Auxiliary Issues in Emotion

Is there such a thing as Emotional Intelligence (EI)?

In short, no (see Locke, 2005). EI has been defined in so many ways and has so many components (on which advocates do not even agree) that it is literally unintelligible. Intelligence is the capacity to grasp abstractions, but you do not need a high IQ to introspect about your emotions. The best terms for what I have been talking about are skill at introspection and the willingness to use that skill. A recent article (Mayer, Salovey, and Caruso, 2008) admits that the term has been defined too broadly. I have read more recent articles and studies on this subject and, sadly, these have only made the confusion worse. EI should be renamed as simply introspective skill. This means there is no need for the term intelligence here at all. It has been used just to give EI cachet. There is no doubt that introspective skill could be taught, and that existing and would-be managers could benefit from such training. This is not to say that introspection is the most important leadership managerial skill. I do not think it necessarily is (see the other chapters in this book), but it is a very useful one for reasons which I think I have made clear.

Emotional experience versus emotional expression

In the literature, emotional expression is called emotional "display" but that sounds rather like making emotions into a peacock. As noted from the last case, sometimes, it is best to suppress the overt expression of an emotion so as not to unduly upset others in the workplace. Here is the way to deal with justified anger without acting too angry. From manager to work team (let us assume that it is still Sandra speaking), "I have just learned that all the subtasks for our project X are behind schedule, even though I have been assured for the past several weeks that everything was on target. Let me say that this makes me quite angry for two reasons. First, I think I have been deceived. Maybe you were afraid I would blow up at you, but even if that were true (which it is not), how does it help to deny reality? It just makes the mess worse. From now on, I want you to tell me if you are having problems right away, and we will work to solve it. If you fail to do this in the future, I will assume you are lacking in moral integrity and will act accordingly. Second, because I was not kept informed, we may end up hurting our reputation with the customer and that reflects badly on us and our company. Now let us discuss how to ensure better information exchange and then how to fix this project."

The proper tone here would be serious and stern but not enraged or intimidating. It is clear that the manager is angry, and she has identified this but has not lost control of her anger. Further, she has explained the *reasons* for the anger and suggested specific actions that should be taken next.

What if the emotion is positive – for example, the company or unit just got a new, much desired contract, or some other good news? Here is a real-life example from Mickey Dresser, CEO of retailer J. Crew (and formerly of The Gap, from which he was fired; Brodie, 2008, p. 56). Mickey likes to use a public address system to communicate with employees. One day in the middle of lunch he was patched through to the office PA system to give this message:

> Hi, everyone, it's Mickey. I'm at Koi [a restaurant], waiting to meet my son for lunch, and I'm seeing a woman wearing our Florentine-print dress. Her friend just asked her where she got it. She said, "J. Crew." It's going to be a great lunch!

Dresser was clearly expressing excitement and joy based on the anticipation of great sales and wanted to share his feelings with his employees. One can guess that most employees were pleased by this announcement. This brings us to another point.

The effect of the manager on the mood of the office

Because managers are in a position of power (see Chapter 15), they can influence the mood of the whole office, especially the mood of people they come into direct contact with (maybe through email too). An angry, condemning mood will incite anxiety and fear in others, because the manager will be seen as a threat (even without making specific threats). In contrast, a manager who projects a benevolent mood will create a happier atmosphere. Of course, a manager has to be businesslike and have firm standards, but this is not incompatible with a pleasant demeanor. This issue brings up another one.

Should you fake emotions?

I agree with those who say: No (e.g. see Grandey, 2008). Employees can readily spot emotions that are not authentic. But how then can you set the mood of the office? Part of the answer lies in selection. Organizations should not choose people as managers who are not nice people (though obviously niceness is far from the only requirement). Some people are temperamentally (and ethically) unsuited to manage other people. But let us say you have personality problems and yet want to set a positive tone with your subordinates.

The first step would be to identify why your mood is predominantly negative; fixing this might require professional help. You may hold subconscious premises (e.g.

no one can be trusted, people are out to get me) that could be changed. (In some cases, medication or therapy may be called for as well.)

The next step would be to learn interpersonal skills – that is, appropriate ways of behaving with others regardless of your emotional impulses. For example, if you are angry that a subordinate has done a bad job, you can make clear what your standards are and learn specific steps to follow to deal with the problem without blowing up, as noted in some earlier examples. Further, you can learn how to encourage subordinates and praise them for doing good work (Chapter 7). You can also learn how to listen, a skill that too many managers lack. You can apply these skills whether your emotions are pushing you in the right direction at a given time or not. (Many executives today have personal coaches that can help them these skills).

Both these steps reflect aspects of emotional control. In addition, you can make sure you are a person of high moral character since character is within the realm of one's choice (Locke, 2018). This will build trust between you and your subordinates, which helps foster high morale, providing you are also competent (see Chapter 17).

What about customer service personnel?

It is generally agreed that being a customer service representative is a stressful job, especially when it involves constantly dealing with complaints. The service reps get the brunt of the anger because they are symbols of the whole company.

The first step is again selection: choose people who like this type of work. The second step involves a secret about emotions that 99% of customer service reps do not seem to know – it concerns how to deal with the customers' anger. Most reps respond to anger or grumpiness (based on hundreds of examples from my personal experience) either by totally ignoring, i.e. by total silence, or asking "So what can I help you with?" or by defensiveness ("Don't blame me."). This simply increases the customer's anger.

Here is the secret: you have to start by *disarming the anger* by acknowledging the emotion and even empathizing with it, viz. "I'm so sorry for the poor service (product, etc.). I don't blame you for feeling disappointed (frustrated, angry)." Because the customer feels *understood emotionally*, the result is that they virtually always calm down and get in a better mood. Then, you need to know what to do to deal with the problem.

Burnout

Burnout means that you no longer enjoy your job and lack enthusiasm for it. There can be many reasons for this which you can discover by introspection – for example, you are told to be selfless and care about everyone but yourself (see, Locke and Kenner, 2009), you never really wanted to be in this type of job in the first place (you chose it based on status or pressures from others or because it was the "in" career at the time, e.g. law); the job does not allow you to grow in your knowledge and expertise (you are stagnating); the job entails never-ending and unresolvable conflicts with others; the people you work with are mean, incompetent, and/or dishonest; the job was not what you expected and desired; stress on the job is unrelenting and you see no way to increase your self-efficacy enough to moderate it, etc. The solution to burnout is usually a job or career change, ideally after you have had time off to reflect about what you want.

Defensiveness

Defensiveness involves trying to protect oneself against perceived attack or criticism. Specifically, what one is trying to protect is one's sense of self-esteem (which may be fragile). Common mechanisms of defense are rationalization (making excuses), lying and denial (I did not do it), and evasion (refusing to consider the issue). The danger of defensives is *that it detaches the mind from reality* and thereby makes the problem impossible to fix.

One of my business heroes in this respect is Ken Iverson, the late CEO of Nucor. Early in its history (after Iverson took over), the company was not doing well, and a stockholder complained at the annual meeting. Iverson did not get defensive. His response was "What can I say? We're a lousy company." Of course, Iverson, unburdened by any desire to fake reality, went on to make Nucor one of the best steel companies in the world. Legendary investor Warren Buffett has the same attitude. When his company has a (rare) bad year, he simply says they did a poor job.

The key principle to sustain high self-esteem and prevent defensiveness is *treat reality (facts) as an absolute.* Former GE CEO, Jack Welch, said that you must face reality as it is, rather than as you want it to be. If you want to change what is (e.g. poor past performance), you have to first acknowledge the facts in front of you, including your own mistakes. Then, you are in a position to fix them.

Note that this policy eliminates the need for defensiveness, because your self-esteem is secure when reality rather than wishes come first. There is no illusion of self-esteem to protect.

Is the Core Role of the Leader Emotional or Rational?

A substantial segment of the leadership literature stresses or implies that the main role of the leader is that of motivator of employees. Although this is a significant role, I believe that it is not the main one and that focusing too heavily on the emotional aspect is very dangerous.

The most important trait of a great leader (over and above ability and integrity), I believe, is *rationality.* (Buffett says this is also the most important trait in a successful investor). Why rationality? Because virtually every decision a leader makes has to be based on looking at the facts, rationally integrating them and drawing conclusions. Many thousands (if not tens of thousands) of decisions have to be made (with or without others' input) in order to run a successful business. (See Introduction to this volume.) These include: what products (and product attributes) to make; where and how to make them; what people to hire and how to assign responsibilities; discovering a competitive strategy; financing the enterprise; managing risk; understanding the law and the economy; projecting trends into the future; anticipating threats; balancing the short term and the long term; constantly changing the organization to meet changing conditions, etc. And this only scratches the surface. Decision-making is hard mental work, leading a company requires a never-ending process of thinking. Motivating people to work hard at doing the wrong thing only hastens the organization's destruction. Thus, cognition must come before motivation.

One of the few top 20 banks that did not deal in subprime loans or invest in high-risk securities was BB&T, a mid-Atlantic regional holding company (see Chapter 20). Its core value: rationality. Its CEO told me a long time before the blowup that what the large banks were doing was irrational. They were making huge short-term profits, undoubtedly accompanied by soaring positive emotions, but the house of cards soon collapsed. Emotion is not rationality.

One's job and careers as a source of life happiness

Most people spend a substantial part of their lives at work. Thus, it is important that, if possible, they pick a job or career that they personally like, preferably love. In times of financial crisis, people can be forced to take jobs that are less than satisfactory, but this should not stop them from looking for something better – even during mid-life or later. To do this, they have to identify what they really like based on trying different things and then introspecting – and then acting. Pleasurable jobs entail mental challenge (Chapter 8), doing something one loves, steady progress in building one's knowledge and expertise, and just rewards.

One of the most common trade-offs people have to consider is money versus the job itself (i.e. the nature of the work). The work that you like the most may not be the type that pays the best. Another is career versus family. One cannot maximize everything. Again, it is important to introspect to identify one's true value hierarchy. But existing value hierarchies do not have to be permanent. They can be chosen – and changed by a process of thought. By choosing and pursuing the right values (including those outside of work) and understanding their relationship to emotion, one can be the agent of one's own success and happiness.

Conclusion

In order not to be the helpless victim of one's emotions, one has to understand their causes. Even though emotions are automatic responses programmed by the subconscious, their causes can be identified and understood. Moreover, emotions can be changed by changing their causes. Further, one has a choice as to how one acts in the face of emotions. There is no innate conflict between reason and emotion. A key to happiness and the harmony of reason and emotion is good introspection.

References

Arnold, M. B. (1960). *Emotion and Personality* (Vol. 1). New York: Columbia University Press.

Binswanger, H. (1991). Volition as cognitive self-regulation. *Organizational Behavior and Human Performance*, 50, 154–178.

Brodie, J. (2008). King of Kool. *Fortune*, September 1, pp. 51–61.

Butler, A. C., Chapman, J. E., Forman, E. M., and Beck, A.T. (2006). The empirical status of cognitive-behavioral therapy: A review of meta-analyses. *Clinical Psychology Review*, 26, 17–31.

Clark, D. A., and Beck, A. T. (1999). *Scientific Foundations of Cognitive Theory of Therapy and Depression.* New York: Wiley.

Grandey, A. A. (2008). Emotions at work: A review and research agenda. To appear in C. Cooper and J. Barling (eds), The *SAGE Handbook of Organizational Behavior* (Vol. 1, pp. 234–261). Thousand Oaks, CA: Sage.

Humphrey, R. H. (2008). *Affect and Emotion.* Charlotte, NC: Information Age publishing.

Locke, E. A. (2005). Why emotional intelligence is an invalid concept. *Journal of Organizational Behavior*, 26, 425–431.

Locke, E. A. (2009). It's Time we brought Introspection out of the Closet. *Perspectives in Psychological Science*, 4, 24–25.

Locke, E. A. (2018). *The Illusion of Determinism. Why Free Will Is Real and Causal.* Edwin A. Locke (Amazon).

Locke, E. A., and Kenner, E. (2009) How altruism undermines mental health and happiness. In A. G. Antoniou, C. L. Cooper, G. P. Chrousos, C. D. Spielberger, and M. W. Eysenck (eds), *Handbook of Managerial Behavior and occupational Health.* Cheltenham, UK: Elgar.

Locke, E. A., and Kenner, E. (2011). *The Selfish Path to Romance.* Doylestown, PA: Platform Press.

Mayer, J. D., Salovey, P., and Caruso, D. R. (2008). Emotional Intelligence. *American Psychologist*, 63, 503–517.

Peikoff, L. (1991). *Objectivism: The Philosophy of Ayn Rand.* New York: Dutton.

Exercises

Privacy should be respected in all exercises, so no one has to reveal anything personal that they do not want to.

Personal

1. This can be done alone as a homework assignment. Think of a recent emotion that you experienced that is worth remembering. It can be positive or negative. First, name the emotion. Then, trace the whole appraisal process. What was the fact or event(s) that triggered the emotion? What stored (subconscious)

knowledge about the triggering event was relevant? What was the subconscious value appraisal(s)? What action impulses did you experience? What did you choose to do? Why did you choose that action rather than another? Did you experience a conflict between your conscious beliefs and the subconscious beliefs behind your emotion? Would you do anything differently if the same event occurred again? What? How would that change the emotion?
2. Do the same thing as #1 but put yourself in the mind of a close friend and analyze their emotion.
3. Search news stories or analyze a story relating to emotions from fiction. Infer what must have gone on.
4. If a close friend has a negative emotion, what could you do to help, assuming they want help, without being bossy or intrusive? (Hint: start by acknowledging their emotion.)

Group

Any of the previous exercises can be done in class.

(*Instructor should strongly urge any member suffering from depression to seek professional help.*)

Discussion Questions

1. Think of the last time you had a strong emotion:
   a. Name the emotion.
   b. What started it (e.g. some event or object)?
   c. What was the subconscious appraisal – for example, stored knowledge and/or value standard – that was responsible?
2. Think of an example of an emotion that led to a felt action tendency or tendencies:
   a. What were they?
   b. How did you finally decide what action to take, if any, from among the various options?

5

Motivate Employee Performance Through Goal Setting

Gary P. Latham

Rotman School of Management, University of Toronto, 105 St. George Street Toronto, Ontario, M5S 3E6
email: *latham@rotman.utoronto.ca*
Fax: 407 340 8873

Goal setting theory (Latham and Locke, 2007, 2018) provides a framework that specifies the most valid and practical ways of increasing employee motivation. This conclusion has been reached by multiple authors working independently (e.g. Earley and Lee, 1992; Miner, 1984; Pinder, 2008). The conclusion is based on the fact that the theory has been used effectively in more than 1000 studies to predict, influence, and explain the behavior of thousands of people in numerous countries (e.g. Australia, Canada, the Caribbean, England, Germany, Israel, Japan, and the United States), in both laboratory and field settings, involving more than 100 different tasks in occupations that included logging, word processing, engineering, and university scholarship (Locke and Latham, 1990; Mitchell and Daniels, 2003). Although developed as a theory of motivation in the workplace, it has been used effectively in leadership, entrepreneurship, sports, negotiations, and to increase creativity as well as the academic performance of university students (Locke and Latham, 2013). The theory has even been found useful for promoting the motivational processes of brain-injured patients (Gauggel, 1999; Prigatano, Wong, Williams, and Plenge, 1997).

Main Principle

The theory states that the simplest most direct motivational explanation of why some people perform better than others is because they have different performance goals (Latham and Locke, 1991). The essence of the theory is fourfold (Locke and

Latham, 1990). First, difficult specific goals lead to significantly higher performance than easy goals, no goals, or even the setting of an abstract goal such as urging people to do their best. Second, holding ability constant, as this is a theory of motivation, and given that there is goal commitment, the higher the goal, the higher the performance. Third, personality traits and incentives influence an individual's behavior, at least in part, to the extent that they lead to the setting of and commitment to a specific difficult goal. Fourth, goal setting, in addition to affecting the three mechanisms of motivation, namely, choice, effort, and persistence, can also have a cognitive benefit. It can influence the motivation to discover ways to attain the goal (Seijts and Latham, 2005; Seijts, Latham, and Woodwark, 2013).

Subprinciples

There are at least four subprinciples necessary for deriving the motivational benefits of goal setting. The goal must be challenging and specific, an individual must have the knowledge and skill to attain it (i.e. ability), feedback must be provided on progress in relation to goal attainment, ways must be found to maintain goal commitment, and resources must be provided for, and obstacles removed to, goal attainment.

Set Challenging Specific Goals

The goal must be both challenging and specific. Given adequate ability and commitment to the goal, the higher the goal, the higher the performance. This is because people normally adjust their level of effort to the difficulty level of the goal. In addition to being targets to attain, goals are the standards by which one judges one's adequacy or success. Challenging goals facilitate pride in accomplishment. People with low goals are minimally satisfied with low performance attainment and become increasingly satisfied with every level of attainment that exceeds their goal. This is also true for individuals with a high goal. To be minimally satisfied, they must accomplish more than those who have a low goal. Consequently, they set a high goal to attain before they will be satisfied with their accomplishment. In short, to be satisfied, employees with high standards must accomplish more than those with low standards. In addition, an employee's outcome expectancies are typically higher for the attainment of high rather than low goals because the outcome one can expect from attaining a challenging goal usually includes such factors as an increase in feelings of self-efficacy, personal effectiveness, recognition from peers, a salary increase, a job promotion, etc. As a result, people, in most instances, readily commit to a high goal if they believe they have the ability to attain it.

Goal specificity facilitates an employee's focus in that it makes explicit what it is the individual should choose to do or try to accomplish. If the goal specifies A, then

B and C will be downplayed. Specificity also facilitates measurement or feedback on progress toward goal attainment. A drawback of an abstract goal such as "do your best" is that it allows people to give themselves the benefit of the doubt concerning the adequacy of their performance (Kernan and Lord, 1998). Thus, their maximum effort is not aroused. For feedback to be used intelligently, it must be interpreted in relation to a specific goal. Goal specificity clarifies for employees what constitutes effective performance.

For goal setting to be maximally effective, the goal and the measure of performance effectiveness must be aligned. Thus, if a logging crew wants to increase productivity by 15%, the performance measure must be the number of trees cut down divided by the hours worked. If the director of an organization's R&D division wishes to increase the client's satisfaction, that is, line management, the goal set can be a specific increase in the frequency of behaviors emitted that have been identified through job analysis as necessary for line management's satisfaction. Goals and the measures of their attainment that have appeared in the scientific literature include physical effort, quantity and quality measures of production, costs, profits, and job behaviors.

Mediators

Challenging, specific goals affect effort and persistence (Latham and Locke, 1991, 2007, 2018). When no time limits are imposed, a specific high goal induces people to work harder or longer than is the case when a low or abstract goal is set. Without time limits, a specific high goal induces people to work until the goal is attained. With time limits, difficult specific goals lead to more effort per unit of time. The American Pulpwood Association found that when paper companies impose quotas on the number of days that they will buy wood from pulpwood crews, the crews cut as much wood in the restricted number of days as they do in a normal five-day work week (Latham and Locke, 1975).

In summary, setting specific challenging goals is important for increasing both job performance and job satisfaction. Job satisfaction is the result of an appraisal of one's performance against one's goals. Job satisfaction is not a result of the person alone or the job alone, but of the person in relation to the job. To the extent that one's job performance is appraised as fulfilling or facilitating the attainment of one's goals, satisfaction is high (Latham and Brown, 2006; Latham, Locke, and Fassina, 2002). For example, in a study conducted in Germany, there were no data to suggest that those who had high goals experienced feelings of exhaustion. Only those employees who perceived their goals were difficult to attain experienced an increase in positive and a decrease in negative affect, an increase in job satisfaction, and perceptions of occupational success over a three-year time frame. An unexpected finding was that lack of goal attainment in one's personal life was related to higher degrees of subjective well-being when the person experienced goal progress on the job (Wiese and Freund, 2005).

MODERATORS

Provide Feedback in Relation to Goals

A truism attributed to the late Mason Haire is "that which gets measured gets done." This is because the act of measurement conveys cogently what the organization truly values versus what it may state that it values. However, the accuracy of Haire's statement is improved through the insertion of the word goals: That which is measured in relation to goals is done. Both goal setting theory and empirical research indicate that in the absence of goal setting, feedback has no effect on performance. This is because feedback is only information; its effect on an individual's actions depends on how it is appraised and what decisions are made with respect to it.

For example, the Weyerhaeuser Company found that engineers and scientists who were urged to do their best after receiving a performance appraisal/feedback performed no better than their counterparts in a control group. A significant increase in performance occurred only among those engineers and scientists who received feedback in relation to their specific high goals (Latham, Mitchell, and Dossett, 1978).

Feedback moderates the positive effect of goal setting. Without feedback, the positive benefit of goal setting on performance is minimized (Erez, 1977). This is because goals direct effort and persistence. Feedback allows people to discern what they should continue doing, stop doing, or start doing to attain the goal.

Gain Goal Commitment

Commitment is the sine qua non of goal setting. Without it, goal setting is a meaningless exercise. Two primary ways to gain commitment are to focus on an individual's *outcome expectancies and self-efficacy* (see Chapter 6)

A downside of setting challenging, specific goals is that people typically obtain tangible evidence that they did not attain them. A teenager may have test scores that provide strong evidence of failure in math. An employee in a consulting firm may have hours and hours of wasted effort, nonbillable hours, on a potential client who subsequently took the business to a competitor. The result can be feelings of loss of control. People learn on the basis of evidence (e.g. revenue, client surveys, staff turnover) that they have failed to attain their goal no matter how much they truly tried to attain it. Through such repeated experiences, they typically "learn" to give up; they learn helplessness. Thus, there are employees who have learned that they cannot increase revenue from existing clients, that they are poor at bringing in new clients, and that they are not able to work effectively with staff. They have tangible evidence to support their conclusions that they should give up their attempts to attain their goals in these three areas.

The solutions for maintaining goal commitment are at least twofold. A first step, as noted earlier, is to focus on *outcome expectancies.* The role of a coach is to help people see the relationship between what they do and the outcome of their actions, and to help people realize the outcomes that they can expect as a result of what they do. An early example of how outcome expectancies affect goal commitment can be found in a study by Lashley (1929). A man, after 900 repetitions, was still unable to master the alphabet. But after he was offered 100 cigarettes if he could learn the alphabet in a week, he proceeded to do so in only 10 trials.

Because the concept of outcome expectancies is as useful in one's personal life as it is in an organizational setting, allow me to share a personal example. I arrived home one day to discover my four children on the front step. They greeted me with the warning not to enter the house as Mom was in a horrific mood. As she had walked across the kitchen floor, her foot had come out of a shoe that had stuck to dried milk. As she fell, her hand braced her from injury as it slipped into an open dishwasher that oozed with leftover breakfast food.

To announce that I will solve the problem would not only have been lunacy on my part, it would have fostered dependence: "Let's wait until Dad gets here; he can fix anything." To look for blame would have been equally fool-hardy on my part: "So what did you do to get your mother in such a bad mood?" "I don't know." "It wasn't me." "She is always in a bad mood." I bet you did something, Dad."

The primary job of a coach is to improve performance rather than focus on blame. This is done through increasing the person's sense of control regarding the attainment of their goals. It is done by helping people to realize the outcomes they can expect from engaging in specific actions. Thus, I simply asked each of them "What can you do within the next 30 seconds to improve Mom's mood?" Setting a goal focuses attention on discovering solutions to its attainment.

One son, likely the guilty party, offered to clean the kitchen, another said he would get us both a drink, and the third said he would make dinner. My daughter quietly ran off to prepare a bath for my wife. The outcome, as expected, was a dramatic upswing in my wife's affect and behavior.

A four-cell empathy box can be used to understand: (i) the outcomes an employee expects from committing to a goal, (ii) the negative outcomes expected from goal commitment, (iii) the positive outcomes expected from sticking with the status quo, and (iv) the negative outcomes expected from doing so. Understanding outcome expectancies enabled a forest products company to shift the dishonest (theft) to honest behavior in the workforce (Latham, 2001). The empathy box is shown in Figure 5.1. The five questions asked are as follows: (i) What positive outcomes do you expect from committing to and pursuing the goal? (ii) What negative outcomes do you expect from committing to and pursuing the goal? (iii) What positive outcomes do you expect from rejecting or ignoring the goal? (iv) What negative outcomes do you expect from rejecting or ignoring the goal? (v) What would have to change for you to commit to the goal (look for answers in cells 2 and 3)?

This empathy box provides a systematic way to "walk in another person's shoes." To the extent that you understand the outcomes an individual or team expects, you will begin to understand their behavior. To the extent that you are able to change the outcomes they expect, you will be able to change their behavior – given the person or team has the confidence they can do so. This leads us to the second concept, self-efficacy.

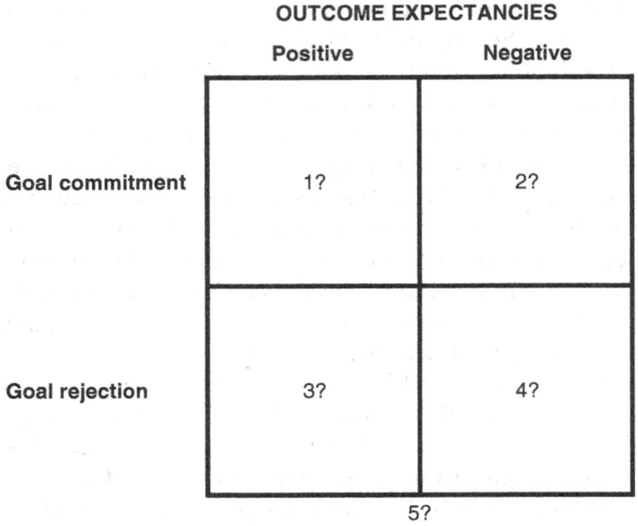

FIGURE 5.1 The empathy box

A second step to maintaining goal commitment is to increase a person's *self-efficacy* (Bandura, 1997, 2001). Self-efficacy is the conviction that one can mobilize one's resources to attain a specific performance level. "I can cause . . . , I can bring about . . . I can make happen. . . ." Self-efficacy is different from self-esteem in that the latter refers to judgments of self-worth: How much does Pat like Pat? Further, self-esteem is a general trait, whereas self-efficacy is domain or task specific. The two are not necessarily related.

Pat may have low self-esteem due to a variety of events that have occurred in Pat's past. Pat has said and done things that are deeply regretted. For these reasons, no one dislikes Pat today more than Pat. Nevertheless, Pat believes (high self-efficacy) that there is no one who is as effective in bringing in new business to the firm. Conversely, Pat may love Pat, yet she may have low self-efficacy in the ability to make a persuasive presentation to a potential client. Furthermore, because self-efficacy is task specific, an individual may have high self-efficacy on ability to work effectively with staff, low self-efficacy on working effectively with clients, and moderate self-efficacy on ability to improve the inner workings of the firm.

People who have problems with self-esteem should be referred to a clinical psychologist. People who have low self-efficacy for attaining a specific, high goal can be coached by you in the workplace.

Bandura (2001) has shown that it is not just our ability that holds us back or propels us forward, but also our perception of our ability. People with low self-efficacy look for tangible evidence to abandon a goal. A failure is confirmation that it is useless to persist in goal attainment. Conversely, people with high self-efficacy commit to high goals. They view obstacles and setbacks to goal attainment as challenges to overcome, as sources of excitement to be savored.

A possible indicator of low self-efficacy is self-denigration of one's ability. Statements such as "I can't deal with a personal computer" may indicate low self-efficacy.

High self-efficacy can be induced in the workplace in at least three ways, enactive mastery, modeling, and persuasion from a significant other. Enactive mastery involves sequencing a task in such a way that all but guarantees early successes for an individual. For example, to increase confidence in the use of a laptop, the following steps should be followed: (i) open/close, (ii) on-off, (iii) keyboard skills, and (iv) save. Early successes through "small wins" build confidence that "I can do this, my goal is indeed attainable."

An effective coach does not abandon an employee during the early stages of learning to attain a goal. To leave the employee to master keyboard skills before teaching the process of "save" is to provide the employee a reason for abandoning the laptop in favor of pen and paper. All that was typed is lost forever when the laptop is turned off in the absence of knowledge of the necessity to "save."

The concepts of outcome expectancy and self-efficacy are often applied together. If the person hates the traditional "snail" mail system, show how hitting a key on the computer will send material any place in the world in seconds. In short, enable the person to see the relationship between mastery of the laptop and the desired outcome the person can expect. Then give the person confidence to do so through the sequencing of the tasks.

A second way to increase self-efficacy regarding goal attainment is through the use of models. The job of coach is to find people with whom the goal setter *identifies* who have either mastered the task, or is in the process of doing so. Note that the word identifies is italicized. Directing a manager who is struggling in the development of staff to another manager who has the "magic touch" with staff may not increase self-efficacy. It may even backfire as a coaching technique if this is all that is done. The person who is struggling may give up after concluding that "I will never acquire that 'magic touch'." Directing this manager to visit an additional colleague who has struggled recently in the past and has subsequently improved the performance of staff is more likely to increase the belief that "if that person can, so can I."

For the same reason, visiting a benchmark company can sometimes be a demotivating experience. The idea underlying benchmarking is to minimize reinventing the wheel on the part of people in other organizations. Through benchmarking, the acquisition of knowledge is accelerated. But, the downside of benchmarking is that visitors can leave full of admiration for what they have witnessed, and demoralized because they are convinced that they do not have the ability to model it: "Their management system is different from ours. Their union contract is nothing like ours. There is no way that we can be like them." To increase their self-efficacy, you must find an organization, in addition to the one that will be used as a benchmark, with whom employees can identify an organization that has previously done poorly but has significantly improved its performance relative to that benchmark, or is in the process of doing so. Finding and visiting this additional organization increases the belief that "if they can, so can we."

The American Pulpwood Association found that *supervisory presence and support* is also a key to goal commitment and productivity (Ronan, Latham, and Kinne, 1973).

When the goal is assigned by a supportive authority figure, goal commitment and performance are high (Latham and Saari, 1979a). These findings are supported by a meta-analysis that showed a 56% average gain in productivity when management commitment to an MBO program is high versus a 6% increase when their commitment is low (Rodgers and Hunter, 1991). Thus, it is not surprising that Bandura (see Chapter 6) found that a third way of increasing self-efficacy is through persuasion from a significant other. People tend to behave in accordance with the expectations of those people who are significant to them. Assigned goals themselves usually lead to high goal commitment because listening to the assignment without objection is in itself a form of consent (Salancik, 1977). Assigning the goal implies that the recipient is capable of attaining it, which in turn increases the person's self-efficacy regarding the task.

Bandura, a past president of the American Psychological Association, and a past honorary president of the Canadian Psychological Association, addressed a classroom of executives as follows:

> We know that intelligence is fixed. You either have it or you don't. We are going to put you through a simulation consisting of tasks that you typically confront as CEOs. I know you will find these tasks frustrating and seemingly impossible.

In an adjoining room, he addressed the other half of the class of executives as follows:

> We know that intelligence is not fixed. Intelligence is the ability to apply what you have learned on previous tasks to present ones. We are going to put you through a simulation consisting of tasks that you typically confront as CEOs. I know that you will find these tasks challenging and fun.

Several hours later, he pushed back the dividing wall. The people in the second group were laughing among themselves as to how similar the simulation was to their daily work lives, and how much they had learned from their experiences that afternoon. The people in the first group were truly angry and frustrated. They demanded to be allowed to go through the same simulation as the second group before their four weeks of executive education at Stanford came to a close. The simulation that they had gone through, they claimed, was not similar at all to what they encountered on their jobs and, hence, was a waste of their time.

In short, both groups behaved in accordance with Bandura's expectations of them, despite the fact that the simulation was identical for both groups. In less than a minute, Bandura's expectations of one group of executives ruined their afternoon, and for the other group, he had the opposite effect.

A coach may or may not be a significant other for the person who is being coached. Thus, a role for you as a coach is to determine the identity of the person's significant other and have that individual or individuals communicate, if true, why they believe the person can attain a specific high goal.

The most powerful significant other is one's self. *Verbal self-guidance* (VSG) or functional self-talk can increase or debilitate self-confidence in goal attainment. We are often our worst enemy. Millman and Latham (2012) trained displaced managers to systematically monitor their self-talk to exclude negative comments and increase positive ones with respect to job attainment. Within nine months, 48% of the people who were trained obtained a job that paid ± $10 000 of their previous job; only one person of eight in the control group was able to do so. The self-efficacy of the participants in the group who were trained in functional self-talk was significantly higher than those in the control group. Similar results have been obtained for Aboriginals in Canada (Latham and Budworth, 2006). Training in VSG also turned highly competitive MBA students into team players (Latham and Brown, 2006) as well as women in Turkey to successfully reenter the job market (Yanar, Budworth, and Latham, 2009)

The order in which these two steps, outcome expectancies and self-efficacy, should be implemented varies by individual. If outcome expectancies are already high, this step may be skipped. Focus immediately on ways of increasing self-efficacy if the person lacks confidence that the goal is attainable.

Provide Resources Needed to Attain the Goal

Goals are unlikely to be attained if situational constraints blocking their attainment are not removed. Thus, the organization needs to ensure that the time, money, staff, and equipment necessary for goal attainment exists. Most importantly, the measurement system must not only allow an accurate tracking of goal progress; it must be aligned with goal attainment.

For example, a newly hired professor may set a goal to receive a mean score of 5 or higher on a seven-point scale of teaching effectiveness rated by students. If the measurement system for promotion and tenure focuses primarily on publications in mainstream academic journals, and resources are provided primarily for conducting research, commitment to this teaching goal may quickly wane.

Arguably, among the most important resources necessary for accruing the positive benefits of goal setting is the employee's ability. Organizations must provide the necessary training to give people the knowledge and skill to attain the goal. This is because the relation of goal difficulty to performance is curvilinear. Performance levels off after the limit of ability has been reached (Locke, Fredrick, Buckner, and Bobko, 1984).

Learning Versus Performance Goals

Consistent with the findings noted earlier regarding an individual's ability are studies by Earley, Connolly, and Ekegren (1989) as well as Kanfer and Ackerman (1989). They found that when people lack the requisite knowledge to master a task, because they are in the early stages of learning, urging them to do their best results in higher performance than setting a specific difficult goal. The reasons are at least threefold (Latham, Seijts, and Crim, 2008). First, such tasks are complex for people. Thus, the direct goal mechanisms of effort, persistence, and choice are no longer sufficient to ensure high performance. This is because people have yet to learn the correct strategy for performing effectively. Second, such tasks require primarily learning rather than motivation. People have no problem-solving processes for these tasks to draw upon. Third, people with specific high goals feel pressure to perform well immediately. As a result, they focus more on their desire to get results than on learning the correct way of performing the task. In short, tasks that are straightforward as well as those that are complex for an individual require attentional resources, but the resource demands of the latter tasks are greater than those of the former (Kanfer, 1990). Where tasks fall within the problem-solving abilities of people, as in cases where they have had experience performing the tasks effectively, specific difficult performance goals readily lead to the development and execution of task specific strategies. Truck drivers at Weyerhaeuser found ways to increase truck loads (Latham and Baldes, 1975) and to decrease truck turnaround time (Latham and Saari, 1982) after being assigned a specific difficult goal. They drew upon the knowledge they already possessed to attain the performance goal.

This was not the case in a study by Winters and Latham (1996) using a new (for the participants) complex class scheduling task developed by Earley (1985). Winters and Latham found a deleterious effect of a specific, difficult goal for performance because the wrong type of goal was set. When a high learning goal was set in terms of discovering a specific number of ways to solve the task, performance was significantly higher than it was when people were urged to do their best or had set a performance outcome goal. This is because a learning goal requires people to focus on understanding the task that is required of them and developing a plan for performing it correctly. As Oppenheimer noted during the development of the atomic bomb, determining how to get to one's destination is often more important than the critical target. Research on goal setting theory shows that high performance is not always the result of high effort or persistence, but rather, high cognitive understanding of the task and strategy or plan necessary to complete it (Seijts and Latham, 2001). A learning goal is especially beneficial for people who score low on cognitive ability (Latham, Seijts, and Crim, 2008). As John D. Rockefeller said years ago, a goal of good management is to show average people how to do the work of superior people. A learning goal can raise the performance of people who score lower on cognitive ability to that of those who score higher on cognitive intelligence.

Environmental Uncertainty

Among the biggest impediments to goal setting is environmental uncertainty (Locke and Latham, 1990). This is because the information required to set learning or outcome goals may be unavailable. And even when such information is available, it may become obsolete due to rapid changes in the environment. Thus, as uncertainty increases, it becomes increasingly difficult to set and commit to a long-term goal.

In a simulation of such a situation, Latham and Seijts (1999) replicated the findings of Earley, Wojnaroski, and Prest (1987) and Kanfer and Ackerman (1989) using a business game where high school students were paid on a piece-rate basis to make toys, and the dollar amounts paid for the toys changed continuously without warning.

Setting a specific high performance goal resulted in profits that were significantly worse than urging the students to do their best. But when *proximal performance goals* were set in addition to the distal goal, profit was significantly higher than in the other two conditions. This is because in highly dynamic situations, it is important to actively search for feedback and react quickly to it (Frese and Zapf, 1994). In addition, Dorner (1991) has found that performance errors on a dynamic task are often due to deficient decomposition of a goal into proximal goals. Proximal goals can increase what Keith and Frese (2005) call error management. Errors provide information to employees as to whether their picture of reality is congruent with goal attainment. There is an increase in informative feedback when proximal or subgoals are set relative to setting a distal goal only.

In addition to being informative, the setting of proximal goals can also be motivational relative to a distal goal that is far into the future. Moreover, the attainment of proximal goals can increase commitment, through enactive mastery, to attain the distal goal (Seijts and Latham, 2001).

Stretch Goals

Do not expect people to willingly stretch themselves by committing to an exceedingly high goal if the outcome they expect is criticism for making an error. One or more errors are bound to occur in the active pursuit of a time-sensitive, exceedingly difficult goal. On tasks that are complex for people, Frese's research (Frese, 2005; Keith and Frese, 2005) shows that performance actually increases if errors are encouraged ("the more errors you initially make, the more you learn").

Use the High Performance Cycle

The usefulness of goal setting theory for everyday applications in work settings is shown in Figure 5.2. The high performance cycle (HPC) (Latham, Locke, and Fassina, 2002; Locke and Latham, 1990) or HPC's usefulness for motivating employees in the public sector was demonstrated by Selden and Brewer (2000). It is a diagnostic tool or framework for understanding why employees are or are not motivated. For example:

1. Demands
   a. Do people have specific high goals?
   b. Are the tasks "drudgery" or growth facilitating?
   c. Do people have the confidence they can attain the goals set (self-efficacy)?
2. Moderators
   a. Have people been trained adequately? Do they have the ability to perform the tasks required of them?
   b. Are they committed to goal attainment?
   c. Do they receive feedback on goal progress?
   d. Do they have the resources to attain the goal or are there situational constraints?

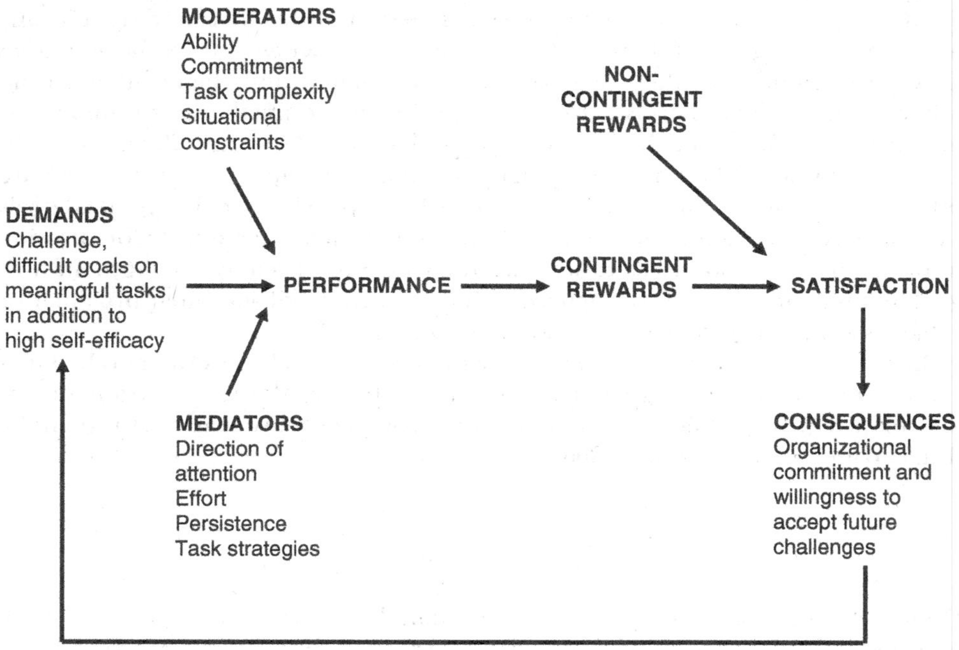

FIGURE 5.2 The high performance cycle

3. Rewards
   a. Are they rewarded for their accomplishments?
      (i) Intrinsically?
      (ii) Extrinsically?
   b. Are they satisfied with their rewards?
4. Attitudes
   a. Are they committed to their organization's effectiveness?
   b. Are they willing to accept future challenges?

Issues in Implementation

For What Should Goals Be Set?

As a theory of motivation, a goal refers to a desired outcome in terms of level of performance to be attained on a task. Goal content refers to the object or result that is sought after (Locke and Latham, 1990). Thus, given ability, performance goals should be set for outcomes that are critical or valued by the individual or the organization in which the person is employed. An employee may have a career goal, a job goal, a financial goal, as well as psychological goals including job satisfaction and self-efficacy. When ability is lacking, a learning goal should be set for discovering the processes and strategies for reaching a desired outcome when the person lacks the knowledge to do so. Behavioral goals, identified through a job analysis, are more effective than a learning goal when the critical behaviors are known, and lack of ability is not an issue (Brown and Latham, 2002). To set a learning goal in this instance is to encourage paralysis through analysis. Behavioral goals are especially appropriate for job satisfaction and self-efficacy.

Because a goal is the object or aim of an action, the completion of a task can be a goal. As noted by Locke and Latham (1990), in most goal setting studies, the term goal refers to attaining a specific standard of proficiency on a given task within a specific time frame. This has resulted in practitioners of goal setting creating the acronym SMART, namely goals that are *s*pecific, *m*easurable, *a*ttainable, *r*elevant, and have a *t*ime frame (Mealiea and Latham, 1996). The framing of a goal is especially important for implementation with regard to the stress that it can cause. Frame the goal positively, for example in terms of something a person can learn to perform well. Do not frame it negatively, as something a person may have difficulty attaining. A negatively framed goal (try not to miss answering 3 of these 15 anagrams) leads to worse performance than a positively framed one (try to make words from 12 or more of the 15 anagrams; Drach-Zahavy and Erez, 2002; Roney, Griggs, and Shanks, 2003).

Who Should Set the Goals?

A seminal study at the General Electric Company (Meyer, Kay, and French, 1965) revealed that it is not so important who sets the goal as it is that a specific challenging goal in fact be set. However, subsequent laboratory and field experiments revealed contradictory findings. Erez and her colleagues (e.g. Erez, 1986; Erez and Arad, 1986; Erez, Earley, and Hulin, 1985) found that goal commitment and subsequent performance is higher when employees participate in the setting of the goal than was the case when the goals were assigned. A series of 11 studies by Latham and his colleagues (e.g. Latham and Saari, 1979a, 1979b; Latham and Steele, 1983) found that when goal difficulty is held constant, goal commitment and performance are the same regardless of whether the goal is assigned or set participatively.

In what is rare if not unique in science, the two antagonists, Erez and Latham, did a series of collaborative studies, with Locke as a mediator, to discover the basis for their conflicting findings (Latham, Erez, and Locke, 1988). They found that their methodology was highly similar in the way that goals were set participatively, yet highly different in the way in which the goals were assigned. In what would be expected, based on Greenberg's organizational justice principles, when the assigned goal was given tersely and without any rationale, it had a negative effect on performance relative to participatively set goals. When an assigned goal from an authority figure included a logic or rationale, it had the same positive effect on goal commitment and performance as did a participatively set goal. (For an overall summary of the research on the effects of participation, see Chapter 11.)

Subsequent research by Latham, Winters, and Locke (1994) revealed that Erez had been correct in arguing the benefit of participation in goal setting, but for the wrong reason. The benefit is primarily cognitive rather than motivational. Employee participation in decision-making has a positive effect on performance to the extent that it increases self-efficacy and the discovery of task relevant strategies. When this does not occur, when these two variables are partialed out, participation in decision-making has a negligible effect on performance.

Training Self-Regulation

The management of oneself lies at the core of goal setting theory. Setting a goal and taking action to attain it is a volitional process. Holding goal difficulty constant, self-set goals are as effective in increasing performance as are goals that are assigned or set participatively (Locke and Latham, 1990). This finding is the basis for training people skills in self-management.

Case Examples

Positive: The University of Washington

The University of Washington trained their maintenance employees (carpenters, mechanics, and electricians) in self-regulation to increase their job attendance (Frayne and Latham, 1987). The training took place in a group setting one hour a week for eight weeks. In the first session, the principles of goal setting were explained to the trainees. In session 2, the trainees generated reasons for their low job attendance. The third session focused on the value of setting behavioral and outcome (days present) goals for attendance. In the fourth session, the importance of self-monitoring one's behavior was discussed. Specifically, the trainees were taught to use charts and diaries to record (i) their own attendance, (ii) the reasons for missing one or more days of the week, and (iii) the steps that were followed to subsequently return to work. The trainees identified rewards and punishers in the fifth session that they would self-administer contingent upon their attendance. In the sixth session, the trainees wrote a behavioral contract with themselves. The contract specified in writing the goal(s) to be attained, the time frame for attaining it, the outcomes of attaining or failing to attain the goal(s), and the task strategies necessary for attaining the goal(s). The seventh session emphasized maintenance. That is, discussion focused on issues that might result in a relapse in absenteeism, planning for such situations should they occur, and developing strategies for dealing with such situations. During the final week of training, the trainer reviewed each technique presented in the program, answered questions from the trainees regarding these skills, and clarified expectations for self-management.

Observe that the training took explicit account of goal setting moderators and subprinciples discussed earlier in this chapter. Goal commitment was the focus of sessions 5 and 6 where rewards and punishers were selected, and a behavioral contract was written. Feedback through self-monitoring was emphasized in session 4. The complexity of the task and the situational constraints were the focus of session 2 where employees specified in writing the behavior that they believed would enable them to get to work, and session 7 where they outlined possibilities for a relapse and what could be done to overcome such issues.

Participatory group discussions occurred throughout the eight weeks of training. The main benefit of participation, as noted earlier, is cognitive; thus, the training focused the attention of each person in the group on identifying effective strategies for overcoming obstacles to attaining the goal. In this way, self-efficacy was increased. Self-efficacy correlated significantly in the study with subsequent job attendance. Three months later, employee attendance was significantly higher in the training than in the control group.

The University of Washington conducted a six-month and a nine-month follow-up study to determine the long-term effects of this training. Employees who had been trained in self-management continued to have higher job attendance than those in the control group. Moreover, when the people in the control group were subsequently given the same training in self-management, but by a different trainer, they too showed the same positive improvement in their self-efficacy with regard to coping with obstacles perceived by them as preventing them from coming to work. Moreover, their job attendance increased to the same level as that which the original training group had achieved three months after it had been trained (Latham and Frayne, 1989).

When are goals ineffective? The answer to this question is given throughout this chapter. For example, both the American Pulpwood Association and Weyerhaeuser found that when the goal is abstract such as urging loggers to do their best, productivity is lower than setting a specific difficult goal (Latham and Kinne, 1974; Latham and Yukl, 1975). They also found that when goals are set and supervisory supportiveness is lacking, turnover is high and people quit (Ronan et al., 1973). When specific challenging performance goals were set before people have acquired knowledge and skill to perform the task, the performance of Air Force cadets dropped (Kanfer and Ackerman, 1989). In short, goals do not work when the principles we have discussed are not applied.

Negative: The Potential Downside of Goal Setting

Setting specific, challenging goals, as is the case with most psychological, not to mention medical techniques, is subject to misuse. For example, a factor analysis of survey data on the job performance of pulpwood producers revealed that a crew's pursuit of high performance goals, in the absence of the supervisor, loaded on the same factor as injuries (Ronan et al., 1973). This may have been due to crew members cutting corners that exceeded their ability to execute safely.

A correlational study of police officers investigated Bandura's (1991) contention that relentlessly pursuing goals that exceed an individual's ability, yet self-worth is judged against attainments of the self-set goals, may be related to despondency and performance debilitation. The results of the study showed that this is not the case for maximum performance, namely, performance on a job promotional exam of police officers (Hrabluik, Latham, and McCarthy, 2012). However, in a second study by the same authors, involving police officers' typical performance as measured by a performance appraisal, excessively high self-set goals were also positively related to performance, but at a cost – emotional exhaustion and low goal disengagement. The latter undoubtedly influenced feelings of exhaustion.

As a follow-up to self-set goals that are perceived as excessively high, Mawritz, Folger, and Latham (2014) conducted a correlational study of goals assigned by managers to supervisors.

Goals perceived by the supervisors as exceeding their ability to attain were related not only to anger and anxiety, but worse, to the abuse of their subordinates. The findings of this and the previous study underserve the necessity of taking into account an individual's ability, a moderator in goal setting theory.

Several experiments conducted by Ordóñez, Schweitzer, Galinsky, and Bazerman (2020) have shown that when (i) an individual's only measure of performance is a self-report, (ii) for which there are no negative consequences for exaggerating how well the task was performed, and a (iii) performance goal as opposed to a learning or behavioral goal is (iv) assigned rather than self-set or set participatively, (v) without taking into account a person's ability, some people may not tell the truth as to how well they performed a laboratory task.

These same researchers have naively generalized their findings to the workplace by citing newspaper articles that describe inappropriate behavior in such companies as Enron, Wells Fargo, and Volkswagen where goals were set. The authors do not cite Doerr, Eaton, and Lewis (2018) who described the impressive gains in performance by Intel, Google, and the Gates Foundation attributed to setting specific, high performance goals. Nevertheless, it is inexcusable for a behavioral scientist to conclude that one variable in an organization, based on newspaper articles and magazines, is the causal agent for the results obtained. There are simply too many confounding variables that prevent reaching such a conclusion (e.g. values of senior management, monetary incentives, organization's culture, and inadequate control systems).

Goals Set in the Subconscious

A limitation of goal setting theory is that it focused solely on consciously set goals. It did not take into account the subconscious, a storehouse of knowledge and values beyond that which is found in awareness at any given point in time. This was a limitation because unlike the conscious mind, the subconscious has an enormous storage capacity. This storage capacity frees the conscious mind to focus on new facts and make new integrations.

In the past decade, extensive research in laboratory and field settings have shown that both performance and learning goals can be primed in the subconscious through the use words and photographs such as those that connote achievement (Chen, Latham, Piccolo, and Itchakov, 2020; Latham, Brcic, and Steinhauer, 2017).

Moreover, field research has shown that setting both conscious and subconscious goals have an additive effect on job performance (e.g. Shantz and Latham, 2009). Moreover, the moderators and mediators that affect the causal relationship of consciously set goals with performance are the same moderators and mediators of unconsciously set goals.

Future Research

Some behavioral ethics researchers, on the basis of laboratory experiments involving college students, claim that setting a specific, high performance goal leads to unethical behavior as defined by an exaggeration of how well they performed the task. However, there were no consequences for a student's erroneous self-report. Moreover, none of the students took money for goal attainment undeservedly even though they were free to do so.

The goals people set and the way they pursue them are a function of their values. To blame a school for assigning grades as the causal link for a student cheating on an exam, or the awards given in professional sports as the causal link for the illegal use of steroids by athletes to enhance their performance is to ignore the causal effect of values on the actions people take. Worse, these researchers have made the inferential leap that their laboratory findings explain the illegal behavior that occurred in companies such as Enron, Wells Fargo, and Volkswagen. Drawing this inference is illogical in that there are too many confounding variables that prevent pinpointing the causal link to the crimes that were committed (e.g. the company's culture, toxic leadership, and the lack of company systems to minimize if not eliminate inappropriate behavior). Future research is needed in field settings to isolate the variables that contribute to unethical behavior.

It is noteworthy that the laboratory experiments of the behavioral ethics researchers involved assigned performance goals. Research is needed to determine whether inappropriate behavior occurs when a goal is self-set or set participatively, and whether it is mitigated when behavioral or learning goals rather than assigned goals are set. Is inappropriate behavior in organizations minimized when both performance and behavioral goals are set?

Conclusion

Specific challenging goals are motivational regardless of whether they are self-set, set participatively, or assigned. If the person has the knowledge and skill necessary to perform the task, performance goals should be set. If the requisite knowledge or skill is lacking, learning goals should be set. If the moderators and subprinciples described in this chapter are taken into account by practitioners of goal setting, the probability that performance and satisfaction will increase is above 0.90 (Locke and Latham, 1990). No other theory of motivation has been found to be as consistently effective in the workplace as goal setting.

References

Bandura, A. (1991). Social cognitive theory of self-regulation. *Organizational Behavior and Human Decision Processes*, 50, 248–287.

Bandura, A. (1997). *Self Efficacy: The Exercise of Control.* New York: Freeman.

Bandura, A. (2001). Social cognitive theory: An agentic perspective. *Annual Review of Psychology*, 52, 1–26.

Brown, T. C., and Latham, G. P. (2002). The effects of behavioural outcome goals, learning goals, and urging people to do their best on an individual's teamwork behaviour in a group problem-solving task. *Canadian Journal of Behavioural Science/ Revue Canadienne des Sciences du Comportement*, 34(4), 276.

Chen, X., Latham, G. P., Piccolo, R. F., and Itzchakov, G. (2020). An enumerative review and a meta-analysis of primed goal effects on organizational behavior. *Applied Psychology: An International Review.* doi:10.1111/apps.12239

Doerr, K., Eaton, D. R., and Lewis, I. A. (2018). Measurement issues in performance-based logistics. In *Handbook of Measurements* (pp. 310–325). Boca Raton, FL: CRC Press.

Dorner, D. (1991). The investigation of action regulation in uncertain and complex situations. In J. Rasmussen, G. Brehmer, and J. Leplat (eds), *Distributed Decision Making: Cognitive Models for Cooperative Work* (pp. 349–356). New York: Wiley.

Drach-Zahavy, A., and Erez, M. (2002). Challenge versus threat effects on the goal-performance relationship. *Organizational Behavior and Human Decision Processes*, 88, 667–682.

Earley, P. C. (1985). Influence of information, choice and task complexity upon goal acceptance, performance, and personal goals. *Journal of Applied Psychology*, 70, 481–491.

Earley, P. C., Connolly, T., and Ekegren, G. (1989). Goals, strategy development and task performance: Some limits to the efficacy of goal setting. *Journal of Applied Psychology*, 74, 24–33.

Earley, P. C., and Lee, C. (1992). Comparative peer evaluations of organizational behavior theories. *Organizational Development Journal*, 10, 37–42.

Earley, C. P., Wojnaroski, P., and Prest, W. (1987). Task planning and energy expended: Exploration of how goals influence performance. *Journal of Applied Psychology*, 72, 107–114.

Erez, M. (1986). The congruence of goal setting strategies with socio-cultural values, and its effect on performance. *Journal of Management*, 12, 83–90.

Erez, M. (1977). Feedback: A necessary condition for the goal setting-performance relationship. *Journal of Applied Psychology*, 62, 624–627.

Erez, M., and Arad, R. (1986). Participative goal setting: Social, motivational, and cognitive factors. *Journal of Applied Psychology*, 71, 591–597.

Erez, M., Earley, P. C., and Hulin, C. L. (1985). The impact of participation on goal acceptance and performance: A two-step model. *Academy of Management Journal*, 28, 50–66.

Frayne, C. A., and Latham, G. P. (1987). The application of social learning theory to employee self-management of attendance. *Journal of Applied Psychology*, 72, 387–392.

Frese, M. (2005). Grand theories and midrange theories: Cultural effects on theorizing and the attempt to understand active approaches to work. In K. G. Smith and M. Hitt (eds), *The Oxford Handbook of Management Theory: The Process of Theory Development*. Oxford, UK: Oxford University Press.

Frese, M., and Zapf, D. (1994). Action as the core of work psychology: A German approach. In H. C. Triandis, M. D. Dunnette, and L. M. Hough (eds), *Handbook of Industrial and Organizational Psychology* (2nd edition) (Vol. 4, pp. 271–340). Palo Alto, CA: Consulting Psychologist Press.

Gauggel, S. (1999). Goal-setting and its influence on the performance of brain-damaged patients. Unpublished doctoral dissertation, Philipps University of Marburg, Germany.

Hrabluik, C., Latham, G. P., and McCarthy, J. M. (2012). Does goal setting have a dark side? The relationship between perfectionism and maximum versus typical employee performance. *International Public Management Journal*, 15(1), 5–38.

Kanfer, R. (1990). Motivation theory and industrial and organizational theory. In M. D. Dunnette and L. M. Hough (eds), *Handbook of Industrial and Organizational Psychology* (pp. 75–170). Palo Alto, CA: Consulting Psychologists Press.

Kanfer, R., and Ackerman, P. L. (1989). Motivation and cognitive abilities: An integrative/aptitude-treatment interaction approach to skill acquisition. *Journal of Applied Psychology*, 74, 657–690.

Keith, N., and Frese, M. (2005). Self-regulation error management training: Emotion control and metacognition as mediators of performance effects. *Journal of Applied Psychology*, 90, 677–691.

Kernan, M. C., and Lord, R. G. (1998). Effects of participative versus assigned goals and feedback in a multitrial task. *Motivation and Emotion*, 12, 75–86.

Lashley, K. S. (1929). *Brain Mechanisms and Intelligence.* Chicago: University of Chicago Press.

Latham, G. P. (2001). The importance of understanding and changing employee outcome expectancies for gaining commitment to an organizational goal. *Personnel Psychology*, 54, 707–716.

Latham, G. P., and Baldes, J. J. (1975). The "practical significance" of Locke's theory of goal setting. *Journal of Applied Psychology*, 60, 122–124.

Latham, G. P., and Brown, T. C. (2006). The effect of learning vs. outcome goals on self-efficacy and satisfaction in a MBA Program. *Applied Psychology: An International Review*, 55, 606–623.

Latham, G. P., and Budworth, M. H. (2006). The effect of training in verbal self-guidance on the self-efficacy and performance of Native North Americans in the selection interview. *Journal of Vocational Behavior*, 68(3), 516–523.

Latham, G. P., and Frayne, C. A. (1989). Increasing job attendance through training in self-management: A review of two studies. *Journal of Applied Psychology*, 74(41), 1–416.

Latham, G. P., and Kinne, S. B. (1974). Improving job performance through training in goal setting. *Journal of Applied Psychology*, 59(2), 187.

Latham, G. P., and Locke, E. A. (1975). Increasing productivity with decreasing time limits: A field replication of Parkinson's law. *Journal of Applied Psychology*, 60, 524–526.

Latham, G. P., and Locke, E. A. (1991). Self regulation through goal setting. *Organizational Behavior and Human Decision Process*, 50, 212–247.

Latham, G. P., and Locke, E. A. (2007). New developments in and directions for goal setting. *European Psychologist*, 12, 290–300.

Latham, G. P., and Locke, E. A. (2018). Goal setting theory: Controversies and resolutions. In D. Ones, N. Anderson, C. Viswesvaran, and H. Sinangil (eds), *The SAGE Handbook of Industrial, Work & Organizational Psychology: Organizational Psychology* (pp. 145–166). Thousand Oaks, CA: Sage.

Latham, G. P., and Saari, L. M. (1982). The importance of union acceptance for productivity improvement through goal setting. *Personnel Psychology*, 35, 781–787.

Latham, G. P., and Saari, L. M. (1979a). The effects of holding goal difficulty constant on assigned and participatively set goals. *Academy of Management Journal*, 22, 163–168.

Latham, G. P., and Saari, L. M. (1979b). The importance of supportive relationships in goal setting. *Journal of Applied Psychology*, 64, 151–156.

Latham, G. P., and Seijts, G. H. (1999). The effects of proximal and distal goals on performance on a moderately complex task. *Journal of Organizational Behavior*, 20, 421–429.

Latham, G. P., and Steele, T. P., (1983). The motivational effects of participation versus goal setting on performance. *Academy of Management Journal*, 26, 406–417.

Latham, G. P., and Yukl, G. A. (1975). Assigned versus participative goal setting with educated and uneducated wood workers. *Journal of Applied Psychology*, 60, 299–302.

Latham, G. P., Brcic, J., and Steinhauer, A. (2017). Toward an integration of goal setting theory and the automaticity model. *Applied Psychology: An International Review*, 66, 25–48.

Latham, G. P., Erez, M., and Locke, E. A. (1988). Resolving scientific disputes by the joint design of crucial experiments by the antagonists: Application to the Erez-Latham dispute regarding participation in goal setting. *Journal of Applied Psychology*, 73, 753–772.

Latham, G. P., Locke, E. A., and Fassina, N. E. (2002). The high performance cycle: Standing the test of time. In S. Sonnentag (ed.), *The Psychological Management of Individual Performance: A Handbook in the Psychology of Management in Organizations* (pp. 201–228). Chichester: Wiley.

Latham, G. P., Mitchell, T. R., and Dossett, D. L. (1978). The importance of participative goal setting and anticipated rewards on goal difficulty and job performance. *Journal of Applied Psychology*, 63, 170–171.

Latham, G. P., Seijts, G., and Crim, D. (2008). The effects of learning goal difficulty level and cognitive ability on performance. *Canadian Journal of Behavioural Science/Revue canadienne des sciences du comportement*, 40(4), 220–229.

Latham, G. P., Winters, D. C., and Locke, E. A. (1994). Cognitive and motivational effects of participation: A mediator study. *Journal of Organizational Behavior*, 15, 49–63.

Locke, E. A., Frederick, E., Buckner, E., and Bobko, P. (1984). Effect of previously assigned goals on self-set goals and performance. *Journal of Applied Psychology*, 69, 694–699.

Locke, E. A., and Latham, G. P. (1990). *A Theory of Goal Setting and Task Performance.* Englewood Cliffs, NJ: Prentice Hall.

Locke, E. A., and Latham, G. P. (2002). Building a practically useful theory of goal setting and task motivation: A 35-year odyssey. *American Psychologist*, 57, 705–717.

Locke, E. A., and Latham, G. P. (2013). *New Developments in Goal Setting and Task Performance.* New York: Routledge.

Mawritz, M. B., Folger, R., and Latham, G. P. (2014). Supervisors' exceedingly difficult goals and abusive supervision: The mediating effects of hindrance stress, anger, and anxiety. *Journal of Organizational Behavior*, 35(3), 358–372.

Mealiea, L. W., and Latham, G. P. (1996). *Skills for Managerial Success: Theory, Experience, and Practice.* Toronto, ON: Irwin.

Meyer, H. H., Kay, E., and French, J. R. P., Jr. (1965). Split roles in performance appraisal. *Harvard Business Review*, 43, 123–129.

Millman, Z., and Latham, G. P. (2012). Increasing re-employment through training in verbal self-guidance. In M. Erez, U. Kleinbeck, and H. K. Thierry (eds), *Work Motivation in the Context of a Globalizing Economy* (pp. 94–104). London: Psychology Press.

Miner, J. B. (1984). The validity and usefulness of theories in an emerging organizational science. *Academy of Management Review*, 9, 296–306.

Mitchell, T. R., and Daniels, D. (2003). Motivation. In W.C. Borman, D. R. Ilgen, and R. J. Klimoski (eds), *Handbook of Psychology: Industrial Organizational Psychology* (Vol. 12, pp. 225–254). New York: Wiley.

Ordóñez, L., Schweitzer, M., Galinsky, A., and Bazerman, M. (2020). Goals gone wild: The systematic side effects of overprescribing goal setting. In Organizational Collaboration (pp. 21–34). Routledge. Organizational Psychology (Vol 1, pp. 103–124). Sage.

Pinder, C. C. (2008). *Work Motivation in Organizational Behavior* (2nd edition). Toronto, ON: Psychology Press.

Prigatano, G. P., Wong, J. L., Williams, C., and Plenge, K. L. (1997). Prescribed versus actual length of stay and inpatient neurorehabilitation outcome for brain dysfunctional patients. *Archives of Physical Medicine and Rehabilitation*, 78, 621–629.

Rodgers, R., and Hunter, J. E. (1991). Impact of management by objectives on organizational productivity. *Journal of Applied Psychology*, 76, 322–336.

Ronan, W. W., Latham, G. P., and Kinne, S. B. (1973). The effects of goal setting and supervision on worker behavior in an industrial situation. *Journal of Applied Psychology*, 58, 302–307.

Roney, C. J. R., Griggs, M., and Shanks, B. (2003). The mediation and moderation of general motivational variables by specific goals that are negatively framed. Unpublished manuscript.

Salancik, G. (1977). Commitment and the control of organizational behavior and belief. In B. M. Staw and G. R. Salancik (eds), *New Directions in Organizational Behavior.* Chicago: St. Clair Press.

Seijts, G. H., and Latham, G. P. (2005). Learning versus performance goals: When should each be used? *Academy of Management Executive,* 19, 124–131.

Seijts, G. H., Latham, G. P., and Woodwark, M. (2013). Learning goals: A qualitative and quantitative review. In E. A Locke and G. P. Latham (eds), *New Developments in Goal Setting and Task Performance* (pp. 195–212). New York, NY: Routledge.

Selden, S. C., and Brewer, G. A. (2000). Work motivation in the senior executive service: Testing the high performance cycle theory. *Journal of Public Administration Research and Theory,* 10, 531–550.

Shantz, A., and Latham, G. P. (2009). An exploratory field experiment of the effect of subconscious and conscious goals on employee performance. *Organizational Behavior and Human Decision Processes,* 109, 9–17.

Wiese, B. S., and Freund, A. M. (2005). Goal progress makes one happy, or does it? Longitudinal findings from the work domain. *Journal of Occupational and Organizational Psychology,* 78, 287–304.

Winters, D., and Latham, G. P. (1996). The effect of learning versus outcome goals on a simple versus a complex task. *Group and Organization Management,* 21, 236–250.

Yanar, B., Budworth, M. H., and Latham, G. P. (2009). The effect of verbal self-guidance training for overcoming employment barriers: A study of Turkish Women. *Applied Psychology: An International Review,* 58, 586–601.

Exercises

Exercise #1

Randomly divide people into three groups. Tell one group (in writing in all cases, so no person will know the others' goals) to think of 14 ways to improve their business (UG or MBA) program or their business unit's effectiveness in two minutes. (Give all subjects actually three minutes to show the effects of persistence of the hard goal: the hard goal group will still be working.) Give a second group the goal of 4 and tell the third group to do their best. Calculate the mean score of each group at the end. It is best to use lined sheets (numbered 1 to 14 or 1 to 4) for the goal groups and a blank sheet for the best group. (This helps prevent people from setting their own personal goals.)

Exercise #2

Give one group a photo of a woman winning a race and give the other group a blank sheet of paper. Ask both groups to come up with as many uses for a coat hanger as they can in two minutes. Count the scores of the two groups. This exercise is designed to measure the effects of subconscious priming.

Exercise #3

Please watch the following video(s):

1. How to achieve your most ambitious goals: https://www.youtube.com/watch?v=TQMbvJNRpLE
2. Why the secret to success is setting the right goals: https://www.youtube.com/watch?v=L4N1q4RNi9I
3. How to break away from habit and follow through on your goals: https://www.youtube.com/watch?v=9ED12INyJgw

Now, form small groups to discuss the video(s) and answer the following questions:

1. What are the major points of the video?
2. How can you use information from the video in your career?
3. Based on the video, what advice do you have for leaders in organizations?

Be prepared to present the ideas from your small group discussion with the class as a whole.

Discussion Questions

1. What is your basic advice to managers regarding how to set goals?
2. Are there any caveats regarding goal setting?
3. What do you do when two different goals conflict with each other?
4. How would you combine goals with rewards?
5. Is goal setting ever a bad idea?

Appendix: Guidelines for Effective Goal Setting in Organizations

By Edwin A. Locke, University of Maryland

Life is a goal-directed process. Organisms that fail to pursue and attain goals that satisfy their needs ultimately perish. In the case of humans, goal setting above the level of the automatically goal-directed functions of the body is a volitional process. Individuals need to make choices constantly as do organizations. An organization with no overarching goal or purpose would achieve nothing. For an organization to succeed, each member of the organization needs to engage in goal-directed action that directly or indirectly furthers the organization's core purpose or vision. What then is required to make goal setting work?

Focus

Goals focus attention and action on certain tasks or outcomes at the expense of others. This is pejoratively called "tunnel vision," but tunnel vision is actually necessary to prevent people from going in ten or a hundred directions at once. Goals need to be specific. Telling people to "work on" customer service or sales is better than nothing, but it is still somewhat vague. One way to make goals specific is to use numbers, for example, make sure customer service ratings are at least X on a 10-point scale, make XX deliveries per day, increase annual sales by XXX%. Tunnel vision only backfires when goals for important outcomes are not set (e.g. focusing on quantity while ignoring quality).

Types of Goals

Most people think of goals at work as being only for performance, for example, sales and profits. But there can also be goals for other actions that help foster good performance. Learning goals are one example. The aim of these is to improve one's skills or expertise through seeking information, experience, coaching, and/or training. There can also be goals for behaviors such as giving others information, warning others of a problem, giving others credit or thanks, treating others with respect, etc. There can also be goals for process such as when meeting a prospective new customer or a complaining customer, go through these six steps. The different types of goals can sometimes be combined. It has been found that one can work to perform well while at the same time learning new skills that will make the outcomes even better.

Prioritization

It may be asked: how many different goals can one person pursue successfully? This depends on the individual's ability, how much help and how much time they have, and the degree to which the goals are logically connected, as when one goal facilitates the achievement of another. Managers can delegate some goals to subordinates, keeping the more important or complex ones for themselves. When there are multiple goals, they need to be prioritized based on importance and urgency. Priorities may change over time based on circumstances, for example, opportunities, emergencies, threat, organizational changes, and the like, so employees need to be constantly updated.

Goals, Difficulty, and Effort

The level of difficulty of the goal affects effort. For a given task, the higher the goal level, the harder people will try (commitment is discussed below). Easy goals lead to low effort. People adjust to what is asked for. If the best performance is wanted, it is advisable NOT to tell people to "do their best" because when told that they usually do not. The term "do your best" is very general and thus interpreted subjectively, and the personal interpretations can vary from easy to hard. A quantitative measure eliminates the ambiguity. But the question remains: how high or hard should the ideal goal be? If the goal is set at an impossibly high level, most people will fail, and employees do not like to be considered inadequate and have to routinely worry about being fired. Furthermore, setting virtually impossible goals will undermine trust and morale. A safer guideline is to assign goals that are challenging yet reachable, for example, average previous performance for that job. (NOTE: In laboratory studies of goal setting, which typically last about an hour, impossible goals may be assigned to some subjects to maximize short-term effort.)

Stretch (Very Hard or Impossible) Goals as an Exception

There are two special circumstances in which setting seemingly impossible goals can be beneficial and not demoralizing. The first would be during an emergency, such as an order that is behind schedule due to unforeseen circumstances, for example, an equipment failure, a supplier failure, employee illnesses or turnover, etc. Employees will usually be willing to pitch in and work extra time to get the job done, especially if they know they will receive a suitable reward such as extra time off. Coping with an emergency can also give people a sense of pride. However, such emergency efforts could wear thin if they become routine and lead to fatigue and burnout. The second exception would be when the organization wants to motivate a major creative breakthrough. Let us say you make magnetic resonance imaging (MRI) machines for hospitals. These machines are expensive to buy, are very noisy, and require many minutes for each test. Goals could be set to think outside the square in order to decrease costs, noise level, or testing time by, say, 50%. The goals might be totally unreachable, but the purpose would be to motivate breakthrough thinking. In the MRI case, an improvement of even 10% might be beneficial. The key principle here is: there should be no penalty for not reaching a stretch goal. Suitable rewards for progress can be decided after the fact.

Goals and Time

Goals themselves can involve meeting deadlines. But goals for results need to involve a time perspective. Long-term goals can be hard to hold in mind. So, it is beneficial to combine proximal (shorter-term) with distal (long-term) goals. The former are a means to the latter, and they allow one to track progress. Proximal goals provide information about the degree to which the long-term strategy is working and can thereby increase confidence. They also help prevent procrastination (waiting until the last minute). Obviously, goal revisions may be necessary as business circumstances change, especially for longer-term goals.

Knowledge and Skill

Successful goal-directed action requires not just desire but also knowledge and skill. Motivation without knowledge will produce effort, but effort has to be guided.

Knowledge and skill come from experience, training, and coaching. It must be stressed that experience alone is not automatically beneficial; people can remain inept and make the same mistakes over and over. The key is what is actually learned from experience.

Feedback

A key type of knowledge needed for goals to work is feedback about progress. Without it, people will not know if they are getting anywhere or whether they are on track to meet a deadline. Feedback may come from many sources, for example, self-tracking, organizational records and monitoring systems, team members, managers, customers, graphic displays, the internet, etc. Useful feedback information must be objective (see the section titled "How to Prevent Cheating" that follows).

Gaining Commitment to Goals

Goal setting does not work unless people are committed to their goals. Four factors play a role. First, it is useful to begin by giving people the organization's reason(s) for the goal, so they do not think it is arbitrary. A second factor is value importance. Many value elements can be come into play here. For example, people are paid to work, so doing what one is asked to do is considered normal and legitimate. Raises and promotions are based on five goal success and repeated failure can lead to dismissal. Further, conscientious employees will take personal pride in their achievements, including expanding their capabilities. Achieving excellence may open up enhanced career opportunities. Leaders and peers may serve as inspiring role models. Team members may encourage success and even demand support. The job may (ideally) engage deeply held personal values, for example, producing life-protecting vaccines. Much depends on selecting employees who show evidence of holding values that fit the organization's vision. A third factor that enhances goal commitment is healthy, reality based (nonpretentious) self-confidence, which is known as self-efficacy in psychology. People will not be motivated to commit to goals they do not think they can attain or work for rewards they do not think they can earn. Selecting and training capable people is important. A fourth factor in commitment is organizational support. We all know that organizations have limited resources, but employees need to know that their efforts are supported. This can include time, money, equipment, space freedom from arbitrary rules, and help from colleagues or assistants. Sincere, verbal expressions of commitment to your projects from higher ups, for example, managers, executives, and the CEO can be inspiring.

Who Sets the Goals?

There are three broad possibilities: participatively set, assigned, and self-set. Contrary to common belief, there is no one method that is always superior to the others. In all cases, the effects depend on the challenge level of the goals that are set and degree of commitment. No one method guarantees the setting of specific, challenging goals. Participatively set goals are set jointly with one's boss. The main benefit of participation is information exchange. Communication is critical in organizations, but this can work in more than one way. For example, subordinates may convince their bosses to agree to easy goals by convincing them that the easy goals they favor are actually hard. This would lead to good rewards but poor performance. (This problem undermined many old-time MBO programs.) In the case of self-set goals, people can set them at whatever level they want, high to low, without anyone's approval. Assigned goals may be the best method of aligning organizational goals with individual goals, but the core requirements for goal effectiveness are the same for all three methods.

How to Prevent Cheating

Virtually everyone wants to succeed in their work and get valued rewards. To many, success is a self-esteem issue. (Studies show that most people view themselves as above average which is obviously not the case.) Thus, it is not surprising that some people may cheat by claiming or reporting achievements that are not theirs or which were faked. Thus, all organizations need a value system, stressing for example, honesty, integrity, and justice. The value system is not just an online list; it is a way of acting. This system has to be driven from the top or top management team, else the organization will descend into anarchy with each group or unit having its own value system. Enforcement requires a series of steps: (i) formulating the value system; (ii) insuring that the higher level managers and CEO are ethical role models in their own behavior; (iii) selecting employees for moral character as well as competence; (iv) communicating the value system to all employees; (v) creating internal control systems, for example, the accounting department, customer feedback, tracking internal complains to prevent or at least detect dishonesty; (vi) incorporating character assessment, including assessments by trustworthy peers, as part of the performance appraisal system; and (vii) dismissing employees who violate the ethics code. Note: ethics violations may be very costly to an organization, not only with respect to reputation but in terms of financial penalties.

Goals and Pay

There is no validated theory within the goal literature regarding the best way to tie goals and pay together. Obviously, people want to be treated justly. But this requires many judgment calls. For example, some people may fail more because they have harder goals than others. Others may have to overcome more obstacles not of their own making than others. Some may get more help than others. Some get great results by abusing subordinates who later burn out or resign. Some make themselves look like heroes by getting out of difficult situations time and time again when their difficulties were actually caused by their own lack of planning. At the same time, the employee who smoothly gains success after success with no drama may be overlooked, even though they are better than the alleged hero. Some people may look good because they take ideas from others with no credit. The bottom line is that managers have to hold a number of context factors in mind. Look not just at who seems to be best but how they got their results.

Goals and Job Satisfaction

Employees are happy when they attain their goals or make progress toward them. Earned success is a source of pride and an incentive to keep striving. Job satisfaction comes from other sources as well, for example, fair pay; recognition; work that ties into one's personal interests; mental challenge; variety; competent, honest leadership; supportive coworkers; competitive benefits; suitable (and safe) working conditions; etc. It is a great challenge to keep people satisfied over time because the world is always changing. A key objective should be to retain as many as you can of your best people, because they are the most critical to organizational success and are also the people that other organizations will most want to poach.

Goals and Teams

The same principles apply here as with individuals, but some new elements are added. Team members can and need to exchange information, thus (if knowledge is distributed) providing a larger pool of information. Members can also encourage and help one another practically and psychologically when there are obstacles. They can also undermine one another, so there need to be rules for team conduct. There is an important caveat: team goals will not work unless all members are committed to the team goals; if there is a conflict, rather than a harmony, between individual and team goals, the process can be undermined. People need to be given credit for contributions to the team. I will not go into organization level goals here, because that is a huge topic in itself – except to say that these need to be driven from the top to start with and require enormous feats of coordination.

Goals and Bullying

What does bullying mean? Using goals as threats; insulting or berating people who have failed through no fault of their own; routinely giving impossible goals which are not used as stretch goals as noted earlier; raising goals arbitrarily but not rewards, etc. Bullying will be perceived as unjust, and employees will resent it and may quietly resist or quit. When word gets around the whole company, the culture can be undermined. Failure needs to be treated as a problem to be solved. There can be many causes: not understanding the goal, not having the needed skills, lack of organizational support, lack of commitment, unwillingness to put forth effort, personal problems, etc. Some failures are outside an employee's control. Termination may be needed (e.g. in the case of clear lack of competence or an ethics violation) but should be preceded by an objective causal analysis. Sometimes employees are assigned to the wrong job and could succeed if placed elsewhere.

Recent Discoveries

Writing About Goals and Values

Recent studies have found that the very process of writing about goals or values leads to more motivation to take goal-directed action. Private goal or value writing sessions can take various amounts of time and sessions can be repeated over time. Longer sessions (e.g. two hours) seem to have more of an effect then shorter ones. Making the written goals specific, including a description of goal strategies seems to facilitate action. The writing is done privately. It is not fully known why writing works.

Subconscious Priming of Goals

Goal setting research has usually focused on conscious goals. However, recent research by Dr. Gary Latham at the University of Toronto and his colleagues has found that goal-directed action can be subconsciously primed. For example, the person may be shown a picture of a runner winning a race and then given a job to perform. The people primed with a picture of a racer (in track) perform better than those shown no picture or a picture of a tree. No deception was involved. It was found that the people shown the racer picture also set themselves higher conscious goals than those shown the tree picture. Much more needs to be learned about how this all works.

Conclusion

Goal setting is a critically important motivational technique, but like all management principles, its benefits depend on how skillfully it is used. Edwin A. Locke is a Professor Emeritus from the R. H. Smith School of Business at the University of Maryland at College Park. With Dr. Latham, he has spent some 50 years developing goal setting theory. A nontechnical article by Locke which makes "Some Observations about Goals, Money, and Cheating in Business" can be found in *Organizational Dynamics*, 48 (2019), pp. 1–5. For those wanting a technical descriptions of goal setting theory and the research behind it, see Locke and Latham's two major books: *A Theory of Goal Setting and Task Performance*, 1990, Prentice Hall, and *New Developments in Goal Setting and task Performance*, 2013, Routledge.

6

Cultivate Self-Efficacy for Personal and Organizational Effectiveness

ALBERT BANDURA

Department of Psychology, Stanford University

EDITORS' NOTE

Albert Bandura died at his home in Stanford on July 26, 2021, from congestive heart failure, at the age of 95. We are indebted to him for his profound impact on organizational sciences.

Human behavior is extensively motivated and regulated through the exercise of self-influence. Among the mechanisms of self-influence, none is more focal or pervading than belief in one's personal efficacy. Unless people believe that they can produce desired effects and forestall undesired ones by their actions, they have little incentive to act or to persevere in the face of difficulties. Whatever other factors may serve as guides and motivators, they are rooted in the core belief that one has to power to produce desired results. That belief in one's capabilities is a vital personal resource is amply documented by meta-analyses of findings from diverse spheres of functioning (Holden, 1991; Holden, Moncher, Schinke, and Barker, 1990; Multon, Brown, and Lent, 1991; Stajkovic and Lee, 2001; Stajkovic and Luthans, 1998). Perceived self-efficacy is founded on the agentic perspective of social cognitive theory (Bandura1997, 2006, 2008a). To be an agent is to influence intentionally one's functioning and life conditions. In this view, people are contributors to their life circumstances not just products of them.

CORE FUNCTIONAL PROPERTIES OF PERCEIVED SELF-EFFICACY

Converging evidence from controlled experimental and field studies verifies that belief in one's capabilities contributes uniquely to motivation and action (Bandura, 1997, 2008b; Bandura and Locke, 2003). Perceived self-efficacy occupies a pivotal role in causal structures because it affects human functioning not only directly, but through its impact on other important classes of determinants. These

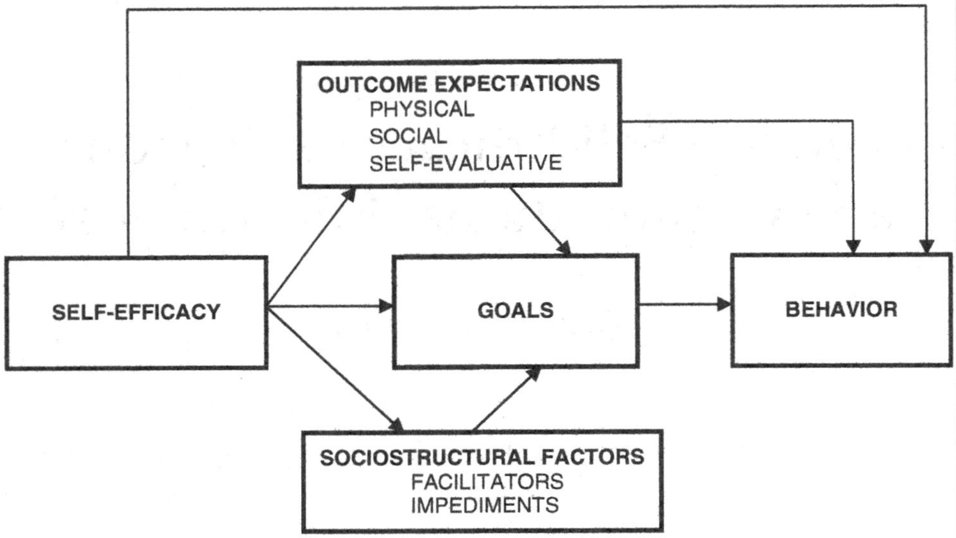

FIGURE 6.1 Structural paths of influence wherein perceived self-efficacy affects motivation and performance attainments both directly and through its impact on goals, outcome expectations, and perception of sociostructural facilitators and impediments

determinants include goal aspirations, incentives and disincentives rooted in outcome expectations, and perceived impediments and opportunity structures in social systems. Figure 6.1 presents the structure of the causal model. Diverse lines of research have verified the various paths in the structural model. Longitudinal research evaluating the full set of determinants confirms that the social cognitive model provides a good fit to the empirical evidence (Plotnikoff, Lippke, Courneya, Birkett, and Sigal, 2008). Among the different determinants, self-efficacy emerges as the strongest predictor.

Efficacy beliefs affect self-motivation and action through their impact on goals and aspirations. It is partly on the basis of efficacy beliefs that people choose what goal challenges to undertake, how much effort to invest in the endeavor, and how long to persevere in the face of difficulties (Bandura, 1997; Locke and Latham, 1990). When faced with obstacles, setbacks, and failures, those who doubt their capabilities slacken their efforts, give up prematurely, or settle for poorer solutions. Those who have a strong belief in their capabilities redouble their effort to master the challenges.

Perceived efficacy likewise plays an influential role in the incentive and disincentive potential of outcome expectations. The outcomes people anticipate depend largely on their beliefs of how well they can perform in given situations. Those of high efficacy expect to gain favorable outcomes through good performance, whereas those who expect poor performances of themselves conjure up negative outcomes. Anticipated outcomes may take the form of material costs and benefits, social commendation and reproof, and self-approving and self-censuring affective reactions.

In theories of motivation founded on the incentives operating through cognized outcomes, such as expectancy-value theories, motivation is governed by the expectation that a given behavior will produce certain outcomes and the value placed on those outcomes. This type of theory includes only one of the two belief systems governing motivation. People act on their beliefs about what they can do, as well as on their beliefs about the likely outcomes of performance. There are countless activities that, if done well, produce valued outcomes, but they are not pursued by those who doubt they can do what it takes to succeed. They exclude entire classes of options rapidly on self-efficacy grounds without bothering to analyze their costs and benefits. Conversely, those of high efficacy expect their efforts to bring success and are not easily dissuaded by negative outcomes.

Rational models of motivation and decision-making that exclude perceived self-efficacy sacrifice explanatory and predictive power. Perceived self-efficacy not only sets the slate of options for consideration, but also regulates their implementation. Having decided on a course of action, one cannot sit back and wait for the performances to appear. Making a decision does not ensure that individuals will mobilize the effort to execute the decided course of action successfully and stick to it in the face of difficulties. A psychology of decision-making requires a psychology of action grounded in enabling and sustaining efficacy beliefs. One must add a performatory self to the decisional self; otherwise, the decider is left stranded in thought.

Beliefs of personal efficacy shape whether people attend to the opportunities or to the impediments that their life circumstances present and how formidable the obstacles appear. People of high efficacy focus on the opportunities worth pursuing and view difficult obstacles as surmountable (Krueger and Dickson, 1993, 1994). Through ingenuity and perseverance, they figure out ways of exercising some measure of control even in environments of limited opportunities and many constraints. Those beset with self-doubts dwell on impediments which they view as obstacles over which they can exert little control. They easily convince themselves of the futility of effort, so they achieve limited success even in environments that provide many opportunities.

Diverse Organizational Impact of Perceived Self-Efficacy

The scope of the organizational applications of perceived self-efficacy will be summarized briefly before presenting the principles for altering efficacy belief systems. The brief review of its scope addresses the challenge of constructing a parsimonious theory of broad generalizability. To begin with, perceived self-efficacy is an influential determinant of career choice and development. The higher the people's perceived efficacy to fulfill educational requirements and occupational roles, the wider the career options they seriously consider pursuing, the greater the interest they have in them, the better they prepare themselves educationally for different occupational careers, and the greater their staying power in challenging career pursuits (Lent, Brown, and Hackett, 1994).

New employees receive training designed to prepare them for the occupational roles they will be performing (see Chapter 4). Those of low perceived efficacy prefer prescriptive training that tells them how to perform the roles as traditionally structured (Jones 1986; Saks, 1995). Employees of high perceived efficacy prefer training that enables them to restructure their roles innovatively by improving the customary practices and adding new elements and functions to them. Self-efficacious employees take greater initiative in their occupational self-development and generate ideas that help to improve work processes (Speier and Frese, 1997).

Organizations that provide their new employees with guided mastery experiences, effective coworkers as models, and enabling performance feedback enhance employees' self-efficacy, emotional well-being, job satisfaction, and level of productivity (Saks, 1994, 1995). Other organizational practices, such as job enrichment and mutually supportive communication, also build employees' perceived efficacy to take on broader functions and a proactive work role (Parker, 1998). Self-efficacy theory provides a conceptual framework within which to study the determinants of effective work design and the mechanisms through which they enhance organizational functioning.

Managers as enabling facilitators of team functioning (see Chapter 15) have also been studied in terms of empowering leadership. It is typically characterized as leading by example, participant decision-making, enabling guidance, and receptivity to members' ideas (Arnold, Arad, Rhoades, and Drasgow, 2000). Empowering leadership has been found to be positively related to team performance, but the mechanisms through which it works have received little attention. Srivastava, Bartol, and Locke (2006) report that empowering leaderships is not directly linked to performance but operates through knowledge sharing and perceived team efficacy.

Work life is increasingly structured on a team-based model in which management and operational functions are assigned to the workers themselves (see Chapter 11). A self-management work structure changes the model of supervisory managership from hierarchical control to facilitative guidance that provides the necessary resources, instructive guidance, and that support that teams need to do their work effectively (Stewart and Manz, 1995). Enabling organizational structures build managers' efficacy to operate as facilitators of productive teamwork (Laschruger and Shamian, 1994). The perceived collective efficacy of self-managed teams predicts the members' satisfaction and productivity (Lindsley, Mathieu, Heffner, and Brass, 1994; Little and Madigan, 1994).

The development of new business ventures and the renewal of established ones depend heavily on innovativeness and entrepreneurship (see Chapter 30). With many resourceful competitors around, viability requires continual ingenuity. At the preparatory level, self-efficacy plays an influential role in the development of entrepreneurial intentions (Zhao, Serbert, and Hills, 2005). Learning experiences and risk propensity had no direct effect on intentions to pursue an entrepreneurial career. They had an impact only to the extent that they raised individuals' beliefs in their efficacy to identify new business opportunities, create new products, think creatively, and commercialize ideas. This is the structural pattern of relations after controlling for prior entrepreneurial intentions. Self-efficacy continues to play an influential role in the undertaking of new ventures.

Entrepreneurs have to be willing to take risks under uncertainty. Those of high efficacy focus on the opportunities worth pursuing, whereas the less self-efficacious dwell on the risks to be avoided (Krueger and Dickson, 1993, 1994). Hence, perceived self-efficacy predicts entrepreneurship and which patent inventors are likely to start new business ventures (Chen, Greene, and Crick, 1998; Markman and Baron, 1999). Venturers who achieve high growth in companies they have founded or transformed those they bought have a vision of what they wish to achieve, a firm belief in their efficacy to realize it, set challenging growth goals, and come up with innovative production and marketing strategies (Baum, Locke, and Smith, 2001; Baum and Locke, 2004).

Effective leadership and workforces require receptivity to innovators that can improve the quality and productivity of organizations. Managers' perceived technical efficacy influences their readiness to adopt electronic technologies (Jorde-Bloom and Ford, 1988). Efficacy beliefs affect not only managers' receptivity to technological innovations, but also the readiness with which employees adopt them (Hill, Smith, and Mann, 1987; McDonald and Seagall, 1992). Efficacy fostered adoption of new technologies, in turn, alters the organizational network structure and confers influence on early adopters within an organization over time (Burkhardt, and Brass, 1990).

Perceived self-efficacy to fulfill occupational demands affects level of stress and physical health of employees (see Chapter 27). Those of low efficacy are stressed both emotionally and physiologically by perceived overload in which task demands exceed their perceived coping capabilities, whereas those who hold a high belief in their efficacy and that of their group are unfazed by heavy workloads (Jex and Bliese, 1999). Perceived self-efficacy must be added to the demand–control model of occupational stress to improve its predictability. It contends that being given control over work activities reduces the stressfulness of work life. High job demands with opportunity to exercise control over various facets of the work environment is unperturbing to jobholders of high perceived efficacy, but stressful to those of low perceived efficacy to manage them (Schaubroeck and Merritt, 1997). Efforts to reduce occupational stressfulness by increasing job control without raising self-efficacy to manage the increased responsibilities will do more harm than good. For the self-efficacious, job underload can be a stressor. Indeed, employees of high efficacy are stressed by perceived underload in which they feel thwarted and frustrated by organizational constraints in developing and using their potentialities (Matsui and Onglatco, 1992). Exposure to chronic occupational stressors with a low sense of efficacy to manage job demands and to enlist social support in times of difficulty increases vulnerability to burnout (Brouwers and Tomic 1999; Leiter, 1992; Salanova, Grau, Cifse, and Lloreus, 2000). This syndrome is characterized by physical and emotional exhaustion, depersonalization of clients, lack of any sense of personal accomplishment, and occupational disengagement with cynicism about one's work.

A resilient sense of efficacy provides the necessary staying power in the tortuous pursuit of innovation and excellence. Yet the very undaunted self-efficacy that breeds success in tough ventures may perpetuate adherence to courses of action that hold little prospect of eventual success. Thus, for example, managers of high perceived efficacy are more prone than those of low efficacy to escalate commitment to unproductive ventures (Whyte and Saks, 2007; Whyte, Saks, and Hook, 1997) and to remain wedded to previously successful practices despite altered realities that place them at competitive disadvantage (Audia, Locke, and Smith, 2000). The corrective for the perils of success is not deflation of personal efficacy. Such a disenabling remedy would undermine aspiration, innovation, and human accomplishments in endeavors presenting tough odds. Individuals who are highly assured in their capabilities and the effectiveness of their strategies are disinclined to seek discordant information that would suggest the need for corrective adjustments. The challenge is to preserve the considerable functional value of resilient self-efficacy, but to institute information monitoring and social feedback systems that can help to identify practices that are beyond the point of utility. Reliable risk analysis, when achievable, is essential in preventing irresponsible ventures that created a global financial crisis. However, one must distinguish between escalative commitment to a failing venture and engagement in deceptive and fraudulent corporate practices. Research on the exercise of moral agency attests to the influential role played by selective moral disengagement in corporate practices that spawn widespread harm (Bandura, 1999; Bandura, Caprara, and Zsolnai, 2002; White, Bandura, and Bero, 2009). As a trader in the midst of the growing financial crisis put it, "I leave my ethics at the door."

It is easy to achieve veridical judgment. Simply punish optimism. The motivational belief system that fosters accomplishments in difficult endeavors combines realism about tough odds, but optimism that through self-development and perseverant effort one can beat those odds. We study intensively the risks of overconfidence, but ignore the more pervasive personal and social costs of underconfidence. This bias probably stems from the fact that the costs of lost opportunities and underdeveloped potentialities are long delayed and less noticeable than those of venturesome missteps. The heavy selective focus on the risk of overconfidence stands in stark contrast to the entrepreneurial spirit driving the modern workplace in the rapidly changing world.

The functional value of veridical self-appraisal depends on the nature of the venture. In activities where the margins of error are narrow and missteps can produce costly or injurious consequences, one is best served by conservative appraisal of one's efficacy. It is a different matter when difficult accomplishments can produce substantial personal or social benefits and the personal costs involve time, effort, and expendable resources. People have to decide whether to invest their efforts and resources in ventures that are difficult to fulfill, and how much hardship they are willing to endure in formidable pursuits that may have huge payoffs but are strewn with obstacles and uncertainties. Turning visions into realities is an arduous process with uncertain outcomes. Societies enjoy the considerable benefits of the eventual accomplishments in the arts, sciences, and technologies of its persisters and risk-takers. Realists trade on the merchandizable products that flow from the creations of innovative persisters. To paraphrase the discerning observation of George Bernard Shaw, reasonable people adapt to the world and unreasonable ones try to change it, so human progress depends on the unreasonable ones.

Social cognitive theory distinguishes among three forms of perceived efficacy depending on the source of control over events. Direct individual efficacy pertains to belief in one's capability to exercise some measure of control over events within one's command. However, in many spheres of functioning, people do not have direct control over conditions that affect their lives. They exercise proxy efficacy through socially mediated influence. They do so by influencing others who have the resources, knowledge, and means to act on their behalf to secure the outcomes they desire. Many of the things that people seek are achievable only by working collaboratively for common purpose through interdependent effort. In the exercise of collective efficacy, they pool their knowledge, skills, and resources and act in concert to shape their future (Bandura, 2000; Gully, Incalcaterra, Joshi, and Beaubien, 2002; Stajkovic and Lee, 2001).

Given the generality and centrality of the self-efficacy mechanism in the causal structures governing diverse aspects of organizational functioning, programs aimed at developing a resilient sense of efficacy can yield significant dividends in performance accomplishments and personal well-being. The principles for developing and strengthening beliefs of personal efficacy are addressed in the sections that follow. Social cognitive theory lends itself readily to personal and social applications in diverse spheres of life. These applications are extensively reviewed elsewhere (Bandura, 1986, 1997, 2004, 2006). The present chapter summarizes the relevant principles for developing a resilient sense of efficacy and illustrates their application in the organizational field.

Principles Governing the Development of Personal and Collective Efficacy

Self-efficacy beliefs are developed by four principal sources of information conveyed enactively, vicariously, persuasively, and somatically. The most effective way of instilling strong efficacy is through enactive mastery experiences structured through graduated attainments. If people experience only easy successes, they come to expect quick results and are easily discouraged by failure. Hence, resilient efficacy requires experience in overcoming obstacles through perseverant effort. The route to high attainments is strewn with failure and setbacks. Success is achieved by learning from mistakes. Resilience must also be built by training in how to manage failure so that it is informative rather than demoralizing.

The second way of developing personal and collective efficacy is by social modeling. Competent models convey knowledge, skills, and strategies for managing task demands. By their example in pursuing challenges, models foster aspirations and interest in activities. Seeing people similar to oneself succeed by perseverant effort raises observers' beliefs in their own abilities.

Social persuasion is the third mode of influence. If people are persuaded to believe in themselves, they will exert more effort. This increases their chances of success. However, credible persuaders must be knowledgeable and practice what they preach. Effective efficacy builders do more than convey faith in others. They arrange situations for others in ways that bring and success. They avoid placing them, prematurely, in situations where they are likely to fail. They measure success by self-improvement, rather than by triumphs over others. Pep talks, without enabling guidance, achieve little.

People rely partly on their physical and emotional states in judging their efficacy. They read their tension, anxiety, and weariness as signs of personal deficiencies. Mood also affects how people judge their efficacy. Positive mood enhances a sense of efficacy, and depressed mood diminishes it. People often misread their fatigue, windedness, aches, and pains as evidence of declining physical efficacy. These physical conditions are often due to a sedentary lifestyle. Efficacy beliefs are strengthened by reducing anxiety and depression, building physical strength and stamina, and changing misrepresentations of bodily states.

As illustrated in the diverse organizational effects cited earlier, efficacy beliefs regulate human functioning through their impact on cognitive, motivational, affective, and decisional processes. They affect whether people think productively, pessimistically, or optimistically and in self-enacting or self-debilitating ways; how well they motivate themselves and persevere in the face of difficulties; the quality of their emotional well-being they achieve and their vulnerability to stress and depression; and the life choices they make, which set the course of their life paths.

Information for judging personal efficacy, whether conveyed enactively, vicariously, persuasively, or somatically, is not inherently informative. It is only raw data. Experiences become instructive through cognitive processing of efficacy information and reflective thought. One must distinguish between information conveyed by events and information as selected, interpreted, and integrated into self-efficacy judgments.

The cognitive processing of efficacy information involves two separate functions (Bandura, 1997). The first is the types of information people attend to and use as indicators of personal efficacy. Social cognitive theory specifies the set of efficacy indictors that are unique to each of the four major modes of influence. These are summarized in Table 6.1. For example, judgments of self-efficacy based on performance attainments will vary depending on people's interpretive biases, the perceived difficulty of the task, how hard they worked at it, how much help they received, the conditions under which they performed, their emotional and physical state at the time, their rate of improvement over time, and biases in how they monitor and recall their attainments.

The indicators people single out provide the information base on which the self-appraisal process operates. The second function in efficacy judgment involves the combination rules or heuristics people use to weight and integrate efficacy information from the diverse sources in forming their efficacy beliefs. The informativeness of the various efficacy indicants will vary for different spheres of functioning. The various sources of efficacy information may be integrated additively, multiplicatively, configurally, or heuristically. This judgmental process is not entirely dispassionate. Strong preconceptions and affective proclivities can alter self-efficacy appraisals positively or negatively.

The multiple benefits of a strong sense of personal efficacy do not arise simply from the incantation of capability. Saying something should not be confused with believing it to be so. A sense of personal efficacy is constructed through a complex process of self-persuasion based on integrating constellations of efficacy information conveyed enactively, vicariously, socially, and physiologically.

Table 6.1 The distinctive sets of factors within each of four modes of efficacy influence that can affect the construction of self-efficacy beliefs

Enactive efficacy information	**Vicarious efficacy information**
Interpretive biases	Model attribute similarity
Perceived task difficulty and diagnosticity	Model performance similarity
Effort expenditure	Model historical similarity
Amount of external aid received	Multiplicity and diversity of modeling
Situational circumstances of performance	Mastery or coping modeling
Transient affective and physical states	Exemplification of strategies
Temporal pattern of successes and failures	Portrayal of task demands
Selective bias in self-monitoring of performance	
Selective bias in memory for performance attainments	
Persuasory efficacy information	**Somatic and affective information**
Credibility	Degree of attentional focus on somatic states
Expertness	Interpretative biases regarding somatic states
Consensus	Perceived source of affective arousal
Degree of appraisal disparity	Level of arousal
Familiarity with task demands	Situational circumstances of arousal

Enablement Through Guided Mastery

Guided mastery provides one of the most effective ways of cultivating competencies. However, a skill is only as good as its execution, which is heavily governed by self-regulatory and motivational factors. Individuals may, therefore, perform poorly, adequately, or well with the same set of skills depending on the beliefs they hold about their capabilities in given situations (Bandura, 1997). Part of the power of guided mastery stems from its use of all four modes of efficacy development.

The method that produces the best gains in both self-efficacy and skill combines three components (Bandura, 1986). First, the appropriate skills are modeled to convey the basic rules and strategies. Second, the learners receive guided practice under simulated conditions to develop proficiency in the skills. Third, they are provided with a graduated transfer program that helps them to apply their newly learned skills in work situations in ways that will bring them success.

Enabling modeling: Modeling is the first step in developing competencies. Complex skills are broken down into subskills, which can be modeled on videotape in easily mastered steps. Subdividing complex skills into subskills produces better learning than trying to teach everything at once. After the subskills are learned by this means, they can be combined into complex strategies to serve different purposes. Effective modeling teaches general rules and strategies for dealing with different situations rather than only specific responses or scripted routines. Voice-over narration of the rules and strategies as they are being modeled and brief summaries of the rules enhances the development of generic competencies.

The execution of skills must be varied to suit changing circumstances. People who learn rules in the abstract usually do a poor job in applying them in particular situations. However, teaching abstract rules with varied brief examples promotes generalizability of the skills being taught by showing how the rules and strategies can be widely applied and adjusted to fit changing conditions. A single lengthy example teaches how to apply the rule in that particular situation but provides no instruction on how to adapt its application to varying situations.

People fail to apply what they have learned, or do so only half-heartedly, if they distrust their ability to do it successfully. Therefore, modeling influences must be designed to build a sense of personal efficacy as well as to convey knowledge about rules and strategies. The impact of modeling on beliefs about one's capabilities is greatly increased by perceived similarity to the models. Learners adopt modeled ways more readily if they see individuals similar to themselves solve problems successfully with the modeled strategies than if they regard the models as very different from themselves. The characteristics of models, the type of problems with which they cope, and the situations in which they apply their skills should be made to appear similar to the trainees' own circumstances.

Guided skill perfection: Factual and strategic knowledge alone will not beget proficient performance. Knowledge structures are transformed into proficient action through a conception-matching process (Bandura, 1986). Enabling modeling provides the guiding conception for a proficient management of one's work life. The feedback accompanying enactments provides the information needed to detect and correct mismatches between the generic conception of requisite skills and action. This comparative process is repeated until a close match is achieved. Putting into practice what one has learned cognitively can also reveal gaps and flaws in the guiding conception. Recognizing what one does not know contributes to the refinement of cognitive representations by further modeling and verbal instruction regarding the problematic aspects of the representation.

In the transformational phase of competency development, learners test their newly acquired skills in simulated situations where they need not fear making mistakes or appearing inadequate. This is best achieved by role rehearsal in which they practice handling the types of situations they have to manage in their work environment. Mastery of skills can be facilitated by combining cognitive and behavioral rehearsal. In cognitive rehearsal, people rehearse mentally how they will translate strategies into what they say and do to manage given situations.

In perfecting their skills, people need informative feedback about how they are doing. A common problem is that they do not fully observe their own behavior. Informative feedback enables them to make corrective adjustments to get their behavior to fit their idea of how things should be done. Videotape replays are widely used for this purpose. However, simply being shown replays of one's own behavior usually has mixed effects (Hung and Rosenthal, 1981). To produce good results, the feedback must direct attention to the corrective changes that need to be made. It should call attention to successes and improvements and correct deficiencies in a supportive and enabling way so as to strengthen perceived efficacy. Some of the gains accompanying informative feedback result from raising people's beliefs in their efficacy rather than solely from further skill development. The feedback that is most informative and achieves the greatest improvements takes the form of corrective modeling. In this approach, the subskills that have not been adequately learned are further modeled, and learners rehearse them until they master them.

Effective functioning requires more than learning how to apply rules and strategies for managing organizational demands. The transactions of occupational life are littered with impediments, discordances, and stressors. Many of the problems of occupational functioning reflect failures of self-management rather than deficiencies of knowledge and technical skills. Therefore, an important aspect of competency development includes training in resiliency to difficulties. As we shall see later, this requires skill in cognitive self-guidance, self-motivation, and strategies for counteracting self-debilitating reactions to troublesome situations that can easily unhinge one.

Gist, Bavetta, and Stevens (1990) augmented a guided modeling training in negotiation skills with a self-management component. In the latter phase, trainees were taught how to anticipate potential stressors, devise ways of overcoming them, monitor the adequacy of their coping approach, and use self-incentives to sustain their efforts. Trainees who had the benefit of the supplemental self-management training were better at applying learned negotiation skills in new contractual situations presenting conflictful and intimidating elements and negotiated more favorable outcomes than trainees who did not. The self-managers made flexible use of the wide range of strategies they had been taught, whereas their counterparts were more likely to persevere with only a few of the strategies when they encountered negative reactions.

Vinokur and his colleagues devised a multifaceted program to immunize laid-off workers against the debilitating effects of job loss and to restore their efficacy to secure employment in quality jobs (Vinokur, van Ryn, Gramlich, and Price, 1991). They were taught, via modeling and rehearsed in role enactments, how to carry out effective job searches. They identified potential impediments and developed problem-solving strategies for generating alternative solutions. They received resilience training by anticipating potential problems and setbacks and developing coping strategies that enabled them to persist despite disappointments during their job search. In follow-up assessments conducted shortly after the program and several years later, the project participants had higher job-seeking efficacy, found jobs more quickly, got better quality jobs, and earned higher wages than did those who did not receive the program. In a meditational analysis, van Ryn and Vinokur (1992) found that the effect of the reemployment program on job search behavior was mediated by perceived self-efficacy.

Job searches in a competitive market require a lot of self-initiative and staying power in face of discouraging rejections. A resilient sense of efficacy is needed to sustain the effort. Yanar, Budworth, and Latham (2008) combined modeling, functional verbal self-guidance, role rehearsal, and proximal goal setting to hasten the reemployment of women in an Islamic society. They face the added obstacle of gender discrimination in the workplace. Compared to women who received didactic instruction in job search, those who had the benefit of the enabling sociocognitive program were more persistent in their job search and more likely to find work in their area of interest. In accord with the findings of Vinokur et al. (1991), self-efficacy completely mediated the effect of the program on job search behaviors. This low-cost/high-benefit approach also enabled aboriginal youth to secure and maintain employment. The higher instilled self-efficacy, the better their employment outcomes (Latham and Budworth, 2006). This research addresses a matter of growing import as societies continue to become more ethnically and culturally diverse.

Transfer training by self-directed success: Modeling and simulated enactments are well suited for creating competencies. But new skills are unlikely to be used for long unless they prove useful when they are put into practice in work situations. People must experience sufficient success using what they have learned to believe in themselves and the value of the new ways. This is best achieved by a transfer program in which newly acquired skills are first tried on the job in situations likely to produce good results. Learners are assigned selected problems they often encounter in their everyday situations. After they try their hand at it, they discuss their successes and where they ran into difficulties for further instructive training. As learners gain skill and confidence in handling easier situations, they gradually take on more difficult problems. If people have not had sufficient practice to convince themselves of their new effectiveness, they apply the skills they have been taught weakly and inconsistently. They rapidly abandon their skills when they fail to get quick results or experience difficulties.

Mastery modeling is now increasingly used, especially in videotaped formats, to develop competencies. But its potential is not fully realized if training programs do not provide sufficient practice to achieve proficiency in the modeled skills or if they lack an adequate transfer program that provides success with the new skills in the natural environment. Such programs rarely include training in resiliency through practice on how to handle setbacks and failure. When instructive modeling is combined with guided role rehearsal and a guided transfer program, this mode of organizational training usually produces excellent results. Because trainees learn and perfect effective ways of managing task demands under lifelike conditions, problems of transferring the new skills to everyday life are markedly reduced.

A mastery modeling program devised by Latham and Saari (1979) to teach supervisors the interpersonal skills they need to work effectively through others is an excellent illustration of this type of approach to competency development. Supervisors have an important impact on the morale and productivity of an organization. But they are often selected for their technical competencies and job-related knowledge, whereas their success in the supervisory role depends largely on their interpersonal skills to guide, enable, and motivate those they supervise.

Latham and Saari (1979) used videotape modeling of prototypic work situations to teach supervisors how to manage the demands of their supervisory role. They were taught how to increase motivation, give recognition, correct poor work habits, discuss potential disciplinary problems, reduce absenteeism, handle employee complaints, and overcome resistance to changes in work practices (Goldstein and Sorcher, 1974). Summary guidelines defining key steps in the rules and strategies being modeled were provided to aid learning and memorability. The group of supervisors discussed and then practiced the skills in role-playing scenarios using incidents they had to manage in their work. They received enabling feedback to help them improve and perfect their skills.

To facilitate the transfer of supervisory skills to their work environment, they were instructed to use the skills they had learned on the job during the next week. They then reviewed their successes and difficulties in applying the skills. If they encountered problems, the incidents were reenacted and the supervisors received further training through instructive modeling and role rehearsal on how to manage such situations. Supervisors who received the guided mastery training performed their supervisory role more skillfully both in role-playing situations and on the job assessed a year later than did supervisors who did not receive the training. Because the skills proved highly functional, the supervisors adhered to them. Weak training programs often rely heavily on platitudinous rules for success delivered in a hyped-up fashion. Any motivational effects rapidly dissipate as the initial burst of enthusiasm fades through failure to produce good results. Latham and Saari found that simply explaining to supervisors in the control group the rules and strategies for how to handle problems on the job without modeling and guided role rehearsal did not improve their supervisory skills. Because this approach provides supervisors with the tools for solving the problems they face, they expressed favorable reactions to it.

Supervisory skills instilled by guided mastery improve the morale and productivity of organizations (Porras and Anderson, 1981; Porras, Hargis, Patterson, Maxfield, Roberts, and Bies, 1982). Compared to the productivity of control plants, the one that received the guided mastery program improved supervisory problem-solving skills and had a significantly lower absentee rate, lower turnover of employees, and a 17% increase in the monthly level of productivity over a six-month period. This surpassed the productivity of the control plants. Mastery modeling produces multiple benefits in sales similar to those in production as reflected in enhanced productivity and a lower rate of turnover in personnel (Meyer and Raich, 1983).

There are no training shortcuts or quick fixes for perceived inefficacy, dysfunctional work habits, and deficient self-regulation and occupational competencies. As is true in other spheres of functioning (Miller, Brown, Simpson, Handmaker, Bien, Luckie, Montgomery, Hester, and Tonigan, 1995), the methods that are least effective are most widely used because they are easy to do, whereas enablement methods of proven value are used less often because they require greater investment of time and effort.

The application of guided mastery for markedly different purposes, such as the elimination of anxiety dysfunctions, further illustrates the power and generality of this approach (Bandura, 1997; Williams, 1992). Talk alone will not cure intractable problems. To overcome chronic anxiety, people have to confront the perceived threats and gain mastery over them. When people avoid what they fear, they lose touch with the reality they shun. Guided mastery provides a quick and effective way of restoring reality testing and disconfirming faulty beliefs. But even more important, mastery experiences that are structured to develop coping skills provide persuasive affirming tests that they can exercise control over what they fear. However, individuals are not about to do what they avoid. Therefore, one must create enabling environmental conditions so that individuals who are beset with profound self-doubt about their coping capabilities can perform successfully despite themselves. This is achieved by enlisting a variety of performance mastery aids (Bandura, 2004). This mode of treatment eliminates anxiety, biological stress reactions, and phobic behavior. It also transforms dream activity and wipes out recurrent nightmares of long standing. The changes endure.

Cognitive mastery modeling: A great deal of professional work involves making decisions and finding solutions to problems by drawing on one's knowledge, constructing new knowledge structures, and applying decision rules. Competency in problem-solving requires the development of thinking skills for how to seek and construct reliable information and put it to good use. People can learn thinking skills and how to apply them by observing the decision rules and reasoning strategies models use as they seek solutions.

Over the years, organizational training relied almost exclusively on the traditional lecture format despite its limited effectiveness (but see Chapter 4). Mastery modeling works much better than lectures (Burke and Day, 1986). With the advent of the computer, talking heads are being replaced by self-paced instructional programs that provide step-by-step instruction, structured drills, and feedback of accuracy. Comparative tests indicate that cognitive modeling may provide a better approach to the development of higher-order cognitive competencies. In teaching reasoning skills through cognitive modeling, performers verbalize their strategies aloud as they engage in problem-solving activities (Meichenbaum, 1984). The thoughts guiding their decisions and actions are, thus, made observable. During cognitive modeling, the models verbalize their thoughts as they analyze the problem, seek information relevant to it, generate alternative solutions, judge the likely outcomes associated with each alternative, and select the best way of implementing the chosen solution. They also verbalize their strategies for handling difficulties and how to manage intrusive thoughts and disruptive emotional reactions, recover from mistakes, and motivate themselves. This enables them to remain task oriented under trying conditions.

Modeling thinking skills along with action strategies can aid the development of reasoning skills in several ways. Watching models verbalize their thoughts as they solve problems commands attention. Hearing the rules verbalized as the action strategies are implemented produces faster learning than only being told the rules or seeing only the actions modeled. Modeling also provides an informative context in which to demonstrate how to go about solving problems. The rules and strategies of reasoning can be repeated in different forms as often as needed to develop generative thinking skills. Varied application of reasoning strategies to fit different circumstances increases understanding of them and their generalizability. Observing models verbalize how they use their cognitive skills to solve problems highlights the capacity to exercise control over one's thought processes, which has been shown to boost observers' sense of efficacy over and above the strategic information conveyed.

Similarity to succeeding models boosts the instructional impact. And finally, modeling how to manage failures and setbacks fosters resilience to aversive experiences.

Gist (1989) taught managers how to generate ideas to improve the quality of organizational functioning and customer service by providing them with guidelines and practice in innovative problem-solving. Cognitive modeling, in which models verbalized strategies for generating ideas, proved superior to presenting the same guidelines solely in the traditional lecture format. Managers who had the benefit of cognitive modeling expressed a higher sense of efficacy and generated considerably more ideas of greater variety. Regardless of the format of instruction, the higher the instilled efficacy beliefs, the more abundant and varied were the generated ideas.

The advantages of cognitive mastery modeling are even more evident when the effectiveness of alternative instructional methods is examined as a function of trainees' preexisting level of perceived efficacy. Gist, Rosen, and Schwoerer (1988) taught managers with a computerized tutorial how to operate a spreadsheet program and use it to solve business problems. Cognitive modeling provided the same information and the same opportunities to practice the computer skills but used a videotape of a model demonstrating how to perform the activity. Videotaped cognitive modeling instilled a uniformly high sense of efficacy to acquire computer software skills regardless of whether managers began the training self-assured or self-doubting of their computer capabilities. A computerized tutorial had weaker effects on efficacy beliefs and was especially ineffective with managers who were insecure in their computer efficacy. Cognitive modeling also promoted a high level of computer skill development. The higher the preexisting and the instilled efficacy beliefs, the better the skill development. The benefits of mastery modeling extend beyond the development of technical skills. Compared to the computer tutorial training, mastery modeling produced a more effective working style, less negative affect during training, and higher satisfaction with the training program. Mastery modeling provides an instructional vehicle that lends itself well for enlisting affective and motivational determinants of competency development.

We have entered a new era in which the construction and management of knowledge and development of expertise relies increasingly on electronic inquiry. Much information is currently available only in electronic rather than print form. The electronic network technologies greatly expand opportunities to attain expertise. Skill in electronic search is emerging as an essential competency. Knowledge construction through electronic inquiry is not simply a mechanical application of a set of cognitive operators to an existing knowledge base. Rather, it is a challenging process in which affective, motivational, and self-regulatory factors influence how information is gathered, evaluated, and integrated into knowledge structures.

Information seekers face an avalanche of information in diverse sources of varying value and reliability. It requires a robust sense of efficacy to find one's way around this mounting volume and complexity of information. People who doubt their efficacy to conduct productive inquiries, and to manage the electronic technology, can quickly become overwhelmed. In developing their cognitive skills for untangling the Web, individuals were taught how to frame the electronic inquiry by selecting key constructs and finding reliable sources, how to broaden the scope and depth of inquiry by using appropriate connectors, and how to sequence the inquiry optimally (Debouski, Wood, and Bandura, 2001). Compared to a group that received a computer tutorial, those who had benefit of cognitive modeling that conveyed the same search rules gained higher perceived efficacy and satisfaction in knowledge construction. They spent less time in errors and redundancies, used better search and sequencing strategies, learned more, and were more successful in constructing new knowledge. Putting a human face with whom one can identify in electronic instructional systems substantially boosts their power.

Belief in one's efficacy to manage electronic technology influences not only how well individuals acquire knowledge by this means, but also their receptivity to electronic innovations, job satisfaction, and productivity (Gist, Rosen, and Schwoltrer, 1988; McDonald and Siegall, 1992). Many organizational activities are now performed by members of virtual teams working together from scattered locations through computer-mediated collaboration. Working remotely with little direct supervision across time, space, and cultural orientations can be quite taxing. Those of high perceived efficacy for remotely conducted collaborative work have more positive job attitudes and achieve higher job performances than those of low perceived efficacy (Staples, Hulland, and Higgins, 1998).

Cultivation of Self-Regulatory Competencies

The capacity for self-regulation through the exercise of self-influence is another core feature of an agentic theory of human motivation and action (Bandura, 2006). The accelerated growth of knowledge and rapid pace of social and technological change are placing a premium on capabilities for self-motivation and self-development (Bandura, 2002). Indeed, to keep up with a world that is rapidly changing, people have to develop, upgrade, and reform their competencies in continual self-renewal. To achieve this, they must develop skills in regulating the cognitive, motivational, affective, and social determinants of their functioning.

Self-management is exercised through a variety of interlinked self-referent processes including self-monitoring, self-efficacy appraisal, personal goal setting, and enlistment of motivating incentives (Bandura, 1986, 1991; Locke and Latham, 1990). Knowledge of how these various subfunctions of self-regulation operate provides particularized guides on how to develop and implement this capability.

People cannot influence their own motivation and actions if they do not keep track of their performances. Neither goals without knowing how one is doing nor knowing how one is doing without any goals is motivating (Bandura, 1991). Success in self-regulation partly depends on the fidelity, consistency, and temporal proximity of self-monitoring. Observing one's pattern of behavior is the first step toward doing something to affect it, but, in itself, such information provides little basis for self-directed reactions.

Goals and aspirations play a pivotal role in the exercise of self-directedness. Goals motivate by enlisting self-evaluative investment in activities rather than directly. Once people commit themselves to goal challenges, they care about how they do. Two types of affective motivators come into play – people seek self-satisfaction from fulfilling valued goals, and are prompted to intensify their efforts by discontent with substandard performances. The goals that are motivating are the types that activate self-investment in the activity. They include explicitness, level of challenge, and temporal proximity. Explicit goals motivate because they specify the type and amount of effort needed to attain them. Many of the goals people set for themselves result in failure because they are too general and personally noncommitting. To create productive involvement in activities, goals must be explicit (see Chapter 9). The amount of effort enlisted and satisfaction that accompany different goal attainments depends on the level at which they are set. Strong interest and self-investment in activities is sparked by challenges. There is no self-satisfaction with easy successes. Nor do goals that are widely out of one's reach bring any satisfying accomplishments and, over time, they can weaken one's sense of efficacy.

The effectiveness of goals in regulating motivation and performance depends on how far into the future they are projected. Long-range goals provide the vision and give direction to one's activities. But they are too distant to serve as current motivators. There are too many competing activities at hand for distant futures to exert much impact on current behavior. It is too easy to put off serious efforts in the present to the tomorrows of each day. Self-motivation is best sustained by attainable subgoal challenges that lead to distant aspirations. Short-term subgoals enlist the strategies and motivators in the here and now needed to get to where one is going. Difficult goal challenges are not achievable at once. Seemingly overwhelming activities are mastered by breaking them into smaller manageable steps. Concentrated effort in the short term brings success in the long term (Bandura and Schunk, 1981; Latham and Brown, 2006; Morgan, 1985).

Goal systems structured along the lines described above function as remarkable robust motivators across diverse activity domains, environmental settings, populations, and time spans (Bandura, 1997; Locke and Latham, 1990). The chapter by Latham (Chapter 9) provides further guidelines on how to structure and implement goal systems for productive engagement in personal and organizational pursuits.

Perceived self-efficacy plays an influential role in the self-regulation of motivation and actions through goal systems. It does so in part by its impact on goal setting. The stronger the people's belief in their capabilities, the higher the goal challenges they set for themselves and the firmer their commitment to them. Graduated subgoals provide a means for building perceived self-efficacy and intrinsic interest where they are lacking (Bandura, 1991, 1997). There are several ways they achieve these effects (Bandura and Schunk, 1981). Sustained effort fostered by proximal goals builds competencies. Subgoal attainments provide clear markers of increasing mastery. Evidence of progress builds self-efficacy. Subgoal attainments also bring self-satisfaction. Satisfying experiences build intrinsic interest in activities. Effective self-regulation is also central to personal management of emotional states and problem behaviors that have a negative spillover on work performance. Employee absenteeism costs US industries billions of dollars annually. It is a serious problem that disrupts work schedules, raises costs, and decreases productivity. Frayne and Latham (1987) provide the elements for an effective self-management system to reduce absenteeism. Employees who often missed work were taught in groups how to manage their motivation and behavior more effectively. They kept a record of their work attendance. They analyzed the personal and social problems that prevented them from getting to work and were taught strategies for overcoming these obstacles. They set themselves short-term goals for work attendance and rewarded themselves for meeting their goals. Training in self-regulation increased employees' beliefs in their efficacy to overcome the obstacles that led them to miss work. They improved their work attendance and maintained these changes over time (Latham and Frayne, 1989). The stronger they believed in their self-management capabilities, the better was their work attendance. A control group of employees who did not receive the program in self-regulation continued their absentee ways.

Conclusion

The guiding principles and applications reviewed in the preceding sections underscore the centrality of perceived self-efficacy as a personal resource that yields dividends in motivation, performance attainments, and emotional well-being. Social cognitive theory embeds perceived efficacy within a broad network of sociocognitive factors. There are several features of social cognitive theory that lends itself readily to widespread social applications. Its key sociocognitive factors are amenable to change; the theory specifies how to alter them, clarifies the mechanisms through which they work, and provides explicit guidelines on how to translate theory into effective practice for personal and social change.

A substantial body of evidence verifies that perceived self-efficacy operates as a common mechanism through which changes are achieved by diverse modes of influence, across markedly diverse spheres of functioning, with heterogeneous populations, and under differing life conditions. This widespread generalizability is in keeping with Occam's maxim advocating theoretical parsimony.

References

Arnold, J. A., Arad, S., Rhoades, J. A., and Drasgow, F. (2000). The empowering leadership questionnaire: The construction and validation of a new scale for measuring leader behaviors. *Journal of Organizational Behavior,* 21, 249–269.

Audia, G., Locke, E. A., and Smith, K. G. (2000). The paradox of success: An archival and a laboratory study of strategic persistence following a radical environmental change. *Academy of Management Journal,* 43, 837–853.

Bandura, A. (1986). *Social Foundations of Thought and Action: A Social Cognitive Theory.* Englewood Cliffs, NJ: Prentice-Hall.

Bandura, A. (1991). Self-regulation of motivation through anticipatory and self-regulatory mechanisms. In R. A. Dienstbier (ed.) *Perspectives on Motivation: Nebraska Symposium on Motivation* (Vol. 38, pp. 69–164). Lincoln: University of Nebraska Press.

Bandura, A. (1997). *Self-Efficacy: The Exercise of Control.* New York: Freeman.

Bandura, A. (1999). Social cognitive theory of personality. In D. Cervone and Y. Shoda (eds.) *The Coherence of Personality: Social-Cognitive Bases of Consistency, Variability, and Organization* (pp. 185–241). New York: Guilford Press.

Bandura, A. (2000). Exercise of human agency through collective efficacy. *Current Directions in Psychological Science*, 9, 75–78

Bandura, A. (2002). Growing primacy of human agency in adaptation and change in the electronic era. *European Psychologist*, 7, 2–16.

Bandura, A. (2004). Swimming against the mainstream: The early years from chilly tributary to transformative mainstream. *Behavioral Research and Therapy*, 42, 613–630.

Bandura, A. (2006). Toward a psychology of human agency. *Perspectives on Psychological Science*, 1, 164–180.

Bandura, A. (2008a). The reconstrual of "free will" from the agentic perspective of social cognitive theory. In J. Baer, J. C. Kaufman, and R. F. Baumeister (eds), *Are We Free? Psychology and Free Will* (pp. 86–127). Oxford: Oxford University Press.

Bandura, A. (2008b). *A Dose of Conditionality and Scientific Probity for the Quest of Negative Self-Efficacy Effects.* Submitted for publication.

Bandura, A., Caprara, G. V., and Zsolnai, L. (2002). Corporate transgressions through moral disengagement. In L. Zsolnai (ed.) *Ethics in the Economy: Handbook of Business Ethics* (pp. 151–164). Oxford: Peter Lang Publishers.

Bandura, A., and Locke, E. (2003). Negative self-efficacy and goal effects revisited. *Journal of Applied Psychology*, 88, 87–99.

Bandura, A., and Schunk, D. H. (1981). Cultivating competence, self-efficacy, and intrinsic interest through proximal self-motivation. *Journal of Personality and Social Psychology*, 41, 586–598.

Baum, J. R., Locke, E. A., and Smith, K. G. (2001) A multi-dimensional model of venture growth. *Academy of Management Journal*, 44, 292–303.

Baum, J. R., and Locke, E. A. (2004). The relationship of entrepreneurial traits, skill and motivation to subsequent venture growth. *Journal of Applied Psychology*, 89, 587–598.

Brouwers, A., and Tomic, W. (1999). Teacher burnout, perceived self-efficacy in classroom management, and student disruptive behavior in secondary education. *Curriculum and Teaching*, 14, 7–26.

Burke, M. J., and Day, R. R. (1986). A cumulative study of the effectiveness of management training. *Journal of Applied Psychology*, 71, 232–245.

Burkhardt, M. E., and Brass, D. J. (1990). Changing patterns or patterns of change: The effects of a change in technology on social network structure and power. *Administrative Science Quarterly*, 35, 104–127.

Chen, C. C., Greene, P. G., and Crick, A. (1998). Does entrepreneurial self-efficacy distinguish entrepreneurs from managers? *Journal of Business Venturing*, 13, 295–316.

Debouski, S., Wood, R. E., and Bandura, A. (2001). Impact of guided exploration and enactive exploration on self-regulatory mechanisms and information acquisition through electronic search. *Journal of Applied Psychology*, 86, 1129–1141.

Frayne, C. A., and Latham, G. P. (1987). Application of social learning theory to employee self-management of attendance. *Journal of Applied Psychology*, 72, 387–392.

Gist, M. E. (1989). The influence of training method on self-efficacy and idea generation among managers. *Personnel Psychology*, 42, 787–805.

Gist, M. E., Bavetta, A. G., and Stevens, C. K. (1990). Transfer training method: Its influence on skill generalization, skill repetition, and performance level. *Personnel Psychology,* 43, 501–523.

Gist, M., Rosen, B., and Schwoerer, C. (1988). The influence of training method and trainee age on the acquisition of computer skills. *Personnel Psychology,* 41, 255–265.

Goldstein, A. P., and Sorcher, M. (1974). *Changing Supervisor Behavior.* New York: Pergamon.

Gully, S. M., Incalcaterra, K. A., Joshi, A., and Beaubien, J. M.. (2002). A meta-analysis of team-efficacy, potency, and performance: Interdependence and level of analysis as moderators of observed relationships. *Journal of Applied Psychology,* 87(5), 819–832.

Hill, T., Smith, N. D., and Mann, M. F. (1987). Role of efficacy expectations in predicting the decision to use advanced technologies: The case of computers. *Journal of Applied Psychology,* 72, 307–313.

Holden, G. (1991). The relationship of self-efficacy appraisals to subsequent health related outcomes: A meta- analysis. *Social Work in Health Care,* 16, 53–93.

Holden, G., Moncher, M. S., Schinke, S. P., and Barker, K. M. (1990). Self-efficacy of children and adolescents: A meta- analysis. *Psychological Reports,* 66, 1044–1046.

Hung, J. H., and Rosenthal, T. L. (1981). Therapeutic videotaped playback. In J. L. Fryrear and R. Fleshman (eds), *Videotherapy in Mental Health* (pp. 5–46). Springfield, IL: Thomas.

Jex, S. M., and Bliese, P. D. (1999). Efficacy beliefs as a moderator of the impact of work-related stressors: A multilevel study. *Journal of Applied Psychology,* 84, 349–361.

Jones, G. R. (1986). Socialization tactics, self-efficacy, and newcomers' adjustment to organizations. *Academy of Management Journal,* 29, 262–279.

Jorde-Bloom, P., and Ford, M. (1988). Factors influencing early childhood administrators' decisions regarding the adoption of computer technology. *Journal of Educational Computing Research,* 4, 31–47.

Krueger, N. F., Jr., and Dickson, P. R. (1993). Self-efficacy and perceptions of opportunities and threats. *Psychological Reports,* 72, 1235–1240.

Krueger, N., Jr., and Dickson, P. R. (1994). How believing in ourselves increases risk taking: Perceived self-efficacy and opportunity recognition. *Decision Sciences,* 25, 385–400.

Laschruger, H. K. S., and Shamian, J. (1994). Staff nurses' and nurse managers' perceptions of job-related empowerment and managerial self-efficacy. *Journal of Nursing Administration,* 24, 38–47.

Latham, G. P., and Brown, T. C. (2006). The effect of learning vs. outcome goals on self-efficacy, satisfaction and performance in an MBA program. *Applied Psychology: An International Review,* 55, 606–623.

Latham, G. P., and Budworth, M. (2006). The effect of training in verbal self-guidance on the self-efficacy and performance of native Americans in the selection interview. *Journal of Vocational Behavior,* 68, 516–523.

Latham, G. P., and Frayne, C. A. (1989). Self-management training for increasing job attendance: A follow-up and a replication. *Journal of Applied Psychology,* 74, 411–416.

Latham, G. P., and Saari, L. M. (1979). Application of social learning theory to training supervisors through behavioral modeling. *Journal of Applied Psychology,* 64, 239–246.

Leiter, M. P. (1992). Burnout as a crisis in self-efficacy: Conceptual and practical implications. *Work and Stress,* 6, 107–115.

Lent, R. W., Brown, S. D., and Hackett, G. (1994). Toward a unifying social cognitive theory of career and academic interest, choice, and performance. *Journal of Vocational Behavior,* 45, 79–122.

Lindsley, D. H., Mathieu, J. E., Heffner, T. S., and Brass, D. J. (1994, April). *Team Efficacy, Potency, and Performance: A Longitudinal Examination of Reciprocal Processes.* Paper presented at the Society of Industrial-Organizational Psychology, Nashville, TN.

Little, B. L., and Madigan, R. M. (1994, August). *Motivation in Work Teams: A Test of the Construct of Collective Efficacy.* Paper presented at the annual meeting of the Academy of Management, Houston, TX.

Locke, E. A., and Latham, G. P. (1990). *A Theory of Goal Setting and Task Performance.* Englewood Cliffs, NJ: Prentice- Hall.

Markman, G. D., and Baron, R. A. (1999, May). *Cognitive Mechanisms: Potential differences Between Entrepreneurs and Non-Entrepreneurs.* Paper presented at the Babson College/Kauffman Foundation Entrepreneurship Conference.

Matsui, T., and Onglatco, M. L. (1992). Career self-efficacy as a moderator of the relation between occupational stress and strain. *Journal of Vocational Behavior,* 41, 79–88.

McDonald, T., and Siegall, M. (1992). The effects of technological self-efficacy and job focus on job performance, attitudes, and withdrawal behaviors. *The Journal of Psychology,* 126, 465–475.

Meichenbaum, D. (1984). Teaching thinking: A cognitive- behavioral perspective. In R. Glaser, S. Chipman, and J. Segal (eds), *Thinking and Learning Skills (Vol. 2): Research and Open Questions* (pp. 407–426). Hillsdale, NJ: Erlbaum.

Meyer, H. H., and Raich, M. S. (1983). An objective evaluation of a behavior modeling training program. *Personnel Psychology,* 36, 755–761.

Miller, W. R., Brown, J. M., Simpson, T. L., Handmaker, N. S., Bien, T. H., Luckie, L. F., Montgomery, H. A., Hester, R. K., and Tonigan, J. S. (1995). What works? A methodological analysis of the alcohol treatment outcome literature. In R. K. Hester, and W. R. Miller (eds), *Handbook of Alcoholism Treatment Approaches: Effective Alternatives* (2nd edition). Boston: Allyn and Bacon.

Morgan, M. (1985). Self-monitoring of attained subgoals in private study. *Journal of Educational Psychology,* 77, 623–630.

Multon, K. D., Brown, S. D., and Lent, R. W. (1991). Relation of self-efficacy beliefs to academic outcomes: A meta-analytic investigation. *Journal of Counseling Psychology,* 38, 30–38.

Parker, S. K. (1998). Enhancing role breadth self-efficacy: The roles of job enrichment and other organizational interventions. *Journal of Applied Psychology,* 83, 835–852.

Plotnikoff, R. C., Lippke, S., Courneya, K. S., Birkett, N., and Sigal, R. J. (2008). Physical activity and social cognitive theory: A test in population sample of adults with type 1 or type 2 diabetes. *Applied Psychology: An International Review*, 57, 628–643.

Porras, J. I., and Anderson, B. (1981). Improving managerial effectiveness through modeling-based training. *Organizational Dynamics*, Spring, 60–77.

Porras, J. I., Hargis, K., Patterson, K. J., Maxfield, D. G., Roberts, N., and Bies, R. J. (1982). Modeling-based organizational development: A longitudinal assessment. *Journal of Applied Behavioral Science*, 18, 433–446.

Saks, A. M. (1994). Moderating effects of self-efficacy for the relationship between training method and anxiety and stress reactions of newcomers. *Journal of Organizational Behavior*, 15, 639–654.

Saks, A. M. (1995). Longitudinal field investigation of the moderating and mediating effects of self-efficacy on the relationship between training and newcomer adjustment. *Journal of Applied Psychology*, 80, 211–225.

Salanova, M., Grau, R., Cifre, E., and Llorens, S. (2000). Computer training, frequency of use and burnout; the moderating role of computer self-efficacy. *Computers in Human Behavior*, 16, 575–590.

Schaubroeck, J., and Merritt, D. E. (1997). Divergent effects of job control on coping with work stressors: The Key role of self-efficacy. *Academy of Management Journal*, 40, 738–754.

Speier, C., and Frese, M. (1997). Generalized self-efficacy as a mediator and moderator between control and complexity at work and personal initiative: A longitudinal field study in East Germany. *Human Performance*, 10(2), 171–192.

Srivastava, A., Bartol, K. M., and Locke, E. A. (2006). Empowering leadership in management teams: Effects on knowledge sharing, efficacy, and performance. *Academy of Management Journal*, 49, 1239–1251.

Stajkovic, A. D., and Luthans, F. (1998). Self-efficacy and work-related performance: A meta-analysis. *Psychological Bulletin*, 124, 240–261.

Stajkovic, A. D., and Lee, D. S. (2001). *A Meta-Analysis of the Relationship between Collective Efficacy and Group Performance*. Paper presented at the national Academy of Management meeting, Washington, DC.

Staples, D. S., Hulland, J. S., and Higgins, C. A. (1998). A self-efficacy theory explanation for the management of remote workers in virtual organizations. *Journal of Computer-Mediated Communication*, 3(4). DOI: https://doi.org/10.1111/j.1083-6101.1998.tb00085.x

Stewart, G. L., and Manz, C. C. (1995). Leadership for self-managing work teams: A typology and integrative model. *Human Relations*, 48, 747–770.

van Ryn, M., and Vinokur, A. D. (1992). How did it work? An examination of the mechanisms through which an intervention for the unemployed promoted job-search behavior. *American Journal of Community Psychology*, 20, 577–597.

Vinokur, A. D., van Ryn, M., Gramlich, E. M., and Price, R. H. (1991). Long-term follow-up and benefit-cost analysis of the jobs program: A preventive intervention for the unemployed. *Journal of Applied Psychology*, 76, 213–219.

White, J., Bandura, A., and Bero, L. A. (2009). Moral disengagement in the corporate world. *Accountability in Research,* 16(1), 41–74.

Whyte, G., and Saks, A. (2007). The effects of self-efficacy on behavior in escalation situations. *Human Performance,* 20, 23–42.

Whyte, G., Saks, A., and Hook, S. (1997). When success breeds failure: The role of perceived self-efficacy in escalating commitment to a losing course of action. *Journal of Organizational Behavior,* 18, 415–432.

Williams, S. L. (1992). Perceived self-efficacy and phobic disability. In R. Schwarzer (ed.), *Self-Efficacy: Thought Control of Action* (pp. 149–176). Washington, D.C.: Hemisphere.

Yanar, B., Budworth, M.-H., and Latham, G. P. (2008). *Training Islamic Women in Verbal Self-Guidance to Overcome Discrimination in Turkey.* Submitted for publication.

Zhao, H., Seibert, S. E., and Hills, G. E. (2005). The mediating role of self-efficacy in the development of entrepreneurial intentions. *Journal of Applied Psychology,* 90, 1265–1272.

Note

Some sections of this chapter contain revised, updated, and expanded material from the book *Self-Efficacy: The Exercise of Control,* 1997, New York, Freeman.

Exercises

1. *Personal* Self-Efficacy Building

Identify a skill of competency that you lack but would like to have. Based on the material in this chapter, design a training program (others may be part of the program) that would increase your self-efficacy in this realm. Include both behavioral and cognitive aspects.

2. *Building* Team Efficacy

Based on your previous work experience in teams, identify a situation in which team efficacy was low.

What competencies did the team lack which undermined their effectiveness? How would you build the needed types of efficacy? What would you do to prevent overconfidence?

7

Pay for Performance

KATHRYN M. BARTOL

Robert H. Smith School of Business, University of Maryland

Our principle is *pay for performance.* This principle involves providing monetary rewards through carefully designed compensation systems that base pay on measured performance within the control of participants. It also includes incorporating appropriate concerns for procedural and distributive justice. In most situations, properly designed pay-for-performance systems will lead to better performance results.

Well-designed pay-for-performance systems make major contributions to performance through two main mechanisms. First, they positively influence the motivation to perform. Second, they impact the attraction and retention patterns of organizations (i.e. who joins and who remains), thereby affecting the caliber of individuals available to perform.

A number of different pay delivery plans qualify as pay-for-performance systems, although they vary widely with respect to how closely they tie pay to performance. Pay-for-performance systems can deliver monetary rewards at the individual, small group/team, and/or division or organizational level. Evidence suggests that pay for performance at each of these levels can positively impact performance.

Individual Level

At the individual level, there are three major types of pay-for-performance systems: *traditional incentive systems, variable pay configurations,* and *merit pay plans.* Traditional incentive plans include *piece-rate plans* and *sales commissions.* With piece-rate incentive plans, an employee is paid a specified rate for each unit produced or each service provided. Mitchell, Lewin, and Lawler (1990) estimate that the proper use of piece-rate plans leads to performance gains in the 10–15% range. Based on their review of the literature, Locke, Feren, McCaleb, Shaw, and Denny (1980) concluded that the median productivity improvement from piece-rate plans is 30%. A meta-analysis involving mainly piece-rate pay found that financial incentives are associated with higher performance in terms of quantity and also found no detrimental impact on quality (Jenkins, Mitra, Gupta, and Shaw, 1998). Perhaps because of the difficulty of objectively assessing individual performance in most jobs, a recent estimate suggests that piece-rate systems are used in less than 4% of private sector jobs (Gerhart, 2017). The other traditional incentive, the commission, is a sales incentive that is typically expressed as a percentage of sales dollars, a percentage of gross profit margins, or some dollar amount for each unit sold (Colletti and Cichelli, 1993). The available research indicates that salespeople tend to prefer commissions over other forms of reward (Lopez, Hopkins, and Raymond, 2006) and can be effectively motivated by them (e.g. Banker, Lee, Potter, and Srinivasan, 1996; Ford, Walker, and Churchhill, 1985; Harrison, Virick, and William, 1996). Such commission systems often include a smaller base salary with the larger commission part depending on meeting some threshold or quota and require careful thought. In recent experiment, a large Swedish retail chain used daily quotas rather than monthly ones to help keep lower-performing salespeople from giving up effort if sales for the month were not going well. However, the change to daily quotes led high-performing salespeople to focus on low-ticket items, which ultimately lowered overall sales and the firm's profits (Chung, Narayandas, and Chang, 2021).

The second major type of individual level pay-for-performance plan is *variable pay*. It is also sometimes referred to as short-term incentive pay and relies on measuring performance for up to one year. Variable pay is performance-related compensation that does not permanently increase base pay and that must be re-earned to be received again. It is typically in the form of a bonus. Because base pay tends to move up more slowly with variable pay plans, the amount of bonus that can be earned needs to be substantial to make up for the fact that part of the pay is "at risk" (Schuster and Zingheim, 1996). The risk stems from the possibility that desired performance might not be achieved and therefore the pay not earned (Bartol and Locke, 2000). The piece-rate and commission pay plans discussed earlier actually constitute forms of variable pay, albeit forms in which a greater proportion of pay is typically tied to performance than is the case with newer forms of variable pay. A growing number of employers are moving to variable pay: The portion of US companies offering one or more variable pay plans rose from 51% in 1991 to 78% in 2005 and to 85% in 2017 (Dean, 2006; Miller, 2017). Research suggests that variable pay plans are useful in boosting performance (e.g. Chung and Vickery, 1976; Lee, 1988; Nyberg, Pieper and Trevor, 2016; Smilco and Van Neck, 2004; Yukl and Latham, 1975).

A form of variable pay that is currently popular is a lump-sum bonus for achieving particular goals. Locke (2004) identifies four methods of linking bonuses to goals: *assigning stretch goals and paying bonuses only if the goals are achieved, having multiple goal levels and corresponding bonuses that increase as higher goals are met, offering bonuses that grow incrementally as performance improves (with no upper limit),* and *setting specific, challenging goals but making decisions about bonuses after the fact so that contextual factors can be taken into account.* For the most part, this line of thinking can also be applied to the sales quotas mentioned earlier. Locke notes that each choice has its pros and cons. For example, bonuses paid only when stretch goals are met, although highly motivating, might also encourage employees to take shortcuts or cheat. Also, they could be discouraging for those who approach but do not reach their goals. Having either multiple or continuous goal and bonus levels (which are similar to piece-rate pay plus goals) may be less likely to result in cheating or gaming, but it is unclear whether such approaches can motivate the highest levels of performance. Setting goals but determining pay after the fact, while accounting for situational factors, requires bosses to understand the full context of employees' performance more than they often can do. An Empsight survey (2020) of mainly large companies indicated that 71.7% of employees are eligible to receive variable pay. Results also showed that lower-level employees receive a much lesser percentage of their pay as a merit bonus compared to middle managers and professionals and especially top managers. Merit bonuses typically depend on a combination of individual, business unit, and company performance. Bonuses at higher levels tend to be more dependent on company performance, presumably because executives are in a stronger position to affect it.

The third major type of individual level pay-for-performance plan, *merit pay*, rewards individuals for past work behaviors and outcomes by adding dollar amounts to their base pay. Merit pay is the most widely used pay system in US organizations (Bretz, Milkovich, and Read, 1992; O'Dell, 1987). Milkovich and Newman (2008) report that at least 90% of US firms reward employees through merit pay (Gerhart and Newman, 2020; Milkovich and Newman, 2008). Based on a review of 25 studies, Heneman (1992) concludes that merit pay plans appear to be moderately effective in influencing performance. Taking a longer-term view, Harris, Gilbreath, and Sunday (1998) provide evidence that the connection between merit pay and performance may be greater than that which short-term studies can detect because the cumulative effects of various types of merit pay adjustments linked to performance, such as those related to promotions, can be substantial. Nyberg et al. (2016) also found a link between merit pay and performance overtime, although the connection between bonus and performance was stronger. The findings of this latter study are consistent with the fact that average company budgets for salary increases (merit pay) in recent years have been holding steady at around 3%, down from 5.5% in 1990, whereas variable pay budgets mainly associated with merit bonuses have been increasing from an average of 4.2% in 1990 to ranges varying around 10–15% recently (Empsight, 2020; Gerhart, 2017; Miller, 2017).

Team Level

In addition to pay for performance at the individual level, there is considerable interest in pay-for-performance plans focused on small groups or teams (Conroy and Gupta, 2016; Parker, McAdams, and Zielinski, 2000). Such pay plans provide monetary rewards based on the measured performance of the group or team. Small work groups or teams are official (designated or recognized by management) multiperson work units composed of individuals who operate interdependently in the performance of tasks that affect others associated within the organization (Hackman, 1987). One survey found that almost 70% of Fortune 1000 companies are using some type of work group or team incentives (Lawler, Mohrman, and

Ledford, 1995). Usage in smaller organizations may be less, with one survey showing that 35% of the 140 companies responding, most of which had 2000 or few employees, reported using team rewards (McClurg, 2001). Evidence suggests that performance gains can be associated with the use of monetary rewards for groups (Cotton and Cook, 1982; Gomez-Mejia and Balkin, 1989; Quigley, Tesluk, Locke, and Bartol, 2007; Super, Li, Ishqaidef, and Guthrie, 2016; Wageman and Baker, 1997). For instance, a meta-analysis involving team-based incentives by Garbers and Konradt (2014) showed that team-based rewards have a positive effect on performance. A meta-analysis by Nyberg, Maltarich, Abdulsalam, Essman, and Cragun (2018) also found a positive effect of incentive-based pay on team performance. But researchers have theorized that the pay results in teams may be influenced by situational factors, such as task complexity, tenure of members of the team, and distribution of expertise (Balkin and Montemayor, 2000; DeMatteo, Eby, and Sundstrom, 1998; Lawler, 2003; Nyberg et al., 2016). It is worth noting that there can be different formats for team incentives, including being utilized as rewards only for the best teams (competition among teams), target based for reaching predetermined goals, and piece-rate systems that reward for incremental additions. Increased interest in team pay is also emerging in the executive suite, particularly with respect to top management teams (Devers, Cannella, Gregory, Reilly, and Yoder, 2007), with some support for a link between pay for performance and firm performance for such top-level teams (Nyberg et al., 2018). Given the complexity of team incentives, more research is needed to better understand the underlying conditions for effective team pay-for-performance.

Organizational Level

At the organizational level, three pay systems that potentially link pay and performance are *gainsharing, profit sharing,* and *stock options. Gainsharing* is a compensation plan in which an organization shares with employees a portion of the added earnings obtained through their collective increases in productivity (Henderson, 1997) or the achievement of other goals, such as customer satisfaction with quality (Gerhart and Rynes, 2003). Such plans usually involve a significant portion of organization's employees and possibly all. In large organizations, plans may apply to plants, divisions, or other significant subsystems of the organization. In recent years, gainsharing has been extending its reach beyond traditional industrial settings to other realms such as health care (Jain and Roble, 2008; Patel, 2006). The available evidence on gainsharing indicates that such plans can lead to positive outcomes (Nyberg et al., 2018) such as gains in productivity (Welbourne and Gomez-Mejia, 1995) or other positive outcomes such as decreases in absenteeism, lower numbers of grievances (Arthur and Jelf, 1999), and improved knowledge transfer by encouraging employees to offer suggestions (Arthur and Aiman-Smith, 2001). There are also indications that the advantages of gainsharing may dissipate over time due to the number of suggestions and ideas for improvement leveling off (Nyberg et al., 2018). Hence, keeping the program running effectively may take considerable effort.

The second type of organizational level pay system aimed at performance is *profit sharing*, which provides payments to employees based on the profitability of the business. Payments can be made through current distribution plans (paid in cash), deferred plans (paid toward retirement), or a combination of both, although most companies establish deferred plans because of the associated tax advantages. According to one estimate, more than 60% of Fortune 1000 companies have profit-sharing plans (Lawler et al., 1995). Data supporting the performance effects of profit-sharing plans are somewhat unclear. Kruse (1993) found that productivity growth in firms using profit sharing was 3.5–5.0% higher than in firms that did not use profit sharing. However, Kim (1998) found that profit-sharing companies tend to have higher labor costs than other companies, thereby erasing any advantage of profit sharing. There are some weaknesses inherent in profit-sharing plans as a direct means of boosting performance. One is that it can be somewhat difficult to establish a clear connection (sometimes referred to as "line of sight") between individual actions and impact on profits, especially in large organizations. Evidence for this is Kruse's (1993) finding that annual productivity growth was greater in smaller profit-sharing companies than in larger ones (11–17% productivity growth in companies having fewer than 775 employees, versus 0.0–6.9% in companies having 775 or more). Another weakness is that accounting and financial management practices and other factors outside employees' control can also impact the bottom line. A recent meta-analysis showed a positive impact of profit-sharing plans on relevant outcomes but also cited evidence that the benefits may lessen over time (Lucifora and Origo, 2015; Nyberg et al., 2018). Other evidence suggests that profit sharing in conjunction with pay-for-performance plans may be helpful in improving employees' performance-reward expectancy, line of sight, and ultimately their performance (Han, Bartol, and Kim, 2015). Finally, the deferred nature of many of these plans may not provide strong valence with respect to motivating performance. Indeed, Kruse (1993) found that productivity growth was higher for plans paying cash rewards than for those making deferred payments. Faced with employees wanting higher hourly pay rates, Walmart has recently scrapped it profit-sharing plan. The plan involved quarterly payment to employees if certain goals were met; however, there were quarters in which goals were not met, and there was no payout to employees from the plan (Nassauer, 2021).

A third type of organizational level reward system is employee *stock ownership*, which is considered a long-term incentive. One study of Fortune 1000 companies showed that 71% had stock ownership programs of some type (Lawler et al., 1995). During the 1990s, the most rapidly growing approach was via stock options, which gives employees the right to purchase a specific amount of stock at a designated price over a specified time period (Brandes, Dharwadkar, Lemesis, and Heisler, 2003). The basic rationale is that employees will be more concerned about the long-term success of the organization and increase their efforts if they can reap the benefits as reflected in the rising price of the organization's stock. Additionally, extending ownership can both attract new talent and enhance perceptions of fairness (and thus retention) in current employees. In 2000, a study of 490 organizations reported that companies with stock option plans that were broadly dispersed (beyond the executive level) performed better and had higher average compensation levels than companies without broad-based plans, and also that increases in productivity seemed to counterbalance any dilution of earnings per share that occurred when the options were exercised (Sesil, Kroumova, Kruse, and Blasi, 2000).

Since 2000, however, conditions have changed significantly. In a much-debated ruling in 2005, the Financial Accounting Standards Board began requiring companies to recognize stock options as a cost on their income statements in the year they were awarded rather than merely list them in the footnotes – a change that diluted earnings per share in the year options were granted and rendered options less attractive to many employers (Deshmukh, Howe, and Luft, 2008). Moreover, the value of options plummeted beginning in 2007, when a crisis in the mortgage markets ultimately led to the historic "Wall Street bailout" by the US government in 2008 and to widespread fear of a steep global recession. When an option is "underwater" (when its exercise price exceeds the current market price), the value is neutralized and employees' anticipated wealth – along with any motivational potential that might have existed in holding the option – evaporates (Delves, 2001). As a result, a number of companies either stopped granting options or only grant them to executives (Gerhart and Newman, 2020). And, even in times of rising stock prices, the effect of stock options may be less than hoped for. One study found that when stock prices have risen above the option price, lower-level employees tend to exercise their options shortly after vesting, a factor that may truncate some of the longer-term motivational potential (Huddart and Lang, 1996). Direct stock awards for employees may be gaining some traction. An executive at KKR, a private equity firm, has been advocating grants of stock to workers in industrial and manufacturing companies, arguing that stock ownership helps to better align the interests of workers with management, encourages worker engagement, and strengthens company culture. Stock awards have been made to workers when a KKR company, Gardner Denver, was developed in 2017 and again when the company merged to create Ingersoll Rand, Inc., a pump and compressor maker owned by KKR. The combined company is doing well, and the lowest-paid worker to receive a grant in 2017 has stock now valued at $35 000. Inspired Harley-Davidson has announced that it also will be making stock awards to employees (Gottfried, 2021)

Overall Effects

There is some debate regarding whether there are best practices that are applicable to most organizations (Gerhart, Trevor, and Graham, 1996; Huselid, 1995), or whether it is important to match pay systems to particular strategies (Montemayor, 1994; Youndt, Snell, Dean, and Lepak, 1996). The weight of evidence seems to be shifting toward the strategy argument (e.g. Shaw, Gupta, and Delery, 2001; Yanador and Marler, 2006). For instance, Gerhart and Newman (2020) note that an innovator strategy might entail new products and short development times that may lead to incentives designed to spur innovation. A cost-cutting strategy might take on an efficiency emphasis and reward productivity increases and process improvements. Yet, a customer-focused strategy may involve delighting customers and include payouts associated with customer satisfaction.

In considering performance-focused pay plans, the direct impact of pay plans on performance is not the only effect to consider. Growing evidence suggests that there are indirect pay plan effects stemming from influences on attraction and retention patterns in organizations. Interestingly, scholars have identified a *sorting* effect such that a change to pay for performance can influence the composition of an organization's associated workforce (Gerhart and Fang, 2014; Gerhart and Rynes, 2003; Lazear, 1986, 2000; Rynes, 1987) (see Gerhart, 2017, p. 122; Williams and Livingstone, 1994). An example is shown in a study by Lazear (2000) in which he found the average level of output per worker in an auto glass factory increased by about 44% after a switch from hourly to piece-rate pay. Further investigation showed that half of the gain reflected an increase in worker productivity. However, in seeking to identify an explanation for the other half of 44%, Lazear discovered a sorting effect, wherein the other half of the gain (22%) was due to lower-productivity workers leaving and being replaced by higher performers. While the other half was due to the gain from new workers who replaced the lower-performing employees who left, the fact that pay-for-performance systems also tend to convey information about relative standing in the organization may also encourage turnover of lower-performing workers (Bartol, Durham, and Poon, 2001).

Relatedly, researchers have also given attention to the issue of horizontal pay dispersion, which occurs when employees doing similar jobs are paid rates that differ. Accumulating evidence suggests that pay dispersion associated with pay for performance, as opposed to dubious reasons, such as favoritism, poorly executed pay plans, or politics (Kepes, Delery, and Gupta, 2009), can have beneficial effects (Gerhart, 2017; Gupta, Conroy, and Delery, 2012). For instance, in a multiway study of independent grocery stores, Shaw (2015) found that with high pay-for-performance pay dispersion was associated with poor performer quit rates, which, in turn, helped boost organizational performance. On the other hand, good performers were found to be more likely to quit when pay was compressed (as opposed to dispersed) and pay-for-performance was not part of the compensation system. Similarly, Tekleab, Bartol, and Liu (2005) found that employee dissatisfaction with the trajectory of their merit raise amounts was associated with employee turnover.

Interestingly, due to the flexibility and control over labor costs that it provides, variable pay may also reduce turnover. By having more money allocated to bonuses or other forms of variable pay, an organization can shrink its payroll costs during downturns rather than downsize. Gerhart and Trevor (1996) provide evidence that variable pay plans lessen organizational employment variability, allowing for greater employment stability for employees and their organizations.

What Is Required to Make the Principle Work?

Define Performance

First, it is essential to identify explicitly what performance is desired. Clearly defining performance, however, requires looking beyond individual jobs and thinking strategically about the organization as a whole. It means developing a business model based on what drives the business (e.g. customer satisfaction), after which goals can be set at the various levels of the organization and determinations made about what will be rewarded. Without a business model (or with the wrong one), management risks setting goals and rewarding employees for the wrong things – and finding its employees doing those wrong things very efficiently, to the organization's detriment. Focusing on what drives the business leads to the setting of appropriate performance goals for individual employees at all the organizational levels. Then, the act of tying incentives to the achievement of those goals will have not only motivational but also informational value, because people will receive a clear message about what specific behaviors and/or outcomes are expected via communications about the reward system. A temptation to resist is that of defining performance in terms of job aspects that are easily quantifiable, thereby ignoring job dimensions that may be critically important but difficult to measure. This can lead an organization to fall into the trap of "rewarding A while hoping for B" (Kerr, 1995). Or the opposite can occur in which high performers end up being given more work (almost a sort of punishment) rather than rewarded in a meaningful way (Skaggs, Manz, Lyle, and Pearce, 2018). For pay for performance to be effective, strategically important job dimensions – even hard-to-measure ones – must be identified, communicated, assessed, and rewarded.

Communicate

Because it is impossible to be motivated by incentives one does not grasp, it is critically important not only to design a pay plan that is understandable but also to communicate both clearly and frequently how the program works and what employees must do to bring about the results that will trigger a payout (Englmaier, Roider, and Sunde, 2017). Communication also implies providing feedback along the way about progress toward targets (Smilco and Van Neck, 2004). Young, Burgess, and White (2007) describe the effects of a failure to communicate in a pay-for-quality project for physicians. Participants found the rules to be complicated, failed to fully understand the plan, and were not sufficiently engaged by meager attempts to explain it. Thus, although 75% of those eligible received a bonus payment in the first year, very few knew whether they had received their payment or, if they did, realized that it was for their performance on the program's quality measures. Some physicians were so unaware of the financial rewards available to them that they discarded, unopened, the mail that included their bonus checks.

Ensure Competence

Employees must have the appropriate knowledge, skills, and abilities (KSAs) and self-efficacy (see Chapter 6) to perform at the desired level. Instituting pay for performance is a futile exercise if employees are unable to perform at the level required to receive the reward. Hiring people who are efficacious and who possess (or can readily obtain through training) the relevant KSAs is essential.

Make Pay Systems Commensurate with Employees' Values

Pay for performance will only work if the rewards being offered are valued and the amount is viewed as sufficient, given what employees are being asked to accomplish. Employers can generally assume that money is a value to their employees, both practically and symbolically. Some employees, however, may not value the incremental gain being offered for high-level performance if the amount is viewed as paltry and, thus, not worth the additional effort. Further, a pay system can fail if it is perceived as undermining employees' other values. For example, individuals may be uninterested in obtaining even a substantial amount of additional pay if they believe that achieving performance goals means sacrificing greater personal values, such as time to pursue their own interests (e.g. family life), a low-stress work environment, or a commitment to high-quality work or to standards of ethical behavior.

Use Nonfinancial Motivators Too

Most employers assume that money is an effective motivator because it enables employees to buy things that they want or need. Also, money is important from a justice standpoint, giving high performers what is due them for their exceptional contributions to the success of organization. Nonetheless, exclusive reliance on financial incentives would be an unwise policy because it would ignore other important sources of work motivation. Nonmonetary motivators include a diverse assortment of activities, such as providing interesting and important work assignments (see Chapter 5), engendering commitment to the realization of a vision (or to a visionary leader; Chapter 16), assigning challenging goals in conjunction with ongoing performance feedback (see Chapter 10), granting autonomy regarding how a job is accomplished (see Chapter 14), providing public and/or private recognition for outstanding contributions (see Chapter 12), or simply enabling one to do work that one loves.

Use Money in Conjunction with Intrinsic Motivation

Amabile (1993) argues that it is possible to achieve "motivational synergy" by encouraging both intrinsic and extrinsic motivation (see Chapter 5). She posits that intrinsic motivation arises from the value of the work itself to the person. It can be fostered through such measures as matching employees to tasks on the basis of their skills and interests, designing work to be optimally challenging, and bringing together diverse individuals in high-performing work teams. Amabile further suggests that, when creativity is particularly important, it may be best to hold off heavily emphasizing extrinsic motivators during the problem presentation and idea generation stages when intrinsic motivation appears to be most important. Extrinsic factors may be particularly helpful during the sometimes-difficult validation and implementation stages. A meta-analytic study (Eisenberger and Cameron, 1996) and a set of laboratory and field studies (Eisenberger, Rhoades, and Cameron, 1999; Fang and Gerhart, 2012) also indicated that tangible rewards can enhance, rather than undermine, the effects of intrinsic motivation. Some (e.g. Ryan and Deci, 2000), however, contest this view. Gerhart (2017) has speculated that part of the reason for the discrepancy in views may be that studies finding undermining have tended to focus on relatively narrow circumstances involving piece-rate systems, which have a low frequency of use in the US.

Promote a Culture of Honesty and Integrity

Locke (2019) notes that care must be taken to ensure that goals and rewards are developed within a culture that emphasizes honesty and integrity. Because it can be difficult to set up incentive systems that work perfectly in every aspect, it can be important to set up control systems, such as obtaining customer feedback, setting up tracking systems to verify elements such as sales, and obtaining feedback from others in the organization. Locke also points to the need for the CEO or head of the organization to be a role model of integrity, the advantage of hiring people with moral character, the value of training and socialization with respect to the organization's value systems, the requirement for the monitoring of compliance, and finally the willingness to terminate people who cheat and are dishonest.

Target the Appropriate Organizational Level

Performance-based pay must be at the appropriate level. Increasingly, firms are rewarding performance at the group and/or organizational levels rather than at the individual level alone, in hopes of boosting organizational performance through enhanced information sharing, group decision-making, and teamwork (Bartol and Hagmann, 1992; Han et al., 2015; Parker et al., 2000). Lawler (1971) argues that the distinction between individual and group pay plans is important because individual and group plans are viewed differently by employees and have different effects. A key decision for management, then, concerns whether incentive pay should be based on individual or group performance. Further, if the organization chooses to reward group performance, decisions must be made about what constitutes a "group" for performance-measurement purposes. For example, will group-based pay be based on the performance of a team, a work unit, a division, or the entire organization?

There has been little actual research to offer guidance regarding the level of performance to which incentives should be tied, although several views have been advanced by compensation experts (e.g. Gomez-Mejia and Balkin, 1992; Mitchell et al., 1990; Montemayor, 1994). Key factors that should be considered when making this important decision include.

- *Nature of the task:* Pay for performance at the individual level is considered most appropriate when the work is designed for individuals, where the need for integration with others is negligible, where group performance means only the sum of members' individual performances, or where the work is simple, repetitive, and stable. For sequential teams that perform various tasks in a predetermined order (necessitating that group performance cannot exceed that of the lowest individual member), it has been recommended that base pay be skill based, and team incentives be team bonuses with payouts distributed as a percentage of base pay. Alternatively, group-based incentive programs, through which all the members receive equal shares of a team bonus, are generally considered appropriate when teams are composed of individuals from the same organizational level, when members have complementary roles and must depend upon each other and interact intensively to accomplish their work, so that group performance is enhanced by cooperation, and when the nature of the technology and workflows allow for the identification of distinct groups that are relatively independent of one another. Some coaching of the team (see Chapter 18) may help the group develop norms that discourage free riding (Hackman and Wageman, 2005), thus enabling accurate work with less decrement in speed.

- *Ability to measure performance:* Good performance measures are critically important in any pay-for-performance plan (Conroy and Gupta, 2016). Pfeffer (1998) argues that performance can often be more reliably assessed at aggregate than at individual levels. He concludes that individual incentive pay should be replaced by collective rewards based on organizational or subunit performance that highlight the interdependence among organizational members. Although many are unwilling to go as far as Pfeffer in discounting the potential value of individual incentives, most agree that group incentives are a suitable alternative when the identification of individual contributors is difficult due to the nature of the task. For gainsharing plans in particular, it is not only necessary that there be good performance measures for the unit or plant, but also that there be a reliable performance history in order to develop a gainsharing formula. When group performance is rewarded with gainsharing, however, it is nonetheless important, particularly in Western cultures, to provide a means for identifying individual contributions to the group effort (e.g. through peer evaluations), so that members keep in mind their accountability at both the individual and group levels.
- *Organizational culture:* Group incentive plans are best suited to situations in which the organizational culture emphasizes group achievements (see Chapter 28). Group incentives work best when free riding is unlikely (e.g. because members hold each other accountable or because employees are professionals who possess high intrinsic motivation). If a corporate culture is strongly individualistic and competitive, group plans such as team incentives will likely encounter considerable resistance from organizational members accustomed to focusing on individual accomplishments and/or may lead to lower levels of cooperative behavior (Hill, Bartol, Tesluk, and Langa, 2009).
- *Management's purpose:* Group incentives are recommended in situations in which there is a need to align the interests of multiple individuals into a common goal, or when management wishes to foster entrepreneurship at the

group level. At the organizational level, profit sharing is often used to communicate the importance of the firm's financial performance to employees, heightening their awareness of the overall financial performance of the organization by making a portion of their pay vary with it. This is thought to be most motivating when employees believe that they can substantially influence the profit measure, such as in smaller organizations and those in which the means by which profits are achieved are well understood.

Some have proposed mixed models, whereby incentive pay is based partially on individual measures of performance and partially on group measures. Wageman (1995), however, found that teams having mixed forms of reward (i.e. rewards based on both the individual and group performances), mixed tasks (i.e. some tasks performed solely by individuals and some by interdependent groups), or both, had lower performance than those with task and pay designs that were clearly either individual level or team level. She proposes that mixed tasks and rewards may lead to inferior performance by adding a group element to what is primarily an individual task, thereby undermining attention to the task. It may also be more difficult to develop supporting norms for cooperation in the team (Quigley et al., 2007). In addition, teams executing mixed tasks may need more time to adjust because of the greater complexity of tasks that have both the individual and group performance components. In fact, one study (Johnson, Hollenbeck, Humphrey, Ilgen, Jundt, and Meyer, 2006) has shown that it even may be more difficult for a team to shift from a competitive to a cooperative reward structure than from cooperative to a competitive one. When a competitive reward structure was shifted to a cooperative one, team members seem to engage in "cutthroat cooperation" in which team members retained much of their competitive behavior within the new reward systems intended to foster cooperation. Another complicating factor is that some workers may prefer individual pay over team-based pay (Cable and Judge, 1994; Haines and Taggar, 2006; Shaw, Duffy, and Stark, 2001). The question remains, then, how best (or when) to mix individual- and group-based incentive plans.

Make Pay Commensurate with the Level of Risk Employees Are Required to Bear

Risk refers to uncertainty about outcomes (Sitkin and Pablo, 1992), and, by definition, pay-for-performance systems involve uncertain outcomes for employees. Individuals tend to be risk-averse concerning pay because they have no way of minimizing their income risk through diversification, as investors are able to do with their stock portfolios.

At least four factors can affect employees' perceptions concerning the riskiness of a pay-for-performance plan. First is the proportion of employee pay that is performance based. Although (as noted earlier) the average percentage of variable pay in the US has ranged from 10–15 recently, the proportion ranges widely from 0 – 70% (and even to 100% for salespersons; Gomez-Mejia and Balkin, 1992).

The higher the proportion of variable pay, the more risk the employee must bear in a trade-off between income security and the potential for higher earnings (Gomez-Mejia, Balkin, and Cardy, 1998). At some point, the level of risk may be perceived as so great that it would be unacceptable to the majority of employees, regardless of the potential for high pay. Some have attributed the recent acute shortage of truck drivers in part to the way in which most truck drivers are paid, which is commonly by the mile. This constitutes a sort of piece-work arrangement but can also involve significant pay volatility because loads are assigned based on availability and location. Moreover, the industry has been slow to award pay increases to help compensate (Conroy, Roumpi, Delery and Gupta 2021; Wolf, 2021). The second factor that influences employees' perceptions of risk is their self-efficacy (see Chapter 6) that they can achieve the performance goals on which pay is contingent. Those who are confident of their ability to perform at a high level should perceive contingent pay as less risky than those who are less confident of their ability. Third, to the extent that the performance measure on which pay is based is influenced by factors outside individual employees' control (e.g. technology or macroeconomic factors affecting profits or stock prices), perceived risk for the employee is increased. For example, CEOs run the risk of losing income (and even employment) if the companies for which they are responsible are unsuccessful – whatever the cause. A fourth factor affecting employee perceptions of risk is the amount of time between performance and the receipt of rewards. Because the future is uncertain, deferred rewards involve more risk than immediate ones. For employees to accept a pay system offering long-term rewards, they must be willing to delay gratification in the hopes of greater (but uncertain) future returns. Research by Shelley (1993) indicates that managers may expect to be compensated for the loss of immediate compensation by the payment of a premium that is far in excess of the amount the time *value of money* would imply – a finding that is probably true of nonmanagerial employees as well.

Possible Exceptions to the Principle of Paying for Performance

It does not make sense for an employer to offer to pay employees more unless the employer will actually get more in the bargain. When, therefore, might it be unwise (or even counterproductive) to offer incentives?

When Employees Are Learning

In learning situations, when employees are attempting to "get up to speed" on a new task, offering performance-based pay may frustrate more than it motivates. Performance failures that are a natural part of learning may be exaggerated in the learner's mind because of failure not only to perform the task but also to obtain the monetary reward. Thus, it is unwise to pay for performance until employees are able to perform at the desired level.

When the Employer Can Monitor

Agency theory (Jensen and Meckling, 1976) suggests that financial incentives are unnecessary when employers can easily monitor employees' behavior (e.g. by direct observation or through information systems) and give them ongoing direction and feedback. In such situations, employees' awareness that they are being monitored may obviate paying for performance.

When Other Motivators Are Sufficient or Compensatory

Some people value other aspects of their jobs more than they value pay – factors such as interesting work, autonomy, desirable location, benefits that meet their needs, or having a boss they love working for. Such individuals will often accept lower pay in order to have what is more important to them in their jobs.

When the Company Is Unionized

Union contracts constrain an employer's pay policies, and thus, under collective bargaining agreements, it may be impossible to pay for performance, especially at the individual level. When incentives are included in a union contract, they are usually group incentives, because group pay is viewed as encouraging cohesion rather than competition among members.

Case Examples

1. Paying for Individual Performance

Wells Fargo Wells Fargo provides an example of the pay-for-performance system gone awry. The bank, the fourth largest in the United States, was forced to pay $3 billion and other fines in 2020 in conjunction with a fake account scandal tied in part to the bank's financial incentive program and related impossible sales goals. Much of the scandal stemmed from the Community Bank Division whose head set high goals for cross-selling, which involved having customers sign up for multiple banking products (Veetikazhi and Krishnan, 2019). When a customer has multiple products, a bank has more information about the customers, allowing the bank to make better decisions about pricing, credit, and other product offerings. Thus cross-selling can aid the profitability of a bank (Tayan, 2019).

During the period 2002–2016, the Division Head set up intense completion, including daily score cards complete with monitoring on an hourly basis. Branch managers were given quotas associated with the number and types of products sold. If they did not meet a particular day's quotas, the deficit was added to the next day's goals. In one example of the type of pressure exerted, an exercise called "running the gauntlet" required managers to run to a whiteboard and write their performance figures. Branch employees received financial incentives for meeting the cross-sell and customer-service targets. Personal bankers could earn bonuses up to 15–20% of their salary, while tellers were eligible for up to 3% (Tayan, 2019). The incentives were tied to meeting minimum goals. Adding to the pressure, starting in 2010, achieving high targets was considered also in employees' annual performance appraisals.

Given the financial incentives and pressure, bank employees began to use fraud to meet the imposed targets. They opened millions of accounts in customers' names, ordered credit cards, and set up bill payment programs mostly without customers' knowledge. To do so, they took actions such as forcing customers to buy into services they did not need, creating fake personal identification numbers, forging signatures, and transferring customers' money across accounts without informing customers and often trying to hide the transactions from them by using their own contact information so that customers did not receive notification (Flitter, 2020; Kelly, 2020). Even though turnover was more than 30%, the Community Bank head dismissed concerns, noting that there was no shortage of applicants for positions.

The practices started to come to light when a story about fraudulent accounts appeared in the *Los Angeles Times* in December 2013, Still, Wells Fargo top management and the board of directors were slow to act, but the scheme began to unravel further as customers filed numerous complaints with government regulatory agencies and the Wells Fargo CEO was called to testify before the US Senate (Veetikazhi and Krishnan, 2019). Various court filings indicated that thousands of employees had been quietly fired in the final five years of fraudulent behavior, and many more were disciplined based on customer complaints. The CEO, Community Bank head and various other managers, along with some board members, ultimately were forced to resign.

2. *Paying for Team Performance*

Children's Hospital of Boston The accounts receivable (AR) department of Children's Hospital in Boston developed a team-based incentive program that led to a greatly reduced billing cycle and aided cash flow for the hospital (Cadrain, 2003). The department had installed a new billing system that was not working as intended, causing problems for employees and leading to low morale in the department. The time to receive payments after bills were sent out was stretching beyond 100 days, and hospital officials were becoming concerned about cash flow. To help improve employee morale and shorten the billing cycle, hospital executives set up an incentive plan aimed at establishing a line of sight that allowed employees to focus on the connections between the number of days a bill spends in AR and the quarterly cash flow of the hospital. Team members were provided with three possible goals stated in terms of the number of days an unpaid bill remained in AR: threshold, target, and optimal. Each goal had a dollar amount attached to it with a provision for a quarterly payment of $500, $1000, or $1500, respectively. Within 30 days of the end of each quarter, each team member would receive a part of the payment prorated to reflect the number of scheduled hours the team member worked, and a progress celebration was held. Once the team members understood the connection between their work and the cash flow at the hospital as well as how their efforts could increase their personal cash flow, they began working closely as a team to follow up with patients, insurers, or the medical records people. By the end of the plan's first fiscal year, employees had succeeded in reducing the average number of days a bill was in AR from 100 to 75.8. Shortly after, they reached the middle 60s. The plan had an added bonus for the hospital because turnover in the AR department plummeted.

3. Paying for Organizational Performance

Handelsbanken Swedish-based Handelsbanken provides an example of profit sharing used effectively to reward performance and instill loyalty among employees (Hope and Fraser, 2003). The bank's stated goal has long been to consistently realize higher profitability than comparable banks, and in 1973 then-CEO Jan Wallander established Octogonen, a foundation through which Handelsbanken shares with employees the "extra profits" made possible through their efforts. Employees are rewarded when company profits exceed the average profits of comparable banks, and almost every year since 1973 the board has allocated a portion of profits to Octogonen. Each full-time employee in the bank's home markets receives an equal part of that year's allocated amount, regardless of position or salary. Distributions are deferred until retirement at age 60. Since Octogonen's beginning, Handelsbanken has performed well, and the profit-sharing system has paid out significant amounts of money. The payments to Octogonen, however, were suspended in early 2019 after the bank detected a significant increase in costs during 2018. The payments were resumed later in 2020 after costs showed significant reductions (Wass, 2021).

The plan, in conjunction with other employee-friendly human resource management practices, is thought to be an incentive for staff to remain with the company (Hammarström, 2007; Handelsbanken, 2007). In one survey, 82% of Handelsbanken staff reported believing they could make a valuable contribution to the bank's success (Times Online, 2007), and 86% reported that they would not leave, even if they had another job offer (Times Online, 2008). The company is viewed as having very motivated employees despite the absence of more common bonus plans (Schwartzkopff, 2020).

Conclusion

Paying for performance works – when done right. It communicates what factors are most important to the company's success and focuses employees' attention and effort on those factors. It is fair, because it pays more to those who contribute more. In turn, it attracts individuals who can perform at high levels and, by recognizing and rewarding them for doing so, makes them want to remain. It is important to remember that many contextual factors can affect the success of pay-for-performance systems. These factors include clearly defining performance, making sure to carefully communicate the parameters of the pay system, ensuring that employees have the skills to be competent, making the payments congruent with employees' values, building in nonfinancial incentives, using money in conjunction with intrinsic motivation, promoting a culture of honesty and integrity, and targeting the appropriate level for the pay-for-performance plan.

References

Amabile, T. M. (1993). Motivational synergy: Toward new conceptualizations of intrinsic and extrinsic motivation in the workplace. *Human Resource Management Review,* 3, 185–201.

Arthur, J. B., and Aiman-Smith, L. (2001). Gainsharing and organizational learning: An analysis of employee suggestions over time. *Academy of Management Journal,* 44, 737–754.

Arthur, J. B., and Jelf, G. S. (1999). The effects of gainsharing on grievance rates and absenteeism over time. *Journal of Labor Research,* 20, 133–145.

Balkin, D. B., and Montemayor, E. F. (2000). Explaining team-based pay: A contingency perspective based on the organizational life cycle, team design, and organizational learning literatures. *Human Resource Management Review,* 10, 249–269.

Banker, R. D., Lee, S.-Y., Potter, G., and Srinivasan, S. (1996). Contextual analysis of performance impacts of outcome-based incentive compensation. *Academy of Management Journal,* 39, 920–948.

Bartol, K. M., Durham, C. C., and Poon, J. M. (2001). Influence of performance evaluation rating segmentation on motivation and fairness perceptions. *Journal of Applied Psychology,* 86(6), 1106–1119. https://doi-org.proxy-um.researchport.umd.edu/10.1037/0021-9010.86.6.1106

Bartol, K. M., and Hagmann, L. L. (1992, November-December). Team-based pay plans: A key to effective teamwork. *Compensation and Benefits Review,* 24–29.

Bartol, K. M., and Locke, E. A. (2000). Incentives and motivation. In S. L. Rynes and B. Gerhart (eds), *Compensation in Organizations.* San Francisco: Jossey-Bass.

Brandes, P., Dharwadkar, R. Lemesis, G. V., and Heisler, W. J. (2003). Effective employee stock option design: Reconciling stakeholder, strategic, and motivational factors. *Academy of Management Executive,* 17(1), 77–93.

Bretz, R. D., Milkovich, G. T., and Read, W. (1992). The current state of performance appraisal research and practice: Concerns, directions, and implications. *Journal of Management,* 18, 321–352.

Cable, D. M., and Judge, T. A. (1994). Pay preferences and job search decisions: A person-organization fit perspective. *Personnel Psychology,* 47, 317–348.

Cadrain, D. (2003). Put success in sight. *HR Magazine,* 48(5), 84–92.

Chung, D. J., Narayandas, D., and Chang, D. (2021). The Effects of Quota Frequency: Sales Performance and Product Focus. *Management Science,* 67(4), 2151–2170. https://doi-org.proxy-um.researchport.umd.edu/10.1287/mnsc.2020.3648

Chung, K. H., and Vickery, W. D. (1976). Relative effectiveness and joint effects of three selected reinforcements in a repetitive task situation. *Organizational Behavior and Human Decision Processes,* 16, 114–142.

Conroy, S. A., and Gupta, N. (2016). Team pay-for-performance: The devil is in the details. *Group & Organization Management,* 4, 32–65.

Conroy, S. A., Roumpi, D., Delery, J. E., and Gupta, N. (2021). Pay volatility and employee turnover in the trucking industry. *Journal of Management,* 1. https://doi-org.proxy-um.researchport.umd.edu/10.1177/01492063211019651

Colletti, J. A., and Cichelli, D. L. (1993). *Designing Sales Compensation Plans: An Approach to Developing and Implementing Incentive Plans for Salespeople.* Scottsdale: American Compensation Association.

Cotton, M. S., and Cook, J. L. (1982). Meta-analyses and the effects of various reward systems: Some different conclusions from Johnson et al. *Psychological Bulletin,* 92, 176–183.

Dean, S. (2006). Why companies are moving to variable pay. *Business and Legal Reports.* Retrieved September 19, 2008, from: http://comp.blr.com/display.cfm?id=155070.

Delves, D. P. (2001). Underwater stock options. *Strategic Finance,* 83(6), 26–32.

DeMatteo, J. S., Eby, L. T., and Sundstrom, E. (1998). Team-based rewards: Current empirical evidence and directions for future research. *Research in Organizational Behavior,* 20, 141–183.

Deshmukh, S., Howe, K. M., and Luft, C. (2008). Stock option expensing: The role of corporate governance. *Journal of Applied Corporate Finance,* 20(2), 122–129.

Devers, C. A., Cannella, Jr., A. A., Reilly, G. P., and Yoder, M. E. (2007). Executive compensation: A multidisciplinary review of recent development. *Journal of Management,* 33, 1016–1072.

Eisenberger, R., and Cameron, J. (1996). Detrimental effects of reward: Reality or myth? *American Psychologist,* 51, 1153–1166.

Eisenberger, R., Rhoades, R., and Cameron, J. (1999). Does pay for performance increase or decrease perceived self-determination and intrinsic motivation? *Journal of Personality and Social Psychology,* 75, 1026–1040.

Empsight (2020). Policies, Practices & Merit Survey Report, New York: Empsight International, LLC.

Englmaier, F., Roider, A., and Sunde, U. (2017). The role of communication of performance schemes: Evidence from a field experiment. *Management Science,* 63, 4061–4080.

Fang, M., and Gerhart, B. (2012). Does pay for performance diminish intrinsic interest? *International Journal of Human Resource Management,* 23(6), 1176–1196. https://doi-org.proxy-um.researchport.umd.edu/10.1080/09585192.2011.561227

Flitter, E. (2020, February 21). The price of Wells Fargo's fake account scandal grows by $3 billion. *The New York Times.* https://www.nytimes.com/2020/02/21/business/wells-fargo-settlement.html. Downloaded on November 3, 2021.

Ford, N. M., Walker, O. C., and Churchhill, G. A. (1985). Differences in the attractiveness of alternative rewards among industrial salespeople: Additional evidence. *Journal of Business Research,* 13, 123–138.

Garbers, Y., and Konradt, U. (2014). The effect of financial incentives on performance: A quantitative review of individual and team-based financial incentives. *Journal of Occupational & Organizational Psychology,* 87(1), 102–137. https://doi-org.proxy-um.researchport.umd.edu/10.1111/joop.12039

Gerhart, G. (2017). Incentives and pay for performance in the workplace. *Advances in Motivation Science,* 4, 910140.

Gerhart, G., and Fang, M. (2014). Pay for (individual) performance: Issues, claims, evidence and the role of sorting effects. *Human Resource Management Review,* 24, 41–52.

Gerhart, G. and Newman, J. M. (2020). *Compensation* (13th edition). New York: McGraw-Hill.

Gerhart, G., and Rynes, S. L. (2003). *Compensation: Theory, Evidence, and Strategic Implications.* Thousand Oaks, CA: Sage.

Gerhart, G., Trevor, C. O., and Graham, M. E. (1996). New directions in compensation research: Synergies, risk, and survival. *Research in Personnel and Human Resources Management,* 14, 143–203.

Gerhart, G., and Trevor, C. O. (1996). Employment variability under different compensation systems. *Academy of Management Journal,* 39, 1692–1712.

Gottfried, M. (2021, February 19). KKR Executive's Push to Spread Employee Stock Ownership Begins to Gain Traction. *Wall Street Journal.* https://www.wsj.com/articles/kkr-executives-push-to-spread-employee-stock-ownership-begins-to-gain-traction-11613730601?mod=Searchresults_pos19&page=3

Gomez-Mejia, L. R., and Balkin, D. B. (1989). Effectiveness of individual an aggregate compensation strategies. *Industrial Relations,* 28, 431–445.

Gomez-Mejia, L. R., and Balkin, D. B. (1992). *Compensation, Organizational Strategy, and Firm Performance.* Cincinnati, OH: South-Western.

Gomez-Mejia, L. R., Balkin, D. B., and Cardy, R. L. (1998). *Managing Human Resources* (2nd edition). Upper Saddle River, NJ: Prentice-Hall.

Gupta, N., Conroy, S. A., and Delery, J. E. (2012). The many faces of pay variation. *Human Resource Management Review,* 22(2), 100–115. https://doi-org.proxy-um.researchport.umd.edu/10.1016/j.hrmr.2011.12.001

Hackman, J. R. (1987). The design of work teams. In J. W. Lorsch (ed.), *Handbook of Organizational Behavior* (pp. 315–342). Englewood Cliffs, NJ: Prentice Hall.

Hackman, J. R., and Wageman, R. (2005). A theory of team coaching. *Academy of Management Review,* 30, 269–287.

Haines, V. Y., and Taggar, S. (2006). Antecedents of team reward attitude. *Group Dynamics: Theory, Research, and Practice,* 10, 194–205.

Hammarström, H. (2007, October). Handelsbanken, Sweden: Make work pay – make work attractive. Retrieved October 12, 2008, from http://www.eurofound.europa.eu/areas/qualityofwork/betterjobs/cases/se04handelsbanken.htm

Han, J. H., Bartol, K. M., and Seongsu Kim. (2015). Tightening up the performance-pay linkage: Roles of contingent reward leadership and profit-sharing in the cross-level influence of individual pay-for-performance. *Journal of Applied Psychology,* 100(2), 417–430. https://doi-org.proxy-um.researchport.umd.edu/10.1037/a0038282

Handelsbanken (2007). *2007 Annual Report.* Retrieved October 12, 2008, from http://www.handelsbanken.com/us

Harris, M. M., Gilbreath, B., and Sunday, J. A. (1998). A longitudinal examination of a merit pay system: Relationships among performance ratings, merit increases, and total pay increases. *Journal of Applied Psychology,* 83, 825–831.

Harrison, D. A., Virick, M., and William, S. (1996). Working without a net: Time, performance, and turnover under maximally contingent rewards. *Journal of Applied Psychology,* 81, 331–345.

Henderson, R. I. (1997). *Compensation Management in a Knowledge-Based World* (7th edition). Upper Saddle River, NJ: Prentice Hall.

Heneman, R. L. (1992). *Merit Pay: Linking Pay Increases to Performance Ratings.* Reading, MA: Addison-Wesley.

Hill, N. S., Bartol, K. M., Tesluk, P. E., and Langa, G. A. (in press). When time is not enough: The development of trust and cooperation in computer mediated teams. *Organizational Behavior and Human Decision Processes.*

Hope, J., and Fraser, R. (2003). New ways of setting rewards: The beyond budgeting model. *California Management Review,* 45(4), 104–119.

Huddart, S., and Lang, M. (1996). Employee stock option exercises: An empirical analysis. *Journal of Accounting and Economics,* 21, 5–43.

Huselid, M. (1995). The impact of human resources management practices on turnover, productivity, and corporate financial performance. *Academy of Management Journal,* 38, 635–672.

Jain, S. H., and Roble, D. (2008, March). Gainsharing in health care: Meeting the quality-of-care challenge. *Healthcare Financial Management,* 72–78.

Jenkins, G. D., Jr., Mitra, A., Gupta, N., and Shaw, J. D. (1998). Are financial incentives related to performance? A meta-analytic review of empirical research. *Journal of Applied Psychology,* 83, 777–787.

Jensen, M., and Meckling, M. (1976). Theory of the firm: Managerial behavior, agency costs and ownership structure. *Journal of Financial Economics,* 3, 305–360.

Johnson, M. D., Hollenbeck, J. R., Humphrey, S. E., Ilgen, D. R., Jundt, D., and Meyer, C. J. (2006). Cutthroat cooperation: Asymmetrical adaptation to changes in team reward structures. *Academy of Management Journal,* 49, 103–119.

Kelly, J. (2020, February 24). Wells Fargo forced to pay $3 billion for the bank's face account scandal. Forbes. https://www.forbes.com/sites/jackkelly/2020/02/24/wells-fargo-forced-to-pay-3-billion-for-the-banks-fake-account-scandal/?sh=60d9737342d2. Downloaded on November 3, 2021.

Kepes, S., Delery, J. E., and Gupta, N. (2009). Contingencies in the effects of pay range on organizational effectiveness. *Personnel Psychology,* 62, 497–531.

Kerr, S. (1995, February). On the folly of rewarding A, while hoping for B. *Academy of Management Executive,* 9, 7–14.

Kim, S. (1998). Does profit sharing increase firms' profits? *Journal of Labor Research,* 19, 351–370.

Kruse, D. L. (1993). *Profit Sharing: Does It Make a Difference?* Kalamazoo, MI: Upjohn Institute.

Lazear, E. P. (1986). Salaries and piece rates. *Journal of Business,* 59, 405–431.

Lazear, E. (2000). Performance pay and productivity. *American Economic Review,* 90, 1346–1361.

Lawler, E. E., III. (1971). *Pay and Organizational Effectiveness: A Psychological View.* New York: McGraw-Hill.

Lawler, E. E., III. (2003). Pay systems for virtual teams. In C. B. Gibson and S. G. Cohen (eds), *Virtual Teams That Work: Creating Conditions for Virtual Team Effectiveness.* San Francisco: Jossey-Bass.

Lawler, E. E., III, Mohrman, S., and Ledford, G. E., Jr. (1995). *Creating High Performance Organizations.* San Francisco: Jossey-Bass.

Lee, C. (1988). The effects of goal setting and monetary incentives on self-efficacy and performance. *Journal of Business and Psychology,* 2, 366–372.

Locke, E. A. (2004). Linking goals to monetary incentives. *Academy of Management Executive,* 18(4), 130–133.

Locke, E. A. (2019). Some observations about goals, money and cheating in business. *Organizational Dynamics*, 48, 100692, 1–4.

Locke, E. A., Feren, D. B., McCaleb, V. M., Shaw, K. N., and Denny, A. T. (1980). The relative effectiveness of four methods of motivating employee performance. In K. D. Duncan, M. M. Gruneberg, and D. Wallis (eds), *Changes in Working Life* (pp. 363–388). London: Wiley, Ltd.

Lopez, T. B., Hopins, C. D., and Raymond, M. A. (2006). Reward preferences of salespeople: How do commissions rate? *Journal of Personal Selling and Sales*, 26(4), 381–390.

Lucifora, C., and Origo, F. (2015). Performance-related pay and firm productivity: evidence from a reform in the structure of collective bargaining. *ILR Review*, 68(3), 606–632. https://doi-org.proxy-um.researchport.umd.edu/10.1177/0019793915570876

McClurg, L. N. (2001). Team rewards: How far have we come? *Human Resource Management*, 40(1), 73–86.

Milkovich, G. T., and Newman, J. M. (2008). *Compensation* (9th edition). New York: McGraw-Hill/Irwin.

Miller, S. (2017, August 7). 3% salary increases put greater focus on variable pay. SHRM Online Compensation. https://www.shrm.org/resourcesandtools/hr-topics/compensation/pages/salary-raises-variable-pay.aspx

Mitchell, D. J. B., Lewin, D., and Lawler, E. E., III. (1990). Alternative pay systems, firm performance, and productivity. In A. S. Blinder (ed.), *Paying for Productivity: A Look at the Evidence*. (pp. 15–94). Washington, D.C.: The Brookings Institution.

Montemayor, E. F. (1994). A model for aligning teamwork and pay. *ACA Journal*, 3(2), 18–25.

Nassauer, S. (September 9, 2021). Walmart to end quarterly bonuses for store workers. Wall Street Journal. https://www.wsj.com/articles/walmart-to-end-quarterly-bonuses -for-store-workers-11631190896

Nyberg, A. J., Maltarich, M. A., Abdulsalam, D. "Dee," Essman, S. M., and Cragun, O. (2018). Collective pay for performance: A cross-disciplinary review and meta-analysis. *Journal of Management*, 44(6), 2433–2472. https://doi-org.proxy-um.researchport.umd.edu/10.1177/0149206318770732

Nyberg, A. J., Pieper, J. R., and Trevor, C. O. (2016). Pay-for-performance's effect on future employee performance. *Journal of Management*, 42(7), 1753–1783. https://doi-org.proxy-um.researchport.umd.edu/10.1177/0149206313515520

O'Dell, C. (1987). *People, Performance and Pay*. Houston: American Productivity Center.

Parker, G., McAdams, J., and Zielinski, D. (2000). *Rewardings Teams: Lessons from the Trenches*. San Francisco: Jossey-Bass.

Patel, A. D. (2006, September). Gainsharing: Past, present, and future. *Healthcare Financial Management*, 124–130.

Pfeffer, J. (1998, May–June). Six dangerous myths about pay. *Harvard Business Review*, 76, 108–119.

Quigley, N., Tesluk, P. E., Locke, E. A., and Bartol, K. M. (2007). The effects of incentives and individual differences on knowledge sharing and performance effectiveness. *Organization Science*, 18, 71–88.

Ryan, R. M., and Deci, E. L. (2000). Self-determination theory and the facilitation of intrinsic motivation, social development, and well-being. *American Psychologist,* 55, 68–78.

Rynes, S. L. (1987). Compensation strategies for recruiting. *Topics in Total Compensation,* 2(2), 185.

Schuster, J. R., and Zingheim, P. K. (1996). *The New Pay: Linking Employee and Organizational Performance.* San Francisco: Jossey-Bass.

Schwartzkopff, F. (2020, July 13). The bank refuses to pay out lavish bonuses, and it's doing just fine. Fortune. https://fortune.com/2020/07/13/this-bank-refuses-to-pay-out-lavish-banker-bonuses-and-its-doing-just-fine/. Download on November 2, 2021.

Sesil, J. C., Kroumova, M. A., Kruse, D. L., and Blasi, J. R. (2000). Broad-based employee stock options in the U.S.: Do they impact company performance? *Academy of Management Proceedings 2000 HR,* G1–G6.

Shaw, J. D. (2015). Pay dispersion, sorting, and organizational performance. *Academy of Management Discoveries,* 1(2), 165–179. https://doi-org.proxy-um.researchport.umd.edu/10.5465/amd.2014.0045

Shaw, J. D., Duffy, M. K., and Stark, E. M. (2001). Team reward attitude: construct development and initial validation. *Journal of Organizational Behavior,* 22, 903–917.

Shaw, J. D., Gupta, N., and Delery, J. E. (2001). Congruence between technology and compensation systems: Implications for strategy implementation. *Strategic Management Journal,* 22, 379–386.

Shelley, M. (1993). Outcome signs, question frames, and discount rates. *Management Science,* 39(7), 806-815.

Sitkin, S. B., and Pablo, A. L. (1992). Reconceptualizing the determinants of risk behavior. *Academy of Management Review,* 17, 9–38.

Skaggs, B. C., Manz, C. C., Lyle, M. C. B., and Pearce, C. L. (2018). On the folly of punishing A while hoping for A: Exploring punishment in organizations. *Journal of Organizational Behavior,* 39, 812–815.

Smilco, J., and Van Neck, K. (2004). Rewarding excellence through variable pay. *Benefits Quarterly,* 20(3), 21–25.

Super, J. F., Li, P., Ishqaidef, G., and Guthrie, J. P. (2016). Group rewards, group composition and information sharing: A motivated information processing perspective. *Organizational Behavior & Human Decision Processes,* 134, 31–44. https://doi-org.proxy-um.researchport.umd.edu/10.1016/j.obhdp.2016.04.002

Tayan, B. (2019 January). The Wells Fargo Cross-Selling Scandal. Stanford Closer Look Series. Corporate Governance Research Initiative. 1–16. https://www.gsb.stanford.edu/faculty-research/publications/wells-fargo-cross-selling-scandal. Downloaded November 3, 2021.

Tekleab, A. G., Bartol, K. M., and Liu, W. (2005). Is it pay levels or pay raises that matter to fairness and turnover? *Journal of Organizational Behavior,* 26(8), 899–921. https://doi-org.proxy-um.researchport.umd.edu/10.1002/job.352

Times Online (2007). Best 100 Companies: 11. Handelsbanken. Retrieved October 12, 2008, from http://www.timesonline.co.uk/tol/life_and_style/career_and_jobs/best_100_companies/article1473616.ece

Times Online (2008). Best 100 Companies: 10. Handelsbanken. Retrieved October 12, 2008, from http://www.timesonline.co.uk/tol/life_and_style/career_and_jobs/best_100_companies/article3478984.ece

Veetikazhi, R., and Krishnan, G. (2019). Wells Fargo: Fall from great to miserable: A case study on corporate governance failures. *Southern Asian Journal of Business and Management Cases,* 8(1), 88–99.

Wageman, R. (1995). Interdependence and group effectiveness. *Administrative Science Quarterly,* 40, 145–180.

Wageman, R., and Baker, G. (1997). Incentives and cooperation: The joint effects of task and reward interdependence on group performance. *Journal of Organizational Behavior,* 18, 139–158.

Wass, S. (2021, February 3). Handelsbanken resumes payments into profit-sharing plan amid progress on costs. S&P Global Market Intelligence. https://www.spglobal.com/marketintelligence/en/news-insights/latest-news-headlines/handelsbanken-resumes-payments-into-profit-sharing-plan-amid-progress-on-costs-62445464. Download on October 30, 2021.

Welbourne, T. M., and Gomez-Mejia, L. R. (1995). Gainsharing: A critical review and a future research agenda. *Journal of Management,* 21, 559–609.

Williams, C. R., and Livingstone, L. P. (1994). Another look at the relationship between performance and voluntary turnover. *Academy of Management Journal,* 37, 269–298.

Wolf, M. (2021). Economic brief: What's behind the truck driver shortage? WSJ. https://deloitte.wsj.com/articles/economic-brief-whats-behind-the-truck-driver-shortage. Downloaded October 23, 2021.

Yanador, Y., and Marler, J. H. (2006). Compensation strategy: Does business strategy influence compensation in high-technology firms? *Strategic Management Journal,* 27, 559–570.

Young, G. J., Burgess, J. F., and White, B. (2007). Pioneering pay-for-quality: Lessons from the Rewarding Results demonstrations. *Health Care Financing Review,* 29(1), 59–70.

Youndt, M. A., Snell, S. A., Dean, J. W., Jr., and Lepak, D. P. (1996). Human resource management, manufacturing strategy, and firm performance. *Academy of Management Journal,* 39, 836–866.

Yukl, G. A., and Latham, G. P. (1975). Consequences of reinforcement schedules and incentive magnitude for employee performance: Problems encountered in an industrial setting. *Journal of Applied Psychology,* 60, 294–298.

Exercises

Analyzing the Pay System at Your Job

1. Think about your current job (or a job you have held in the past). Circle the types of pay you receive in this job:
   Non-performance-based pay: Salary Hourly pay
   Individual level: Piece-rate Sales commission Other variable pay Merit pay

Team level: Team-based pay
Organizational level: Gainsharing Profit sharing Stock ownership (or options)

2. Use a scale from 0 to 4 to answer a–c. *(Circle your ratings.)*
   a. How well does the pay plan contribute to your *motivation to perform at a high level?*
      Performance: Not at all motivating 0 1 2 3 4 Extremely motivating
   b. How well does the pay plan contribute to *your motivation to collaborate with or help fellow employees accomplish their work goals?*
      Collaboration: Not at all motivating 0 1 2 3 4 Extremely motivating
   c. How well does the pay plan contribute to your *motivation to remain with the organization?*
      Retention: Not at all motivating 0 1 2 3 4 Extremely motivating
3. What (if any) aspects of the plan are demotivating or demoralizing to you?
4. (a) What is one change your employer could make to the pay system that would enhance your motivation to perform well and stay with the organization? (b) What potential pitfalls or risks (to you, your fellow employees, or the organization) would be associated with this proposed change?
5. Please watch the following video(s):
   a. Hourly employees vs. pay for performance: https://www.youtube.com/watch?v=Fa6uXjX8o30
   b. Why you should know how much your coworkers are making: https://www.ted.com/talks/david_burkus_why_you_should_know_how_much_your_coworkers_get_paid/footnotes?referrer=playlist-how_to_run_a_company_like_a_vi
   c. Pay for performance and intrinsic motivation: https://www.youtube.com/watch?v=yeRuruYV7rE

Now form small groups to discuss the video(s) and answer the following questions:

1. What are the major points of the video?
2. How can you use information from the video in your career?
3. Based on the video, what advice do you have for leaders in organizations?

Be prepared to present the ideas from your small group discussion with the class as a whole.

Discussion Questions

1. Why should organizations pay for performance?
2. What are some creative pay-for-performance programs you have seen in organizations?
3. Are there any downsides to pay for performance?
4. What are your recommendations for a manager wishing to start a pay-for-performance program?

8

Promote Job Satisfaction Through Mental Challenge

TIMOTHY A. JUDGE[1], RYAN KLINGER[2], AND MENG LI[3]

[1] The Ohio State University
[2] Old Dominion University
[3] Kincentric

The most popular definition of job satisfaction was supplied by Locke (1976), who defined it as "... a pleasurable or positive emotional state resulting from the appraisal of one's job or job experiences" (p. 1304). There are many possible influences on how favorably one appraises one's job, and numerous theories of job satisfaction have attempted to delineate these influences. Empirical evidence, however, has suggested only one clear attribute of the work itself that consistently influences job satisfaction – the cognitive challenge of the work. This leads to the general principle that will be the focus of this chapter – that mentally challenging work is the key to job satisfaction. Thus, the most effective way an organization can promote the job satisfaction of its employees is to enhance the mental challenge in their jobs, and the most consequential way most individuals can improve their own job satisfaction is to seek out mentally challenging work.

Before discussing this principle in more detail, however, it is important to demonstrate the importance of the principle. Scores on a valid measure of job satisfaction are the most important pieces of information organizations can collect, not only as one measure of management effectiveness, but because, as we will note, job satisfaction scores predict a wide range of individual and organizational levels of outcomes.

Some of the outcomes that job satisfaction has been linked to are as follows:

Job performance: The relationship between job satisfaction and performance has an interesting history. In 1985, a quantitative review of the literature suggested that the true correlation between job satisfaction and performance was quite small (Iaffaldano and Muchinsky, 1985). However, more recent evidence reveals that the relationship is larger than was previously thought. A comprehensive review of 300 studies determined that when the correlations are corrected for the effects of sampling error and measurement error, the average true score correlation between overall job satisfaction and job performance is 0.30 (Judge, Thoresen,

Bono, and Patton, 2001). Thus, it does appear that a happy worker is more likely to be a productive one. Evidence also exists for a relationship at the organizational level – companies listed in the "100 Best Companies to Work for in America" outperformed their peers on several financial outcomes. They generated 2.3–3.8% higher annual stock returns and exhibited 0.32% higher earnings announcement returns from 1984 to 2011 (Edmans, 2012). Of course, the relationship between satisfaction and performance may be reciprocal. Not only may employees who are happy with their jobs be more productive, but performing a job well may lead to satisfaction with the job, especially if good performance is rewarded (see Chapters 8 and 7).

Withdrawal behaviors: Job satisfaction displays relatively consistent, negative correlations with absenteeism and turnover. Job dissatisfaction also appears to display negative correlations with other specific withdrawal behaviors, including unionization, lateness, drug abuse, and retirement. Furthermore, Harrison, Newman, and Roth (2006) and Fisher and Locke (1992) have shown that when these specific behaviors are aggregated as indicators of a general withdrawal syndrome, job satisfaction is quite predictive.

Life satisfaction: Evidence indicates that job satisfaction is also moderately to strongly related to one outcome that individuals find particularly important – life satisfaction (Tait, Padgett, and Baldwin, 1989). Since the job is a significant part of life, the correlation between job and life satisfaction makes sense – one's job experiences spill over on to life. Thus, people who have jobs that they like are more likely to lead happy lives.

Thus far, job satisfaction has been defined, and it has been shown that job satisfaction matters. Thus, any principle that reveals how to best promote job satisfaction is important to understand. With this foundation, in the next section of this chapter, the model that best describes the principle – that job satisfaction is best achieved through mentally challenging work – will be reviewed.

Job Characteristics Model

The theory that best describes the role of the work environment in providing mentally challenging work is the Job Characteristics Model (JCM). JCM argues that the intrinsic nature of work is the core underlying factor causing employees to be satisfied with their jobs. The model, in its full explication by Hackman and Oldham (1980), focuses on five core job characteristics that make one's work challenging and fulfilling: (i) *Task identity* – degree to which one can see one's work from beginning to end; (ii) *Task significance* – degree to which one's work is seen as important and significant; (iii) *Skill variety* – degree to which the job allows employees to do different tasks; (iv) *Autonomy* – degree to which employee has control and discretion for how to conduct their job; and (v) *Feedback* – degree to which the work itself provides feedback for how the employee is performing the job. According to the theory, jobs that are enriched to provide these core characteristics are likely to meet individuals' needs for mental challenge and fulfillment in their work and, thus, will be more satisfying and motivating to employees.

Measurement of Job Characteristics

There are various ways intrinsic job characteristics can be measured. Arguably the most common approach relies on the Job Diagnostic Survey (JDS) to measure the extent to which the five core intrinsic job characteristics are present in the job (for an alternative approach, see Morgeson and Humphrey's [2006] Work Design Questionnaire). Items from the JDS appear in Table 8.1. When responding to items in the table, individuals circle the number (from 1 to 7) that is the most accurate description of their job. The JDS can be used to rate almost any type of job. Ideally, one would give the JDS to a number of people in an organization within a job type

Table 8.1 Measurement of intrinsic job characteristics: the Job Diagnostic Survey

1. How much *autonomy* is there in your job? That is, to what extent does your job permit you to decide *on your own* how to go about doing the work?

   1———2———3———4———5———6———7

   Very little; the job gives me almost no personal "say" about how and when the work is done.
   Moderate autonomy: many things are standardized and not under my control, but I can make some decisions about work.
   Very much; the job gives me almost complete responsibility for deciding how and when the work is done.

2. To what extent does your job involve doing a *"whole" and identifiable piece of work*? That is, is the job a complete piece of work that has an obvious beginning and end? Or is it only a small *part* of the overall piece of work, which is finished by other people or by automatic machines?

   1———2———3———4———5———6———7

   My job is only a tiny part of the overall piece of work; the results of my activities cannot be seen in the final product or service.
   My job is a moderate-sized "chunk" of the overall piece of work; my own contributions can be seen in the final outcome.
   My job involves doing the whole piece of work, from start of finish; the results of my activities are easily seen in the final product or service.

3. How much *variety* is there in your job? That is, to what extent does the job require you to do many different things at work, using a variety of your skills and talents?

   1———2———3———4———5———6———7

   Very little; the job requires me to do the same routine things over and over again.
   Moderate variety. Very much; the job requires me to do many different things, using a number of different skills and talents.

(Continued)

Table 8.1 (Continued)

4. In general, how *significant or important* is your job? That is, are the results of your work likely to significantly affect the lives or well-being of other people?

   1————2————3————4————5————6————7

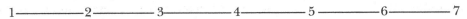

   Not very significant; the outcomes of my work are *not* likely to have important effects on other people.
   Moderately significant. Highly significant; the outcomes of my work can affect other people in very important ways.

5. To what extent does *doing the job itself* provide you with information about your work performance? That is, does the actual *work itself* provide clues about how well you are doing – aside from any "feedback" coworkers or supervisors may provide?

   1————2————3————4————5————6————7

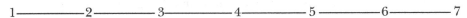

   Very little; the job is set up so I could work forever without finding out how well I am doing.
   Moderately; sometimes doing the job provides "feedback" to me; sometimes it does not.
   Very much; the job is set up so that I get almost constant feedback as I work about how well I am doing.

Source: Hackman, J. R., and Oldham, G. R. (1980). *Work Redesign.* Reading, MA: Addison-Wesley.

to get a reliable measurement of the job characteristics. The JDS is not copyrighted and, thus, is free to use. However, care must be taken in administering the JDS. The reader interested in measuring intrinsic job characteristics should consult Hackman and Oldham (1980), who provide all of the JDS items, along with an excellent discussion of administrative issues.

Research Support

There are several indirect pieces of evidence supporting Hackman and Oldham's model. First, when individuals are asked to evaluate different facets of their job such as pay, promotion opportunities, coworkers, and so forth, the nature of the work itself generally emerges as the most important job facet (Jurgensen, 1978). Second, of the major job satisfaction facets – pay, promotion opportunities, coworkers, supervision, and the work itself – satisfaction with the work itself, far and away, best predicts overall job satisfaction (Rentsch and Steel, 1992). Thus, if we are interested in understanding what causes people to be satisfied with their jobs, the nature of the work (intrinsic job characteristics) is the first place to start. Unfortunately, managers often think employees are most desirous of pay to the exclusion of other job attributes such as challenging work. For example, a 1997 survey indicated that, out of 10 job attributes, employees ranked interesting work as the most important job attribute (good wages was ranked fifth), whereas when it came to what managers thought employees wanted, good wages ranked first while interesting work ranked fifth (Kovach, 1997).

Research directly testing the relationship between workers' reports of job characteristics and job satisfaction has produced consistently positive results. Humphrey, Nahrgang, and Morgeson (2007) meta-analyzed the results of over 250 studies of work characteristic job outcome relationships. All five intrinsic job characteristics were strong predictors of employee job satisfaction. Moreover, these core characteristics were generally found to be significant predictors of other attitudinal criteria, such as organizational commitment and work motivation, as well as behavioral, job performance outcomes. The empirical data suggest that intrinsic job characteristics are the most consistently significant situational predictor of job satisfaction.

How to Increase Mental Challenge in Jobs

Ever been in a car accident? If you have, you probably remember picking up the phone to call your insurance company and, inevitably, talking to many different people, recounting the details of your accident several times. It may be weeks or even months before your claim is settled and, if you ever happen to call to inquire about the status of your claim, you may discover that your claim is buried somewhere in the system. As a customer in this situation, you probably feel irritated and poorly served, being passed around like a hot potato. But have you ever wondered what the implications of such a system are for employees? When each employee specializes in processing one part of the claim, the mental challenge afforded by the job suffers. Over and over, the same person may answer the phone from customers, take down basic details of the accident, and then pass on the claim to someone else, never to see it again. Even the job of claims adjuster can be broken into segments that are very specialized. When individuals repeatedly perform narrow and specialized tasks, they are unlikely to see their work as very challenging or intrinsically motivating.

As an example of how to diagnose and change a work system in this situation, assume that we have administered the JDS to several customer service representatives (CSRs) and managers of a local branch office of an insurance company. Assume that the average JDS scores for each job characteristic are as depicted in Figure 8.1. From this figure, you can determine where the problems are and, if one is to improve CSR attitudes, where changes need to be made. Specifically, as compared to managers, CSRs report especially low levels of skill variety, task identity, and autonomy. Under such circumstances, you would expect the average CSR to report a low level of job satisfaction. But what can be done about it? How can the profile of a CSR job be made to look more like that of the manager? Before specifically addressing this question, let us consider some general ways of increasing intrinsic job characteristics:

Job rotation: Job rotation entails employees performing different jobs; typically, rotation occurs once employees have mastered their present job and are no longer challenged by it. Many companies use job rotation to increase flexibility – i.e. having employees capable of performing a wide variety of jobs allows adjustments

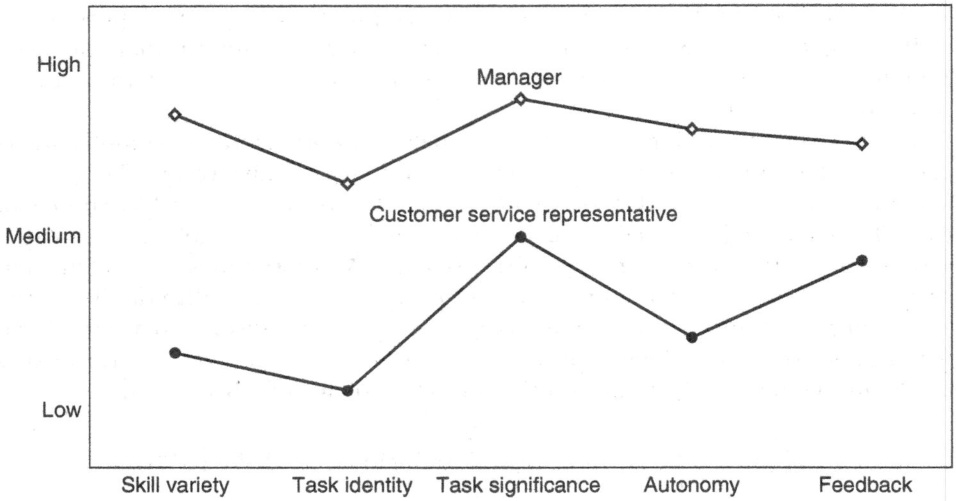

FIGURE 8.1 Job characteristics profiles for job of customer service representative and manager

to be made due to absenteeism, injury, or changes in product demand. By allowing substitution, job rotation can be particularly useful when an employer faces skill shortages (Berry, 2008). However, there are also substantial satisfaction benefits. Many employees enjoy trying their hand at different jobs and appreciate the broader perspective it provides (such as when Southwest Airlines ticket agents try loading bags on the plane). Some companies even pay people for successfully rotating into new jobs; such pay systems are referred to as "skill-based pay."

Job enlargement: Job enlargement, sometimes called horizontal loading, involves expanding the number of tasks associated with a particular job. The difference between job enlargement and job rotation may seem subtle. The difference is that with job rotation, jobs are not really redesigned. Employees simply systematically move from one job to another, but while they are performing a job, the nature of the work has not changed. Job enlargement is a more fundamental intervention because it involves actually changing the job. For example, an assembly line worker who formerly performed one discrete operation (bolting the seat to the floor of a car) may instead be part of a team that performs many phases of the assembly operation. Another example would be workers in a grocery store who may work at the checkout counter, stock shelves, or clean, depending on what needs to be done.

Job enrichment: Job enrichment, sometimes referred to as vertical loading, involves increasing the *responsibilities* of the job. Compared to job enlargement, the increase in the variety in the work of an enriched job may be no more than of an enlarged job, but the responsibility (and often autonomy) of the job is increased. For example, self-managed work teams may take on responsibilities such as staffing, scheduling, and performance appraisal formerly assigned to the team's supervisor. One example of job enrichment occurred at the Duncan Hines angel food cake factory in Jackson, Tennessee. Workers who combine the ingredients for the cake mix are given letters from customers who have had problems with the cake mix. Employees may call up customers to help them solve their problems and, in the meantime, perhaps learn how to make better mixes or provide clearer instructions (Johns, 1996). A similar job enrichment program was undertaken in a totally different industry. Saturn relied on enriched production work teams which were "self-directed and empowered with the authority, responsibility, and resources necessary to meet their day-to-day assignments and goals, including producing budget, quality, housekeeping, safety and health, maintenance, material and inventory control, training, job assignments, repairs, scrap control, vacation approvals, absenteeism, supplies, record keeping, personnel selection and hiring, work planning, and work scheduling" (Saturn Memorandum of Agreement, 1985).

Job feedback: Job feedback pertains to the degree to which employees obtain direct and clear information about the effectiveness of their performance. Such feedback can be obtained through the design of the job (e.g. receive a satisfaction rating from a customer right after a call) or be delivered by supervisors or coworkers (e.g. performance feedback conversations). It is worth noting that such a mechanism of immediate feedback has been adopted by the video game industry to create addictive and engaging games for decades (e.g. the exciting "Ding" when you hit a coin as Mario). By making job feedback a part of job design, the knowledge of results can be increased, mistakes can be quickly corrected, and achievements can be celebrated and recognized in a timely manner. Providing performance feedback to employees was also found to significantly improve employees' feelings of empowerment and, intrinsic motivation (Gagné, Senecal, and Koestner, 1997). The positive effects are stronger when the employees have high propensity to seek and utilize feedback (Gabriel, Frantz, Levy, and Hilliard, 2014).

Now let us return to our insurance company example. Having learned about the ways in which intrinsic job characteristics can be increased, how could we redesign the CSR job? Rotating CSRs through different specialties could increase skill variety. Providing CSRs with feedback on the resolution of each claim could raise task identity. Giving CSRs more latitude in servicing customers could increase autonomy. Though each of these piecemeal changes may have merit, a deeper approach would be to assign CSRs' responsibility for entire claims. Although there are some aspects of the job that a CSR may not be able to accomplish on their own, these could be referred to a claims adjuster, or CSRs could be trained to take on some of the duties of a claims adjuster. By assigning an employee responsibility for the entire claim, both horizontal loading and vertical loading are increased. Horizontal loading is enhanced because the CSR may need to arrange a rental car for the customer, determine whether a check has been processed, or negotiate with another insurance company representative about payment on a claim. Vertical loading is increased by giving the CSR discretion to make decisions about various aspects of the claim (e.g. whether to provide a loaner car for a particular claim, prioritizing claims, etc.). The downsides of redesigns such as this come in the form of training costs and the recognition that there are some employees who do not welcome challenging work. In addition, more mentally challenging jobs may require more intelligent employees and, subsequently, higher compensation costs. However, research indicates that the benefits of job redesign generally outweigh these costs (Cascio, 1991).

Criticisms and Limitations

JCM has amassed a great deal of support in the research literature. Despite the support, there have been several criticisms of the model. Two of the most important concerns are reviewed below.

Measurement of Job Characteristics

JCM assumes that job characteristics cause job satisfaction. It is important to remember that the measures of intrinsic job characteristics typically are perceptual. According to some researchers, perceptual measures are susceptible to biasing influences such as mood. If employees' mood at the time of rating their job characteristics and job satisfaction affects both ratings, the correlation between perceptions of job characteristics and job satisfaction would be inflated (i.e. the real relationship would be lower than it appears). Furthermore, there are concerns that the relationship is not solely from job characteristics to job satisfaction; job satisfaction may also (or instead) cause perceptions of job characteristics. Although some research has supported these criticisms, other research has shown that when these limitations are remedied (e.g. using objective measures of job characteristics), a relationship between job characteristics and job satisfaction still exists (Glick, Jenkins, and Gupta, 1986; Judge, Bono, and Locke, 2000). Thus, while these criticisms are important to keep in mind, they do not undermine the model.

Motivational Versus Mechanistic Work Design Approaches

Motivational approaches to work design, grounded in industrial and organizational psychology and exemplified by JCM, aim to capitalize on the motivational and attitudinal benefits that accrue from a challenged and psychologically fulfilled workforce. In contrast, mechanistic approaches, as advocated by classical industrial engineers, emphasize increased efficiency through factors such as work skill simplification and task specialization. The mechanistic approach would seem to conflict with job design endorsed by the JCM: the former emphasizes efficiency in production (high output levels, low error rates, etc.), the latter emphasizes the advantages of a satisfied and motivated workforce (Campion, 1988; Edwards, Scully, and Brtek, 2000).

Subsequent research by Campion, Morgeson, and colleagues (Campion, Mumford, Morgeson, and Nahrgang, 2005; Morgeson and Campion, 2002), however, suggests that steps can be taken to minimize these efficiency–satisfaction trade-offs. For instance, utilizing a *level separation approach*, one might design organizational structures based on the mechanistic principles of standardization and simplification and still implement the core motivational characteristics within individual jobs. Thus, "basic efficiencies are built into the flow of the work, yet individual jobs are satisfying" (Campion et al., 2005, p. 371). Or *a sequential approach* could be implemented in which both approaches are applied in succession. For instance, after tasks are specialized, management may take steps to increase autonomy and feedback.

Moderators

Employees with Low Growth Need Strength

In considering the recommendation that organizations should increase the mental challenge of jobs, one might wonder whether everyone seeks mental challenge in their work. Indeed, the relationship between intrinsic job characteristics and job satisfaction depends on employees' growth need strength (GNS). GNS is employees' desire for personal development, especially as it applies to work. High-GNS employees want their jobs to contribute to their personal growth and derive satisfaction from performing challenging and personally rewarding activities. One of the ways GNS is measured is by asking employees, with a survey, to choose between one job that is high on extrinsic rewards (such as pay) and one that is high on intrinsic rewards. For example, one item asks the employee to choose between "A job where the pay is very good" and "A job where there is considerable opportunity to be creative and innovative." Individuals who strongly prefer the latter job are likely to be high on GNS – all else equal, high-GNS people prefer jobs that are challenging and interesting, which allow them to work autonomously and use a number of skills, over jobs that are otherwise rewarding (high pay, good supervision, pleasant coworkers, etc.). According to the model, intrinsic job characteristics are especially satisfying for individuals who score high on GNS. In fact, research supports this aspect of the theory. As shown in Figure 8.2, across the 10 studies that have investigated the role of GNS in the relationship between intrinsic job characteristics and job satisfaction, the relationship tends to be stronger for employees with high GNS (average $r = 0.68$) than for those with low GNS (average $r = 0.38$). However, as the figure shows, it is important to note that intrinsic job characteristics are related to job satisfaction even for those who score low on GNS (Frye, 1996).

Employees Who Value Other Job Attributes

Thus far, we have established that job satisfaction is best promoted through intrinsically challenging work because most employees value the work itself more than other job attributes. One exception to this principle is that employees who do not care about intrinsic job characteristics (low GNS) will be less satisfied by challenging work. A more generalized means of considering this exception is through values.

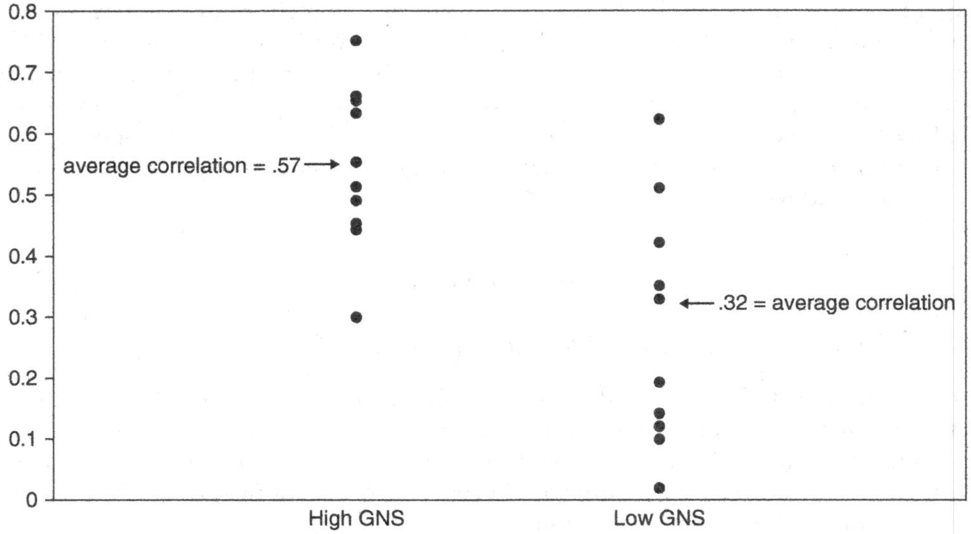

FIGURE 8.2 Studies of the correlation between intrinsic job characteristics and job satisfaction for individuals with high and low growth need strength

It may not be that only employees with low GNS will respond less favorably to intrinsic job characteristics, the exception would also apply to employees who value other job or organizational attributes. Following his definition of values as that which one desires or considers important, Locke (1976) argued that individuals' values would determine what satisfied them on the job. Only the unfulfilled job values that were important to the individual would be dissatisfying. Thus, value-percept theory predicts that discrepancies between what is desired and received are dissatisfying only if the job facet is important to the individual. Because as a general rule individuals value work more than other job attributes, Locke's argument is consistent with the general principle described in this chapter. Thus, if intrinsic job characteristics were the most important job facet to most individuals, then Locke's theory would predict that increasing the level of intrinsic job characteristics (thus reducing the have-want discrepancy with respect to intrinsic characteristics) would be the most effective means of raising employees' job satisfaction. However, it must be recognized that when an employee does not value challenging work, other values must be fulfilled to satisfy the person.

Personality

Implicit in Locke's definition of job satisfaction is the importance of both feeling and thinking. People's evaluation of their jobs is a process of rational thought (how is my pay relative to my peers, is my work as challenging as I would like?), but it is also influenced by people's dispositional outlook. Research has shown that unhappy children become dissatisfied workers later in life (Staw, Bell, and Clausen, 1986). There is even evidence that job satisfaction is partly heritable (see Arvey, Carter, and Buerkley, 1991). Thus, part of the reason we like or dislike our jobs has nothing to do with the jobs. Rather, it is due to our dispositional outlook that derives from our genes and early childhood experiences. Judge, Locke, Durham, and Kluger (1998) have found that the key dispositional factor leading to job satisfaction is core self-evaluations – if we have a positive self-regard, we are likely to see our jobs positively and undertake jobs that are challenging. Evidence indicates that core self-evaluations are related to job satisfaction through various processes, including that those with positive core self-evaluations both attain more challenging work, and perceive their work as more challenging and interesting (Judge et al., 2000). Individuals with positive core self-evaluations are also more likely to work toward goals for reasons that are consistent with their values (Judge, Bono, Erez, and Locke, 2005).

The fit between one's level of openness to experience and job characteristics was also found to predict one's job crafting behaviors, where employees voluntarily make meaningful adaptations and adjustments to their tasks (Kim, Baek, and Shin, 2019). Moreover, openness to experience is also found to moderate the relationship between job characteristics (i.e. skill variety) and job satisfaction (De Jong, Van Der Velde, and Jansen, 2001).

Dispositions are important in understanding job satisfaction. To a large extent, they are what cause two people with the same job to be differentially satisfied by it. The main practical implication of the dispositional source of job satisfaction is that if employers wish to raise satisfaction levels of their workforce, they need to select applicants with positive dispositions. However, the dispositional source of job satisfaction does not invalidate the general principle presented in this chapter; it merely explains why the general principle does not account for all the variation in job satisfaction. Over and above dispositional factors and mental challenge, people also value being treated fairly (Montañez-Juan, García-Buades, Sora-Miana, Ortiz-Bonnín, and Caballer Hernández, 2019), pay, and social support for others at work (Morgeson and Humphrey, 2006).

Other Moderators

In addition to the boundary conditions mentioned earlier, management wishing to capitalize on the potential benefits of mentally challenging work should consider several moderators that impact the success of job redesign. For instance, any time new tasks or skill requirements are added to a job, one should consider issues such as:

- Do the employees possess excess cognitive capacity to handle the additional job demands (Phillips, 2008)? If not, then increasing the job demands might overload the employees.
- Do the employees believe they can successfully perform the new job? If not, the organization may consider techniques designed to increase employee self-efficacy (see Chapter 6) before or during the implementation of the new job.

- Are the employees intrinsically interested in the new demands or tasks? Employee satisfaction is unlikely to increase when the challenge comes from tasks or jobs which are not personally interesting, e.g. studying the law is mentally challenging but many people have no interest at all in it (Holland, 1997).

Case Examples

1. Job Redesign at Volvo's Manufacturing Plants

In the early 1990s, the Volvo corporation was experiencing high levels of employee absenteeism and turnover in their manufacturing facilities due to dissatisfaction with the "mass production environments dominated by . . . Tayloristic work practices" (Wallace, 2008, p. 113). In manufacturing plants across Sweden and the UK, Volvo attempted to combat these issues by experimenting with alternatives to the traditional assembly line–style manufacturing work design. As one production manager put it, a change was needed in order to "give all employees the chance to develop as a whole person, to take more responsibility for their work environment, to have more space to decide on what work they will do and to have more control on their working environment" (Wallace, 2008, p. 115).

Following the job redesign initiative, rather than being assigned one particular activity along an assembly line, employees were grouped into autonomous work teams and given responsibility for the overall production of the vehicles (*high task identity*). Employees were afforded the opportunity to utilize a *variety of skills* as they rotated job tasks, from foundry work to machine maintenance to painting and detailing, etc., depending on situational demands or personal preferences (Thompson and Wallace, 1996). For instance, at the Tuve plant, workers were allowed to rotate jobs as frequently as once every four hours (Thompson and Wallace, 1996), with no approval from upper management necessary (*high autonomy*). Each team was also responsible for inspecting their finished products, providing members with *feedback* concerning the quality of their work. These changes resulted in significant perceptual adjustments as employees no longer felt that they were merely "machine operators" but rather "car manufacturers" (*increased task significance*).

Volvo's commitment to making automobile assembly a more intrinsically motivating occupation resulted in several positive work outcomes. In its Kalmar plant, turnover dropped from 24–5% following reorganization (Jones, 1991). Furthermore, in the Volvo Truck Corporation plants, absenteeism fell from 15–12% and machine tool efficiency increased by 40–90% in some units (Thompson and Wallace, 1996). The time required to manufacture automobiles was reduced by two to four hours per vehicle and overall production costs decreased as well (Wallace, 2008).

Despite the overwhelmingly positive outcomes experienced across several Volvo plants, by 2004, nearly all had been reconfigured to more similarly reflect previous assembly line structures. Critics postulated that this move was "not totally based on logical overarching decisions or rational decision management . . ." (Engstrom, Blomquist, and Holmstrom, 2004, p. 836), but rather reflected three shortcomings. First, Volvo's desire to seek more international ventures put pressure on the corporation to adopt the lean processing approach that had become the dominant paradigm in the automobile industry (Wallace, 2008; Womack, Jones, and Roos, 1991). Second, as pointed out by Wagner (see Chapter 11), efficient work techniques and other valuable information residing within the autonomous work teams were not being successfully distributed across the organization, thus hindering Volvo's ability to capitalize on team-level innovations and remain competitive in a global industry. Finally, although Volvo committed heavily in the technological aspects of the job redesign, experts point out that its commitment to the social/managerial aspects was inadequate (Engstrom et al., 2004). Human resource (HR) functions such as employee selection, training, compensation, and performance evaluation were never properly redesigned to reflect the changed nature of the work. For instance, many employees lacked the prerequisite skills to accomplish their new tasks, resulting in considerable variation in the effectiveness of the autonomous work teams. In sum, altering the nature of work to increase intrinsic satisfaction is one tool organizations can use to influence employee attitudes and behaviors. However, as the Volvo case illustrates, job redesign must be considered in terms of internal (e.g. HR practices) and external (e.g. global competition) factors to capitalize on the potential benefits of mentally challenging work.

2. A Case of Resolving Boredom at Work in the Catering Sector

The hospitality and catering industry in the UK employs over three million people and monotony (repetitive tasks) and boredom at work have become a significant problem. For the customer service providers, not only are the work repetitive, the outputs or their work are often intangible, perishable, and variable (Tsai, 2016).

For over 200 catering staff from the University Catering at a British university, job boredom seems to be less of an issue. Their daily tasks do not differ much from typical catering staff – involving either counter service of food or table clearing and cleaning. Both tasks are highly repetitive and can be very intense during peak times.

Tasks for staff who serve food at the counter involve fetching and placing up to five kinds of food based on customers' requests. These tasks often involve the same stimuli, events, and body movements. During peak hours, the catering assistants repeat the same routine every 7 to 18 seconds. For table clearing and cleaning staff, they walk around the tables to collect used dishes and take them to the cleaning point, which requires little thought or attention. The dish cleaning crew probably have the most monotonous tasks. Their responsibilities include clearing trash from plates, placing plates and cutlery in the dishwashing machine, taking washed items out of the machine, and trash disposal. Each crew member only takes on one or two tasks – just like working on an assembly line (Tsai, 2016). Despite the monotonous nature of the tasks, crew members never express any feelings of boredom. This is largely due to three main aspects of the job: employee characteristics, job rotation system, and management strategy.

Employee characteristics: Many of the workers who found the job not boring also like the predictability of the job. It allows them to settle in their job, perform tasks correctly, and know what is expected of them. Many mentioned that their favorite aspect of the job is to meet and talk to people during work hours. Meanwhile, all employees who are interviewed expressed interests in working in service industries, while the majority mentioned need for money, supportive management, good welfare, and teamwork as reasons for remaining interested in their jobs.

Job rotation system: The supervisors' plan the shifts in a way each employee can perform a different job each day (e.g. work on the counter for one day then move on to cleaning) or work in a different unit regularly (e.g. switch from the cafeteria to the coffee bar). Such practice helped employees to improve their capabilities to perform different tasks and gave employees psychological security over their diversified knowledge and skills.

Supervisory and organizational support: University Catering created plans to offer training and development for all employees to provide better customer service and give financial rewards for good performance. More importantly, the organization offer leadership training for supervisors, especially on offering positive verbal feedback and nonverbal actions to motivate others. They learned to encourage and praise staff members daily and let them know that they did a good job. They also learned to be present and share their subordinates' workload (e.g. help employees clean the tables during peak hours). As one employee mentioned in the interview, "They (the managers) won't leave you alone, they never stand around . . . you find them clearing up tables, pushing trolleys together with you. . . . I feel very happy when they come . . . because it makes you realize that they know the job is very important" (Tsai, 2016, p. 222).

Questions: What principles of the chapter are discussed in these cases? How do the solutions deployed by cases match the principles that are found to improve mental challenges of a job?

Conclusion

Job satisfaction matters. Employees who are satisfied with their jobs tend to perform better, withdraw less, and lead happier and healthier lives. Organizations whose employees are satisfied with their jobs are more likely to be productive and profitable. The single most effective way organizations can achieve a satisfied workforce is to provide their employees with mentally challenging work. In this chapter, we discussed various ways to provide employees with mentally challenging work to improve their job satisfaction, such as providing job rotation, job enlargement, job enrichment, and job feedback. However, we should also keep in mind that the impact of job characteristics on job satisfaction can be affected by individual factors such as one's GNS, individual preference for job attributes, and personality.

References

Arvey, R. D., Carter, G. W., and Buerkley, D. K. (1991). Job satisfaction: Dispositional and situational influences. *International Review of Industrial and Organizational Psychology*, 6, 359–383.

Berry, M. (Sept. 4, 2008). Skills commission to investigate how to maximise staff potential. *Personnel Today* (retrieved from http://www.personneltoday.com on Sept. 4, 2008).

Campion, M. A. (1988). Interdisciplinary approaches to job design: A constructive replication with extensions. *Journal of Applied Psychology*, 73, 467–481.

Campion, M. A., Mumford, T. V., Morgeson, F. P., and Nahrgang, J. D. (2005). Work redesign: Eight obstacles and opportunities. *Human Resource Management*, 44, 367–390.

Cascio, W. F. (1991). *Costing Human Resources: The Financial Impact of Behavior in Organizations*. Boston: PWS-Kent.

De Jong, R. D., Van Der Velde, M. E., and Jansen, P. G. (2001). Openness to experience and growth need strength as moderators between job characteristics and satisfaction. *International Journal of Selection and Assessment*, 9, 350–356.

Edmans, A. (2012). The link between job satisfaction and firm value, with implications for corporate social responsibility. *Academy of Management Perspectives*, 26, 1–19.

Edwards, J. R., Scully, J. A., and Brtek, M. D. (2000). The nature and outcomes of work: A replication and extension of interdisciplinary work design research. *Journal of Applied Psychology*, 85, 860–868.

Engstrom, T., Blomquist, B., and Holmstrom, O. (2004). Reconstructing the history of the main Volvo Tuve plant. *International Journal of Operations and Production Management*, 24, 820–839.

Fisher, C. D., and Locke, E. A. (1992). The new look in job satisfaction research and theory. In C. J. Cranny, P. C. Smith, and E. F. Stone (eds), *Job Satisfaction* (pp. 165–194). New York: Lexington.

Frye, C. M. (1996). New evidence for the Job Characteristics Model: A meta-analysis of the job characteristics-job satisfaction relationship using composite correlations. Paper presented at the Eleventh Annual Meeting of the Society for Industrial and Organizational Psychology, San Diego, CA.

Gabriel, A. S., Frantz, N. B., Levy, P. E., and Hilliard, A. W. (2014). The supervisor feedback environment is empowering, but not all the time: Feedback orientation as a critical moderator. *Journal of Occupational and Organizational psychology*, 87, 487–506.

Gagné, M., Senecal, C. B., and Koestner, R. (1997). Proximal job characteristics, feelings of empowerment, and intrinsic motivation: A multidimensional model. *Journal of Applied Social Psychology*, 27, 1222–1240.

Glick, W. H., Jenkins, G. D., Jr., and Gupta, N. (1986). Method versus substance: How strong are underlying relationships between job characteristics and attitudinal outcomes? *Academy of Management Journal*, 29, 441–464.

Hackman, J. R., and Oldham, G. R. (1980). *Work Redesign*. Reading, MA: Addison-Wesley.

Harrison, D. A., Newman, D. A., and Roth, P. L. (2006). How important are job attitudes? A meta-analytic comparison of integrative behavioral outcomes and time sequences. *Academy of Management Journal*, 49, 305–325.

Holland, J. L. (1997). *Making Vocational Choices: A theory of Vocational Personalities and Work Environments.* Odessa, FL: Psychological Assessment Resources.

Humphrey, S. E., Nahrgang, J. D., and Morgeson, F. P. (2007). Integrating motivational, social, and contextual work design features: A meta-analytic summary and theoretical extension of the work design literature. *Journal of Applied Psychology,* 92, 1332–1356.

Iaffaldano, M. R., and Muchinsky, P. M. (1985). Job satisfaction and job performance: A meta-analysis. *Psychological Bulletin,* 97, 251–273.

Johns, G. (1996). *Organizational Behavior.* New York: HarperCollins.

Jones, H. G. (1991). Motivation for higher performance at Volvo. *Long Range Planning,* 24, 92–104.

Judge, T. A., Bono, J. E., Erez, A., and Locke, E. A. (2005). Core self-evaluations and job and life satisfaction: The role of self-concordance and goal attainment. *Journal of Applied Psychology,* 90, 257–268.

Judge, T. A., Bono, J. E., and Locke, E. A. (2000). Personality and job satisfaction: The mediating role of job characteristics. *Journal of Applied Psychology,* 85, 237–249.

Judge, T. A., Locke, E. A., Durham, C. C., and Kluger, A. N. (1998). Dispositional effects on job and life satisfaction: The role of core evaluations. *Journal of Applied Psychology,* 83, 17–34.

Judge, T. A., Thoresen, C. J., Bono, J. E., and Patton, G. K. (2001). The job satisfaction—job performance relationship: A qualitative and quantitative review. *Psychological Bulletin,* 127, 376–407.

Jurgensen, C. E. (1978). Job preferences (What makes a job good or bad?). *Journal of Applied Psychology,* 50, 479–487.

Kim, M., Baek, S. I., and Shin, Y. (2019). The effect of the congruence between job characteristics and personality on job crafting. *International Journal of Environmental Research and Public Health,* 17, 1–20.

Kovach, K. A. (September 26, 1997). Do you know your staff? *Industry Trends.* Locke, E. A. (1976). The nature and causes of job satisfaction. In M. D. Dunnette (ed.), *Handbook of Industrial and Organizational Psychology* (pp. 1297–1343). Chicago: Rand McNally.

Locke, E. A. (1976). The nature and causes of job satisfaction. In: Dunnette, M. D. (ed), *Handbook of Industrial and Organizational Psychology,* Vol. 1 (pp. 1297–1349). Chicago, IL: Rand McNally.

Montañez-Juan, M. I., García-Buades, M. E., Sora-Miana, B., Ortiz-Bonnín, S., and Caballer Hernández, A. (2019). Work Design and Job Satisfaction: The moderating role of organizational justice. *Revista Psicologia Organizações e Trabalho,* 19, 853–858.

Morgeson, F. P., and Campion, M. A. (2002). Minimizing tradeoffs when redesigning work: Evidence from a longitudinal quasi-experiment. *Personnel Psychology,* 55, 589–612.

Morgeson, F. P., and Humphrey, S. E. (2006). The Work Design Questionnaire (WDQ): Developing and validating a comprehensive measure for assessing job design and the nature of work. *Journal of Applied Psychology,* 91, 1321–1339.

Phillips, J. M. (2008). The role of excess cognitive capacity in the relationship between job characteristics and cognitive task engagement. *Journal of Business and Psychology,* 23, 11–24.

Rentsch, J. R., and Steel, R. P. (1992). Construct and concurrent validation of the Andrews and Withey Job Satisfaction Questionnaire. *Educational and Psychological Measurement*, 52, 357–367.

Saturn Memorandum of Agreement. (1985). Saturn Corporation, Detroit, MI.

Staw, B. M., Bell, N. E., and Clausen, J. A. (1986). The dispositional approach to job attitudes: A lifetime longitudinal test. *Administrative Science Quarterly*, 31, 437–453.

Tait, M., Padgett, M. Y., and Baldwin, T. T. (1989). Job and life satisfaction: A reevaluation of the strength of the relationship and gender effects as a function of the data of the study. *Journal of Applied Psychology*, 74, 502–507.

Tsai, C. J. (2016). Boredom at work and job monotony: An exploratory case study within the catering sector. *Human Resource Development Quarterly*, 27, 207–236.

Thompson, P., and Wallace, T. (1996). Redesigning production through teamworking. *International Journal of Operations and Production Management*, 16, 103–118.

Wallace, T. (2008). Cycles of production: From assembly lines to cells to assembly lines in the Volvo Cab plant. *New Technology, Work, and Employment*, 23, 111–124.

Womack, J., Jones, D., and Roos, D. (1991). *The Machine that Changed the World.* New York: Harper-Perennial.

Exercises

1. Identifying Factors Related to Job Satisfaction

The National Opinion Research Center at the University of Chicago surveyed over 50 000 Americans to determine which occupations scored the highest and lowest in terms of overall job satisfaction. Whereas firefighters and physical therapists were generally very satisfied employees, roofers and cashiers were generally unsatisfied with their jobs.

Use the Department of Labor's Occupational Information Network (O*NET; http://online.onetcenter.org) to compare job descriptions and relevant knowledge, skills, abilities, and other characteristics of: (i) firefighters, (ii) physical therapists, (iii) roofers, and (iv) cashiers. In terms of the core characteristics of JCM, which occupations inherently have high levels of task identity, task significance, skill variety, autonomy, and feedback? Judging from these four jobs, do higher values of JCM core characteristics appear to correlate with higher job satisfaction? What other factors might impact the satisfaction scores?

2. Redesigning Jobs to Increase Mental Challenge

Identify three separate jobs. These can be current jobs, jobs you have held in the past, and/or jobs that you are familiar with. Use JDS (see Table 8.1) to assess each job's motivating potential. Formulate a plan to redesign the jobs that will increase their motivating potential. While working, think about the following issues:

1. How will redesigning your jobs impact other jobs within the organization?
2. What HR functions (recruitment, selection, training, performance appraisal, compensation, etc.) will be impacted by the redesigned jobs? What can you do to realign HR functions with your new jobs?

3. Are some jobs easier to redesign than others? What factors make a job easy or hard to redesign?
4. Is it easier to increase some core JCM characteristics than others? What core JCM characteristics are easy or hard to adjust?
5. What are the costs associated with your job redesign plans? Given these costs, do you think an organization would benefit from implementing your changes?

Think about a past job experience. Rate that job with the short version of JDS. How does this job score? Discuss your tasks and responsibilities with the class and provide an example or two on why you scored the way you did on a few of the job characteristics described in the survey.

Please watch the following video(s):

1. https://www.ted.com/talks/michael_c_bush_this_is_what_makes_employees_happy_at_work/transcript
2. https://www.ted.com/talks/shawn_achor_the_happy_secret_to_better_work?referrer=play_list-shawn_achor_work_happier
3. https://www.ted.com/talks/dan_ariely_what_makes_us_feel_good_about_our_work?refer_rer=playlist-7_talks_to_help_you_find_the_r

Now form small groups to discuss the video(s) and answer the following questions:

1. What are the major points of the video?
2. How can you use information from the video in your career?
3. Based on the video, what advice do you have for leaders in organizations?

Be prepared to present the ideas from your small group discussion with the class as a whole.

Discussion Questions

1. What are the most important job characteristics for your ideal job? How would these characteristics affect your attitudes toward your job? Which job characteristic(s) would you trade for a relatively satisfactory job?
2. What other factors do you think are more important to you than intrinsic job characteristics discussed in this chapter? Why?

9

Follow the Science to Make Training Work

EDUARDO SALAS,[1] AND KEVIN C. STAGL,[2]

[1] Allyn R. & Gladys M. Cline Professor of Psychology, Rice University
[2] Department of Psychology, George Mason University

The fight for talent to seize competitive advantage has raged for decades, but there is a renewed urgency to attract, develop, and retain top performers post pandemic (Dowd, 2021). Iconic US brands such as Goldman Sachs adaptively reorganized via distributed performance arrangements to retain partners and managing directors migrating to geographic locations with more accommodative personal and business environments. In this example, changes in latitudes are driven by changes in attitudes about securing and sustaining sector dominance via talent.

The flow of talent is not localized to Manhattan's financial district, as surveyed NYC employers reported 57% of employees will likely return to the office three days per week by January 2022, while 21% permanently remain remote (Partnership for New York City, 2021). One-third of Big Apple employers reported downsizing five-year office space lease plans. This talent shift is contributing to a Great Resignation of 8.7 million US employees who quit their jobs during August and September 2021, a record for the Labor Department's Job Openings and Labor Turnover metric.

Unfortunately, a national education crisis, employment levels topping 94%, a growing retiree bubble, and the rapid rise of emerging market opportunities are draining an already shallow domestic talent pool. And the scarcity of workers with cultural competence, interpersonal savvy, and quantitative proficiency is not just a US problem, as 41% of 37000 employers across 27 countries report experiencing human capital difficulties (Manpower, 2007).

The business imperative to sustain excellence while ramping-up agile production and service capacity to meet volatile customer demand also requires developing a talented workforce. US organizations invest $177 billion annually on training and development initiatives of an astounding $1T+ allocated domestically to training and higher education (Carnevale, Strohl, and Gulish, 2015). Employers make massive investments in training because it can be a powerful lever for structuring and guiding experiences to facilitate the attainment of affective, attitudinal, behavioral, and cognitive (AABCs) learning outcomes by employees (Kraiger, Ford, and Salas, 1993). In turn, attained knowledge and proficiency can horizontally transfer to the workplace and over time transfer vertically to impact team and organizational outcomes (Kozlowski, Brown, Weissbein, Cannon-Bowers, and Salas, 2000). In fact, building bench strength by energizing employees to realize their full potential via rigorous training can improve multiteam systems, interorganizational alliances, and entire national economies (Aguinis and Kraiger, 2009).

While trillions are spent annually worldwide on training activities, 52% of employers still report struggling to rapidly develop skills and only 13% claim to have a very clear understanding of the capabilities required to succeed (IBM, 2008). Moreover, only 27% find web-based training, and a mere 17% virtual classroom training, to be effective at meeting their needs (IBM). Perhaps this is not surprising given prior estimates suggest only 10% of training expenditures transfer to the job (Georgenson, 1982) and a meager 5% of solutions are evaluated in terms of organizational benefits (Swanson, 2001). It seems now, more than ever before, there is a requirement for actionable guidance to make training work and endure via learning science.

Fortunately, the science of training has benefited from an explosion of research activity since the "golden age" of training during the 1990s and has much to contribute to ensuring the vitality of employers and the domestic and global economies they fuel (Bisbey, Reyes, Traylor, and Salas, 2019). For example, Salas and Cannon-Bowers (2000), and then Salas and Stagl (2009), harnessed the science of training to extract core principles and advance targeted guidance for designing and deploying training in the first and second editions of this vaunted book series.

A decade later, this chapter continues the tradition by providing evidenced theoretics, practical wisdom, and actionable guidelines for stakeholders charged with fostering more effective individuals, teams, and organizations via systematic training initiatives. Our discussion follows a four-phase process to optimizing blended training solutions. We draw upon our own experiences facilitating learning, and heavily upon the science of training, to advance phase-specific guidelines for analyzing, developing, deploying, and evaluating training solutions (see Figure 9.1 and Tables 9.1–9.4). Next, we describe the success of team training in the aviation industry and discuss the lessons learned from a failure to develop a sales force. We conclude by offering a few scenario-based exercises, a set of discussion questions, and media resources advanced to impart knowledge about the specification, administration, and evaluation of impactful learning solutions.

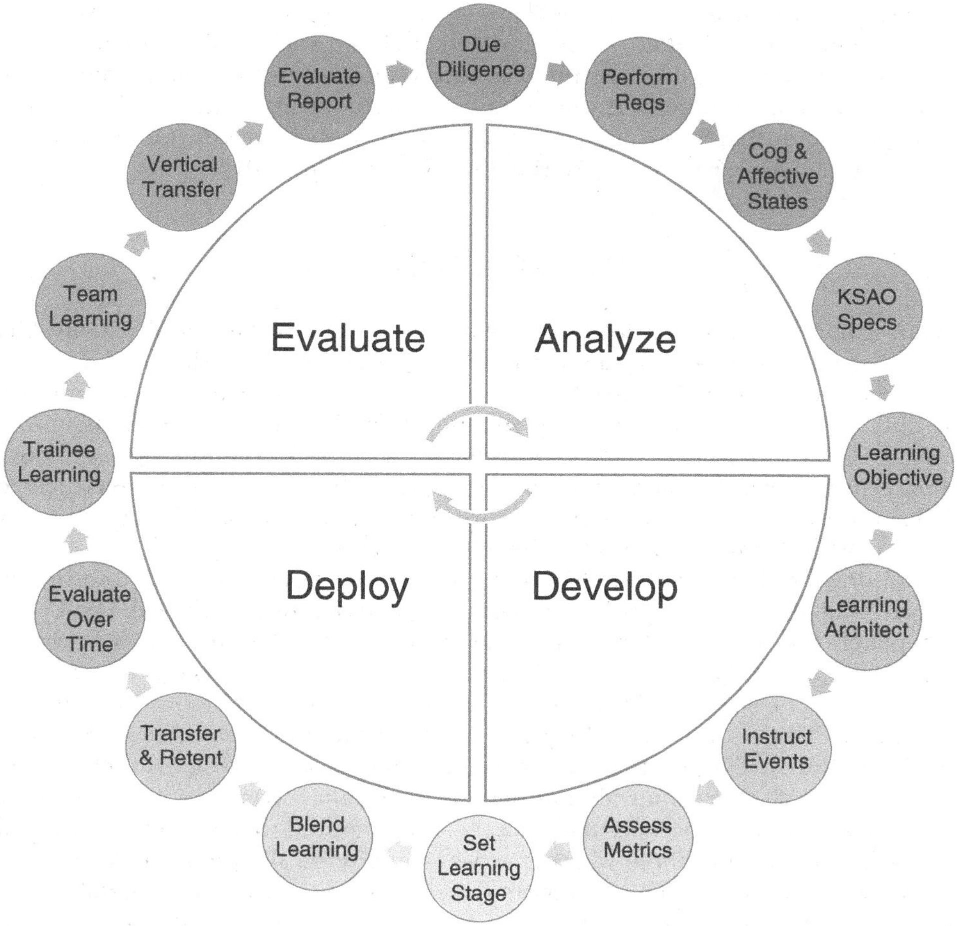

FIGURE 9.1 Select training optimization considerations

Analyze Training Needs

Training needs analysis can be the most important phase of training design because its success depends on an intensive collaborative partnership between key stakeholders. The mandate of this partnership is to clarify the purposes of training, illuminate the organizational context with an emphasis on its affordances and constraints, define effective performance and its drivers, and begin to cultivate a climate of learning and transfer. Essential activities conducted during the needs analysis phase include: (i) executing training due diligence, (ii) defining performance functions and processes, (iii) defining affective and cognitive states, (iv) defining a person specification attribute model, and (v) delineating learning objectives. Training guidelines for each of the principles of the training analysis phase are in Appendix A. When executed with care, these activities can help ensure that the remaining phases yield a meaningful learning solution. In fact, recent meta-analytic research findings suggest that a thorough needs analysis process increases trainee learning and transfer (Lacerenza, Reyes, Marlow, Joseph, and Salas, 2017).

Execute Due Diligence

Training methods and techniques are not interchangeable or universally applicable, as evidenced by recent meta-analytic findings (Salas, DiazGranados, Klein, Burke, Stagl, Goodwin, and Halpin, 2008). For example, the same learning solution may be differentially effective if it is implemented to address immediate versus downstream business objectives. Hence, effective instruction in one setting may prove counterproductive elsewhere or at a different time. This speaks to why it is critical to describe the specific challenges and opportunities training will address, and thereby defining what, for whom, and when benefits will accrue.

Training requires fixed and variable startup and recurring costs for a downstream return. Due diligence is a process for clarifying and quantifying the expected costs and benefits from training for individuals, teams, and higher-level units (division, organization, and society). One critical question that must be answered is whether the organization has sufficient bench strength to sustain operations by assuming the responsibilities of trainees during training execution (Hughes, Zajac, Spencer, and Salas, 2018). The front-end analysis may also involve auditing instructional infrastructure such as learning laboratories and media analysis to identify affordances. The purpose of the process is to collect the data required to have an objective and dispassionate dialogue about whether or when a solution should be deployed. And the conversation must encompass more than just productivity and profitability concerns, as training can also be a powerful lever for enhancing performance-related factors such as employee satisfaction, team cohesion, social capital, organizational reputation, and customer retention.

A core component of the due diligence process is a pretraining transfer analysis (Hughes, Zajac, Spencer, and Salas, 2018). The analysis helps describe the dimensions targeted for horizontal transfer, the emergent processes of vertical transfer, and the contextual factors that may promote or impinge on the transfer process. For example, the number, scope, and nature of the salient nesting arrangements in an organization must be mapped to determine their potential effects on nested variables (Mathieu, Maynard, Taylor, Gilson, and Ruddy, 2008). Designers should be careful to distinguish between objective situational characteristics and social-psychological perceptions of organizational factors as well as evaluate the embeddedness or bond strength of key dimensions (Kozlowski and Salas, 1997).

Senior organizational leaders and direct supervisors can actively contribute to a climate for learning and transfer (Grossman and Salas, 2011) or passively inhibit the replication of learned behaviors in the workplace. It is imperative, for example, to set the tone for an inclusive learning experience as recent research findings suggest that older employees may evoke negative stereotypes when training to operate information technology that ultimately degrade interaction quality during training and decrease post-training performance proficiency evaluations (McCausland, King, Bartholomew, Feyre, Ahmad, and Finkelstein, 2015). A thorough stakeholder analysis can identify champions of training and provide a transparent forum for airing concerns and asking questions to prepare for the opportunity (Bisbey, Traylor, and Salas, 2020). This is critical because training, like all initiatives, involves the allocation of limited financial resources, which some may feel are better allocated to the production of goods or services, media campaigns, infrastructure improvements, and/or technology upgrades. Yet, in order for training to be successful, there must be both sufficient financial and personal support. Hence, parties on both sides of the a isle are best identified and persuaded in advance. Favorable projections of the net present value of training relative to other capital investments can be persuasive evidence when financial estimates are based on realistic and conservative inputs.

Define Performance Requirements

A second training needs analysis activity involves defining performance requirements. Established taxonomies of performance processes and multilevel theories of performance should be leveraged to precisely define the nature of performance (Cannon-Bowers and Bowers, 2011; Campbell and Kuncel, 2002; Marks, Mathieu, and Zaccaro, 2001; Salas, Stagl, Burke, and Goodwin, 2007). This involves illuminating, describing, disaggregating, and contextualizing the taskwork and teamwork processes that are critical to effective performance. Observation, behavioral- and cognitive-oriented task inventories, critical incident interviews, focus groups, and card sorts can help nuance key constructs. Protocol analysis whereby experts verbalize their thoughts during problem-solving is also a useful technique for eliciting decision-making processes in natural settings (Ericsson, 2009). Training designers should also take steps to model and minimize the systematic and random sources of error inherent to job analysis data.

Once key performance dimensions are defined, they should be bracketed by mapping their antecedents and moderators within and outside the focal level of interest (Hackman, 1999). For example, the effectiveness of team coordination can be predicated upon motivated members at an individual level and investments in acquiring collaborative information technologies at an organizational level. The relative importance of these operative phenomena to alternative tactical and strategic business scenarios should also be illuminated, so specific criteria can be better targeted for improvement. It is also essential to map and model the projected trajectory of trainee change in learning outcomes over time. For example, n-dimensional learning curve response surfaces can be generated to inform learning experience design. Describing the transitional multidimensional maturational change process of learning signatures from novice to competent to expert provides insight into how training should be developed, delivered, and evaluated.

Define Cognitive and Affective States

Taskwork and teamwork processes are not executed in isolation. As employees enact performance processes (e.g. situation assessment), they dynamically draw upon and revise their cognitive (e.g. mental models and situation awareness) and attitudinal (e.g. self-efficacy and motivation) states, structures, stores, and systems. Designers charged with creating training solutions must describe and frame these states, specify why and how they enable effective performance, and forge learning experiences that target them for development. For example, both the content (e.g. declarative knowledge and procedural knowledge) and types of mental models (e.g. situation, task, and equipment) should be delineated. An event-based knowledge-elicitation protocol can be used to provide information that helps identify the states that should be targeted for development by training (Fowlkes, Salas, Baker, Cannon-Bowers, and Stout, 2000).

Once essential states are identified, it is important to determine if, and the extent to which, cognition and affect must be shared or complimentary to enable effective performance in the workplace. This is a particularly acute concern in team training settings because scholars often invoke shared mental models and shared affect to explain how collectives execute both routine and adaptive team performance (Burke, Stagl, Salas, Pierce, and Kendall, 2006). Moreover, cultivating shared affect via training simulations can help prepare teams to navigate even unprecedented challenges (Klein, Stagl, Salas, Parker, and Van Eynde, 2007). The unfolding compositional or compilational process via which the content and structure of affect and cognition emerge to the unit level should also be clearly specified because it provides insight about the instructional methods, features, and tools required to cultivate and sustain team states. Robust state recursively enabling and episodically refined is a differentiator of expert teams relative to the much more common team of experts (Salas, Cannon-Bowers, and Johnston, 1997).

Define Knowledge, Skills, and Abilities (KSA) Attributes

In addition to framing the core processes and cognitive and affective states that collectively comprise effective performance, training practitioners must also define an attribute model. Attribute models specify the direct determinants of performance such as KSAs. Training designers should leverage structured attribute inventories, knowledge tests, skill repositories, and production records to shed light on the KSAs that should be targeted for development by a training solution. For example, the declarative (i.e. what), procedural (i.e. how), and strategic (i.e. why) knowledge required to effectively execute performance processes must be defined. Strategic knowledge is especially important because it allows trainees to understand why and when to apply declarative knowledge (Kozlowski, Gully, Brown, Salas, Smith, and Nason, 2001). This example illustrates that KSAs must first be identified and then ordered in a sequence from those that are more fundamental to those that are more complex in order to maximize the benefit of sequenced learning opportunities.

Training designers should be cognizant that not all of the myriad of characteristics and capabilities can be targeted for development via a single training solution, and that not all KSAs are best developed via training approaches or specific techniques (Campbell and Kuncel, 2002). Rather, the needs analysis process should allow for the identification and prioritized specification of those KSAs that are most essential to performance at multiple levels with greater emphasis given to dimensions that are most amenable to change via a learning experience as it is projected to be introduced in a particular organizational setting. The ratings, constructed responses, and implicit learner model-based insights of subject matter experts and past trainees can help practitioners hone in on key attributes. Multiple stakeholder perspectives should be elicited when illuminating the most critical KSAs to organizational success given alternative business models.

Delineate Learning Objectives

The final step in analyzing training needs involves delineating learning objectives. The information gathered from the prior steps of need analysis process must be translated into training objectives, learning objectives, and enabling objectives. In practice, task statements are often transformed into learning objectives by supplementing them with contextual information, conditions, and standards. It is important to remember, however, that designers should not force learning objectives into behaviorally based statements of employee actions, as cognitive and affective learning objectives are equally important to fostering effective performance (Kraiger, 2002). Suitable learning objectives are clear, concise, and measurable. To the extent these three criteria are met, training content will be more targeted, engaging, and ultimately more useful.

Develop Training Content

The second phase of designing a training solution involves a series of activities executed in support of developing and integrating training content in a unified active learning experience, including: (i) designing a learning architecture, (ii) creating instructional experiences, and (iii) developing assessment tools and feedback systems. Training guidelines for each of the principles of the training development phase are in Appendix B. For the purposes of the present discussion, it is assumed that training is not confined to classroom walls, in-house, or otherwise, but rather is delivered via a blended learning solution that encompasses multiple mediums and locations. While blended learning solutions typically include a dedicated block of instructor-led time, they also include other instructional mediums such as mobile-delivered, web-based learning modules, and sometimes even full-task simulators. Interestingly, the findings of a survey of 400 human resource executives across 40 countries suggest that blended learning solutions are considered the most effective approach for meeting training needs (IBM, 2008). The specific content of training will vary widely across settings given employer objectives, talent bench strength, performance proficiency requirements, conditionalized standards, legacy media, and financial constraints.

Design Learning Architecture

A learning architecture is comprised of several integrated systems, software applications and hardware components, which collectively provide the capability to plan, select, author, sequence, push, store, secure, mine and model, and evaluate learning content, techniques, assessment algorithms, KSA profiles, and performance records. An intelligent scenario management system with an experience adjustable programmable interface should be engineered to provide senior training stakeholders, instructional designers, instructors, and trainees with the access, tools, and guidance required to nimbly create and change content to reflect emerging operational challenges (Zachary, Bilazarian, Burns, and Cannon-Bowers, 1997).

An intuitive dashboard interface (a graphical user interface with drop down menus) with simple navigation can be designed to control the content by dynamically resequencing modules or ramping instructional intensity. For example, employees with limited time for training may occasionally need access to quick refresher tutorials rather than more intensive mastery-learning-driven lessons. This example hints at the power of computer-adaptive training to provide efficiencies by both decreasing cost and time inputs while increasing proficiency output yields. The computing power to fulfill this quest is both readily available and increasingly affordable, so learning architectures should be designed to track and account for learner differences in goals, abilities, competence, and learning signatures over time to adjust the experience accordingly.

With sufficient development time and psychometric expertise, architectures can be programmed to capitalize on the stretched exponential gains in learning that can result from accounting for aptitude-treatment interactions (Cronbach and Snow, 1977). Embedded tools can help assess a trainee's expertise, abilities, self-efficacy, and goal orientation and tailor training structure, content, feedback, and guidance to maximize the benefits accrued by learners. While the costs of such an approach are front-loaded, often requiring substantially more content to be generated, scaled, and sequenced, the horizontal and vertical rewards of computer-adaptive training will ultimately deliver the knockout blow to static, out-of-the-box solutions.

Learning architectures can also incorporate additional useful features like text-to-speech conversion, speech recognition, information visualization, perceptual contrasts, and playback. A system that is comprised of several subsystems can highlight important events and cues (Stout, Salas, and Fowlkes, 1997) and pose questions and hints to learners (Lajoie, 2009), thereby prompting trainee self-regulatory activities while pursuing individual-level and team-level goals (Bell and Kozlowski, 2002; DeShon, Kozlowski, Schmidt, Milner, and Wiechmann, 2004). The encoding and storage capabilities of some architectures can also dynamically capture instructor ratings, comments, and debriefing markers (Smith-Jentsch, Zeisig, Acton, and McPherson, 1998). Systems can also capture and upload information on an Intranet or the Internet, so learners can leverage on-demand tutors, chat rooms, asynchronous post forums, and lessons learned archives.

Forge Instructional Experiences

The most important step of developing training content involves forging and blending quality instructional experiences as it is not how fast you train but how well you train fast. The process includes outlining an instructional management plan, instructor guides, and when necessary detailed scripts for instructors and training confederates. This stage is another important juncture at which instructional designers can lean on and learn from present or past trainees to help illuminate the multiple branching paths trainees may take when pursuing the attainment of learning objectives (Lajoie, 2009). Mapping the potential paths, including some of those less traveled, is essential to accurately forecasting when trainees are likely to falter, crafting meaningful learning experiences, timing assessment, and tailoring appropriate guidance.

When a myriad of branching paths precludes precisely defining a single overarching chronology of experiences, the most effective alternative event timelines should be mapped to help inform scenario sequencing, assessment, and feedback. Content in even high learner control environments must be sequenced to some extent because the development of knowledge structures and complex performance processes is contingent on the prior acquisition and chunking of more fundamental knowledge and skills (Anderson, 1993). It can be beneficial to impart the capabilities underlying component tasks prior to developing KSAs underpinning linking tasks (Goldstein and Ford, 2002). For example, materials presenting general rules and principles should precede those highlighting the structural, functional, and physical relationships among systems. Scenarios, and the experiences they impart, can be sequenced to reflect increasingly complex operational realities (Gagné, Briggs, and Wager, 1988).

When instructional content is integrated and orchestrated, it serves to foster holistic, meaningful experiences for trainees. For example, contextually grounded scenarios help trainees better understand their learning experience by replicating a familiar workplace. Unfortunately, stakeholders are too often preoccupied with representing, to the greatest degree possible, the operational context via high fidelity technologies. This can be a mistake because physical fidelity is often a secondary concern to the psychological fidelity induced by instructional experiences. The primacy of psychological fidelity is seen in the effectiveness with which computer-based training solutions can supplement, and for some soldiers substitute, for the large-scale military exercises conducted at the US Army's National Training Center

(Chatham, 2009, A). A similar distinction between mundane realism and experimental realism is often made during experiments with synthetic stimuli and environments. Mundane realism is concerned with whether an experiment situation is similar to the situations people are most likely to encounter outside the special purpose setting of a controlled training event. Experimental realism is concerned with whether a participant experiences the experimental situation as intended by the experimenter. Mundane realism may be inconsequentially low, whereas experimental realism may be critically high, thereby enhancing external validity evidence for the findings of a training evaluation study.

Forging effective instructional experiences requires a systematic consideration of the methods via which information and other cues are delivered in training settings. Three of most common means of packaging training content are via information presentation, demonstration, and practice. For example, lectures, resource readings, exercises, case studies, and serious games can be used to present information to trainees. In terms of demonstrating or modeling key skills, role-plays, motion pictures, closed-circuit television, and interactive multimedia are useful. Trainee attention to and learning from behavioral models can be increased by matching models to trainee biodata, varying model competence, and sequencing positive and negative models.

The science of learning also informs training scheduling. Initially slating time for massed practice followed by a variable practice schedule can be effective for developing the capabilities to perform complex tasks. Interleaving or providing information, demonstration, and practice across multiple mediums on a cluster of similar tasks is more effective than blocking practice on separate tasks (Bjork, 2009). Designers should also ensure sufficient spacing between separate modules and between lessons and learner assessment. This further underscores the importance of quantitatively longitudinally tracking training investment yields as well as proficiency outcomes.

In terms of the types of practice scenarios that instructional developers should craft, novice learners should be exposed to routine obstacles that must be navigated. As trainees move along the trajectory of development, practice difficulty can be increased to simulate complex challenges in increasingly incongruent environments. This requires the designers of training to systematically specify the dimensions along which training scenarios will become more complex and fluid. Finally, emergency situations and crisis events should be designed so that trainees are forced to persevere through adversity as their expertise accrues (McKinney and Davis, 2003). For example, research findings suggest expert modeling during difficult scenarios dispatched by cybersecurity incident response dyads comprised of experts and novices can markedly enhance the knowledge and proficiency attained by novices (Zaccaro, Dalal, Tetrick, and Steinke, 2016).

Develop Assessment Tools

Once meaningful instructional experiences have been forged, assessment tools and techniques must be developed to operationalize key learning constructs, such as trainee reactions, learning, behavior, and results. Specific constructs from each of these training outcome taxons should be assessed as meta-analytic findings suggest that the training effectiveness evidence is contingent upon the criterion operationalized (Arthur, Bennett, Edens, and Bell, 2003). A comprehensive treatment of the application of psychometric theory to create assessment tools used to assess learner processes and outcomes is beyond the scope of the present discussion. Rather, only broad prescriptions are presented. Training designers are strongly encouraged to seek the consultation of subject matter experts when designing assessments, as poorly designed or improperly timed metrics can make even great training appear bad and bad training turn ugly.

The most straightforward guidance is to develop standardized measures of unitary constructs, assess multiple learning outcomes and performance processes, and triangulate the measurement of outcomes via multiple assessment methods (Nunnally and Bernstein, 1998). Following these truisms helps yield the tools required to understand the effects of training. For instance, the findings of an evaluation study may suggest trainees acquired a great deal of factual information (viz., declarative knowledge) but have no concept of why and when to apply specific facts in context (viz., strategic knowledge). Without reliable measures of different knowledge types, stakeholders evaluating the training solution would be left pondering why transfer failed.

Fortunately, comprehensive guidance for designing and applying assessment tools in training initiatives is available to interested readers. For example, recent reviews of assessing learning outcomes have discussed the use of concept maps, card sorts, and pairwise comparisons for scaling trainee's knowledge structures (Stagl, Salas, and Day, 2007). The benefits of situational judgment tests for training needs assessment, content delivery, and evaluation have also been discussed exhaustively elsewhere (Fritzsche, Stagl, Burke, and Salas, 2006).

Deploy Training

Deployment is a key phase in the training process in part because it is tightly bound to the organizational system in which training is executed. There are three core activities comprising training deployment, including: (i) setting the stage for learning, (ii) delivering a blended learning solution, and (iii) supporting transfer and maintenance. The former and latter actions are taken to foster a climate for learning and transfer (Grossman and Salas, 2019). Training guidelines for each of the principles of the training deployment phase are in Appendix C.

Set the *Stage* for Learning

Setting the stage for learning begins by ensuring that trainers are properly prepared to facilitate the delivery of instruction, recognize and assess learning, and reinforce proficient performance when it occurs. There are several approaches to preparing trainers to perform their duties such as rater error training, frame of reference training, and the mental simulation of instructor activities. For example, the frame of reference training increases the awareness and skill of trainers to identify and assess competency and performance dimensions when they are displayed during training.

The second step in setting the stage for learning involves preparing the trainee for the attainment of KSAs. This includes measuring and increasing a trainee's motivation to learn, self-efficacy, and self-regulatory activity (Colquitt, LePine, and Noe, 2000). It is also critical to de-emphasize preexisting power and demographic differences, engage less verbal learners, and display an individualized interest in the development of each employee during group training.

Once trainers and trainees are adequately prepared to engage in learning, the purpose and objectives of training must be stated and explained. This is an opportunity to frame training as both a privilege and a necessity by describing why it is instrumental to securing valued outcomes for individuals and their employers. It is also a time to provide a realistic preview of training, and advanced organizers of the learning experience can help guide this candid conversation.

The next step in setting the stage for learning involves stating conditionalized learning and performance standards so that trainees have appropriate benchmarks against which to gauge their development and self-regulate accordingly. In addition to setting standards, trainers should discuss how trainees should pursue goals. For example, performance goals are often sufficient when training is concerned with skill automaticity for simple tasks; however, mastery goals, that emphasize learning rather than the demonstration of ability, are typically more useful for facilitating proficiency in complex task domains. Trainees should also be engaged in helping to set their own proximal and distal training goals as this can increase trainee motivation to learn.

A final step involves providing trainees with learning tips. For example, attentional advice, learning strategies, and preparatory information about stressors can alert trainees to important aspects of instruction. Learners must be encouraged to explore, experiment, and actively construct meaning from training (Edmondson, 2008). For example, errors should be framed as opportunities to reflect and delineate lessons that can be transferred to the workplace (Keith and Freese, 2008). Trainees may require instruction on how to learn from failures (Argyris, 1992). One of the critical lessons learned from a recent initiative executed to develop cybersecurity incident response teams is that error management training can increase admission, discussion, and learning from errors, mistakes, and failures (Zaccaro et al., 2016).

Deliver the Blended Learning Solution

The second stage in deploying training involves delivering the blended learning solution. There are three primary mechanisms for delivering content including information presentation, modeling, and practice. Information can be presented via the use of lectures, reading assignments, case studies, and open discussions. The specific content of what is discussed is dictated by the particular KSAs targeted for development but should also include descriptions of effective and ineffective performance, common workplace errors, and tactics for meeting business challenges.

Trainees must be encouraged to actively construct, integrate, and associate facts rather than treated as passive recipients of instructional content (Schwartz and Bransford, 1998). Couching lessons in contrasting cases comprised of alternative equally compelling explanations for an event or dilemma is a powerful approach for motivating the active construction and attainment of proficiency. Likewise, perceptual contrasts or alternative pictorial depictions help trainees notice the subtle features of visualized information (Bransford, Franks, Vye, and Sherwood, 1989)

Prior to practice, trainees should be asked to engage in symbolic rehearsals or mental simulations of the processes they intend to enact during training. During practice, trainees should be given ample opportunity to repeatedly engage in the cognitive and behavioral actions targeted for development to the point of overlearning. It is important to note, however, that repeated practice is often not sufficient to develop learning outcomes and may even be counterproductive to skill generalization. Rather, trainers should guide trainees through deliberate practice by requiring repetitions on gradually modified tasks (Ericsson, 2009). For example, difficulties, obstacles, and equipment malfunctions can be gradually introduced to ramp instructional intensity and content complexity as learners develop competence in navigating routine challenges.

When training content is delivered, instructors, an intelligent learning architecture or a combination of the two, must assess the progress of learners and deliver timely, accurate, and actionable feedback. For example, evaluative and interpretative feedback can be used to provide trainees adaptive guidance (Bell and Kozlowski, 2002). While novice learners may need more, and more immediate feedback, over time diagnostic information should be faded and delivered more intermittently to gradually remove the scaffolding inherent to training solutions.

Support Transfer and Maintenance

Training is often concluded when presentation, practice, and assessment are complete. This is unfortunate because the post-practice stage provides a window of opportunity to enhance learning transfer and maintenance. For example, after action reviews both debrief and educate. Trainers should empower trainees to drive this dialogue by soliciting and reinforcing comments while withholding input for clarifications (Tannenbaum, Smith-Jentsch, and Behson, 1998). Asking trainees to generate explanations for their actions during training is critical to the process.

Once the debriefing session is complete, trainers should offer final guidance to learners. Trainees, in conjunction with their managers and leaders, should be prompted to set proximal and distal goals for applying newly acquired capabilities in the workplace (Taylor, Russ-Eft, and Chan, 2005). It is also important to advise trainees to reflect over their training experiences and to continually refresh their learning to sustain retention and avoid performance proficiency decay. For example, peer-to-peer rehearsals, communities of practice, and online discussion forums can each contribute to facilitating the long-run maintenance of learning.

The final step of training deployment involves intervening in the workplace to help ensure transfer. Engaging a trainee's network to encourage, recognize, and reward the display of newly attained KSAs can help foster a climate for learning and transfer (Grossman and Salas, 2011). In fact, recent meta-analytic evidence supports the centrality of organizational support, supervisor support, and peer support to helping to cultivate trainee motivation to transfer and thereby transfer and retention (Hughes, Zajac, Woods, and Salas, 2020). Preemptive steps should also be taken to minimize the delay between training and operational use of new capabilities.

Evaluate Training

The final phase in optimizing systematic training involves evaluating training effectiveness and, more importantly, why it was effective or ineffective to inform improvements. Unfortunately, many organizations do not evaluate training effectiveness because evaluation can be costly, complex, and resource intensive. It often requires specialized expertise and a team of people who can collect, analyze, and interpret performance data. However, organizations often fail to consider that inefficient training can be far more costly downstream, in terms of substandard performance, errors, and missed opportunities, than a relatively inexpensive evaluation effort. Training guidelines for each of the principles of the training evaluation phase are in Appendix D.

Execute Evaluation Planning

The first step in evaluating training involves determining the purpose of evaluation as well as the sophistication of the consumers of evaluation study findings (Kraiger, 2002). The balanced objectives of the multiple stakeholders to the training enterprise often inform the research questions asked and studies performed to answer training evaluation questions. Rigorous experimental, quasi-experimental, and nonexperimental designs are available to evaluate training, and the strengths and weaknesses of a specific design should be identified and addressed before it is used to evaluate training (Shadish, Cook, and Campbell, 2002). There are quasi-experimental designs that also afford procedural and statistical controls useful for evaluation given that situational constraints preclude formal true experimentation (Sackett and Mullen, 1993). For example, cross-sectional quasi-experimentation research designs can be employed to collect trainee reactions and evidence training effects on trainee learning. Other technical considerations include modeling contextual factors, levels of analysis and aggregation, and optimizing multiwave longitudinal designs to maximize the benefits of training evaluation.

Gauge *Trainee* and Team Learning

Affective and utility reactions, the AABCs of learning, and performance proficiency for a host of teamwork and taskwork processes are assessed during training evaluation. Evaluators can scale affective, utility, and difficulty reactions to program objectives, content and materials, delivery methods and technologies, instructors, duration, and environment (Alliger, Tannenbaum, Bennett, Traver, and Shotland, 1997;

Lee and Pershing, 1999; Sitzmann, Brown, Casper, Ely, and Zimmerman, 2008). Assessing trainee and team learning with reliable measures is also essential to triangulating development. Seek to assess affective states such as self-efficacy and potency as well as knowledge, skill proceduralization, compilation and automaticity, and team proficiency.

Gauge *Organizational* Impact

A key question is whether the purpose of training is to effect change or help trainees achieve a performance standard. Analytic techniques for conceptualizing and gauging change are available (Day and Lance, 2004), whereas less rigorous designs are useful in the latter case. There are unique issues inherent to each training objective. For example, pretraining levels of performance may not increase from training executed to effect change, as assessed during or post practice, and yet workplace performance improves markedly. This result can occur when errors and difficulties are injected to ramp instructional intensity. Training that is too easy can maximize AABC change sans subsequent transfer, generalization, and retention (Bjork, 2009). This demonstrates the importance of evaluators ensuring the consistency of the level of the focal variables and contextual factors, research design, psychometric stimuli, aggregation rules, descriptive and inferential statistical analysis, and interpretation (Kozlowski et al., 2000). This is also vital to accurately estimating training impact on organizational performance via return on investment, cost benefit, and net present value analyses.

Case Examples

1. A *Success:* The Aviation Experience

Teamwork improves performance in some jobs; in others, it is imperative. For example, teamwork in the cockpit is essential – lives depend on it. We know that 60–80% of the accidents or mishaps in aviation are due to human error, and a large percentage of those are caused by coordination and other teamwork problems in the cockpit.

Research on team training has developed many methods and techniques to enhance teamwork in complex environments such as the cockpit. These approaches are pervasive in the aviation industry. In fact, both the military aviation community and the commercial airlines implement systematic team training (Weiner, Kanki, and Helmreich, 1993). The US Department of the Navy (DON) has designed and delivered team training for its aviation platforms for many years. For example, engagement simulations, which provide a forum and format for group experiential learning, helped the DON increase its superiority in air-to-air combat by a factor of 12 in one year (Chatham, 2009, B). This training continues to be refined and scaled to reach more people via live, virtual, and constructive simulation (Brannick, Prince, and Salas, 2005).

Training scientists and learning specialists, in partnership with subject matter experts, developed an approach that systematically helps instructional developers design and deliver crew resource management training for the DON (Salas, Prince, Bowers, Stout, Oser, and Cannon-Bowers, 1999). This approach illustrates how to apply the four phases outlined in this chapter. It begins with an identification of operational and mission requirements and the required competencies and performance processes (i.e. needs analysis). Extensive interviews and observations were conducted in order to ensure that the required KSAs for coordination were identified. The literature was reviewed and a theory-based framework developed.

In parallel to this process, the scientists, sponsors, users, and industry representatives met on an ongoing basis to discuss organizational procedures and policies that needed to be in place as the methodology evolved. In the end, this proved to be a very valuable dialogue – it prepared the US Navy for the training. Specifically, it created a learning climate – before the training was implemented, during and after. Once training objectives were derived and validated by subject matter experts (SMEs), the methodology called for designing and creating opportunities for practice and feedback, developing measurement tools for feedback, and implementing the training. The approach ended with suggestions for ensuring a multicomponent evaluation protocol is built into training.

This approach has been translated into a detailed set of specifications. These are a set of step-by-step instructions that can be used by instructional designers to develop curriculum and supporting materials. The evaluation of communities following this approach suggest that crews react better to the instruction, learn more about teamwork, and exhibit more teamwork behaviors in the cockpit as a result of the training (Salas, Fowlkes, Stout, Milanovich, and Prince, 1999).

In sum, this approach has been implemented and tested in several communities – and it works. It works because the approach uncovers the required KSAs and performance processes, prepares the organization for the training, relies on theories of learning, and applies sound pedagogical and andragogical principles to the design of team training. It works because the training seeks to diagnose and remedy specific deficiencies. It works because the implementation process sets the right climate for learning and transfer and evaluates its impact. It works because the methodology guides the instructional developer through a systematic process incorporating all the phases outline here, and utilizes the best information that the science of training can offer.

2. A *Failure:* Training the Sales Force

Sales at a large media company were down for the third consecutive quarter. Management reviewed several reliable strategies to improve sales and concluded that one solution would be to improve training for the large, dispersed sales force. For the sake of expediency, the training department began using a needs analysis they performed several years before to enhance training. Their plan was first to update the original needs analysis and then to develop new training approaches. They also searched for new training technologies as a possible means to decrease training delivery costs. Unfortunately, however, management was so intent on doing something quickly that training directors were ultimately pressured to acquire a generic, off-the-shelf training package by a local vendor. One of the features of the package that appealed to management was the web delivery medium, saving the time and expense of sales force travel to the main office to participate in the training. Hence, even though the package was costly to purchase, the company believed it a bargain relative to the fixed and recurring expenses of developing a new package in-house and delivering it in person to each member of the sales force.

Sales were, six months post training, still declining, and the executive team turned to the training department for answers. In the haste, no reliable measures of training effectiveness had been designed, so the training administrators had insufficient quantitative evidence to diagnosis. For lack of a better idea, members of the training department began questioning the sales force to determine why the training was not working. Several sales associates reported that training was slow and boring, and that it did not teach new sales techniques. They also complained that, without an instructor, it was impossible to clarify the facts and processes they did not fully understand. Moreover, they reported sales were off not because they needed basic sales technique training, but because so many new products were being introduced to customers and they could not keep up. In fact, many sales people recently requested updated product briefings with design engineers. The training department reported these findings to management and requested a mandate and resources to design a new training solution, beginning with a fresh front-end analysis.

So how could this employer have avoided this costly mistake? Our contention is, had they engaged in systematic training due diligence, design, and delivery processes, they would have optimized effective training and not invested in a useless product. For example, a careful needs analysis would have revealed specific performance deficiencies. A better assessment of the training delivery – especially as it related to trainee motivation – would have indicated that the course may not have been the best choice. Unfortunately, cases like this occur all too frequently, but can easily be avoided if systematic training design, delivery, and evaluation processes are executed.

Conclusion

As recently as the 1990s, the transformative power of training and education was not fully appreciated in some circles, as typified by Jack Welch's statement "We want only A players. Don't spend time trying to get C's to be B's. Move them out early" (Slater, 1998, p. 157). Today, "the people make the place" (Schneider, 1987, p. 437), and there is an intensifying mandate to gain competitive advantage by developing and retaining top talent. In fact, 75% of 400 human resource executives across 40 countries view leader development as mission critical (IBM, 2008).

There was a time from World War II until the 1960s when the training literature was voluminous but largely ". . . nonempirical, nontheoretical, poorly written and dull" (Campbell, 1971, p. 565). Today, the science of training has much to offer to the development of individuals, teams, and organizations. In this chapter, we offered a translation mechanism for stakeholders charged with optimizing training. The theoretics, principles, guidelines, and practices discussed can be applied to develop and deploy meaningful learning experiences via training solutions.

Acknowledgments

This work was partially supported by the National Science Foundation (Grants 1853528 and 1842894) to Rice University, as well as the National Aeronautics and Space Administration (Grants NNX16AP96G and NNX17AB55G) to Rice University. We thank Scott Tannenbaum for his insights on the principles discussed herein.

References

Aguinis, H., and Kraiger, K. (2009). Benefits of training and development for individuals and teams, organizations, and society. *Annual Review of Psychology*, 60, 451–474.

Alliger, G. M., Tannenbaum, S. I., Bennett, W., Traver, H., and Shotland, A. (1997). A meta-analysis of the relations among training criteria. *Personnel Psychology*, 50, 341–358.

Anderson, J. R. (1993). Problem solving and learning. *American Psychologist*, 48, 35–44.

Argyris, C. (1992). *On Organizational Learning*. Blackwell.

Arthur, W., Bennett, W., Edens, P. S., and Bell, S. T. (2003). Effectiveness of training in organizations: A meta-analysis of design and evaluation features. *Journal of Applied Psychology*, 88, 234–245.

Bell, B., and Kozlowski, S. W. (2002). Adaptive guidance: Enhancing self-regulation, knowledge and performance in technology-based training. *Personnel Psychology*, 55, 267–306.

Bisbey, T. M., Reyes, D. L., Traylor, A. M., and Salas, E. (2019). Teams of psychologists helping teams: The evolution of the science of team training. *American Psychologist*, 74, 278–289. http://dx.doi.org/10.1037/amp0000419.

Bisbey, T. M., Traylor, A., and Salas, E. (2020). Implications of the changing nature of work for training. In B. J. Hoffman, M. K. Shoss and L. A. Wegman (eds), *The Cambridge Handbook of the Changing Nature of Work* (pp. 364–382). Cambridge University Press. https://doi.org/10.1017/9781108278034.

Bjork, R. A. (2009). Structuring conditions of training to achieve elite performance: Reflections on elite training programs and related themes in chapters 10–13. In K. A. Ericsson (ed.), *The Development of Professional Expertise: Toward Measurement of Expert Performance and Design of Optimal Learning Environments* (pp. 312–329). Cambridge University Press.

Brannick, M. T., Prince, C., and Salas, E. (2005). Can PC-based systems enhance teamwork in the cockpit? *The International Journal of Aviation Psychology*, 15, 173–187.

Bransford, J. D., Franks, J. J., Vye, N. J., and Sherwood, R. D. (1989). New approaches to instruction: Because wisdom can't be told. In S. Vosniadou and A. Ortony (eds.), *Similarity and Analogical Reasoning* (pp. 470–497). Cambridge University Press.

Burke, C., Stagl, K., Salas, E., Pierce, L., and Kendall, D. (2006). Understanding team adaptation: A conceptual analysis and framework. *Journal of Applied Psychology*, 91, 1189–1207.

Campbell, J. P. (1971). Personnel training and development. *Annual Review of Psychology*, 22, 565–603.

Campbell, J. P., and Kuncel, N. R. (2002). Individual and team training. In N. Anderson, D. S. Ones, H. K. Sinangil and C. Viswesvaran (eds.), *Handbook of Industrial, Work and Organizational Psychology* (pp. 272–312). Sage.

Cannon-Bowers, J. A., and Bowers, C. (2011). Team development and functioning. In S. Zedeck (ed.), *APA Handbook of Industrial and Organizational Psychology* (Volume 1, pp. 597–650). Washington, DC: American Psychological Association.

Carnevale, A. P., Strohl, J., and Gulish, A. (2015). *College is Just the Beginning: Employers' Role in the $1.1 Trillion Postsecondary Education and Training System* (Report No. ED558166). Washington, DC: Georgetown University Center on Education and the Workforce. Retrieved from https://files.eric.ed.gov/fulltext/ED558166.pdf

Chatham, R. E. (2009, A). Toward a second training revolution: Promise and pitfalls of digital exponential training. In K. A. Ericsson (ed.), *The Development of Professional Expertise: Toward Measurement of Expert Performance and Design of Optimal Learning Environments* (pp. 215–246). Cambridge, UK: Cambridge University Press.

Chatham, R. E. (2009, B). The 20th century revolution in military training. In K. A. Ericsson (ed.), *The Development of Professional Expertise: Toward Measurement of Expert Performance and Design of Optimal Learning Environments* (pp. 27–60). Cambridge, UK: Cambridge University Press.

Colquitt, J. A., LePine, J. A., and Noe, R. A. (2000). Toward an integrative theory of training motivation: A meta-analytic path analysis of 20 years of research. *Journal of Applied Psychology*, 85, 678–707.

Cronbach, L. J., and Snow, R. E. (1977). *Aptitudes and Instructional Methods: A Handbook for Research on Interactions.* Irvington.

Day, D., and Lance, C. (2004). Understanding the development of leadership complexity through latent growth modeling. In D. Day, S. J. Zaccaro and S. M. Halpin (eds), *Leader Development for Transforming Organizations.* Mahwah, NJ: Erlbaum Associates.

DeShon, R. P., Kozlowski, S. W. J., Schmidt, A. M., Milner, K. A., and Wiechmann, D. (2004). A multiple-goal, multilevel model of feedback effects on the regulation of individual and team performance. *Journal of Applied Psychology*, 89, 1035–1056.

Dowd, T. (2021, June 16). Talent wars: The post-pandemic hiring race for a competitive advantage. *Forbes.* https://www.forbes.com/sites/forbeshumanresourcescouncil/2021/06/16/talent-wars-the-post-pandemic-hiring-race-for-a-competitive-advantage/?sh=4b87b7df5ca4

Edmondson, A. C. (2008). The competitive imperative of learning. *Harvard Business Review*, 86(8), 60–67.

Ericsson, K. A. (2009). Enhancing the development of professional performance: Implications from the study of deliberate practice. In K. A. Ericsson (ed.), *The Development of Professional Expertise: Toward Measurement of Expert Performance and Design of Optimal Learning Environments* (pp. 405–431). Cambridge, UK: Cambridge University Press.

Fowlkes, J. E., Salas, E., Baker, D. P., Cannon-Bowers, J. A., and Stout, R. J. (2000). The utility of event-based knowledge elicitation. *Human Factors*, 42, 24–35.

Fritzsche, B. A., Stagl, K. C., Salas, E., and Burke, C. S. (2006). Enhancing the design, delivery, and evaluation of scenario-based training: Can situational judgment tests contribute? In J. A. Weekley, and R. E. Ployhart (eds), *Situational Judgment Tests.* Erlbaum.

Gagné, R. M., Briggs, L. J., and Wager, W. W. (1988). *Principles of Instructional Design* (3rd edition). Holt, Rinehart and Winston.

Georgenson, D. L. (1982). The problem of transfer calls for partnership. *Training and Development Journal,* 36, 75–78.

Goldstein, I. L., and Ford, J. K. (2002). *Training in Organizations* (4th edition). Wadsworth Thompson Learning.

Grossman, R., and Salas, E. (2011). The transfer of training: What really matters. *International Journal of Training and Development,* 15, 103–120.

Hackman, J. R. (1999). Thinking differently about context. In R. Wageman (ed.), *Research on Managing Groups and Teams: Groups in Context.* JAI Press.

Hughes, A. M., Zajac, S., Spencer, J. M., and Salas, E. (2018). A checklist for facilitating training transfer in organizations. *International Journal of Training and Development,* 22(4), 334–345.

Hughes, A. M., Zajac, S., Woods, A. L., and Salas, E. (2020). The role of work environment in training sustainment: A meta-analysis. *Human Factors,* 62, 166–183. https://doi.org/10.1177/0018720819845988

IBM (2008). *Unlocking the DNA of the Adaptable Workforce, the IBM Global Human Capital Study.* IBM.

Keith, N., and Freese, M. (2008). Effectiveness of error management training: A meta-analysis. *Journal of Applied Psychology,* 93, 59–69.

Klein, C., Stagl, K. C., Salas, E., Parker, C., and Van Eynde, D. (2007). Returning to flight: Simulation-based training for the US National Aeronautics and Space Administration's Mission Management Team. *International Journal of Training and Development,* 11, 132–138.

Kozlowski, S. W. J., Brown, K. G., Weissbein, D. A., Cannon-Bowers, J. A., and Salas, E. (2000). A multilevel perspective on training effectiveness: Enhancing horizontal and vertical transfer. In K. J. Klein and S. W. J. Kozlowski (eds), *Multilevel Theory, Research, and Methods in Organizations* (pp. 157–210). Jossey-Bass.

Kozlowski, S. W. J., Gully, S. M., Brown, K., Salas, E., Smith, E., and Nason, E. (2001). Effects of training goals and goal orientation traits on multidimensional training outcomes and performance adaptability. *Organizational Behavior and Human Decision Processes,* 85, 1–31.

Kozlowski, S. W. J., and Salas, E. (1997). An organizational system approach for the implementation and transfer of training. In J. K. Ford and Associates (eds), *Improving Training Effectiveness in Work Organizations* (pp. 247–90). LEA.

Kraiger, K., Ford, J. K., and Salas, E. (1993). Application of cognitive, skill-based, and affective theories of learning outcomes to new methods of training evaluation. *Journal of Applied Psychology,* 78, 311–328.

Kraiger (2002). Decision-based evaluation. In K. Kraiger (ed.), *Creating, Implementing and Maintaining Effective Training and Development: State-of-the Art Lessons for Practice* (pp. 331–375). Jossey-Bass.

Lacerenza, C. N., Reyes, D. L., Marlow, S. L., Joseph, D. L., and Salas, E. (2017). Leadership training design, delivery, and implementation: A meta-analysis.

Journal of Applied Psychology, 102(12), 1686–1718. http://dx.doi.org/10.1037/apl0000241

Lajoie, S. P. (2009). Developing professional expertise with a cognitive apprenticeship model: Examples from avionics and medicine. In K. A. Ericsson (ed.), *The Development of Professional Expertise: Toward Measurement of Expert Performance and Design of Optimal Learning Environments* (pp. 61–83). Cambridge, UK: Cambridge University Press.

Lee, S. H., and Pershing, J. A. (1999). Effective reaction evaluation in evaluating training programs. *Performance Improvement*, 38, 32–39.

Manpower (2007). Talent shortage study: 2007 global results. http://files.shareholder.com/downloads/MAN

Marks, M. A., Mathieu, J. E., and Zaccaro, S. J. (2001) A temporally based framework and taxonomy of team process. *Academy of Management Review*, 26, 356–376.

McCausland, T. C., King, E. B., Bartholomew, L., Feyre, R., Ahmad, A., and Finkelstein, L. M. (2015). The technological age: The effects of perceived age in technology training. *Journal of Business and Psychology*, 30, 693–708. doi:10.1007/s10869-014-9390-5

McKinney, E. H., and Davis, K. J. (2003). Effects of deliberate practice on crisis decision performance. *Human Factors*, 45, 436–444.

Nunnally, J., and Bernstein, I. (1994). *Psychometric Theory*. McGraw Hill.

Sackett, P. R., and Mullen, E. J. (1993). Beyond formal experimental design: Towards an expanded view of the training evaluation process. *Personnel Psychology*, 46, 613–627.

Partnership for New York City (2021). Return to Office Results Released – November, News article, Available at https://pfnyc.org/news/return-to-office-results-released-november/

Salas, E., and Cannon-Bowers, J. A. (2000). Design training systematically. In E. A. Locke (ed.), *The Blackwell Handbook of Principles of Organizational Behavior* (pp. 43–59). Blackwell.

Salas, E., Cannon-Bowers, J. A., and Johnston, J. H. (1997). How can you turn a team of experts into an expert team?: Emerging training strategies. In C. Zsambok and G. Klein (eds), *Naturalistic Decision Making* (pp. 359–370). Lawrence Erlbaum.

Salas, E., DiazGranados, D., Klein, C., Burke, C. S., Stagl, K. C., Goodwin, G. F., and Halpin, S. M. (2008). Does team training improve team performance? A meta-analysis. *Human Factors*, 6, 903–933.

Salas, E., Fowlkes, J. E., Stout, R. J., Milanovich, D. M., and Prince, C. (1999). Does CRM training improve teamwork skills in the cockpit? Two evaluation studies. *Human Factors*, 41, 327–343.

Salas, E., Prince, C., Bowers, C. A., Stout, R. J., Oser, R. L., and Cannon-Bowers, J. A. (1999). A methodology for enhancing crew resource management training. *Human Factors*, 41, 61–72.

Salas, E., and Stagl, K. C. (2009). Design training systematically by following the science of training. In E. A. Locke (ed.), *The Handbook of Principles of Organizational Behavior: Indispensable Knowledge for Evidence-Based Management* (pp. 59–84). Sussex, UK: Wiley.

Salas, E., Stagl, K. C., Burke, C. S., and Goodwin, G. F. (2007). Fostering team effectiveness in organizations: Toward an integrative theoretical framework of team performance. In J. W. Shuart, W. Spaulding, and J. Poland (eds), *Modeling Complex Systems: Motivation, Cognition, and Social Processes* (pp. 185–243). Nebraska Press.

Schneider, B. (1987). The people make the place. *Personnel Psychology*, 40, 437–453.

Schwartz, D. L., and Bransford, J. D. (1998). A time for telling. *Cognition and Instruction*, 16, 475–522.

Shadish, W. R., Cook, T. D., and Campbell, D. T. (2002). *Experimental and Quasi-Experimental Designs for Generalized Causal Inference.* Boston, MA: Houghton, Mifflin and Company.

Sitzmann, T., Brown, K. G., Casper, W. J., Ely, K., and Zimmerman, R. (2008). A meta-analysis of the nomological network of trainee reactions. *Journal of Applied Psychology*, 2, 280–295.

Slater, R. (1998). *Jack Welch and the GE Way: Management Insights and Leadership Secrets of the Legendary CEO.* McGraw-Hill.

Smith-Jentsch, K. A., Zeisig, R. L., Acton, B., and McPherson, J. A. (1998) Team dimensional training: A strategy for guided team self-correction. In J. A. Cannon-Bowers and E. Salas (eds), *Making Decisions Under Stress: Implications for Individual and Team Training.* APA Press.

Stagl, K. C., Salas, E., and Day, D. V. (2007). Assessing team learning outcomes: Improving team learning and performance. In V. I. Sessa and M. London (eds), *Work Group Learning: Understanding, Assessing, and Improving How Groups Learn in Organizations* (pp. 369–392). Taylor and Francis.

Stout, R. J., Salas, E., and Fowlkes, J. E. (1997). Enhancing teamwork in complex environments through team training. *Group Dynamics: Theory, Research and Practice*, 1, 169–182.

Swanson, R. A. (2001). *Assessing the Financial Benefits of Human Resource Development.* Perseus.

Taylor, P. J., Russ-Eft, D. F., and Chan, D. W. L. (2005). A meta-analytic review of behavior modeling training. *Journal of Applied Psychology*, 90, 692–709.

Tannenbaum, S. I., Smith-Jentsch, K. A., and Behson, S. J. (1998) Training team leaders to facilitate team learning and performance. In J. A. Cannon-Bowers and E. Salas (eds), *Making Decisions Under Stress: Implications for Individual and Team Training.* APA.

Weiner, E. L., Kanki, B. J., and Helmreich, R. L. (1993). *Cockpit Resource Management.* Academic.

Zaccaro, S. J., Dalal, R. D., Tetrick, L., and Steinke, J. A. (2016). *The Psychosocial Dynamics of Cyber Security.* Routledge.

Zachary, W., Bilazarian, P., Burns, J., and Cannon-Bowers, J. A. (1997). Advanced embedded training concepts for shipboard systems. *Proceedings of the 19th Annual Interservice / Industry Training, Simulation and Education Conference* (pp. 670–679). National Training Systems Association.

Appendix A

Table 9.1 Analyze training needs phase: principles and guidelines

Training phase	*Guiding principle*	*Training guidelines*
Analyze training needs	Conduct due diligence	Describe an organization's mission, strategy, structure, context, and desired outcomes
		Articulate the benefits for individuals, teams, and higher-level units (division, organization, and society)
		Link solutions to specific organizational outcomes (performance, effectiveness, and profitability)
		Consider the impact on organizational performance-related factors (satisfaction, reputation, and social capital)
		Frame cross-level effects of contextual factors on motivation, learning, and transfer
		Specify how individual results emerge to impact unit- or organization-level outcomes (vertical transfer)
		Conduct a stakeholder analysis to identify and understand parties advocating for and against training
		Estimate the expected net present value of proposed training solutions
	Define performance requirements	Leverage established theories of performance and taxonomies of processes to guide criteria specification
		Disaggregate dependent variables to illuminate the specific aspects of performance targeted by training
		Use task inventories, cognitive task analysis, and critical incident interviews to nuance key factors
		Conduct probed protocol analysis to elicit the stimuli, goals, and actions of experts in natural situations
		Map the trajectory of change from novice to expert performance
		Describe the relative importance of taskwork and teamwork processes during performance episodes

(*Continued*)

Table 9.1 (Continued)

Training phase	*Guiding principle*	*Training guidelines*
	Define cognitive and affective states	Frame individual-level cognitive (mental models and situation awareness) and affective (self-efficacy) states
		Describe the types of mental models (equipment, task, and team) targeted for development
		Use event-based knowledge-elicitation techniques with subject matter experts to describe shared states
		Model the compositional or compilational emergence of cognitive and affective states
		Determine the relative importance of sharedness and accuracy of cognitive and affective states
	Define KSA attributes	Specify the direct determinants of the processes and emergent states comprising effective performance
		Leverage knowledge and skill inventories, skill repositories, and performance records
		Describe the declarative, procedural, and strategic knowledge applied to enact performance processes
		Describe the attitudes that can be changed as a result of the learning process
		Identify short-, mid-, and long-term competency requirements given alternative performance requirements
	Delineate learning objectives	Translate training needs into training objectives, learning objectives, and enabling objectives
		Contextualize task statements by describing appropriate performance standards
		Delineate behavior-, cognitive-, and affective-based learning objectives
		Ensure learning objectives are clear, concise, and link to measurable learning outcomes

Appendix B

Table 9.2 Develop training content phase: principles and guidelines

Training phase	*Guiding principle*	*Training guidelines*
Develop training content	Design learning architecture	Develop an intelligent scenario management system that allows instructors and users to author content
		Design a dashboard interface that can be used to control training content, sequence, and pace
		Program systems to provide tailored training features based on aptitude-treatment interactions
		Design the capacity to manipulate action tempo and compress the arrival time of events
		Design the capacity to vary the predictability and difficulty of contexts, tasks, events, and situations
		Program intelligent tutors to dynamically monitor, assess, diagnose, intervene, and remediate performance
		Create the capacity to compile performance records and for an on-demand lesson learned repository
	Forge instructional experiences	Develop an instructional management plan, instructor guides, and scripts
		Map the branching paths learners can take and forecast where trainees are likely to encounter difficulties
		Construct a chronological timeline of training events
		Craft instructional content that has psychological fidelity as well as physical fidelity
		Include opportunities for trainees to discover knowledge and relationships for themselves

(*Continued*)

Table 9.2 (Continued)

Training phase	*Guiding principle*	*Training guidelines*
		Develop lectures, exercises, games, reading lists, and illustrative case studies
		Leverage role-plays, motion pictures, closed-circuit television, and interactive multimedia to display models
		Increase stimulus variability by manipulating the character and competence of models
		Ramp practice difficulty by including multiple levels and increasingly incongruent environments
		Incorporate routine obstacles, emergency situations, and crisis events trainees must navigate
	Develop assessment tools and metrics	Develop tools to assess multiple dimensions of trainee learning and performance
		Construct multiple-choice and situational judgment tests to assess knowledge and skill
		Develop concept maps, card sorts, and pairwise comparison ratings to illuminate knowledge structures
		Assess the fragmentation, structure, and accessibility of knowledge chunks
		Triangulate measurement by leveraging multiple elicitation and representation techniques
		Create tools to dynamically capture trainee key strokes, communication, and perceptual movements

Appendix C

Table 9.3 Deploy training phase: principles and guidelines

Training phase	*Guiding principle*	*Training guidelines*
Deploy training	Set the stage for learning	Provide trainers with frame of reference and rater error training if ratings are used to evaluate trainees
		Measure and take steps to increase motivation to learn
		Prepare trainees to engage in meta-cognitive and self-regulatory processes
		Provide advanced organizers of learning points
		Prompt trainees to explore, experiment, and actively construct explanations in their training environment
		Frame errors as a natural part of training that contribute to learning
		Ask trainees to reflect over the informative aspects of errors when they occur
	Deliver blended solution	Use information presentation techniques such as reading assignments, lectures, and discussions
		Prompt learners to generate knowledge and skills that are targeted for acquisition
		Require trainees to integrate and associate various facts and actions into coherent mental models
		Pose difficult and structured reflection questions after case studies
		Ask trainees to integrate information and discern common themes provided in contrasting cases
		Explore the lessons learned from case studies of effective and ineffective performance

(*Continued*)

Table 9.3 (Continued)

Training phase	*Guiding principle*	*Training guidelines*
		Guide trainees through deliberate practice by asking them to repeat similar tasks with gradual modifications
		Encourage trainees to persist in practice to the point of over-learning/automaticity
	Support transfer and maintenance	Conduct training debriefings organized around key events and learning objectives
		Guide self-correction by keeping the debriefing discussion focused and modeling effective feedback skills
		Reserve instructor input for times when trainees cannot generate input or when clarifications are required
		Identify lessons learned and areas for continued improvement to guide self-development efforts
		Prompt trainees to set proximal and distal goals for applying new capabilities
		Identify and implement solutions to accelerate the cycle time required to realize training benefits
		Schedule shorter booster sessions after the main training initiative is complete

Appendix D

Table 9.4 Evaluate training phase: principles and guidelines

Training phase	*Guiding principle*	*Training guidelines*
Evaluate training	Execute evaluation plan	Determine the purposes, needs, and sophistication of the consumers of training evaluation findings
		Identify an appropriate experimental, quasi-experimental, or passive-observational training design
		Consider alternatives when rigorous experimental designs are not feasible in a given setting
		Review controls for factors that affected the inferences drawn from training evaluation
		Compile subjective evaluations and objective indices of multiple training criteria
		Ensure consistency between the level of focal variables, contextual factors, design, aggregation, and analysis
		Consider the relative efficacy of various approaches to measuring longitudinal change
	Gauge trainee learning	Measure the extent trainees' expectations were fulfilled as proximal indicators of reactions and learning
		Differentiate between affective and utility reactions
		Assess learning in terms of affective, behavioral, and cognitive outcomes
		Measure short-term retention immediately after training and long-term retention
		Gauge transfer by examining generalization to the job context and maintenance of learning over time
		Plot a maintenance curve and determine reasons for any decrements in maintenance over time

(*Continued*)

Table 9.4 (Continued)

Training phase	*Guiding principle*	*Training guidelines*
		Consider the interactions of work characteristics and time on the application of skills in the workplace
	Gauge team learning	Model unit-level outcomes as the mean of individual-level change when vertical transfer is compositional
		Evaluate both individual-level and unit-level outcomes when vertical transfer is compilation-based
		Use longitudinal designs when evaluating vertical transfer based on compilation emergence models
		Use techniques applicable to analyzing nonlinear configural relationships when emergence is compilational
	Gauge organizational impact	Estimate the cross-level relationships of improved individual performance on organizational performance
		Determine whether the costs of training were recouped
		Estimate the return on investment from training
		Estimate the utility or economic impact of a training solution over time
	Disseminate training results	Provide trainees with a copy of training evaluation reports
		Ensure the information collected from the transfer context is available to other designated parties
		Ensure designated parties have a clear understanding of the implications of evaluation findings
		Implement solution process changes suggested by the findings of formative evaluations
		Implement changes in the talent management system suggested by summative evaluations

Exercises

1. *Training* Planning

A large computer manufacturer experienced declining revenues during FY21. After careful analysis, the executive team determined that global competitors were squeezing their market share by offering a suite of comprehensive technical support services for their computers. A mandate was issued from the C-suite to recruit and develop the human capital required to offer similar services. As the chief learning officer, it is your charge to ensure that your organization has proficient people in place by the close of the second quarter 2022. To accomplish your objectives, develop a plan for what forms of training will executed, why training will be administered, and how proposed solutions will contribute to meeting the immediate, mid-range, and long-run requirements of your organization. Be precise in specifying what internal and external resources and support are required to design and deploy the solution in a timely manner.

2. *Training* Evaluation

A management consultancy was contracted by a medical supply firm to evaluate an in-house training solution for medical representatives. Discouraged by the findings that medical reps were apparently not learning during training (as measured by post-training reactions and declarative knowledge), yet seemed to be performing very effectively in the workplace, the consulting house turned to you as a subject matter expert to review their training evaluation study results. Describe the steps you will take to help the consultants uncover the true impact of the training solution. Think through training design, criterion identification, change measurement, and data analysis issues. State your recommendations for conducting a stronger evaluation.

Discussion Questions

1. How can training stakeholders energize and sustain active learning processes?
2. What are the benefits of tracking the transfer, generalization, and retention of performance proficiency post training using repeated measures and longitudinal designs?
3. How can documenting and modeling trainee learning curve response surfaces inform training duration, the delivery of adaptive training experiences, and employee remediation?

Training Media Resources

1. https://www.youtube.com/watch?v=Omc9ldssFNw
2. https://www.youtube.com/watch?v=r-8ryTWMp48
3. https://www.youtube.com/watch?v=DcnapnW7zjk
4. https://www.youtube.com/watch?v=mJur0jefARE
5. https://www.youtube.com/watch?v=d72rm5iUKqc

10

Embed Performance Appraisals into Broader Performance or Management Systems

Maria Rotundo and Kelly D. Murumets

Joseph L. Rotman School of Management, University of Toronto

A performance appraisal provides an assessment of the extent to which the employee completes the work that is agreed in a manner that is consistent with the organization's values and that motivates employee performance improvement and growth. Historically, performance appraisals are conducted once a year and have formed an essential part of the performance management process, whereby the information obtained from these assessments has informed decisions that organizations and its leaders take. The performance management process is ongoing and encompasses more than just the appraisal. There is a vast literature on the benefits and drawbacks of performance appraisals and performance management more broadly along with factors to consider in their design and implementation. Nevertheless, a comprehensive review of these two processes and their literatures is not the focus of this chapter. Rather, this chapter outlines some key components of a performance appraisal and some steps that leaders can take throughout the performance cycle to motivate employee performance improvement and growth.

There are at least four assumptions underlying the two sections in the chapter. Two of these assumptions relate to the purpose of the performance appraisal. The first assumption is that organizations have an interest in designing and implementing these systems to motivate and improve performance with a focus on employee growth. A performance management process, of which the performance appraisal is one part, that is designed for the sole purpose of documenting performance could include different steps than one that seeks to motivate performance and growth. Second, in this chapter, emphasis is placed on communication during the appraisal and in the time period in between assessments, since this period is where the opportunity lies for motivating performance and growth. The role that the leader as coach plays in this communication process is paramount as it is the important step of preparing leaders for this role.

The third assumption is that organizations and its leaders have conceptualized employee performance in light of the organization's goals and values that support its strategic plan. The workplace continues to evolve and has seen significant change in the nature of work, jobs, and roles, as well as in the employee experience at work and, consequently in the behaviors that facilitate effective performance. Further, an organization's values indicate expectations for "how" the work is to be done (e.g. with honesty and integrity; in a collaborative, respectful, and inclusive environment). Thus, the tools that are discussed in this chapter form part of the systems that embed values throughout the organization (as per Chapter 28).

The fourth assumption relates to the organization context. This chapter provides suggestions to guide organizations and its leaders. Nevertheless, a well-designed system should be tailored to the specific work and context within which the organization operates, so it is important to take these into consideration. Some suggestions are provided throughout the chapter. As one example, more frequent assessments that capture shorter performance cycles are preferred over one annual assessment, if the work (e.g. short-term project-based work), context, and resources permit. Further, organizational structures that are flat and designed around primarily self-managed teams versus more traditional hierarchical organizational structures based on functional departments, divisions, or global regions may present different opportunities or challenges for performance appraisals. Nevertheless, the two sections of this chapter offer guidelines for leaders and employees.

The first section titled *Components of a Performance Appraisal* offers three tools to facilitate a discussion and evaluation of what employees achieve in the specified performance cycle. One tool is the *Individual Objectives Attainment,* which is a discussion about the employee's achievements relative to an agreed set of performance objectives. The objectives were established by the employee in a team setting (when applicable), the objectives were discussed at meetings throughout the performance period, and the objectives are measurable and under the control of the individual. It should be a straightforward component of the process. The second tool, *Behavior-Based Appraisal,* is a discussion between the leader and the employee about the alignment of the employee's behaviors relative to the values of the organization. As will be explored in this chapter, there are assessment tools that can improve the impartiality of this assessment and that may involve feedback from various sources. The third tool is the employee's *Personal Development Plan.* All meetings should include a discussion between the leader and the employee about the employee's personal development (i.e. how the employee would like to professionally and personally grow and develop to realize their potential), where they see their career leading, and how they can make the greatest impact on this organization and/or on the world).

The second section titled *How to Improve Individual and Organizational Performance* offers four tools to motivate performance and growth throughout the performance cycle. One tool is *Goal Setting* that is initiated by employees and works in junction with objectives setting. Jointly through these processes, employees specify that which they strive to achieve that is under their control and for which they are accountable during the respective performance cycle. The second tool, *Leader as Coach,* focuses on the important role that the leader plays throughout the year in guiding, motivating, and inspiring employees as they work to achieve their goals. This role is focused heavily on ongoing communication whereby the leader sets clear expectations, provides developmental feedback, supports the employee as they work through obstacles, and facilitates career planning, among other behaviors. The third tool, *Multisource Feedback*, recognizes that performance information oftentimes is available from other sources with whom the employee interacts. To the extent that this information is accessible and that organizations can invest in well-designed tools to solicit this information from relevant sources, it can provide useful information. The fourth tool is *Training* on how to use the tools to maximize their effectiveness. The training should raise awareness of the challenges associated with these processes and explain how the tools are designed to mitigate these challenges. It should involve discussion, practice, incorporate feedback, and allow for follow-up.

We offer one last observation before we transition to the chapter sections, which is to recognize the importance of designing practices and processes to enable organizations and their members to be adaptable and responsive to changing and sometimes challenging external environments. We write this chapter during a pandemic that continues to impact everyone globally. It is the work of incredible talent that has seen us through these very difficult times. Although many scholars and practitioners have written about the need to be agile, nothing has made this more salient than the times in which we find ourselves. Leaders and employees pivoted in unbelievable ways to keep people safe and to provide them with access to essential services. It is with the spirit of partnership, collaboration, and community that we write this chapter. Although the pandemic is an extreme example, it reminds us that we should build flexibility into these practices.

Components of a Performance Appraisal

The performance appraisal is a complex, ongoing process. It no longer entails a "supervisor" assessing their "subordinate's" attendance, punctuality, appearance, and attire, or any other subjective metrics. The purpose of a performance appraisal is no longer about simply following administrative protocols or risk mitigation in the court system. Performance appraisals, when most effectively administered, are designed to help employees realize their potential, ensure that feedback is central to the system, strengthen the corporate culture, and improve the organization's results and its delivery of its strategy.

Various tools have been incorporated in the performance appraisal process to help leaders evaluate employees and coach performance. They can be focused on assessing the work that has been completed, how the work was completed, and whether the work is consistent with the company's values. They should focus attention on actions and behaviors that are under the control of the individual (Campbell and Wiernik, 2015). Some of the tools can mitigate concerns about criterion contamination or criterion deficiency and can be used to inform the design of training initiatives or multisource feedback systems. Some tools are better for evaluation while others for coaching especially if developing employees is of interest, and so their choice can be based on their intended purpose.

Criterion contamination occurs when factors other than performance are reflected in the appraisal. For example, leaders' impressions about employees may be influenced by biases, likeability, and idiosyncratic tendencies, to name just a few factors, which can distort their appraisals. Criterion deficiency occurs when the appraisal has not considered all of the relevant dimensions of work performance. For example, an appraisal that is based solely on absenteeism does not reflect the quantity and quality of work performed although absenteeism may impact some of these factors. Thus, an appraisal tool should focus leaders' attention on the critical work that needs to be completed and on the desired behaviors that underly the achievement of this work in line with the organization's values. Such a tool would mitigate concerns that the appraisal suffers from criterion contamination or deficiency.

This section discusses three tools that can facilitate the performance appraisal process. They are Individual Objectives Attainment, Behavioral-Based Appraisal Tools, and Personal Development Plan. There are three common denominators to all three of these tools. First, all three tools include discussion between the leader and the employee. Second, all three tools include decisions being logged to ensure that follow-up is never contingent on the memory of one or both parties. Finally, all three tools include accountability of the employee and of the leader. The leader and the employee are "partners" in the employee's performance appraisal process. These tools are described in further detail as follows.

Individual Objectives Attainment

The most effective organizations establish a corporate strategy and, subsequently, corporate objectives that are aligned with this strategy. The strategy may have a three-, four-, or five-year horizon, while the corporate objectives have a shorter time frame. Once the organization's objectives are set, there should be a process whereby teams establish their respective sets of objectives, aligned with the corporate objectives and, de facto, the corporate strategy (Drucker, 1954; Reddin, 1971). These objectives are related to outputs of the role, specific, time bound, measurable, and weighted, one relative to the other, based on priority. The highest performing organizations see their teams setting their team and team member objectives. Such a process ensures that there is vertical alignment, but also horizontal alignment. The greatest outcome of this process is that each team member leaves the objective-setting meeting understanding their team's, their colleagues', and their own objectives. As a result, employees are not handed a performance agreement; instead, they meet with their leader to sign off on the performance agreement that they, themselves, developed.

As a result of this powerful process, employees are able and, in fact, asked to self-assess. Before meeting with their leader for a performance appraisal meeting, the employee completes the performance appraisal for their own Individual Objectives Attainment. The leader completes the same prework. In the performance appraisal meeting, the leader and the employee share their prework with one another. A final performance appraisal of the Individual Objectives Attainment component of the process is the consensus of the two parties. It should be clear to both parties those individual objectives that were exceeded, met, partially met, or not met.

The critical portion of this meeting is the discussion between the leader and the employee. What could the employee have done differently? What could the leader have done differently? It is the occasion for each party to give the other feedback. It is a coaching opportunity for the leader. While the Individual Objectives Attainment discussion is a look back, the focus of the meeting is on the future, and the steps that both parties will take to improve performance going forward. The leader's success is dependent on the success of the employee and, so, the discussion is very much two-way. The relationship between the leader and the employee is tantamount to success. This meeting is about building that relationship and developing deeper bonds of trust and openness. The more candid the discussion, the greater the revelations about performance and the greater the opportunities for improvement.

Behavior-Based Appraisal

How organizations and its leaders conceptualize work performance that is aligned with the values of the organization informs the content of the tools discussed in this chapter including behavior-based appraisal tools. Current conceptualizations of work performance consider positive discretionary and negative discretionary performance behaviors in addition to the traditional emphasis on task performance (e.g. Rotundo and Sackett, 2002). Positive discretionary behaviors like organizational citizenship behaviors (also referred to as contextual performance, extra-role behaviors, among other terms) contribute in a positive way to the social and psychological environment at work (e.g. sharing information and cooperation; Organ, 2018), reflect positive behavioral examples of "how" to accomplish work goals, and are assessed favorably. Negative discretionary behaviors or counterproductive work behaviors (also referred to as deviance; Bennett and Robinson, 2000) contribute in a negative way to individuals and organizations, are discouraged, and result in lower performance assessments (e.g. production deviance, theft, and workplace aggression; Gruys and Sackett, 2003; Rotundo and Spector, 2017). Negative discretionary behaviors also take into consideration actions that reflect unethical conduct that can arise during the process of attaining work performance (e.g. misuse of information or resources) and indicate behaviors that are the opposite of acting with honesty and integrity and that can undermine trust. Although these three components of performance are related, they are distinct elements of employee performance (Dalal, 2005; Sackett, Berry, Wiemann, and Laczo, 2006) and have been incorporated into behavior-based appraisal tools and weighted differentially (Rotundo and Sackett, 2002) given their importance to individuals and organizations.

Behavioral-based performance tools define the performance components that have been identified as most applicable for the given work (or role) in light of the organization's values using behavioral statements. Typically, the behavioral information for these instruments is obtained from a critical incident work analysis and is informed by the organization's values. However, some organizations have consolidated their jobs into broader roles, which can, in turn, inform the content of these tools. This process can involve input from multiple sources and ensures that leaders, employees, and any other potential users of the tool all have a common understanding of what the dimensions are and of the behaviors that are expected (Bracken and Rotolo, 2019). Two examples are Behavioral Observation Scales (BOS) and the Behaviorally Anchored Ratings Scales (BARS). These formats vary in how the scale anchors are presented. The BOS asks the leader to rate the frequency of each very specific behavioral statement that has been deemed critical for effective performance using a Likert scale (e.g. "1" almost never to "7" almost always). The BARS defines each scale anchor (e.g. low performance "1" all the way to high performance "7") with a list of the behaviors for the respective dimension that reflect each performance level. Thus, both formats include behavioral phrases but differ in how they are presented.

Research shows support for behavioral-based tools. Employees reported favorable reactions to an appraisal system and high goal clarity and goal specificity for the BOS (Tziner, Joanis, and Murphy, 2000). Research has also reported within-person performance improvement before and after the use of a BOS (Tziner, Kopelman, and Livneh, 1993). Other research findings also suggest that the BOS is useful for making within-person comparisons and for developing and coaching employees (Cambon and Steiner, 2015). These tools provide clear and specific behavioral examples of what employees need to do to achieve high performance (Tziner and Kopelman, 2002), which can facilitate the leader as coach role by identifying strengths and weaknesses. In contrast, a system that is focused on differentiating people or making between-person comparisons is designed typically for evaluative purposes and not necessarily development (Cambon and Steiner, 2015). The BOS and other behavioral-based appraisal tools can be very time intensive and costly to create and implement, which should be weighed in light of the purpose for which the appraisal system is designed.

Personal Development Plan

During the Personal Development Plan portion of the performance appraisal meeting, the employee kicks off the discussion. They share their feelings about personally and professionally growing during the performance period. The leader asks questions to clarify, understand, and probe. The leader asks about the blockages to the employee's definition of success and asks how they can help to remove blockages. The leader's role is to listen and to provide coaching.

An employee sharing their professional and personal goals is a vulnerable exercise. The leader must create a trusting environment for the discussion. Trust is created by allowing for open and honest two-way communication without either party interrupting the other and by genuinely listening and trying to understand. Trust is created by asking relevant questions that demonstrate understanding and/or a desire to understand.

While it is the leader's role to help remove blockages to the employee's personal and professional growth plans, it is acceptable for the leader to identify areas where they are not able to assist and, if possible, give the rationale for this truth. Some of the best coaching may come from the leader helping the employee to identify ways that they can remove their blockages themselves. Excellent coaching is a skill that must be learned. Leader training is almost certainly a "must."

Summary

The first half of this chapter outlined three tools to support leaders and employees as they conduct the annual performance appraisal. These tools include Individual Objectives Attainment, Behavioral-Based Assessment Tool, and a Performance Development Plan and involve input from employees, leaders, and other sources, as well as extensive discussion between the employee and the leader. The appraisal reflects the accomplishments of the employee in the respective performance cycle and covers the objective components of performance, the desired behaviors, along with the learning and growth that occurred. As a package, these tools can provide a more comprehensive assessment of performance than either tool on its own. Nevertheless, the performance appraisal takes place at a specific point in time, and so it is important to also discuss some tools that organizations can use in the intervening months to increase the success of employees, leaders, and in turn the organization. These tools, which include Goal Setting, Leader as Coach, Multisource Feedback, and Training will be the focus of the second half of the chapter.

How to Improve Individual and Organizational Performance

The critical period for motivating performance is the months in between performance assessments. This is the time when employees create and test strategies to get their work done and manage the challenges and distractions that they encounter along the way, which explains in part day-to-day within-person fluctuations in performance (Dalal, Alaybek, and Lievens, 2020). Goal Setting, discussed next, is one tool that can help focus employees' attention on goal-relevant actions and behaviors. This is also the time when leaders are receiving information and updates from other organizational leaders, employees, and many other sources. These updates and information can also inform decisions to refocus effort as appropriate (e.g. Rotundo, Sackett, Enns, and Mann, 2012). These moments present important opportunities for leaders to communicate any adjustments and troubleshoot. Thus, the Leader as Coach role can facilitate communication and keep everyone on track and aligned with the organization's goals. Multisource Feedback systems, to the extent that they are appropriate for the context and well designed and implemented, can provide useful input on whether goals are being achieved and in line with the organization's values. Training is another tool that is available to prepare everyone on how to appraise performance and how to manage the time in between assessment periods to achieve high performance. These four tools will be elaborated in this section.

Goal Setting

Goal setting can be incorporated in the performance appraisal process (Locke and Latham, 1990) jointly with objectives setting when planning for the next performance cycle. Together they state what you are striving to achieve from which the actions that are needed to achieve them are established. This process aims to provide individuals with clarity and to focus their effort and attention on that which is needed to attain success. This can be especially useful when individuals are presented with competing demands on their time, many of which can be unrelated and even impediments to goal attainment. Further, goal setting theory assumes that individuals have the requisite knowledge and experience to achieve the goals; otherwise, training should take place before the goal setting process to fill any gaps.

The goal setting process has been associated with improved performance (e.g. Kleingeld, van Mierlo, and Arends, 2011; Locke and Latham, 1990) especially when implemented with at least five fundamentals (Latham and Locke, 2006; Locke and Latham, 2019). Goals that are specific and challenging but attainable have been associated with higher performance. Specific goals seek to reduce ambiguity and direct individuals' attention to a set of actions that are under their control and more closely associated with attainment of the goals. They can make something that appears otherwise abstract more tangible and actionable especially when specified in behavioral terms (Locke, 2019). When goals are broad, subgoals can be specified that connect specific actions and behavior to broader goals. Challenging but attainable goals can motivate individuals to push themselves to achieve more than they would if they set "do-your-best" goals. Since the goals are attainable rather than impossible, challenging goals can be associated with increased rather than diminished self-efficacy (i.e. confidence that you can achieve the goal; see Chapter 5). Furthermore, specific and challenging but attainable goals have been proposed to mitigate unethical or dishonest conduct that can arise if goals are impossible and failure to achieve them has negative or punitive consequences (Locke, 2019). Allowing for choice in the goal setting process can restore a sense of control to a situation that is often otherwise lacking of it and has been associated with increased self-efficacy and higher goal commitment (e.g. Latham, Winters, and Locke, 1994). Allowing for participation in the process can have beneficial effects especially as it relates to the quality of the strategies that individuals use to achieve their goals, which in turn increases their self-efficacy and performance (Latham et al., 1994). Relatedly, learning goals can create a similar state, whereby individuals are open to exploring novel solutions rather than sticking to the status quo and have been associated with improved performance. Learning goals have also been associated with less concern in failing to achieve the goal or preventing failure and, in turn, less unethical behavior (Welsh, Bush, Thiel, and Bonner, 2019). Goal setting effectiveness relies on the feedback process, whereby individuals take primary responsibility for checking progress against goals with potential input from the leader and other sources, which are discussed in the next sections.

Leader as Coach

This section discusses the role that coaching by a leader can play in facilitating employee performance, well-being, and growth (Bachkirova, Spence, and Drake, 2016; Beattie, Kim, Hagen, Egan, Ellinger, and Hallin, 2014; Dahling, Taylor, Chau, and Dwight, 2016; Gregory and Levy, 2011; McCarthy and Milner, 2013; Kinicki, Jacobson, Peterson, and Prussia, 2013; Schleicher, Baumann, Sullivan, Levy, Hargrove, and Barros-Rivera, 2018; Steelman, and Wolfeld, 2018). It refers to the coaching that occurs through the day-to-day communication and exchange that leaders have with employees and not to professional coaches who are hired to work with leaders on their own self-development. Although both can be effective, this section focusses on the former. Coaching has long been recognized as a responsibility of leaders. A facet of transformational leadership espouses the importance of listening, advising, developing, and coaching (e.g. individualized consideration; Avolio and Bass, 1995) and has been found to predict subsequent employee performance (Bormann and Rowold, 2016). Scholars and organizations have identified dimensions of coaching (Beattie et al., 2014) that characterize effective managers and that are valued by employees even over technical dimensions (Bryant, 2011; Garvin, 2013). Scholars have found support for the positive association between leaders' coaching behaviors and employee attitudes or outcomes (e.g. Dahling et al., 2016; Kinicki et al., 2013; Liu and Batt, 2010; Steelman, and Wolfeld, 2018). Nevertheless, coaching has not always been prioritized by organizations and leaders due to organizational, economic, individual, or other factors. Large spans of control can limit the time and attention that leaders have to devote to coaching activities, economic circumstances may favor technical performance dimensions, leaders themselves do not always feel confident in their coaching skills, and not all leaders believe that employee performance is coachable, to name a few. Not surprisingly, research and practice have lagged in studying coaching and in developing the coaching skills of leaders (Bachkirova et al., 2016; Beattie et al., 2014; Heslin, VandeWalle, and Latham, 2006; Hagen and Aguilar, 2012; McCarthy and Milner, 2013; Milner, McCarthy, and Milner, 2018; Schleicher et al., 2018). Nonetheless, this section offers some evidence-based tips for coaching employees.

The working relationship between leaders and their employees is one of the most important elements of the coaching process (deHaan, and Gannon, 2016; McCarthy and Milner, 2013). A strong relationship takes time to develop but can facilitate the leaders' efforts to coach employees. A coaching relationship that is based on mutual trust, respect, empathy, and effective communication has been associated with more positive coaching experiences by employees (Anseel, Lievens, and Schollaert, 2009; Gregory and Levy, 2011; Gregory and Levy, 2012).

Establishing clear performance expectations is fundamental to coaching. Setting objectives helps employees direct their time and effort and helps them prioritize among competing demands. It is equally important to make clear the standards of performance that are expected. Organizations or its members can differ in what they see to be superior performance compared to average performance, and employee experiences can be varied especially with greater job mobility.

A meta-analysis of reactions to performance appraisals reported a positive association between clear performance standards and favorable employee reactions (Pichler, Beenen, and Wood, 2020). It also reported that feedback frequency was associated with more favorable reactions when the knowledge of performance standards was high. Further, performance can differ in relation to whether objectives are achieved in accordance with the organization's values (e.g. Maylett, 2019). Some employees may achieve high outcomes but compromise interpersonal relationships along the way or engage in conduct that poses long-term risks for the organization (e.g. unethical conduct; Locke, 2019). Thus, it important for leaders to set these expectations upfront along with employees and their teams, ensure that they understand them, and communicate whether employees are meeting them throughout the cycle (Kinicki et al., 2013; Losch, Traut-Mattausch, Mühlberger, and Jonas, 2016; Schleicher et al., 2018; Steelman and Wolfeld, 2018). Addressing performance difficulties as they arise is part of the process (Gregory and Levey, 2011; Steelman and Wolfeld, 2018), can present learning opportunities if properly handled, and can motivate the employee to make adjustments rather than continue to falter. Acknowledging and recognizing strong performance is equally important (Liu and Batt, 2010). Thus, clear expectations with appropriate follow-up are fundamental to coaching.

Developmental feedback can be an important part of effective coaching (Schleicher et al., 2018). High-quality feedback that is intended for development rather than evaluation, exchanged in a respectful manner in real time, and focused on awareness, learning, and growth are facets of a strong feedback environment (Steelman and Williams, 2019; Steelman and Wolfeld, 2018). These facets have been associated with favorable perceptions of the coaching relationship (Gregory and Levy, 2011). Further, feedback has been found to moderate the relationship between challenging developmental assignments and leadership skills development (DeRue and Wellman, 2009). In this research, individuals who reported less access to feedback experienced less skills development as the assignments became more challenging. In contrast, individuals who had access to more feedback reported higher skills development. It is well established that negative information can be experienced as a threat and be negatively associated with important outcomes (e.g. Byron, Khazanchi, and Nazarian, 2010; Fredrickson, 2001). Negative feedback can have a detrimental effect on problem-solving and creativity especially when it is top-down (Kim and Kim, 2020), which is counter to the purpose for which feedback is intended. Thus, how feedback is communicated is as important to the coaching relationship as whether it is exchanged at all. Thus, careful attention should be given to establishing a feedback environment that encourages communication and is focused on development.

An important part of coaching is supporting employees as they work through problems (Bormann and Rowold, 2016; Dahling et al., 2016). Obstacles can derail even the most motivated and capable performers. Employees develop strategies to accomplish their work and can become very efficient and effective at it. However, these strategies can also become impediments when the work changes or new processes are introduced. Guiding them to consider new ways to approach problems can facilitate the learning process and help them stay on track. Questions that prompt them to think differently and to reflect on the work are encouraged (McCarthy and Milner, 2013). Enlisting the help of coworkers, team members, and mentors and directing them to other learning resources are additional tools and can also foster a collaborative environment. Coaching is not about solving problems for employees but rather facilitating the learning process for employees as they focus on the solution.

Coaches can facilitate career planning (Dahling et al., 2016; Gregory and Levy, 2012). New and challenging work experiences can encourage skills development and bring about self-awareness. Employees can discover their strengths and the kind of work that energizes them, as well as work roles they may find less fulfilling. In partnership with the other organizational functions and career resources, these experiences can help coaches create career paths for employees that exploit their strengths and see them progressing into roles in which they are more likely to thrive. However, the process of self-discovery can be filled with highs and lows. Thus, a leader needs to want to help others, believe in them, and be able to instill confidence through the journey (Anseel et al., 2009; Bryant, 2011; Heslin et al., 2006).

Coaching has been associated with favorable individual and group outcomes (Hagen and Aguilar, 2012). In a study involving call center agents, coaching frequency predicted better subsequent performance (i.e. shorter time on call with customer), and this effect was stronger in settings that used group-based rewards (Liu and Batt, 2010). A study of sales representatives reported that the coaching skills of the district manager had a positive effect on end of year sales goal attainment (Dahling et al., 2016). This relationship was partially mediated by role clarity. Higher coaching skill was positively related to role clarity, which in turn had a positive effect on sales. In contrast, the findings regarding coaching frequency were unexpected. Coaching frequency had a negative effect on sales goal attainment when coaching skill was low and no effect when coaching skill was high. This last finding draws a distinction between the importance of the quality and not just quantity of the coaching experience. Other research also found support for the association between coaching and role clarity (Kim, Egan, Kim, and Kim, 2013). In this research, role clarity in turn mediated the relationship between coaching and satisfaction and coaching and job performance. Coaching also had an indirect association with commitment through its relationship with work satisfaction. Given the limited research on coaching, there have been calls for stronger research designs that consider both the processes and outcomes of coaching (Greif, 2016). Nevertheless, there is some initial evidence supporting its positive relationship with important attitudes, experiences, and outcomes.

Coaching has been associated with favorable outcomes in educational settings. In an experiment involving the procrastination behavior of university students, students in the one-on-one coaching condition reported higher satisfaction with the experience, higher goal attainment, and less procrastination behavior compared to a control group (Losch et al., 2016). The first two effects occurred through the mediators of autonomy and intrinsic motivation, which were associated with the one-on-one coaching. In another field experiment involving students, the receipt of coaching that was administered via text messages throughout an academic semester related to higher reports of student well-being at the end of the semester (i.e. greater sense of belonging and support) and greater use of student success strategies (i.e. more help-seeking and meetings with instructors and tutors; Oreopoulos, Petronijevic, Logel, and Beattie, 2020). This research found no significant relationships between coaching and academic outcomes (i.e. grades). These findings highlight the range of benefits that coaching can have.

Multisource Feedback

Although leaders are an important source to appraise employees' performance, they are not the only ones who can provide input. Multisource feedback, commonly referred to as 360-degree feedback, is a process whereby input about an employee's performance is sought from individuals who work with the employee or have interacted with the employee during the completion of some part of their work. Typically, the sources are coworkers, customers, the leader, the employee themself, employees who report to them, and team members, among other potential sources. Multisource feedback was introduced to support the development of employees as they prepared to assume leadership roles or to support their development while in leadership roles. It is believed that by obtaining a broader perspective on the employee's performance, a more complete picture emerges of their strengths, preferences, and opportunities for growth. These insights can inform specific goals for coaching sessions, the choice of mentors and trainers, or other developmental opportunities. Indeed, research has reported the existence of meaningful variance in performance that can be attributed to a specific source of the assessment (Hoffman and Woehr, 2009).

Traditionally, multisource feedback does not form part of the annual appraisal when it is implemented solely for development purposes and is conducted at a different time from when annual appraisals are conducted. These features are designed to focus attention on the growth opportunities rather than on it as an evaluation. This perspective is believed to motivate sources to provide honest assessments. More recently, however, some organizations have incorporated multisource feedback into the appraisal process, thereby changing its primary purpose and potentially altering its developmental role. Concerns have been raised that shifting the purpose may negatively influence the quality of the assessments provided by other sources. Notwithstanding, recent research suggests that organizations may realize beneficial individual and organizational outcomes even when both purposes are pursued (Kim, Atwater, Patel, and Smither, 2016; Maylett, 2019). Nevertheless, the decision to invest in a multisource feedback process, irrespective of the purpose(s), should be taken based on whether it supports the organization's strategy and values and whether the organization is prepared to invest the significant time and resources that are needed to design the instruments and implement the process appropriately, effectively integrate it with other systems, and train the feedback sources on the multisource system (Church, Bracken, Fleenor, and Rose, 2019).

A leader can assess the performance of their direct reports on many work responsibilities, but depending on several factors such as the work arrangement and span of control, to name a few, leaders do not always have sufficient information to provide an assessment on all components nor is this information readily available through alternative means such as technology (Maylett, 2019). A majority of work is done in teams, through exchanges with coworkers, clients, contractors, consumers, or some combination of sources. These interactions can provide useful data on the quality and quantity of performance beyond objective outputs or what is observed by the leader. The extent to which the employee demonstrates effective team behaviors, acts with honesty and integrity, is prepared for team meetings, shares information with coworkers, or conveys accurate product knowledge during a sale are the types of behaviors that other sources may be able to comment on. Leaders often obtain the employee's perspective on these interactions through their day-to-day communication. However, it does not always reflect the view of all parties (Hoffman and Woehr, 2009) and may limit opportunities to identify problems early enough to permit adjustments before they escalate. Relatedly, it is recommended that information be obtained anonymously and from multiple individuals within each source for it to be useful, provided that these two criteria are feasible. Research has shown that employees and peers demonstrate greater halo (e.g. lower variation) and leniency (e.g. higher average assessment score) in their assessments of leaders when compared to assessments made by the leader's leader even when the multisource assessments are intended for developmental purposes (Ng, Koh, Ang, Kennedy, and Chan, 2011). Assuring anonymity may encourage more honest responses but relies on there being a sufficient number of assessors within each source. Thus, assessors from different sources can be invited to contribute anonymous data based on the performance dimensions they are best equipped to assess and relatively close to when the exchanges occur.

Just as leaders may differ in their interpretation of how a performance dimension is defined or in their interpretation of what excellent versus average performance entails, peers or other sources can be just as susceptible to the same deviations. Some of these deviations operate at the individual level, whereby there are deviations within the group of peers (i.e. peers differ from one another in what they expect from a team member), while other deviations are a function of the "peer" role in comparison to the "leader" role (i.e. peers may differ in what they expect from a team member compared to what leaders expect; Hoffman and Woehr, 2009; Maylett, 2019; Ng et al., 2011). Consumers can have different standards for what they consider to be effective customer service. Thus, it is important to design instruments for multisource feedback that are tailored to the source, define performance in specific and observable actional and behavioral terms, and that reflect levels of performance (Bracken and Rotolo, 2019; Heidemeier and Moser, 2009; Locke, 2019; Vecchio and Anderson, 2009). Similarly, if narrative statements are invited, it should be clear as to what performance dimensions are being assessed (David, 2013).

One of the challenges of using multisource feedback is in interpreting the data provided from multiple sources, since there can be variation within sources as well as between different sources as noted earlier. This variation does not always mean that there is a problem with the assessment or the instrument. That is, peers may provide assessments that differ from each other or that differ from a leader or customer assessments. It is entirely feasible that an employee has different quality of exchanges with some team members than others. These deviations may even be expected depending upon the performance dimensions they are assessing. Further, these deviations can provide exactly the type of information that is needed to identify growth areas. When multisource feedback is used for developmental purposes, the value is in learning how these exchanges are perceived and why, so that an employee can continue to grow, excel at their goals, and pursue their career plans. This may seem odd to some readers since they tend to group employees into categories of effective performers or not based on limited information without appreciating that employees may not excel at all parts of work. Once the data are aggregated, it is important to look for any trends in the data that indicate strengths or opportunities for growth. It is best to uncover these needs early and facilitate development through appropriate channels. For example, an organization that implemented a multisource feedback system in a manufacturing plant for strategic reasons and to supplement the annual top-down appraisal provided by the leader found a low correlation between assessments provided by the leader and those obtained from the newly implemented multisource assessment (Maylett, 2019). More specifically, the multisource assessment focused on "how" the employees did the work (e.g. interpersonal skills, integrity, and teamwork) and incorporated input from peers, the employee, and other sources, while the annual top-down appraisal provided by the leader focused on "what" the employee achieved in accordance with key performance indicators. Although there were some similarities in the assessments, they did not overlap as had originally been expected. In fact, some of the top performers on the "what" received significantly lower scores on the "how." Thus, this process provided useful information for development.

Research supports a positive relationship between feedback obtained from multiple sources and performance. Scholars reported that developmental feedback (e.g. high quality, focused on social norms, and future oriented) was positively related to the performance of newcomers (Li, Harris, Boswell, and Xie, 2011). More specifically, when supervisors provided feedback, it was related to more helping behavior of the employee, and when peers provided the feedback, it was related to higher task performance of the employee. They also found that the newcomer's proactive personality (e.g. propensity to demonstrate personal initiative) moderated some of the findings. That is, the effect of supervisors' feedback was stronger for individuals who reported a low score on proactive personality. In contrast, feedback provided by peers was related to more helping behavior for newcomers who scored high on proactive personality. These findings support the potential benefit that this type of feedback can have early in one's career, while they still have ample opportunity to incorporate it into their future work selves. Research also supports a positive association between multisource feedback and productivity. A multilevel study on firms in South Korea found a positive association between the use of multisource feedback and employee ability and knowledge sharing, which in turn mediated the relationship between multisource feedback and workforce productivity (e.g. sales per employee; Kim et al., 2016). They found that the mediation effect of knowledge sharing was stronger when multisource feedback was used for both developmental and administrative purposes compared to when it was used for only one purpose.

Training

Training should play an important part in the implementation and maintenance of the performance appraisal process and the tools associated with improving individual and organization performance (Bachkirova et al., 2016; Church et al., 2019; Locke, 2019; McCarthy and Milner, 2013; Roch, Woehr, Mishra, and Kieszczynska, 2012). A survey of US human resources executives indicated that 76% provide leaders with performance appraisal training (Gorman, Meriac, Roch, Ray, and Gamble, 2017). A survey of human resources professionals in Canada reported that performance appraisal training was positively associated with perceptions of the effectiveness of the performance management process (Haines and St-Onge, 2012). Further, receipt of training has been positively associated with leaders feeling more prepared for appraising performance (Speer, Prewett, and Siver, 2020). With regard to coaching, a survey of leaders in Australia revealed that although their organization supported them in professional development training, over 40% wanted more intensive training focused specifically on coaching (Milner et al., 2018). Thus, training should be considered in the implementation of these practices. Although the discussion here is on leader training, which has been the focus of most research, it is important that other sources involved in providing performance-related information (i.e. peers and employees) are given guidance on the processes and tools they use whether through training or other resources. Further, writing goals and objectives that are indeed specific, challenging, and measurable can benefit from guidance and practice (Locke, 2019). This section discusses training separately for appraising performance and training designed to improve leader coaching.

A well-researched program for training leaders on the use of behavior-based performance appraisal tools is frame-of-reference (FOR) training (Chirico, Buckley, Wheeler, Facteau, Bernardin, and Beu, 2004). This approach helps leaders develop common prototypes or schemas for categorizing employees based on performance-relevant information (Gorman and Rentsch, 2009; Woehr, 1994). Leaders are believed to rely on these prototypes when they appraise employees (Roch et al., 2012). FOR training begins with how work performance is conceptualized with the consideration of the organization's values. The aim is to agree on what constitutes work performance so that leaders' attention is focused on these dimensions when they observe and assess employees rather than on characteristics that are unrelated to work. The purpose of the second step is to establish performance standards defined in behavioral terms that differentiate a high score on the assessment scale (e.g. score of 7 on a seven-point Likert scale) from an average or low score. This step aims to align leaders when they evaluate the performance-relevant behaviors. Once leaders complete the first two steps, they are given the opportunity to practice appraising hypothetical individuals. The program relies on rich media such as videos that illustrate different levels of actual performance for the participants to evaluate. Participants are given feedback on their evaluations afterward. Typically, the training takes place with a group of leaders in a highly interactive session that includes discussion throughout. In the survey noted earlier (Gorman et al., 2017), FOR training was the most common training reported by human resources professionals followed by a program that focused solely on the first two steps (i.e. typically referred to as performance dimension training).

Frame-of-reference training has been associated with improved appraisal outcomes in the way of accuracy (e.g. Roch et al., 2012), and these effects generalized to an assessment center context when outcomes were assessed two weeks after the training (Gorman and Rentsch, 2017). Further, in a study of call center customer service representatives, some of the same principles described in FOR training were incorporated into the performance appraisal process through the use of calibration meetings (Speer, Tenbrink, and Schwendeman, 2019). That is, leaders first completed a pre-assessment of employees and then discussed their assessments in a meeting that was led by members of the department and human resources group. One of the purposes of the meeting was to develop a common frame-of-reference for when the leaders completed the actual performance assessments after the meeting. Researchers found that the assessments completed after the meeting demonstrated a stronger association with other performance metrics that were collected by the organization (i.e. call time, upselling, customer satisfaction) compared to the assessments that were done before the meeting. Nevertheless, this training focuses on the evaluation component and ensuring consistency among leaders in what they are assessing and on standards of performance. It does not prepare leaders for the day-to-day coaching that takes place throughout the cycle and where the real opportunity lies to facilitate employee performance, growth, and development.

Training leaders on effective coaching is an important part of motivating performance and growth (Bachkirova et al., 2016). As employees ascend to senior positions, priority is typically placed on demonstrating technical expertise, even though leaders are increasingly called upon to coach employees on a day-to-day basis. Nevertheless, there has been relatively little attention given to preparing leaders for the coaching role. This lack of preparation can exacerbate real or perceived deficiency and insecurity in coaching others. As discussed earlier, effective coaching is a complex process that involves interpersonal and cognitive elements. Demonstrating empathy and caring, communicating effectively, establishing performance expectations, and creating a motivating and supportive feedback environment that facilitates learning, growth, and development are elements of effective coaching. However, these elements are not always realized in the most coaching experiences, which can have detrimental effects. Research has shown that poor coaching skill is associated with less favorable outcomes even when coaching frequency is high (Dahling et al., 2016). Further, research has shown that some leaders are less inclined to coach others due to their implicit beliefs that employee attributes are not amenable to development (Heslin et al., 2006). However, these same leaders increased their willingness to coach after training. Thus, organizations are encouraged to invest in preparing leaders on how to coach others.

Summary

The second half of this chapter described four tools that can help leaders motivate employee performance and growth. These tools include Goal Setting, the role of Leader as Coach, Multisource Feedback, and Training. These tools emphasize the importance of preparing employees and leaders for their respective roles and setting them up to succeed. These tools encourage open communication and dialogue between employees and leaders on an ongoing bases as well as input from multiple sources, with the aim of facilitating developmental feedback, fostering employee growth, and in turn motivating high employee performance. Together, these tools provide employees and leaders with a solid basis for the performance appraisal.

Case Examples

The cases described next are some examples of how performance appraisals have been experienced by employees. Readers can discuss the case examples beginning with the first one. Readers are encouraged to identify what worked and what did not work in each case, and to share insights about how they might feel in each case example as, first, the employee and, second, as the leader.

Example A

Pat is a programmer at a software company. Connor is the leader, responsible for a team of five people. Pat is the only programmer on the team. Connor's background does not include programming; Connor has always worked in project management, and this is Connor's first role as a leader.

Pat's performance appraisal meeting is scheduled with Connor for next Wednesday at 3 p.m. Pat is feeling anxious about the meeting. Pat has not yet received an agenda for the meeting and does not know the expectations of the meeting.

On Wednesday at 3 p.m., Pat arrives at Connor's office. Connor does not welcome Pat into the office until 3:10 p.m. Connor sits in the office chair and invites Pat to take a seat in the chair across from the desk. Connor then proceeds to refer to various pieces of paper with type- and hand-written notes on them.

Connor begins the meeting, letting Pat know that Pat has done a very good job over the last year. No examples and no further clarification are given.

Connor cites one example of when Pat submitted an assignment one day late. The example was from six months ago. Connor does not cite any other examples of late work. Connor then proceeds to talk about how it is difficult to know exactly what Pat has produced. Pat is writing code. It seems that Pat is debugging a great deal of the time. It seems that Pat is working very diligently. However, Connor has noticed that Pat did arrive to the office 10–15 minutes late back in January. Connor then hands Pat the performance appraisal document that indicates an assessment. Connor thanks Pat and asks if there are any questions. Pat is not certain what to say and, in the end, says that there are no questions.

Pat is excused. The meeting is finished within 15 minutes.

Post-meeting, Pat is confused, uninspired, and frustrated, and Connor is relieved that the meeting is over.

Example B

Avery is a buyer of apparel for a local department store. Campbell is the leader. Campbell manages a team of five people, each with a different area of focus. Campbell has only been at the department store for two years. For the last three jobs, a team of people have been reporting to Campbell. In each of these leadership roles, Campbell has received leadership training.

For the last two years, Avery has met with Campbell once per week for a one-on-one coaching session. At the meeting, they update one another, they review issues and successes, and, together, they discuss how best to remove blockages to performance. More formally, once per year, at mid-year, they meet for a Checkpoint meeting; the agenda of which is designed to discuss all elements of a performance appraisal meeting, identify if Avery is on track for year-end performance, and problem-solve about how best to remove any blockages to performance. Given that these discussions occur weekly, and coaching is ongoing, there are no surprises at the Checkpoint meeting.

Avery has a performance appraisal meeting with Campbell in two weeks' time. Today, Campbell sent an email reminding Avery of the one-hour meeting and letting Avery know that Campbell looks forward to it. Campbell also reminds Avery to do the prework for the meeting of which Avery is aware. The prework includes an Individual Objectives Attainment component, Behavioral Performance component, and a Personal Development Plan component. Avery knows that Campbell will complete the same prework.

At the scheduled date and time, Avery and Campbell meet at the round table in Campbell's office. There are no papers on the table, except the prework that both have completed. They discuss Avery's performance one component at a time. During the Individual Objectives Attainment component of the meeting, Avery shares their assessment of the first objective, after which Campbell shares the assessment of the first objective. They discuss the objective and spend extra time if, for some reason, their assessments differ. They proceed in this fashion, one objective by one objective, until they have discussed the entire performance agreement. For each objective, they talk about what each of them could have done differently to ensure a better result and they agree on how they will operate for the year ahead. They, then, turn their attention to the Behavioral Performance component of the performance appraisal; again, reviewing the criteria one-by-one. Avery will share the prework first, followed by Campbell's assessment. Campbell may be able to share feedback from various sources, dependent on the assessment tool(s) used. Finally, the two review Avery's Personal Development Plan. They discuss Avery's professional and personal growth over the last year and, then, turn their attention to the year ahead. At the conclusion of the discussion of the Personal Development Plan,

Campbell asks Avery if there is any other feedback Avery has for Campbell. Campbell then asks if there is anything else that they should discuss as it relates to Avery's performance, the job, the team, or the organization.

The two agree that they have covered all topics related to the performance appraisal and jointly call the meeting to a close.

There should not be any surprises at the performance appraisal meeting, given that Avery and Campbell have discussed all performance matters at weekly and, formally, at the Checkpoint meeting, and given Campbell's ongoing coaching of Avery.

Post-meeting, Avery is clear on direction, feels heard, and is motivated, and Campbell is confident that Avery will deliver even better results in the next performance period.

Conclusion

The performance appraisal process and the time period in between assessments requires significant time and resources to design and implement well as suggested throughout this chapter. The success of these processes in motivating performance and growth should not be taken as a given and depends upon many factors. Although a thorough discussion is beyond the scope of this chapter, it offers some tools to facilitate their effectiveness. These tools take into consideration the importance of the entire performance period rather than the appraisal event alone and presume an interest on the part of the organization, its leaders, and employees themselves in employee growth and development and not just in evaluation. Furthermore, these processes work in tandem with the recruitment and selection, compensation and incentives, and other processes, practices, and systems, which should be all aligned and integrated for maximum effectiveness.

References

Anseel, F., Lievens, F., and Schollaert, E. (2009). Reflection as a strategy to enhance task performance after feedback. *Organizational Behavior and Human Decision Processes,* 110, 23–35.

Avolio, B. J., and Bass, B. M. (1995). Individual consideration viewed at multiple levels of analysis: A multi-level framework for examining the diffusion of transformational leadership. *The Leadership Quarterly,* 6(2), 199–218. doi:http://dx.doi.org.myaccess.library.utoronto.ca/10.1016/1048-9843(95)90035-7

Bachkirova, T., Spence, G., and Drake, D. (2016). *The SAGE Handbook of Coaching.* SAGE Publications Ltd, https://www-doi-org.myaccess.library.utoronto.ca/10.4135/9781473983861

Beattie, R. S., Kim, S., Hagen, M. S., Egan, T. M., Ellinger, A. D., and Hamlin, R. G. (2014). Managerial coaching: A review of the empirical literature and development of a model to guide future practice. *Advances in Developing Human*

Resources, 16(2), 184–201. doi:http://dx.doi.org.myaccess.library.utoronto.ca/10.1177/1523422313520476

Bennett, R. J., and Robinson, S. L. (2000). Development of a measure of workplace deviance. *Journal of Applied Psychology,* 85(3), 349–360. doi:http://dx.doi.org.myaccess.library.utoronto.ca/10.1037/0021-9010.85.3.349

Bormann, K. C., and Rowold, J. (2016). Transformational leadership and followers' objective performance over time: Insights from German basketball. *Journal of Applied Sport Psychology,* 28(3), 367–373. doi:http://dx.doi.org.myaccess.library.utoronto.ca/10.1080/10413200.2015.1133725

Bracken, D. W., and Rotolo, C. T. (2019). Can we improve rater performance? In A. H. Church, D. W. Bracken, J. H. Fleenor, and D. S. Rose (eds), *The Handbook of Strategic 360 Feedback; The Handbook of Strategic 360 Feedback* (pp. 255–289, Chapter xiii, 562 Pages) Oxford University Press, New York, NY. doi:http://dx.doi.org.myaccess.library.utoronto.ca/10.1093/oso/9780190879860.003.0015 Retrieved from http://myaccess.library.utoronto.ca/login?qurl=https%3A%2F%2Fwww.proquest.com%2Fbooks%2Fcan-we-improve-rater-performance%2Fdocview%2F2477697793%2Fse-2%3Faccountid%3D14771

Bryant, A. (March 12, 2011). Google's quest to build a better boss. *New York Times.* Retrieved (August 10, 2021): https://www.nytimes.com/2011/03/13/business/13hire.html

Byron, K., Khazanchi, S., and Nazarian, D. (2010). The relationship between stressors and creativity: A meta-analysis examining competing theoretical models. *Journal of Applied Psychology,* 95(1), 201–212. doi:http://dx.doi.org.myaccess.library.utoronto.ca/10.1037/a0017868

Cambon, L., and Steiner, D. D. (2015). When rating format induces different rating processes: The effects of descriptive and evaluative rating modes on discriminability and accuracy. *Journal of Business and Psychology,* 30(4), 795–812. doi:http://dx.doi.org.myaccess.library.utoronto.ca/10.1007/s10869-014-9389-y

Campbell, J. P., and Wiernik, B. M. (2015). The modeling and assessment of work performance. *Annual Review of Organizational Psychology and Organizational Behavior,* 2, 47–74. doi:http://dx.doi.org.myaccess.library.utoronto.ca/10.1146/annurev-orgpsych-032414-111427

Chirico, K. E., Buckley, M. R., Wheeler, A. R., Facteau, J. D., Bernardin, H. J., and Beu, D. S. (2004). Note on the need for true scores in frame-of-reference (FOR) training research. *Journal of Managerial Issues,* 16(3), 382–395. Retrieved from http://myaccess.library.utoronto.ca/login?qurl=https%3A%2F%2Fwww.proquest.com%2Fscholarly-journals%2Fnote-on-need-true-scores-frame-reference-training%2Fdocview%2F620566901%2Fse-2%3Faccountid%3D14771

Church, A. H., Bracken, D. W., Fleenor, J. H., and Rose, D. S. (2019). *The Handbook of Strategic 360 Feedback.* Oxford University Press, New York, NY. doi:http://dx.doi.org.myaccess.library.utoronto.ca/10.1093/oso/9780190879860.001.0001 Retrieved from http://myaccess.library.utoronto.ca/login?qurl=https%3A%2F%2Fwww.proquest.com%2Fbooks%2Fhandbook-strategic-360-feedback%2Fdocview%2F2477700754%2Fse-2%3Faccountid%3D14771

Dahling, J. J., Taylor, S. M., Chau, S. L., and Dwight, S. A. (2016). Does coaching matter? A multilevel model linking managerial coaching skill and frequency to sales goal attainment. *Personnel Psychology*, 69(4), 863–894. https://doi.org/10.1111/peps.12123

Dalal, R. S. (2005). A meta-analysis of the relationship between organizational citizenship behavior and counterproductive work behavior. *Journal of Applied Psychology*, 90(6), 1241–1255. doi:http://dx.doi.org.myaccess.library.utoronto.ca/10.1037/0021-9010.90.6.1241

Dalal, R. S., Alaybek, B., and Lievens, F. (2020). Within-person job performance variability over short timeframes: Theory, empirical research, and practice. *Annual Review of Organizational Psychology and Organizational Behavior*, 7, 421–449. doi:http://dx.doi.org10.1146/annurev-orgpsych-012119-045350

David, E. M. (2013). Examining the role of narrative performance appraisal comments on performance. *Human Performance*, 26(5), 430–450. doi:http://dx.doi.org.myaccess.library.utoronto.ca/10.1080/08959285.2013.836197

de Haan, E., and Gannon, J. (2016). The coaching relationship. In T. Bachkirova, G. Spence, and D. Drake, *The SAGE Handbook of Coaching* (pp. 195–216). SAGE Publications Ltd. https://www-doi-org.myaccess.library.utoronto.ca/10.4135/9781473983861.n11

DeRue, D. S., and Wellman, N. (2009). Developing leaders via experience: The role of developmental challenge, learning orientation, and feedback availability. *Journal of Applied Psychology*, 94(4), 859–875. doi:http://dx.doi.org.myaccess.library.utoronto.ca/10.1037/a0015317

Drucker, P. F. (1954). *The Practice of Management*. New York: Harper & Row.

Fredrickson, B. L. (2001). The role of positive emotions in positive psychology: The broaden-and-build theory of positive emotions. *American Psychologist*, 56(3), 218–226. doi:http://dx.doi.org.myaccess.library.utoronto.ca/10.1037/0003-066X.56.3.218

Garvin, D. A. (2013). How Google sold its engineers on management. *Harvard Business Review*, 91(12), 74–82.

Gorman, C. A., Meriac, J. P., Roch, S. G., Ray, J. L., and Gamble, J. S. (2017). An exploratory study of current performance management practices: Human resource executives' perspectives. *International Journal of Selection and Assessment*, 25(2), 193–202. doi:http://dx.doi.org.myaccess.library.utoronto.ca/10.1111/ijsa.12172

Gorman, C. A., and Rentsch, J. R. (2009). Evaluating frame-of-reference rater training effectiveness using performance schema accuracy. *Journal of Applied Psychology*, 94, 1336–1344.

Gorman, C. A., and Rentsch, J. R. (2017). Retention of assessment center rater training: Improving performance schema accuracy using frame-of-reference training. *Journal of Personnel Psychology*, 16(1), 1–11.

Gregory, J. B., and Levy, P. E. (2011). It's not me, it's you: A multilevel examination of variables that impact employee coaching relationships. *Consulting Psychology Journal: Practice and Research*, 63, 67–88.

Gregory, J. B., and Levy, P. E. (2012). Employee feedback orientation: Implications for effective coaching relationships. *Coaching: An International Journal of Theory, Research and Practice*, 5, 86–99.

Greif, S. (2016). Researching outcomes of coaching. In T. Bachkirova, G. Spence, and D. Drake, *The SAGE Handbook of Coaching* (pp. 569–588). SAGE Publications Ltd, https://www-doi-org.myaccess.library.utoronto.ca/10.4135/9781473983861.n31

Gruys, M. L., and Sackett, P. R. (2003). Investigating the dimensionality of counterproductive work behavior. *International Journal of Selection and Assessment*, 11(1), 30–42. doi:http://dx.doi.org.myaccess.library.utoronto.ca/10.1111/1468-2389.00224

Hagen, M., and Aguilar, M. G. (2012). The impact of managerial coaching on learning outcomes within the team context: An analysis. *Human Resource Development Quarterly*, 23(3), 363–388. doi:http://dx.doi.org.myaccess.library.utoronto.ca/10.1002/hrdq.21140

Haines, V. Y., and St-Onge, S. (2012). Performance management effectiveness: Practices or context? *The International Journal of Human Resource Management*, 23, 1158–1175.

Heidemeier, H., and Moser, K. (2009). Self-other agreement in job performance ratings: A meta- analytic test of a process model. *Journal of Applied Psychology*, 94, 353–370.

Heslin, P. A., VandeWalle, D., and Latham, G. P. (2006). Keen to help? Managers' implicit person theories and their subsequent employee coaching. *Personnel Psychology*, 59, 871–902.

Hoffman, B. J., and Woehr, D. J. (2009). Disentangling the meaning of multisource performance rating source and dimension factors. *Personnel Psychology*, 62(4), 735–765. Retrieved from http://myaccess.library.utoronto.ca/login?qurl=https%3A%2F%2Fwww.proquest.com%2Fscholarly-journals%2Fdisentangling-meaning-multisource-performance%2Fdocview%2F220145636%2Fse-2%3Faccountid%3D14771

Kim, K. Y., Atwater, L., Patel, P. C., and Smither, J. W. (2016). Multisource feedback, human capital, and the financial performance of organizations. *Journal of Applied Psychology*, 101(11), 1569–1584. doi:http://dx.doi.org.myaccess.library.utoronto.ca/10.1037/apl0000125

Kim, S., Egan, T. M., Kim, W., and Kim, J. (2013). The impact of managerial coaching behavior on employee work-related reactions. *Journal of Business and Psychology*, 28(3), 315–330. doi:http://dx.doi.org.myaccess.library.utoronto.ca/10.1007/s10869-013-9286-9

Kim, Y. J., and Kim, J. (2020). Does negative feedback benefit (or harm) recipient creativity? the role of the direction of feedback flow. *Academy of Management Journal*, 63(2), 584-612. doi:http://dx.doi.org.myaccess.library.utoronto.ca/10.5465/amj.2016.1196

Kinicki, A. J., Jacobson, K. J. L., Peterson, S. J., and Prussia, G. E. (2013). Development and validation of the performance management behavior questionnaire. *Personnel Psychology*, 66(1), 1–45. doi:https://doi.org/10.1111/peps.12013

Kleingeld, A., van Mierlo, H., and Arends, L. (2011). The effect of goal setting on group performance: A meta-analysis. *Journal of Applied Psychology*, 96(6), 1289–1304. doi:http://dx.doi.org.myaccess.library.utoronto.ca/10.1037/a0024315

Latham, G. P., and Locke, E. A. (2006). Enhancing the benefits and overcoming the pitfalls of goal setting. *Organizational Dynamics,* 35(4), 332–340. doi:http://dx.doi.org.myaccess.library.utoronto.ca/10.1016/j.orgdyn.2006.08.008

Latham, G. P., Winters, D. C., and Locke, E. A. (1994). Cognitive and motivational effects of participation: A mediator study. *Journal of Organizational Behavior,* 15(1), 49–63. doi:http://dx.doi.org.myaccess.library.utoronto.ca/10.1002/job.4030150106

Li, N., Harris, T. B., Boswell, W. R., and Xie, Z. (2011). The role of organizational insiders' developmental feedback and proactive personality on newcomers' performance: An interactionist perspective. *Journal of Applied Psychology,* 96(6), 1317–1327. doi:http://dx.doi.org.myaccess.library.utoronto.ca/10.1037/a0024029

Liu, X., and Batt, R. (2010). How supervisors influence performance: A multilevel study of coaching and group management in technology-mediated services. *Personnel Psychology,* 63, 265–298. doi: 10.1111/j.1744-6570.2010.01170.x

Locke, E. A. (2019). Some observations about goals, money and cheating in business. *Organizational Dynamics,* 48(4), 5. doi:http://dx.doi.org.myaccess.library.utoronto.ca/10.1016/j.orgdyn.2018.11.004

Locke, E. A., and Latham, G. P. (1990). *A Theory of Goal Setting and Task Performance.* Englewood Cliffs, NJ, US: Prentice-Hall, Inc

Locke, E. A., and Latham, G. P. (2019). The development of goal setting theory: A half century retrospective. *Motivation Science,* 5(2), 93–105. https://doi.org/10.1037/mot0000127

Losch, S., Traut-Mattausch, E., Mühlberger, M. D., and Jonas, E. (2016). Comparing the effectiveness of individual coaching, self-coaching, and group training: How leadership makes the difference. *Frontiers in Psychology,* 7, 17. doi:http://dx.doi.org.myaccess.library.utoronto.ca/10.3389/fpsyg.2016.00629

Maylett, T. M. (2019). The journey from development to appraisal: 360 feedback at general mills. In A. H. Church, D. W. Bracken, J. H. Fleenor and D. S. Rose (eds), *The Handbook of Strategic 360 Feedback* (pp. 327–341, Chapter xiii, 562 Pages), Oxford University Press, New York, NY. doi:http://dx.doi.org.myaccess.library.utoronto.ca/10.1093/oso/9780190879860.003.0018 Retrieved from http://myaccess.library.utoronto.ca/login?qurl=https%3A%2F%2Fwww.proquest.com%2Fbooks%2Fjourney-development-appraisal-360-feedback-at%2Fdocview%2F2477701851%2Fse-2%3Faccountid%3D14771

McCarthy, G., and Milner, J. (2013). Managerial coaching: Challenges, opportunities and training. *Journal of Management Development,* 32(7), 768–779. doi:http://dx.doi.org.myaccess.library.utoronto.ca/10.1108/JMD-11-2011-0113

Milner, J., McCarthy, G., and Milner, T. (2018). Training for the coaching leader: How organizations can support managers. *Journal of Management Development,* 37(2), 188–200. doi:http://dx.doi.org.myaccess.library.utoronto.ca/10.1108/JMD-04-2017-0135

Ng, K. Y., Koh, C., Ang, S., Kennedy, J. C., and Chan, K. Y. (2011). Rating leniency and halo in multisource feedback ratings: Testing cultural assumptions of power distance and individualism-collectivism. *Journal of Applied Psychology,* 96, 1033–1044.

Oreopoulos, P., Petronijevic, U., Logel, C., and Beattie, G. (2020). Improving non-academic student outcomes using online and text-message coaching. *Journal of*

Economic Behavior & Organization, 171, 342–360. doi:http://dx.doi.org.myaccess.library.utoronto.ca/10.1016/j.jebo.2020.01.009

Organ, D. W. (2018). Organizational citizenship behavior: Recent trends and developments. *Annual Review of Organizational Psychology and Organizational Behavior,* 5, 295–306. doi:http://dx.doi.org.myaccess.library.utoronto.ca/10.1146/annurev-orgpsych-032117-104536

Pichler, S., Beenen, G., and Wood, S. (2020). Feedback frequency and appraisal reactions: A meta-analytic test of moderators. *The International Journal of Human Resource Management,* 31(17), 2238-2263. doi:http://dx.doi.org.myaccess.library.utoronto.ca/10.1080/09585192.2018.1443961

Reddin, W. J. (1971). *Effective Management by Objectives; The 3-D Method of MBO.* New York: McGraw-Hill.

Roch, S. G., Woehr, D. J., Mishra, V., and Kieszczynska, U. (2012). Rater training revisited: An updated meta-analytic review of frame-of-reference training. *Journal of Occupational and Organizational Psychology,* 85(2), 370–395. doi:http://dx.doi.org.myaccess.library.utoronto.ca/10.1111/j.2044-8325.2011.02045.x

Rotundo, M., and Sackett, P. R. (2002). The relative importance of task, citizenship, and counterproductive performance to global ratings of job performance: A policy-capturing approach. *Journal of Applied Psychology,* 87(1), 66–80. doi:http://dx.doi.org.myaccess.library.utoronto.ca/10.1037/0021-9010.87.1.66

Rotundo, M., Sackett, P. R., Enns, J. R., and Mann, S. (2012). Refocusing effort across job tasks: Implications for understanding temporal change in job performance. *Human Performance,* 25(3), 201–214. doi:http://dx.doi.org.myaccess.library.utoronto.ca/10.1080/08959285.2012.683905

Rotundo, M., and Spector, P. E. (2017). New perspectives on counterproductive work behavior including withdrawal. In J. L. Farr and N. T. Tippins (eds), *Handbook of Employee Selection* (2nd edition, pp. 476–508). New York, NY: Routledge, Taylor & Francis.

Sackett, P. R., Berry, C. M., Wiemann, S. A., and Laczo, R. M. (2006). Citizenship and counterproductive behavior: Clarifying relations between the two domains. *Human Performance,* 19(4), 441–464. doi:http://dx.doi.org.myaccess.library.utoronto.ca/10.1207/s15327043hup1904_7

Schleicher, D. J., Baumann, H. M., Sullivan, D. W., Levy, P. E., Hargrove, D. C., and Barros-Rivera, B. (2018). Putting the *system* into performance management systems: A review and agenda for performance management research. *Journal of Management,* 44(6), 2209–2245. doi:http://dx.doi.org.myaccess.library.utoronto.ca/10.1177/0149206318755303

Speer, A. B., Prewett, M. S., and Siver, S. R. (2020). Frequency and effects of performance appraisal training in applied settings. *International Journal of Selection and Assessment,* 28(2), 209–214. doi:http://dx.doi.org.myaccess.library.utoronto.ca/10.1111/ijsa.12286

Speer, A. B., Tenbrink, A. P., and Schwendeman, M. G. (2019). Let's talk it out: The Effects of calibration meetings on performance ratings. *Human Performance,* 32(3–4), 107–128. doi:10.1080/08959285.2019.1609477

Steelman, L. A., and Williams, J. R. (2019). Using science to improve feedback processes at work. In L. A. Steelman and J. R. Williams (eds), *Feedback at Work;*

Feedback at Work (pp. 1–7, Chapter xi, 288 Pages). Springer Nature Switzerland AG, Cham. doi:http://dx.doi.org.myaccess.library.utoronto.ca/10.1007/978-3-030-30915-2_1 Retrieved from http://myaccess.library.utoronto.ca/login?qurl=https%3A%2F%2Fwww.proquest.com%2Fbooks%2Fusing-science-improve-feedback-processes-at-work%2Fdocview%2F2555995599%2Fse-2%3Faccountid%3D14771

Steelman, L. A., and Wolfeld, L. (2018). The manager as coach: The role of feedback orientation. *Journal of Business and Psychology,* 33(1), 41–53. doi:http://dx.doi.org.myaccess.library.utoronto.ca/10.1007/s10869-016-9473-6

Tziner, A., Joanis, C., and Murphy, K. R. (2000). A comparison of three methods of performance appraisal with regard to goal properties, goal perception, and ratee satisfaction. *Group & Organization Management,* 25(2), 175–190.

Tziner, A., and Kopelman, R. E. (2002). Is there a preferred performance rating format?: A non-psychometric perspective. *Applied Psychology: An International Review,* 51(3), 479–503. doi:http://dx.doi.org.myaccess.library.utoronto.ca/10.1111/1464-0597.00104

Tziner, A., Kopelman, R. E., and Livneh, N. (1993). Effects of performance appraisal format on perceived goal characteristics, appraisal process satisfaction, and changes in rated job performance: A field experiment. *The Journal of Psychology: Interdisciplinary and Applied,* 127(3), 281–291. doi:http://dx.doi.org.myaccess.library.utoronto.ca/10.1080/00223980.1993.9915562

Vecchio, R. P., and Anderson, R. J. (2009). Agreement in self-other ratings of leader effectiveness: The role of demographics and personality. *International Journal of Selection and Assessment,* 17(2), 165–179.

Welsh, D., Bush, J., Thiel, C., and Bonner, J. (2019). Reconceptualizing goal setting's dark side: The ethical consequences of learning versus outcome goals. *Organizational Behavior and Human Decision Processes,* 150, 14–27. doi:http://dx.doi.org.myaccess.library.utoronto.ca/10.1016/j.obhdp.2018.11.001

Woehr, D. J. (1994). Understanding frame-of-reference training: The impact of training on the recall of performance information. *Journal of Applied Psychology,* 79(4), 525–534. https://doi.org/10.1037/0021-9010.79.4.525

Exercises

Conduct a Self-Appraisal or Group Appraisal

Use the suggestions outlined in this chapter to assess your performance or your group's performance since the last appraisal. Next, prepare a performance and development plan to cover the next performance period. Make note of the challenges that you encountered during this exercise and be prepared to discuss these challenges with classmates or workshop participants.

This exercise can be used to help individuals think more carefully about the work for which they are accountable, generate a discussion about the challenges associated with each step in the process, and emphasize the extent of preparation and information required to effectively utilize each tool.

Video Analysis and Discussion

Please watch the following video(s):

1. Don't bury the annual performance review: https://www.youtube.com/watch?v=-2Cn8LWLdak
2. Bad performance appraisal: https://www.youtube.com/watch?v=GVFB_MoHF54

Now form small groups to discuss the video(s) and answer the following questions:

1. What are the major points of the video?
2. How can you use information from the video in your career?
3. Based on the video, what advice do you have for leaders in organizations?

Be prepared to present the ideas from your small group discussion with the class as a whole.

Discussion Questions

1. Evaluate a performance appraisal process that you experienced personally at your current or former place of employment against the process steps outlined in this chapter including the time period in between the performance assessments.
2. As an employee, to receive a fair performance appraisal, what process steps mentioned in the chapter are most important to you and why?
3. As a leader, what three skills would you need to learn and practice to effectively administer a performance appraisal and coach employees?

11

Use Participation to Share Information and Distribute Knowledge

JOHN A. WAGNER III

Michigan State University

Participation is a process in which decision-making, problem-solving, action planning, or similar activities are shared and performed jointly by hierarchical superiors and their subordinates. To participate, superiors and subordinates work together to identify alternatives, consider preferences, and finalize judgments. Defined in this manner, participation differs from direction, in which superiors follow autocratic procedures and act alone (Wagner, 1982). Participation also differs from consultation, in which superiors ask subordinates for their inputs and opinions but then weigh alternatives and make a final choice on their own (Vroom and Yetton, 1973). Less obviously, perhaps, participation differs from delegation, in which superiors remove themselves and cede complete authority to their subordinates. Whereas participation requires that outcomes reflect needs and interests shared across hierarchical levels, delegation is more likely to allow subordinates the autonomy to act in accordance with personal interests (Leana, 1987).

Social theorists have long suggested that participation influences human behavior by (i) involving participants directly in ongoing processes, thereby securing their commitment to participatory outcomes through the "sense of ownership" stimulated by their personal involvement, or by (ii) providing participants the opportunity to exchange and collect information, and to become more fully informed and knowledgeable about ongoing activities and participatory results (Pateman, 1970). Organizational researchers have similarly speculated that participation might influence behavior in organizations through two distinct mechanisms, one termed *motivational* and the other *cognitive* (Bartlem and Locke, 1981; Locke and Schweiger, 1979; Miller and Monge, 1986; Schweiger and Leana, 1986; Wagner, Leana, Locke, and Schweiger 1997). Research on the two mechanisms sheds light on each mechanism's ability to predict and explain likely outcomes of participatory processes and, thus, holds important implications for the management of organizational behavior.

Participation Does Not Always Motivate, and the Lack of it Does Not Always Demotivate

The motivational mechanism is thought to affect behavior in organizations through the heightened sense of personal commitment to, or acceptance of, participatory outcomes that comes from having a say in participatory processes and a part in shaping the outcomes of those processes. According to this explanation, participation stimulates a sense of commitment that motivates participants to support and implement participatory resolutions. Behavior is motivated and satisfaction is experienced as participants strive to see their resolutions through to completion.

Research on the motivational mechanism extends back to a series of studies conducted, during the 1920s and 1930s, at Western Electric's Hawthorne Plant, located near Chicago, IL. In reviewing analyses of the effects of factors such as factory lighting, incentive payment, and supportive supervision on workforce satisfaction and performance, Hawthorne researchers noticed a pattern of results that seemed to indicate that workers were influenced by social conditions – specifically, by desires to satisfy needs for companionship and support at work – and that such conditions might have strong motivational effects. This led them to suggest that participatory involvement, in providing the opportunity to satisfy social needs, might motivate increased task performance and stimulate greater acceptance of organizational policies (Roethlisberger and Dickson, 1939).

Following up on this speculation, Coch and French (1948) performed a study of textile pieceworkers that appeared to indicate that workers would accept changes in job practices more readily if involved in the design and implementation of those practices. The authors identified participatory processes as effective in encouraging acceptance of and commitment to changed standards and procedures. They also characterized participation as a potentially powerful method of reducing personal frustration and aggression attributable to resistance to change.

Subsequent analyses of the motivational effects of participation focused increasing attention on *participation defined as a process of influence sharing* and on the heightened personal commitment thought to accompany the redistribution and equalizing of influence and authority in organizations. Theorists identified participatory processes as likely to have strong positive effects on workforce morale and satisfaction, feelings of involvement and commitment, and employee motivation and performance (e.g. Anderson, 1959; Dickson, 1981; McMahon, 1976; Patchen, 1964). Research first seemed to support this assertion (Fox, 1957; McCurdy and Eber, 1953; Pennington, Haravey, and Bass, 1958; Vroom, 1960), but as further evidence amassed, it became apparent that participation's motivational effects were neither as strong nor as generalizable as originally proposed. Some studies reported zero or near-zero relationships between participation and motivation, commitment, or performance (Alutto and Belasco, 1972; Castore and Murnighan, 1978; Ivancevich, 1977; Jenkins and Lawler, 1981; Rosenbaum and Rosenbaum, 1971), and others reported evidence of negative relationships between participation and the same outcome variables (Gibb, 1951; Green and Taber, 1980; Latham and Saari, 1979).

In the wake of these conflicting findings, Wagner and Gooding (1987) used a statistical technique called meta-analysis to aggregate the results of 70 published studies of participation, in order to estimate the strength of participation's general effects. After removing the effects of a troubling research artifact, percept-percept inflation (Crampton and Wagner, 1994), Wagner and Gooding discovered that participation correlated, on average, 0.11 with performance, 0.11 with satisfaction, and 0.10 with acceptance (i.e. commitment). Although a subsequent reanalysis of Wagner and Gooding's data appeared to contradict their findings (Erez, Bloom, and Wells, 1996), an additional analysis showed the contradictory interpretation to be invalid (Wagner and Lepine, 1999). Other studies have produced findings similar to and supportive of Wagner and Gooding's results (e.g. Locke, Feren, McCaleb, Shaw, and Denny, 1980; Wagner, 1994). After considering the available evidence, Locke, Alavi, and Wagner (1997) concluded that participation's likely correlations with performance and satisfaction are both on the order of 0.11. Changing levels of participation (i.e. from direction to participation), therefore, explain only about 1% of the concurrent change in performance or satisfaction. This conclusion offers little general support for the use of participation as a motivational technique in the workplace.

Moderators: When Is Participation Most Likely to Motivate?

Despite documenting participation's limitation, in general, as a motivational tool, Wagner and Gooding (1987) also discovered situational conditions under which participation might have more substantial effects. In particular, their analysis suggested that *participation is more likely to be related to employee satisfaction when participation takes place in smaller groups* – typically, groups of 12 or fewer members. Implied by this finding is the possibility that participants are unable to develop a sense of personal connection to or ownership of participatory outcomes in larger group settings, due perhaps to the fact that many people share in the creation of those outcomes, and thus, each participant fails to derive satisfaction from participatory processes or results. In small groups, however, participation and satisfaction are correlated at the level of 0.25 on average, indicating that about 6% of the change in satisfaction can be attributed to participation's effects. The size of this relationship suggests that group size is an important situational condition and that participation in small groups has limited, but nonetheless noteworthy, utility as a practical means of stimulating workplace satisfaction.

Wagner and Gooding (1987) also reported that *differences in task complexity have effects on the strength of relationships between participation and both satisfaction and acceptance.* In each relationship, the effect is stronger when tasks are less complex, meaning more behaviorally routine and less cognitively demanding. Suggested is the possibility that participation can be used to enrich – make more challenging – otherwise oversimplified work. Participation's relationship with satisfaction is again somewhat modest, with an average correlation of 0.26 revealed in the presence of simple tasks, but its relationship with acceptance is more substantial, as evidenced by an average correlation of 0.32 under simple task conditions. Indicated by the latter finding is a fairly strong enrichment effect, in which increasing participation by individuals who otherwise perform simple tasks explains just over 10% of the corresponding increase in acceptance of the results of participatory processes.

Primary Causal Mechanism: Participation Disseminates Information

In contrast to the motivational mechanism's definition of participation as a process of influence sharing, within the framework of the cognitive mechanism, the focus is on *participation defined as a process of information sharing.* From this perspective, participation's effects on organizational behavior are thought to be a function of the increased knowledge and deeper understanding afforded by participatory information sharing. Researchers have proposed that participatory information sharing might influence participant behaviors in several ways, for example: (i) knowing how to do a job increases the opportunity to do the job productively (Lawler and Hackman, 1969; Scheflen, Lawler, and Hackman, 1971); (ii) understanding how a job fits into the larger picture of work group interdependence and organizational mission enables effective adjustment to changing work conditions (Ledford and Lawler, 1994; Williams, 1982); (iii) sharing knowledge and insights encourages common understanding and greater cooperation (Dickson, 1981; Marrow and French, 1946); and (iv) being able to access and make use of the collective information of an organization's membership increases the likelihood of successful organizational innovation and creativity (Stewart, 1997; Tannenbaum, 1968).

Research on the cognitive mechanism has sought to determine whether participation does, in fact, promote information sharing, and whether such sharing can have beneficial consequences for the performance of individuals, groups, or organizations. In one study, Latham, Winters, and Locke (1994) allowed some subjects in a laboratory experiment to share and discuss strategies for attaining assigned goals on a class scheduling task, but prohibited other subjects from participating in similar discussions. Results of the experiment indicated that individuals who participated in strategy discussions formed better task strategies, felt more able to succeed in the task, and performed better on the task than did subjects barred from participation. Moreover, differences in strategy quality were found to explain much of the effect of participation on performance, indicating that participation improved performance by helping participants discover better performance strategies – a cognitive rather than motivational effect.

In another study, Scully, Kirkpatrick, and Locke (1995) manipulated the knowledge held by supervisors and subordinates in two-person laboratory groups. In one-third of the groups in the study, supervisors had the correct information needed to do their tasks, in one-third they had incorrect information, and in one-third they had no information whatsoever; subordinates were also split in thirds and assigned the same three levels of information, and half of the groups engaged in participatory information sharing while the other half did not. Results indicated that participation alone had no effect on subjects' performance, but that participation had beneficial effects on performance if the subordinate had the correct information and the supervisor had none. In addition, performance suffered if the supervisor lacked correct information or if either or both members of a pair had incorrect information.

In a third study, Quigley, Tesluk, Locke, and Bartol (2007) distributed knowledge differentially within dyads of laboratory partners, then examined motivational factors expected to influence the degree of knowledge sharing between partners and the effects of this sharing on partner performance. Among the results of this study is the finding that group-oriented incentives motivated sharing more than did individualized incentives, especially when norms between partners supported knowledge exchange, and that knowledge sharing enhanced partner performance, especially when high self-efficacy and trust in dyad partner led to the development of difficult self-set performance goals. These results suggest that participation might exert an indirect motivational effect by encouraging knowledge sharing within groups or teams. An effect of this sort differs from the direct motivational effects assessed in prior participation research and described earlier and appears worthy of further consideration.

In sum, these studies and others like them indicate that participatory processes can be used to share or redistribute information, and that such redistribution can have positive effects on performance when it provides otherwise uninformed individuals with ready access to requisite knowledge and insights (Bartlem and Locke, 1981; Bass, Valenzi, Farrow, and Solomon, 1975; Lowin, 1968; Tsai, 2001). Also highlighted are motivational boundary conditions that influence the strength and utility of these effects. Supported is the principle that participation will be beneficial when some individuals possess or can discover pertinent information and use participatory processes to disseminate it to others (Durham, Knight, and Locke, 1997).

Moderators: When Is Participation Most Able to Inform?

In addition to confirming participation's effectiveness in distributing information, Scully et al. (1995) also provided evidence of an important situational condition – information impactedness, or the degree to which information is *differentially* distributed among people – that appears able to determine whether participation will improve participant cognition and performance. Participation's effects appear stronger in instances where information is impacted, that is, in the possession of some but not all individuals, since participatory information exchange allows participants to break down information disparities and increase the extent to which knowledge is shared and generally accessible. Conversely, participation's effects are weaker when information is already available to all, since additional information sharing is unnecessary and consumes resources more profitably devoted to other activities (Bass and Valenzi, 1974; Latham and Yukl, 1975; Williams, 1982).

Beyond the effects of impactedness, speculation and the results of prior research suggest several additional situational conditions that might also affect the workings of the cognitive mechanism. One of these, *interdependence*, concerns the degree to which participants must work together to perform and succeed. Under conditions of low interdependence, individuals, groups, or organizations can perform successfully by working alone, while under conditions of high interdependence, individuals, groups, or organizations must work together to succeed. Differences in interdependence exert situational influence on participation's efficacy by affecting the amount of information required to coordinate ongoing relationships. While individuals performing independent tasks need not exchange much information to do their work, individuals performing interdependent tasks must share a great deal of information, including messages about what has been done, what must be done next, what adjustments need to be made in response to changing conditions, and so forth. To the extent that this information flow must be ongoing, that is, occurring as coordination problems emerge (as opposed to taking place on an occasional basis or through a supervisory intermediary), participatory "mutual adjustment" contributes to successful coordination and enhanced performance (Durham et al., 1997; Lawler, 1982; Sashkin, 1976).

Another situational condition, *complexity*, also appears likely to exert contingency effects on relationships between participation and performance. Complexity reflects the degree to which a task, objective, or situation is understandable, with low complexity referring to conditions that are simple and readily understood, and high complexity alluding to conditions that are complicated or intricate, therefore, difficult to interpret and comprehend. Successful performance in the presence of lower complexity is possible without additional information or insight. However, success under conditions of higher complexity requires access to the additional information needed to render the complex understandable. To the degree that participatory information exchange is able to provide such access, participation may produce little benefit when combined with low complexity but should provide appreciable benefit when paired with high complexity (e.g. Anderson, 1959; Singer, 1974). Note that this pattern is exactly opposite the configuration of effects revealed in research on the motivational mechanism, described earlier, wherein participatory enrichment improved performance on simple tasks.

Finally, the situational condition of change concerns *the extent to which tasks, group conditions, and organizational contexts are stable, consistent, and predictable*, under conditions of low change, versus dynamic, variable, and unpredictable, in situations of high change. In the presence of low change, success can be achieved by following familiar procedures, without modifying customary ways of doing things. In contrast, high amounts of change require that variability first be sensed, and that modifications then be made to existing plans and processes to match them to the demands of changing conditions. Such sensing and modification normally require information about the nature of change and the state of changed conditions. To the extent that such information is available to some but not necessary all participants, participation can facilitate information dissemination and lead to successful adaptation and continued productivity (e.g. Abdel-Halim, 1983; Jermier and Berkes, 1979; Koch and Fox, 1978; Schuler, 1976).

Implementation: Structuring Participation Can Make it More Effective

In thinking about participation, the first picture to come to mind is often that of a group of participants, seated casually around a table and engaged in spontaneous conversation. In fact, much research on participatory processes uses a physical arrangement that closely resembles this configuration. However, studies on group processes have indicated that grouping people together and asking them to suggest ideas and state opinions in front of others can stifle input into ongoing discussions. In particular, when personal statements are readily attributable to individual participants, ideas and opinions that might be considered even the least bit controversial may remain unstated (e.g. Diehl and Stroebe, 1987).

To deal with this problem, researchers have suggested structuring group discussion sessions so that innovation or judgment is done individually and discussion occurs only to clarify the interpretation of information and brainstorm additional alternatives. Using the *nominal group technique* (NGT), for instance, a group of individuals convenes around a table with a session coordinator and receives a description of the problem to be dealt with or issue to be addressed. Next, working alone, each participant writes down whatever ideas come to mind. The coordinator then asks each participant to share his or her ideas and writes them on a public display. Subsequently, participants discuss each other's ideas to clarify and expand on them and then evaluate them as a group. Finally, participants rank the ideas privately, and the idea that ranks the highest among the participants is chosen as the group's final recommendation (Moore, 1987).

As an alternative to using discussion structuring such as the NGT, Locke et al. (1997) suggested that emerging information technologies – specifically groupware technologies – might be used to improve the effectiveness of participatory information exchange. For example, an *electronic meeting support system* can be used in a room of participants to display each individual's comments – typed in on personal computer terminals – anonymously on a projected screen. This manner of computer-mediated communication reduces the reluctance that participants might have to present unfavorable information or state controversial opinions. As a result, more information and information of higher quality can be exchanged among participants, and participants report more satisfaction with participatory processes and outcomes (Alavi, 1993; Alavi and Palmer, 2000; see also Chapter 11, this volume).

In addition, *videoconferencing* can be used to bring together participants from several different sites. Although anonymity may be lost, participation is able to nullify some of the negative effects of physical separation and encourage information sharing across great distances. Asynchronous approaches can also be used to structure participatory information exchange without the requirement of simultaneous presence. For instance, website bulletin boards and chat rooms can be set up for groups of participants, allowing them to share information and disseminate knowledge without requiring that everyone be available at the same time. Corporate email systems can also be used to channel and catalog information exchanged among participants separated by both time and distance. Using such procedures, the prototypical face-to-face group is replaced by technological mediation (Locke et al., 1997).

Case Examples

1. Volvo

To illustrate some of the costs and benefits of encouraging participation in the workplace, consider the differing experiences of Volvo and Toyota. Well-known as a Swedish producer of cars, trucks, and marine engines, Volvo's automotive operations were hailed, during the 1970s and 1980s, as among the foremost examples of progressive industrial participation (e. g., Jenkins, 1976). Assembly employees often worked in groups as direct participants in personnel decision-making (what group members to hire, reward, or fire), job design procedures (how to accomplish the group's work, how to divide and assign this work as individualized tasks, and when to rotate among task assignments), and similar activities. Employees also elected worker representatives to serve on management committees charged with such tasks as ensuring workplace health and safety, establishing corporate environmental policies, overseeing training programs, and assessing proposed product innovations. In addition, an employee representative sat on Volvo's corporate board of directors. Finally, newer plants at sites, including Kalimar and Skovde, were designed and built to support team-based manufacturing and, at the same time, reduce hierarchical distinctions between managers and workers by placing open management offices on the shop floor, providing central cafeterias to be used by all employees, and creating "small workshop" areas wherein individual teams could produce complete subassemblies without substantial outside intervention.

By the mid-1970s, Volvo's labor costs had grown to become among the highest in the automotive industry (Gyllenhammar, 1977). Although some of this expense could be attributed to the cost of complying with Sweden's social welfare regulations then in effect, as much as a 15% falloff in productivity appeared due to the redirection of workforce energy away from shop floor production and toward participatory interaction (Swedish Employers' Confederation, 1975). As long as Volvo was able to command premium prices for its cars, due to the high perceived quality and durability of its products, the company was able to offset production costs and compete in the world marketplace. However, with the introduction of such Japanese lines as Lexus, Infiniti, and Acura, Volvo's position as a quality leader deteriorated and the company's ability to offset its high internal costs declined.

Initially, Volvo attempted to meet market challenges by implementing cost control measures that included shutting down most major operations at Kalimar, Skovde, and other newer plants, and cutting back on participatory programming in its older locations. By 1994, however, rumors within the automotive industry suggested that Volvo was seeking a friendly merger to stave off bankruptcy or dissolution (Taylor, 1994). After considering several possible partners, in early 1999 Volvo sold its automotive business to the Ford Motor Company. In 2008, after several failed attempts to cut costs and create profitable operations, Ford put Volvo up for sale with the hope of recouping enough money to offset the costs of a decade of inefficiency. Chinese manufacturer Geely Holding Group acquired Volvo in 2010 and continues as its owner.

2. Toyota

As Volvo's market position declined during the late 1970s and 1980s, the position of Toyota, another automotive manufacturer, improved dramatically. Toyota typifies the approach used in Japanese-based companies of that era to organize shop floor operations and structure managerial affairs. Its production facilities were set up as traditional assembly line operations, and written, standardized instructions regulated most production processes (Shingo, 1981). Centralized, directive, and sometimes secretive management practices controlled company operations (Sethi, Namiki, and Swanson, 1984). In contrast to Volvo's attempts to involve workers in all the phases of corporate management, Toyota's higher level managers reserved the prerogative to lead the company without significant input from below.

Within this general structure, however, such practices as Quality Circles and *ringi* decision-making introduced a degree of participation into the shop floor and lower managerial ranks. Quality Circles consist of groups of operative employees that meet with their immediate supervisors on a regular basis, typically every week or two, for an hour or two at a time to discuss problems with production scheduling, product quality, shop floor safety, and so forth. Circle participants work together to suggest solutions and improvements, which are then sent up the management hierarchy for further study and possible adoption (Ferris and Wagner, 1985). *Ringi* decision-making is a system in which proposed decisions are circulated among management subordinates and their hierarchical superiors for deliberation and approval. Often proposals are originated by senior managers and sent through the subordinate ranks for further refinement, although on occasion junior managers initiate the process with proposals of their own that are sent upward for approval (Cole, 1971).

In contrast to Volvo's experience, Toyota was able to control production costs and, at the same time, produce cars perceived by consumers to be of high quality and reasonable price. In an age of oil embargoes and environmental concerns, the company produced small, fuel-efficient cars that came to dominate the North American market. In the 1980s, Toyota introduced larger cars and, later, the Lexus line of luxury automobiles. The company also expanded its production facilities worldwide and branched into the Scion line of affordable small cars (discontinued in 2017 due to decreasing market interest). All the while, efforts to control costs and improve quality allowed Toyota to gain increasing market share at home and abroad. During the first quarter of 2008, Toyota's sales figures surpassed those of General Motors, up to that time the largest automotive company in the world. Based on 2020 sales, Toyota continued as the foremost auto producer, ahead of Volkswagen.

In comparing Volvo's situation with Toyota's, there are obvious differences in the scope of participation implemented in the two companies, since at Volvo participatory processes were central to corporate governance while, at Toyota, they played an ancillary role. This difference alone seems to explain Toyota's greater relative efficiency as a producer of automobiles, since the same kinds of resources that were consumed in participation at Volvo were expended in production at Toyota. Yet, beneath this conspicuous difference lies a deeper explanation, originating in differences in the primary reasons why participation was enacted within the two firms to begin with.

At Volvo, participation was seen mainly as a way of restoring the ability of otherwise routinized manufacturing tasks to satisfy human needs, encourage commitment to the company and its products, and motivate attendance and successful performance (Aguren, Bredbacka, Hansson, Ihregren, and Karllson, 1985; Nicol, 1975). The fact that participation could encourage information exchange was acknowledged by Volvo's management, but this exchange was thought to be valuable more for the commitment and motivation that would be aroused than for the increased understanding or cognitive gain that might also occur (Gyllenhammar, 1977). Volvo's approach was clearly designed to activate participation's motivational mechanism.

At Toyota, in contrast, participation was used to redistribute information that would otherwise remain buried on the shop floor or hidden among lower level managers (Dore, 1973). Motivation at Toyota, as in other large firms in Japan, was presumed by management to come from a combination of deference to authority and cultural collectivism that tied each employee's welfare to the well-being of the employer. Such "Japanese management" practices as lifetime employment and seniority-based pay were used to remind employees of the permanence of their relationship with their employer and of the importance of working hard to bring honor to their company and its management (Wagner, 1982). The primary aim of participation was consistent – and at Toyota remains consistent to the present day – with the cognitive mechanism's focus on information sharing and improved understanding.

As suggested by Toyota's experiences, participation can serve as an effective method of managing information and distributing knowledge. Although all of Toyota's achievements in the world marketplace cannot be attributed to the effects of participation alone, in facilitating the redistribution of information and sharing of knowledge among employees, participation has contributed significantly to the company's continuing success.

Conclusion

Studies of participation's motivational effects continue to report positive results (e.g. Behravesh, Abubkar, and Tanova, 2020; Saha and Kumar, 2017), but each such study is subject to the percept-percept artifact described previously, leading to doubts about claims of participation's motivational efficacy. More generalizable evidence, reviewed in this chapter, suggests that participation's usefulness as a motivational tool is often quite limited. Only in small groups or in combination with simple tasks is participation likely to have appreciable effects, and even then only on the outcomes of satisfaction or acceptance. Managers facing problems with workforce motivation are better advised to look for solutions in such practices as goal setting, job redesign, and incentive payment.

Although the collection of studies performed specifically to assess the cognitive mechanism is considerably smaller than the stream of research conducted on the motivational mechanism, a stronger case can be made for using participation to influence performance through its effects on the distribution of information among subordinates and their hierarchical superiors. Especially when information is unevenly distributed and the work being performed incorporates significant interdependence, complexity, or change, participation should yield substantial increases in participant knowledge and insight, which, in turn, should enhance performance and effectiveness in the workplace. Structuring participatory sessions specifically to encourage the exchange of information should have additional positive effects. Managers seeking ways to improve the distribution of information and knowledge are well advised to consider participatory processes.

References

Abdel-Halim, A. A. (1983). Effects of task and personality characteristics on subordinate responses to participative decision making. *Academy of Management Journal*, 26, 477–484.

Aguren, S., Bredbacka, C., Hansson, R., Ihregren, K., and Karlsson, K. G. (1985). *Volvo Kalimar Revisited: Ten Years of Experience.* Stockholm: Efficiency and Participation Development Council.

Alavi, M. (1993). An assessment of electronic meeting systems in a corporation setting. *Information and Management*, 25, 175–182.

Alavi, M., and Palmer, J. (2000). Use information technology as a catalyst for organizational change. In E. A. Locke (ed.), *The Blackwell Handbook of Principles of Organizational Behavior* (pp. 404–417). Oxford, UK: Blackwell Publishers Ltd.

Alutto, J. A., and Belasco, J. (1972). A typology for participation in organizational decision making. *Administrative Science Quarterly*, 17, 117–125.

Anderson, R. C. (1959). Learning in discussions: A resume of authoritarian-democratic studies. *Harvard Education Review*, 29, 210–215.

Bartlem, C. S., and Locke, E. A. (1981). The Coch and French study: A critique and reinterpretation. *Human Relations*, 34, 555–566.

Bass, B. M., and Valenzi, E. R. (1974). Contingent aspects of effective management styles. In J. G. Hunt and L. L. Larson (eds), *Contingency Approaches to Leadership* (pp. 75–123). Carbondale, IL: Southern Illinois University Press.

Bass, B. M., Valenzi, E. R., Farrow, D. L., and Solomon, R. J. (1975). Managerial styles associated with organizational, task, personal, and interpersonal contingencies. *Journal of Applied Psychology*, 66, 720–729.

Behravesh, E., Abubakar, A. M., and Tanova, C. (2020). Participation in decision-making and work outcomes: Evidence from a developing economy. *Employee Relations*, 43, 610–621.

Castore, C. H., and Murnighan, J. K. (1978). Determinants of support for group decision. *Organizational Behavior and Human Performance*, 22, 75–92.

Coch, L., and French, J. R. P., Jr. (1948). Overcoming resistance to change. *Human Relations*, 1, 512–532.

Cole, R. E. (1971). *Japanese blue collar.* Berkeley, CA: University of California Press.

Crampton, S. M., and Wagner, J. A. III (1994). Percept-percept inflation in microorganizational research: An investigation of prevalence and effect. *Journal of Applied Psychology*, 79, 67–76.

Dickson, J. W. (1981). Participation as a means of organizational control. *Journal of Management Studies*, 18, 159–176.

Diehl, M., and Stroebe, W. (1987). Productivity loss in brainstorming groups: Toward the solution of a riddle. *Journal of Personality and Social Psychology*, 53, 497–509.

Dore, R. (1973). *British Factory – Japanese Factory*. Berkeley, CA: University of California Press.

Durham, C. C., Knight, D, and Locke, E. A. (1997). Effects of leader role, team-set goal difficulty, efficacy, and tactics on team effectiveness. *Organizational Behavior and Human Decision Processes*, 72, 203–231.

Erez, A., Bloom, M. C., and Wells, M. T. (1996). Random rather than fixed effects models in meta-analysis: Implications for situational specificity and validity generalization. *Personnel Psychology*, 49, 275–306.

Ferris, G. R., and Wagner, J. A. III (1985). Quality circles in the United States: A conceptual reevaluation. *Journal of Applied Behavioral Science*, 21, 155–167.

Fox, W. M. (1957). Group reaction to two types of conference leadership. *Human Relations*, 10, 279–289.

Gibb, C. A. (1951). An experimental approach to the study of leadership. *Occupational Psychology*, 25, 233–248.

Green, S. G., and Taber, T. D. (1980). The effects of three social decision schemes on decision group processes. *Organizational Behavior and Human Performance*, 25, 97–106.

Gyllenhammar, P. G. (1977). *People at Work*. Reading, MA: Addison-Wesley.

Ivancevich, J. M. (1977). Different goal setting treatments and their effects on performance and job satisfaction. *Academy of Management Journal*, 20, 406–419.

Jenkins, D. (1976). *Job Power*. Garden City, NY: Doubleday.

Jenkins, G. D., and Lawler, E. E. III (1981). Impact of employee participation on pay plan development. *Organizational Behavior and Human Performance*, 28, 111–128.

Jermier, J. M., and Berkes, L. J. (1979). Leader behavior in a police command bureaucracy: A closer look at the quasi-military model. *Administrative Science Quarterly*, 24, 1–23.

Koch, J. L., and Fox, C. L. (1978). The industrial relations setting, organizational forces, and the form and content of worker participation. *Academy of Management Review*, 3, 572–583.

Latham, G. P., and Saari, L. M. (1979). Importance of supportive relationships in goal setting. *Journal of Applied Psychology*, 64, 151–156.

Latham, G. P., and Yukl, G. A. (1975). Assigned versus participative goal setting with educated and uneducated woods workers. *Journal of Applied Psychology*, 60, 299–302.

Latham, G. P., Winters, D., and Locke, E. A. (1994). Cognitive and motivational effects of participation: A mediator study. *Journal of Organizational Behavior*, 15, 49–63.

Lawler, E. E. III (1982). Increasing worker involvement to enhance organizational effectiveness. In P. S. Goodman (ed.), *Change in Organizations: New Perspectives on Theory, Research, and Practice* (pp. 33–70). San Francisco, CA: Jossey-Bass.

Lawler, E. E. III, and Hackman, J. R. (1969). Impact of employee participation in the development of pay incentive plans: A field experiment. *Journal of Applied Psychology*, 53, 467–471.

Leana, C. P. (1987). Power relinquishment versus power sharing: Theoretical clarification and empirical comparison of delegation and participation. *Journal of Applied Psychology*, 72, 228–233.

Ledford, G. E., Jr., and Lawler, E. E. III (1994). Research on employee participation: Beating a dead horse. *Academy of Management Review*, 19, 633–636.

Locke, E. A., Alavi, M., and Wagner, J. A. III (1997). Participation in decision making: An information exchange perspective. In G. R. Ferris (ed.), *Research in Personnel and Human Resources Management* (Vol. 15, pp. 293–331). Greenwich, CT: JAI Press.

Locke, E. A., Feren, D. B., McCaleb, V. M., Shaw, K. N., and Denny, A. T. (1980). The relative effectiveness of four methods of motivating employee performance. In K. D. Duncan, M. M. Gruneberg, and D. Wallis (eds), *Changes in Working Life* (pp. 363–388). London, UK: John Wiley & Sons.

Locke, E. A. and Schweiger, D. M. (1979). Participation in decision making: One more look. In B. M. Staw (ed.), *New Directions in Organizational Behavior* (Vol. 1, pp. 265–339). Greenwich, CT: JAI Press Inc.

Lowin, A. (1968). Participative decision making: A model, literature critique, and prescription for research. *Organizational Behavior and Human Performance*, 3, 68–106.

Marrow, A. J., and French, J. R. P., Jr. (1946). A case of employee participation in a nonunion shop. *Journal of Social Issues*, 2, 29–34.

McCurdy, H. G., and Eber, H. W. (1953). Democratic vs. authoritarian: A further investigation of group problem-solving. *Journal of Personality*, 22, 258–269.

McMahon, J. T. (1976). Participative and power-equalized organizational systems: An empirical investigation and theoretical integration. *Human Relations*, 29, 203–214.

Miller, K. I., and Monge, P. R. (1986). Participation, satisfaction, and productivity: A meta-analytic review. *Academy of Management Journal*, 29, 727–753.

Moore, C. M. (1987). *Group Techniques for Idea Building*. Beverly Hills, CA: Sage.

Nicol, G. (1975). *Volvo*. London, UK: William Luscombe Publisher Limited.

Patchen, M. (1964). Participation in decision making and motivation: What is the relation? *Personnel Administrator*, 27, 24–31.

Pateman, C. (1970). *Participation and Democratic Theory*. London, UK: Cambridge University Press.

Pennington, D. F., Haravey, F., and Bass, B. M. (1958). Some effects of decision and discussion on coalescence, change, and effectiveness. *Journal of Applied Psychology*, 42, 404–408.

Quigley, N. R., Tesluk, P. E., Locke, E. A., and Bartol, K. M. (2007). A multilevel investigation of the motivational mechanisms underlying knowledge sharing and performance. *Organization Science*, 18, 71–88.

Roethlisberger, F. J., and Dickson, W. J. (1939). *Management and Morale*. Cambridge, MA: Harvard University Press.

Rosenbaum, L. L., and Rosenbaum, W. (1971). Morale and productivity consequences of group leadership style, stress, and type of task. *Journal of Applied Psychology*, 55, 343–348.

Saha, S, and Kumar, S. P. (2017). Influence of participation in decision making on job satisfaction, group learning, and group commitment: Empirical study of public sector undertakings in India. *Asian Academy of Management Journal*, 22, 79–101.

Sashkin, M. (1976). Changing toward participative management approaches: A model and methods. *Academy of Management Review*, 1, 75–86.

Scheflen, K. C., Lawler, E. E. III, and Hackman, J. R. (1971). Long-term impact of employee participation in the development of pay incentive plans: A field experiment revisited. *Journal of Applied Psychology*, 55, 182–186.

Schuler, R. S. (1976). Participation with supervisor and subordinate authoritarianism: A path-goal theory reconciliation. *Administrative Science Quarterly*, 21, 320–325.

Schweiger, D. M., and Leana, C. R. (1986). Participation in decision making. In E. A. Locke (ed.), *Generalizing from Laboratory to Field Settings* (pp. 147–166). Lexington, MA: Lexington Books.

Scully, J. A., Kirkpatrick, S. A., and Locke, E. A. (1995). Locus of knowledge as a determinant of the effects of participation on performance, affect, and perceptions. *Organizational Behavior and Human Decision Processes*, 61, 276–288.

Sethi, S. P., Namiki, N., and Swanson, C. L. (1984). *The False Promise of the Japanese Miracle*. Marshfield, MA: Pitman.

Singer, J. N. (1974). Participative decision making about work: An overdue look at variables which mediate its effects. *Sociology of Work and Occupations*, 1, 347–371.

Singo, S. (1981). Study of the Toyota production systems. Tokyo: Japan Management Association.

Stewart, T. A. (1997). *Intellectual Capital: The New Wealth of Organizations*. New York: Currency Doubleday.

Swedish Employers' Confederation (1975). *Job Reform in Sweden*. Stockholm: Swedish Employers' Confederation.

Tannenbaum, A. S. (1968). *Control in Organizations*. New York: McGraw Hill.

Tsai, W. (2001). Knowledge transfer in intraorganizational networks: Effects of network position and absorptive capacity on business unit innovation and performance. *Academy of Management Journal*, 44, 996–1004.

Taylor, A. III (1994). New ideas from Europe's automakers: Managing the crisis at Volvo. *Fortune*, December 12, 168.

Vroom, V. H. (1960). *Some Personality Determinants of the Effects of Participation*. Englewood Cliffs, NJ: Prentice Hall.

Vroom, V. H., and Yetton, P. W. (1973). *Leadership and Decision-Making*. Pittsburgh, PA: University of Pittsburgh Press.

Wagner, J. A. III (1982). Individualism, collectivism, and the control of organization. Unpublished dissertation, University of Illinois, Department of Business Administration, Urbana-Champaign IL.

Wagner, J. A. III (1994). Participation's effects on performance and satisfaction: A reconsideration of research evidence. *Academy of Management Review*, 19, 312–330.

Wagner, J. A. III, and Gooding, R. Z. (1987). Shared influence and organizational behavior: A meta-analysis of situational variables expected to moderate participation-outcome relationships. *Academy of Management Journal*, 30, 524–541.

Wagner, J. A. III, Leana, C. R., Locke, E. A., and Schweiger, D. A. (1997). Cognitive and motivational frameworks in research on participation: A meta-analysis of effects. *Journal of Organizational Behavior*, 18, 49–65.

Wagner, J. A. III, and LePine, J. A. (1999). Participation's effects on performance and satisfaction: Additional evidence from U.S. research. *Psychological Reports*, 84, 719–725.

Williams, T. A. (1982). A participative design for dispersed employees in turbulent environments. *Human Relations*, 35, 1043–1058.

Exercises

1. Demonstrating the effectiveness of participation as a method of sharing information

Materials: Index cards and pen or pencil.

Preparation: Form teams of six members and select one member to serve as leader. For each team, prepare a deck of eight cards as follows:

Facts [each one on a card with the card number (1, 2, 3, 4, 5, 6, 7, or 8) on the back]:

1. Provider B offers low prices with proven technology but never finishes a job on time or without errors.
2. Provider C does very good work with proven technology but is typically quite expensive.
3. Provider D is going to offer new yet inexpensive technology in its bid. Only two other companies have used it but have no complaints. The system worked and was on time.
4. Provider E has never been late on a project and its prices are reasonable but almost always its systems take two weeks to work seamlessly.
5. Company A headquarters is adamant about the project being completed on time and that it work perfectly within two days.
6. The company (A) has been barely profitable in the last two years and headquarters is very cost conscious.
7. Blank.
8. Blank.

Procedure: The team of one leader plus five members work for company A. Company A headquarters wants to install a new telephone system and has delegated the project to the team. The team is looking at bids from competing companies (B, C, D, and E) for the telephone system. Each team member and the leader have spent several months doing research related to the decision (different people have worked on different things). The project leader makes the final decision. Complete each of the following three trials.

Trial 1

The leader gets cards 1, 2, and 5. Team members get 3, 4, and 6–8. The leader makes the decision without talking to the members. The decision is recorded without further discussion.

Trial 2

Distribute the cards as in Trial 1. The leader can talk to *one* member about what is on the member's card. A blank card allows another choice. The leader then makes the decision. The decision is recorded without further discussion.

Trial 3 (Suggested time for this part: about 10 minutes)

Cards 1–6 are randomly distributed, one per person (Cards 7 and 8 are not used in this trial). There is full discussion, allowing all members (including the leader) to report the contents of their cards and fully argue their views. Then, the leader makes the final decision. The decision is recorded.

Questions for discussion:

1. Which trial yielded the best decision? Why?
2. What happens when leaders do not seek information from followers, as in Trial 1? Knowing this, why do you think that leaders often not seek information from their followers?
3. Why do subordinates sometimes choose to not speak up even when they have relevant information?
4. In light of what you have learned in this exercise, what can be done in organizations to ensure the distribution of knowledge and information?

[Teaching note: The best choice is Provider D. B is too unreliable. C is too expensive. E is almost never on time. By design, Trial 3 is supposed to yield the correct decision without fail.]

2. Choosing the most appropriate process

Form groups of four to six members and talk about the following in small-group discussions and then report the results of these discussions back to the entire class in a large-group discussion:

1. Thinking about where you work, describe an instance in which top-down processes were used to make a major decision. How quickly was the decision made? Was it the right decision? How well was the decision accepted by those individuals it affected?
2. Next, describe an instance in which participatory processes were used to make a major decision. How quickly was the decision made? Was it the right decision? How well was the decision accepted by those individuals it affected?

3. Finally, describe an instance where delegation was used to make a major decision. How quickly was the decision made? Was it the right decision? How well was the decision accepted by those individuals it affected?
4. Based on your answers to Questions 1–3, when are each of the three decision-making processes – top-down, participatory, and delegation – likely to be most effective? When will each be least effective? What do your answers have to say about the strengths and limitations of participation as a decision-making process?

3. Video analysis and discussion

Please watch the following video(s):

1. The emerging work world in the participation age: https://www.youtube.com/watch?v=ewA2BqbWhUQ
2. Frientorsip: The Solution to Employee Engagement: https://www.youtube.com/watch?v=IBHjUVFhFjA

Now form small groups to discuss the video(s) and answer the following questions:

1. What are the major points of the video?
2. How can you use information from the video in your career?
3. Based on the video, what advice do you have for leaders in organizations?

Be prepared to present the ideas from your small-group discussion with the class as a whole.

Discussion Questions

1. Explain how information sharing can increase the performance of individuals and groups in organizations. Would participation be an effective way to improve performance in situations where everyone is already fully informed? Why or why not? Would participation have a large effect in situations where work is simple and jobs are independent? Why or why not?
2. If you were a consultant advising a client to use participation to disseminate information, what would you say to the client to encourage adoption of participatory processes?
3. Teams, or groups of highly interdependent members, are often formed to accomplish complex tasks beyond the abilities of individuals working alone. If you were the manager of a team, what would you do to encourage its members to keep one another fully informed?

12

Recognizing Employees

Jean M. Phillips, Kathryn E. Dlugos, Hee Man Park, Kameron M. Carter, and Dorothea Roumpi

School of Labor and Employment Relations, Penn State University

Employee recognition is the explicit acknowledgment and praise of employee behavior, outcome, or achievement that appreciates, rewards, and motivates them. Providing recognition to employees outside of the employer's financial compensation system for exceptional performance, for demonstrating behaviors consistent with organizational culture and values, or for making sustained contributions to their workgroups or to the employer can enhance motivation and engagement. Although competitive pay and bonuses are important motivators, recognition, in its many forms, is another essential motivator desired by employees. Recognition from the employer, supervisor, peers, and even customers can improve customer service, profits, and employee retention (Peterson and Luthans, 2006). Effective recognition programs help to not only increase employee satisfaction and retention, but also improve organizational productivity and performance (Appelbaum and Kamal, 2000). Thus, recognition programs are of strategic importance for organizations and are often viewed as one of the core elements of a high-performance work system (Chuang and Liao, 2010). As one expert explains, "Recognition is often invisible in nature and yet priceless in value. You can give recognition without giving a reward. You should never give a reward without giving recognition" (Saunderson, 2013). Recognition has long been identified as a precursor of motivation (Dutton, 1998, Saunderson, 2004) and self-identity, as well as an important element of meaningful work (MOW, 1987). The absence of recognition is a known workplace risk factor for turnover (Waters, Bortree, and Tindall, 2013) and psychological distress (Kaushal, 2020).

Rewards, one of the manifestations of recognition, can be monetary or nonmonetary. Monetary rewards are a type of compensation that influence extrinsic motivation (Porter and Lawler, 1968) or the external rewards received from doing the job. Nonmonetary rewards, on the other hand, are a type of recognition that enhances intrinsic motivation (Porter and Lawler, 1968) by increasing a job's internal rewards including pride, fulfilling a purpose, and feeling appreciated. Although feedback and monetary rewards are also important to intrinsic motivation, the focus of this chapter is on nonmonetary recognition.

Employee recognition can occur through formal programs created and run by the employer, such as employee of the month programs, or can occur informally such as when coworkers or customers spontaneously express appreciation for a job well done. Informal recognition occurs when informal acknowledgment or appreciation is given to an employee, such as a supervisor's praise for going the extra mile with a customer or a coworker's genuine thanks for assistance with a task. Effective recognition can reinforce an employer's culture and values and enhance the alignment between organizational and individual performance goals. For example, if an organization valuing collaboration creates a teamwork award, this signals to employees that collaboration is not only important but valued and appreciated.

Done well, employee recognition programs can reinforce employee performance, align employee behaviors with organizational culture and values, improve employee motivation and retention, and increase organizational performance (Stajkovic and Luthans, 1997, 2001, 2003). Research notes that recognition granted in the form of awards that are more public is also likely to strengthen the loyalty relationship between organizations and employees; supervisors granting such recognition signal their desire for a relational bond with the employee, and employees accepting recognition indicate their approval and internalization of the company's goals (Gallus and Frey, 2016). When created and implemented poorly, however, employee recognition programs can have the opposite effect. Because recognition may lead to favorable performance evaluations and promotions, if it is misused, it can negatively influence an employer's internal labor market and the quality of its talent pipeline to leadership positions. When creating and managing employee recognition programs, it is important to start with an understanding of why recognition is effective or ineffective, what should be recognized, and the roles the organization, supervisors, coworkers, and even nonorganizational stakeholders play in this process.

Why Recognition Works

The fundamental reason that recognition works is that even without a financial component (although monetary rewards further strengthen its benefits; Stajkovic and Luthans, 2003), appreciation is an intrinsically motivating reinforcer that makes the receiver more likely to continue the recognized behavior. For example, if an employee does something well and is recognized for it formally or informally, they likely feel positively about what they did and are likely to repeat it due to the reinforcement. Recognition is also a social reinforcer because it confirms that the recipient's work is valued by others. A field experiment on gratitude found that managers' simple expression of gratitude increased the number of calls made by university fundraisers due to enhanced social worth (Grant and Gino, 2010). Receiving recognition also tends to reduce individuals' tendency to engage in such counterproductive behaviors as denigration because recognition increases perceived social worth (Cho and Fast, 2012). Social recognition can be verbal or nonverbal – even a smile of thanks from a customer or coworker can feel good and reinforces the employee's behavior and effort. Reinforcement is also consistent with social cognitive theory (Bandura, 1986), which focuses on the interaction between external factors including rewards and punishments and internal factors including attention and motivation.

Recognition also works through reciprocity. The reciprocity norm is the social norm that when someone does something for you, it creates an obligation to return the favor. Essentially, people tend to give back after they have been given to. This ethic of reciprocity is present in all cultures and religions (Deckop, Cirka, and Andersson, 2003). Employees who feel valued reciprocate with positive work behaviors including helping others or going beyond job requirements in fulfilling one's role. Research has found that employees are more likely to help colleagues after receiving help themselves (Deckop et al., 2003). When an employer, boss, colleague, or customer positively recognizes an employee, the employee instinctively wants to reciprocate in some way. Because recognition fulfills our psychological needs for respect, appreciation, and competence and is positively received, employee engagement and motivation increase due to the employees' desire to reciprocate the positive treatment.

The most effective employee recognition programs appreciate and recognize employees in ways that are meaningful to them. Some employees, including those higher in extroversion, might be very proud of being featured on a wall plaque recognizing them as a customer service leader. Others might be even more proud of their colleagues nominating them for a teamwork award. Few employees would be motivated by cheap watches or poor-quality award plaques. Because employees with families are also rewarded by the positive reaction and pride of their families when they are positively recognized at work, involving the recipient's family in an appreciation or recognition event can further enhance its motivational effect.

What and Who Should Be Recognized

As summarized in Figure 12.1, the process of recognition begins with identifying what warrants recognition, deciding how the recognition should occur, identifying when the targeted behaviors take place, providing the recognition, measuring the effectiveness of the recognition, and monitoring the recognition system as needed to accomplish the goals identified in the first step. Recognition should be strategically used to appreciate and reinforce desired employee behaviors. Exceptional performance is an obvious choice for recognition, and exemplary performance is often best identified by the recipient's coworkers or supervisor, or even by customers and communicated via customer service surveys. Engaging in behaviors reflective of important organizational values can also be recognized and reinforced, as well as behaviors reflecting important aspects of the organizational culture. For example, a company valuing integrity and ethical behavior might have a peer-nominated ethics award. Peers are often in the best position to observe many coworker behaviors and to recognize when someone has gone the extra mile for a coworker or customer or

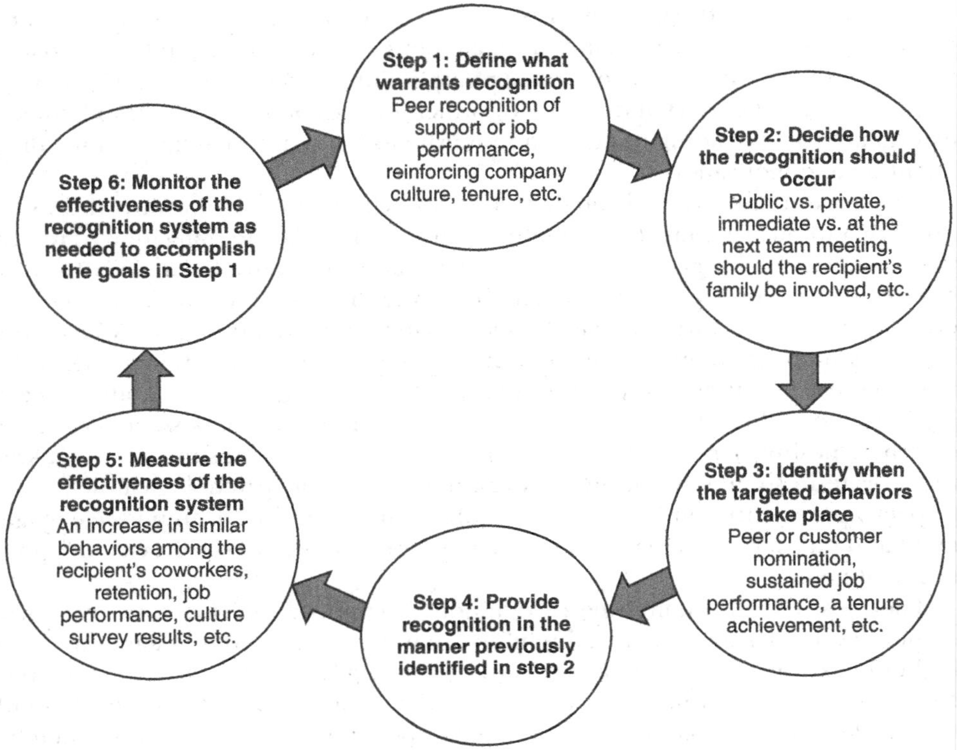

FIGURE 12.1 The recognition process

consistently displayed behaviors consistent with the organization's values and culture. Many organizations also recognize sustained employee contributions to their workgroup or to the organization with length of service or sustained contribution awards. This is particularly strategic for employers desiring long employee tenures as it signals to all employees that the organization appreciates and values long-term employee contributions. Acknowledging and appreciating employees who stay with the organization for a period of time can improve retention and strengthen the employer's internal talent pipeline.

It is important to note that recognized behaviors differ across jobs and across organizations, and what an employer or supervisor decides to recognize can vary both within and across organizations. Supervisors have teams with different dynamics and needs. For example, some younger teams might benefit from a teamwork award, whereas older, high-performing teams might find this awkward. Supervisors can strategically use recognition by identifying subordinates who most need it. Employees' needs for recognition also vary on a daily basis (Tepper, Dimotakis, Lambert, Koopman, Matta, Man Park, and Goo, 2018). Informal recognition programs under the discretion of supervisors and not managed by the human resource management department or company leaders enables lower-level leaders to implement the best recognition programs for their needs.

Recognition can occur at the individual, team, or even business unit level, and the choice should match the organization's goals and the degree to which individual or team behaviors are relevant. Singling out a single member of an interdependent team that just landed a big contract after considerable creativity and effort would likely undermine the performance of the other team members if they had contributed similarly to the accomplishment. If one or two team members were disproportionately responsible for a team's achievement, however, then recognizing at the team level is likely to foster resentment and frustration. If there is already a clear outperformer, a recognition program is also unlikely to motivate anyone including the top performer to improve their performance as the outcome seems predetermined. Furthermore, switching from individual-based recognition to cooperative team-based recognition might have initial negative consequences of poor information sharing and lowered team performance (Johnson, Hollenbeck, Humphrey, Ilgen, Jundt, and Meyer, 2006). In addition, if an employee feels they did not receive equitable recognition compared to their peers, their motivation and performance might decrease. It is important to always monitor for unintended consequences of a recognition program as even purely symbolic awards have been found to create motivations to game the award and decrease employees' attention to and performance on other important tasks (Gubler, Larkin, and Pierce, 2016).

What should be recognized also differs depending on whether the recognition program is formal or informal. Formal programs have clear objectives and rules that allow participating employees to understand what they must do and how they must do it to earn the recognition (e.g. a safety streak or total sales value recognition award). The goals of a formal recognition program and what can be measured to evaluate progress toward these goals drive what is recognized. If an employer wants to reward quality customer service, then a certain number of positive customer feedback surveys might trigger a verbal commendation. If retention is the goal, then recognition and appreciation are given after certain periods of service. If behaviors and performance cannot be identified or measured, it is difficult to incorporate them in a formal recognition program. Research also suggests that recognition works best when provided somewhat exclusively to several top performers rather than solely to the top performer or to all eligible employees (Bradler, Dur, Neckermann, and Non, 2016). Unintended consequences of the recognition should always be considered. For example, employee of the month programs might lower the morale of other high-performing employees who were not selected, and programs that create competition among coworkers for the desired recognition can undermine teamwork and morale. Safety streak recognition programs might motivate employees to not report accidents or injuries, which is inconsistent with the employer's safety goals and could violate Occupational Safety and Health Administration (OSHA) regulations.

Informal recognition can be given at regular intervals or spontaneously at the discretion of supervisors, coworkers, and customers. Informal recognition should happen as soon as possible when it is warranted, even for relatively small behaviors. Being recognized a year after a behavior or milestone occurs is not as impactful as receiving it soon after the contribution is made. More immediate and consistent gestures help to reinforce a positive work environment and show employees that what they do is appreciated and valued. Giving employees thank you cards, buttons, or something else to give to coworkers to show appreciation is an example of informal recognition. Supervisors can also choose to frequently acknowledge the contributions and performance of subordinates and thank them publicly or privately. By publicly showing appreciation, supervisors can signal which behaviors or accomplishments are aligned to organizational goals and strategy. Supervisors may also take advantage of such public recognition for enhancing team learning by encouraging the recognized employees to share how they accomplished goals. Informal recognition tends to be more effective when it is easier to observe and identify coworker behaviors and performance. Because it is harder to identify critical performance-related behaviors in service organizations, for example, the effect of informal recognition programs is higher in manufacturing than in service organizations (Stajkovic and Luthans, 1997).

It is important to note that informal recognition has different appropriateness in different cultures. Cultural differences, including power distance and collectivism, influence the appropriateness of employee recognition. For example, one culturally sensitive supervisor effectively used different recognition systems for different locations. Public recognition for high performance was given to Greeks and Italians, but Germans and Scandinavians received a formal email rather than public recognition. Furthermore, public recognition for individual accomplishment may not be effective and could even create some discomfort in highly collectivistic cultures. Because collectivists prioritize the performance of collective units (e.g. the team or organization) over individual performance, receiving individual recognition in a public setting may undermine in-group harmony. In addition, national culture should inform the choice between monetary and nonmonetary recognition. In collectivist cultures and cultures characterized by high power distance, nonmonetary recognition is considered more appropriate (Mendonca and Kanungo, 1990). Organizations should be sensitive to the culture-based preferences of their employees around the world when designing recognition programs, and managers may need to be flexible as to how they recognize employees with different cultural backgrounds in a single location. The national culture context influences also what should be recognized. In more feminine cultures, for instance, there is more emphasis on recognizing work-related factors such as building strong interpersonal relationships, whereas more masculine cultures are more focused on recognizing more output-based performance outcomes (Newman and Nollen, 1996; Sparrow and Wu, 1998).

In addition to recognizing job-related behaviors, recognition programs can also reinforce corporate culture and values. For example, Disney has created a variety of recognition programs that continually let the Cast Members that influence Guest experiences at their parks and resorts know how valued and appreciated they are. Disney even encourages Guests to compliment deserving Cast Members on social media, at Guest Relations, or by phone (Muscaro, 2020).

It is important to try to recognize all employees who meet the recognition criteria, if there is no need to restrict an award to just one person, do not restrict it. Leaving a deserving employee out of a recognition event is likely to undermine their motivation and even prompt them to leave. Similarly, be as sure as possible that an employee is deserving of recognition before giving it. Recognizing an undeserving employee is also undermining to motivation. In addition, if it is impossible to establish objective criteria likely to be accepted by all eligible employees, it may be best not to create a recognition program for that behavior or performance.

How Recognition Should Occur

One of the most important things to remember about recognizing employees is that they should be recognized in ways that are meaningful to them. Insincere praise or appreciation not linked to the performance of a positive behavior, such as a supervisor telling a team "good job" after a typical meeting, is not as motivational as praise for a specific behavior or accomplishment. To maximize the alignment of the employer's reinforcement goals with employees' needs and values, company leaders should clarify the organizational goals that are to be reinforced and then involve employees from all organizational levels in identifying what they want to be recognized for and how. Leader support and involvement in recognition programs is critical to employees' perceptions of the sincerity and authenticity of the acknowledgment. Incorporating both daily or weekly informal and longer-term formal recognition programs can help employees view the formal recognition programs as sincere rather than as a form of manipulation. Providing informal recognition to employees who experience high challenge stressors such as time pressure and a heavy workload as well as uncertainty in their work can be particularly effective because those subordinates are more likely to seek positive input such as intellectual inspiration and respect for their personal feelings from their leaders (Tepper et al., 2018). Occasionally or regularly starting or ending meetings with a recognition of recent individual or team behaviors or performance can boost employee motivation. The scarcity of a type of recognition or award also matters. If an award is seen as too commonly awarded or insignificant by employees, it could undermine their motivation and even become something employees would rather not receive because it is meaningless to them. In essence, managing the timing and the frequency of recognition is an important task for effective managers.

It is also important that recognition be given by the people most impacted by and aware of the behavior being recognized. A sincere smile and "thank you" from a customer, supervisor, or coworker after an employee goes above and beyond the call of duty or performs their job extremely well can be incredibly meaningful. Internal customers such as other departments or groups in the organization that are affected by the employee or team being recognized can also acknowledge a job well done. Supervisor recognition of employees' performance and contributions communicates their knowledge of what employees are doing as well as their appreciation for a job well done. Supervisors are important providers of recognition as it is their job to evaluate and motivate their subordinates. Like all recognition messages, supervisors' recognition should be clear and consistent. For example, supervisors, who understand the role of each employee's work in a larger organizational context, can recognize subordinates' accomplishments by specifically explaining how their work contributes to organizational success. All managers should simultaneously engage

Table 12.1 Creative types of recognition

Entries into a raffle for prizes such as a day off or a free lunch
A small but meaningful item such as a stuffed company mascot that is visible in the employee's workspace; it could rotate to different employees being recognized for anything from peer appreciation to reinforcing a company value
A catered or potluck lunch to recognize a team
To promote peer recognition, enter the name of every referring employee into a drawing for a small prize to encourage employees to recognize deserving coworkers
Company branded clothing or merchandise
A shout-out on the organization's social media page
Celebrate Employee Appreciation Week
Make a donation to the recipient's favorite charity in their name

in goal-based recognition as a part of formal recognition programs to send a strong message about what the employer values and how it appreciates the efforts and talents of its employees. This might require training supervisors in how to effectively recognize employees and how to do so without bias in addition to effective communication skills. Table 12.1 highlights some creative types of recognition.

Again, it is important to monitor recognition programs to identify and prevent unintended consequences and ensure that it is being implemented as the organization intends. Some supervisors might manipulate recognition programs to perpetuate abuse toward some subordinates or think they are too busy to recognize others. For example, a supervisor might give an award to a favorite employee rather than to the most deserving subordinate, or "punish" a deserving but unliked employee by not nominating them for a formal recognition program. This behavior is a form of abusive supervision and should be looked out for to avoid demotivating valued employees. Organizations may discourage such unfortunate situations of supervisors not recognizing deserving employees by providing training or a brief intervention. For example, research shows that supervisor support training (e.g. training focusing on benevolence, sincerity, and fairness) can significantly reduce abusive supervision (e.g. nonrecognition of good work or taking credit for subordinates' work) in the long term (Gonzalez-Morales, Kernan, Becker, and Eisenberger, 2018).

Choosing between public and private recognition is important. Public recognition is visible to the recipient's coworkers, the entire company, and even the public if done through a company-wide communication or social media. Private recognition is a more personal message from the sender to the recipient, such as in a text, email, or private conversation. If there is a chance the recipient would prefer that the recognition be kept private, even if they are proud and excited about the acknowledgment, private recognition is best. If the accomplishment being recognized reinforces the employer's core goals or values or is related to organizational performance, this information might be even more impactful if shared with the company and even the public. In addition to signaling to employees across the organization that a particular accomplishment is valued in light of company goals, public recognition might serve to reduce gender disparities within companies. Indeed, recent experimental research exploring the effect of a recognition intervention has explored this possibility, while both private and public recognition enhanced the likelihood that both men and women working in Science, Technology, Engineering and Math (STEM) fields will contribute their ideas, public recognition boosted women's confidence in their work and helped close the "gap" in contributions between genders (Gallus and Heikensten, 2020).

Including employees' families in recognition events can also enhance their effectiveness. The families of high-performing employees are often aware of the hard work and trade-offs a recognized employee makes in balancing their work and home lives. Including employees' families in recognition can take several forms. It can be as simple as sending an email/letter/flowers to the employees' partner or parents and letting them know that the organization recognizes the employee's high performance and contribution as well as the importance of the support this employee has received from their family environment. Another form of involving employees' families can be letting families attend and even be involved in and acknowledged during recognition ceremonies, which can reinforce the employer's appreciation and further strengthen the employees' pride and the reinforcement of the recognition.

At What Level Should the Recognition Happen

Formal and informal recognition programs can be created at the organizational, supervisor, coworker, or customer level. Different types of recognition and appreciation are most relevant and effective at each level.

Organizational level recognition: At the organizational level, recognition can be given in a variety of ways. The methods chosen to acknowledge individuals, teams, and business units should be consistent with the employer's culture and values as well as employee preferences. Employee surveys, exit interviews, and anonymous feedback on recognition system satisfaction especially during pilot and early roll-out stages can increase the appeal of a formal recognition program to the employees it is intending to motivate.

Supervisor recognition: Supervisors are often in the best position to know what needs improvement in their specific workgroup. Teamwork and helping behaviors in addition to other team-level behaviors that enhance team performance and reinforce the organization's culture are often effectively acknowledged by the supervisor, whose role is to enhance team effectiveness.

In addition, some leaders try not to let subordinates look better than them, undermining the goals of formal recognition programs. Denied or unsupported recognition requests can undermine the goals of an organization's formal recognition program.

Coworker recognition: Peer recognition and appreciation is best used for behaviors and accomplishments that the supervisor is not able to observe as readily but has identified as important for the team. Appreciation notes, peer awards, and other types of recognition are often very well received by employees, as peers who work closely with a deserving employee are most aware of the time, effort, and enthusiasm or commitment put forth by the recognized employee on a given task or project. It is important to monitor peer recognition programs to ensure that the recognition is not just given to popular employees but is actually linked to important criteria. The possible occurrence of biases and even intentional discrimination should be monitored, especially with peer recognition programs. Anonymous feedback programs can help employers understand what is working and what might need to be addressed in all types of recognition programs.

Customer recognition: Customer recognition, both inside and outside the organization, helps employees derive greater meaningfulness and significance from their work as they learn how they are positively impacting others through their behaviors and performance. Customer feedback surveys are commonly used to evaluate and recognize employee performance. However, there may be some things that customers can reinforce that the company may not want them to. For example, an employer might want employees to follow company rules regarding product returns or other customer treatment, but if breaking these rules and being more lenient leads to positive customer recognition that then influences future raises or promotions, employees might be motivated to break these rules. Threats about giving negative feedback create pressure for employees to pursue customer rather than employer goals and can undermine the intent of the recognition program. Employees might also be motivated to abuse the recognition program by treating customers who receive a randomly generated feedback survey invitation on their receipt differently than those who do not. Because secret shoppers for one restaurant chain always ask for a receipt to be reimbursed for their meal, employees have learned to treat the minority of customers asking for a receipt particularly well rather than giving all customers the same high level of service.

The Role of Recognition Beyond Employee and Organization Outcomes

If recognition is done well, there are clearly numerous benefits for recognized employees, other employees who observe their peers being recognized, and the organization more broadly. However, it is likely that employee recognition also plays a role beyond boosting employee performance, motivation and engagement, and retention. How recognition occurs within organizations has the potential to impact not only the more immediate attitudinal and behavioral reactions from employees that organizations seek, but also the overall functioning of their internal labor markets. For instance, whether recognition occurs as part of a formal program or occurs more informally on a day-to-day basis is likely to influence the degree to which recognition, awards, or honors are used in performance reviews or promotion decisions. If some supervisors within an organization choose to provide different forms of recognition or recognize employees more or less frequently or publicly, some employees might be given an advantage in advancement decisions or developmental opportunities despite exhibiting similar behaviors to those less-recognized employees.

Additionally, whether and how supervisors provide recognition is also likely to influence the extent to which employees throughout the company are attracted to those supervisors. For example, supervisors who are known as providing recognition to their employees in specific ways may experience greater (or lesser) interest from other employees hoping to work with them in the future. This is similar to research which has shown that managers who are more open to employee voice experience higher levels of attraction from other employees at the organizations (McCarthy and Keller, 2020). This further highlights the importance of thoughtfully considering how recognition is implemented within organizations and for whom.

While recognition is likely to impact a company's internal labor market, it might also affect external constituents. For example, if the company or the recognized employee highlight such recognition to the general public (primarily via news articles and social media), that recognition is visible to external job seekers and customers, as well as the company's competitors. Seeing a given company recognize their employees for various behaviors or achievements may signal to employees external to the company that the organization values their workers, as well as their contributions, increasing external workers' desire to join that company. In a similar vein, current and potential customers might appreciate that a company whose products or services they enjoy is recognizing their workers for a job well done and publicly highlighting their contributions. Finally, the organization's competitors are likely to take note of employee recognition occurring at other companies and seek to similarly implement recognition programs for the benefit of employees and the company alike.

Case Examples

To better understand the power of recognition, we will look at how Disney appreciates and motivates their *Cast Members,* which is what they call their employees working at the Disney Store or at Disney Parks, through a variety of programs.

Recognition at Walt Disney World

Dee Hansford, former Manager of Cast Recognition at Disney, stated, ". . . companies are realizing that in order to gain a competitive advantage, they must have a system in place to reinforce the mission and business goals through recognition. Higher compensation and incentives are short term solutions; recognition is a lasting solution" (Recognition Professionals International, 2021). Lee Cockerell, retired Executive Vice President of Operations for the Walt Disney World Resort, believes that recognition, encouragement, and appreciation drive high employee performance (Clayton, 2020). Cockerell believes, "It is a no-brainer that when people feel respected and valued for the talents and skills they bring to the team, they feel more motivated and inspired, which leads to commitment" (Clayton, 2020). Cast Members are regularly reminded of their importance to the "show" experienced by Guests when they visit a Walt Disney hotel or theme park, regardless of the role they play.

Given the importance of Cast Member engagement to memorable Guest experiences, recognition plays an important role in recognizing and motivating Walt Disney World Cast Members. Blue name tags identify recipients of the prestigious Walt Disney Legacy award, given to Cast Members nominated by their peers for embodying the values of "dream, create, and inspire" (Clayton, 2020). The #castcom pliment program even allows Guests to recognize Cast Members via Twitter. The tweets are not only put on Twitter for all Twitter users to see, but also go in the Cast Member's formal record, enabling leadership to also see the recognition (Clayton, 2020). One of the most coveted award at the park is the Spirit of Fred Award. Named for a long-term employee who made his way up the ranks by exemplifying Disney values, Fred makes the awards himself, including The Lifetime Fred Award and the annual Spirit of Fred Awards (Windust, 2016). By recognizing and appreciating employees for their reinforcement of Disney's cultural values in addition to business outcomes, Disney has created an environment in which employees are motivated, engaged, and committed to creating great Guest experiences, which drive Disney's strong business results.

Discussion Questions:

1. Referring to Figure 12.1, how did Disney implement its employee recognition program?
2. Why do you think the recognition methods used by Disney were appropriate or inappropriate for its goals and targeted employees?
3. If you were Disney, how else might you recognize Cast Members for reinforcing Disney's cultural values?

Recognition Errors

A supervisor in an organization lacking a formal recognition program decided to implement one of their own to appreciate and motivate their high-performing team of nine employees. All nine employees were very hard working and consistently exceeded customer expectations while reinforcing the organization's values around high-quality customer service and teamwork. The team worked very interdependently in getting their work done and consistently supported each other whenever necessary.

In thinking about what to recognize, the supervisor remembered a customer who had called a couple of weeks earlier to praise the exceptional customer service they had received from the team in resolving their issue. The supervisor decided to recognize that event at the next weekly team meeting by singling out the employee they thought was probably the most responsible for the special treatment.

At the beginning of the meeting, the supervisor described the customer's message and asked for a round of applause for the team member's exceptional service performance. Unexpectedly, the team, including the employee being recognized, seemed surprised and not nearly as positive as the supervisor had thought they would be. The supervisor noticed a decline in team morale following the meeting and wondered what they had done wrong.

Discussion Questions:

1. What could have explained the team's negative reaction to the recognition?
2. What could have explained the recognition recipient's negative reaction to the recognition?
3. What would be a more appropriate way for the supervisor to recognize and motivate this team?

References

Appelbaum, S. H., and Kamal, R. (2000). An analysis of the utilization and effectiveness of non-financial incentives in small business. *The Journal of Management Development*, 19, 9/10, 733–763.

Bandura, A. (1986). *Social Foundations of Thought and Action: A Social Cognitive Theory*. Upper Saddle River, NJ: Prentice Hall.

Bradler, C., Dur, R., Neckermann, S., and Non, A. (2016). Employee recognition and performance: A field experiment. *Management Science*, 62(11), 3085–3099.

Cho, Y., and Fast, N. J. (2012). Power, defensive denigration, and the assuaging effect of gratitude expression. *Journal of Experimental Social Psychology*, 48(3), 778–782. https://doi.org/10.1016/j.jesp.2011.12.016

Chuang, C. H., and Liao, H. U. I. (2010). Strategic human resource management in service context: Taking care of business by taking care of employees and customers. *Personnel Psychology*, 63(1), 153–196.

Clayton, R. (2020). 3 keys to employee performance from Disney. *Psychology Today*, February 6. Retrieved from https://www.psychologytoday.com/us/blog/work-life-insights/202002/3-keys-employee-performance-disney.

Deckop, J. R., Cirka, C. C., and Andersson, L. M. (2003). Doing unto others: The reciprocity of helping behavior in organizations. *Journal of Business Ethics*, 47(2), 101–113.

Dutton, G. (1998). The Re-enchantment of Works. *Management Review*, 87(2), 51–54.

Gallus, J., and Frey, B. S. (2016). Awards: A strategic management perspective. *Strategic Management Journal*, 37(8), 1699–1714.

Gallus, J., and Heikensten, E. (2020). Awards and the gender gap in knowledge contributions in STEM. *AEA Papers and Proceedings*, 110, 241-44.

Gonzalez-Morales, M. G., Kernan, M. C., Becker, T. E., and Eisenberger, R. (2018). Defeating abusive supervision: Training supervisors to support subordinates. *Journal of Occupational Health Psychology*, 23(2), 151–162. https://doi.org/10.1037/ocp0000061

Grant, A. M., and Gino, F. (2010). A little thanks goes a long way: Explaining why gratitude expressions motivate prosocial behavior. *Journal of Personality and Social Psychology*, 98(6), 946.

Gubler, T., Larkin, I., and Pierce, L. (2016). Motivational spillovers from awards: Crowding out in a multitasking environment. *Organization Science*, 27(2), 286–303.

Johnson, M. D., Hollenbeck, J. R., Humphrey, S. E., Ilgen, D. R., Jundt, D., and Meyer, C. J. (2006). Cutthroat cooperation: Asymmetrical adaptation to changes in team reward structures. *Academy of Management Journal*, 49(1), 103–119.

Kaushal, N. (2021). Respect and recognition of the work as building blocks of the workplace: A work-psychological perspective. *The Palgrave Handbook of Workplace Well-Being* (pp. 1–24). New York: Palgrave-Macmillan.

McCarthy, J. E., and Keller, J. (2021). How Managerial Openness to Voice Shapes Internal Attraction: Evidence from UNITED STATES School Systems. *ILR Review*, DOI: 10.1177/00197939211008877.

Mendonca, M., and Kanungo, R. N. (1990). Work culture in developing countries: Implications for performance management. *Psychology and Developing Societies*, 2(2), 137–164.

MOW International Research Team (1987). *The Meaning of Working*. London: Academic Press.

Muscaro, T. J. (2020). #CastCompliment – How to thank a Disney Cast Member. *Insidethemagic.net*. Retrieved from https://insidethemagic.net/2020/07/cast-compliment-tm1/.

Newman, K. L., and Nollen, S. D. (1996). Culture and congruence: The fit between management practices and national culture. *Journal of International Business Studies*, 27(4), 753–779.

Peterson, S. J., and Luthans, F. (2006). The impact of financial and nonfinancial incentives on business-unit outcomes over time. *Journal of Applied Psychology*, 91, 156–165.

Porter, L., and Lawler, E. (1968). *Managerial Attitudes and Performance*. Homewood: Irwin.

Recognition Professionals International (2021). Frequently asked questions. Retrieved from https://www.incentivemarketing.org/RPI/About/FAQs/RPI/About/FAQs.aspx?hkey=d52e6e21-6830-4538-84dc-88af5a153894.

Saunderson, R. (2004), Survey findings of the effectiveness of employee recognition in the public sector. *Public Personnel Management*, 33(3), 255–276.

Saunderson, R. (2013). Top 10 Differences Between Rewards and Recognition. *Northstar Meetings Group*. Retrieved from https://www.northstarmeetingsgroup.com/Incentive/Strategy/Top-10-Differences-Between-Rewards-and-Recognition?inc=1.

Sparrow, P., and Wu, P. C. (1998). Does national culture really matter? Predicting HRM preferences of Taiwanese employees. *Employee Relations*, 20(1), 26–56.

Stajkovic, A. D., and Luthans, F. (1997). A meta-analysis of the effects of organizational behavior modification on task performance, 1975-95. *Academy of Management Journal*, 40, 1122–1149.

Stajkovic, A. D., and Luthans, F. (2001). The differential effects of incentive motivators on work performance. *Academy of Management Journal*, 4, 580–590.

Stajkovic, A. D., and Luthans, F. (2003). Behavioral management and task performance in organizations: Conceptual background, meta-analysis, and test of alternative models. *Personnel Psychology*, 56, 155–194.

Tepper, B. J., Dimotakis, N., Lambert, L. S., Koopman, J., Matta, F. K., Man Park, H., and Goo, W. (2018). Examining Follower Responses to Transformational Leadership from a Dynamic, Person–Environment Fit Perspective. *Academy of Management Journal*, 61(4), 1343–1368. https://doi.org/10.5465/amj.2014.0163

Waters, R. D., Bortree, D. S., and Tindall, N. T. (2013). Can public relations improve the workplace? Measuring the impact of stewardship on the employer-employee relationship. *Employee Relations*, 35(6), 613–629.

Windust, J. (2016). Walt Disney and the 4 performance management tools. *LinkedIn*. Retrieved from https://www.linkedin.com/pulse/walt-disney-4-performance-management-tools-jon-windust.

Exercises

Imagine that you are the manager of a restaurant with the business strategy of providing high-quality meals and customer service while charging a premium price. Employees are expected to be knowledgeable about the food and wine, attentive to diners' needs, and professional while working collaboratively with each other to provide the best possible customer experience. Employees are paid an above-market base wage and all tips are shared equitably among the staff. You want to create a recognition program to better motivate employees to work collaboratively, maximize sales, and provide the best possible customer experience. What low- or no-cost recognition program will you implement?

Now imagine that you are the manager of a fast casual restaurant with the strategy of providing good-quality food to customers as cheaply as possible and as quickly as possible. Employees are expected to work efficiently in fulfilling orders and meeting customers' needs. Employees are paid a market wage and rarely receive tips. As a result, turnover is higher than you would like and needing to continually train new hires decreases the restaurant's efficiency. You want to create a recognition program to better motivate employees to work quickly and accurately and to stay with the restaurant for a longer period of time. What low- or no-cost recognition program will you implement?

Video Analysis and Discussion

Please watch the following video(s):

"The Power of Appreciation: Mike Robbins at TEDxBellevue" (18:06) https://www.youtube.com/watch?v=a3wX8nmvlZ0&ab_channel=TEDxTalks

Now form small groups to discuss the video(s) and answer the following questions:

1. How does Mike Robbins explain the difference between appreciation and recognition?
2. What is the role of both appreciation and recognition at work?
3. As a manager, how can you both effectively appreciate and effectively recognize your employees?
4. What difference do you think it will make if you appreciate and recognize your employees?

Be prepared to present the ideas from your small group discussion with the class as a whole.

Discussion Questions

1. Could a single low- or no-cost recognition program be implemented equally effectively in both restaurants? If so, what recognition would be appropriate?
2. What is an example of a recognition program that would not be equally effective in both restaurants? Why would it not be equally effective?
3. How should the decision about the two recognition programs be made?
4. What could be some unintended consequences of a recognition program in either of the two restaurants?

13

Sustain Organizational Performance Through Continuous Learning, Change, and Realignment

MICHAEL BEER

Harvard Business School and TruePoint

Hierarchy makes it hard for lower levels to reveal the whole truth in conversations with those at the top, research and experience tells us (Argyris, 1985; Detert and Edmondson, 2011; Morrison and Milliken. 2000). And there is evidence that the inability to have honest conversations that reveals the whole truth stands in the way of organizational learning and change (Argyris and Schon, 1996; Beer, 2020). Consider recent ethical and performance failures at Boeing, Wells Fargo Bank, and Volkswagen among many equally devastating failures in other companies around the world. In all cases, lower-level people knew of the problems that ultimately caused reputational and financial damage, but there was no means for them to have an honest conversation with those at the top.

Honest organization-wide conversations are only possible if leaders at the top are ready to lead them. Their personal readiness for the conversation has proven to be the single best predictor of whether they will decide to lead such an honest conversation and change process and its effectiveness. That is in part a function of the extent to which they are dissatisfied with the status quo – the effectiveness and performance of their organization. It is also dependent on the extent they are secure and confident and consequently give people a voice and involve them in decisions (Beer, 2020).

We are living in a world in which the only constant is change. Companies must respond to rapid changes in markets and technology if they are to survive and prosper. To enable organizational adaptation, senior executives must lead a process of change that develops their own and peoples' dissatisfaction with the status quo and realigns the organization as a total system with new business realities.

Consider the case of Apple Computer (Beer and Gibbs, 1990). Founded by Steve Jobs and Steve Wozniak in a garage in Silicon Valley in 1977, the company was the first to develop and produce a personal computer. The Apple II and its successor, the Macintosh, led the industry in technology, design, and user friendliness. In 1980, the company had virtually 100% of the market. It had grown 100% a year and was among the fastest growing companies in the world. In 1990, its revenues reached $5.5 billion, and employment reached 14500. By 1997, however, the company's market share was down to 3%, and its revenues and number of employees were shrinking. It was also losing money and had lost the race to dominate the personal computer market to Dell, Compaq, and IBM.

Apple's dominance in the computer market declined even though in 1983 John Scully, at the time president of PepsiCo, was brought in as Apple's new CEO to enable the company to cope with new competitive realities. As we shall see throughout this chapter, Scully failed to lead an organizational learning and change process from which he and his top team could learn about barriers to organizational and leadership effectiveness. To succeed in competing with low-cost personal computers, Scully would have had to mobilize energy for change among senior executives by creating dissatisfaction with the status quo and then develop a new organization – structure, systems, people, processes, and culture – needed to compete with its low-cost competitors. Such changes would have enabled Apple to develop organizational capabilities and behaviors Apple, whose success had been based on innovation, did not possess. Though the company had talented and creative technical people, it lacked several essential organizational capabilities associated with success in uncertain and rapidly changing environments (Beer, 2020; Kotter and Heskett, 1992; Lawler, 1997; Lawrence and Lorsch, 1967; Miles and Snow, 1978). They are: [1]

Honest conversations that enabled people at all levels to voice their views to top managers about the effectiveness of the organizational capabilities discussed as follows. The capability to have an honest conversation is essential in an uncertain and rapidly changing environment (Beer, 2020). For this type of dialogue to occur, trust and skills in dialogue are needed as is courage of leaders to hear potentially embarrassing truths.

The conversation follows the following pattern. Top management communicates to lower level its intended direction and lower levels communicate to top management if they believe the direction is flawed and identify organizational barriers to successful implementation of the new strategic or values direction. At Apple, lower-level managers that saw the need for lower-cost computers were ignored. Similarly, differences between key functions – at Apple Research and

[1]The term *behavior* incorporates the description of actual behaviors as well as the description of attitudes and skills that are proxies for behavior.

Development (R&D) and Marketing – were never discussed in a way that would enable R&D to understand threats Marketing perceived.

Coordination between functions, businesses, and geographic regions around businesses and/or customers is essential for speed of response to customer needs and a cost-effective operation. Apple's individualistic culture and lack of cross-functional teams made coordination between Marketing, Sales, and R&D difficult. Consequently, the company failed to recognize and respond to a rapidly growing business market that demanded new and lower-cost products.

Commitment to customer needs and an economically successful business is essential for any enterprise. Without that commitment, employee's interests are not aligned with the purpose of business. Apple's people were committed to technical innovation not meeting customer needs in a changing market. This blinded them to the possibility that a less elegant and lower-cost technical solution being introduced by competitors (low-cost PC's with a DOS operating system) might succeed.

Competence in the activities most critical to success, as well in management and leadership are both essential. Some companies rely on selling or distribution for success and others on merchandising. Still others may rely on technical skills in R&D, the capability that made Apple a success in its early years. But without effective leadership and management, firms like Apple cannot mobilize technical and functional competencies into a coordinated effort and results. That was certainly true of Apple Computers. As a result of its rapid growth, Apple's technically excellent people were promoted to key positions, but they lacked leadership and management skills to develop the coordination Apple desperately needed to succeed.

Creativity and *innovation* in both technical and administrative matters are essential for a business to retain its competitive edge. Apple succeeded largely based on its creativity and innovation in technology. But it lacked the capacity to innovate and change its approaches to organizing and managing people, something that was essential if it was going to succeed in a changing marketplace.

Leading organizational change is about defining a new strategic direction for the business and realigning its structure, management processes, systems, people skills, and culture so that needed organizational capabilities required to implement the new direction emerge. Of course, implementing the new direction typically also leads to redefinition of direction as the organization learns through the process of implementation what works and what does not work. That is why the behaviors mentioned earlier, particularly open communication and creativity, are so essential to the capacity of the organization to adapt and renew itself. The effectiveness of an effort to lead change should be judged by the extent to which it develops the five Cs – the organizational capabilities listed earlier, *and* the extent to which it develops the capacity of the organization to renew itself in the future.

The story of Apple illustrates the tendency of all organizations to stop learning and changing in the face of success. Why does this happen to organizations? What are the essential principles of organizational change that leaders in John Scully's position should follow if they are to overcome the natural tendency of organizations to maintain the status quo?

Basic Facts About Organizational Behavior and Change

This section presents basic facts managers must understand about organizational behavior and change if they are to succeed in the difficult task of leading change. They explain why organizations resist change and what is needed to change them (Beer, Eisenstat, and Spector, 1990; Katz and Kahn, 1978; Pfeffer, 1997; Schein, 1990).

Organizations Are Complex Open Systems

A variety of organizational facets – structure, human resource policies, management processes, values and skills of people, and the leadership behavior of top management – conspire to produce an organization's distinctive pattern of behavior. These facets are interdependent and are continuously engaged in a process of mutual adaptation to achieve "fit" or congruence with the organization's chosen strategy (Lawrence and Lorsch, 1967). By an open system, we mean that the organization is subject to influence by the external environment, largely through the influence of markets, society, and/or the larger corporate organization (if the organization is a subunit of a larger corporation).

Figure 13.1 illustrates the key dimensions that must fit together – be aligned – for an organization to be effective. It suggests that organizational behavior is shaped by four forces – the organization's environment and the emergent strategic task the organization must manage to succeed, the organization's design, the people

FIGURE 13.1 Organizational alignment model

selected and promoted, and the behavior of leaders and their top team. Organizations naturally evolve toward an equilibrium state in which these elements fit tightly. In the short term, fit leads to organizational effectiveness. The organization has developed certain behaviors required for its success and has developed leadership behavior, structures, and systems to cause these behaviors consistently. When the environment changes and places new demands on the organization, leaders must realign the organization to fit new circumstances.

Implicit in this formulation is a contingency perspective. It holds that the best way to organize and manage people depends on the nature of the situation and strategy (Lawrence and Lorsch, 1967; Miles and Snow, 1978). We know, for example, that the optimal structure of an organization depends on the nature of the environment and strategy (Miles and Snow, 1978; Nadler and Tushman, 1988). At the same time, there is growing evidence that sustainable advantage depends on organizing and managing people around a set of values and principles including the use of teams, collaboration, symbolic egalitarianism, training and development for employees, and open communication (Beer, 2009; Pfeffer, 1998). The five Cs listed earlier reflect these findings. The implication is that the change process itself must be aligned with these principles if they are to become embedded in the organization.

Organizational Alignment Develops a Distinctive and Persistent Culture

Culture is defined as the assumptions, beliefs, values, and resultant behavior leaders invent or discover to solve problems in the external and internal environment. It is what these leaders teach new members as the correct way of perceiving, thinking, and acting to solve problems (Schein, 1985). The tendency of managers to attract, select, and promote people based on how similar they are to those already in the organization increases the strength of the culture (Schneider, 1994). Under the leadership of its founder Steve Jobs, Apple Computer attracted, selected, and promoted employees who were individualistic and committed to elegant technology. This created a strong culture that demanded conformity to these values and eschewed more pragmatic business considerations.

That companies develop a persistent culture and have difficulty in adapting is evident in the low survival rate of companies (Foster and Kaplan, 2001; Miller, 1990). A substantial number of the Fortune 500 companies 20 years ago – Gulf Oil, Digital Equipment, International Harvester, Scott Paper, US Steel, and Westinghouse – no longer exist.

Organizations vary in the strength of their culture, however. Moreover, subcultures typically exist in various parts and subunits of the organization. Organizational change involves confronting the persistent pattern of behavior that is blocking the organization from higher performance, diagnosing its consequences, and identifying the underlying assumptions and values that have created it. That process must go on at the corporate level as well as in multiple businesses and operating units, each with a different strategic task and subculture.

Organizational Behavior Is Resistant to Change

Fundamental organizational change calls into question existing patterns of management – the authority, decision rights, and values of existing managers and departments. When a changing environment threatens an organization's capacity to survive, top management is challenged to redefine how it will compete. It must define new objectives and a new strategic task. It should not be surprising that making these changes is painful. Key members of the organization will experience psychological and sometimes material losses (Beer, 1991). Their power and status may diminish. Past relationships may be disrupted. New skills may be required threatening employees' sense of competence and self-esteem as well as their careers and job security. The perception of these potential losses leads to resistance. For example, R&D – the technical function at Apple Computer – stood to lose some of its influence in designing products if Apple were to compete more aggressively in selling personal computers to the business market. Consequently, careers, self-esteem, and the very sense of identity and meaning technical people derived from work were also threatened.

All human beings employ emotional and cognitive processes to defend themselves against threat (Argyris and Schon, 1996). Moreover, people make sense of past behavior by forming beliefs that rationalize them and by escalating commitment to them. These common human characteristics prevent managers from learning that their actual behavior – their theory in action – is inconsistent with their stated aspiration – their espoused theory. These human characteristics cause organizational policies, management practices, and leadership behavior and style to persist in the face of new realities unless skills and norms of inquiry and constructive conflict resolution are developed (Argyris and Schon, 1996). All attempts to change organizations must overcome the defensiveness of individuals and groups, cause learning to occur, or result in the replacement of individuals not capable of learning. Effective change efforts maximize the amount of learning and minimize the need for replacement. This enables the organization to retain the wealth of company specific knowledge about customers, products, and technology and retain commitment that is otherwise lost when key people are replaced.

Substantial evidence exists that many efforts to change organizations fail in making a fundamental transformation in organizational culture (Beer et al., 1990; Hall, Rosenthal, and Wade, 1993; Schaffer, 1988). They produce only superficial change since underlying assumptions and beliefs about the business and how it should be managed are not confronted. These change efforts are characterized by wave after wave of programs – education and training initiatives for all employees, continuous changes in structure, the development of mission, and value statements or initiatives such as reengineering and total quality management.

Consider a large industrial enterprise whose financial performance lagged the industry. Management felt that the cause was the ineffectiveness of its managers. With the help of a new senior human resource executive hired from a company known for its best human resource practices, a four-week management education program was launched to change the company. The program's faculty was world class and the content highly relevant including a module on competition and strategy, organizational effectiveness, leadership, and interpersonal skills. The last module of the program involved participants working on analyzing and making recommendations to top management about an important corporate problem. Participants were so enthusiastic about the potential of the program for changing the company that they asked top management to go through the program. They were certain that if the company was to adopt the ways of thinking and doing embedded in the program, the corporation would regain its competitive edge. Top management agreed to go through the program. Despite the enthusiasm of all parties involved in the program (faculty, students, and top management), three years later, top management and managers who went through the program indicated in interviews and surveys that very little change had occurred in the company's pattern of management.

John Scully's efforts to change Apple Computer also suffered from programmatic change, thereby delaying a dialogue about the real underlying problems. During a five-year period, Scully changed the organization's structure four times but coordination between Marketing, Sales, and R&D and communication between top management and lower levels did not improve, nor did Apple's performance live up to expectations.

Programs fail when the top management team delegates the task for change to a staff group or consultants. In this way, they avoid the difficult task of confronting the underlying causes of the problems faced by the firm. These are often connected to their own and other managers' assumptions and beliefs about the nature of the business and the best means for organizing and managing people. It is far easier for a CEO to obtain agreement from key people to a program or initiative than it is to breach defenses that block learning about deeper underlying problems. These require leadership – the hard work of confronting problems and developing commitment to change and making difficult decisions about people who will not or cannot change. It should come as no surprise that the capacity to confront conflict has been found to be associated with a firm's ability to succeed in highly uncertain and turbulent environments where the rate of change has to be rapid and continuous (Lawrence and Lorsch, 1967).

Forces for Organizational Change: Dissatisfaction and Leadership

Given the natural tendency of all management to defend the past and resist change, it has been observed that change does not seem to occur unless a sense of urgency exists among the organization's leaders (Kotter, 1997; Kotter, 2008). This does not typically occur unless they become highly dissatisfied with the status quo (Beer, 1991). Dissatisfaction with the status quo arises naturally because of problems that threaten the firm's performance and even survival. Financial losses, a long and protracted decline in stock price, shrinking market share, loss of a major customer, high employee turnover, or a union strike are all forces that can bring management to a realization that change is needed. The more severe the crisis, the higher the dissatisfaction with the status quo and the more energy will be released to act. And it takes enormous amounts of human energy to confront entrenched assumptions and practices.

Severe problems may not be enough, however. As we saw in the case of Apple Computer, management was able to ignore dramatic changes in their markets and a shrinking market share. The missing ingredient was leadership (Beer, 1991; Kotter, 1997). John Scully was unable to mobilize the commitment to change of key people, particularly his top team. He lacked the courage to engage people in a dialogue about historic assumptions, practices, and norms of behavior. Change leaders, it has been found, possess the capacity to confront difficult issues. Indeed, companies that succeed in transforming themselves appear to do so because of changes in their top team (Virany, Tushman, and Romanelli, 1992). Leaders, typically new leaders, develop a top management team that is like minded about the need for and the direction of change (Beer and Eisenstat, 1996). A united and effective top team results in improvements in coordination and thereby consistent action across all parts of the organization. Without this, lower-level employees perceive an inconsistency between the new direction espoused by top management and their actual behavior. This raises doubts about top management's commitment and makes it unlikely that commitment to change at lower levels will develop.

Consistency Between Means and Ends

There is great variation in the consistency between change ends and means chosen by leaders. To the extent the means contradict the values and practices leaders intend to embed in the future organizational state, people question management's true commitment to the values and practices they espouse. Trust between leaders and lower-level people declines. Lowered trust makes it more difficult for leaders to engage people and mobilize commitment to change.

Leaders who intend to develop high-performance organizations characterized by the behavior and practices discussed earlier (good coordination and teamwork, high creativity, open communication, high commitment, and good interpersonal and leadership skills) are not successful unless they *involve people in the change process* (Beer et al., 1990). Contradictions between words and deeds are inevitable, of course, in any complex organizational change process. But a strong bias toward involvement appears to be necessary. Just as importantly, *management's willingness and skills in encouraging lower levels to raise issues of inconsistency* between their (management's) words and their actions builds the trust and partnership with lower-level high-performance organizations typically embody.

How to Lead Change: Seven Steps for Successful Change

The dynamics of organizational behavior and change discussed earlier translate into *seven steps* a general manager must take to lead change in his or her organization. These steps assume that the leader is dissatisfied with the status quo and feels that change is needed to cope with new competitive realities. Effective leaders are always on the lookout for a discontinuity in the organization's environment, says Andrew Grove, CEO of Intel. His book *Only the Paranoid Survive* (Grove, 1996) captures well the need for constant vigilance.

Unfortunately, incumbent top managers are often slow to recognize the need for change and/or are too timid in confronting managers and workers below them with the need for change. Under these circumstances, change cannot take place until the leader is replaced. The price of not being vigilant can be seen in statistics for Fortune 500 CEO tenure. Average CEO tenure in 2008 is 3.2 versus in 2008 versus 10.5 years in 1990. Leaders who are not dissatisfied with the status quo are removed by boards of directors, so significant organizational change can occur. Even new managers, however, can fail to manage change if they do not understand and/or are unskillful in leading change. As a new CEO John Scully had nine years to change Apple Computer. He failed because he did not take the following steps.

1. Mobilize energy for change

Energy for change must be mobilized in the top management team as well as in key managers at lower levels. It is mobilized by creating dissatisfaction with the status quo as was noted above. The following three actions can mobilize energy for change (Beer, 1991).

- *Demanding improved performance and behavior:* Leaders can energize organizational members by articulating demanding goals and standards for behavior. When Jack Welch took over General Electric in the early 1980s, he told all business unit managers that they had to get their business units to be number 1 or 2 in their industries or the business would be sold. Stan Mahlik, executive vice president for Manufacturing at Goodyear Tire and Rubber energized his 100 plant managers around the world to change their operations by demanding that, unless their tires met certain quality standards, they would become scrap. This energized them to search for new technology and management approaches. Percy Barnevik, CEO of ABB, articulated new performance goals and behavioral standards at a world-wide meeting of the top 500 executives in the company within weeks after a merger that formed the new company. About behavior, acting even if it is wrong, he said, is better than not acting at all.
- *Exposing the top team and employees to feedback:* A general manager who is dissatisfied with the status quo has come by this view through awareness of low quality, high cost, poor profits, dissatisfied customers, or unhappy shareholders. Exposing managers and workers to this information through presentations as well as direct experience is a powerful way to unleash energy for change. When Louis Gerstner took over IBM after it had fallen on hard times in the early 1990s, he asked all top executives to visit at least one customer a month. These visits gave them new insights into what was happening in the industry and how IBM needed to respond. Likewise, staff groups in corporations have been energized to become more effective when they have been exposed to feedback from line organizations they serve. Manufacturing plant managers faced with a resistant work force and union have taken workers and union leaders on trips to see customers, displayed competitive products in the lobby of the building, and informed employees about the plant's financial performance through presentations and display of information on bulletin boards.

- *Exposing employees to model organizations:* Exposing managers and lower levels to radically different practices in other companies or within the same company can unleash energy. This has been referred to as benchmarking best practice. A visit to an innovative team-based manufacturing plant unleashed energy in managers, workers, and union leaders to transform Navigation Products, their business unit, to a similar model of management, one that promised to improve coordination across functions, build trust, and improve communication (Beer et al., 1990). In the early 1980s, the automobile companies sent managers by the hundreds to Japan to learn about manufacturing methods that gave Japanese manufacturers a significant edge in quality, though in this instance what they learned failed to be translated into change rapidly enough given the state of the automobile industry in 2008.

2. Develop a new compelling direction – Strategy and values

Feedback and information are not enough. A new direction must be developed. To develop this direction, change leaders orchestrate a series of discussions in their management team to develop an understanding of what this information means for change in the company's direction. Exactly how successful is the organization being in its product or service offering? Why is it not successful? How committed are people? How effective is the organization? What is the implication for the future survival and success of our organization? What should be the new objectives and strategy? What should be the guiding values of the organization? What are the implied priorities? Discussing these questions in the light of the feedback and data to which managers have been exposed can lead to a new understanding and sense of urgency.

Jerry Simpson, general manager of Navigation Products, held a series of meetings with his top team that led them to defining new and ambitious goals for the business and a new direction (Beer et al., 1990). A study of 25 business units undergoing change found that units that had changed the most were more likely than lagging units to have established a clear and broadly understood link between business problems and the need for change (Beer et al., 1990). Making the link is what makes the new direction compelling to members of the organization. It is quite important that leaders involve the whole top team in the formulation of the new objectives and strategy. And it is important for that top team to involve other key managers in discussing and critiquing their new strategy. This builds the commitment needed to implement the new direction.

Moreover, the general manager or CEO can use the work of developing a new direction to develop their top team's effectiveness. Research shows that effective strategy formulation and implementation depends on top team effectiveness (Beer and Eisenstat, 2000; Eisenhardt, 1989). Team effectiveness is developed through encouraging new behavior, coaching, and if needed replacement of those key executives who do not play a constructive role in the team and/or do not become committed to the new direction.

3. *Identify organizational barriers to implementing the new direction*

Often the resistance to change is at the highest levels of the company (Finkelstein, 2003; Miller, 1990). Hierarchy insulates top management teams from the effects of their behavior and policies. Exposing top management to feedback about what employees perceive as barriers to implementing a new strategy further creates dissatisfaction and identifies what changes in organization and behavior are needed to implement the new strategy. John Scully began his belated and ultimately unsuccessful effort to change Apple Computer after an attitude survey showed strong negative sentiments in the company about the lack of strategic clarity and problems with top management's leadership. Eisenstat and I (Beer and Eisenstat, 2000) asked top teams, as part of a planned effort to develop an organization capable of strategy implementation, to appoint tasks forces of eight of their best employees. Task force members interviewed organizational members one or two levels below the top about barriers to strategy implementation. Task forces then fed back their findings to top teams using a carefully crafted process that enabled the task force to be honest and management to be nondefensive (Beer and Eisenstat, 2004). Six barriers were consistently identified across many organizations, and, not surprisingly, they were the reverse of the principles for an aligned organization and the change principles discussed in this chapter. The barriers were:

- Unclear strategy and conflicting priorities
- An ineffective top team
- A general manager who was either too autocratic or too laissez-faire (not confronting problems)
- Poor coordination
- Poor vertical communication
- Inadequate leadership and management and its development at lower levels

Because these barriers were known to everyone but were not discussable, we called them the "silent killers." Like hypertension, they can cause an organizational heart attack – organizational failures in implementing strategy. Until a commitment is developed by top teams to overcome the fundamental management problems represented by the silent killers, it is unlikely that a new strategic direction can be implemented, or the organization aligned with that strategy. Many change initiatives fail because underlying management problems are not confronted and overcome. Change leaders should, therefore, try to collect data about barriers perceived by lower levels, so plans for change can incorporate their voice about leadership and organizational problems. Efforts to change organizations without this step lead to cynicism and low commitment. Of course, this requires top manager openness to learning about their own role in the organization's performance problems. If this does not happen, as it often does not, a new general manager or CEO will be appointed when the silent killers and their consequences begin to affect performance in a significant way.

4. Develop a vision of how the business will be organized for success

Having heard the voice of lower-level employees regarding barriers to achieving the new strategic direction, the top team must work together to fashion a vision of the organization' future state (see Chapter 16). They will have to envision how the elements in the organizational model presented in Figure 13.1 will need to change to enable a change in organizational behavior. The following questions will have to be answered.

- How should the organization be redesigned to ensure the appropriate coordination between value creating activities that must work together to implement the strategic task defined earlier in step 2? Redesign of the organization will include changes in structure, systems, and planning process. These changes are intended to change roles, responsibilities, and relationships so that the new strategy can be implemented. For example, business, customer, or product and project teams may be created; change from a decentralized divisional structure to a matrix structure may be necessary; the number of hierarchical layers may be reduced; and the size and role of corporate staff may change.
- How will the top team's own leadership behavior change to enable the new organization to function effectively? These changes may include modification in the CEOs style and or changes in the frequency and focus of top management meetings and work. For example, the CEO of Becton Dickinson received feedback from an employee task force that he too closely supervised the corporate strategic planning process and that there were too many meetings. He responded by delegating more responsibility to his sector presidents and changing the focus and content of his top team's management work (Beer and Williamson, 1991).
- What changes in peoples' skills will be needed to ensure that the new organization works effectively? Changes in human resource policies and practices will be needed to ensure that the right people with the right skills occupy the new roles designated by the reorganization.

5. Communicate and involve people in implementation

The new organizational vision must be communicated to the whole organization. People in the organization should be told why a new strategy is needed and how the new organizational arrangements will help shape new behavior and better performance. Articulating the links between new competitive realities and the new organization will enable people to commit to the changes.

Consider what Don Rogers, the general manager of the Electronic Products, a division at Allentown Materials Corporation, did in this regard (Beer and Weber, 1998a). Rogers' top team had just decided to implement cross-functional new product development teams to enhance product development success, a strategic imperative for them to compete in their industry. Rogers and his whole top team visited 13 locations over a two-month period to communicate with every salaried employee how the new organization would work and why they were adopting it. The why included telling all employees about competitive problems that led to change and organizational barriers that had been uncovered through a survey and diagnosis of the division, including problems people perceived in Rogers' own leadership. Communication was two-way. After Rogers and his team presented their change plan employees met in small groups to discuss what they heard. They then assembled to raise questions and challenge management. A *dialogue* between top and bottom is essential for top management to learn about potential problems they will encounter in implementation so that they can make changes in their action plans accordingly. And that dialogue must be continuous and ongoing for change to succeed.

6. Support behavior change

After the new organization is implemented, employees, particularly those whose roles and responsibilities have been most impacted by the organizational changes, will need support to develop needed skills and attitudes. This is often done through consultants who coach individuals and teams. It can also be done through training and education programs. In the Electronic Products Division mentioned earlier, consultants sat in on all team meetings for the first six months and coached the teams and their leaders in how to work in these new unfamiliar arrangements. Moreover, consultants brought together key managers in pairs of departments whose relationships were blocking coordination and facilitated a discussion that led to improvements. The purpose was to change behavior and skills within teams, thereby increasing the probability of their success.

7. Monitor progress and make further changes

Organizational change is an action learning process. As the new organizational arrangements are enacted, much is learned about how to modify structure, systems, policies and practices, and behavior to achieve intended results. Top- and lower-level managers discover how to carry out their new roles and responsibilities and gain insights into how their own styles and skills need to be changed. Those who cannot adapt decide to leave on their own or are asked to leave. As time goes on, the organization begins to function more effectively, and this is translated into better performance. Because the business environment and strategy are constantly changing, survival requires organizations to recycle these seven steps periodically and so that the organization can be realigned with new realities.

Orchestrating Corporate-Wide Strategic Change

A large organization is typically made up of many interdependent – subunits – divisions, each a business unit, regional and country organizations, or operating units such as manufacturing plants, stores, and offices. Leading the organization through the seven steps discussed earlier is the responsibility of unit leaders at every level.

Corporate-wide change requires top management to play two roles (Beer, 1991; Ghoshal and Bartlett, 2000). They must *lead a change process within the top management unit.* This process would define how the corporate whole will coordinate the activities of the corporation's many subunits to achieve the wider purpose of the corporation. But that is not enough. Corporate leaders must also *orchestrate a process that encourages leaders in each of the corporation's subunits to lead their own seven-step learning and organizational alignment process* (Beer and Eisenstat, 1996). Innovations in organizing and managing will occur from such a process, and it is top management's role to orchestrate the diffusion of managerial innovations in leading units through conferences, visits to leading edge units, and, most importantly, through the transfer of successful leaders from leading edge to lagging units (Beer et al., 1990).

Where should corporate-wide change start? Sometimes subunit change comes about naturally at the periphery, in business units, manufacturing facilities, or stores far from headquarters. Often these are subunits offering quite different products or services from the parent. It is in these units that managers are faced with different competitive demands and/or have the freedom to innovate and lead change. Under these circumstances, changes are only adopted by other organizational subunits if top management actively works to move the innovations and the managers who led them to other parts of the large company (Beer et al., 1990; Walton, 1987).

Clearly, corporate-wide change will occur much more quickly if top management has conviction that change is needed. Top management's role is to encourage, even demand, that managers of independent business units, manufacturing plants, retail stores, or country organizations (in global companies) lead change in their units (Beer et al., 1990; Ghoshal and Bartlett, 2000). Jack Welch who led General Electric through a major transformation in the 1980s and 1990s *required* key managers to employ Work-Out, a process that required leaders to listen to key people about barriers to effectiveness, to assess their root causes and realign it for greater effectiveness (Ulrich, Kerr, and Ashkenas, 2002). Top management's role is not to drive change through corporate staff and consultant led programs. As discussed earlier, these will fail to mobilize energy and leadership at the unit level needed for change to succeed. Moreover, corporate programs prevent top management from discovering who of their subunit managers are able to lead the seven-step organizational learning and change process, an indicator of their leadership potential.

Case Examples

I will first briefly summarize the case of Apple Computer used throughout this chapter to illustrate an unsuccessful effort to lead change. I then review two successful change efforts.

Apple Computer: A case of failure

John Scully did not restore Apple to its former dominant market position. He was unable to develop sufficient dissatisfaction with the status quo to produce the energy needed for change. He never created a top team capable of agreeing on Apple's new strategic direction. As late as 1988, he appointed to a key top management position an executive whose strategic vision was diametrically opposite to one that Apple had to take to cope with new competitive realities. His inclination to avoid conflict prevented him from confronting key strategic and organizational issues. And he never led a change process that enabled his top team to discover and discuss the silent killers that blocked them from realigning their organization with their intention to succeed in selling Apple's offering to the business market, one quite different from the education market where they had been successful. Consequently, shareholders, customers, and employees failed to derive the value (stock price, lower-cost products, and career opportunities, respectively) that a successful enterprise would otherwise have yielded. Apple's success in the late 1990s to the present under the leadership of CEO Steve Jobs represents a new strategic era enabled by a "new" CEO (Jobs was Apple's founder and first CEO but was replaced by Scully). After Scully's departure, Jobs articulated a new strategy and successfully aligned the organization with it.

Hewlett Packard's Santa Rosa Systems Division (HP/SRSD): Successful unit-level change

The Hewlett Packard Santa Rosa Systems Division is a case of successful change at the business unit level but failure by HP's top management to spread innovation to other units (Beer and Rogers, 1997). In 1992, HP/SRSD was formed to manage and grow a new measurement systems business for HP. By 1994, the division was experiencing many problems and its performance did not meet top management's expectations. There were numerous reasons for this. The division had organized itself and was being managed in a manner like HP's traditional test and measurement divisions. Yet the systems business was significantly different, particularly with respect to the need to customize systems. The mismatch between the traditional approach to organizing and managing and the demands of a very different business environment and strategy created many tensions between functions and between the top team and the remainder of the organization.

Data collected by a task force of the division's best employees revealed that the six silent killers described earlier were blocking organizational effectiveness. Employees perceived the general manager' style was laissez-faire. He was not engaging his top team in a discussion of conflicting strategies and priorities perceived by lower levels. Consequently, coordination between several functions essential for successful execution of two interdependent strategies was not occurring. Section managers who had been assigned to lead cross-functional teams were ineffective in gaining consensus in their teams in part because they lacked experience and skills needed to lead teams and in part because they lacked formal authority. And, while everyone in the division knew of these problems and complained about them to each other in private conversations, they did not give voice to their frustrations to the top team. The division manager and his staff were also aware of tensions and knew the division was failing, but without feedback from lower levels, they did not quite understand the urgency for change that lower-level managers felt.

With the encouragement of his human resource executive, the division manager hired an external consultant, who, using a process called the Strategic Fitness Process (Beer and Eisenstat, 2004), helped the top team go through the seven-step change process. This enabled these issues to be surfaced for discussion and diagnosis. As a result, the top team identified their own ineffectiveness as a team, the general manager's style, and the ineffectiveness of cross-functional teams in coordinating functional departments as the root cause of poor performance. In that same meeting, they agreed to reorganize the division as a matrix structure to facilitate coordination, defined new roles for key people and teams in the new structure, and defined a new role for the top team, one that fit the new structure, and created new ground rules for how the top team should operate and how decision would be made.

Data collected a year later by the same task force and an employee survey showed significant improvement though some issues persisted. Sales had tripled and profits went up 250%. While the division's management attributed some of the improvements in the division's performance to an upturn in the market they served, they felt that they would not have been able to take advantage of market demand without the changes in organizing and managing they had made. The division manager and his team also decided to lead the seven-step task alignment process once a year as a way of fostering continuous change. Five years later, HP's top management felt that SRSD, which had lagged its sister divisions in performance and effectiveness, was now a model to which other divisions could look. Division management had successfully led change and innovated when they adopted the Strategic Fitness Process for fast change.

ASDA: Successful corporate-wide strategic change

ASDA, a UK grocery chain, offers an example of excellent top management leadership of strategic change (Beer and Weber, 1998b). With the company 1.5 billion pounds in debt and near bankruptcy, Archie Norman was appointed as CEO to turn around the company. Upon arriving in December of 1991, he met with his top team and quickly resolved to make changes in its membership. He also announced that while he did not have any preconceived ideas about what the problems were or how to solve them, he would insist on debate and transparency. He also announced that a "renewal store" would be identified where managers would be given license to innovate in the retail proposition, the physical space, and in the way people were organized and managed. He promptly began an assessment of the company's situation by making unannounced visits to many of the company's 200 stores. There he talked to lower-level workers and store management asking them to tell him about barriers to company performance. They quickly informed him that for years, headquarters, particularly the trading (purchasing) department, had not been listening to stories about what products the stores thought would sell.

Within months, he began to reshape the way the top team worked together and in the way the trading department at corporate headquarters communicated with and incorporated store views into their buying decisions. He told everyone that stores were to be "loved" and listened to. He established multiple mechanisms for communication between headquarters and the stores, and between store management and customers and employees. Within nine months, a totally new approach to retailing and organizing and managing a store was created in the "renewal store" by the store manager and his top team working with a corporate cross-functional team. Sales increased immediately, as did morale. Over a six-year period, virtually every store in the company had gone through the renewal process. Sales and profits not only improved, but also improved at a faster rate than its competitors. By 1998, the stock price had multiplied eight folds.

The success of the renewal program – the heart of the change effort – rested on top management's recognition that it had to spread innovation in the first renewal store to all 200 stores. What enabled this to happen was top management's decision to withhold financial resources for a given store's renewal until its management had exhibited the behavior, and values of teamwork, delegation, and communication top management thought were critical to store performance. It also became clear to store managers that their career success was now dependent on leading a renewal process in their own store. A "Driving Test" – an assessment of the extent to which each store's management had turned barriers like the "silent killers" into organizational and managerial strengths – was employed to assess a store's senior team's readiness to lead change. In stores where this did not happen quickly enough, they replaced the store manager. Six years after the change effort began over 50% of store managers had been replaced with leaders who would and could lead store renewal.

Exceptions and Moderators: How Universal Are These Change Guidelines?

So long as the objectives of organizational change are the development of organizational capabilities for sustained competitive advantage over time, the principles and guidelines offered in this chapter hold. If, however, the objectives are short-term improvements in shareholder value without regard to developing organizational capability for the long term, the guidelines for change proposed in the chapter do not apply. Management that wants to obtain short-term improvements in stock price are much more likely to succeed by drastic restructuring, cost reductions, and layoffs. Considerable evidence exists that such steps enhance the stock price of companies in the short term, but do not create alignment and sustained high commitment and high performance (Cascio, 2002). This is precisely what Al Dunlap did in just a few years as CEO of Scott Paper. What was not downsized was sold. The company no longer exists today.

There are, of course, many instances where top management wants to build organizational capability for the long term, but the company's performance is so poor that drastic steps must be taken to reduce cost in the short run. Under these circumstances, there are two options (Beer and Nohria, 2000). The first option is to phase the change process so that restructuring (selling businesses that could not be turned around), productively improvements, cost reduction, and layoffs come first, followed by the action steps outlined in this chapter. That is what Jack Welch did at General Electric with great success. The second option is to press forward with both cost reduction and layoffs while also following the guidelines in this chapter for a change process that builds organizational capability. There is evidence that such a dual strategy, cost reduction and investment in building organizational capability, can lead to successful change (Beer et al., 1990; Beer and Nohria, 2000). Companies that emphasized cost reduction at the expense of the steps described here did not successfully change their culture.

Embedded in the change process recommended here is an assumption that leaders value excellence, people, involvement, teamwork, and learning, including learning about themselves. Autocratic, controlling, and defensive leaders are unlikely to be able to implement the seven-step change and alignment process. These steps require a commitment to building organizational capability, organizational learning, and to empowering leaders throughout the organization to lead change in their subunits. The somewhat slower pace of capability building change demands that leaders buy time by managing expectations of capital markets. Again, the case of ASDA described earlier is an excellent example of what can be done in this regard. By telling financial markets that they would not make major improvements in performance for three years, CEO Norman bought the time he needed to begin to rebuild organizational capabilities.

Conclusion

Organizations are complex multifaceted systems of organizing, managing, and leading developed from successes the business has had in dealing with past challenges. It is threats to power, status, esteem, and security and competence that are felt when the system needs to change that creates resistance to change. Fear leads to defensiveness and the inability to learn about what is no longer working, consider new alternatives, and develop a new system of organizing, managing, and leading.

Organizational change requires leaders who are ready to change the organization and their role as leaders. They use poor performance to develop dissatisfaction with the status quo among key people in the organization. When people come to believe that the organization's future is endangered, energy for change is released. Successful change managers lead a process that approximates the seven steps described in this chapter. They mobilize energy for change, develop a new compelling direction, identify organizational barriers to implementing the new strategy, develop a vision of how the organization will operate in the future, communicate the vision and involve people, support behavior change through coaching, and recycle learning and change to monitor progress and make new changes whenever the business faces new strategic inflections.

In large multiunit corporations, the responsibility for change lies with leaders at every level, not just with corporate top management. Top management's responsibility is to demand that unit managers lead change consistent with the competitive task faced by the company and by their unit. They then spread change to all parts of the larger organization through the transfer of managers from leading edge to lagging units. They must also lead change in the top management unit. Change can start anywhere but will be slow to spread, if it spreads at all, without a top management team committed to transforming the company and its many subunits.

The capacity to lead an organization through change is increasingly important as the pace of competition and change increases. It requires leaders who are ready to learn what is not working and lead change in their organization and how their own leadership. Adaptive organizations develop a disciplined process of organizational learning and change, replace leaders who are not ready to employ such processes, and develop and promote leaders who are.

References

Argyris, C. (1985). *Strategy, Change and Defensive Routines.* London: Pitman.

Argyris, C., and Schon, D. A. (1996). *Organizational Learning II: Theory, Method and Practice.* Reading, MA: Addison-Wesley.

Beer, M. (1980). *Organization Change and Development: A Systems View.* Santa Monica, CA: Goodyear.

Beer, M. (1991). *Leading Change.* Boston, MA, Harvard Business School Note, Boston, MA, Harvard Business School Press.

Beer, M. (2009). *Building High Commitment and High Performance Organizations.* San Francisco, CA: Jossey-Bass.

Beer, M. (2020). *Fit to Compete: Why Honest Conversations About Your Organization's Capabilities is the Key to a Winning Strategy.* Boston: Harvard Business Review Press.

Beer, M., Eisenstat, R. A., and Spector, B. (1990). Why change programs don't produce change. Harvard Business Review, November-December, 112–121.

Beer, M., and Eisenstat, R. (1996). Developing an organization capable of strategy implementation and learning. *Human Relations,* 49, 597–619.

Beer, M., and Eisenstat, R. A., (2000). The silent killers of strategy implementation and learning. Sloan Management Review, 41(4), 29–40.

Beer, M., and Eisenstat, R. (2004) How to have and honest conversation about your strategy. *Harvard Business Review,* November.

Beer, M., and Gibbs, M. (1990). *Apple Computer (Abridged): Corporate Strategy and Culture.* Boston, MA: Harvard Business School Case, Harvard Business School Press.

Beer, M., and Nohria, N. (eds) (2000) *Breaking the Code of Change,* Boston, MA: Harvard Business School Press.

Beer, M., and Rogers, G. A. (1997). *Hewlett Packard's Santa Rosa Systems Division.* Harvard Business School Case. Boston, MA: Harvard Business School Press.

Beer, M., and Weber, J. (1998a). *Allentown Materials Corporation: The Electronic Products Division (B).* Harvard Business School Case. Boston, MA: Harvard Business School Press.

Beer, M., and Weber, J. (1998b). *ASDA (A) (A1) (B) (C).* Harvard Business School Case. Boston, MA: Harvard Business School Press.

Beer, M, and Williamson, A. (1991). *Becton Dickinson: Corporate Strategy and Culture. Harvard Business School Case.* Boston, MA: Harvard Business School Press.

Beer, M., Eisenstat, R., and Spector, B. (1990). *The Critical Path to Corporate Renewal.* Boston, MA: Harvard Business School Press.

Cascio, W. F. (2002). *Responsible Restructuring: Creative and Profitable Alternatives to Layoffs.* San Francisco: Berrett-Koehler Publishers, Inc.

Detert, J., and Edmondson, A. (2011). Implicit voice theories: Taken-for-granted rules of self-censorship at work. *Academy of Management Journal,* 54(3), 461–488.

Eisenhardt, K. M. (1989). Making fast strategic decisions in high velocity environments. *Academy of Management Journal,* 32, 543–576.

Finkelstein, S. (2003). *Why Smart Executives Fail.* London: Portfolio.

Foster, R., and Kaplan, S. (2001). *Creative Destruction: Why Companies that are Built to Last Underperform the Market – And How to Transform Them.* New York: Doubleday.

Ghoshal, S., and Bartlett, C. A. (2000). Building behavioral context; A blueprint for corporate renewal. To appear in M. Beer and N. Nohria (eds), *Breaking the Code of Change.* Boston, MA: Harvard Business School Press.

Grove, A. (1996). *Only the Paranoid Survive.* New York, NY: Doubleday.

Hall, G., Rosenthal, J., and Wade, J. (1993). How to make reengineering really work. *Harvard Business Review,* Nov.–Dec.

Katz, D., and Kahn, R. L. (1978). The social psychology of organizations. New York: John Wiley & Sons.

Kotter, J. (1997). *Leading Change.* Boston, MA: Harvard Business School Press.

Kotter, J. (2008). *A Sense of Urgency.* Boston, MA: Harvard Business School Press.

Kotter, J., and Heskett, J, (1992). *Corporate Culture and Organizational Performance.* New York, NY: The Free Press.

Lawler, Edward III. (1997). *The New Logic of Organizations.* San Francisco, CA: Jossey-Bass.

Lawrence, P. R., and Lorsch, J. W (1967). *Organization and Environment.* Boston, MA: Division of Research, Graduate School of Business Administration, Harvard University.

Miles, R. E., and Snow, C. C. (1978). *Organizational Strategy, Structure and Process.* New York: McGraw Hill

Miller, D. (1990). *The Icarus Paradox: How Exceptional Companies Bring About Their Own Downfall.* New York: Harper Business.

Morrison, E. W., and Milliken, F. (2000). Organizational silence: A barrier to change and development in a pluralistic society. *Academy of Management Review,* 25(4), 706–725.

Nadler, D., and Tushman, M. L. (1988). *Strategic Organizational Design.* Homewood, IL, Scott Foresman.

Pfeffer, J. (1997). *New Directions for Organization Theory.* New York, NY: Oxford University Press.

Pfeffer, J. (1997). New directions for organization theory: Problems and prospects. Oxford, England: Oxford University Press.

Pfeffer, J. (1998). *The Human Equation.* Boston, MA: Harvard Business School Press.

Schaffer, R. H. (1988). *The Breakthrough Strategy: Using Short Term Successes to Build the High Performance Organization.* Cambridge, MA: Ballinger.

Schein, E, (1985). *Organizational Culture and Leadership.* San Francisco, CA: Jossey-Bass.

Schien, E. (1990). Organizational culture and leadership. New York: John Wiley & Sons.

Schein, E. H. (1990). Organizational culture. *American Psychologist,* 45, 109–119.

Schneider, B. (1994). The people make the place. *Personnel Psychology,* 40, 437–454.

Ulrich, D., Kerr, S., and Ashkenas, R. (2002). *GE Work-Out: How to Implement GE's Revolutionary Method for Busting Bureaucracy and Attacking Organizational Problems – Fast.* New York: McGraw-Hill.

Virany, B., Tushman, M., and Romanelli, E. (1992). Executive succession and organization outcomes in turbulent environments: An organization learning approach, *Organizational Science,* 3, 72–91.

Walton, R. E. (1987). *Innovating to Compete: Lessons for Diffusing and Managing Change in the Workplace.* San Francisco: Jossey-Bass.

Exercises

Assess the effectiveness of your MBA program and diagnose reasons for misalignment and ineffectiveness

1. Teams of three students will discuss what they expect to obtain from the MBA or EMBA education.
2. Each team develops a strategic statement of direction of three outcomes they expect from their MBA and three values they hope will guide individual and instructor behavior. e three or less primary goals of students is craftcrafte (30 minutes).
3. The goals will serve as the strategy statement for the remainder of the exercise.
4. Each trio will have the following task:
   a. Students interview each other about shortfalls they see in achieving student aspirations for the program and the barriers they see to their achievement (30 minutes).
   b. Each trio develops a consensus about three strengths of the program and three weaknesses or barriers to achieving desired outcomes (30 minutes).
   c. Each trio diagnoses the root causes for the success or failure of the MBA program in achieving strategic goals (45 minutes).
5. Two trios meet to share what they have learned about MBA program strengths and weaknesses.

Develop a change plan that will align the MBA program with strategic goals articulated in the first exercise

Each trio meets to develop an action plan for change in the MBA program (30 minutes).

1. Each group arrives at barriers to change they anticipate (20 minutes).
2. Each group develops recommendations for a change strategy the dean should employ (30 minutes).
3. Group reports: What are the barriers to change and their implications for leading change in the MBA program (30 minutes).
4. Instructor leads a discussion of reports.

Video Analysis and Discussion

Please watch the following video(s):

1. Six barriers to becoming a high-performance organization: https://youtu.be/L6zPYdpOqL8
2. Fit to compete: https://www.dropbox.com/s/5jumqeg0bczi3nq/Fit_to_Compete__Why_Honest_Conversations_About_Your_Company___s_Capabilities_are_the_Key_to_a_Winning_Strategy_v2_%28SD_Small_-_WEB_MBL_%28H264_900%29%29.mp4?dl=0

Now form small groups to discuss the video(s) and answer the following questions:

1. What are the major points of the video?
2. How can you use information from the video in your career?
3. Based on the video, what advice do you have for leaders in organizations?

Be prepared to present the ideas from your small group discussion with the class as a whole.

Discussion Questions

(i) What were key strengths of the MBA and key weaknesses or barriers to achieving your goals for the MBA program?
(ii) What are the key barriers to change?

14

Empowerment's Pivotal Role in Enhancing Effective Self- and Shared Leadership

JAY A. CONGER[1] AND CRAIG L. PEARCE[2]

[1]Kravis Leadership Institute Claremont McKenna College
[2]Pennsylvania State University

Empowerment is an essential building block of today's expressions of leadership. Its role has become particularly salient as our old notion of leadership as the responsibility of an individual at the top of an organization is being challenged. With the rise of knowledge workers, today's employees demand more than simply a good job and a paycheck. They expect to make more meaningful contributions through empowered self-leadership and team-based shared leadership (Pearce and Manz, 2005).

Empowerment and the latter forms of leadership are intertwined. For example, at the individual level of analysis, empowerment is experienced when followers engage in effective self-leadership (Houghton, Neck, and Manz, 2003; Manz and Sims, 1980), where self-leadership is defined as "a process through which people influence themselves to achieve the self-direction and self-motivation needed to perform" (Houghton et al., 2003, p. 126). The empirical evidence suggests that empowerment has a powerful positive influence on an individual's capacity to lead themselves (e.g. Liden, Wayne, and Sparrowe, 2000; Spreitzer, 1995; Spreitzer, Kizilos, and Nason 1994). Moving to the group level of analysis, empowerment is experienced when a group effectively practices shared leadership (Pearce and Conger, 2003; Pearce, 2004, 2008), where shared leadership is defined as "a dynamic, interactive influence process among individuals in groups for which the objective is to lead one another to the achievement of group or organizational goals or both" (Pearce and Conger, 2003, p. 1). Here again, the empirical evidence is fairly robust regarding the positive influence of empowerment (e.g. Ensley, Hmeileski, and Pearce, 2006; Pearce and Sims, 2002; Pearce, Yoo, and Alavi, 2004, Seibert, Wang, and Courtright, 2011).

THE EMPOWERMENT PROCESS

In recent decades, there has been a steady increase in interest in empowerment as a motivational tool in both the academic (e.g. Conger and Kanungo, 1988; Houghton et al., 2003; Liden and Arad, 1995; Mills and Ungson, 2003; Pearce and Sims, 2002; Thomas and Velthouse, 1990) and practitioner literature (e.g. Block, 1987; Conger, 1989; Manz and Sims, 1989, 2001; Pearce, 2008). The essence of empowerment, at the individual level of analysis, entails granting autonomy to individuals to perform tasks, while simultaneously enhancing their task-related self-efficacy (Bandura, 1986, 1997). Naturally, empowerment needs to be founded on appropriately set goals (Locke and Latham, 1990).

The actual process of empowerment can be viewed along six stages that include the psychological state of an empowering experience, its antecedent conditions, and its behavioral consequences. The six stages are shown in Figure 14.1. The first stage is the diagnosis of conditions within individuals and their organizations that are responsible for feelings of disempowerment. Following the diagnosis of disempowerment, leaders may employ certain strategies indicated in stage 2. The employment of these strategies is aimed not only at removing some of the conditions responsible for disempowerment, but also (and more importantly) at providing subordinates with empowerment information for stage 3. Individuals then interpret this information in stage 4 according to personal styles of assessment. If these styles assess the information as empowering, then an individual will feel empowered and the behavioral effects of empowerment will be observed in stage 5, where individuals become effective self-leaders (Manz and Sims, 1980). Beyond these five stages for the individual, empowerment can spread among group members and lead to group

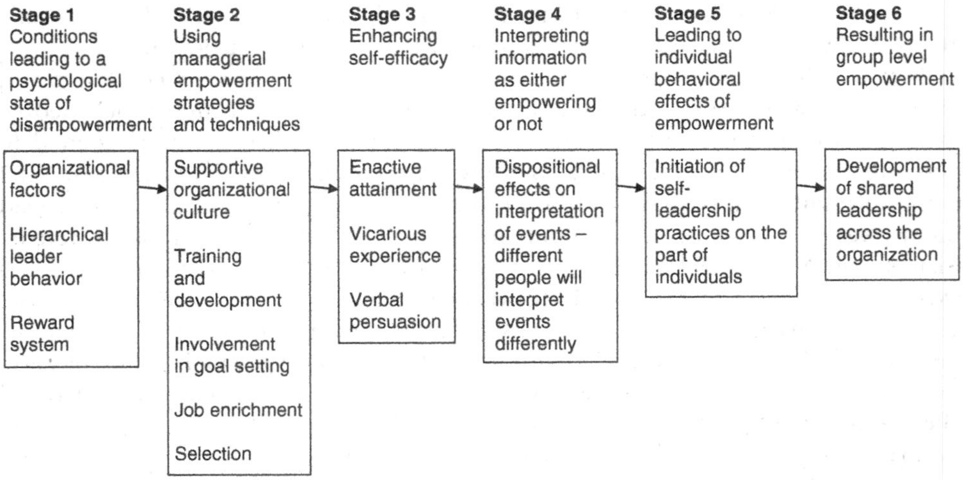

FIGURE 14.1 Stages of the empowerment process
Source: Adapted from Conger and Kanungo (1988).

empowerment, whose result is the display of shared leadership in stage 6 (Bligh, Pearce, and Kohles, 2006).

Stage 1

Starting with the first stage (the context), there are specific individual and contextual factors that contribute to the lowering of empowerment feelings among organizational members (Block, 1987; Conger, 1989; Kanter, 1979, 1983; Thomas and Velthouse, 1990). From the standpoint of organizational factors, Table 14.1 identifies some of the principal factors that influence and hinder empowerment outcomes. These are organized into four categories: (i) organizational, (ii) hierarchical leader behavior, (iii) reward systems, and (iv) job design. For instance, organizations with high levels of formalization and impersonal control systems can stifle member initiative, meaningfulness, and a sense of responsibility. Aversive and directive hierarchical leader behavior can strip control and discretion from organizational members (Pearce, Sims, Cox, Ball, Schnell, Smith, and Trevino, 2003: Pearce and Manz, 2005). Rewards may not be allocated on the basis of members' competence or innovative behavior, but rather on their blind compliance with formalized control from the top. When organizations do not provide rewards that are valued by members, and when the rewards are not based on member competence, initiative, and innovative job behavior, employees' sense of disempowerment increases (Sims, 1977; Szilagyi, 1980). Reward systems that emphasize innovative/unusual performance and high incentive values have a significant probability of fostering a greater sense of empowerment, while those that do not tend to disempower (Kanter, 1979; Kanungo, 1987; Lawler, 1971, 1977). Finally, when jobs provide very little challenge and meaning, and when they involve role ambiguity, role conflict, and role overload, employees can feel a crippling sense of disempowerment (Lawler and Finegold, 2000).

Stage 2

To address conditions of disempowerment (stage 2), there are a number of management practices that can restore or heighten a sense of empowerment. For example, at the organizational level, company policies and cultures can emphasize self-determination, internal collaboration over competition, high performance standards, nondiscrimination, and meritocracy. In addition, organizations that provide multiple sources of loosely committed resources at decentralized or local levels, that structure open communications systems, and that create extensive network-forming devices are more likely to be empowering (Kanter, 1983). Jobs that provide task variety, personal relevance, appropriate autonomy and control, low levels of established routines and rules, and high advancement prospects are more likely to empower subordinates (Block, 1987; Hackman, Oldham, Janson, and Purdy, 1975; Kanter, 1979; Oldham, 1976; Strauss, 1977).

TABLE 14.1 Context factors leading to potential lowering of empowerment beliefs

Organizational factors
- Significant organizational changes/transitions
- Competitive pressures
- Impersonal bureaucratic climate
- Poor communications/network-forming systems
- Highly centralized organizational resources

Hierarchical leader behavior
- Directive (high control)
- Aversive (emphasis on fear)
- Negativism (emphasis on failure)
- Lack of reason for actions/consequences

Reward systems
- Noncontingency (arbitrary reward allocation)
- Low incentive value of rewards
- Lack of competence-based rewards
- Lack of innovation-based rewards

Job design
- Lack of role clarity
- Lack of training and technical support
- Unrealistic goals
- Lack of appropriate authority/discretion
- Low task variety
- Limited participation in programs, meetings, and decisions that have a direct impact on job performance
- Lack of appropriate/necessary resources
- Lack of network-forming opportunities
- Highly established work routines
- High rule structure
- Low advancement opportunities
- Lack of meaningful goals/tasks
- Limited contact with senior management

Source: Adapted from Conger and Kanungo (1988).

The practices mentioned earlier can be viewed from the different perspectives of either formal/organizational mechanisms or individual/informal techniques. Organizations require both types to effectively instill a context of empowerment. For example, when organizations engage in participation programs, they establish formal systems that empower organizational members through the sharing of information, formal power, and authority.

In order for this sharing of power to be effective at the individual level, however, employees must perceive it as increasing their sense of self-efficacy – which is accomplished largely through the more informal practices of individual leaders and in their one-on-one interactions with subordinates and coworkers (Conger and Kanungo, 1998). Empowerment initiatives that rely on a singular approach, such as the delegation of decision-making, usually prove to be ineffective. Rather, initiatives must be supported on multiple levels and by multiple interventions. In the ideal case, they would involve a highly supportive organizational culture; training and developmental experiences that heighten one's sense of competence; involvement in goal setting or, especially, in the means to achieve goals, job designs that are highly meaningful to employees; the selection of managers open to empowerment approaches and proactive in their use; and the selection and promotion of employees whose interpretative schemes are biased toward constructive and enabling self-assessments (Liden and Arad, 1995; Spreitzer et al., 1994).

Stage 3

In order to be effective, the empowerment practices outlined earlier must directly provide information to employees about personal efficacy, a sense of choice, meaningfulness of the task, and impact (stage three). For example, on the dimension of competence or self-efficacy, Bandura (1986, 1997) has identified four sources of such information: enactive attainment, vicarious experience, persuasion/feedback, and emotional arousal state. Personal efficacy gained through enactive attainment refers to an individual's authentic mastery experience directly related to the job. For example, a leader can allocate or structure tasks that provide an empowering experience for an individual. When subordinates are trained to perform complex tasks or are given more responsibility in their jobs, they have the opportunity to increase their efficacy and to receive positive feedback. Initial success experiences (through successively moderate increments in task complexity and responsibility along with training to acquire new skills) can make one feel more capable and, therefore, more empowered.

Empowerment information can also come from the vicarious experiences of observing similar others, i.e. coworkers, who perform successfully on the job. Very often, a leader's exemplary behaviors empower subordinates to believe that they can behave in a like manner or that they can at least achieve some improvement in their performance. In addition, words of encouragement, performance feedback, mentoring advice, and other forms of social persuasion are often used by leaders, managers, and group members to raise efficacy and provide empowerment information to subordinates and coworkers (Conger, 1989; Pearce and Sims, 2002). For instance, leaders may use annual meetings to provide empowering information in the form of praise and encouragement for exceptional performance. Through positive performance evaluations, managers may similarly foster an empowered state. Naturally, this does not imply that one should raise the performance evaluations of direct reports irrespective of their actual performance. Falseness breeds distrust.

Leadership practices that have been identified as empowering include (i) expressing confidence in subordinates accompanied by high performance expectations (Burke, 1986; Conger, 1989; House, 1977; Neilsen, 1986); (ii) fostering opportunities for subordinates to participate in decision-making and goal setting or to create their own jobs (Block, 1987; Burke, 1986; Conger, 1989; Erez and Arad, 1986;

House 1977; Kanter, 1979; Neilsen, 1986; Strauss, 1977); (iii) providing autonomy from bureaucratic constraints and encouraging independent action (Block, 1987; Ensley et al., 2006; Kanter, 1979; Pearce and Sims, 2002); (iv) setting inspirational and/or meaningful goals (Bennis and Nanus, 1985; Block, 1987; Conger and Kanungo, 1998; McClelland, 1975; Tichy and Devanna, 1986); and (v) encouraging self-development and opportunity thinking (Houghton et al., 2003; Manz and Sims, 1989, 2001).

Finally, personal competence expectations are affected by one's emotional arousal state. Individuals are more likely to feel competent when they are not experiencing strong negative arousal. Emotional arousal states that result from dysfunctional levels of stress, fear, anxiety, depression, and so forth, both on and off the job, can lower self-efficacy expectations. Therefore, empowerment strategies that provide information in the form of emotional support for subordinates and that create a supportive and trusting group atmosphere (Neilsen, 1986) can be effective in strengthening self-efficacy beliefs. For example, employees' stress, anxiety, and tension on the job can be reduced by managers clearly defining employees' roles, reducing information overload, and offering them technical assistance to accomplish job tasks. Similarly, the impact of depression and self-doubt on subordinates as a result of failures on the job could be lessened by their supervisor attributing such failures to external and unstable factors (assuming there are valid reasons for doing so) such as task difficulty, inadequate support systems, and so forth, rather than attributing it to the individual's efforts or abilities (Weiner, 1985). Employees, of course, must learn to take personal responsibility for what they can control.

Stages 4–6

As a result of receiving the above forms of information, employees will interpret this information according to their individual styles of assessment in stage 4. In other words, personal interpretations will determine whether the information is seen as empowering or not. Depressed individuals, for example, are less likely to see successes as indicative of their own competence. Others may have irrational standards of perfection that, in turn, reduce perceptions of personal empowerment. For these very reasons, a careful selection of employees is necessary. In the next section where we discuss exceptions, we will describe this assessment process in greater depth since it directly affects the success of any empowerment initiative.

If information is indeed interpreted as empowering, then the individual will enter a state of psychological empowerment – and the behavioral effects of empowerment will be noticed in stage 5 – followers becoming effective self-leaders (Manz and Sims, 1980). Beyond the behavioral effects of empowerment on individuals are the effects on groups. As individuals display effective self-leadership, the creation of shared leadership is the logical next step (stage 6). According to Bligh et al. (2006, p. 20), "the development of the self-leadership capabilities of team members sets into motion the meso-level processes that result in higher collective-levels of trust, potency, and commitment, which in turn facilitate the sustained sharing of mutual influence within the team that comprises shared leadership."

Boundary Conditions/Moderators

We do not advocate empowerment as a new panacea for all organizational woes or to address leadership challenges or gaps. Clearly, there are limitations regarding the efficacy of empowerment. As Locke (2003) has indicated, there are certain tasks that are the responsibility of the most senior leader. For example, Locke (2003, p. 278) noted that "core values must be pushed from the top down." In fact, we believe there are situations in which empowerment is actually harmful, (e.g. it could create anarchy with respect to core values). Further, empowerment could produce a state of overconfidence in leaders and their followers and, in turn, misjudgments on the part of both. Because of a sense of false confidence in positive outcomes, employees might persist in efforts that, in actuality, are tactical or strategic errors.

Similarly, followers might overextend themselves through tasks that are largely impossible to accomplish. Leaders also might use such practices to garner commitment to tasks that are unethical. The positive personal effects that are felt by followers during empowering experiences may blind them to the leader's own pragmatic (whatever works for me today), non-value-driven agenda or the nefarious manipulation of others. (Self-interest is a good thing if it is tied to proper values.)

There may also be situations where leaders and organizations have little latitude to increase a sense of empowerment. For example, some jobs are highly mechanistic and routine. No matter what attempts are made at redesign, the jobs remain essentially the same. Serious economic downturns or intense competitive situations may limit an organization's ability to provide inspiring goals or appealing rewards other than simple job security. Trapped in autocratic cultures, leaders wishing to empower may find themselves constrained by the larger system – their efforts at empowerment largely negated by the overriding culture or design elements of the organization.

Finally, there is the crucial issue of individual differences. For instance, some individuals may not have the requisite skills, ethical disposition, or conscientiousness necessary for empowerment. Further, during the process of empowerment, individuals are making subjective assessments about information and specific tasks. One individual may assess the same information quite differently from another. For example, some styles of assessment are properly self-enhancing, and others are self-debilitating (Peale, 1954). As such, what might be an empowering experience for one individual may be a disempowering or nonempowering one for another. In the latter case, an individual may have set dysfunctional standards in the form of absolutistic "musts" concerning tasks. They may have the personal standard of "Perfection [outside of any rational context] is my goal on all dimensions of this task." Such standards tend to reduce a person's assessment of their success since anything short of perfection is seen as failure (Thomas and Velthouse, 1990). Followers can also get trapped in these self-reinforcing cycles. Low personal assessments of their competence can lead to low initiative and inactivity, which further reinforces perceptions of low success and a sense of low competence (Thomas and Velthouse, 1990).

Followers' rational confidence in themselves clearly plays a central role. The motivation to undertake any new activity requires a measure of self-confidence on the part of individuals and a sense of potency (Bligh et al., 2006; Gully et al., 2005), or collective confidence, on the part of groups. If an individual has a strong foundation of belief in themselves, they are likely to be more optimistic than others when engaging in activities where information about task assessments is uncertain or cloudy (Thomas and Velthouse, 1990). In addition, followers vary to the degree in which they invest themselves psychologically in tasks. Termed "global meaningfulness," this concept describes an individual's overall level of caring or commitment to tasks. People differ considerably along this dimension (Solomon and Patch, 1970). Individuals with low levels of global meaningfulness tend to experience alienation and are less likely to believe that new tasks will be meaningful (Thomas and Velthouse, 1990).

Given the psychological dynamics discussed earlier, empowerment interventions must take into careful consideration the individuals, groups, and tasks involved. For some, their psychological outlook may prove a serious barrier to empowerment. Instead, it will be their capacity for self-reflection and learning that will determine, over the long term, whether they can at some point experience empowerment. At the same time, extended and persistent efforts at empowerment on the part of leaders will be required under such circumstances. With some individuals, there may be little that a leader or coworker can, or should, do to empower them. This is especially true for followers who are in a psychologically unbalanced state. Outside professional help – for example, psychotherapy – may be the only possible option. For this very reason, careful selection and placement are critical factors.

Case Examples

To understand how empowerment works in the real world, we will look first at two positive examples and one negative/positive example. Each will be drawn from case studies of actions undertaken by senior organizational leaders to empower their workforces.

Richard Branson, the Virgin Group

As chief executive officer of the Virgin Group (a diversified British company encompassing entertainment/communications businesses and an airline), Richard Branson employs a variety of means to empower members of the company. At an organizational level, he preserves an entrepreneurial atmosphere through a Japanese-style keiretsu structure whereby the 40 companies operating in 35 countries under the Virgin Group operate quasi-independently but collaboratively in a global network (Kets de Vries and Dick, 1995). Once a company reaches a certain size, it is split into several organizations so that employees retain their sense of identity with their organization and a small-company, entrepreneurial atmosphere is preserved. At the individual level, each unit is led by a managing director who has considerable freedom to lead the business as they see fit and who has an equity position in the company. Decision-making within the company is, therefore, decentralized. At the same time, senior managers have access to Branson for advice and guidance and can reach him 24 hours a day (Kets de Vries and Dick, 1995).

To further promote individual entrepreneurship within the company, employees with attractive ideas for new ventures are provided with seed capital and ownership. As a result, many of the Virgin companies are the product of employee ideas. A bridal service division called Virgin Bride, for example, was the idea of a Virgin Airways stewardess to whom Branson provided "venture capital." The company's new ventures allow Branson to stretch and develop employees by creating more opportunities for upward mobility and greater responsibility (Kets de Vries and Dick, 1995).

A central tenet of the company's culture is the importance of employees. Branson's maxim is staff first, customers second, and shareholders third, and Branson clearly keeps an eye on these results. As a result, he has created a culture which is egalitarian, nonbureaucratic, friendly, and family-like in atmosphere. The culture is one where people enjoy their work and have fun. It is also one which emphasizes proactivity. As Branson likes to say, "We can decide on something in the morning and have it in operation by the afternoon" (Kets de Vries and Dick, 1995). Taken together, the corporate culture, the company's organizational design/reward systems, and Branson's leadership style work effectively to create a cadre of empowered managers.

Julie Morath, Children's Hospital and Clinics of Minneapolis

Hired in May of 1999 as the chief operating officer of the Children's Hospital and Clinics of Minneapolis, Julie Morath launched a major initiative to improve patient safety at the hospital (Tucker, Edmondson, and Roberto, 2007). She introduced changes in the hospital's systems, processes, and culture all to stimulate learning and to empower the workforce of physicians, nurses and administrators. Among her early initiatives was the extensive use of confidential focus groups. These were designed to give these critical stakeholders voice and ownership of the safety initiative. Rather than build the case for greater safety by herself, she employed the focus groups to gather data on the current state of patient safety and to identify and dismantle the barriers that prevented individuals from discussing medical accidents. These sessions generated grassroots' enthusiasm for the safety initiative. Fundamental to her approach to empowerment was the transformation of the organization's culture around medical errors and accidents. Historically, a serious error resulted in "finger pointing" where individuals were singled out and blamed for the failures and then disciplined. Julie wanted to establish an environment where everyone was focused instead on learning from past mistakes and generating solutions to address errors. She explained that only rarely were accidents the product of one person's poor decision. Rather, most medical errors were the result of a series of small breakdowns in complex systems. To reinforce this perspective, she introduced a new system for reporting medical accidents, which she called "blameless reporting." Individuals could communicate accidents confidentially and anonymously without being punished. The goal was to surface as many accidents as possible and determine their underlying causes. This system empowered nurses and doctors to not only deeply examine the root causes of safety issues but to focus on truly effective solutions generated by the care givers themselves rather than through the bureaucracy. She also created forums for all of Children's employees to come together and learn about the current state of research on medical safety. These educational forums encouraged many individuals to learn more about the science of improving safety in complex systems. One outcome was the creation of "safety action teams" where cross-functional teams of eight employees would meet monthly to discuss medication safety issues. These teams would generate ideas and recommendations that were then shared across the hospital. These action teams proved to be a powerful source of frontline empowerment. They rooted out unnecessary complexity and policy barriers that had prevented nurses and physicians from providing safe care to patients.

To and from the Depths of Despair

Part A This is the tale of an organization on the brink of disaster and of deep disempowerment. The company was known, for decades, as the standard bearer of quality in their industry. They were a commercial powerhouse in engineering and manufacturing. Under the rule of a dictatorial leader, however, the company systematically fell apart. This case is focused on just one of their facilities, located in the mid-Atlantic United States, which was an exemplar of the company's woes. This facility had approximately one million square feet under roof and employed approximately 5000 individuals. Then, corporate leadership decided that payroll expenses were too high and that workforce reductions were an effective solution. First, they outsourced one of the main product lines of the facility. As a result, the remaining workers felt deep discontent and disempowerment. A by-product was the decline in quality – the very dimension that differentiated the organization in the marketplace. Soon to follow was a downturn in profitability. According to the general manager of the facility, "We began to hemorrhage."

Following the outsourcing campaign, the corporate leaders decided that they wanted to break the union in order to lower wages and restore profitability. Accordingly, they transferred a third of the work to a different state, a right-to-work state. The union did not take that action lying down. They ultimately organized a union in the new location. According to the president of the union, "We took that action because the company had thrown down the gauntlet. And the fight began. The company was fighting their own workforce . . . and we won."

Soon on the heels of the transfer of work to the right-to-work state were contract negotiations with the union, and the company feared a walkout. This precipitated what came to be known as "the strike bank incident." The strike bank incident involved the company ordering employees to work mandatory overtime in order to build up a reserve of parts to tide them through in the event of a strike. According to the general manager, "It was chaos. We had parts hanging from the ceiling. And of course, quality went to hell, and we further alienated the workforce."

The upshot of all of these draconian management actions were several bomb threats, which caused the evacuation of the massive facility and continued disruption to the operations. Meanwhile, the organization continued to tally up record losses. The facility hit rock bottom when they experienced a murder and a suicide attempt.

Part B Organizations, just like people, often need to hit rock bottom before they change, and this is exactly what happened in this case. Following the last incident, the general manager and the president of the union got together and decided to bring in an outside consulting firm to help them get back on course. The general manager stated, "We decided to focus on quality as a way to rebuild our relationship with employees. Nobody can argue with quality." The president of the union was in complete agreement, stating, "We didn't want to fight. We never wanted to fight. We wanted to have pride in our work."

Thus, they focused on workforce empowerment through several initiatives. It started with 20 hours of training for every single employee. The training focused on such things as problem-solving, decision-making, communication, and teamwork skills. The initial training was done by the consulting firm. From there out, the training was conducted by volunteers, from the shop floor.

Employees were formed into dozens of what they called Quality Action Teams. The teams were empowered to take on the quality problems facing the firm. Naturally, the transition was not easy for all of the managers (now called team leaders) involved. For example, the general manager recalled, "We had three guys who just couldn't make the transition. We told them 'No more hard ass, now you're a coach and a facilitator.' They just didn't want to make the adjustment. And lucky for them, we were able to give them early retirement."

Over time, the transition to an empowered workforce took hold. The plant saw steady rises in quality, productivity, and profitability. About a year into the process, one incident marked the turning point. The general manager recounted, "We started up a machine – it didn't work – it shut down our assembly plant. So we put together a team, and these guys were incredible. They were truly a super team. Every one of those guys showed real leadership, and in the end they had the machine back up and running. I put their success story up on the marquee, at the entrance to the plant to give them some recognition. That's when everybody realized what a little teamwork could do."

According to the union president, "In the past, common sense never entered into the picture. It was 'Do it the way we're telling you to do it because we're the managers and you're the employees.' Now each member of the team is expected to contribute to the leadership of the team. We've come a long way." One of the shop floor employees summarized the transition to empowerment the best by stating, "I finally feel liberated . . . yeah liberated, that's the word for it. For all these years I was just doing what I was told to do. Now Bob [the team leader] asks me what I think we should do. My ideas finally matter, and it feels great!"

In the end, quality was improved by a factor of 10, the workforce was positively engaged, and the company returned to solid profitability. In fact, they ultimately, after about three years onto the road to empowerment, won their State Senate Productivity Award – analogous to the Malcolm Baldridge Award at the national level – an award the general manager and union president alike credit their success to the empowerment of the workforce.

Conclusion

As readers will have realized by now, empowerment holds remarkable opportunities when it comes to leadership. We believe that we are in an era that is demanding far more self- and shared leadership, where power is truly distributed across a greater number of individuals, as well as up and down the hierarchy. Only when we have achieved a greater appreciation for the positive outcomes associated with the role of empowerment in promoting leadership and a real understanding of the many ways in which it contributes to enhancing the quality of leadership, will we be able to harness its full potential to contribute to organizational performance. Only then, will our traditional notions of leadership – as personified in the solitary individual in a position of authority where followers are simply interchangeable "parts" – become a thing of the past.

References

Abramson, L. Y., Garber, J., and Seligman, M. E. P. (1980). Learned helplessness in humans: An attributional analysis. In J. Garber and M. E. P. Seligman (eds), *Human Helplessness: Theory and Applications* (pp. 3–34). New York: Academic Press.

Abramson, L., Scligman, M., and Tcasdale, J. (1978). Learned helplessness in humans: Critique and reformulation. *Journal of Abnormal Psychology*, 87, 19–74.

Bligh, M., Pearce, C. L., and Kohles, J. (2006). The Importance of self and shared leadership in team based knowledge work: Toward a meso-level model of leadership dynamics. *Journal of Managerial Psychology*, 21(4), 296–318.

Bandura, A. (1986). *Social Foundations of Thought and Action: A Social-Cognitive View.* Englewood Cliffs, NJ: Prentice-Hall.

Bandura, A. (1997). *Self-Efficacy: The Exercise of Control.* New York: W. H. Freeman.

Bennis, W., and Nanus, B. (1985). *Leaders.* New York: Harper & Row.

Block, P. (1987). *The Empowered Manager.* San Francisco: Jossey-Bass.

Burke, W. (1986). Leadership as empowering others. In S. Srivastra (ed.), *Executive Power* (pp. 5177). San Francisco: Jossey-Bass.

Conger, J. A. (1989). Leadership: The art of empowering others. *Academy of Management Executive*, 33, 17–24.

Conger, J. A., and Kanungo, R. N. (1988). The empowerment process: Integrating theory and practice. *Academy of Management Review*, 31, 471–482.

Conger, J. A., and Kanungo, R. N. (1998). *Charismatic Leadership in Organizations.* Thousand Oaks, CA: Sage Publications.

Ensley, M. D., Hmieleski, K. M., and Pearce, C. L. (2006). The importance of vertical and shared leadership within new venture top management teams: Implications for the performance of startups. *Leadership Quarterly*, 17(3), 217–231.

Erez, M., and Arad, R. (1986). Participative goal setting: Social, motivational, and. cognitive factors. *Journal of Applied Psychology*, 71(4), 591–597.

Hackman, J. R., Oldham, G. R., Janson, R., and Purdy, K. (1975). New strategy for job enrichment. *California Management Review*, 17(4), 57–71.

Houghton, J. D., Neck, C. P., and Manz, C. C. (2003). *Self-leadership and SuperLeadership: The Heart and Art of Creating Shared Leadership in Teams* (pp. 123–135). In C. L. Pearce and J. A. Conger (eds), *Shared leadership: Reframing the Hows and Whys of Leadership*, Thousand Oaks, CA: Sage Publications.

House, R. J. (1977). A 1976 theory of charismatic leadership. In J. G. Hunt and L. L. Larson (eds), *Leadership: The Cutting Edge* (pp. 189–207). Carbondale: Southern Illinois University Press.

Kanter, R. M. (1979). Power failure in management circuits. *Harvard Business Review*, 57(4), 65–75.

Kanter, R. M. (1983). *The Change Masters*. New York: Simon & Schuster.

Kanungo, R. N. (1987). Reward management: A new look. In S. L. Dolan and R. S. Schuler (eds), *Canadian Readings in Personnel and Human Resource Management* (pp. 261–275). St. Paul: West.

Kets de Vries, M. F. R., and Dick, R. J. (1995). *Branson's Virgin: The Coming of Age of a Counter-Cultural Enterprise*. Fontainebleau, France: INSEAD.

Lawler, E. E. (1971). *Pay and Organizational Effectiveness: A Psychological View*. New York: McGraw-Hill.

Lawler, E. E. (1977). Reward systems. In J. R. Hackman and L. J. Suttle (eds), *Improving Life at Work: Behavioral Science Approaches to Organizational Flange* (pp. 163–226). Santa Monica, CA: Goodyear.

Lawler, E. E., and Fingold, D. (2000). Individualizing the organization: Past, present and future. *Organizational Dynamics*, 29(1), 1–15.

Liden, R. C., and Arad, S. (1995). A power perspective of empowerment and work teams: Implications for human resource management research. *Research in Personnel and Human Resource Management*, 14.

Liden, R. C., Wayne, S. J., and Sparrowe, R. T. (2000). An examination of the Mediating role of psychological empowerment on the relations between the job, interpersonal relationships, and work outcomes. *Journal of Applied Psychology*, 85(3), June, 407–416.

Locke, E. A. (2003). Leadership. In C. L. Pearce and J. A. Conger (eds), *Shared Leadership: Reframing the Hows and Whys of Leadership* (pp. 271–283). Thousand Oaks, CA: Sage Publications.

Locke, E. A., and Latham, G. (1990). *A Theory of Goal Setting and Task Performance*. New York: Prentice Hall.

Manz, C. C., and Sims, H. P., Jr. (1980). Self-management as a substitute for leadership: A social learning theory perspective. *Academy of Management Review*, 5(3), 361–367.

Manz, C. C., and Sims, H. P., Jr. (1989). *Superleadership: Leading Others to Lead Themselves*. New York: Prentice Hall Press.

Manz, C. C., and Sims, H. P., Jr. (2001). *The New Superleadership*. San Francisco: Berrett-Koehler.

McClelland, D. C. (1975). *Power: The Inner Experience*. New York Irvington Press.

Mills, P. K., and Ungson, G. R. (2003). Reassessing the limits of structural empowerment: Organizational constitution and trust as controls. *Academy of Management Review, 28*, 143–153.

Neilsen, E. (1986). Empowerment strategies: Balancing authority and responsibility. In S. Srivastra (ed.), *Executive Power* (pp. 78–110). San Francisco: Jossey-Bass.

Oldham, G. R. (1976). The motivational strategies used by supervisors' relationships to effectiveness indicators. *Organizational Behavior and Human Performance*, 15, 66–86.

Peale, N. V. (1954). *The Power of Positive Thinking.* New York: Prentice-Hall.

Pearce, C. L. (2004). The future of leadership: Combining vertical and shared leadership to transform knowledge work. *Academy of Management Executive*, 18(1), 47–57.

Pearce, C. L. (July 7, 2008). Follow the leaders. *Wall Street Journal*, B8, 12

Pearce, C. L., and Conger, J. A. (eds) (2003). *Shared leadership: Reframing the Hows and Whys of Leadership.* Thousand Oaks, CA, Sage Publications.

Pearce, C. L., and Sims, H. P. (2002). Vertical versus shared leadership as predictors of the effectiveness of change management teams: An examination of aversive, directive, transactional, transformational, and empowering leader behaviors. *Group Dynamics: Theory, Research, and Practice*, 6(2), 172–197.

Pearce, C. L., Sims, H. P., Jr., Cox, J. F., Ball, G., Schnell, E., Smith, K. A., and Trevino, L. (2003). Transactors, transformers and beyond: A multi-method development of a theoretical typology of leadership. *Journal of Management Development*, 22(4), 273–307.

Pearce, C. L., Yoo, Y., and Alavi, M. (2004). Leadership, social work and virtual teams: The relative influence of vertical vs. shared leadership in the nonprofit sector. In R. E. Riggio and S. Smith-Orr (eds), *Improving Leadership in Nonprofit Organizations* (pp. 180–203). San Francisco: Jossey Bass.

Pearce, C. L., and Manz, C. C. (2005) The new silver bullets of leadership: The importance of self- and shared leadership in knowledge work. *Organizational Dynamics*, 34(2), 130–140.

Seibert, S. E., Wang, G., and Courtright, S. H. (2011) Antecedents and consequences of psychological and team empowerment in organizations: A meta-analytic review. *Journal of Applied Psychology*, 96(5), 981–1003.

Sims, H. P. (1977). The leader as a manager of reinforcement contingencies. In J. G. Hunt and L. L. Larson (eds), *Leadership: The Cutting Edge* (pp. 121–137). Carbondale: Southern Illinois University Press.

Solomon, P., and Patch, V. D. (1970). *Handbook of Psychiatry* (2nd edition). Los Angeles: Lange Medical Publications.

Spreitzer, G. M. (1995). Individual empowerment in the workplace: Dimensions, measurement, and validation. *Academy of Management Journal*, 38, 1442–1465.

Spreitzer, G. M., Kizilos, M. A., and Nason, S. W. (1994). A dimensional analysis of the relationship between psychological empowerment and effectiveness, satisfaction, and strain. Paper presented at the Western Academy of Management Meetings.

Strauss, G. (1977). Managerial practices. In J. R. Hackman and L. J. Suttle (eds), *Improving Life at Work: Behavioral Science Approaches to Organizational Change* (pp. 297–363). Santa Monica, CA: Goodyear.

Szilagyi, A. D. (1980). Causal inferences between leader reward behavior and subordinate goal attainment, absenteeism, and work satisfaction. *Journal of Occupational Psychology*, 53, 195–204.

Thomas, K. W., and Velthouse, B. A. (1990). Cognitive elements of empowerment. *Academy of Management Review*, 15, 666–681.
Tichy, N. M., and Devanna, M. A. (1986). *The Transformational Leader*. New York: Wiley.
Tucker, A., Edmondson, A., and Roberto, M. A. (2007). *Children's Hospital and Clinics (A)*. Boston: Harvard Business School Publishing.
Weiner, B. (1985). An attributional theory of achievement motivation and emotion. *Psychological Review*, 92, 548–573.

Exercises

Your empowerment profile

Step 1: Complete the following questionnaire.

For each of the following items, select the alternative with which you feel more comfortable. Although you may feel both a and b describe you in some items or neither is ever applicable in others, you should select the alternative that better describes you most of the time.

1. When I have to give a talk or write a paper, I
__ a. base the content of my talk or paper on my own ideas
__ b. do a lot of research, and present the findings of others in my paper or talk.
2. When I read something I disagree with, I
__ a. assume my position is correct
__ b. assume what's presented in the book or article is correct.
3. When someone makes me extremely angry, I
a. ask the other person to stop the behavior that is offensive to me
b. say little, not quite knowing how to state my position.
4. When I do a good job, it is important to me that
a. the job represents the best I can do
b. others take notice of the job I've done.
5. When I buy new clothes, I
__ a. buy what looks best on me
__ b. try to dress in accordance with the latest fashion.
6. When something goes wrong, I
__ a. try to solve the problem
__ b. try to find out who's at fault.
7. As I anticipate my future, I
a. am confident I will be able to lead the kind of life I want to lead
b. worry about being able to live up to my obligations.
8. When examining my own resources and capacities, I
__ a. like what I find
__ b. find all kinds of things I wish were different.
9. When someone treats me unfairly, I
__ a. put my energies into getting what I want
__ b. tell others about the injustice.

10. When someone criticizes my efforts, I
 __ a. ask questions in order to understand the basis for the criticism
 __ b. defend my actions or decisions, trying to make my critic understand why I did what I did.
11. When I engage in an activity, it is very important to me that
 __ a. I live up to my own expectations
 __ b. I live up to the expectations of others.
12. When I let someone else down or disappoint them, I
 __ a. resolve to do things differently next time
 __ b. feel guilty and wish I had done things differently.
13. I try to surround myself with people
 __ a. whom I respect
 __ b. who respect me.
14. I try to develop friendships with people who
 __ a. are challenging and exciting
 __ b. can make me feel a little safer and a little more secure.
15. I make my best efforts when
 __ a. I do something I want to do when I want to do it
 __ b. someone else gives me an assignment, a deadline, and a reward for performing.
16. When I love a person, I
 __ a. encourage him or her to be free and choose for himself or herself
 __ b. encourage him or her to do the same thing I do and to make choices similar to mine.
17. When I play a competitive game, it is important to me that I
 __ a. do the best I can
 __ b. win.
18. I really like being around people who
 __ a. can broaden my horizons and teach me something
 __ b. can and want to learn from me.
19. My best days are those that
 __ a. present unexpected opportunities
 __ b. go according to plan.
20. When I get behind in my work, I
 __ a. do the best I can and don't worry
 __ b. worry or push myself harder than I should.

Step 2: Score your responses as follows:

Total your a responses:__________ Total your b responses: __________

(If you score higher on "a" in comparison to "b," you feel relatively empowered. If you score higher on "b" than "a," you feel relatively disempowered. The difference between the two scores indicates the relative amount of empowerment (or disempowerment) you feel.)

Step 3: Discussion. In small groups or with the entire class, answer the following questions:

DESCRIPTION

1. Look at the two totals. Which score is highest? Which is lowest?
2. Do your scores describe you well? Why or why not?

DIAGNOSIS WITH A PARTNER

3. Discuss some experiences you have had that confirm your score.
4. Discuss some experiences you have had that disconfirm your score.
5. How does this information help you to act more effectively in organizations?
6. Discuss this with the class as a whole.

Source: "The Empowerment Profile" from *The Power Handbook* by Pamela Cuming. Copyright © 1980 by CBI Publishing. Reprinted by permission of Van Nostrand Reinhold Co. Inc.

Analysis of the Film Dead Poets Society

Instructions:

The film, ideally, should be assigned to be viewed outside of class time. During class, the instructor will queue up several scenes to prompt discussion. Below is a list of discussion questions to guide the interpretation of the film:

- Under what conditions are individuals willing and motivated to accept empowerment?
- What is the effect of individual differences in empowerment?
- What are the effects of specific leader behaviors on followers, and do the effects differ by follower?
- What is the importance of background factors, such as the norms in place in the institution or the role of other influential individuals to the process?
- How does leadership come to be shared and how do the roles transition between various characters?
- How can empowerment go awry if followers do not have sufficient skills to make sound judgment, and how can you attempt to prevent this from happening?
- How do we apply the principles we have been discussing to organizations?

Film description:

The film *Dead Poets Society* (DPS) is set at a private school – the Welton Academy for boys. During their first class with their English teacher, Mr. Keating, the boys are taken out into the hallway, where he tells them they are bright individuals, with the power to choose their own path – to essentially become self-leaders. This is in stark contrast to the teaching norms at the academy. As such, Mr. Keating clearly demonstrates empowering leader behavior. As the movie progresses, we steadily see the boys take on this newfound empowerment and become effective self-leaders.

One day, one of the boys finds an old yearbook with Mr. Keating in it, where Mr. Keating listed the DPS as one of his important school activities. When questioned about it, Mr. Keating replies that the DPS was dedicated to finding transcendental meaning and that the members would sit in a cave near a pond and recite poetry. Subsequently, the boys decide to start up the DPS once again, ultimately demonstrating effective shared leadership in the process.

Unfortunately, we also get to witness empowerment gone awry, when the boys abuse their empowerment and begin drinking, smoking, going to parties, and otherwise running amok. Upon finding out about this, Mr. Keating counsels the boys to be wise, not foolish, with their empowerment.

In a plot twist, Mr. Keating is inappropriately made a scapegoat when one of the boys commits suicide, and he is terminated from his position. When Mr. Keating enters the classroom for the final time, several of the boys stand on their desks and call him "O Captain! My Captain!" as a way of demonstrating their sincere appreciation for how he empowered them to grow and expand their lives. The final message of the film is that people should think for themselves and be capable self-leaders, while empowering others in a similar way.

Discussion Questions

1. What is empowerment?
2. What is self-leadership?
3. What is shared leadership?
4. Under what conditions would you advise empowering individuals to engage in self-leadership and groups to engage in shared leadership?
5. What are the caveats for empowerment, self-leadership, and shared leadership?

15

Effective Use of Power and Influence Tactics in Organizations

GARY YUKL

State University of New York at Albany

INTRODUCTION

The concept of "power" has been very useful for understanding how people in organizations are able to influence each other (Mintzberg, 1983; Pfeffer, 1981, 1992; Yukl, 2013). Power is usually defined as potential influence over people and events. In this chapter, the focus is on the potential influence of one person (the "agent") on the work-related attitudes and behavior of one or more members of an organization ("target persons"). There are different types of power, and an agent usually has more of some types than of other types. This chapter will describe each type of power and how it is relevant for effective job performance in organizations.

Proactive influence tactics are specific behaviors used in organizations to influence a target person to carry out a work-related request or to support a proposed change. This chapter describes 11 different types of proactive influence tactics that may be used by a leader or other member of an organization. The relevance, feasibility, and effectiveness of each type of proactive tactic depend in part on several aspects of the situation, including the influence objective and the agent's power over the target person.

SOURCES OF INDIVIDUAL POWER

Social scientists usually differentiate between position power and personal power (French and Raven, 1959; Yukl and Falbe, 1991). Position power is the potential influence derived from the agent's position and role in the organization, and it is determined by organizational policies, rules, and regulations, formal reward systems, legal constraints, and labor union contracts. The specific types of position power include legitimate authority, reward power, coercive power, and information power. Personal power is potential influence derived from agent characteristics and some aspects of the relationship between the agent and a target person. Expert power and referent power are specific types of personal power. This first section of this chapter will describe each specific type of power and how it is relevant for effective performance by members of an organization.

Legitimate Power

Legitimate power is derived from the perceived authority and right of the agent to influence specified aspects of a target person's behavior. The underlying basis for legitimate power is the agreement by members of an organization to comply with rules and legitimate requests in return for the benefits of membership (March and Simon, 1958). Legitimate power is strengthened by an internalized value of the target person that it is proper to obey authority figures and carry out formal agreements.

The scope of authority for a leader or other member is usually specified in writing by documents (e.g. organization charter, bylaws, job description, and employment contract). The legitimate authority for the top executives of an organization usually includes their right to determine formal policies, rules, pay and benefits programs, and performance criteria for members. A manager or other designated leader usually has more legitimate power over subordinates than over other people in the organization. The formal policies may include the right to request necessary information, technical advice, and assistance from other subunits of the organization, but some ambiguity about an individual's authority over peers may remain (Davis, 1968).

When legitimate authority is the basis for a request, making a polite request is usually more effective than an arrogant demand, especially for a target person who is likely to be sensitive about status differentials and authority relationships. Nevertheless, a legitimate request should usually be made in a firm, confident manner to avoid giving the impression that it is not proper or appropriate (Sayles, 1979). In an emergency situation, to express doubts or appear confused risks, a loss of influence over target persons and a direct order in a command tone of voice is sometimes necessary (Mulder, Ritsema van Eck, and de Jong, 1970).

A request or task assignment that does not appear legitimate may be ignored or otherwise resisted by the target person, especially if the requested activity is also tedious, dangerous, or controversial. Doubts about legitimacy are more likely for an unusual request or requests made by an agent with no clear authority over the target person. If the legitimacy of a request is not obvious, it should be verified by the agent.

Reward Power

Reward power is derived from agent control over resources and rewards desired by target persons. This type of power is increased when a target person is highly dependent on the agent for attaining an important reward and cannot get it another way. Reward power is derived in part from an agent's formal authority, which varies greatly across organizations and from one type of position to another within the same organization. The higher a person's position in the authority hierarchy of an organization, the more reward power the person is likely to have. Reward power over subordinates is usually much stronger than reward power over peers or superiors. One form of reward power over subordinates is influence over their compensation, benefits, and career advancement. Many managers are authorized to give pay increases, bonuses, or other rewards to deserving subordinates. Reward power is also derived from control over other tangible benefits such as a promotion, a better job, a better work schedule, a larger operating budget, a larger expense account, formal recognition (e.g. awards and commendations), and status symbols such as a larger office or a reserved parking space.

Lateral reward power is potential influence over other people in the organization who depend on the agent for resources and assistance not clearly specified by the formal authority system or formal agreements. Access to a powerful person inside or outside the organization may provide an opportunity to get benefits desired by other members who lack such access, thereby providing some reward power over them. Trading of favors needed to accomplish task objectives is a common form of influence among peers in organizations, and research indicates that it is important for the success of middle managers (Cohen and Bradford, 1989; Kaplan, 1984; Kotter, 1985).

Upward reward power is very limited in most organizations. Unless a leader is elected by the subordinates, they seldom have much direct influence over the leader's career success. Sometimes subordinates are able to enhance the reputation and career of their boss if they perform their jobs well and speak favorably about the boss (Mechanic, 1962). Some individuals may also derive upward reward power from their unique ability to acquire important resources and benefits from outside sources.

An agent's reward power can be used to influence a target person to carry out an unusual request by making an explicit or implicit offer to provide something desired by the person. Compliance is most likely if the reward is something valued by the target person, and the agent is perceived as a credible source for it. Thus, it is essential for an agent to identify the rewards valued by a target person, and agent credibility should not be risked by making unrealistic promises or failing to deliver on a promise after target compliance occurs.

The use of reward power involves some risks. When rewards are based on a target person's job performance, the person may neglect important aspects of the work that are not clearly specified and closely monitored by the agent. How reward power is used often involves issues of fairness and ethical behavior, and even a large reward may not have the desired effect if it is seen as a bribe to get a target person to do something improper or unethical.

Coercive Power

Coercive power over subordinates is derived from the authority to punish them for the violation of rules and policies or failure to comply with legitimate orders and requests. The formal authority system of an organization usually specifies the legitimate use of punishment, and it varies greatly for different types of organizations. A leader may have many types of punishment to use with a subordinate, including dismissal, suspension, demotion, reassignment to a less desirable job, or a decrease in pay or benefits.

Lateral coercive power over a peer (e.g. a coworker in the same subunit or someone in another subunit of the organization) is usually very limited. The agent can threaten to complain to the superior of a peer who refuses to carry out a legitimate request, or the agent may threaten to withhold future cooperation with the person. However, since mutual dependencies usually exist in lateral relations between different subunits, coercion is likely to elicit retaliation and escalate into a conflict that is not good for either subunit.

Upward coercive power is also very limited in most organizations. Subordinates may be able to damage the reputation of their boss by restricting production, sabotaging operations, initiating grievances, holding demonstrations, or making complaints to higher management (Mechanic, 1962). In organizations with elected leaders, subordinates or followers may be able to remove the leader from office or prevent the leader's re-election.

Coercive power can be invoked by communicating a threat or warning that target persons will suffer undesirable consequences for refusing to comply with a request, rule, or policy. The threat may be explicit, or it may be only a hint that the target person will be sorry for failing to do what the agent wants. The likelihood of compliance is greatest when the threat is perceived to be credible, and the target person strongly desires to avoid the threatened punishment. Sometimes it is necessary for an agent to verify coercive power by demonstrating the ability to use it. However, even a credible threat may be unsuccessful if the target person refuses to be intimidated or believes that it is possible to avoid agent detection of noncompliance by the target person.

A limitation of coercion is that it may cause undesirable outcomes such as anger, resentment, and retaliation by target persons. In work organizations, the most appropriate use of coercive power is to deter behavior that is detrimental to the organization, such as illegal activities, theft, violation of safety rules, reckless acts that endanger others, and willful disobedience of legitimate requests that are important.

Information Power

Access to important information and control over its distribution provide another source of power in organizations (Pfeffer, 1981). Information power is a potential source of agent power over subordinates, peers, or bosses. Control over information makes it easier to interpret events for people in a way that serves the agent's interests. Control over information about an agent's own job performance can be used to make exaggerated reports of successful performance and to cover up mistakes and poor decisions, or delay their discovery. Control over information about the cause of a problem and the feasibility of potential solutions can be used to influence decisions made by people who rely on this information. A leader who controls the distribution of information to subordinates can make it difficult for them to challenge the leader's decisions. Control over the upward flow of information to superiors can be used to influence their decisions (Mechanic, 1962; Pettigrew, 1972).

People with exclusive access to important information and control over its distribution may be tempted to use information power in unethical ways for their own personal benefit. However, when an agent is no longer viewed as a credible source of important information, the agent's control over the information may be removed.

Expert Power

Expert power is derived from the dependence of target persons for advice and assistance from an agent who has more expertise in solving problems and planning task activities that are important to the target persons (French and Raven, 1959; Hickson, Hinings, Lee, Schneck, and Pennings, 1971; Patchen, 1974). Expert power can be acquired by demonstrating competence, such as by making decisions or initiating changes that prove successful, or by giving advice or making predictions that prove to be correct. However, some people are able to convey a false impression that they have exceptional expertise or that their expertise extends beyond the specific type of problem or task for which they actually have special skills or knowledge.

A request made by an agent who has substantial expert power is more likely to be carried out without any need for an explanation of the reasons for the request. However, for an unusual or controversial request or proposal, the agent may need to explain why it is important and feasible. Successful influence depends on the leader's credibility and persuasive communication skills in addition to technical knowledge and analytical ability. Explanations should be made in a clear, confident manner, and the agent should avoid making inconsistent statements. However, the agent should be careful to avoid flaunting superior expertise in an arrogant way or dismissing any target person's concerns in a way that implies the target person is ignorant. Even when an agent is acknowledged to have more expertise, the target person usually has some relevant information, ideas, and concerns that should be considered.

Referent Power

Referent power is derived from the desire of target persons to please an agent toward whom they have strong feelings of affection, admiration, and loyalty (French and Raven, 1959). Referent power is usually greater when there is a strong personal friendship, or when the agent is strongly admired and respected by the target person. The strongest form of referent power involves the influence process called personal identification. A person who identifies with an agent and wants to gain and maintain the agent's approval and acceptance is more likely to do what the agent asks, imitate the agent's behavior, and develop attitudes similar to those expressed by the agent. Someone who is well liked and admired by others can have considerable influence by setting an example of proper and desirable behavior for them to imitate. However, people may also imitate undesirable behavior in someone they admire, and it is important to avoid this potential problem. Referent power is an important source of influence for members of an organization who are able to acquire it, but it has limitations and can be lost if used to exploit and manipulate other people.

Power and Leadership Effectiveness

Most of the power research conducted in organizations has involved the influence of appointed or elected leaders, and this research shows that power is related to leadership effectiveness in complex ways (Yukl, 2013). How much power is needed for successful leadership will depend in part on the situation, including the type of organization and leader, the leader's objectives, and the leader's skill in using power. To achieve and maintain a high level of performance for a group or organization, leaders usually need enough authority to make necessary changes, reward competent members, and deter reckless or destructive behavior by a member. More position power is needed to implement major changes, especially when there is strong opposition to change. Efforts to influence the decisions and actions of others are also enhanced by a leader's strong expert and referent power.

The possession of strong position and personal power involves risks as well as benefits for leaders, and it is important to avoid these risks. A leader with substantial power may be tempted to rely on it too much. The notion that power corrupts is especially relevant for position power. Leaders with strong position power are more likely to perceive subordinates as objects of manipulation, to devalue their worth, to maintain more social distance from them, and to attribute the cause of subordinate achievements to the leader's power rather than to the intrinsic motivation and voluntary efforts of subordinates (Kipnis, 1974). Thus, a moderate amount of position power is probably optimal in most situations.

Extreme amounts of personal power can also corrupt a leader. Initial success in resolving problems and gaining the respect and admiration of others may cause a leader to assume more wisdom and expertise than is warranted. A leader with substantial expert and referent power may be tempted to act in reckless ways (McClelland, 1975; Zaleznik, 1970). Although strong personal power can provide important benefits, it should be used in an ethical and supportive way.

Outcomes of Specific Influence Attempts

Up to now, the chapter has described the different sources of power and their relevance for effective performance by leaders and other members of organizations. To understand how members of an organization can influence each other, it is also helpful to examine how the use of different proactive influence tactics affects the outcome for a specific influence attempt.

Three different types of outcomes are useful for describing the success of an influence attempt with a single target person (Yukl, 2013). Commitment means the target person is enthusiastic about the request and makes a strong effort to do it effectively. Commitment is the best outcome for requests that require the target person to take initiative in dealing with problems and continue to perform a task in the face of setbacks and difficulties. Compliance means that the person is indifferent about the request and makes only a minimum effort. However, compliance is often a sufficient outcome for a simple, routine type of request. Resistance means the target person is opposed to carrying out the request and tries to avoid doing it. Resistance usually indicates a failed influence attempt, although sometimes it is useful if it reveals that the agent's plan or proposal is unlikely to achieve the desired objectives.

A common form of influence behavior in organizations is to make a "simple request" that does not involve the use of a proactive influence tactic. A simple request is most likely to be successful if it appears legitimate, it is clearly relevant for the work unit, and it is something the target person knows how to do. However, even when a simple request is perceived to be legitimate, it often results in subordinate compliance rather than commitment. For a request or proposal that is not considered appropriate, important, necessary, and feasible by the target person, the agent will need to use one or more of the proactive influence tactic to attain a favorable outcome.

Proactive Influence Tactics

Over the past quarter century, several researchers have attempted to identify distinct types of proactive influence tactics (e.g. Kipnis, Schmidt, and Wilkinson, 1980; Schilit and Locke, 1982; Yukl and Tracey, 1992; Yukl, Seifert, and Chavez, 2008). The research has identified 11 proactive influence tactics that are distinct and relevant for understanding the outcomes of influence attempts made by an agent with a target person in the organization. Each tactic will be explained briefly, and the conditions favoring its use will be described.

Rational Persuasion

Rational persuasion involves the use of explanations, logical arguments, and factual evidence that a proposal or request will provide important benefits for the organization, team, or mission. A strong form of rational persuasion that includes a detailed explanation of the importance and feasibility of a request or proposed change and documentation of supporting evidence is much more likely to be effective than a weak form of rational persuasion that only includes a brief explanation and assertions made without any supporting evidence. Rational persuasion is relevant when the agent and the target person have the same task objectives, but the target person does not recognize that the agent's request or proposal is a good way to attain these objectives. Rational persuasion is unlikely to be useful if the target person opposes the agent's objectives.

An agent's expert power, information power, and referent power can all enhance the effectiveness of rational persuasion. Agent expertise and technical knowledge are the source of facts and explanations relevant for making a persuasive case, and strong communication skills help an agent use relevant knowledge effectively. Rational persuasion is also more effective when the agent is perceived to be a credible and trustworthy source of information and advice.

Apprising

Apprising involves the explanation of reasons why a request or proposal will benefit the target person as an individual. The agent may explain how a request will improve the person's skills, make the person's job easier or more satisfying, or help advance the target person's career. Unlike rational persuasion, apprising does not involve benefits for the team or organization. Unlike exchange, the agent is not offering to give the target something, but is only pointing out that an assignment or proposed course of action will provide some personal benefits desired by the target person. Apprising can be effective when the agent is a credible source of information about likely personal benefits, the benefits are not already known to the target person, and the benefits are sufficient to justify the time and effort needed for the target person to carry out a request or assignment. As with rational persuasion, the effectiveness of apprising is enhanced by the agent's expert power, information power, referent power, and communication skills.

Inspirational Appeals

An inspirational appeal is an attempt to develop enthusiasm and commitment by arousing strong emotions and linking a request or proposal to the target person's values, hopes, and ideals. Examples of ideals that may be used include patriotism, freedom, justice, and humanitarianism. The agent may appeal to a target person's desire to accomplish something worthwhile, to make an important contribution, to perform an exceptional feat, to be a member of the best team, or to work on a special project that will save many lives.

Inspirational appeals vary in complexity from a brief explanation of the ideological justification for a proposed project or change to a major speech that articulates an appealing vision of what the group or organization could accomplish or become. The complexity of an inspirational appeal depends in part on the size of the task to be undertaken, the amount of effort and risk involved, and the extent to which people are asked to deviate from established, traditional ways of doing things. To identify an appropriate type of inspirational appeal requires insight into the values, hopes, and fears of the person or group to be influenced. The effectiveness of an inspirational appeal also depends on the agent's credibility and communication skills, such as the ability to use vivid imagery and metaphors, manipulate symbols, and employ voice and gestures to generate enthusiasm and excitement.

Consultation

Consultation is an attempt to increase the target person's commitment to carry a request or support a proposal by involving the person in determining how it will be done. Consultation can take different forms when used as an influence tactic. One form is to present a proposed project or change to a target person who will be involved in implementing it to find out if the person has any doubts, concerns, or suggestions about it. In the discussion that follows, which may involve some negotiation and joint problem-solving, the agent considers ways to modify the original request or proposal so that it takes into account the target person's suggestions and concerns. Another form of consultation is to present only a general strategy or objective rather than a detailed proposal and ask the target person to help plan how to attain the objective or to suggest specific action steps for implementing the strategy. For consultation to be feasible, the target person must agree that the objective is worthwhile. A target person will not be enthusiastic about suggesting ways to attain an objective that is undesirable.

Exchange Tactics

Exchange tactics involve an explicit or implicit offer by the agent to reward the target person for doing what the agent requests. The effective use of exchange tactics requires agent control over the distribution of some rewards or benefits that are desired by the target person, and the agent must be perceived as trustworthy enough to actually provide them. Thus, exchange tactics are facilitated by an agent's reward power and credibility.

Exchange tactics are especially appropriate when the target person is indifferent or reluctant about complying with a request. In effect, the agent offers to make it worthwhile to comply by promising to provide a reward that is desired by the target person. Examples of potential rewards include recommending a pay increase or promotion for the person or offering to share some of the tangible benefits from a proposed project or activity. A clear explanation of promised rewards is usually more effective than an implicit promise to provide an unspecified reward at a future time. Exchange tactics can be moderately effective for influencing subordinates and peers, but it is difficult to use them for influencing superiors, because a subordinate seldom has control over important rewards to offer bosses.

Collaboration

Collaboration involves an offer by the agent to provide resources or assistance needed by the target person to carry out a request or task assignment. Examples of this tactic include offering to show the target person how to do a requested task, offering to provide the equipment or technical assistance needed to perform a requested task, and offering to help the target person deal with a problem that would be caused by carrying out the request. Unlike exchange tactics, collaboration does not involve an offer to provide personal benefits to the target person.

Collaboration is very effective when the target person perceives that the agent's request is not feasible without additional resources and assistance that the agent is able to provide. The use of this tactic communicates that the agent considers the request to be important, and it also shows consideration for the difficulties the target person would have in carrying out the request. Collaboration is most useful when the agent understands the obstacles faced by the target person in carrying out a request and the agent has sufficient expertise and resources to help the target overcome these obstacles. An agent's expert power and information power enhance the value of advice about how to carry out a request, and agent position power enhances access to relevant resources needed by the target person to carry out a request.

Personal Appeals

A personal appeal involves asking someone to do a favor based on friendship or loyalty to the agent. This tactic is one way to enact referent power, although when referent power is very strong, a personal appeal may not be necessary. A common type of personal appeal is for an agent to describe what is wanted and then ask the target person to do it as a special favor. However, sometimes an agent will ask for a personal favor before saying what the favor actually is.

A personal appeal is only relevant when the agent has a friendly relationship with the target person, and the tactic is only appropriate for a limited range of requests. A difficult request may be ignored by the target person if it is not clearly important to the agent, or if it seems like an improper attempt to take advantage of their friendship. Personal appeals are sometimes useful for influence attempts with a peer or outsider, but they are seldom necessary for influencing subordinates and they are difficult to use with bosses.

Ingratiation Tactics

Ingratiation is behavior that makes a target person feel accepted and appreciated by the agent. Examples include giving compliments, showing respect, and acting especially friendly and helpful before making a request. Ingratiation is commonly used as an impression management tactic to improve relationships with people and gain more referent power, but sometimes it can be used as a proactive influence tactic (Liden and Mitchell, 1988; Wayne and Ferris, 1990). For example, the agent may explain why the target person is uniquely qualified to carry out a difficult request. An ingratiation tactic that appears to be sincere can make a target person more willing to consider a request. However, compliments made just before asking a powerful target person for something may appear insincere and manipulative. Ingratiation is a more useful proactive tactic when the target person is a subordinate or peer rather than a boss.

Legitimating Tactics

Legitimating tactics involve attempts to establish the authority or right to make a task-related request. A legitimating tactic can be useful when the agent's authority is ambiguous or the legitimacy of a request or command is not clear. Examples of legitimating tactics include providing evidence of prior precedent, showing consistency with organizational policies and rules, or reminding the target that the request is consistent with a prior contract or agreement. Useful documents for verifying legitimacy include written rules, policies, charters, contracts, job descriptions, or work orders. Legitimating tactics are not necessary for routine requests to subordinates but may be relevant when trying to implement a major change or deal with an unusual crisis. This proactive tactic may also be relevant for an unusual request to a peer or outsider who is likely to doubt that it is legitimate.

Pressure Tactics

Pressure tactics include threats, warnings, or demands by the agent, and repeated checking with the target person to see if a request has been carried out. An example of a hard form of pressure tactic is a strongly worded threat about the punishment that will occur if the target person does not comply with a request. An example of a softer form of pressure tactic is a reminder that the deadline is approaching for a task the target person has agreed to do. Sometimes a soft form of pressure is sufficient to induce compliance with a request, particularly if the person is just lazy or apathetic rather than strongly opposed to it. An explicit warning or strong threat is sometimes necessary to get compliance with legitimate requests or rules and policies that are unpopular. The hard pressure tactics require some coercive power and are more likely to result in compliance if the target person believes the agent is able and willing to carry out threats of punishment. A limitation of most hard pressure tactics is that they are likely to undermine working relationships and may lead to resistance, avoidance, or retaliation by the target person. For this reason, hard pressure tactics should not be used except as a last resort when the influence objective is important and other proactive tactics have failed to elicit compliance by the target person.

Coalition Tactics

Coalition tactics involve the assistance of other people in an effort to influence a target person. The coalition partners may be peers, subordinates, superiors, or outsiders (e.g. clients and suppliers). The agent may only mention important people who support the agent's request or proposal, or the agent may ask those people to directly express their support to the target person. The appropriate type of coalition tactic depends on the influence objective, the agent-target relationship, and the amount of resistance expected or encountered.

Coalition tactics are usually combined with other types of proactive influence tactics used by the agent and coalition partners. For example, the agent and a coalition partner may both use rational persuasion to influence the target person. Sometimes the agent and a coalition partner will use different tactics to influence the target person. Coalition tactics can be effective for influencing a peer or superior to support a proposed change or innovation if the coalition partners are able to provide credible evidence that it is desirable and feasible. The coalition tactic called an "upward appeal" involves getting assistance from the boss of the target person, and it is sometimes used after earlier attempts by the agent to influence the target person are unsuccessful.

Effectiveness of Single and Combined Tactics

Research comparing the effects of different proactive tactics indicates that some individuals are usually more effective than others (Falbe and Yukl, 1992; Yukl, Kim, and Falbe, 1996; Yukl and Tracey, 1992; Yukl et al., 2008). The proactive tactics most likely to result in target person commitment to carry out a request or support a proposal are rational persuasion, inspirational appeals, consultation, and collaboration. Apprising and exchange tactics can be moderately effective for influencing compliance by subordinates, peers, or outsiders, but these tactics seldom result in target commitment and are difficult to use with superiors. Pressure, legitimating tactics, ingratiation, and personal appeals are unlikely to elicit commitment, but they can be useful in some situations for eliciting compliance, which may be a sufficient outcome to achieve the agent's influence objective. The need to include coalition partners in an influence attempt usually indicates that some target person resistance is expected, and the outcome will depend on the credibility, power, and influence skills of the coalition partners.

The effectiveness of an influence attempt can be increased by using more than one type of tactic at the same time or sequentially (Falbe and Yukl, 1992). When using different tactics in the same influence attempt, the agent should select tactics that are mutually compatible. For example, rational persuasion is a very flexible tactic that is usually compatible with most of the other proactive tactics. Strong pressure tactics are not compatible with ingratiation because they weaken target feelings of friendship and loyalty, which ingratiation is intended to strengthen. When tactics are used sequentially, some types (e.g. ingratiation and consultation) are more suitable for an initial influence attempt, whereas other types (e.g. exchange and pressure) are more appropriate for a follow-up influence attempt (Yukl, Falbe, and Youn, 1993).

Even though some tactics are generally more useful than others, success is not guaranteed for any individual tactic or combination of tactics. The effectiveness of each proactive tactic depends in part on the type of situation in which it is used and the outcome (commitment or compliance) considered to be necessary for the influence attempt to be successful. Other determinants of the outcome include the type of agent-target relationship, the agent's position and personal power, the interpersonal skills of the agent, and how the request is perceived by the target person. A tactic is more likely to be successful if it is a socially acceptable form of influence behavior, if it is used for a request that is legitimate and relevant, if the agent has sufficient position and personal power to use the tactic effectively, if the tactic can improve target person attitudes about the desirability and feasibility of the request, if the tactic is used in a skillful way, and if it is consistent with the target person's values and needs (Yukl and Gardner, 2020; Yukl and Tracey, 1992).

Case Examples

Positive Case: Restview Hospital

Mary Carter is the manager of accounting and billing records at Restview Hospital, a large residential health care facility. Jack Morelli, the facility administrator, wanted to modernize Restview's system of accounts billing, and he asked Mary to investigate the available software packages. Jack explained that the Restview board of directors would like to decide which software package to purchase at their next quarterly board meeting.

Mary quickly learned that there were three vendors with a software system for accounts billing. One was Standard Software Systems, the company that provided the software currently used to process the Restview payroll. Mary knew that the president of the company was a close personal friend of Jack. Mary contacted a sales representative from each company to get information about their software. She also contacted managers at some other hospitals that were already using one of the three billing software packages to get firsthand information about any difficulties experienced in installing and using it. Her investigation revealed that the three software packages were about the same price, but Standard's was less flexible and user-friendly than the other two. The software package from Reliable Computer was clearly the best one for Restview's needs.

Mary prepared a short report with a recommendation to purchase the software package from Reliable Computers and a summary of the reasons for her recommendation. Mary did not know most of the Restview directors, but she offered to present her findings to them the following week at their meeting. However, Jack said he could handle the presentation by himself. After the board meeting, Jack informed Mary that the board members had decided to purchase the software package from Standard Software. He explained that they wanted to reward Standard for the excellent customer service provided to Restview. A year after the decision to purchase the Standard Software, it was still not operating smoothly, and it had caused some costly problems for the hospital.

Negative Case: Jeff Skilling and the Rise and Fall of Enron

Enron, under the leadership of CEO Jeff Skilling, became known as a juggernaut of success before it failed disastrously. Skilling epitomizes the negative use of power. He was universally considered charismatic, demonstrating referent power. He was clearly an expert in creating complex financial instruments, i.e. he had expert power. By virtue of his role – CEO – he had legitimate power. His use of reward and punishment power, however, are what distinguish him as a leader in the negative use of power.

Skilling transformed Enron from a company focused on energy resources into a financial trading company credited with the creation of a financial term called "mark-to-market." The mark-to-market concept enabled Enron to recognize potential "profits" from long-term financial trades in the current period, thereby distorting their financial statements to enable the distribution of enormous rewards to executives and traders at the company (reward power). At the same time, executives and traders that did not deliver such transactions were ostracized and eliminated (punishment power), using what employees called the "rank and yank" system.

The dubious trades and financial instruments, using mark-to-market, could be covered, as long as true profitability was on the rise. Nonetheless, as deals began to fail, Skilling relied upon his expert power in complex financial instruments to create "special purpose entities" to hide such loses and to appear to Wall Street as continuing to meet or exceed analyst expectations.

Skilling transformed the culture of Enron (referent power) from a company delivering value to one creating financial instruments, which were difficult to decipher, where the appearance of short-term financial results was the only thing that mattered. Ultimately, the house of cards created by Skilling's abuse of power resulted in one the largest bankruptcies in US history (it was the largest bankruptcy to date when it occurred). The bankruptcy totaled more than $65 Billion and resulted in nearly 30,000 employees losing their jobs at Enron. The Enron bankruptcy had follow-on disruptive effects at other major employers as well (e.g. Arthur Andersen also lost nearly 30,000 employees).

With power comes responsibility. Some leaders rise to the occasion. Others abuse their power. Jeff Skilling clearly falls into the latter camp – he was sentenced to 24 years in prison, which was later reduced to 14 years, for his abuse of power and fraudulent activities.

Conclusions

Effective job performance usually requires cooperation and support from other people in the organization. It is important to have an appropriate amount and type of position power, and it is also desirable to develop and maintain a substantial amount of expert and referent power. However, an individual's power should be used in a way that is ethical and appropriate for the situation, or it is likely to engender resentment and resistance.

The outcome of an influence attempt made by an agent with a target person depends in part on what tactics are used, how skillfully they are used, and the context in which they are used. The four "core tactics" that are usually the most effective for eliciting target person commitment are consultation, inspirational appeals, collaboration, and strong forms of rational persuasion. The other tactics are useful in some situations to elicit target person compliance, but they are much less likely to elicit target commitment. Using a combination of relevant and compatible proactive tactics is usually a more effective influence strategy than using only a single tactic. Before making an influence attempt that involves an important objective, it is essential to diagnose the situation carefully and select tactics that are relevant and mutually compatible.

References

Cohen, A. R., and Bradford, D. L. (1991). *Influence Without Authority.* New York: John Wiley and Sons.

Davis, K. (1968). Attitudes toward the legitimacy of management efforts to influence employees. *Academy of Management Journal,* 11, 153–162.

Falbe, C. M., and Yukl, G. (1992). Consequences for managers of using single influence tactics and combinations of tactics. *Academy of Management Journal,* 35, 638–653.

French, J. R. P., and Raven, B. H. (1959). The bases of social power. In D. Cartwright (ed.), *Studies of Social Power* (pp. 150–167). Ann Arbor, MI: Institute for Social Research.

Hickson, D. J., Hinings, C. R., Lee, C. A., Schneck, R. S., and Pennings, J. M. (1971). A strategic contingencies theory of intra-organizational power. *Administrative Science Quarterly,* 16, 216–229.

Kaplan, R. E. (1984). Trade routes: The manager's network of relationships. *Organizational Dynamics,* Spring, 37–52.

Kipnis, D. (1974). *The Powerholders.* Chicago: University of Chicago Press.

Kipnis, D., Schmidt, S. M., and Wilkinson, I. (1980). Intra-organizational influence tactics: Explorations in getting one's way. *Journal of Applied Psychology,* 65, 440–452.

Kotter, J. P. (1985). *Power and Influence: Beyond Formal Authority.* New York: Free Press.

Liden, R. C., and Mitchell, T. R. (1988). Ingratiatory behaviors in organizational settings. *Academy of Management Review,* 13, 572–587.

March, J. G., and Simon, H. A. (1958). *Organizations.* New York: Wiley.

Mechanic, D. (1962). Sources of power of lower participants in complex organizations. *Administrative Science Quarterly*, 7, 349–364.
McClelland, D. C. (1975). *Power: The Inner Experience.* New York: Irvington.
Mintzberg, H. (1983). *Power in and Around Organizations.* Englewood Cliffs, NJ: Prentice Hall.
Mulder, M., Ritsema van Eck, J. R., and de Jong, R. D. (1970). An organization in crisis and noncrisis conditions. *Human Relations*, 24, 19–41.
Patchen, M. (1974). The locus and basis of influence on organizational decisions. *Organizational Behavior and Human Performance*, 11, 195–221.
Pettigrew, A. (1972). Information control as a power resource. *Sociology*, 6, 187–204.
Pfeffer, J. (1981). *Power in Organizations.* Marshfield, MA: Pittman.
Pfeffer, J. (1992). *Managing with Power: Politics and Influence in Organizations.* Boston, MA: Harvard Business School Press.
Sayles, L. R. (1979). *What Effective Managers Really Do and How They Do It.* New York: McGraw-Hill.
Schilit, W. K., and Locke, E. A. (1982). A study of upward influence in organizations. *Administrative Science Quarterly*, 27, 304–316.
Wayne, S. J., and Ferris, G. R. (1990). Influence tactics, affect, and exchange quality in supervisor-subordinate interactions: A laboratory experiment and field study. *Journal of Applied Psychology*, 75, 487–499.
Yukl, G. (2013). *Leadership in Organizations* (8th edition). Englewood Cliffs, NJ: Prentice Hall.
Yukl, G., and Falbe, C. M. (1991). The importance of different power sources in downward and lateral relations. *Journal of Applied Psychology*, 76, 416–423.
Yukl, G., Falbe, C. M., and Youn, J. Y. (1993). Patterns of influence behavior for managers. *Group and Organization Management*, 18, 5–28.
Yukl, G., and Gardner, W. L. (2020). *Leadership in Organizations* (9th edition). Boston, MA, Pearson Education.
Yukl, G., Kim, H., and Falbe, C. M. (1996). Antecedents of influence outcomes. *Journal of Applied Psychology*, 81, 309–317.
Yukl, G., Seifert, C., and Chavez, C. (2008). Validation of the extended influence behavior questionnaire. *Leadership Quarterly*, 19(5), 609–621.
Yukl, G., and Tracey, B. (1992). Consequences of influence tactics when used with subordinates, peers, and the boss. *Journal of Applied Psychology*, 77, 525–535.
Zaleznik, A. (1970). Power and politics in organizational life. *Harvard Business Review*, 48, 47–60.

Exercises

Exercise 1

Describe a successful attempt by a boss or coworker to influence you during the past few months, and identify the specific influence tactics used by the person. Then, describe an unsuccessful attempt by the same person or someone else in the organization to influence you, and identify the tactics used by that person. Analyze the reasons for the success or failure of each influence attempt. Consider the agent's position and personal power, the relevance of the influence tactics for the situation, and your initial attitudes about the objective of the influence attempt.

Exercise 2

Think about an influence attempt that you need to make or would like to make in the near future. Plan an appropriate influence strategy, taking into account your power bases, the agent-target relationship, the target's attitudes about the influence objective, and your knowledge and influence skills. Select some specific influence tactics that would be appropriate for this influence attempt and consider the best way to sequence them (e.g. initial tactics and what you would do if the initial effort is unsuccessful).

Video Analysis and Discussion

Please watch the following video(s):

1. Why ordinary people need to understand power: https://www.youtube.com/watch?v=Cd0JH1AreDw
2. 3 things that make a meaningful vision: https://www.youtube.com/watch?v=zpzZumZCdWA

Now form small groups to discuss the video(s) and answer the following questions:

1. What are the major points of the video?
2. How can you use information from the video in your career?
3. Based on the video, what advice do you have for leaders in organizations?

Be prepared to present the ideas from your small group discussion with the class as a whole.

Discussion Questions

1. Describe the types of power Mary, Jack, and the Restview board have in this situation.
2. Explain how the power of the different parties could explain the software decision.
3. What could Mary have done that may have given her more influence over the decision?

16

Engage in Visionary Leadership

David A. Waldman

Arizona State University

It is often quoted from the Bible that "where there is no vision, the people perish." While this quote was never meant to depict business or organizations, it certainly applies to effective leadership in the work world. But before I get to visionary leadership in organizations, I want to share a personal experience of visionary leadership that I received from a medical doctor a number of years ago. I was playing tennis with a friend who was much more adept at the sport compared to me, a feat that is not too hard to realize. The individual hit a passing shot that I ran to get to, but the tennis ball went past me. While I was still running and looking toward my friend, the ball had evidently hit a backstop at the end of the court and came straight back in the direction toward which I was running. Without seeing the ball, my right foot stepped on it squarely and twisted in an inward and outward motion. I went down in pain and actually passed out for probably 30 seconds or so.

My friend managed to get me to an emergency room where my ankle got wrapped, and I received crutches. The next day, I went to see an orthopedic specialist, who told me that nothing was broken, but I had a relatively severe sprain. I then proceeded to commiserate and whine about how I was in so much pain and emotional distress, and I just knew that I would never be the same. In other words, I let the doctor know that I felt like my ankle would never heal correctly, I would not be able to run or play various sports again, and I might not even be able to walk correctly. In short, I had no vision of a positive future. The doctor calmed me down and told me exactly what I would need to do over the next several weeks and months, such as work with his physical therapist. He said that if I did those things and managed to not reinjure the ankle, I would be just fine in several months and would be able to do everything that I did prior to the injury. In a word, he restored my vision. To make a long story short, I followed his instructions, did not reinjure the ankle, and in the years that have passed, I have been able to do all of the physical activities about which I originally had no optimistic vision. Fortunately, I was wrong, and fortunately, I was able to experience the comforting and insightful guidance of this physician.

The point of this opening story is twofold. First, it shows what vision is all about, as well as why it is so important. Although the story pertains to one leader and one follower, vision can also be conceived at a collective level (i.e. teams, organization, and society). In a nutshell, vision is important because it energizes people emotionally, stimulates them intellectually, and can bring people together to pursue collective efforts. This chapter will explain the nature of vision and visionary leadership, as well as their importance. Second, the opening story of this chapter demonstrates that vision is not just the purview of organizational leaders; people in many occupations or walks of life can – and should – demonstrate vision. With that said, in this chapter, I will focus on visionary leadership in organizations. The following topics will be covered:

1. The background of visionary leadership in the literature
2. What visionary leadership is all about
3. Contextual and personal qualities driving visionary leadership
4. Case examples
5. Conclusion

In addition, I will provide a few self-analysis exercises in Appendix A and B at the end of the chapter. These exercises will allow you to better consider how you personally stack up in terms of potential for visionary leadership. First, let us briefly examine how visionary leadership has been considered in the academic literature.

Background in the Literature

Prior to the 1990s, decades of leadership literature had considered leadership effectiveness in largely "managerial" terms. That is, effective leaders were thought of as individuals who planned, organized, and provided some degree of socioemotional support to followers. But in the 1990s, various authors began to examine visionary leadership more carefully (Baum, Locke, and Kirkpatrick, 1998). For example, House and colleagues (House and Aditya, 1997; House and Shamir, 1993) considered how leaders could have extraordinary qualities (e.g. charisma) and act in extraordinary ways (e.g. provide vision). Indeed, theories of transformational and charismatic leadership emerged with vision as a central component (Bass and Avolio, 1995; Baum et al., 1998). However, larger conceptualizations of extraordinary leadership (i.e. beyond vision), especially charismatic and transformational leadership, have come under attack on both conceptual and methodological grounds (van Knippenberg and Sitkin, 2013).

Visionary leadership provides a good example of the basis for such criticisms. The Multifactor Leadership Questionnaire (MLQ) (Bass and Avolio, 1995) has been a key measure of transformational leadership over the years. Several subfactors compose the transformational leadership construct, including idealized influence, attributed charisma, inspirational motivation, individualized consideration, and intellectual stimulation. Van Knippenberg and Sitkin (2013) argued that the conceptual linkages among these factors were never made clear. Moreover, in the

MLQ, visionary leadership is measured through a single item in the inspirational motivation scale, "articulates a compelling vision of the future." This item confounds the behavior (i.e. providing vision) with an outcome (i.e. compelling).

Accordingly, van Knippenberg and Sitkin (2013) acknowledged that aspects of the transformational/charismatic leadership framework could be useful, particularly visionary leadership. However, the nature of visionary leadership remains a somewhat elusive issue that I will attempt to clarify in this chapter. That said, I must acknowledge up front that I conceive visionary leadership as different from organizational vision. The strategic leadership literature sometimes confounds these two concepts (e.g. Finkelstein, Hambrick, and Cannella, 2009). Organization vision is a formal statement that might be listed on annual reports, boardroom walls, and other forms of corporate advertisement. Visionary leadership involves not only statements that may or may not be written down, but also the behaviors or acts (e.g. verbal communication) of individual leaders. Perhaps most importantly, visionary leadership matters; organizational vision, not so much. In other words, what matters are the people who espouse and implement vision, not potentially empty or symbolic words that might be framed on a boardroom wall. In the sections that follow, we will see exactly what visionary leadership is all about and why it is so essential for leaders and their organizations.

What Visionary Leadership Is All About

At its core, leadership involves influencing others in a targeted manner. The targeting can be relatively short versus long term in nature. Visionary leadership is all about understanding and taking action (e.g. communicating to others) based on a long-term perspective. In other words, it entails influencing others through forward-looking thinking and behavior. Visionary leadership can be understood along several dimensions: (i) frequency of visionary behavior, (ii) vision content in terms of boldness and idealism, (iii) bright versus dark vision, and (iv) singular versus shared vision formation. I examine each of these dimensions next.

Frequency of Visionary Behavior

At its core, visionary leadership can be considered in terms of the extent to which an individual displays an understanding of the future and can clearly and easily articulate what that future might look like (Kim, Waldman, Balthazard, and Ames, 2019; Stam, Lord, van Knippenberg, and Wisse, 2014). Some individuals have a difficult time thinking about and articulating the future, while for others, it seems to come naturally. In a later section, I outline a number of examples of visionary leaders, including Michael Crow, president of Arizona State University (ASU). Crow has been notorious for easily and frequently making future-oriented articulations about ASU (Waldman and O'Reilly, 2022).

There are a number of personal factors that may preclude a high frequency of such futuristic articulations and behavior on the part of a leader. I will also address these factors later in the chapter. For now, go to Appendix A of this chapter to gain some insight into the extent to which you are visionary with regard to your own personal future.

Boldness and Idealism

Despite the importance of simply engaging in future-oriented understanding and actions, there is a qualitative nature to what makes visionary leadership different from other forms of influence. *First,* vision can be distinguished from relatively mundane or incremental goals, for example, increase market share by 1%. Instead, as compared to goals, vision is bold, oriented toward radical change, and less tangible. Moreover, visionary leaders communicate their bold visions with both passion and energy. As a classic example of leader vision, in 1961, President John Kennedy went in front of the Congress of the USA and the American public and passionately spoke about how he envisioned the country putting a man on the moon, and returning him back to the earth safely, by the end of the decade. In their book, *Built to Last: Successful Habits of Visionary Companies,* Collins and Porras (1994) coined the acronym "BHAG," which stands for "big hairy audacious goal." A BHAG largely characterizes what vision is all about. It is both long term and bold, but, at the same time, within a conceivable realm of possibility. If President Kennedy had proclaimed that the United States should put a man in space and return him to Earth, it would have been neither long term nor bold, since, at the time, the country was on the edge of already doing so. But the idea of putting a man on the moon was a bold and daring stretch of individuals' imaginations.

That said, there can be a fine line between vision and what might be viewed by others as simply insanity. Vision extends one's perspective in ways that can seem far-fetched and highly risky. But if a leader's vision goes too far, it can seem ridiculous and not worth considering. If President Kennedy had said that by the end of the 1960s, the USA should commit itself to putting a man on Mars, and returning him safely to Earth, people would have thought that Kennedy was either joking or had lost his mind. In short, while a vision stretches the imaginations, it should nevertheless be seen as possible and, thus, acceptable. Interestingly, leaders such as Elon Musk in more recent times are espousing vision that includes the colonization of Mars, and potentially returning visitors to Mars safely back to Earth. Such vision, although quite bold in nature, is now seen as possible to attain and within a latitude of acceptance on the part of others.

Second, vision tends to be based in values and high ideals that provide meaning and are energizing to others. For example, vision can be based on values/ideals pertaining to innovation, and how the realization of the vision will serve customers and society. Steve Jobs stressed such a vision with the development of the Macintosh in the 1980s. I will say more about Steve Jobs as a case example of visionary leadership later in this chapter.

Perhaps more broadly, vision can be socialized in terms of the betterment of a range of constituent groups (Galvin, Waldman, and Balthazard, 2010). In other words, vision is often based on socialized values. Indeed, Sully de Luque, Washburn, Waldman, and House (2008) demonstrated that CEOs who emphasize stakeholder values in their decision-making (i.e. concerns for employees, the environment, and the community) are more likely to be viewed as visionary and inspirational, as compared to leaders who simply stress economic values (i.e. concern for controlling costs, increasing market share, and profits). In turn, Sully de Luque et al. (2008) showed how leaders with strong stakeholder values stand a better chance of realizing positive outcomes (e.g. financial outcomes) for their firms.

Two lessons can be learned through their research. First, if leaders want to be viewed as visionary or inspiring, they should emphasize stakeholder values in their decision-making. Second and ironically, the strong pursuit of economic values is actually likely to go unrequited. That is, if a leader emphasizes economic values over stakeholder values, that person is not as likely to actually maximize the financial goals of his or her firm. Instead, stakeholder values as personified through vision are more likely to lead to positive outcomes – including financial outcomes. To see how you personally stack up on stakeholder versus economic values (or priorities), complete the measure that is shown in Appendix B of this chapter.

Bright Versus Dark Vision as Part of Change Processes

In many ways, vision is all about change because visionary leadership becomes more relevant when change is occurring or needs to occur. As an example, Kotter (1996) talked about systematic organizational change through an eight-step process. As part of the process, Kotter (1996) emphasized forming a bright or positive vision of where change might lead an organization. Indeed, this positive framing is very much in line with traditional ways of conceiving leader vision (e.g. House and Aditya, 1997; House and Shamir, 1993). That said, before the positive vision is formed and widely communicated, the very first step of planned organizational change should be to create a sense of urgency for change. One way that this sense of urgency can be accomplished is for the leader to articulate a darker vision of what might happen in the future (e.g. organizational collapse) if change is not pursued.

The point here is that there are roles for both brighter and darker sides of vision. Sometimes, the darker side of vision is necessary in order to jolt people or organizations away from the status quo and toward change. But obviously without a brighter vision of hope and optimism, the darker vision will only serve to scare people or drive in fear to an organization. Thus, darker vision should be used sparingly and only in conjunction with the presentation of a brighter vision.

Singular Versus Shared Vision Formation

Many people think of the visionary leader as the lone savior who has the unique and special foresight of what will be in the future. Accordingly, since the visionary leader has such special abilities, that person is given deference and power – and perhaps even characterized as a prophet. This is a key reason for why *visionary* and *charismatic* leadership are terms that are often used in the same breath (House and Shamir, 1993). There is no denying that some individuals are more prone to visionary leadership and, thus, might be viewed in such a manner. However, the reality is that for the most part, nobody can predict the future with 100% accuracy, and visionary leadership capabilities are relatively widespread. Accordingly, there is no inherent reason as to why vision formation should be the domain of a singular leader, and indeed, there are reasons to believe that the shared formation of vision is optimal.

The notion of formal leadership working in unison with shared leadership is not a new concept in the literature (e.g. see Pearce and Sims, 2002; Zhang, Waldman, and Wang, 2012). Berson, Waldman, and Pearce (2016) applied the concept to the co-creation of vision. The basic idea is that vision formation could be jointly pursued by both formal leaders and followers. Although multiple paths to co-creation are possible, one process might be that a formal leader "floats" an initial vision to followers, who then consider and through dialogue, make suggestions for additions or revisions. The formal leader then reformulates vision and again engages in dialogue with followers. Eventually, consensus is formed around a shared vision. An advantage of such a process is that less time might need to be devoted to "selling" the vision to followers, and there might be less resistance to the change that is typically associated with new vision. That is, the co-creation of vision helps to ensure commitment to later implementation, and that it is not simply "the leader's vision" *per se.* Interestingly, according to Kotter (1996), the second step of planned organizational change is to form a powerful coalition. It might be easier to form such a coalition by involving followers or other constituents (e.g. key customers) early on in vision creation.

In addition, to realize shared vision and implementation, it is important that once formed, vision is shared widely and pieced out individually. Followers and other constituent groups need to take the vision to heart, so to speak. Specifically, they need to understand how the vision applies to their own work or their organizational units. In other words, if a vision is to ultimately be implemented, a wide swath of followers must understand and be emotionally committed to that vision. In the case of President Kennedy's vision to put a man on the moon in the 1960s, various units of NASA, the military (e.g. the US Navy), and private organizations (e.g. contractors for NASA) each had their own parts to play to ensure the realization of the vision.

What Drives Visionary Leadership Behavior?

Like many aspects of organizational behavior, visionary leadership is driven by two overall dimensions: (i) context and (ii) individual qualities. Context provides the impetus for new vision. When aspects of context change, new vision may become necessary. These aspects include technological change, major shifts in government regulation, and competitive pressures. As an example, consider the recent COVID-19 pandemic. To some degree, the pandemic warranted incremental or short-term change (e.g. restaurants shifting from in-store dining to increased take-out service), and thus, vision as defined in this chapter is not relevant. However, the pandemic has also led to more long-term considerations, such as new visions regarding how work might be designed (e.g. more telecommuting, less need for office space, and so forth).

While changes in the context or environment of an organization can spawn the need for new vision, it is only people who can create and implement it. But why are some people more prone to visionary behavior than others? It takes courage as a leader, as well as a strong sense of self, to engage in visionary behavior. With regard to courage, the idea is relatively simple. If an individual projects out into the future in terms of bold or idealistic vision, there is a good chance that the vision will not be realized (at least in its original form) or even attempted. Accordingly, the visionary individual risks credibility as a leader. On the other hand, if a leader simply attempts to maintain the status quo, there is less risk to the individual's credibility.

To be visionary, one must have a strong sense of self, perhaps even an inflated view of oneself, and a belief that he or she has an inherent right to lead. Narcissism is all about a strong sense of self and the perception on the part of the individual that he or she has a special right or privilege to lead other people (Ames, Rose, and Anderson, 2006; Galvin et al., 2010). Not surprisingly, Maccoby (2003, 2004) considered the connection between narcissism and visionary leadership. Thus, while there is an obvious downside to narcissism on the part of leaders, there may also be a silver lining in terms of a propensity toward visionary behavior. Interestingly, Owens, Wallace, and Waldman (2015) showed how leaders who are able to paradoxically combine narcissism and humility are likely to produce favorable outcomes. Consider how this combination might align with the consideration of shared vision formation discussed earlier. A leader with narcissistic tendencies might formulate a bold new vision. But then optimally, based on the simultaneous possession of humility, that leader would realize that he or she can learn from others and, thus, allow input or honing of the vision on the part of others (e.g. followers and customers) – that is, shared visionary leadership. Maccoby (2004) referred to such individuals as "productive narcissists."

Neural Underpinnings of Visionary Leadership

The field of organizational neuroscience is emerging as a means of forming a better understanding of organizational phenomena. The basic idea is that concepts like leadership can be considered more thoroughly, in terms of both measurement and theoretical understanding, with a neurological lens. Through the use of quantitative electroencephalogram technology, visionary leadership tendencies have been linked to electrical activity in the brain. For example, Waldman, Balthazard, and Peterson (2011) considered how right frontal activity is correlated with visionary leadership. Kim, Williams, Balthazard, and Ames (2019) presented evidence that a broader network in the brain, the default mode network (DMN), is predictive of visionary leadership.

These results are promising in that they do indicate a link between neural activity and visionary leadership behavior. On the other hand, such linkages should be understood with caution. Specifically, it is not as simple as saying that there is a neural basis for leader cognition and behavior. Instead, the context, both short and long term, can come into play. Waldman, Wang, Hannah, and Balthazard (2017) showed how electrical activity in the DMN was related to ethical ideology and behavior. Thus, when taken in combination with the work of Kim et al. (2019), the DMN appears to be related to multiple aspects of effective leadership. However, the research of Waldman et al. (2017) also revealed how different job types were also associated with neural differences based on the DMN. Leaders who were identified as having strong leadership potential at the upper ranks of the US army (e.g. lieutenant colonels who were being targeted for the rank of full colonel) showed patterns of DMN activity that were most consistent with ethical leadership. Conversely, individuals enrolled in an executive MBA program (e.g. largely middle-level managers in business corporations) showed a much more negative DMN profile that was consistent with a lack of ethical leadership.

Why might there be such categorical differences between work types/contexts? The answer may lie in how different work types or contexts either attract certain types of individuals (e.g. more ethical or visionary) or reinforce such leadership behavior over time. Indeed, as speculated by Waldman et al. (2017), it is even possible that over time, certain work types or contexts may gradually alter neural structures of individuals to be in line with various forms of leadership – such as visionary leadership. But at this point, such thinking must remain speculative. The bottom line is that like so many other forms of behavior, visionary leadership is likely to be a function of both the individual (e.g. through neural activity) and that person's context.

Case Examples

In this section, I will share a number of case examples of visionary leaders. Visionary leadership is extraordinary, and the same can be said for all of these leaders. They come from different walks of life, sectors, and time periods. In addition, they are not necessarily in formal, organizational leadership roles. For example, the orthopedic doctor mentioned in the opening example of this chapter clearly practiced visionary leadership. Each of the following leaders in his or her own way represents aspects of visionary leadership as described in this chapter. Several of these case examples are also described in Waldman and O'Reilly (2022).

Martin Luther King

Martin Luther King is perhaps the consummate or prototypical visionary leader. His "I have a dream" speech in Washington, DC in 1963 encapsulates what leader vision, and its communication, is all about.[1] The speech includes vibrant images and language, such as "I have a dream that little children will one day live in a nation where they will not be judged by the color of their skin but by the content of their character."

[1] See http://www.analytictech.com/mb021/mlk.htm

Not only did the speech contain such inspirational rhetoric, it was delivered in a passionate, energetic manner. It also did what so many effective visionaries are known for; specifically, connecting the past, present, and future. Visionary leaders tend to have a deep perspective that connects the past, present, and future in a vivid and persuasive manner (Kim et al., 2019).

Mary Kay Ash

Women have for years strived for equality in the workplace, including equality with regard to pay and earnings capability. However, when Mary Kay Ash founded and grew her cosmetics firm in the 1960s and 1970s, the earning power of women was actually much lower than current times. She founded her firm not so much on the premise of making better cosmetics than competitors, but rather with the purpose and vision of helping women (i.e. her employees) achieve a better footing with men in terms of the ability to make money. At the time, that vision was very bold, as well as socialized (i.e. oriented toward serving the needs of a broader stakeholder group) and based on high ideals.

Steve Jobs

Like other visionary leaders, Steve Jobs developed a reputation, especially in his early years at Apple, as being somewhat controversial. His narcissistic demeanor and sometimes caustic, and even abusive, behavior contributed to setbacks in his career. Nevertheless, Jobs was also the consummate visionary leader (Isaacson, 2011). At the heart of his visionary leadership was the ability to foresee how advanced technology could be made simple and usable for the typical consumer. As an example, although more technically oriented engineers developed mouse technology for computers, Jobs was able to envision possibilities in its use for personal computing on the part of the average consumer.[2] Further, Jobs identified with his role as a visionary leader. In his hindsight regarding the original development of the Macintosh computer, Jobs saw his special role in the project as maintaining and reinforcing the vision (Isaacson, 2011). He did so by continually reminding fellow team members on the Macintosh project of the ultimate vision for the machine, even during setbacks and doubts on the part of those members (Isaacson, 2011).

Hugh Pace

Prior the 1990s, Goodyear-Oxo operated as an independent subsidiary within the Goodyear organization. Headquartered in Mexico City, its mission was to produce and sell tires within Mexico. However, in the 1990s, the economic landscape started

[2] See https://zurb.com/blog/steve-jobs-and-xerox-the-truth-about-inno

to change dramatically in North America in general, and Mexico more specifically. That is, the combined advent of NAFTA and recurring devaluation of the peso combined to present an opportunity for Goodyear-Oxo to become an exporter of tires to markets in other countries, especially the USA and Canada.

As described by Youngdahl, Waldman, and Anders, 1998, Hugh Pace became the chief executive at Goodyear-Oxo in the early 1990s. Given the evolving economic context, Pace attempted to develop new vision at Goodyear-Oxo. Specifically, he worked from the framework of total quality management, which was a popular mechanism in the 1990s for improving quality and customer-based management. Together with other top executives at Goodyear-Oxo, they formed a shared vision that blended quality, concern for employee welfare and development, and the pursuit of global markets. The key here is that new vision was not created solely by Hugh Pace, but instead was co-formulated by multiple individuals. As the chief executive, Pace took a hands-on approach with various units of Goodyear-Oxo to help facilitate their respective implementation of the company's new vision (Youngdahl et al., 1998). In some ways, this approach was similar to the "keeper of the vision" role played by Steve Jobs in the development of the Macintosh.

John Mackey

John Mackey is the founder and CEO of Whole Foods, now owned by Amazon. Like other visionary leaders, Mackey is not without controversy. For example, he received much criticism for anonymous postings over several years on a Yahoo chat forum that demeaned a rival, Wild Oats Markets Inc.[3] Nevertheless, Mackey pioneered the concept of conscious capitalism, which envisions a form of capitalism, whereby firms truly attempt to understand and value the interconnected needs of a range of stakeholders – not just shareholders. In so doing, firms demonstrate a higher sense of purpose beyond simply being money-making entities.

Elon Musk

Elon Musk certainly represents yet another unique and controversial figure as a leader. But one thing that is clear is his vision tendencies.[4] Whether the vision involves electric cars or even the colonization of Mars,[5] Musk has shown no hesitancy to think and communicate boldly about the future. And like many other visionary leaders, Musk exudes a charismatic persona that tends to land him in the limelight, as exemplified by his appearance on NBC's *Saturday Night Live* in 2021.

[3] See https://www.reuters.com/article/us-wholefoods-ftc/john-mackey-panned-wild-oats-on-web-idUSN1133440820070712

[4] see https://www.inc.com/john-eades/in-just-9-words-elon-musk-shows-us-how-to-be-visionary-leaders.html

[5] see http://www.businessinsider.com/elon-musk-colonization-of-mars-sxsw-2018-3

Michael Crow

From the start of his tenure, Michael Crow stressed the future, even looking as much as 40 years down the road. A frequent theme was that for Phoenix, AZ (i.e. the home base of ASU) to be a world-class city, it had to have a world-class university – something that ASU was not in 2002. In the early portion of his tenure, Crow stressed this fact and his vision repeatedly in front of different audiences (e.g. students, faculty, community members, legislators, and so forth). Repeated communication of this nature is essential because new vision implies change, and people tend to be very hesitant about change, and resist it, for a number of reasons (Kotter, 1996). These reasons include the notion that people become comfortable in their routines, and change can involve the need for additional resources or shifts in how resources are obtained. As an example, in order to move the university toward his vision in a context of dwindling investment from the state of Arizona, Crow pushed for dramatic increases in tuition in the early part of his tenure. Not surprisingly, these increases were met with resistance from students, parents, and other members of the community. In order to overcome resistance to change, it is important for a leader to communicate the vision widely and often, and in the process, provide a clear rationale for the change that would need to accompany new vision. In line with Crow's original vision, over time, ASU has come closer to world-class status as a university (see Waldman and O'Reilly, 2022).

Blockbuster Vision: From the Heights of Success to Bankruptcy

While Blockbuster, the brick and mortar, retail giant, created a robust and compelling vision in the mid-1980s that enabled them to dominate the video rental market, it was that vision that was ultimately their undoing. At their height, in the mid-2000s, Blockbuster had more than 9000 stores and more than 80,000 employees. They grew to dominate the sector with a close-to-the-customer vision: They established retail outlets where customers could browse through video titles and select material for home viewing. They had outlets in nearly every community throughout the United States and began aggressive international expansion. The vision served them well for about two decades.

The market began to shift as the Internet became more powerful, however, enabling customers to browse for videos in the comfort of their homes. While executives at Blockbuster dabbled into this online world, it came too little and too late. To wit, Blockbuster had an opportunity to buy their up-and-coming rival Netflix in 2002 for $50 million but turned down the opportunity. Now Netflix dominates the sector, and the in-store retail experience has been supplanted by Red Box, which offers self-service kiosks for video rentals. Blockbuster filed for bankruptcy in 2010.

Psychologists use the term "escalation of commitment" to describe what happened at Blockbuster. Escalation of commitment is a situation where people become increasingly committed to a vision simply because they have historically been committed to that particular vision. Escalation of commitment can be a tremendous tool, if the vision is effective and the environment remains the same. On the other hand, if the vision has served people well in the past, and the environment suddenly shifts, rendering the vision obsolete, escalation of commitment to the vision can destroy an organization, as it did with Blockbuster.

Conclusion

As suggested by the opening principle of this chapter, visionary leadership is all about forward-looking thinking and communication. While there may be aspects of a leader's context or environment that could engender more visionary behavior on the part of individuals, leaders' own predispositions are largely responsible for whether such behavior will be shown. This raises the age-old issue of whether visionary leaders are born versus nurtured. It might seem like, as compared to other aspects of effective leadership, visionary leadership is something with which a person is either born or not. In other words, it would seem that it is all about nature, not nurture.

That said, it is possible that visionary leadership could be nurtured through the type of developments in neuroscience that were considered earlier in this chapter. Specifically, perhaps a technique known as neurofeedback could be used to help develop visionary tendencies on the part of leaders. Through operant feedback protocols, neurofeedback involves the systematic altering of electrically based brain structures to be more in line with healthy or more effective behavior. Although the technique has been used primarily as a non-pharmaceutical alternative to maladies like ADD, Waldman et al. (2011, 2017) considered the potential of neurofeedback in the realm of peak performance behavior like leadership. As suggested earlier, research is beginning to identify unique, electrical neural structures associated with visionary leadership (e.g. Kim et al., 2019). The idea would be to use neurofeedback technology to condition a leader's brain to be in line with known (i.e. through systematic research) neurological structures associated with visionary leadership.

To better understand this approach, let us compare it to the type of training that goes into a competitive sport. Take, for example, professional football. For any given position in that sport, physical conditioning is a necessary ingredient for success. But beyond such conditioning, players must be trained how to properly execute their particular positions. With regard to leadership development, the latter is commonly recognized, while the former has been largely ignored. That is, much thought has been put into how traditional techniques like motivational speakers, case analyses, exercises, and so forth might help to stimulate visionary behavior on the part of leaders. However, little thought has previously gone into the type of conditioning that may be necessary, specifically, neurological conditioning through neurofeedback. I am not attempting to suggest that neurofeedback might be a "magic bullet" for the development of visionary leadership. Nevertheless, as we move forward into the future, such innovative approaches to leadership development should certainly be considered and explored.

References

Ames, D. R., Rose, P., and Anderson, C. P. (2006). The NPI-16 as a short measure of narcissism. *Journal of Research in Personality*, 40, 440–450.

Bass, B. M., and Avolio, B. (1995). *Multifactor Leadership Questionnaire (MLQ)*. Palo Alto, CA: Mind Garden.

Baum, J. R., Locke, E. A., and Kirkpatrick, S. A. (1998). A longitudinal study of the relation of vision and vision communication to venture growth in entrepreneurial firms. *Journal of Applied Psychology*, 83, 43–54. https://doi.org/10.1037/0021-9010.83.1.43

Berson, Y., Waldman, D. A., and Pearce, C. L. (2016). Enhancing our understanding of vision in organizations: Toward an integration of leader and follower processes. *Organizational Psychology Review*, 171–191.

Collins, J., and Porras, J. I. (1994). *Built to Last: Successful Habits of Visionary Companies*. New York: Harper Business.

Finkelstein, S., Hambrick, D. C., and Cannella, A. A., Jr. (2009). *Strategic Leadership: Theory and Research on Executives, Top Management Teams, and Boards*. New York: Oxford University Press.

Galvin, B., Waldman, D. A., and Balthazard, P. A. (2010). Visionary communication qualities as mediators of the relationship between narcissism and follower perceptions of charismatic leadership. *Personnel Psychology*, 63, 509–537.

House, R. J., and Aditya, R. (1997). The social scientific study of leadership: Quo vadis? *Journal of Management*, 23, 409–474.

House, R. J., and Shamir, B. (1993). Toward an integration of transformational, charismatic and visionary theories of leadership. In M. Chemmers and R. Ayman (eds), *Leadership: Perspectives and Research Directions* (pp. 81–107). New York: Academic Press.

Isaacson, W. (2011). *Steve Jobs: The Exclusive Biography*. New York: Simon & Schuster.

Kim, J. Williams, R., Balthazard, P. A., and Ames, J. (2019). Neural foundations of visionary leadership. Paper presented at the meeting of the Academy of Management, Boston, August 2019.

Kim, J. J., Waldman, D. A., Balthazard, P. A., and Ames, J. B. (2022). Leader self-projection and collective role performance: A consideration of visionary leadership. *The Leadership Quarterly*, doi.org/10.1016/j.leaqua.2022.101623

Kotter, J. P. (1996). *Leading Change*. Boston, MA: Harvard Business School Press.

Maccoby, M. (2003). *The Productive Narcissist: The Promise and Peril of Visionary Leadership*. New York, NY: Broadway Books.

Maccoby, M. (2004). Narcissistic leaders: The incredible pros, the inevitable cons. *Harvard Business Review*, 82, 92–101.

Owens, B. P., Wallace, A. S., and Waldman, D. A. (2015). Leader narcissism and follower outcomes: The counterbalancing effect of leader humility. *Journal of Applied Psychology*, 100, 1203–1213.

Pearce, C. L., and Sims, H. P. Jr. (2002). Vertical versus shared leadership as predictors of the effectiveness of change management teams: An examination of aversive, directive, transactional, transformational, and empowering leader behaviors. *Group Dynamics: Theory, Research, and Practice*, 6, 172–197.

Stam, D., Lord, R. G., van Knippenberg, D., and Wisse, B. (2014). An image of who we might become: Vision communication, possible selves, and vision pursuit. *Organization Science*, 25, 1172–1194.

Sully de Luque, M., Washburn, N. T., Waldman, D. A., and House, R. J. (2008). Unrequited profit: How stakeholder and economic values relate to subordinates' perceptions of leadership and firm performance. *Administrative Science Quarterly*, 53, 626–654.

Van Knippenberg, D., and Sitkin, S. B. (2013). A critical assessment of charismatic—transformational leadership research: Back to the drawing board? *Academy of Management Annals*, 7(1), 1–60.

Waldman, D. A., Balthazard, P. A., and Peterson, S. (2011). The neuroscience of leadership: Can we revolutionize the way that leaders are identified and developed? *Academy of Management Perspectives*, 25(1), 60–74.

Waldman, D. A., and O'Reilly, C. (2022). *Leadership for Organizations* (2nd edition). Boston, MA: FlatWorld.

Waldman, D. A., Wang, D., Hannah, S. T., and Balthazard, P. A. (2017). A neurological and ideological perspective of ethical leadership. *Academy of Management Journal*, 60, 1285–1306.

Youngdahl, W., Waldman, D. A., and Anders, G. (1998). Leading the total quality transformation at Goodyear-Oxo, Mexico: An interview with Hugh Pace. *Journal of Management Inquiry*, 7, 59–65.

Zhang, Z., Waldman, D. A., and Wang, Z. (2012). A multilevel investigation of leader-member exchange, informal leader emergence, and individual and team performance. *Personnel Psychology*, 65, 49–77.

Appendix A

Future Orientation Scale

For each item below, please rate yourself honestly as you actually are, rather than how you might hope to be. Use the below scale:

1. = not at all
2. = once in a while
3. = sometimes
4. = fairly often
5. = frequently, if not always

____ 1. I make plans and take actions based on future goals.
____ 2. I have a clear understanding of where I am heading in life.
____ 3. I can clearly articulate my personal vision for my future.
____ 4. I talk about the future easily.
____ 5. I talk about the future frequently.

Scoring. Add your scores across these items and divide by 5. A score of 4 or more represents a strong future orientation. A score between 3 and 4 would be moderate. A score of less than 3 would be low.

Now form groups of two and discuss your results. Answer the following questions:

1. What is future orientation?
2. How do you think future orientation is likely to affect you at work?
3. Are people with different types of future orientations suited to different types of work?

Discuss your answers with the class as a whole.

Appendix B

Strategic Decision-Making Values

1 = represents a *top* priority for you; 2 = represent a *secondary* priority for you

In all of your following rankings, answer as you think you would actually prioritize if you were running a business, rather than as you hope you would prioritize. In other words, what would be your actual priorities?

Respond to items 1 and 2 by imagining that you are running a business. Use the scale shown earlier.

____1. The well-being of my employees.
____2. Maintaining profit margins.

Respond to items 3 and 4 by imagining that you are running a business. Use the scale shown earlier.

____3. Ensuring operational efficiencies.
____4. The environmental impact of my firm.

Respond to items 5 and 6 by imagining that you are running a business. Use the scale shown earlier.

____5. Making sure that my firm serves the greater community.
____6. Securing greater market share or sales.

Respond to items 7 and 8 by imagining that you are running a business. Use the scale shown earlier.

____7. Controlling costs.
____8. The well-being of my customers or clients.

Add up your scores on items as follows:

Economic values	*Stakeholder values*
2	1
3	4
6	5
7	8

Note that the possible score for each column can range from 4 to 8, and both columns should add up to 12 in total. For each column:

Score of 4 and 5 = strong priority
Score of 6 = moderate priority
Score of 7 and 8 = weak priority

Now form groups of two and discuss your results. Answer the following questions:

1. How are your results similar?
2. How are your results different?
3. What advice do you have for your partner?
4. What advice do you have for leaders in general when it comes to strategic decision-making values?

Now be prepared to share your results with the class as a whole.

Video Analysis and Discussion

Please watch the following video(s):

1. Power of a Vision: https://www.youtube.com/watch?v=66DXqosfZSQ
2. 3 Things that Make a Meaningful Vision: https://www.youtube.com/watch?v=zpzZumZCdWA

Now form small groups to discuss the video(s) and answer the following questions:

1. What are the major points of the video?
2. How can you use information from the video in your career?
3. Based on the video, what advice do you have for leaders in organizations?

Be prepared to present the ideas from your small group discussion with the class as a whole.

Discussion Questions

1. What is visionary leadership?
2. Why do we care about vision?
3. What is the difference between a "good" and a "bad" vision?
4. How does one enable people to *share* a vision?

17

Foster Trust Through Ability, Benevolence, and Integrity

Jason A. Colquitt[1] and Michael D. Baer[2]

[1] University of Notre Dame
[2] Arizona State University

Editors' Note

Earlier versions of this chapter were authored by Sabrina C. Salam, who died tragically in a car accident on April 4, 2005. The current authors are indebted to Sabrina for all her contributions to the foundation of this work.

Concerns about trust are woven into many aspects of working life. Encounters with new coworkers, leaders, or followers are dominated by questions about trust, setting the tone for future interactions. As relationships develop, trust serves as a guide that paces the openness, investment, and spontaneity of the interactions between individuals at work. As individuals navigate their way through hierarchical relationships, trust influences decisions about whether to cooperate with directives at the risk of exploitation. Finally, trust takes on a renewed importance in times of organizational crisis, as it can help maintain a sense of confidence and optimism during tough times.

The academic literature defines trust as the willingness of a trustor to be vulnerable to the actions of a trustee based on positive expectations about the trustee's characteristics, behaviors, and intentions (Mayer, Davis, and Schoorman, 1995). When employees trust their supervisors, they would be prepared to grant them influence over important issues by – for example – disclosing sensitive or personal information (Mayer and Davis, 1999; Schoorman, Mayer, and Davis, 2007). Note that trust in this example is not the actual disclosing of the information; it is the psychological state that makes the employee willing to do it. The disclosing of information represents risk-taking, which can be viewed as one behavioral expression of trust (Mayer et al., 1995).

The *Oxford English Dictionary* defines trust as confidence in, or reliance on, some quality or attribute of a person. Several qualities or attributes are capable of inspiring trust in leaders. For example, research has examined attributes like competence, loyalty, concern, consistency, reliability, honesty, openness, and value congruence (Butler, 1991; Butler and Cantrell, 1984; Mayer et al., 1995). Research examines these attributes under the heading of "trustworthiness," grouping them into three distinct categories or concepts. One of the three concepts is *ability*. If they want their followers to trust them, leaders must know what they are talking about, meaning they must possess relevant job knowledge and skills (Mayer et al., 1995). Only then will followers be confident that the leader's ideas are worth taking seriously. Of course, ability is often domain specific (Zand, 1972). Actions that reveal an expertise in one area (e.g. running the advertisement campaign for a new product) does not necessarily signal competence in another (e.g. determining the overall strategy for the entire organization).

The other two aspects of trustworthiness are less domain specific, reflecting more on the person and character of the leader. *Benevolence* entails the degree to which a leader has a sense of goodwill toward followers, showing concern and loyalty to them for reasons that are not egocentric or solely motivated by profits (Mayer et al., 1995). One could contrast benevolent leaders with narcissistic leaders or Machiavellian leaders who simply want to "use" people as means to their own personal ends. This facet of trustworthiness is evident in good mentor-protégé relationships, where a dyadic bond exists that goes beyond the formalized relationships reflected in an organizational chart.

Integrity, the third component, captures the degree to which a leader adheres to sound ethical and moral principles (Mayer et al., 1995). Leaders who have integrity keep their promises, exhibit consistent actions and behaviors, and adhere to values such as honesty and openness. Integrity also conveys an alignment between a leader's words and a leader's deeds (Simons, 2002). From this perspective, integrity can be gauged by asking whether leaders "do what they say they will do."

When discussing trust in leaders in organizations, what they most want to know is how to increase trust within their units. If followers do not trust leaders, they react to the leader's words with skepticism, spending time monitoring the leader, checking up on them, and creating contingency plans if things go wrong (Mayer and Gavin, 2005). Such reactions amount to a "distrust tax" that can reduce the speed and efficiency of the actions, behaviors, and decisions within organizational units (Covey, 2006). In addition, a sense of distrust can undermine communication and cooperation within the unit while increasing the potential for damaging forms of group conflict. With that in mind, this chapter focuses on using the concepts of ability, benevolence, and integrity as a means of increasing trust.

The Benefits of Trust

Before examining our focal principle in more depth, it is useful to review the importance of trust within work units. That discussion will reveal that leaders should foster trust within their work units because it leads to many beneficial outcomes in organizational life (Colquitt, Scott, and LePine, 2007; Dirks and Ferrin, 2002). Those outcomes include the following.

Redefining the Work Relationship

The most effective work relationships involve employees who are willing to go beyond the strict definitions of their work roles (Graen and Scandura, 1987). When a leader asks a follower to "go the extra mile," the follower must have confidence that those efforts will eventually be rewarded, despite the absence of any formalized schedule or agreement. Followers who trust their leaders are willing to engage in those extra actions because they trust that their leader will eventually reciprocate (Blau, 1964). Put differently, they trust that their leaders will, over the long term, engage in a fair exchange relationship (see Chapter 11 for more on this issue). The end result of that trust is a work relationship built on evolving role definitions and requirements rather than bureaucratically defined lists of job duties.

Creativity and Innovation

Employees face other risks in their working lives, even apart from the extra-mile sorts of behaviors alluded to earlier. Among those risks is the decision to do their work in a creative and innovative fashion. Being innovative and creative usually entails a greater danger of making mistakes than following tradition. After all, novel ideas and solutions are not always functional and are not always accepted by an employee's peers. Despite those dangers, followers may accept the risks involved in creativity and innovation if they trust in the leader's ability, benevolence, and integrity. When followers view a leader as trustworthy, they know the leader will not take advantage of honest mistakes in a manner that will harm the employee.

Job Performance

Trust enhances employee job performance for several reasons. Many employees cannot perform their jobs at a truly effective level without the extra-role and risk-taking behaviors that can be fostered by trust. However, trust also impacts an employee's ability to focus on the task at hand (Mayer and Gavin, 2005). If employees are spending too much time "covering their backsides," worrying about politics, and drawing up contingency plans, they will not be able to focus enough attention on their job duties. Even if they can somehow remain focused on their jobs, the additional monitoring and backing up chores will heighten their stress level.

Communication

The amount of trust that exists between a leader and a follower affects the communication between them, including the amount of information exchange and the accuracy and efficiency of that exchange. Followers who trust their leaders will share facts and information with them more frequently and will be less likely to be guarded or secretive in the information that is conveyed. The effectiveness of a work unit often depends on followers being willing to share "bad news" without fears the leader will "shoot the messenger" (i.e. react punitively and destructively). Trust can enable candor, lessening the likelihood that news will be "spun" in an inaccurate manner. Indeed, the ability of trust to encourage undistorted communication and collaboration is especially important in times of organizational crisis (Zand, 1972). Furthermore, a distrustful employee may even withhold good news, thinking in some way it will work to their disadvantage if others somehow claim credit for it.

Commitment to Decisions

When a leader is successful in creating trust in employees, these employees are likely to be more committed to decisions developed jointly with the leader and to decisions made by the leader alone (Frost and Moussavi, 1992; Tyler and Degoey, 1996; Zand, 1972). Commitment to decisions is important in order to ensure their successful implementation. Many change programs in organizations, for example, fail because the majority of employees do not trust the motives or do not know the reasons behind them; thus, the employees are not committed to the desired changes and do not implement them in their daily work. Employees revert to the "old way of doing things" with the only difference that they are now using, for example, more expensive tools and systems. Because trust encourages commitment to decisions, developing greater trust in the leader encourages the implementation of changes in the work unit.

Commitment to the Organization

The reasons employees leave an organization are very frequently related to their direct superiors and, specifically, the trust these employees develop toward their superiors. For example, whether a leader follows up on promises made to the employee, whether a leader provides competent instruction to the employee, and whether a leader keeps promises are all influential in a subordinate's decision to stay with an organization. Employees may develop an emotional bond with trustworthy leaders (McAllister, 1995) or may feel a sense of obligation to remain with them to further the organization's work. Regardless of the underlying reasons, retaining such employees is critical to avoid the expense associated with turnover while protecting the knowledge and expertise of the work unit.

Implementing the Principle

How can organizational leaders implement our focal principle by using ability, benevolence, and integrity to foster trust? We will describe several actions that flow from the top of the organization – as represented by its culture – down to the leaders themselves, particularly in terms of their traits and skills. Once leaders are told about the principle, the importance of ability, benevolence, and integrity may seem obvious in hindsight. Nevertheless, many leaders fail to act in a trustworthy fashion, either because they lack valuable aptitudes and skills, they have poor moral character, they lack concern for the employees, or they become distracted by daily challenges. Besides managing their followers, leaders need to monitor competitor movements, new product developments, government regulations, and technical and process issues in their supply chain. Because those challenges are numerous, organizations need to emphasize issues of trustworthiness throughout their management and staffing decision-making.

Create a Culture of Trustworthiness

Organizational culture is the shared values (i.e. what is important; see Chapter 30) and beliefs (i.e. how things work) that interact with an organization's processes, structures, and control systems to create behavioral norms (i.e. how things are done around here) (Uttal, 1983). Developing and maintaining the "right" kind of organizational culture is a complex process that depends on multiple factors. The founders of an organization often set the tone for the culture, while actively managing staffing decisions so that the right people are selected and promoted over time. The leaders in an organization become the agents of that culture and, therefore, need to exhibit consistent actions that model the beliefs and values reflected in the culture. After all, employees look to the actions of the leader to understand the beliefs and values that are rewarded in the organization. If leaders' actions and words conflict with one another, it is likely that the actions will loom larger in the minds of followers than the words as they seek to understand the "true" culture.

There are several organizational activities that leaders can undertake to create a culture of trustworthiness in their organization. Probably one of the most crucial steps is to communicate and formalize the ethical principles that underlie integrity by creating fair and consistent procedures and ensuring that adherence to those procedures is transparent to every member of the organization. This can be aided through the involvement of at least some of the affected and involved employees whenever an organization makes critical decisions, plans activities, or initiates changes. Furthermore, the decision procedures that precede and accompany any organizational changes should be communicated widely so that employees can review these procedures whenever desirable.

Additionally, during the planning and implementation of any organizational changes, employees should often have the opportunity to have a dialogue with the decision-makers of the organization. This includes the opportunity to voice disagreements with organizational practices and the willingness of management to listen to disagreements. That sort of exchange will give leaders the opportunity to highlight the ethical standards and business considerations that have guided the organizational change and its implementation. Without that level of two-way communication, employees may react based on mistaken impressions that undercut perceptions of trustworthiness.

A culture of trustworthiness can also be created by emphasizing competence throughout the organization. One of the first steps in such an effort is gaining a more complete and valid understanding of the knowledge, skills, abilities, and other factors that are vital to success in the various jobs in the organization. Extensive job analyses should be conducted, with the results flowing into specific and accurate job descriptions. Unfortunately, many organizations suffer from unclear roles and responsibilities, which leads to an unclear definition of job functions. Colleagues, supervisors, or employees may develop distrust toward particular individuals because they expect them to have skills in areas that are not part of their job descriptions. Every member of the organization needs to understand their own roles and responsibilities, and those of their colleagues.

Emphasizing competence within the culture also requires leaders to identify the incompetent behaviors of employees and demonstrate that such behaviors will not be tolerated or rewarded in the organization. One means of accomplishing this goal is utilizing the results of job analyses to inform the development and use of performance evaluation procedures (see Chapter 10). That practice will ensure that leaders are knowledgeable about what it means to "do a good job" in a particular area. In cases where performance behaviors are not adequate, the organization should implement training and development programs that increase the right kinds of competencies (see Chapter 9). Such programs need to be comprehensive, long term, and available to all employees who need them. Furthermore, a process needs to be in place where the programs are continuously updated based on changes in the organization, the market, relevant technologies, consumer demands, and so forth.

Increase Leader Ability

Having emphasized the importance of the larger organizational culture, we now focus on the leaders themselves. A leader's trustworthiness can depend on both technical skills and general managerial competencies. Technically speaking, a leader needs to possess the competence, knowledge, and skills to perform certain actions and make certain decisions in their area of expertise. That ability is needed for followers to accept leader decisions and commit to them. Leaders, therefore, need extensive training in both technical and managerial skills. In addition to that training, leaders need to keep up to date with the most recent developments in their area, committing to employee development and continuous learning activities. This is something that is increasingly difficult given the high frequency of innovations and changes in any business area. Of course, leaders who are high in general intelligence will be more likely to attain and maintain high levels of technical ability (see Chapter 1).

Aside from their technical skills, however, leaders need to maintain high levels of general managerial competencies. Those competencies include being able to plan a career path with followers, setting the right kinds of goals with followers, evaluating follower performance accurately, providing coaching and development, and effectively managing conflict within the unit. Those competencies also include interpersonal skills, such as developing a knowledge and understanding of one's employees and their unique abilities. In many units, these managerial competencies have a stronger impact on unit performance than the leader's own technical skills.

Successfully managing ability levels requires leaders to show self-awareness and a realistic judgment about their strengths and weaknesses. Overestimating one's ability often results in failure, which can hamper the development of trust among followers. Thus, leaders should demonstrate to followers that they know what they do (and do not) know. It is a sign of objectivity to know when to ask for help and input in a particular task. Leaders should strive to approach followers who possess helpful knowledge and abilities to solve a particular problem, admitting that they would not be able to accomplish this task successfully alone. This sort of participative leadership can effectively capitalize on the variations in information and competencies across followers within a work unit (see Chapter 11).

One of a leader's most important roles is allocating rewards and resources, such as pay, promotions, and assignments. As leaders make those decisions, followers are assessing whether the leader demonstrates competency in that role. One visible and important aspect of allocation decisions is whether the procedure begins and concludes within a reasonable time frame (Outlaw, Colquitt, Baer, and Sessions, 2019). When leaders make decisions in a timely fashion – neither too fast nor slow – they demonstrate their decisiveness and organizational skills (Eisenhardt, 1990). Followers interpret this behavior as an indication of the leader's managerial ability, contributing to increased trust in the leader (Outlaw et al., 2019). Accordingly, as leaders make allocation decisions, they would be wise to consider the timeliness of those decisions in addition to their fairness.

Build Leader Benevolence

Although followers can judge a leader's ability rather quickly and reliability, gauging a leader's benevolence requires more time and attention. One way to demonstrate benevolence is to be supportive – to show concern for follower welfare, to consider follower needs, and to help followers on work tasks when necessary (Mayer and Davis, 1999). Managerial training can emphasize the importance of leader supportiveness, and relevant personality traits could also be considered in the context of selection and placement decisions. For example, leaders who are particularly Machiavellian or narcissistic are unlikely to engage in the kinds of behaviors needed to build a sense of benevolence.

Over time, continued demonstrations of benevolence can deepen the trust felt by a follower for a leader. Eventually, the dyad becomes characterized by a mutual investment of time and attention, and a mutual sense of fondness and respect. Role definitions become broadened, with the follower willing to "back up" the leader if necessary, or "stick their neck out" to support the leader (Graen and Uhl-Bien, 1995). Because it depends on frequent demonstrations of goodwill and frequent interactions between the leader and follower, this deepened sense of trust may only develop in a few select work relationships (Lewicki and Bunker, 1995;

McAllister, 1995). Still, if it does develop, it can serve as a robust and long-lasting foundation for extra-role and risk-taking behaviors within those relationships.

Demonstrate Leader Integrity

As with benevolence, gauging a leader's integrity can be difficult for employees in the early days and weeks of a working relationship. One way for a leader to demonstrate integrity is to show full consistency between words and deeds (Simons, 2002). In simple terms, leaders need to keep their promises – to "walk the walk," not just "talk the talk." Unfortunately, several factors can result in a disconnect between a leader's words and deeds. For example, some leaders are too quick to revise their espoused values and aspirations in response to fads, fashions, and changes. Those tendencies can result in a sense of confusion on the part of followers, damaging leader credibility (Simons, 2002). Some leaders are also too quick to make promises that they cannot keep, which further undermines credibility.

Another way for leaders to demonstrate integrity is to adhere to sound ethical principles. Although several principles are relevant to integrity, principles of organizational justice are particularly strong drivers of trust levels (for a review, see Colquitt, Greenberg, and Zapata-Phelan, 2005). Procedural justice, for example, encompasses a number of principles that describe how decision-making procedures should be structured. Such procedures should be accurate, consistent, unbiased, correctable, and provide opportunities for employee voice and input. Whenever followers see a leader engage in decision-making – whether in the context of a hiring decision, a performance evaluation, a conflict resolution procedure, or some other event – they can gauge adherence to these principles as evidence of trustworthiness (Colquitt and Rodell, 2011; Lind, 2001; Tyler and Lind, 1992).

Other justice principles describe how procedures should be communicated and discussed with employees as decision-making occurs (Bies and Moag, 1986). Interpersonal justice encompasses two principles – that communication should be respectful and that it should refrain from improper or prejudicial statements. Informational justice also encompasses two principles – that communication should be honest and trustful and that adequate explanations should be offered for key decisions (note that scholars have debated whether it is appropriate to classify interpersonal and informational justice as forms of "justice" per se). For more on that debate, see Locke (2003), Bies (2005), and Colquitt, Greenberg, and Scott (2005). When leaders speak to followers disrespectfully or use derogatory remarks, followers will rightly question the standards and principles that guide leader behaviors. When leaders are dishonest about decision-making procedures, or remain guarded and tight-lipped about their details, followers may similarly begin to doubt or question the integrity and character of the leader (Colquitt and Rodell, 2011).

Indeed, giving honest information may be particularly relevant to integrity because honesty is so fundamental in discussions of trustworthiness (Butler, 1991; Butler and Cantrell, 1984). Unfortunately, leaders are often reluctant to tell the truth. During times of crisis and change, business leaders often are faced with the challenge of either telling an uncomfortable truth, remaining silent, or downplaying the severity of the situation. There are plenty of other situations in which, in the short term, it may be more comfortable not to tell the truth to followers. Ultimately, however, even dishonesty that was meant to protect employee morale will eventually be exposed, undermining trustworthiness at a time when commitment to the organization is most vital. Even concerted efforts at secrecy can backfire, as employees may simply "fill in the gaps" in their understanding with their own theories about the leader's behavior. Therefore, leaders need to take steps to explain the true reasons for their decisions to those individuals affected by it, leaving less room for negative interpretations of leader behavior.

Fostering Trustworthiness Through Alternate Means

Thus far, our suggestions for fostering trustworthiness have focused on ways that a leader can provide "hard data" about their ability, benevolence, and integrity to their followers. This approach assumes that followers' perceptions of a leader's trustworthiness are based on rational, systematic assessments of the data they have gathered about the leader (Kramer, 1999). Yet, followers often make trustworthiness assessments before they have had an opportunity to gather these data, such as when they are new to the organization. In these situations, followers must draw on less conscious, implicit cues to infer a leader's trustworthiness (Baer and Colquitt, 2018). For example, newcomers perceive their organizations as more trustworthy when the work environment is aesthetically pleasing, leading to higher trust and enhanced learning (Baer, van der Werff, Colquitt, Rodell, Zipay, and Buckley, 2018). Leaders could benefit from followers' reliance on this implicit, heuristic processing by creating a pleasing physical work environment. Leaders might also harness the "power of a smile," as smiling sends an implicit signal that the person is more competent, caring, and honest (for a review, see Baer and Colquitt, 2018).

The rational approach to trust assumes that an employee will base their trust in a colleague on how that specific colleague has treated them in past interactions. Research indicates, however, that an employee's perception of a particular colleague can also be temporarily impacted by how the employee is treated by their *other* colleagues (Baer, Matta, Kim, Welsh, and Garud, 2018). As an employee goes throughout the day, they are gathering information about whether people, in general, are trustworthy. For example, consider an employee whose colleague – Regina – is helpful and kind to them during a morning meeting. This positive treatment from Regina leads the employee to form a short-term heuristic that *people* are generally altruistic and reliable. Throughout the rest of the day, this heuristic will tend to influence how the employee perceives the trustworthiness of their other coworkers, such as Jim, Maria, and Collin. This research suggests that leaders can start a beneficial cascade of trustworthiness in a workgroup by modeling and encouraging helpful and kind behavior.

Exceptions to the Principle

Are there times when increasing ability, building benevolence, and demonstrating integrity will fail to foster trust? Research has repeatedly supported the impact of the three trustworthiness aspects on employee trust (Colquitt et al., 2007). However, there are times when taking steps to increase trustworthiness will have a weaker impact on actual trust levels. Three factors comprise relevant exceptions to our focal principle.

Visibility of the Leader's Behavior

Increases in ability, benevolence, and integrity will only result in increases in trust when those efforts are noticed. For a follower to assess a leader's trustworthiness, the follower must be aware of and familiar with the leader's actions and decisions. Increasing the visibility of a leader's behavior is, therefore, necessary for the fostering of trust. The leader can ensure visibility through frequent contact and exchange of information with followers. Such contact can be face to face or through other means (e.g. telephone, memos, email, etc.). However, greater face-to-face contact leads to richer and more high-quality information exchanges, which can only encourage the building of trust (Salam, 1998).

When leaders communicate face to face rather than through other means, they can convey information in greater detail, thereby preventing any misinterpretations by followers. Moreover, face-to-face communication allows followers to ask for immediate clarification. This, in turn, may trigger further explanations of a situation by the leader, which increases the overall quality of communication. In this way, data that are relevant to ability, benevolence, and integrity can be described, discussed, and explained. Face-to-face communication also allows the leader to directly demonstrate competence in a particular task and offer shows of support, both of which make leader trustworthiness more salient.

Personality of Followers

Individuals differ in their tendency to trust others. Trust propensity is a personality trait that affects the amount of trust an individual feels toward others (Mayer et al., 1995). Individuals who are dispositionally trusting have a general belief that the words and promises of others can be relied upon. Individuals who are dispositionally suspicious are fundamentally skeptical of "human nature," doubting the trustworthiness of others as a sort of default position. Trust propensity is an important factor that affects trust early on in a relationship, before valid data on ability, benevolence, and integrity have been gathered.

Negative personal experiences, where individuals learned that trusting others can have adverse consequences, can lead to the development of a low trust propensity. Similarly, positive experiences where trust has been rewarded can lead to a high trust propensity. Early childhood experiences are particularly impactful to trust propensity, as it is believed to be one of the first personality traits to develop within individuals. National culture also has an impact, as some cultures have a higher general level of trust propensity than others. Although this trait is difficult to change, experiences over a long period of time that are incompatible with the existing disposition can lead to a modification of the trait.

An individual's trust propensity likely serves as somewhat of an anchor that binds their trust around a particular level. If a leader takes steps to increase ability, build benevolence, or demonstrate integrity, trust levels may adjust around that anchor. Still, even large increases in trustworthiness may have minimal impact on individuals who are dispositionally suspicious. Such individuals may react to such efforts with skepticism, looking for hidden motives behind leader actions or alternative explanations for the relevant changes.

Follower Information Processing

The development of trust depends on how the followers perceive their environment and what attributions they make based on these perceptions (Kramer, 1996). Although leaders might have an "objective" level of trustworthiness, trust depends on a personal assessment of trustworthiness by the follower. In other words, although clear and visible data about the leader's past and current actions may be available, the development of trust depends on how the follower processes and interprets this information.

There is a large stream of research studying attribution theory (Weiner, 1974). One lesson learned from this research is that cognitions and mental frameworks affect what individuals perceive and how the vast amount of information relevant to social interactions is interpreted. Theory and research on decision-making also identifies how individuals differ in their "mental accounting" (Kramer, 1996). For example, how certain scenarios are framed is likely to affect the perceptions of trustworthiness in an individual. Thus, aside from influencing what the follower knows about the leader's actions, the leader can also influence how the follower processes that information by providing the appropriate framing. For example, a leader's actions may not seem consistent until the leader informs the employee that these actions are leading toward a common goal.

Case Examples

We provide the following real-life examples from businesses where trust has been a major issue determining the success of various endeavors. These examples illustrate how the principle explained in this chapter can be translated into real business situations. The first case illustrates factors that influence trust in interpersonal relationships, while the second case illustrates factors that influence trust at an organizational level.

1. Moving from a Functional to a Product-Oriented Structure

A department of a large European logistics and transportation company, responsible for three products, used to be organized according to technical expertise. The department had one director. Three functional groups – mechanical, information technology, and hydraulics – reported to this director. Several technicians and operators worked within each of the functional groups. This operational structure, however, often functioned poorly in terms of cost and quality of service, so a new structure was put in place. In this new structure, teams were organized around product lines rather than functions. The restructuring led to the formation of three teams with newly appointed leaders. These leaders were each given responsibility for an entire product line and the management of a multifunctional team.

After six months of operation, the results varied widely between the teams, with none of them functioning according to the outlined principles. The director was surprised at the high degree of operating disparity between the teams, particularly because her trust in the different team leaders was inconsistent with the actual performance of the teams. Furthermore, the atmosphere within the teams ranged from motivated and productive to dissatisfied and demoralized. The explanation for this confusing situation lies in the different types of behaviors the team leaders exhibited toward their supervisors versus their subordinates.

Although product team 1 had the highest performance, the director was not happy with the team's leader. As a result, she did not have faith that the favorable results would last. This lack of trust could be attributed to several factors. Product team 1's leader was new in the role and had no prior experience writing management reports. Consequently, she avoided submitting regular reports and communications to her director. The leader's lack of experience and poor communication skills led the director to question the leader's ability. Moreover, the director interpreted the lack of communication from the leader of team 1 as low concern for the director's needs, harming perceptions of benevolence.

In contrast, the members of product team 1 had high trust in their team leader. The leader organized many occasions for communication and information exchange within the team. Those actions fostered exchanges of helpful information and increased intrateam support. Furthermore, the team leader demonstrated high ability in the work content while providing team members with some decision-making power over their work. The leader also utilized fair performance evaluations and demonstrated support and concern for member needs. These actions fostered perceptions of integrity and benevolence, making the leader appear trustworthy to the team.

The performance of product team 2 was lower than that of product team 1. Nevertheless, the director trusted the leader of product team 2. In the director's opinion, it was only because of the leader that product team 2 achieved good results. The director's higher trust in the leader of product team 2 than the leader of product team 1 can be explained by perceptions of trustworthiness. The leader of product team 2 provided regular and detailed management reports to the director. Furthermore, the team leader frequently met with the director, both formally and informally, to apprise her of the team's work. The team leader told the director that the team's poor results were due to low performance of the operators on the team. The team leader noted that he often had to jump in and do the operators' jobs to compensate for their low performance. These actions painted a favorable picture of the leader's technical and managerial abilities. In addition, the director felt that the leader was demonstrating his integrity by honestly communicating the team's problems and demonstrating his benevolence by personally assisting the team with its workload.

Within product team 2, however, there was very little trust in the team leader. The operators in the team felt that the team leader unfairly provided all the bonuses to his former colleagues – the mechanics on the team. This fostered conflict between the operators and the mechanics, which reduced trust between the operators and the leader and between the operators and the mechanics. In contrast, the mechanics felt fairly treated, as they believed the team leader rightfully evaluated them more favorably than the operators. The leader also spent more time coaching the mechanics than the operators, resulting in differential perceptions about the leader's benevolence. Taken together, the leader's disparate treatment of these two groups of employees created a division that lowered team performance.

Product team 3 had the worst performance of all three teams. Nevertheless, the director trusted the management capabilities of the leader of product team 3, revealing a further disconnect between the director's assessment of leader trustworthiness and the actual performance of the three teams. The leader of product team 3 was skilled at monitoring performance and writing very detailed and informative reports. The leader was also very skilled in managing his budget, planning resources, and in setting performance goals. The director greatly appreciated this detailed information and consistent demonstration of management skills, which contributed to her positive impression of the leader of team 3.

Within product team 3, however, the atmosphere was very strained, as all members of the team had very low perceptions of his trustworthiness. These perceptions could be attributed to the leader's poor interpersonal, communication, and coaching skills. The leader was also managing a product that he did not understand. Compounding his lack of skill and knowledge, the leader actively avoided communicating with his team members. Rather than directly helping the team, the team leader sequestered himself doing paperwork and preparing detailed reports for management. These actions led team members to doubt the leader's managerial abilities and technical expertise. The leader's perceived apathy toward the team's well-being also lowered their perceptions of his benevolence.

This case illustrates several important aspects of building trust. First, both followers and leaders are sensitive to cues about a person's ability, benevolence, and integrity. In this scenario, the director and the team members were receiving different signals about the team leaders' trustworthiness. The trust-relevant data that the director observed were different than the trust-relevant data that the team members observed. The director also prioritized different aspects of ability than the team members. Taken together, these variations resulted in a disconnect in perceived trustworthiness between the director and the team members. Indeed, perceptions of trustworthiness even varied within teams, with some factions perceiving favoritism that undermined integrity, whereas other factions felt that treatment was fair and just. As leaders strive to effectively build trust, they should take care to convey positive information about their trustworthiness upward, downward, and laterally within the organization.

2. Managing Organizational Change

An international chemical company has recently implemented an enterprise resource planning (ERP) system, in the hope that the system would improve efficiency and productivity in its supply chain. A few months after the implementation of this tool, however, none of the desired results had been achieved. Processes were still ineffective, employees resisted implementation of the new system, morale was low, and employees were increasingly distrustful of management. Detailed interviews with employees indicated that they did not understand why this change was necessary and perceived the new system as something that was unilaterally imposed on them by their leadership team. This lack of perceived control made employees feel both unsupported and unfairly treated, which in turn triggered doubts about leadership's benevolence and integrity.

The management team also neglected to educate employees about how and why their roles and responsibilities would be changing due to the new system. Employees also did not understand that the new ERP system was part of a broader initiative to "future proof" their technology and better integrate with suppliers and buyers. Management's failure to clearly convey this information triggered perceptions that management was incompetent. Employees also interpreted this lack of communication as an unfair disregard for their well-being, wondering if management cared that these changes were time-consuming and stressful for employees. Additionally, employees were upset that although management stated they were open to employee feedback, employees' opinions about the ERP system were never solicited or considered. This disconnect between management's words and deeds was upsetting to employees. In sum, management's actions led employees to doubt the leadership team's ability, benevolence, and integrity.

This case further illustrates how ability, benevolence, and integrity combine to influence employees' trust in leadership. More importantly, the case reveals how the importance of trustworthiness becomes magnified in times of organizational change. Change efforts create a great deal of uncertainty and insecurity among employees. Those feelings prompt employees to take a fresh, careful, and sometimes skeptical look at their work environment (Lind, 2001). Any data that convey questionable levels of trustworthiness will be noticed and discussed among employees, restricting their trust at precisely the time when management needs them to take risks by utilizing new methods or procedures. As a result, leaders need to take extra steps to showcase their ability, benevolence, and integrity during times of change.

Conclusion

Ability, benevolence, and integrity are critical to followers' trust in their leader. Ability reflects the knowledge, skills, and aptitudes of a leader; it is fostered by demonstrating expertise in technical areas and general management competencies. Benevolence reflects a desire to be considerate of the follower; it is fostered by displays of concern and support. Integrity captures an adherence to moral and ethical principles; it is fostered by aligning words with deeds and adhering to standards of organizational justice. Followers who trust their leaders tend to exhibit several beneficial behaviors. For example, followers are more likely to engage in beneficial extra-role behaviors, such as unsolicited helping and making useful suggestions for change. A sense of trust also allows followers to take the risks needed to engage in creative and innovative behaviors. Likewise, followers' job performance tends to improve, as they are free to focus on the tasks at hand rather than worrying about politics, contingency plans, and watching their backs. High levels of trust also improve communication, as followers feel freer to share sensitive information. Finally, trust increases follower commitment to leaders' decisions while enhancing their desire to stay with the organization.

References

Baer, M. D., and Colquitt, J. A. (2018). Why do people trust? Moving toward a more comprehensive consideration of the antecedents of trust. In S. Sitkin, R. Searle, and A.-M. Nienaber (eds), *The Routledge Companion to Trust* (pp. 163–182). New York: Routledge.

Baer, M. D., Matta, F., Kim, J. K., Welsh, D., and Garud, N. (2018). It's not you, it's them: Social influences on trust propensity and trust dynamics. *Personnel Psychology*, 71, 423–455.

Baer, M. D., van der Werff, L., Colquitt, J. A., Rodell, J. B., Zipay, K. P., and Buckley, F. (2018). Trusting the "look and feel": Situational normality, situational aesthetics, and the perceived trustworthiness of organizations. *Academy of Management Journal*, 61, 1718–1740.

Bies, R. J. (2005). Are procedural justice and interactional justice conceptually distinct? In J. Greenberg and J. A. Colquitt (eds), *The Handbook of Organizational Justice* (pp. 85–112). Mahwah, NJ: Erlbaum.

Bies, R. J., and Moag, J. F. (1986). Interactional justice: Communication criteria of fairness. In R. J. Lewicki, B. H. Sheppard, and M. H. Bazerman (eds), *Research on Negotiations in Organizations* (Vol. 1, pp. 43–55). Greenwich, CT: JAI Press.

Blau, P. M. (1964). *Exchange and Power in Social Life.* New York: Wiley.

Butler, J. K. (1991). Toward understanding and measuring conditions of trust: Evolution of a conditions of trust inventory. *Journal of Management*, 17, 643–663.

Butler, J. K. Jr., and Cantrell, R. S. (1984). A behavioral decision theory approach to modeling dyadic trust in superiors and subordinates. *Psychological Reports*, 55, 19–28.

Colquitt, J. A., Greenberg, J., and Scott, B. A. (2005). Organizational justice: Where do we stand? In J. Greenberg and J. A. Colquitt (eds), *The Handbook of Organizational Justice* (pp. 589–619). Mahwah, NJ: Erlbaum.

Colquitt, J. A., Greenberg, J., and Zapata-Phelan, C. P. (2005). What is organizational justice? A historical overview. In J. Greenberg and J. A. Colquitt (eds), *The Handbook of Organizational Justice* (pp. 3–56). Mahwah, NJ: Erlbaum.

Colquitt, J. A., and Rodell, J. B. (2011). Justice, trust, and trustworthiness: A longitudinal analysis integrating three theoretical perspectives. *Academy of Management Journal*, 54, 1183–1206.

Colquitt, J. A., Scott, B. A., and LePine, J. A. (2007). Trust, trustworthiness, and trust propensity: A meta-analytic test of their unique relationships with risk taking and job performance. *Journal of Applied Psychology*, 92, 909–927.

Covey, S. M. R. (2006). *The Speed of Trust: The One Thing That Changes Everything.* New York: The Free Press.

Dirks, K. T., and Ferrin, D. L. (2002). Trust in leadership: Meta-analytic findings and implications for research and practice. *Journal of Applied Psychology*, 87, 611–628.

Eisenhardt, K. M. (1990). Speed and strategic choice: How managers accelerate decision making. *California Management Review*, 32, 39–54.

Frost, T. F., and Moussavi, F. (1992). The relationship between leader power base and influence: The moderating role of trust. *Journal of Applied Business Research*, 8, 9–14.

Graen, G. B., and Scandura, T. (1987). Toward a psychology of dyadic organizing. In L. L. Cummings and B. M. Staw (eds), *Research in Organizational Behavior* (Vol. 9, pp. 175–208). Greenwich, CT: JAI Press.

Graen, G. B., and Uhl-Bien, M. (1995). Relationship-based approach to leadership: Development of leader-member exchange (LMX) theory of leadership over 25 years: Applying a multi-level multi-domain perspective. *Leadership Quarterly*, 6, 219–247.

Kramer, R. M. (1996). Divergent realities and convergent disappointments in the hierarchic relation: Trust and the intuitive auditor at work. In R. M. Kramer and T. R. Tyler (eds), *Trust in Organizations: Frontiers of Theory and Research* (pp. 216–245). Thousand Oaks, CA: Sage Publications.

Kramer, R. M. (1999). Trust and distrust in organizations: Emerging perspectives, enduring questions. *Annual Review of Psychology*, 50, 569–598.

Lewicki, R. J., and Bunker, B. B. (1995). Trust in relationships: A model of development and decline. In B. B. Banker and J. Z. Rubin (eds), *Conflict, Cooperation, and Justice* (pp. 133–173). San Francisco, CA: Jossey-Bass.

Lind, E. A. (2001). Fairness heuristic theory: Justice judgments as pivotal cognitions in organizational relations. In J. Greenberg and R. Cropanzano (eds), *Advances in Organizational Justice* (pp. 56–88). Stanford, CA: Stanford University Press.

Locke, E. A. (2003). Good definitions: The epistemological foundation of scientific progress. In J. Greenberg (ed.), *Organizational Behavior: The State of the Science* (pp. 415–444). Mahwah, NJ: Lawrence Erlbaum Associates.

Mayer, R. C., and Davis, J. H. (1999). The effect of the performance appraisal system on trust for management: A field quasi-experiment. *Journal of Applied Psychology*, 84, 123–136.

Mayer, R. C., Davis, J. H., and Schoorman, F. D. (1995). An integrative model of organizational trust. *Academy of Management Review*, 20, 709–734.
Mayer, R. C., and Gavin, M. B. (2005). Trust in management and performance: Who minds the shop while the employees watch the boss? *Academy of Management Journal*, 48, 874–888.
Mayer, R. C., and Norman, P. M. (2004). Exploring attributes of trustworthiness: A classroom exercise. *Journal of Management Education*, 28, 224–249.
McAllister, D. J. (1995). Affect- and cognition-based trust as foundations for interpersonal cooperation in organizations. *Academy of Management Journal*, 38, 24–59.
Outlaw, R., Colquitt, J. A., Baer, M. D., and Sessions, H. (2019). How fair versus how long: An integrative theory-based examination of procedural justice and procedural timeliness. *Personnel Psychology*, 72, 361–391.
Salam, S. (1998). *The Effects of Subordinate Competence, Leader Competence, Leader Integrity, and Technology on Subordinate Participation Seeking, Performance, Satisfaction, and Agreement.* UMI Dissertation Information Service, Ann Arbor, Michigan.
Schoorman, F. D., Mayer, R. C., and Davis, J. H. (2007). An integrative model of organizational trust: Past, present, and future. *Academy of Management Review*, 32, 344–354.
Simons, T. (2002). Behavioral integrity: The perceived alignment between managers' words and deeds as a research focus. *Organization Science*, 13, 18–35.
Tyler, T. R., and Degoey, P. (1996). Trust in organizational authorities: The influence of motive attributions on willingness to accept decisions. In R. D. Kramer and T. R. Tyler (eds), *Trust in Organizations: Frontiers of Theory and Research* (pp. 331–356). Thousand Oaks, CA: Sage Publications.
Tyler, T. R., and Lind, E. A. (1992). A relational model of authority in groups. In M. Snyder (ed.), *Advances in Experimental Social Psychology* (Vol. 25, pp. 115–192). New York: Academic Press.
Uttal, B. (1983). The corporate culture vultures. *Fortune*, Oct. 17.
Weiner, B. (1974). *Achievement Motivation and Attribution Theory.* Morristown, NJ: General Learning Press.
Zand, D. E. (1972). Trust and managerial problem-solving. *Administrative Science Quarterly*, 17, 229–239.

Exercises

1. Appraising the Trustworthiness of Others

One valuable exercise for teaching students about trust requires them to consider how they weigh information on ability, benevolence, and integrity. Students should try to think of a classmate or work colleague that fits each of the following profiles:

1. Particularly low levels of ability but seemingly acceptable levels of benevolence and integrity
2. Particularly low levels of benevolence but seemingly acceptable levels of ability and integrity
3. Particularly low levels of integrity but seemingly acceptable levels of ability and benevolence

After thinking about these three classmates or colleagues, students are asked to rate how comfortable they would be turning over important duties and responsibilities to each one. Differences in that rating can then be used to explore the relative importance of the three trustworthiness facets.

2. Reacting to Trustworthy and Untrustworthy Leaders

Another valuable exercise asks students to consider their experiences with trustworthy and untrustworthy leaders. Students are first asked to picture a leader who is particularly trustworthy – having a strong mix of ability, benevolence, and integrity. In thinking about this leader, students should consider:

1. How did that high level of trustworthiness affect their motivation?
2. How did that high level of trustworthiness affect their tendency to take risks on the job?

Next, students should picture the opposite sort of leader – an untrustworthy leader with a particularly weak mix of ability, benevolence, and integrity. The same two questions should be considered in reference to that leader. Comparing how the students answered these questions in reference to the trustworthy versus untrustworthy leaders provides insight into how substantially trustworthiness impacts followers' reactions to leadership.

Video Analysis and Discussion

Please watch the following video(s):

1. First why, and then trust: https://www.youtube.com/watch?v=4VdO7LuoBzM
2. What we do not understand about trust: https://www.youtube.com/watch?v=1PNX6M_dVsk

Now form small groups to discuss the video(s) and answer the following questions:

1. What are the major points of the video?
2. How can you use information from the video in your career?
3. Based on the video, what advice do you have for leaders in organizations?

Be prepared to present the ideas from your small group discussion with the class as a whole.

Discussion Questions

1. When you have started a new job or role, what are some of the ways you have tried to convey to your leader that you have high levels of ability, benevolence, and integrity? Which approaches do you feel have been most effective and least effective?

2. Assume your company has a policy that states when an employee is late to work, the leader should formally record that offense in the employee's "permanent record." Now assume that you arrive late to work because there was a massive accident that extended your commute by an hour. On the one hand, the leader would be demonstrating benevolence by giving you a break and not recording your late arrival. On the other hand, the leader would, to some extent, be demonstrating low integrity by not following the company's rule. How should leaders handle situations that seemingly put aspects of trustworthiness into conflict with each other?

18

Teamwork in Organizations

The Best Teams Learn, Adapt, and Are Resilient

ALLISON M. TRAYLOR[1], SCOTT TANNENBAUM[2], ERIC J. THOMAS[3,4], AND EDUARDO SALAS[5]

[1] Department of Psychology, Clemson University
[2] The Group for Organizational Effectiveness
[3] The Mcgovern Medical School at the University of Texas Health Science Center Houston
[4] The University of Texas At Houston – Memorial Hermann Center for Healthcare Quality and Safety
[5] Department of Psychological Sciences, Rice University

Teams have long been essential to organizations. However, in the wake of massive technological advancement, rapidly evolving workforce demographics, and increasingly complex challenges facing today's organizations, today's teams must work more efficiently and effectively than ever before. In dynamic, challenging environments, a team cannot sustain success unless they effectively *learn, adapt,* and *demonstrate resilience.* Teams must be positioned to reflect on their past behavior to make improvements, change their course of action when challenges arise, and bounce back quickly when they experience setbacks. Without this, a team may manage to produce a short-term win, but it is unlikely to demonstrate long-term effectiveness and almost certainly will not become a great team.

Team learning, adaptation, and resilience are distinct, but interconnected capabilities that help teams assess, overcome, and improve in the face of challenges. *Team learning* describes an ongoing process of reflection and action characterized by asking questions, seeking feedback, experimenting, reflecting, and discussing errors or unexpected outcomes (Edmondson, 1999). Learning enables teams to become more effective over time. Even the best teams make mistakes or otherwise have room for improvement. Expert teams are explicit in taking time to debrief, reflect on performance, and integrate feedback to learn from their mistakes and improve over time. As a result, these teams are less likely to make the same mistakes again and are more likely to identify inefficiencies or better ways to approach tasks or challenges to improve their performance the next time they work together.

Effective teams are also able to adapt to challenges as they occur. *Team adaptability* is defined as a change in teamwork in response to a salient cue that leads to a functional outcome for the team (Burke, Stagl, Salas, Pierce, and Kendall, 2006). Adaptation requires two components: that a team identifies a challenge and that the team effectively responds to the challenge by modifying the way they think, feel, and behave. Adaptable teams have superior situation awareness – they constantly monitor their internal and external resources and any potential threats to team effectiveness. In addition, when they do identify challenges or other factors that require them to change their behavior, adaptable teams can do so quickly by identifying which aspects of teamwork need to change and making decisions quickly and accurately.

Finally, *team resilience* describes a team's capacity to withstand and overcome stressors in a way that enables sustained performance (Alliger, Cerasoli, Tannenbaum, and Vessey, 2015). Whereas team adaptability is focused on behaviors that allow a team to identify and respond to challenges as they occur, resilience encompasses a broader set of capabilities that concern how a team minimizes challenges before they occur, manages teamwork in the face of a challenge, and recovers in the aftermath of a challenge. Team learning and adaptation are important components for managing and recovering from challenges, but resilience is focused on a broader capability and key behaviors aimed at maintaining effectiveness before, during, and after a setback occurs. In addition, resilience captures aspects of the well-being of a team. Whereas learning and adaptation tend to be more task focused, resilience requires team members to be attentive to each other's needs as they address stressors and recover from setbacks together.

Although teamwork looks quite different across contexts, the importance of learning, adaptation, and resilience to success is fairly universal. For example, in heath care, surgical team members working together for the first time may need to learn to anticipate each other's needs, such as which instrument to hand the surgeon at a particular time or who on the team is most adept at performing a particular aspect of a procedure. It is also likely that surgical teams will face challenges that require them to adapt. For example, a surgical team may find that their original plan for excising a malignant tumor is insufficient. As a result, they need to be able to quickly determine that the original plan will no longer work and formulate a new plan that will lead to a better outcome for the patient. Finally, it is imperative that the surgical team be able to demonstrate resilience. Even if the surgical team can adapt and generate a new plan for excising a patient's tumor, the new plan may require more hours, expertise, or attention that place stress on the team. A resilient surgical team can take these challenges in stride, anticipating each other's needs to offer breaks where possible, offering backup or expertise where possible, and reallocating roles and resources to ensure the team can recover quickly.

Learning, adaptation, and resilience may look different in the office than in an operating room, but these principles are still paramount in driving team effectiveness. For example, in product innovation teams, teams can learn by soliciting feedback from external stakeholders on their ideas, prototypes, or products. After a prototype for a product is developed, the team may discuss improvements to the prototype itself, but it is also vital that the team discuss what went well – and not so well – in the process of developing the prototype. Engaging in conversations about teamwork can help members understand what they can do more effectively next time, from how to better communicate an idea to how to streamline an important process so that it goes more smoothly in the next iteration. Finally, the best product innovation teams demonstrate resilience. A team that is able to anticipate potential bottlenecks in their supply chain, like a part for a prototype that may take months to produce, could avert a major delay by ordering the part several months before it is needed. If the part would still arrive much too late, the team could try to manage the issue by finding a workaround, such as an alternative way of building the prototype that will suffice until the part is available. Finally, if the bottleneck due to the delayed part is unavoidable, a resilient team may recover lost time by pivoting and moving on to a phase of the project that is unaffected by the missing part.

Teamwork is also essential beyond Earth's atmosphere. Scientists at NASA find that learning, adaptability, and resilience are key to effective astronaut teamwork (Landon, Slack, and Barrett, 2018). Astronauts work in an extremely high-stakes environment where a small error could turn catastrophic. Both in their training and during their missions, regular debriefs provide them with a structured opportunity to discuss areas where mistakes were or could have been made so that they are avoided in the future. Astronaut teams are likely to face unpredictable challenges that require them to adapt quickly. In this context, adaptation not only requires immense expertise on behalf of team members, but also the ability to adapt how the team works together. For example, members may temporarily take on a part of another team member's role to allow them time to handle an emergent challenge. The same skills enable astronaut teams to demonstrate resilience. To minimize or manage a challenge, a crew may need to coordinate with mission control, where team members on the ground who often have additional information and insight into the nature of a problem can offer potential workarounds to help them manage a challenge when it occurs. The best astronaut teams can also bounce back quickly when they do face challenges by reallocating resources as necessary or by providing backup support to team members who may need to recover.

Whether in the operating room, office, or outer space, the best teams learn, adapt, and are resilient. Although these principles look different across these diverse contexts, the principles remain the same. In the following section, we discuss drivers of learning, adaptation, and resilience.

Key Determinants of Effective Teamwork

A team made up of individual medical, innovation, or astronaut experts will not necessarily perform together as an expert team. Expertise is necessary but insufficient for team effectiveness. Fortunately for these teams, the ability to learn, adapt, and be resilient can be developed over time. Over the past 30 years, researchers have investigated the drivers of effective teamwork. In this section and in Table 18.1, we summarize these drivers – the seven Cs of teamwork (Tannenbaum and Salas, 2020) – and explore how they enable teams to learn, adapt, and build resilience more effectively.

Table 18.1 Summary of the seven drivers of team learning, adaptability, and resilience

Driver	*Definition*	*Recommendations for teams*
Conditions	Features of a team's environment, and these features can greatly facilitate or inhibit teamwork	Ensure organizational design and incentives promote teamwork Provide opportunities for team learning at the organization level Set teams up for success by providing the flexibility and resources for adapting and bouncing back from setbacks
Capability	A team's collective knowledge, skills, and abilities	Ensure that the team's KSAs align with the task at hand Select team members high in learning orientation who will be invested in improving their KSAs Encourage collective orientation in team members to help maintain a team-centered focus Identify individuals who are high in emotional intelligence to help promote team resilience
Cooperation	Attitudes and beliefs that emerge as a team works together	Focus on building trust among team members over time Build cohesion to help the team focus on the collective when experiencing stress Instill a high level of team potency among team members Promote psychological safety by remaining humble and receptive to feedback and new ideas
Cognition	A team's shared understanding of the team's vision, priorities, roles, tasks, expertise, and situation	Promote team situation awareness to improve the team's ability to identify and respond to environmental challenges Build and maintain accurate shared mental models Conduct regular check-ins with team members to promote situation awareness and shared mental models

Table 18.1 (Continued)

Driver	*Definition*	*Recommendations for teams*
Communication	The process of sharing knowledge and information to promote effective team performance	Focus on communication quality over communication quantity Engage in closed-loop communication to ensure that information shared is accurate and complete
Coordination	The core set of behaviors, including team monitoring, that underlie team effectiveness	Conduct regular team check-ins to identify new challenges Provide backup behavior and emotional support to team members who need help
Coaching	Guidance, support, and feedback provided to a team by its leader, members, or an outside facilitator	Encourage shared leadership among team members Promote psychological safety in the coaching process

Figure 18.1 depicts how the drivers of teamwork work together to facilitate learning, adaptability, and resilience. A team's conditions, capabilities, cognitions, and communications are inextricably linked to a team's ability to coordinate actions effectively. In turn, this set of behaviors shapes and is shaped by team cooperation, or what team members feel and believe about working together. Team coaching influences the other drivers of teamwork by providing teams with the structure and

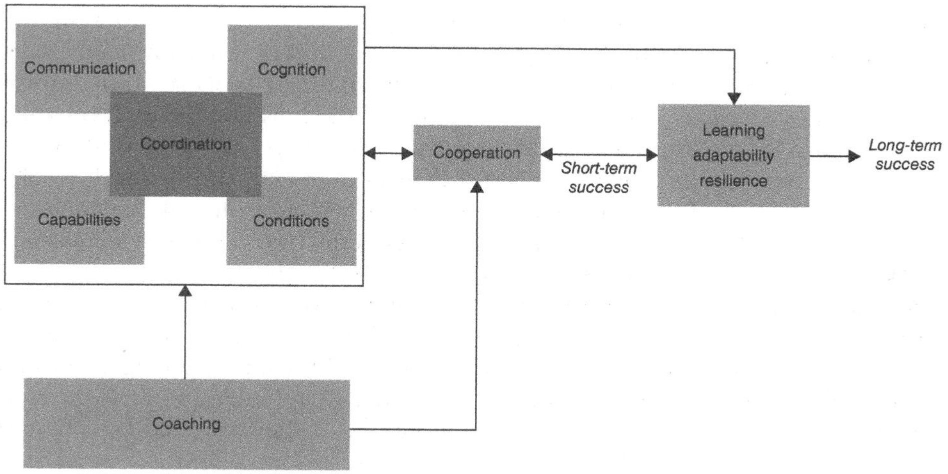

FIGURE 18.1 The seven drivers of team learning, adaptability, and resilience
Source: Adapted from Tannenbaum and Salas (2020).

feedback necessary to improve how members work together. In the short term, the seven Cs alone may generate successful short-term outcomes. However, teams that use the seven Cs to drive learning, adaptability, and resilience are also able to garner longer-term success.

Create the Conditions *for Team Success*

It may come as some surprise that a bedrock of team learning, adaptation, and resilience lies outside the team. *Conditions* describe features of a team's environment, and these features can greatly facilitate or inhibit teamwork (Salas, Shuffler, Thayer, Bedwell, and Lazzara, 2015). In general, teams can perform most effectively when their organization provides structures and systems that support teamwork. Incentive systems, culture and values, and organizational structure can greatly influence teamwork. For example, an organization that relies strictly on individual performance to determine bonuses or to decide who gets promoted may send a signal that collaboration is not valued. In contrast, if the organization also tied rewards, promotions, and work opportunities to collaborative behaviors, team outcomes, and teamwork competencies, it may be more likely to encourage individuals to work together and feel invested in their collective success. In the same way that organizational conditions can promote teamwork in general, organizations can also create conditions to promote learning, adaptation, and resilience.

Organizations can create conditions for learning through both formal and informal avenues. For example, developing a high-quality team training program focused on helping teams build their teamwork capabilities and then recognizing and supporting employees who engage in training can encourage team members to build the competencies necessary to succeed at teamwork (Salas, DiazGranados, Klein, Burke, Stagl, Goodwin, and Halpin, 2008). Informal mechanisms, such as organizational culture, can also promote learning. For example, in organizations that have a culture where feedback is expected and valued, it is easier for teams to engage in ongoing learning. When reflection and learning are well-established norms for individuals, teams are more likely to engage in them as well. In such organizations, it might be the normal to conduct a team debrief session at the midpoint of a project or after a performance episode. Teams that engage in feedback seeking and debriefing – whether among team members or with outside stakeholders – are more likely to identify alternative approaches, generate more creative solutions to problems, and reach their potential (Keiser and Arthur, 2001).

Similarly, organizational conditions can stimulate or reduce team adaptation. For example, a highly bureaucratic culture can inhibit flexibility and adaptation. If a team needs to seek approval in order to make relatively simple changes, they are less likely to make ongoing adjustments. An organization looking to promote team adaptability should give teams adequate autonomy, so they can change course in response to emergent challenges. Highly capable teams are able to strategize and generate creative solutions to challenges quickly and effectively, but without the ability to implement their solutions, they are unlikely to be able to adapt.

Finally, organizations can provide conditions that boost team resilience by ensuring that their teams have the resources they need to minimize and manage challenges and to bounce back after they face a setback. In the same way that providing flexibility and autonomy can help teams adapt, these features of an organization can help teams respond to and recover from challenges autonomously. To promote recovery – and to protect a team from setbacks – organizations can also promote resilience by focusing on well-being. Focusing on well-being helps buffer teams from experiencing the detrimental effects of burnout (Bakker, Emmerik, and Euwema, 2006). For example, after a particularly intense period of work when a team had to work through a draining experience, an organization could provide team members with additional time off, allow members to rotate responsibilities, or assign a less challenging task to the team to provide them with a reprieve before taking on the next big challenge. Ensuring that conditions promote well-being can help enable teams to bounce back quickly.

Ensure Teams Have the Right Mix of Capabilities

The next driver of team learning, adaptation, and resilience is a team's *capabilities*, or a team's collective knowledge, skills, and abilities (KSAs). A team's knowledge may consist of their understanding of a system the team works with or how to complete a task at hand. A team's skills may consist of members' experiences conducting a certain type of task. A team's abilities can refer to things like cognitive or physical ability. In most teams, members possess a range of different KSAs, and variety in KSAs is often beneficial for performance. For example, in a heath care team, having physicians, nurses, pharmacists, physical therapists, and other ancillary members with expertise in different aspects of medicine can help them generate the best solutions for patient care and ensure that the team is considering all the aspects of a patient's well-being. However, having overlap in team member KSAs can also be beneficial. For example, if a project demands change and one team member has more on their plate than others, a team member with similar expertise could step in and back up their teammate, enabling the team to continue to perform its mission.

A team's capabilities should align with the task at hand. Does the team possess the capabilities it needs to complete key work tasks effectively? A group of managers who are forming a number of new project teams might consider conducting a team task analysis (Arthur, Edwards, Bell, Villado, and Bennett 2005), which can help them understand the mix of KSAs the teams must possess to achieve their goals. Although some team capabilities can be improved through training or on-the-job experience, establishing the right team composition initially can greatly increase a team's opportunity for success. Although a team task analysis may be more practical if an organization is forming several of the same type of teams, a scaled-down version of this activity can be helpful to clarify a one-of-a-kind team's compositional needs. Taking the time to consider the mix of KSAs required for a team to succeed can help a manager understand how to compose that team.

Importantly, possessing the right mix of KSAs to accomplish a task is necessary but insufficient to promote learning, adaptability, and resilience. Team members must also have the propensity to learn, adapt, and promote resilience. For example, teams that are learning oriented are better able to learn and adapt as they work together. Learning orientation describes a team's propensity to encourage learning and competence development among their members (Bunderson and Sutcliffe, 2003). Teams high in learning orientation engage in behaviors like feedback giving and seeking, reflection, and debriefing that allow a team to recognize areas for improvement and to implement improvements as they work together, thus bolstering later performance.

In order to effectively adapt, teams must have enough members with a collective orientation or the propensity to work collaboratively in team settings (Driskell, Salas, and Hughes, 2010). Teams with members who are collectively oriented achieve higher performance, in part due to their improved ability to adapt to changing or stressful conditions. When teams face stressful challenges, members have a tendency to lose focus on the team and instead focus on their individual goals and perspectives (Driskell, Johnston, and Salas, 2001). Collective orientation can help keep members' focus on the team when stressors arise, enhancing the team's ability to generate team-focused workarounds to challenges.

Finally, teams whose members have higher levels of emotional intelligence may be more resilient to challenges. Emotional intelligence describes one's ability to perceive, manage, understand, and integrate their emotions (Zeidner, Matthews, and Roberts, 2004). Higher emotional intelligence helps team members appraise stressors as less threatening, and it buffers members from both negative emotions and physiological responses in reaction to stress (Schneider, Lyons, and Khazon, 2013). When teams have members with high levels of emotional intelligence, they may be better able to facilitate the processes of mitigating and managing challenges.

In sum, capabilities serve as a necessary foundation for team learning, adaptation, and resilience. The best teams not only possess the right mix of KSAs to succeed, but also the willingness to adjust in their roles and gain new knowledge that will allow the team to tackle unexpected challenges.

Promote Cooperation *Among Team Members*

While conditions and capabilities are features that are relatively fixed at the time a team is formed, cooperation encompasses a variety of attitudes and beliefs that emerge as a team works together. Generally, cooperation describes how team members feel and what they believe about their team, their teammates, and their work together. Teams with higher levels of cooperation are able to disagree more constructively and feel positively about working together. Although there are some personal characteristics of team members that can make cooperation easier – like agreeable personalities and a team orientation – cooperation is more strongly influenced by one's experience working on a specific team. An individual may not like working in teams in general but can feel positively about working on a team where they like and trust their team members. Many aspects of cooperation are important to team performance generally and more specifically to learning, adaptability, and resilience in teams.

First, cooperative teams trust each other. Team trust has both cognitive components, which focus on how team members *think* about working together, and affective components, which focus on how team members *feel* about each other (Webber, 2008). Cognitive and affective trusts are related to overall team performance and are particularly important for team adaptation and resilience. When teams face challenges and need to quickly change their course of action, it is imperative that they trust the information given to them by their teammates as well as the decisions made by teammates or team leaders. For example, in a space crew facing an unexpected mechanical issue on their spacecraft, team members must trust that their team members on the ground in mission control are providing them with accurate information and have their best interest in mind. In this situation, the space crew may not have access to the full set of information about their equipment and surroundings available in mission control, but having trust in their Earth-bound team members enables them to adapt their roles and tasks accordingly.

Similarly, teams that possess a sense of cohesion tend to be better at adaptation and resilience. Cohesion describes the extent to which team members are committed to the team and the task (Evans and Dion, 2012). This commitment is what helps teams focus when they need to pivot in the face of a challenge, and to address the needs of their team members in the aftermath of a stressful event. In stressful situations, individuals have a natural tendency to narrow their focus, losing sight of the collective and fixating on their own tasks and immediate needs in isolation. A strong sense of cohesion can help a team sustain focus on the collective, maintain the big picture, and commit to the team's success as a whole, rather than their own personal needs.

Cooperative teams are also psychologically safe. Psychological safety describes the shared sense that team members can take interpersonal risks (Edmondson, 1999). In other words, team members feel safe speaking up, asking questions, sharing their opinions, or admitting to mistakes without fear of reprisal from their team leader or fellow members. Psychological safety is especially vital for team learning, a process that is driven by a team's ability to share and discuss feedback. In psychologically safe teams, members feel safe sharing mistakes or near misses, and acknowledging their own limitations, turning these events into opportunities for learning. When team members feel like they will be chastised for admitting to a concern, they are unlikely to speak up, thus preventing the team from learning from their mistakes.

Psychological safety can also help teams overcome *groupthink*, or the tendency for groups to adhere to norms that bolster morale at the expense of critical thinking (Janis, 1997). In teams with low psychological safety, members may be less likely to speak up about information that counters the group's majority views or share unique information that others do not have. As a result, teams can exhibit groupthink by making a decision that is based on incomplete information. In psychologically safe teams, members understand that their unique perspective may be what is needed to help the team make the best decision possible, even if that means disrupting the team's harmony temporarily.

Finally, teams must possess a general sense of confidence in their collective abilities, or team potency (Collins and Parker, 2010). Team potency is an important ingredient to a team's effectiveness, but too much confidence can undermine team success. For example, envision a team of new home builders. While this team may possess some knowledge of how to build various parts of a house, their skills may be rudimentary if the majority of team members are relatively inexperienced. If team potency in this scenario were too high, the members may decide they are capable of building an intricate mansion in a very short time, a task they would almost definitely not succeed in accomplishing. However, if team potency in this scenario were too low, the team might set their sights too low, electing to build a shed with simple electricity and plumbing. In this case, the team might succeed in achieving their goal, but would not reach their full potential. The best teams – those with a balance between confidence and caution – are able to accurately assess their KSAs, ensuring that the team's goals are a match for the team's capabilities (or seeking to boost their capabilities) and that team members are engaging in tasks suited to their own abilities.

Taken together, cooperative attitudes and beliefs help teams learn, adapt, and maintain resilience in many ways. Teams that openly provide feedback and admit mistakes are better able to learn. Those that trust each other in times of stress and are able to keep the team's goals in mind under pressure can more quickly and effectively adapt to changing circumstances. Finally, teams that have high levels of trust and who are committed to both the team and the task at hand are better able to demonstrate resilience by managing challenges as they occur and helping support their team to recover in their aftermath.

Establish Shared Cognition *Among Team Members*

Team cognition refers to team members' shared understanding of the team's vision, priorities, roles, tasks, expertise, and situation (DeChurch and Mesmer-Magnus, 2010). In other words, team cognition captures whether a team is "on the same page" about key aspects of the team, task, or situation at hand. Team cognition is vital for learning, adaptation, and resilience because it serves as a precursor to recognizing challenges in the team's environment and having the capacity to change course.

The aspect of team cognition that captures how teams identify challenges and ways to adapt to those challenges is situation awareness. Situation awareness describes a team's shared understanding of what is going on in their environment related to team performance (Salas, Prince, Baker, and Shrestha, 1995). Situation awareness encompasses *perception* or being aware of what the team is experiencing; *comprehension,* or making sense of what the team is experiencing; and *projection,* or trying to anticipate what will happen next. Teams with high levels of situation awareness have a strong sense of how their team is doing, what resources are available to the team or are becoming scarce, and what factors in the team's environment might affect performance. They then use this information to make sense of their environment and anticipate what will happen next. For example, being aware of available supplies might help the team understand that they are about to face a challenge related to scarce resources.

Once a challenge has been identified, teams rely on accurate shared mental models to adjust their behavior. Shared mental models describe a team's shared vision, shared understanding of things like roles and responsibilities, as well as a shared understanding of their environment (Mathieu, Heffner, Goodwin, Salas, and Cannon-Bowers, 2000). Shared mental models can relate to situation awareness but are focused on whether team members have similar assessments of their environment. Shared mental models do not occur automatically. Expert teams engage in regular check-ins with their team to build and maintain shared mental models. Practices like team meetings before a project begins to discuss roles, workflows, and responsibilities or the establishment of a team charter help get team members on the same page. Similarly, checking in to verify shared understanding of a situation helps teams ensure that their shared mental model is accurate and up to date. Possessing a shared vision is an especially important component of a team's shared mental model and is especially crucial for team learning, adaptation, and resilience. Indeed, Pearce and Ensley (2004) demonstrate that a team's innovation effectiveness is inextricably linked with having a shared vision.

Both situation awareness and shared mental models are vital sources of information for team learning. Teams that have a shared understanding of their team and their environment are better able to learn together. In addition, the same practices that can help build shared mental models, such as checking in with the team and discussing the team's environment, can help bolster shared mental models.

Situation awareness and accurate shared mental models are even more important for team adaptability and resilience. The two fundamental abilities involved in team adaptability are recognizing a potential threat, opportunity, or challenge in the team environment and altering teamwork to respond accordingly. Situation awareness helps teams identify a potential threat or opportunity by keeping members abreast of the resources available in their environment and anticipating needs before they arise. Shared mental models fuel a team's ability to efficiently change course when a challenge has been identified. Teams with accurate shared mental models have a clear picture of where expertise lies within the team, what resources are available to the team, and who should perform which roles within the team. This shared understanding allows teams to generate workarounds involving task flows or team personnel more quickly and to accurately shift to an adjusted mental model together. In a sense, shared cognitions facilitate learning and adaptation and, in turn, must be reset when a team successfully engages in learning and adaptation.

Similarly, team cognition helps fuel team resilience. The minimizing and managing phases of resilience require that teams have an accurate understanding of their environment, so they can do whatever possible to minimize a challenge before it comes to fruition and to manage the challenge when it occurs to reduce its impact on the team. Teams with high levels of situation awareness are able to assess challenges more quickly and accurately, and teams with accurate shared mental models can pivot seamlessly to work together to minimize or manage a conflict when it occurs. In addition, team cognition can help teams bounce back after a challenge. Teams with high levels of situation awareness and accurate shared mental models are in tune with each other. They have a shared understanding of who on their team may need additional support or backup to recover from a challenge and are able to find ways to help the teams recharge.

Facilitate Effective Communication

Beyond how teams think and feel, teams also behave. One form of behavior that drives team effectiveness is team communication, which refers to how teams share knowledge and information to promote effective team performance. Effective communication is central to team learning, adaptability, and resilience, but there is often more to team communication than meets the eye. Fortunately, team scientists across a number of industries, including aviation, aerospace, and the military, have helped clarify when and how team communication drives team performance, learning, adaptability, and resilience.

The best teams are not those that communicate the most. Instead, teams that focus on sharing unique information tend to outperform teams that simply communicate frequently (Marlow, Lacerenza, Paoletti, Burke, and Salas, 2018). Team cognition can help explain why effective teams do not necessarily need to be in constant communication. Instead of communicating constantly, these teams check in when necessary and share the information most relevant to their work. Imagine two business teams where members meet frequently to discuss a project. The first team hosts hour-long meetings in which multiple members often reiterate the same information over and over. In the second team, members are strategic in facilitating the discussion, redirecting conversation when the same points are brought up and asking team members for unique perspectives or any additional information that has not been shared that may be relevant to decision-making. Although teams have a natural tendency to discuss commonly known rather than unique information, a team that is explicit about surfacing and sharing unique information is likely to make better decisions and find more creative workarounds to problems.

Effective teams also engage in closed-loop communication (Salas, Wilson, Murphy, King, and Salisbury, 2008). If a person shares unique information, but other team members misunderstand what was communicated, the information can be useless or even detrimental to performance. That is why closed-loop communication is important. Closed-loop communication has three parts: the information sender's initial communication, the information recipient conveying their understanding of the communication, and a confirmation (or correction) from the sender that the recipient understands what was said. Closed-loop communication can be done quickly in face-to-face conversations as well as virtual interactions.

Effective communication supports team learning, adaptability, and resilience. Closed-loop communication supports learning by ensuring that team members are checking in on understanding as they work together. Feedback cannot be effective unless it is understood by a recipient. To promote team learning, members and leaders should engage in closed-loop communication during debriefs or when receiving feedback. For example, providing feedback, asking the recipient to share what they took away from the feedback, and then providing confirmation that the recipient's impression is accurate promotes learning and subsequent adaptation.

Effective communication also facilitates adaptability and resilience. As a team changes their behaviors and workflow to adjust to changing conditions, effective communication is key. Sharing unique information is vital when teams are assessing their environments, identifying challenges, and making decisions about how to change their behaviors. By focusing on unique information, teams can generate a broader understanding of their environment and ensure that they are making decisions with a more complete and accurate set of information. Closed-loop communication is important when teams share information to verify that the information received is accurate. In addition, closed-loop communication helps teams execute changes to processes effectively, supporting coordination and ensuring that team members maintain an accurate shared mental model.

Coordinate *Teamwork to Drive Effectiveness*

Team cooperation and cognition are integrally related to team coordination – the broad set of behaviors that underlie team effectiveness. Effective coordination behaviors are at the heart of effective teamwork and play a central role in team adaptation and resilience. Coordination begins with team monitoring, or the behaviors required to maintain an understanding of the happenings within and outside of the team (Marks, Mathieu, and Zaccaro, 2001). Teams that engage in effective monitoring check in with each other on a regular basis to help identify challenges as they arise and to provide additional support to team members who need it. Monitoring is what enables the situation awareness component of cognition that we discussed previously.

Using the information provided by monitoring and situation awareness, teams are better able to coordinate their efforts and achieve their goals. For example, a team member might coordinate by providing backup or support to a colleague who is overloaded with responsibilities or needs help completing a task. This type of coordination ensures that the team's resources are allocated effectively. In essence, providing backup is a form of in-the-moment team adaptation.

Team members can also take actions to help one another sustain healthy emotions. Monitoring one's teammates by checking in on how they are doing can help identify when a team member is distressed or feeling negatively about working with the team in some way. In response, the team might adjust they person's workflow or provide the team member with the socioemotional support they need to succeed.

Coordination is especially vital to team adaptation. Team monitoring behaviors allow the team to identify challenges within the team or in their environment. For example, team monitoring might uncover a bottleneck in the team's workflow. Without taking the time to check in, the team may not have realized that one of their members was having trouble completing a specific task that was necessary to move the team forward. After the team identifies the bottleneck, they are able to engage in adaptation by identifying how the team can change their workflow to support the team member, mitigate the bottleneck, and move the team forward. Team monitoring also supports the process of change in this scenario – a team that has engaged in regular check-ins is likely to have a better understanding of the problem space and the range of available solutions.

The aspects of coordination that support adaptation also support resilience, but a team's resilience is also bolstered by the affect-based benefits of team coordination. A critical aspect of team resilience is maintaining a team's emotional state by minimizing and managing challenges to buffer stress and helping rebuild emotional stability and energy after the team experiences a setback. For example, a team that is able to quickly assess a challenge and generate a plan to respond is likely to be better able to maintain a positive mood and avoid an anxious or other negative emotional response to a challenge. Teams that engage in effective coordination focus both on person- and task-oriented monitoring. Checking in on how a team member is feeling can be as important to coordination as checking in on whether a team member can successfully complete a task. The information gained via monitoring how team members are doing provides the opportunity for teams to provide socioemotional and other support to team members who are feeling exhausted or burned out.

Although many teams engage in these coordination processes implicitly, some commonly used tools can help teams explicitly work through the process of detecting, managing, and learning from adversity. Team prebriefs, huddles, and debriefs provide teams with dedicated opportunities to check in with each other. Prebriefs are typically focused on situation awareness and preparatory coordination, and they take place before a team engages in a new task or project. Huddles are quick touch-bases that allow a team to coordinate in the midst of completing a task or addressing a challenge and can be especially helpful for maintaining team affect and situation awareness. Finally, team debriefs occur after a team has completed a task or performance episode. Debriefs provide a structured opportunity for a team to surface lessons learned and plan how they can better coordinate in their future.

In sum, team coordination describes a wide array of behaviors that facilitate team learning, adaptation, and resilience. Teams can engage in these behaviors implicitly – by checking in on teammates and staying attentive to their surroundings. Many of the most effective teams supplement implicit coordination with explicit interventions to support coordination including team prebriefs, huddles, and debriefs.

Promote Team Effectiveness with Coaching

The final driver of team learning, adaptability, and resilience is coaching. As teams face obstacles or setbacks, they need a leader (and often other team members) to provide guidance, support, and feedback. Coaching can be provided by individuals in both formal and informal positions (Hackman and Wageman, 2005). A formally assigned manager may serve in a coaching role, as might an external coach who is an expert in teamwork but who is not a part of the team itself. Team members may also provide informal peer coaching, for example, by providing a teammate with advice or holding one another accountable.

The responsibility for coaching can also be shared among team members through *shared leadership* (D'Innocenzo, Mathieu, and Kukenberger, 2016), which occurs when team members share leadership responsibilities. Shared leadership is especially relevant and necessary in environments with rapidly changing circumstances and conditions that make it difficult for a formal leader to manage all of the leadership tasks on the team. In teams that engage in shared leadership, members share the responsibility of engaging in coaching or other leader behaviors in response to their current situation, seamlessly stepping into and out of a leadership role as necessary. For example, in a project team, one team member may lead the team through the process of setting goals and deadlines and reassessing those deadlines as challenges that hinder the team's progress arise. Another team member may lead the team through an informal debriefing process, helping the team to reflect on their past performance and identify areas for improvement.

Coaching behaviors can boost overall teamwork, in part because of their positive impact on team learning, adaptability, and resilience. As discussed in the section on cooperation, psychological safety is vital to team learning (Edmondson, 1999). Leaders play an outsized role in setting norms around psychological safety on a team. By responding to feedback openly, admitting to their own mistakes, and encouraging all team members to feel safe speaking up – all helpful coaching behaviors – a leader creates a safe environment for team learning. In medicine, where hierarchy makes psychological safety more difficult to develop, a physician who has open discussions with their team about what could have gone better and who responds constructively when lower-ranked team members speak up makes it easier for the team to engage in ongoing learning.

Coaching behaviors can also be used as an avenue for promoting team adaptability. A team leader or team member who maintains a "birds eye view" of the team can identify bottlenecks or other types of challenges that are difficult to perceive when focusing on one's own role on the team. Helping the team identify areas for improvement or challenges as they arise can promote quicker and more efficient adaptation. In addition, a leader can facilitate debriefing sessions that surface needs and promote team adaptation. Similarly, an external coach can provide the outside perspective and feedback necessary to pivot when a challenge arises.

Team coaching behaviors can also promote team resilience in some of the same ways that they help facilitate adaptation. To promote resilience, leaders can help their team to identify and minimize challenges before they occur and to sustain teamwork in the midst of a challenge. By maintaining a broader understanding of team functioning and workflow, a leader can help their team redistribute work among members, identify members who have the necessary expertise to solve a problem that has arisen, or make quick decisions in the face of uncertainty. In addition, they can play an important role in fueling the well-being of team members, both by buffering them from the stressors associated with experiencing a challenge and by helping them bounce back in the aftermath.

Case Examples

1. Effective Teamwork in the Operating Room

The 1999 report *To Err is Human* shed light on the large number of medical errors occurring every year in hospitals. Further investigation indicated that many of these errors occurred due to ineffective teamwork. In most medical teams, members possess the basic KSAs necessary to achieve success. However, human error is still possible, and without effective teamwork, errors are much more likely to occur.

Envision a surgical team working together in the operating room on an appendectomy – a routine and relatively straightforward procedure. All of the members of this team had performed several appendectomies previously, and its members find value in working in a team in the operating room. On this surgical team, members have excellent shared cognition – the scrub tech is ready to hand the surgeon her scalpel before she asks for it. This behavior is possible not only because the scrub tech is well-versed in the steps required for an appendectomy, but because the tech and the surgeon have a shared mental model for what tools the surgeon prefers to perform certain aspects of their procedure. This is a quiet operating room wherein members share new and relevant information, but do not need to communicate constantly because of team members' shared cognition. When team members do speak up, their questions are respected, and no one is belittled. For example, when the medical student observing the procedure asks the attending surgeon a question about why they chose to close the patient's incision with a particular type of stitch, the surgeon responds respectfully and uses the opportunity as a teaching moment rather than belittling the trainee.

This surgical team is effective in implementing many, if not all, of the seven drivers of teamwork. As a result, the team is prepared to succeed not only in performing a routine appendectomy, but also in a more complicated procedure or a surgery with unexpected complications. For example, because members of this team feel comfortable speaking up when they notice a potential mistake, the team is better able to learn how to anticipate and avoid the error in the future. The team's strong shared mental model can help them adapt seamlessly as they pivot to a new approach – for example, the scrub tech may hand the surgeon a different instrument as the surgeon's approach changes. Members are knowledgeable not only about their contribution to the procedure, but they can anticipate the needs of other members even when a complication arises, promoting adaptability. Finally, the team's ability to coordinate effectively minimizes the likelihood that an adverse event will occur, reduces the effects of an unanticipated stressor on the team, and allows team members to provide necessary backup and support to promote recovery and promote resilience. As a result, the team will find success not only in straightforward surgical cases, but also in more complex or risky scenarios.

2. Ineffective Project Team

In offices around the world, leaders increasingly look to teams to solve their most complex and pressing problems. While effective teams can seamlessly generate innovative and effective solutions, teams that struggle to implement the seven drivers of teamwork often fall short.

Envision a project team at an advertising agency working on developing an ad campaign for a new line of cosmetic products. A few of the team members had worked together on a previous ad campaign, so they assumed that getting started working together would be a breeze. Instead, the team came across a number of challenges. Although the team members all had experience working on ad campaigns in the health and beauty space and had worked at the advertising agency for a number of years, some of the team's members regularly express their preferences to work independently and tend to overfocus on their own parts of the campaign, leaving the rest of the team behind. Other team members have at times been disagreeable. When the team huddles early on to pitch concepts for the ad campaign, one particularly vocal member of the team is quick to shut down other team members' ideas. As a result, team members became afraid to share their ideas for new directions and avoid interacting with each other unless absolutely necessary, squelching the team's creative potential.

Because this team has been ineffective in engaging in the drivers of team effectiveness, they struggle with learning, adaptability, and resilience. After their colleague shot down so many ideas in the concept planning meeting and members stopped speaking up in subsequent interactions, the team stopped surfacing critical information that would have helped them anticipate and adjust to any challenges in developing the ad campaign. For example, as a result of low psychological safety, the team developed an entire set of mock-up advertisements for a new fragrance in the cosmetics line that was not being brought to market. Due to ineffective teamwork, the team was unable to pivot away from their efforts in developing advertisements for the discontinued fragrance, and it became difficult for the team to meet their deadlines to develop mock-ups for the remaining products in the line. As a result, the team was months behind on achieving the deadline for the ad campaign, disappointing both the client and leaders in the advertising agency.

Conclusion

In today's ever-changing workplace, teams cannot demonstrate sustained effectiveness without ongoing learning, adaptation, and resilience. Fortunately, researchers have now spent decades working to understand what drives effective teamwork. The seven Cs of teamwork outlined in this chapter provide insights about how to promote team learning, adaptation, and resilience. From the office to outer space, teams in vastly different contexts rely on the same principles to promote effective teamwork. A team's conditions and capabilities lay the groundwork for effective teamwork. Team cooperation and cognition, or how teams feel and think about working together, allow teams to engage in effective coordination and communication. In turn, practices like debriefing that support coordination and communication can help bolster cooperation and cognition. Finally, team coaching facilitated by a leader or team members helps guide team behavior and provide them with the feedback they need to learn, adapt, and be resilient.

Acknowledgment

This work was partially supported by the Center for Clinical and Translational Sciences (UT Health Science Center, Houston, TX), which is funded by the National Institutes of Health Clinical and Translational Award UL1 TR003167 from the National Center for Advancing Translational Sciences. The content is solely the responsibility of the authors and does not necessarily represent the official views of the National Center for Advancing Translational Sciences or the National Institutes of Health. Rice University and University of Texas Health Sciences Center Houston are partners in this grant. This work was also partially supported by National Science Foundation grant 1853528 to Rice University, and also received support from the US Army Research Institute for the Behavioral and Social Sciences, accomplished under Cooperative Agreement Number W911NF-19-2-0173.

References

Alliger, G. M., Cerasoli, C. P., Tannenbaum, S. I., and Vessey, W. B. (2015). Team resilience: How teams flourish under pressure. *Organizational Dynamics*, 44(3), 176–184. https://doi.org/10.1016/j.orgdyn.2015.05.003

Arthur, W., Jr, Edwards, B. D., Bell, S. T., Villado, A. J., and Bennett, W. Jr. (2005). Team task analysis: Identifying tasks and jobs that are team based. *Human Factors*, 47(3), 654–669. https://doi.org/10.1518/001872005774860087

Bakker, A. B., Emmerik, H. V., and Euwema, M. C. (2006). Crossover of burnout and engagement in work teams. *Work and Occupations*, 33(4), 464–489. https://doi.org/10.1177/0730888406291310

Bunderson, J. S., and Sutcliffe, K. M. (2003). Management team learning orientation and business unit performance. *Journal of Applied Psychology*, 88(3), 552–560. https://doi.org/10.1037/0021-9010.88.3.552

Burke, C. S., Stagl, K. C., Salas, E., Pierce, L., and Kendall, D. (2006). Understanding team adaptation: A conceptual analysis and model. *Journal of Applied Psychology*, 91(6), 1189–1207. https://doi.org/10.1037/0021-9010.91.6.1189

Collins, C. G., and Parker, S. K. (2010). Team capability beliefs over time: Distinguishing between team potency, team outcome efficacy, and team process efficacy. *Journal of Occupational and Organizational Psychology*, 83(4), 1003–1023. https://doi.org/10.1348/096317909X484271

DeChurch, L. A., and Mesmer-Magnus, J. R. (2010). The cognitive underpinnings of effective teamwork: A meta-analysis. *Journal of Applied Psychology*, 95(1), 32–53. https://doi.org/10.1037/a0017328

D'Innocenzo, L., Mathieu, J. E., and Kukenberger, M. R. (2016). A meta-analysis of different forms of shared leadership–team performance relations. *Journal of Management*, 42(7), 1964–1991. https://doi.org/10.1177/0149206314525205

Driskell, J. E., Johnston, J. H., and Salas, E. (2001). Does stress training generalize to novel settings? *Human Factors*, 43(1), 99–110.

Driskell, J. E., Salas, E., and Hughes, S. (2010). Collective orientation and team performance: Development of an individual differences measure. *Human Factors*, 52(2), 316–328.

Edmondson, A. (1999). Psychological safety and learning behavior in work teams. *Administrative science quarterly*, 44(2), 350–383. https://doi.org/10.2307/2666999

Evans, C. R., and Dion, K. L. (2012). Group cohesion and performance: A meta-analysis. *Small Group Research*, 43(6), 690–701. https://doi.org/10.1177/1046496412468074

Hackman, J. R., and Wageman, R. (2005). A theory of team coaching. *Academy of Management Review*, 30(2), 269–287. https://doi.org/10.5465/amr.2005.16387885

Janis, I. L. (1997). Groupthink. In R. P. Vecchio (ed.), *Leadership: Understanding the dynamics of power and influence in organizations* (pp. 163–176). University of Notre Dame Press. (Reprinted from "*Psychology Today*," Nov 1971, pp. 43, 44, 46, 74–76.)

Keiser, N. L., and Arthur, W., Jr. (2021). A meta-analysis of the effectiveness of the after-action review (or debrief) and factors that influence its effectiveness. *Journal of Applied Psychology*, 106(7), 1007–1032. https://doi.org/10.1037/apl0000821

Landon, L. B., Slack, K. J., and Barrett, J. D. (2018). Teamwork and collaboration in long-duration space missions: Going to extremes. *American Psychologist*, 73(4), 563–575. https://doi.org/10.1037/amp0000260

Marks, M. A., Mathieu, J. E., and Zaccaro, S. J. (2001). A temporally based framework and taxonomy of team processes. *Academy of Management Review*, 26(3), 356–376. https://doi.org/10.5465/amr.2001.4845785

Marlow, S. L., Lacerenza, C. N., Paoletti, J., Burke, C. S., and Salas, E. (2018). Does team communication represent a one-size-fits-all approach? A meta-analysis of team communication and performance. *Organizational Behavior and Human Decision Processes*, 144, 145–170. https://doi.org/10.1016/j.obhdp.2017.08.001

Mathieu, J. E., Heffner, T. S., Goodwin, G. F., Salas, E., and Cannon-Bowers, J. A. (2000). The influence of shared mental models on team process and performance. *Journal of Applied Psychology*, 85(2), 273–283. https://doi.org/10.1037/0021-9010.85.2.273

Pearce, C. L., and Ensley, M. D. (2004). A reciprocal and longitudinal investigation of the innovation process: The central role of shared vision in product and process innovation teams (PPITs). *Journal of Organizational Behavior*, 25(2), 259–278. https://doi.org/10.1002/job.235

Salas, E., DiazGranados, D., Klein, C., Burke, C. S., Stagl, K. C., Goodwin, G. F., and Halpin, S. M. (2008). Does team training improve team performance? *A meta-analysis. Human Factors*, 50(6), 903–933. https://doi.org/10.1518/001872008X375009

Salas, E., Prince, C., Baker, D. P., and Shrestha, L. (1995). Situation awareness in team performance: Implications for measurement and training. *Human Factors*, 37(1), 123–136. https://doi.org/10.1518/001872095779049525

Salas, E., Shuffler, M. L., Thayer, A. L., Bedwell, W. L., and Lazzara, E. H. (2015). Understanding and improving teamwork in organizations: A scientifically based practical guide. *Human Resource Management*, 54(4), 599–622. https://doi.org/10.1002/hrm.21628

Salas, E., Wilson, K. A., Murphy, C. E., King, H., and Salisbury, M. (2008). Communicating, coordinating, and cooperating when lives depend on it: tips for teamwork. *The Joint Commission Journal on Quality and Patient Safety*, 34(6), 333–341. https://doi.org/10.1016/S1553-7250(08)34042-2

Schneider, T. R., Lyons, J. B., and Khazon, S. (2013). Emotional intelligence and resilience. *Personality and Individual Differences*, 55(8), 909–914. https://doi.org/10.1016/j.paid.2013.07.460

Tannenbaum, S., and Salas, E. (2020). *Teams that work: the seven drivers of team effectiveness.* Oxford University Press.

Webber, S. S. (2008). Development of cognitive and affective trust in teams: A longitudinal study. *Small Group research*, 39(6), 746–769. https://doi.org/10.1177/1046496408323569

Zeidner, M., Matthews, G., and Roberts, R. D. (2004). Emotional intelligence in the workplace: A critical review. *Applied Psychology*, 53(3), 371–399. https://doi.org/10.1111/j.1464-0597.2004.00176.x

Exercises

Exercise 1

Team debriefing can be a powerful tool to promote team learning, adaptability, and resilience. Debriefs are effective because they provide teams with the opportunity to reflect on how well they have executed the drivers of teamwork. Consider a team you have worked with on a class project, internship, or job. Assume the role of a debrief facilitator tasked with helping a team understand how they can improve their performance. Create a debriefing guide for your team that promotes reflection. Include questions that probe at each of the seven drivers of team effectiveness.

Exercise 2

Consider the case of ineffective teamwork in the project team provided earlier. Assume the role of a new team leader stepping in to help improve the team's learning, adaptability, and resilience. Which of the drivers of teamwork would you focus on improving to facilitate learning, adaptability, and resilience in this scenario? What guidance would you give your team to help them improve these drivers? What type of feedback would you deliver to individual team members?

Video Analysis and Discussion

Please watch the following video(s):

1. Working together to make things happen: https://www.youtube.com/watch?v=Fd_nkBHgX8s

Now form small groups to discuss the video(s) and answer the following questions:

1. What are the major points of the video?
2. How can you use information from the video in your career?
3. Based on the video, what advice do you have for leaders in organizations?

Be prepared to present the ideas from your small group discussion with the class as a whole.

Discussion Questions

- How have learning, adaptability, and success helped drive performance in the teams you have been a part of?
- Have you ever worked in a team that has struggled with any of the seven drivers of team effectiveness? What could your team have done to strengthen teamwork in this area?
- How do the seven drivers of teamwork help promote learning, adaptability, and resilience in teams?
- Which of the seven drivers of teamwork do you think is most important for facilitating learning, adaptability, and resilience? Why?
- What can leaders do to help their teams improve on the seven drivers of teamwork?

19

Compose Teams to Ensure Successful External Activity

Deborah Ancona[1], Henrik Bresman[2], and David Caldwell[3]

[1] MIT Sloan School of Management
[2] Insead
[3] Santa Clara University

We propose the fundamental principle that teams should be composed of individuals who can effectively carry out external boundary activity. The central argument is that teams need people who can bridge to the outside – people who can get resources, negotiate agreements, and know who to contact for expertise. Many studies (e.g. Ancona, 1990; Ancona and Caldwell, 1992; Bresman, 2010; Gladstein, 1984; Marrone, Tesluk, and Carson, 2007) have shown that external boundary activity is a crucial predictor of team performance. Therefore, an essential element in a team's composition should be ensuring that such activity takes place.

This principle is very broad. In our view, it applies most directly to temporary teams or task forces that are created for a particular purpose and then transfer their work product to others within the organization or the broader market. Typically, these teams draw on resources and information inside and outside the organization and often must gain the support of other entities within the organization if they are to be successful. The greater the complexity of the work and the higher the interdependence with other organization units, the more the team will need to engage in a complex web of external relationships to manage the coordination, knowledge transfer, and political maneuvering necessary to get its tasks accomplished (Cummings, 2004). As organizations get flatter, more global, cross-functional, and depend more on virtual work solutions, fewer teams can remain isolated and focus solely on internal activity and work (Malone, Bresman, Zellmer-Bruhn, and Beaver, 2016). The increasing reliance on multiteam systems – a network of interdependent component teams that coordinate their efforts to pursue their own goals in tandem with the larger system's goal – has served to accelerate this trend further (Luciano, DeChurch and Mathieu, 2018). Thus, sensitivity to external issues is becoming increasingly important to a wide range of teams.

Justification of the Principle

We assert that the external activities of interdependent organization teams are related to their performance. Although relatively little research has directly addressed this issue – in part because many of our theories of group activities were developed using laboratory groups that do not have external links – the notion that groups require effective interaction with external systems has its roots in the writings of early social psychologists (c.f., Homans, 1950; Lewin, 1951). This general idea was expanded throughout the 1970s and early 1980s by open systems theorists (Katz and Kahn, 1978), researchers studying boundary-spanning behavior (Roberts and O'Reilly, 1979; Tushman, 1977), and writings on autonomous workgroups (c.f., Cummings, 1978). In addition, those studying innovation have written extensively about the transfer of technical information across boundaries (Allen, 1971, 1984; Aldrich and Herker, 1977; Katz and Tushman, 1979). In general, those results showed that in R&D teams with uncertain tasks, boundary-spanning activity was related to performance. More recently, similar results have been found for teams engaged in other types of development projects (e.g. Bresman and Zellmer-Bruhn, 2013).

We also assert that it is not just the frequency of external communication that is important but rather the content of that communication. Frequent contact with outsiders may be necessary for effective boundary management, but it alone is not sufficient. The content and quality of interactions with outsiders will determine whether the team can tap into the power structure of the firm, understand and manage how the team's outputs fit into the broader workflow of the organization, and gain the information and the expertise from outside the team's boundaries that are necessary for success. In a study of 45 product development teams, we found that team members engaged in different activities in dealing with outside groups, and it was the extent to which team members were involved in these activities that was related to team performance. We found that product development effectiveness was most likely when team members engaged in two sets of activities: (i) those designed to promote the team and secure resources and (ii) those that led to tighter links with other groups linked through the workflow. The frequency of communication with outsiders as such was unrelated to the performance of the teams.

Interestingly, we also found that performance was negatively related to the frequency with which groups engaged in broad scanning of the environment, particularly when these activities were done late in the project (Ancona and Caldwell, 1992). Once the product idea was developed, the more successful teams cut down on broad, general communication and increased the number of exchanges aimed at acquiring specific information or coordinating distinct tasks. Less successful teams continued to seek out general information about markets and technologies. In another study of 62 drug development teams, we found that teams seeking to learn vicariously from other teams, based on their prior related experiences, were more likely to perform better – but only when they took the time to carefully reflect on how to apply lessons learned (Bresman, 2010). Teams that did not take the time to engage in this collective reflection process often used the wrong lessons or applied them in the wrong way.

Mechanisms for Meeting External Demands

How does one compose a team to meet external demands? Three aspects of team composition seem particularly relevant: (i) the background characteristics of individual team members, particularly the functional area to which the individuals are assigned; (ii) the connections of team members to relevant networks inside and outside the organization; and (iii) the configuration and nature of team members' assignments on the team. Although background characteristics have been studied extensively in prior research, we examine their effects on external linkages as well as internal dynamics. Network connections are the ties members have to individuals outside the group. Such ties represent the potential resources team members can access. The third component, team configuration, represents the level of involvement individual members have with the team.

The first step in designing a team to meet external demands is to understand the essential resources members must acquire from other groups, learn the expectations others have for the group, and understand how the group's product fits into broader strategic initiatives of the firm. In part, this means acquiring knowledge about the political "structure" of the organization as well as the location of information and resources that will benefit the group. Clearly, some individuals can "map" this network of information and resources better than others, and this mapping is a source of power for individuals who have it and teams that can harness it (Krackhardt, 1990).

Once the critical links between the team and outside groups have been identified, the team can be formed to create these vital connections. Three design variables can be used to manage these connections with other groups. We begin by describing the variables and then lay out some of the issues to be considered in applying these variables to team design.

Diversity in Function

The first mechanism for designing a team that can effectively manage its boundaries is to select people who can represent and have expertise in the diverse functional areas that will contribute to the group's ultimate product. Research has focused on several team diversity dimensions, such as demographic and cognitive diversity, and evidence suggests a nuanced link between diversity and team performance (Horwitz and Horwitz, 2007). However, based on a thorough review, Williams and O'Reilly (1998) conclude that teams that exhibit diversity in functional expertise generally perform at a higher level than teams that do not have that diversity.

For example, functionally diverse top management teams are more successful in making administrative innovations (Bantel and Jackson, 1989) and responding to environmental shocks (Keck and Tushman, 1993) than less diverse teams. There seem to be both an internal and external rationale for the superior performance of functionally diverse teams. Internally, such teams have a greater range of viewpoints and more information exchange (Glick, Miller, and Huber, 1993) than do less diverse teams. This broader range of shared knowledge and experience should allow the group to make more creative decisions than when the group has less information at its disposal. Functionally diverse teams are also likely to communicate with those outside the group and have more links to external resources than less diverse groups (Ancona and Caldwell, 1992). Studies of functional diversity have focused primarily on differences in team members' functional assignments; however, functional diversity can also be intrapersonal. That is, individuals can vary in the number of different functions in which they have worked. Some research suggests that groups of individuals who have experience in different functions can have the same, or even greater, advantages of functionally diverse teams (Bunderson and Sutcliffe, 2002).

Members' Connections to Other Groups and Individuals

A second tool for managing team boundaries is including individuals on the team who have connections or relationships with others outside the group. The connections or ties between individuals in organizations can vary in strength. A strong tie describes a close relationship in which the individuals spend time together, know one another well, and are likely to have helped each other in the past. A weak tie is a more superficial relationship. Individuals know one another but do not have the level of closeness as is present when there is a strong tie (Granovetter, 1973). There are several things to keep in mind about ties to understand how they can affect boundary activities. First, because strong ties require more time and effort to build and maintain than weak ties, individuals can have many more weak ties than strong ties (Burt, 1992). Second, individuals can vary in the pattern of ties they have with others. Some individuals will develop a large number of weak ties but few or no strong ties. Other people may develop a few very strong ties but not have an extensive range of weak ties.

The strong and weak ties team members have with outsiders can help the team effectively manage its boundaries, but they do so in different ways (Hansen, 1999). Suppose team members have extensive networks of weak ties throughout the organization. In that case, it is relatively easy for the team to learn about developments in other areas, resources available to the team, and who might have specialized expertise that could help the team. Simply picking up the telephone and calling an acquaintance in a different part of the company can help the team acquire valuable outside information.

However, sometimes a deeper involvement by an outsider is necessary for helping the team complete its job. For example, sharing detailed information or assisting a team in adopting new technology for their project often requires a substantial effort by the outsider. An individual is likely to be more willing to expend this effort to aid the team if they have a close, meaningful relationship with a team member – in other words, if there is a strong tie – than if the relationship is superficial. Thus, if extensive help is needed from some outsiders, having strong ties with those individuals can increase the chance that the team will get the help they need.

Team Configuration

A third approach to composing a team that effectively manages its boundaries is configuring team members' roles. Most models of teams – particularly those based on laboratory research – assume equal involvement and commitment of all team members to the effort. We do not believe this assumption holds true for most teams in organizations. Composing teams assuming that individual members will make differential contributions to the team's effort provides an effective option for dealing with boundary management issues.

When teams must deal with many external entities or draw information from many sources, there are alternatives in how the team could be composed. The team could contain members who represent all these important groups. Doing so can eliminate much of the need for boundary activity at the expense of creating a very large team. On the other hand, a smaller team would not have direct representation from all relevant groups and would, therefore, require greater boundary activity to guarantee success. An effective way of dealing with the need for including representation without expanding the team's size is through configuring team member roles. Team members can be assigned limited roles on a team yet still provide external information or links to other groups.

There are several ways to do this (Ancona and Bresman, 2007; Ancona and Caldwell, 1997). One approach is to bring experts into the team for a limited time or a particular project aspect. This allows the team to use critical information or expertise without integrating those individuals into the group. A second approach is to shift team membership over time. Individuals who have specific information or external contacts can temporarily join the team based on the boundary activities necessary at a particular time and then leave when their work is complete. A third approach is to have some members be part-time on the team. Individuals whose expertise or contacts are needed over the length of the project but who may have other demands on their time or somewhat limited knowledge of broader project issues could serve on the team on a part-time basis. Finally, the decision-making roles of team members could be differentiated. For teams working on highly complex, interdependent projects, the need for information and coordination with other groups may be too high to be accomplished exclusively through boundary management or some members' part-time or part-cycle involvement. Such situations may require the expansion of the team. However, as the team grows in size, difficulties in decision-making and coordination may arise. One response to this is developing a two-tiered membership made up of a relatively small number of core members – who play a significant role in decision-making – and a larger number of peripheral members – who play a more limited role but are nonetheless full-fledged team members.

Applications of the Principle: Using Functional Diversity, Ties, and Team Configuration for Team Composition

Before deciding who to put on a team, it is important to identify the critical external contacts the team must rely on to succeed. In a real sense, this involves developing a "map" of the external environment, both inside and outside the organization (Ancona and Bresman, 2007). This map should not simply identify the direct contacts the team must have – for example, a process improvement team must coordinate with the information technology function – but also identify sources of general information that can help the team understand the issues it will face. Once a map has been developed, the tools we described can be applied.

First, the team should contain individuals from various functions responsible for the product or process under development. In particular, if the team needs to engage in ongoing coordination around specifications or schedules, including people from the affected functional areas will make the coordination easier.

A second design principle is to include members on the team who have appropriate connections to others in the organization. Selecting team members based on their network connections may offer advantages over simply choosing people based on the function they are in. First, it may not always be possible to select based on function, given the need for individuals to have particular skills necessary for the project. Second, function may be a rough index of the person's network, and considering the team members' connections may allow for a more precise ability to deal with specific external issues than simply selecting based on function (Reagans, Zuckerman, and McEvily, 2004).

In our view, team members should collectively have a mix of strong and weak ties with other individuals. It is important to have individuals on the team who understand the knowledge and resources that may be spread out through the organization and even outside the organization. This implies that the team needs members connected to a wide range of networks both inside and outside the organization. In other words, the team needs an extensive set of weak ties. However, it is at least as important that the team have deep connections with the groups with whom it must directly interface and work to solve problems. This implies that the team includes members who have strong ties with other individuals in positions to provide resources or information to the group. Without a strong tie to a team member, an outsider may not be willing to help the team meet its goals. Weak interunit ties help a project team search for useful knowledge in other subunits and organizations but may not facilitate the transfer of complex knowledge and large-scale assistance.

Finally, configuring individuals' roles is a valuable tool for enhancing other decisions. Effectively applying this concept requires understanding when and how individuals will make critical contributions to the team's work. This requires a detailed map of the environment and a clear understanding of the project. If a team needs extensive information, but only at a particular time, including individuals on the team, but in a limited way may allow the "external resources" of the team to be expanded without permanently increasing the size of the team. Individuals can be assigned to different team roles, whether by having a limited role in decision-making or serving on the team for a limited time. Team membership can also shift over time. This approach is taken by many research and development teams, which is to shift the team's membership as the project's technical challenges evolve.

Moderators and Limitations

Our central principle is that teams should be composed to maximize external boundary-spanning activity. Is this always the case? In answering this question, we think there are two things that must be considered. First, there are moderating factors that must be considered. Second, the principle must be applied appropriately.

An obvious moderating factor to our general principle is the assumption that the *team members are competent* to complete the task. Without competent and motivated people, the team is not likely to succeed, no matter how boundaries are managed. Making staffing decisions exclusively on the ability to bridge boundaries is likely to lead to failure. Drawing from a set of in-depth case studies, Ericksen and Dyer (2004) report that the leaders of low-performing development teams selected team members primarily on "political" attributes such as representing the team to various stakeholders rather than on competencies and skills. In contrast, leaders of high-performing teams consider skill and motivation as well as an ability to manage external boundaries.

A second important moderating factor is the nature of the *group's task*. Consider four types of team tasks that vary in the complexity of *both* the external or boundary activities and the internal or cooperative activities they must accomplish to be successful (see Figure 19.1). Along one axis are internal coordination demands that can be categorized as high or low. High demands require that team members frequently interact to exchange information and coordinate work, while low demands do not require such interaction. Along the other axis are external coordination and political demands that can also be high or low. High demands require that teams interact extensively with people external to the team to access information,

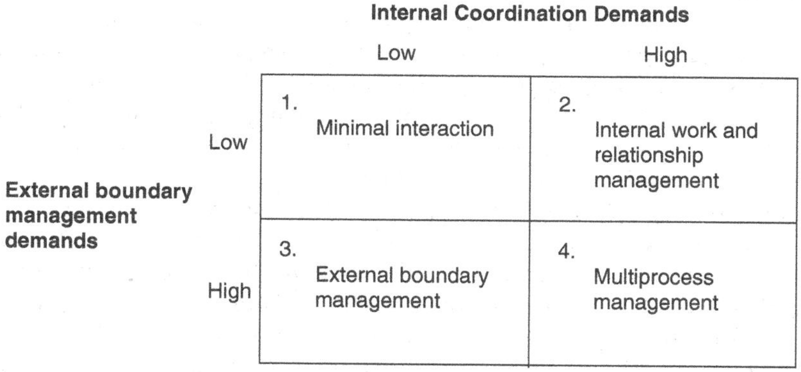

Internal Coordination Demands
Low
High
External boundary management demands
Low
High
1.
Minimal interaction
2.
Internal work and relationship management
3.
External boundary management
4.
Multiprocess management

FIGURE 19.1 Critical processes for team performance

Source: Based on a model found in Ancona and Nadler (1989).

coordinate work, and acquire resources and support. Low demands do not require this depth or complexity of external interaction.

Increasingly, as organizations become flatter and more flexible, as work becomes more complex, and knowledge workers take on complex tasks in teams, more teams will be found in cells 3 and 4, where external demands are higher than in the past. It is for these types of teams that our principle holds. Cell 1 is hardly even a team, but rather more of a set of people who have some aggregated output divorced from others in the organization. Cell 2 could represent teams that are configured to brainstorm creative ideas or solve a very circumscribed problem. Here, all the necessary information resides in the team, and there is little need to have others implement the team's ideas. In each of these two cases, external interactions are minimal, and our principle would not apply. Instead, the team would need to be designed with internal demands being dominant. The focus would be to find the optimal number of people with appropriate information and skills and the motivation to work together (e.g. Campion, Medsker, and Higgs, 1993). In contrast, cell 3 teams need to focus almost exclusively on external boundary management, while cell 4 teams need to carry out multiprocess management – internal work management, relationship management, and external boundary management. Our principle holds for cell 3, while cell 4 requires that both internal and external demands be considered. In our view, more and more teams are moving toward cell 4 because organizations are increasingly using teams to replace formal structures and systems. Because of this, we believe that selecting team members based on their ability to bridge to outsiders while still sharing information, handling conflict, and coordinating work with other team members will grow in importance.

The second issue has to do with applying these ideas appropriately. While the matrix presented earlier presents teams as having a single task, most teams have tasks that change over time so that teams may move from one cell to another over their lives. For example, product development teams move from: (i) exploring product ideas to; (ii) prototyping and exploiting technological achievements to; and (iii) exporting the product to others for manufacturing and marketing. Research has shown that while external boundary management is important throughout this process, it is more important for the exploration and exportation stages and less important during the prototyping and exploiting stage. At a more general level, the task demands at each stage of work need to be assessed, and the team composition needs to shift accordingly. It is because of these changing task demands that team configuration is so important. Through part-cycle membership, the use of experts, and shifting roles, shifting external demands can be met.

Although we argue that staffing a team to deal effectively with external groups is key to team success, the team must also be able to develop effective internal processes. A team needs to create an identity that affords some separation from the larger organization (Yan and Louis, 1999). This may be a somewhat delicate balance. As Alderfer (1976) points out, teams with too much boundary activity may find it hard to set and keep that "separateness" and maintain the cohesion necessary to work as a team. On the other hand, a team with too much cohesion and too strong an identity may be less likely to productively engage external groups than are teams without such cohesiveness (Janis, 1982). Thus, composition needs to be based on external demands while ensuring internal communication and cohesion. Designing a team to meet external demands may lead to a very heterogeneous group. This, in turn, may increase conflict among team members and make coordination problematic. Although different perspectives about the team's task may ultimately increase performance, if these are too great or lead to conflict that is "personal" in nature, performance may suffer (Pelled, Eisenhardt, and Xin, 1999; Reagans and Zuckerman, 2001). To prevent this, it may be useful to do things to enhance the ability of the team members to work together. This can be achieved by having some homogeneity or similarity among team members (e.g. having people with similar tenure to facilitate communication, ensuring a shared goal among team members, etc.). It may also be facilitated by introducing management practices that create an identity and facilitate conflict resolution (Jehn, 1995).

Case Examples

Case 1

Two teams in the same multinational integrated oil company illustrate the role of composition in managing external activities and how the projects' ultimate success was affected by decisions about composition. One of the major problems faced by integrated oil companies is the depletion of reserves obtained using traditional extraction techniques. Both the teams were formed to address different aspects of this problem.

The alpha project team was created to develop new exploration methods for a specific geographic area. The team was also to identify specific tracts in that area that the company should try to acquire because they showed the promise of large reserves.

The alpha project team consisted of 17 members from three different geographic-based organizations in the company who represented many departments based on different geological and geophysical disciplines. Traditionally, these discipline-based departments had worked sequentially on problems rather than as a part of the team. Our interviews indicated that many individuals were skeptical of this team approach. Team members were chosen for their technical expertise and were assigned to the project on a full-time basis. A group of three managers from one of the geographic organizations was created to oversee the team's efforts.

Although there was initial skepticism from some team members, the group quickly developed effective processes for working together. The team held several seminars and went on field excursions to observe the geological area they were investigating. As is true of many large teams, alpha team members worked on different parts of the task in cross-functional subgroups and used a shared database to track the numerous activities' status. There was a great deal of informal communication between team members. Although they had limited experience working in teams, they soon found that combining their knowledge led to solving critical problems. Team members developed strong ties with one another.

Besides biweekly meetings with the steering committee and informal contacts with other experts in their respective fields, the team had little external contact. Team members spent so much time with one another and so little with their functional departments that others outside the team commented that the team tended to isolate itself from the rest of the company. The team leader took on nearly all the external activities of the team, particularly those with management. Team members primarily confined their external activities to exchanging technical information with others.

How successful was the alpha team? The alpha team's two goals were to develop new exploration technologies and apply these technologies to exploration of a new field. As might be expected, based on the points we have made previously, the team successfully found new and effective ways to evaluate potential hydrocarbon prospects. Still, it was not as successful in getting their ideas accepted and utilized within the organization.

In the oil industry, companies may submit competitive applications to the government to obtain a license to further explore and develop a field. Once a license is obtained, there is further exploration and, potentially, the development and the construction of a site. Deciding when to bid on a site and gain government approval requires careful analysis of the site and accurate projections of the oil extracted using various technologies. Once technology decisions were made, the alpha team left it to the steering committee to "transfer" the conclusions of their work to top management and the other groups responsible for developing and submitting competitive applications. Unfortunately, the transfer was problematic, and it took a very long time for the team's results to disseminate within the organization. Because of the delays and lack of broad support, the company could never obtain licenses for the areas the alpha team studied and for which they developed the technology. Some good did come out of the alpha team. Once the team was disbanded and members transferred to other teams, some consulted on a similar project. On this new assignment, the old alpha team members could bring information and contacts into the new team, allowing the alpha technology to be successfully applied. The old alpha team members filled critical boundary roles in the new project.

Case 2

At about the same time the alpha team was formed, a second team, the beta team, also came into being. Like the alpha team, the beta team was created to develop innovative ways to explore new areas. The beta team differed from the alpha team in two important ways. First, it was responsible for developing a new exploration technology and completing a bid on a specific project. In other words, it took on the next phase of work and had to implement its findings. Second, the beta team included members from two other firms with whom a joint application would be prepared. (In the oil industry, companies often partner with one another for competitive advantage or to undertake a large bid.)

The team was composed of 15 experts from the company and one from each of the partner companies. The beta team, like the alpha team, contained members with different areas of geological expertise. Like the alpha team, team members also worked full time on the project and shared common space. The team even used a similar process as the alpha team, dividing the task and working in cross-functional subgroups. Like alpha, the beta team was able to develop innovative technical solutions to problems in exploration.

Unlike the alpha team, this one added a new member six months after its formation. This new member was a field development expert who would eventually work on the application and develop the chosen site. Initially, he joined project meetings as an observer but later moved on to be an active contributor. Also, unlike the alpha team, this team did not have its external links handled by a manager; instead, the team made numerous presentations to top management about project organization, cross-functional teams, alliances between oil companies, and their results. Despite its colocation, the beta team was not seen by others in the organization as isolated.

The beta team was able to move quickly from technical problems to the application phase. Although the first application bid prepared by the beta team was rejected, the team continued and prepared a new application that was accepted. The beta team was ultimately held up as a role model of collaboration between functions and across company boundaries.

How did composition contribute to the outcomes of the alpha and beta teams? In both cases, the teams were composed of individuals from different functional areas. Both teams were co-located and had full-time members. There were substantial differences between the teams, however. The alpha team members were selected strictly based on their technical expertise. Beta team members, especially those from the other companies, were selected both for their technical skills and connections to important networks throughout the organizations of which they were members. The beta team also shifted its membership by bringing in a specialized expert midway through its work and assigning this individual a specialized role. Perhaps most important, the beta team did not "delegate" boundary activity to one person, as did the alpha team. Completing the types of projects alpha and beta were assigned frequently requires more boundary management activity than can be accomplished by one or a small group of individuals. Finally, the internal processes of the two groups were somewhat different. The alpha group worked extensively with one another, usually to the exclusion of external activities. This was not the case in the beta team.

Conclusion

Compared to other areas of investigation of small groups, composition has been relatively neglected despite its obvious importance. Even the research that has been done has not led to systematic conclusions. In a summary of research on composition, Moreland, Levine, and Wingert note that ". . . few researchers study group composition, and no general theory guides their work. Progress toward understanding group composition has thus been slow and sporadic" (1996, p. 11). Unfortunately, relatively little has changed in the last few decades.

In our view, much of this lack of progress has come about because much of the research has been done with groups that do not have meaningful external connections. Such groups do not reflect the true nature of most organizational groups. For most groups in organizations, links with other groups and the external environment are critical for success. Information and resources must be imported if teams are to make effective decisions and the output of the group must be transferred to others. We propose that selecting group members based on their ability to facilitate these boundary activities can be an important element in team success. Importantly, if an entire system of teams does so collectively, it may help the organization as a whole become more agile and nimble (Ancona, Backman, and Isaacs, 2019; Luciano et al., 2018).

References

Alderfer, C. P. (1976). Boundary relations and organizational diagnosis. In M. Meltzer and F. Wickham (eds), *Humanizing Organizational Behavior* (pp. 142–175). Springfield, IL: Charles Thomas.

Aldrich, H. E., and Herker, D. (1977). Boundary spanning roles and organization structure. *Academy of Management Review,* 2, 217–230.

Allen, T. J. (1971). Communications, technology transfer, and the role of the technical gatekeeper. *R&D Management,* 1, 14–21.

Allen, T. J. (1984). *Managing the Flow of Technology: Technology Transfer and the Dissemination of Technological Information within the R&D Organization.* Cambridge, MA: MIT Press.

Ancona, D. G. (1990). Outward bound: Strategies for team survival in an organization. *Academy of Management Journal,* 33, 334–365.

Ancona, D., and Bresman, H. (2007). *X-Teams: How to Build Teams That Lead, Innovate, and Succeed.* Boston, MA: Harvard Business School Press.

Ancona, D. G., and Caldwell, D. F. (1992). Bridging the boundary: External activity and performance in organizational teams. *Administrative Science Quarterly,* 37, 634–665.

Ancona, D. G., and Caldwell, D. F. (1997). Rethinking team composition from the outside in. In M. E. Neale, E. A. Mannix, and D. H. Gruenfeld (eds), *Research on Managing Groups and Teams* (Vol. 1, pp. 21–37). Stamford, CT: JAI Press.

Ancona, D. G., and Nadler, D. A. (1989). Top hats and executive tales: designing the senior team. *Sloan Management Review,* 31, 19–28.

Ancona, D., Backman, E., and Isaacs, K. (2019). Nimble Leadership. *Harvard Business Review,* July–August.

Bantel, K., and Jackson, S. (1989). Top management and innovations in banking: Does the composition of the team make a difference? *Strategic Management Journal,* 10, 107–124.

Bresman, H. (2010). External learning activities and team performance: A multimethod field study. *Organization Science,* 21, 81–96.

Bresman, H., and Zellmer-Bruhn, M. (2013). The structural context of team learning: Effects of organizational and team structure on internal and external Learning. *Organization Science,* 24, 1120–1139.

Bunderson, J. S., and Sutcliffe, K. M. (2002). Comparing alternative conceptualizations of functional diversity in management teams: Process and performance effects. *Academy of Management Journal,* 45, 875–893.

Burt, R. (1992). *Structural Holes: The Social Structure of Competition.* Cambridge, MA: Harvard University Press.

Campion, M., Medsker, G., and Higgs, A. (1993). Relations between work group characteristics and effectiveness: Implications for designing effective work groups. *Personnel Psychology,* 46, 823–847.

Cummings, J. N. (2004). Work groups: Structural diversity, and knowledge sharing in a global organization. *Management Science,* 50, 352–364.

Cummings, T. G. (1978). Self-regulating work groups: A socio-technical synthesis. *Academy of Management Review,* 3, 624–634.

Ericksen, J., and Dyer, L. (2004). Right from the start: Exploring the effects of early team events on subsequent project team development and performance. *Administrative Science Quarterly,* 49, 438–471.

Gladstein, D. (1984). Groups in context: A model of task group effectiveness. *Administrative Science Quarterly,* 29, 499–517.

Glick, W., Miller, C., and Huber, G. (1993). The impact of upper echelon diversity on organizational performance. In G. Huber and W. Glick (eds), *Organizational Change and Redesign* (pp. 176–224). New York: Oxford University Press.

Granovetter, M. S. (1973). The strength of weak ties. *American Journal of Sociology,* 78, 1360–1380.

Hansen, M. T. (1999). The search-transfer problem: The role of weak ties in sharing knowledge across organization subunits. *Administrative Science Quarterly,* 44, 82–111.

Homans, G. (1950). *The Human Group.* New York: Harcourt Brace Jovanovich.

Horwitz, S. K., and Horwitz, I. B. (2007). The effects of team diversity on team outcomes: A meta-analytic review of team demography. *Journal of Management,* 33, 987–1015.

Janis, I. (1982). *Victims of Groupthink: A Psychological Study of Foreign Policy Decisions and Fiascos.* Boston: Houghton-Mifflin.

Jehn, K. A. (1995) A multimethod examination of the benefits and detriments of intragroup conflict. *Administrative Science Quarterly,* 29, 499–518.

Katz, D., and Kahn, R. (1978) *The Social Psychology of Organizing.* New York, NY: Wiley.

Katz, R., and Tushman, M. (1979). Communication patterns, project performance, and task characteristics: An empirical evaluation and integration in an R&D setting. *Organizational Behavior and Human Performance,* 23, 139–162.

Keck, S., and Tushman, M. (1993). Environmental and organizational context and executive team structure. *Academy of Management Journal,* 36, 1314–1344.

Krackhardt, D. (1990). Assessing the political landscape: Structure, cognition, and power in organizations. *Administrative Science Quarterly,* 35, 342–369.

Lewin, K. (1951). *Field Theory in Social Science: Selected Theoretical Papers.* D. Cartwright (ed.). New York: Harper and Brothers Publishers.

Luciano, M. M., DeChurch L. A., and Mathieu, J. E. (2018). Multiteam systems: A structural framework and meso-theory of system functioning. *Journal of Management,* 44, 1065–1096.

Malone, MM., Bresman, H., Zellmer-Bruhn, M. E., and Beaver, G. R. (2016). Contextualization and context theorizing in teams research. *Academy of Management Annals*, 10, 891–942.

Marrone, J. A., Tesluk, P. E., and Carson, J. B. (2007). A multilevel investigation of antecedents and consequences of team member boundary-spanning behavior. *Academy of Management Journal*, 50, 1423–1439.

Moreland, R., Levine, J., and Wingert, M. (1996). Creating the ideal group: Composition effects at work. In E. Witte and J. Davis (eds), *Understanding Group Behavior: Small Group Processes and Interpersonal Relations* (Vol. 2, pp. 11–35). Hillsdale, NJ: Lawrence Erlbaum.

Pelled, L. H., Eisenhardt, K. M., and Xin, K. R. (1999). Exploring the black box: An analysis of work group diversity, conflict, and productivity. *Administrative Science Quarterly*, 44, 1–28.

Reagans, R., and Zuckerman, E. (2001). Networks, diversity and productivity: The social capital of corporate R&D teams. *Organization Science*, 12, 502–517.

Reagans, R., Zuckerman, E., and McEvily, B. (2004). How to make the team: Social networks vs. demography as criteria for designing effective teams. *Administrative Science Quarterly*, 49, 101–133.

Roberts, K., and O'Reilly, C. (1979). Some correlates of communication roles in organizations. *Academy of Management Journal*, 22, 42–57.

Tushman, M. (1977). Special boundary roles in the innovation process. *Administrative Science Quarterly*, 22, 587–605.

Williams, K., and O'Reilly, C. (1998). Demography and diversity in organizations: A review of 40 years of research. In B. Staw and R. Sutton (eds), *Research in Organizational Behavior* (Vol. 20, pp. 77–144). Stamford, CT: JAI Press.

Yan, A., and Louis, M. R. (1999). The migration of organizational functions to the work unit level: Buffering, spanning, and bringing up boundaries. *Human Relations*, 52, 25–47.

Exercises

The following exercises ask you to apply the concepts to a real team. The first exercise is most appropriate if you served on a "project" team. This could be at work or a committee you have served on at school (e.g. organizing a food drive). The second exercise is a tool for planning your next assignment. This could be a team project in a class or some project at work.

Exercise 1

Think about a team you are familiar with – perhaps a team you are now on or were on in the past. Try to identify the key external groups or individuals that could potentially help the team. For example, some groups might be able to provide information or resources to your team. Other groups or individuals might help your team understand and respond to political or strategic issues within the organization.

Still, other groups might be responsible for evaluating your team's work or integrating your work into their own. For each stakeholder, determine whether information, resources, political alignment, or task interdependence needs to be managed. Identify a team member who will interact with each stakeholder. If there are no team members with the skills or connections to manage these activities, think about who you might recruit from outside the team, whether full-time or part-time, to help manage these interactions.

Exercise 2

Based on reading this chapter, think about how you might approach your next team assignment. What would you need to know to "map" the environment? How would you staff the team? What do you need to consider besides the functional competencies required to do the task?

Video Analysis and Discussion

Please watch the following video(s):

1. How to turn a group of strangers into a team: https://www.youtube.com/watch?v=3boKz0Exros
2. Team boundaries: https://www.youtube.com/watch?v=WWWbqEhMOC4

Now form small groups to discuss the video(s) and answer the following questions:

1. What are the major points of the video?
2. How can you use information from the video in your career?
3. Based on the video, what advice do you have for leaders in organizations?

Be prepared to present the ideas from your small group discussion with the class as a whole.

Discussion Questions

1. What advice do you have for team leaders regarding team member selection?
2. What "rules" would you suggest for team composition?
3. How, as a team leader, would you engage in external activity?
4. How, as a team leader, would you adjust team members to engage in external activity?
5. How, as a team leader, would you engage in external activity? Be very specific.

20

Manage Intrateam Conflict Through Collaboration

LAURIE R. WEINGART[1], KAREN A. JEHN[2], AND KORI L. KRUEGER[3]

[1]Tepper School of Business, Carnegie Mellon University
[2]Melbourne Business School, University of Melbourne
[3]Tepper School of Business, Carnegie Mellon University

Intrateam conflict occurs when team members hold discrepant views or have interpersonal incompatibilities. This is especially likely in organizational teams comprised of members from different functional areas, disciplines, or diverse backgrounds. There has been debate in organizational research regarding whether conflict within teams is advantageous for overall performance. While recent large-scale analyses of prior research on team conflict (i.e. meta-analyses) found that, on average, *relationship* conflicts based on personality clashes and interpersonal antagonism are detrimental to team performance and morale, *task* conflicts can have positive or negative effects depending on other characteristics of the group (DeChurch, Mesmer-Magnus, and Doty, 2013; De Dreu and Weingart, 2003; De Wit, Greer, and Jehn, 2012; O'Neill, Allen, and Hastings, 2013). Importantly, conflict researchers have found that task conflicts can be beneficial if managed collaboratively (Amason, 1996; Ensley and Hmieleski, 2005; Jehn, 1995, 1997; Liang, Liu, Lin, and Lin, 2007; Matsuo, 2006; Olson, Parayitam, and Bao, 2007). *Our central principle is that intrateam conflict can be leveraged through collaboration to reach positive team outcomes by increasing the availability of task-relevant information and reducing negative emotions that may hamper team functioning.*

Collaboration is a joint endeavor, involving two or more people working together to complete a task. Collaboration includes teamwork – the coordination of efforts of a group of people around a stated purpose. It involves constructive discussion and effective expression of conflict among team members. Teamwork is focused on groups in which members have common goals, thus making collaboration a key component to successful team outcomes. When embedded in the culture of an organization, this can be more than coordination and cooperation, but rather a continuous partnering of people based on shared values (Haskins, Liedtka, and Rosenblum, 1998).

There are three fundamental steps in leveraging team conflict via collaboration. The first step is to identify the type of intrateam conflict. The second is to engage a productive collaboration strategy using effective approaches to conflict expression and conflict management. The third step is to cultivate conditions that promote collaboration strategies. We address each step below.

Identifying the Type of Intrateam Conflict

The first step in dealing with intrateam conflict collaboratively is to determine the type of conflict. There are two basic categories to consider: performance-related conflict, including task and process conflict, and interpersonal conflict, including relationship and status conflict.

Performance-related conflict involves disagreements among team members on task-related activities. Some of these activities relate to what to do (the task itself) and others are about how to do it – that is, the process of performing the task or delegating resources and duties. *Task conflicts* are disagreements among group members regarding ideas and opinions about the task being performed, such as disagreement regarding an organization's current hiring strategies or determining the information to include in the annual report. Task conflicts include debates over facts (driven by data, evidence) and opinions (De Dreu, Harinck, and Van Vianen, 1999). *Process conflicts* are about logistical and delegation issues such as how task accomplishment should proceed in the work unit, who's responsible for what, and how things should be delegated (Jehn, 1997). They are often about the coordination of the task (e.g. three subtasks need to be completed) or coordination of the people involved (e.g. we should meet at 3 p.m. each day to update; Behfar, Mannix, Peterson, and Trochim, 2011). This type of process conflict, named logistical conflicts, involves discussions of resources and how to approach tasks (Behfar et al., 2011). They can distract team members from the task and decrease task clarity, which reduces coordination and performance. At times process conflict can also feel quite personal, especially when a person's worth or expertise is challenged as a result of the way work is allocated within the group (Greer and Jehn, 2007; van den Berg, Curseu, and Meeus, 2014). This type of process conflict, labeled "contribution conflict," is about equity in the distribution of work and equality of effort (Behfar et al., 2011). These types of process conflicts are more likely to evoke negative emotions and result in lower satisfaction.

Interpersonal conflict involves tensions or discord between team members, including those due to relational issues between team members or those due to social position or status within the team. *Relationship conflicts* are interpersonal disagreements, tensions, and incompatibilities among group members about personal issues that are directed at the person rather than focused on the task. Relationship conflicts frequently reported are about social events, gossip, clothing preferences, political views, and hobbies (Jehn, 1997). *Status conflicts* encompass conflict over members' position or stature relative to one another within the team's social hierarchy (Bendersky and Hays, 2012). For example, members might have conflict over who should be in charge or fight over resources that indicate high status.

Take an R&D team: when the different researchers disagree about data interpretation and the meaning of the results, they are experiencing task conflict. If they argue about who's responsible for writing up the final report and who will make the presentation, they are having a process conflict. Disagreements about automobile gas mileage requirements by the governor, politics, and religion or personal attacks on the intelligence level of anyone who refuses the COVID vaccine are relationship conflicts. Disagreements about the relative value of members' contributions (e.g. who is more important to the group) are status conflict. We focus here on how task and process conflict can be effectively leveraged using collaboration strategies and how relationship and status conflict can be managed. As status conflict is a relatively new area of study, there is less evidence to draw from regarding its consequences and management.

The majority of research examining the consequences of conflict has focused on task, process, and relationship conflicts. Results from a relatively recent meta-analysis of 116 studies of task, process, and relationship conflict provide a nice summary of their effects on team outcomes (De Wit et al., 2012). Their results show that teams with more conflict of any of the three types have lower levels of trust and commitment to the team. In addition, process and relationship conflict have more negative effects on team cohesion and satisfaction than does task conflict. The negative effects of process conflict may partly be due to the potential personal implications of some process conflicts. In fact, both process and relationship conflicts are likely to interfere with group performance. Process conflict is associated with lower work quality and productivity (Jehn, Greer, Levine, and Szulanski, 2008), especially when it occurs early in a group's interaction and is not resolved (Greer, Jehn, and Mannix, 2008). Relationship conflict interferes with task performance by diverting time away from task performance, thus reducing functioning and effectiveness (De Dreu and Weingart, 2003; Murnighan and Conlon, 1991). In contrast, task conflict has been shown to have both positive and negative effects on team performance depending on the study (De Wit et al., 2012). Research shows that it can improve decision quality, strategic planning, learning, and creativity (Amason and Schweiger, 1994; Cosier and Rose, 1977; De Dreu, 2006; Jehn and Rupert, 2008; Todorova, Bear, and Weingart, 2014) when it is not accompanied by high levels of relationship conflict. And although there is less research on status conflict, research has shown that it negatively affects team performance and conflict resolution (Greer and Van Kleef, 2010; Tiedens and Fragale, 2003).

Conflict that is expressed within a team provides information about existing inconsistencies between members, which can increase information exchange and trigger emotional reactions (Cronin and Bezrukova, 2019; Weingart, Behfar, Bendersky, Todorova, and Jehn, 2015). Performance-related conflicts have the potential to provide useful information about the task, the process, or the people involved and their capabilities (see Chapter 10). The differing views discussed add to the group's overall store of knowledge. The information from task conflict in particular has the potential to motivate deliberate, careful assessment of alternatives. When task conflict involves a useful give and take among members, the consultative interaction and problem-solving, and the increased information exchanged enhance performance. In contrast, the information from process conflict is difficult to leverage – conflict over logistics makes it more difficult to coordinate and harms performance, whereas conflict regarding the equity of work distribution harms satisfaction with the team (Behfar et al., 2011). Finally, relationship and status conflicts are least likely to have an informational advantage (Cronin and Bezrukova, 2019). In fact, relationship and status conflicts have been shown to reduce information sharing (Bendersky and Hays, 2012; Humphrey, Aime, Cushenbery, Hill, and Fairchild, 2017).

Interpersonal conflicts are also characteristically more emotional than performance-related conflicts. Because they are personal, they can lead to strong negative emotions such as frustration, anger, and stress (DeChurch et al., 2013; Greer and Jehn, 2007). These negative emotions arise because interpersonal conflicts often involve threats to people's self-identity or self-esteem – the conflicts are often deeply value laden (e.g. De Wit et al., 2012; Jehn et al., 2008). For example, a conflict over whether a woman or minority could make a good US president taps into deeply held values and can be very personal both to men and women and majority and minority members. In addition, the competition associated with status conflict (Pai and Bendersky, 2020) may evoke negative emotions like anger and stress. In contrast, performance-related conflict, particularly task conflict, is less personally threatening and involves less negative emotions (Jehn, 1997). However, that is not to say that performance-related conflict is never emotional. Conflict over task performance can get very heated – often because both sides believe they are right and have strong convictions to their opinions (Cronin and Bezrukova, 2019; Jehn, 1997). In addition, process conflicts often evoke negative emotions (e.g. frustration) and can transform into relationship conflict (Greer et al., 2008) when a person's personal worth or expertise is challenged (Greer and Jehn, 2007; van den Berg et al., 2014).

People can also experience positive emotions in response to conflict (Chen and Ayoko, 2012; Todorova et al., 2014). Consider a debate about an organization's strategy that is stimulating and energizing. Many positive emotions can accompany those performance-related conflicts – happiness, elation, and positive challenge. Research suggests that task conflict elicits active positive emotions including enthusiasm and feeling active, interested, and energetic, whereas relationship conflict is more likely to decrease positive emotions (Todorova et al., 2014).

Engaging an Effective Collaboration Strategy

We assert that intrateam conflict can be successfully leveraged by engaging an effective collaboration strategy – by expressing conflict directly and with low intensity and by using a collaborative conflict management approach.

Use a Collaborative, Problem-Solving Approach

Collaborative approaches to conflict resolution incorporate the needs of others into solutions via problem-solving, yielding, and compromising. Yielding does this while sublimating one's one interests, whereas compromising (i.e. meeting in the middle) and problem-solving (searching for solutions that meet everyone's needs) do not. In contrast, more individualistic processes focus on one's own outcomes without concern for others and include approaches like avoiding and forcing or competing (see Deutsch, 2002, for a discussion). Perhaps not surprisingly, collaborative approaches are associated with higher performance and increased satisfaction and trust, and avoiding and competing are associated with lower performance, satisfaction, and trust in the team (DeChurch et al., 2013). The avoidance or suppression of disagreement has been shown to interfere with team performance. When members avoid presenting dissenting viewpoints, superior alternatives may be overlooked and performance may suffer (Janis, 1982; also see Chapter 20 in this volume). Putting pressure on dissenters, self-censorship, and collective justifications (all associated with groupthink) increase defective decision-making.

A problem-solving approach that surfaces information and identifies underlying interests may be ill-suited for relationship conflicts. Relationship conflicts that have their roots in deeply held values and assumptions are often impossible to resolve in the workplace where activities are primarily task-focused. Thus, trying to get at true underlying interests for relationship conflicts may result in even more intractable disputes, distracting from task performance and escalating negativity. When relationship conflicts have a low potential for resolution, they are sometimes better to avoid (De Dreu and Van Vianen, 2001; Druckman, 1994; Von Glinow, Shapiro, and Brett, 2004).

Interestingly, characteristics of the conflict may steer team members toward specific forms of conflict management. Task conflict (as compared to relationship conflict) has been shown to lead to more collaborative conflict management approaches such as problem-solving, yielding, and compromising (Todorova, Goh, and Weingart, 2021). And people engage in competitive and individualistic conflict management approaches in response to relationship conflict versus task conflict (Maltarich, Kukenberger, Reilly, and Mathieu, 2018; Todorova et al., 2021).

Key Collaboration Behaviors

Collaboration is enacted through group member behavior. Thus, it is important to identify the behaviors that constitute collaboration. We focus on four that are central to the process: express conflict directly and with low oppositional intensity, exchange information, use packaging and trade-offs, and work to break the chain of conflict escalation. The last three behavioral recommendations come from the negotiation literature that examines problem-solving strategies for resolving disputes and transactions where negotiators are simultaneously motivated to cooperate (to create shared value and reach a decision) and compete (to claim value for themselves). This literature has identified *integration of interests* as a collaborative strategic approach for managing conflict (see Chapter 24). The integration of interests includes increasing the availability of resources (thus, "expanding the pie") as well as sharing in the distribution of those resources. Thus, integrative negotiation is a collaborative problem-solving process in which there are divergent interests and can provide insights into collaboration processes.

Express Conflict Directly and with Low Oppositional Intensity Regardless of conflict type, disagreements or dissenting views that are expressed directly and with low oppositional intensity are more likely to convey information, evoke more positive emotional reactions, and (in the case of task conflict) enhance team performance (Todorova et al., 2014; Tsai and Bendersky, 2016; Weingart et al., 2015). Low-intensity, direct communication of conflict has been shown to be more effective in work and personal interactions (Overall and McNulty, 2017).

Conflict expressions are more direct when the sender explicitly indicates that there is a problem, makes it clear what position he or she is taking, and expresses it directly to the other party. In contrast, indirect expressions may cue the existence of opposition, but leave it to the receiver to figure out what the problem actually is. Disputes that are unclear are difficult to resolve because people are unsure where the problem lies and, therefore, what to do about it.

Conflict expressions are less intense when the sender communicates openness to others' perspectives and flexibility in how to resolve the disagreement while expressing their opposition. Debates and deliberation among people are typically low intensity (and direct). They may include a simple acknowledgment of emotion (e.g. "What you said about me makes me angry"; see Chapter 4) and are less likely to elicit a heated exchange, but rather a discussion of causes and attempts to repair. In contrast, conflict expressions that are more intense tend to be more subversive of others or entrenched in their positions and are more emotionally charged. Intense conflict expressions are more likely to escalate because they convey threat and closemindedness. They may be communicated verbally by arguing for one's positions, or nonverbally by yelling, crying, banging fists, slamming doors, or having an angry tone. When conflicts escalate and negative emotions run high, collaboration between the disputants might not be possible. Team members may feel defensive (e.g. Thiel, Harvey, Courtright, and Bradley, 2017) and become less willing to seek out, receive, and share information (Humphrey et al., 2017; Weingart et al., 2015). Collaboration requires a high level of interdependence and willingness to work together. Team members that feel animosity, frustration, anger, or distrust are not likely to be willing to rely on one another. Thus, it is important to engage in direct and low-intensity conflict expression in order to clearly convey information, avoid escalation, and increase the likelihood of positive outcomes.

Exchange Information A key component of collaboration is the exchange of accurate information. Exchanging information increases insight into the other party's preferences and priorities and the probability that negotiators will find integrative agreements, if a zone of agreement exists (Pruitt, 1981; Putnam and Jones, 1982). The benefit of sharing information varies depending on the type of information that is shared and how it is used. Sharing factual information, like constraints or costs, can be used to merely inform the other party (a collaborative application) or to substantiate one's position in an attempt to persuade the other party (a less collaborative approach). Sharing information about preferences for a given issue (i.e. what you want and why you should have it your way) can be more confrontational in nature and does not necessarily improve the quality of an agreement (Weingart,

Hyder, and Prietula, 1996). In contrast, exchanging information about priorities across issues (i.e. the relative importance of the issues to a negotiator and why) represents an effective, collaborative type of information exchange as it involves multiple issues and can facilitate trade-offs across issues (Pruitt and Lewis, 1975; Thompson, 1991).

Package Issues and Make Win-Win Trade-offs It is not uncommon for discussions of multi-issue conflicts to progress one issue at a time – with the group resolving one issue before moving to the next. The problem with this approach is that trade-offs cannot be made across issues. Win-win trade-offs occur when both parties make concessions on less important issues (to themselves) to gain advantage on others that are more important to them (Pruitt, 1981). This tactic is effective at reconciling interests when parties have differing priorities on issues when each party gains more than they lose in the trade-off (see Chapter 24).

When team members are unwilling to share this information (because they fear the other party might not reciprocate, putting themselves at an information disadvantage), effective trade-offs can be identified by exchanging multi-issue offers (i.e. packaging). When issues are packaged together, instead of being considered independently and sequentially, it is easier to arrange trades or concessions as negotiators search for packages that are mutually beneficial (Thompson, Mannix, and Bazerman, 1988; Weingart, Bennett, and Brett, 1993). Discovering trade-offs through the exchange of packaged offers is a more indirect method in that team members must infer other's priorities by stated package preferences (Adair, Weingart, and Brett, 2007).

Work to Break the Chain of Conflict Escalation One of the most difficult aspects of successfully managing conflict is trying to balance the cooperative and competitive components of mixed-motive situations. Once a conflict intensifies or takes on a competitive or personal tone (i.e. transforms into a relationship conflict), it is very difficult to shift it to a more cooperative task-focused interaction, as the conflict can escalate into a destructive cycle. One way to break the chain of contentious behavior is to respond with integrative, collaborative responses (Behfar, Peterson, Mannix, and Trochim, 2008; Brett, Shapiro, and Lytle, 1998; Greer et al., 2008; Putnam and Jones, 1982). Collaboration is then more likely to continue when that collaborative behavior is reciprocated than when it is not (Weingart, Prietula, Hyder, and Genovese, 1999). Another method for breaking conflict spirals is explicitly labeling the contentious reciprocation as unproductive during the interaction. When a conflict is contentious and one party identifies the process as such, the other party would be hesitant to continue in a contentious manner without appearing irrational. Directly responding to a threat by identifying it ("Are you threatening me?") demonstrates that the threat was not effective and may cause the party making the threat to shift tactics or refocus onto the process (Brett et al., 1998).

Third parties can be used to break the chain of conflict escalation. When task conflict escalates, people often take negative comments about their task performance or ideas personally, they become more emotional, and the conflict shifts from focusing on the task to focusing on the people. The resultant relationship conflict may be handled by an outside party to sort through the negative emotions and ascribe more positive attributions to team members' behavior (Eaton and Sanders, 2012; Giebels and Janssen, 2005). Another option is for team members who are not emotionally inflamed to take the disputants off-site, such as into a social setting for drinks, or a walk, where they can reestablish their interpersonal bonds and discuss their concerns. If the negative emotions are so inflamed between two members that they are not willing to talk, we recommend having two members who are closest to each of the adversaries talk, collaboratively, with each of the parties. Then, the two facilitators (i.e. third and fourth parties) can talk and try to bring all four together. Finally, a trusted outsider to the team (e.g. manager or colleague) could help high negative emotion teams get to the point where they can engage in collaboration and constructive conflict without assuming the worst of others (Römer, Rispens, Giebels, and Euwema, 2012; Thiel, Griffith, Hardy, Peterson, and Connelly, 2018). When possible, irrational team members can be replaced.

Cultivate Conditions That Promote Collaboration

Collaboration is effective in managing conflict in that it sets a positive, team-oriented tone for the group (Mintzberg, Dougherty, Jorgensen, and Westley, 1996). However, collaboration does not just happen. Collaboration within teams must be fostered by putting the right conditions in place – creating a team-oriented environment and selecting team members who have the propensity to collaborate.

Create a Team-Oriented Environment

For a team to be collaborative, its atmosphere must support interdependence, reliance, respect, trust, open communication, and collective efficacy (see Chapter 21). While a team orientation can be considered a precondition for effective collaboration, it will also improve as the group experiences successful collaborative events. In this way, norms are developed which perpetuate interdependence, reliance on, and respect for one another.

Creating a team orientation involves framing the group's activities as belonging to the team rather than solely as a set of individual accomplishments. With a team orientation, there is a sense that although we are *each* responsible for our individual contributions to the group, "we" are *jointly* responsible for the group's final product. Team-oriented members take personal pride in the team's performance and feel personally successful when the team is successful. Below, we identify several ways to cultivate a team orientation.

Team Goals A shared group goal can reinforce a superordinate team identity that pulls teams together (see Chapters 5 and 18). When team goals and individual goals support one another, teams that focus on a superordinate or team goal are more likely to have constructive conflict management (Jehn and Bezrukova, 2010;

Somech, Desivilya, and Lidogoster, 2008; Thatcher and Jehn, 1998). This is in contrast to the case where individuals focus *only* on their own contribution, claiming (or denying) responsibility for the overall group's performance.

Develop Collective Efficacy Collective efficacy refers to a group's shared belief in its capabilities to perform a task (in this case, resolve a conflict) (Bandura, 1997; also see Chapter 6). Often what is most important in predicting high performance is that team members feel they have the capabilities to resolve the task and relationship conflicts at hand (Jehn et al., 2008). If members feel they, or others in the group, have the capabilities to constructively manage the conflict, they will engage in positive discussions with one another relying on the competence of the group to reach a satisfactory resolution consistent with the group goal.

Collective efficacy is driven both by the team's beliefs about its ability to work as a unit as well as team members' beliefs about their own and others' capabilities. Self-efficacy (held by an individual) can be raised using several mechanisms (Bandura, 1997; and, as noted, see Chapter 6), three of which are also relevant to collective efficacy in teams. First, collective efficacy can be raised through "enactive mastery experiences," in our case, prior successes at managing similar, challenging conflicts that required effort and perseverance to overcome (Jehn et al., 2008; Rodriguez-Sanchez, Hakanen, and Salanova, 2021). Through experience, team members learn effective strategies for diagnosing and managing conflict, which increases their confidence for managing future conflicts that might arise. Second, collective efficacy can be raised through observing and modeling other teams' collaboration strategies. Teams that can observe similar teams' inner workings and subsequent performance can use that information as a comparator to determine where they stand relative to others. They can also learn from the other team's success and failures. Third, collective efficacy can be raised via collective engagement and positive affect – when others express confidence in the team's capabilities, dedication to the team, and enthusiasm (Rodriguez-Sanchez et al., 2021; Salanova, Llorens, and Schaufeli, 2011).

Affective Integration: Fostering Trust and Respect A key component in collaborative approaches to conflict resolution is the attitudes members have toward one another. Affective integration is a group-level concept representing the feelings that team members hold for one another, specifically in terms of their interpersonal trust, respect, and liking (Cronin, Bezrukova, Weingart, and Tinsley, 2011; Weingart, Cronin, Houser, Cagan, and Vogel, 2005). These attitudes influence the beliefs about behavioral inclinations members have toward each other. Trust evokes beliefs that others can be relied upon (Rotter, 1971). This is often called "trustworthiness," and it leads to the willingness to be confident in another person's competence, integrity, and goodwill (see Chapter 17). Respect, on the other hand, evokes beliefs about the intrinsic value of others and liking implies a general attraction to others (Chaiken, 1987), and at the group level, this is often conceptualized as cohesion (Festinger, 1950).

Affective integration is associated with higher team performance and has been shown to enhance the positive effects of collaboration (Chen and Zhang, 2021).

Affective integration increases the likelihood that team members' assets (knowledge, skills, and abilities [KSAs]) are actually used by the team while collaborating. Both trust and respect play a key role. Trust influences the willingness to share information and receive information as accurate (Carnevale and Lawler, 1986; Kimmel, Pruitt, Magenau, Konar-Goldband, and Carnevale, 1980). Without trust, team members will be unwilling to rely on the KSAs of others for fear teammates might not follow through on their promises or work to undermine teammates' interests. Respect is what leads people to a priori assume potential utility in the ideas of others. People will devote more attention to these ideas in order to find the value that they assume exists.

Affective integration also buffers against the stresses and strains that often arise as a result of team conflict. Trust decreases the likelihood that task conflicts will be perceived as attacking or personal in nature (Choi and Cho, 2011; De Jong and Elfring, 2010; Simons and Peterson, 2000) because of the implied benevolence in those who are trusted. When people respect each other, they take great care not to violate fairness norms regarding how people should behave toward one another (Bies and Moag, 1986). Respect has been shown to relate to (perceptions of) fair treatment as well as the inclination to acknowledge others' status and dignity (Tyler, Degoey, and Smith, 1996; Tyler and Lind, 1992). Finally, liking and its resultant cohesion can serve to prevent people from withdrawing from each other in the face of conflict.

Open and Constructive Conflict Culture Collaboration requires norms for the expression of performance-related conflict that support freedom to disagree and to constructively respond. This is in contrast to norms that support dominating or competing or are discouraging or avoidant of those exchanges (Gelfand, Leslie, Keller, and De Dreu, 2012). Collaborative conflict cultures are psychologically safe, such that people perceive the risk of dissenting to be low (Edmondson and Lei, 2014). If group members feel that it is appropriate and acceptable to discuss their differing opinions, disagreements are more likely to have a positive effect on group process and performance than if these disagreements are discouraged or avoided (Lovelace, Shapiro, and Weingart, 2001). However, openness must be accompanied by restraint and respect for others' contributions so that conflicts do not escalate and become more emotional, relationship conflicts. Openness can be communicated by using an inquiry approach to group decision-making (Garvin and Roberto, 2001). This includes allowing others to make their point without interruption, asking questions to improve your understanding, and engaging in active listening (i.e. repeating back what others have said in your own words to ensure that you heard and understood what they said) (Rogers and Farson, 1979). The ideal culture for a group is to have conflict norms that will allow constructive, open task-related debates but not critical, personal attacks detrimental to performance.

When task conflict is suppressed, the lines of communication will need to be opened for collaboration to be successful. Openness and trust must be nurtured within these teams (Choi and Cho, 2011; Simons and Peterson, 2000). Trust must be allowed to develop over time – through positive experiences, group members will grow more comfortable engaging in collaboration. The team leader can play an important role in setting the norms for open conflict communication in the team (see Chapter 21). Research shows that teams with leaders who are rated to be effective experience more constructive conflict, more freedom to express doubts, and are more innovative (Lovelace et al., 2001; Manz, Barstein, Hostager, and Shapiro, 1989; Van de Ven and Chu, 1989). In addition, providing the team with collaborative skills through training can aid in successful conflict management.

Select Team Members with a Propensity to Collaborate

An important way to promote collaboration is to select team members that have a high propensity to collaborate with others. A team member's propensity to collaborate will be higher when he/she is motivated to work hard toward improving outcomes for oneself and for other members of the team. This requires a cooperative orientation (focus on self and others; Van Lange, 1999) and epistemic motivation (the desire develop and hold a rich and accurate understanding of the world; Kruglanski, 1989). A cooperative orientation provides a focus on collaboration whereas epistemic motivation provides the drive (De Dreu and Carnevale, 2003). While we discuss the two separately, both a cooperative motive and high epistemic motivation are necessary for team members to effectively collaborate (De Dreu, Beersma, Stroebe, and Euwema, 2006). Team members who hold the goal of maximizing individual and group gain *and* are motivated to process information thoroughly are most likely to engage in problem-solving behaviors and effectively resolve disagreements.

Select Team Members Who Are Cooperatively Oriented Team members who are cooperatively oriented place value on maximizing outcomes for all team members and tend to engage in more collaboration as a means to this end (De Dreu, Weingart, and Kwon, 2000; Messick and McClintock, 1968). People who only care about themselves (individualistically oriented) have less interest in collaboration (Gelfand et al., 2001; Messick and McClintock, 1968).

Cooperative orientations influence the quality of agreements through their effect on group member behavior (DeDreu et al., 2000; Weingart et al., 1993). Cooperatively motivated team members tend to engage in more integrative/problem-solving tactics (e.g. truthful information exchange about preferences and priorities, multi-issue offers, and trade-offs) and fewer contentious tactics (e.g. threats, arguing one's position, and power tactics) than do team members who are only individualistically motivated. However, there are two caveats. First, groups comprised of individualistic members sometimes shift to problem-solving when they hit an impasse because they realize that they need to satisfy their teammates interests in order to reach their own goals (i.e. "enlightened self-interest"; Rubin, 1991; Schei, Rognes, and De Dreu, 2008). Second, cooperative groups can become *too* cooperative, resulting in compromise (giving in rather than problem-solving or groupthink) and suboptimal agreements. This is most likely to occur when they do not have a strong reason to resist yielding, for example, when they are under time pressure, have low aspirations, have bad alternatives, or are not accountable to others (De Dreu, Koole, and Steinel, 2000; Pruitt and Rubin, 1986). To remedy each of these situations, individualistically motivated group members can adopt problem-solving to achieve their goals as a way to avoid impasse and cooperative group members may adopt more competitive strategies to protect themselves from being dominated by individualists who do not want to cooperate.

Whereas these orientations (called "social value orientations" in the research literature) are treated as relatively stable individual differences, situational cues can also influence one's propensity to collaborate (De Dreu, Nijstad, and van Knippenberg, 2008). As such, moving a group toward collaboration would require either changing the composition of the team to all cooperative members (via turnover and selection) or providing strong cues about the collaborative nature of the task and the cooperative motives of others. Team members can be instructed to adopt a cooperative approach or incentivized, making cooperation in everyone's self-interest. Instructions from a supervisor or rewards for high joint value agreements have been shown to be effective. The expectation that team members will continue to interact on cooperative tasks in the future ("expected cooperative future interaction") has also been shown to increase cooperative motives (De Dreu et al., 2000). Finally, team members can adjust their motives in response to the behaviors of others in the group. Cooperative actions by others can serve as a signal of willingness to collaborate, but individualistically oriented members also need assurances that cooperation is in their own self-interest (Locke, Tirnauer, Roberson, Goldman, Latham, and Weldon, 2001).

Select Team Members with Epistemic Motives People with high epistemic motivation have a desire to gain knowledge, think deeply, and more thoroughly process information. They engage in more deliberative and systematic processing (De Dreu and Carnevale, 2003). In that people with high epistemic motivation process information more thoroughly and are more likely to revise their view of a given situation (De et al., 2000), it is likely they would make strong contributions to collaborative teams.

People with low epistemic motivation are believed to solve problems and make decisions using heuristic processing, which is relatively quick and effortless. Low epistemic motivation has been shown to impede the quality of information processing and the collaborativeness of group decision-making. Research on negotiation shows that low epistemic motivation increases reliance on stereotypes and irrelevant anchoring information (De Dreu et al., 1999). Small groups composed of members with high need for closure have been found to be less egalitarian in their decision-making and more tolerant of an authoritarian leader (De Grada, Kruglanski, Pierro, and Mannetti, 1999), both of which run counter to collaboration.

Like a cooperative orientation, epistemic motivation is jointly determined by individual differences and situational cues. People with low epistemic motivation are likely to have a high need for closure (Webster and Kruglanski, 1994). The internal pressure to quickly complete the task at hand associated with a high need for closure tends to limit the motivation to deeply process information. Similarly, external time pressure has been shown to limit team members' epistemic motivation (De Dreu et al., 1999).

To increase the odds that a team includes epistemically motivated members, one could screen people in terms of their need for closure or for cognition. In addition, epistemic motivation can be induced by reducing time pressure (reducing the need for closure) or making them accountable for their process. Process accountability has been shown to increase epistemic motivation because when people expect to be observed and evaluated by others regarding the processes they engage, they are more likely to use a more thorough process (Lerner and Tetlock, 1999).

Summary

Conflict does not have to derail team performance. Its negative effects can be neutralized, or even turned positive, when teams engage in effective collaboration strategies. A collaborative approach to conflict involves low-intensity, direct communication of opposition combined with open information exchange and creative problem-solving that reduces the likelihood of conflict escalation. Organizations can cultivate conditions to promote collaboration. Comprising teams with members who already have a propensity to collaborate and then creating a team-oriented environment will pave the way for more effective collaboration and conflict management.

Case Examples

In order to illustrate the use of collaboration in teams, we present two case examples of team conflict: one managed ineffectively, the other effectively. These examples are compilations of conflicts we have observed in our research on teams in organizations. Both examples involve task conflict within cross-functional product development teams working to design a high-quality, low-cost automobile that will meet customers' preferences and desires. These teams are comprised of many parties (including marketing representatives and suppliers), but here we will focus on two central parties – designers and engineers. Each subgroup has its own concerns. The designers are responsible for the brand image and appearance of the car. The engineers are responsible for the functioning of the car and its components and have primary responsibility for keeping costs within budget. Unfortunately, these interests are not always in line with one another.

Dysfunctional Cross-Functional Product Development Team

Consider a cross-functional product development team designing a subsystem of a new model of an automobile. This team is responsible for the design of the car's interior. They are at mid-stage in the design process. Many decisions have been made about the design and functionality of the interior. Models have been developed and general layouts for components (e.g. the console, instrument panel, etc.) have been determined. Engineering feels it has worked out most of the major functionality issues and was able to remain within budget, but just barely. Then, design comes in with a change in styling. In order to maintain brand identity, the shape and flow from the instrument panel to the console needs to change. Engineering is furious. Implications for this change are large. The changes will require a redesign of the placement of internal components within the instrument panel and console. To make these changes will be costly – it will require money that is not there. Design is indifferent to these concerns – they believe that the aesthetic component is what sells the car – and their job is to make sure the automobile sends a coherent message to the customer.

Each group sees the problem from its own perspective, and neither is willing to give ground. Engineering tells design, "it can't be done." Design grows tired of engineering's "no can do" attitude and makes disparaging comments about them behind their backs. Design starts putting pressure on engineering through back channels, trying to force engineering to "make it work." Several meetings occur in which engineering and design try to convince the other on the merits of their positions. Arguments get heated, tempers flare. Little progress is made. Eventually, a compromise solution is reached which moves away from the design intent, compromises functionality, and increases cost.

This conflict can be characterized as a task conflict with low-resolution potential (i.e. team members have low collective efficacy). It involved an important aspect of their task performance and needed to be resolved, but neither side believed they had the ability to do so. There was no sense of a shared fate – rather than focus on developing the best product, each side focused on its own concerns. Conflict norms were more toward blaming and attacking (dominating) than listening and building (collaborating). Opposition was expressed with high intensity in both direct and indirect ways. Such expressions were subversive and undermining, led to negative emotional reactions and little information exchange, and ultimately resulted in an escalatory conflict spiral and less than optimal outcome. What transpired was a contentious conflict, pitting "us" against "them," resulting in a solution that neither party was especially happy with. Was there another way out of this conflict? What could the team have done to find a better solution?

Collaborative Integrated Product Development (IPD) Team

Consider another design team working on the same component. This team faces the same change in styling. But this time, design presents the change in terms of a shared problem – they take responsibility for the change and are willing to consider its implications. Engineering is then willing to collaborate with design to try to make the change possible. The IPD team has a frank discussion about the implications of the change. Design tries to come up with less expensive and less disruptive ways to change the console and instrument panel while maintaining design intent. Engineering tries to develop innovative ways to fit the internal components in the new space. They also start looking for additional sources of funding for the change from the overall vehicle budget. Some discussions grow heated, but because frustration is focused on the problem rather than one another, tension is quickly dispersed. Several potential solutions are developed. A dominant option emerges, which includes a slight design modification that provides adequate space for a key component and some additional funding is found.

This conflict situation differed in several ways from the previous example. While the conflict was just as important and difficult to resolve, collective efficacy was high. Both engineers and designers believed a solution was possible. They viewed themselves as a team tackling a shared problem. As such, members were cooperatively oriented and epistemically motivated to work hard to find a mutually beneficial solution. Conflict norms were collaborative, and conflict was expressed directly and with low oppositional intensity, supporting open information exchange and constructive discussions. Emotions remained under control (see Chapter 4). An integrative solution evolved because the entire IPD team "owned" the problem and worked together, collaboratively, to develop a solution. They trusted one another's expertise, motives, and information in a way that allowed them to reach a mutually satisfactory solution. A team orientation, trust in one another, and a belief that a jointly beneficial solution was possible motivated the team to search together for a solution. This search involved direct and low-intensity conflict expression, sharing information, creativity, some trade-offs, and an effort to avoid turning task frustration into personal attacks and status battles. In addition to a high-quality agreement, this successful conflict resolution process reinforced the team's belief in its ability to solve problems and will make the team more willing to tackle similar problems in the future.

Summary of Cases

The first team's conflict was very contentious, plagued by low affective integration and individualistic orientations – an "us versus them" framing of the problem. Their conflict behavior was characterized by high-intensity expressions of opposition – obstructive, dismissive, and attacking behavior. In contrast, the collaborative team shared the ownership of the problem and developed solutions that recognized the concerns and interests of all parties involved. Their conflict behavior was expressed directly, but in a way that allowed for reflective responses and an openness to integrative solutions. The first team was not willing to openly share information, nor did they trust the information that was received. The information exchange that did occur served the purpose of bolstering a priori positions. In contrast, the collaborative team used information to develop understanding and potential solutions. Because motives were cooperative, it was easier to trust the information provided. In addition, they worked hard at processing the information made available to them, signaling high epistemic motivation. Finally, where the first team was very positional in making demands ("my way is the only way") resulting in a stalemate, the collaborative team used creativity and trade-offs to develop potential solutions. What resulted for the noncollaborative team was a time-consuming, contentious, and sometimes emotional and personal conflict and an unsatisfactory solution. The collaborative team was able to succeed because it managed the conflict by focusing on team goals, exchanging truthful information, developing trust, and using tradeoffs and creativity to find integrative solutions that satisfied both engineering and design's concerns.

Conclusion

The literature on teamwork, negotiation, collaboration, and conflict provided the foundation for this chapter. The key principle gleaned from this prior research demonstrates that conflict can be successfully leveraged through the use of collaboration strategies to obtain information and minimize negative emotions. Collaboration strategies include expressing conflict directly and with low intensity and using collaborative conflict management approaches. The use of collaboration strategies is fostered when a team-oriented environment is cultivated and when team members with a high propensity to collaborate are selected. The management of conflict is often difficult because crucial information is not shared between team members and negative emotions are easily evoked such as defensiveness, anger, and frustration. Collaboration provides a way to increase information exchange and reduce negative emotions, which allows team members to focus more objectively on the task at hand and integrate conflicting perspectives.

References

Adair, W., Weingart, L. R., and Brett, J. (2007). The timing and function of offers in U.S. and Japanese negotiations. *Journal of Applied Psychology*, 92, 1056–1068.

Amason, A. (1996). Distinguishing effects of functional and dysfunctional conflict on strategic decision making: Resolving a paradox for top management teams. *Academy of Management Journal*, 39, 123–148.

Amason, A., and Schweiger, D. M (1994). Resolving the paradox of conflict, strategic decision making, and organizational performance. *International Journal of Conflict Management*, 5, 239–253.

Bandura, A. (1997). *Self-Efficacy: The Exercise of Control.* NY: W. H. Freeman.

Behfar, K., Mannix, E., Peterson, R., and Trochim, W. (2011). Conflict in small groups: The meaning and consequences of process conflict. *Small Group Research*, 42, 127–176.

Behfar, K. J., Peterson, R. S., Mannix, E. A., and Trochim, W. M. (2008). The critical role of conflict resolution in teams: A close look at the links between conflict type, conflict management strategies, and team outcomes. *Journal of Applied Psychology*, 93(1), 170–188.

Bendersky, C., and Hays, N. A. (2012). Status conflict in groups. *Organization Science*, 23(2), 323–340.

Bies, R. J., and Moag, J. S. (1986). Interactional justice: Communication criteria of fairness. In Lewicki, R. J., B. H. Sheppard, and M. H. Bazerman (eds), *Research on Negotiation in Organizations* (Vol. 1, pp. 43–55). Greenwich, CT: JAI Press.

Brett, J., Shapiro, D., and Lytle, A. (1998). Breaking the bonds of reciprocity in negotiations. *Academy of Management Journal*, 41, 410–424.

Carnevale, P., and Lawler, E. (1986). Time pressure and the development of integrative agreements in bilateral negotiations. *Journal of Conflict Resolution*, 30, 639–659.

Chaiken, S. (1987). The heuristic model of persuasion. In M. P. Zanna, and J. M. Olson (eds), *Social Influence: The Ontario Symposium* (Vol. 5, pp. 3–39). Hillsdale, NJ: Lawrence Erlbaum Assoc., Inc.

Chen, M. J., and Ayoko, O. B. (2012). Conflict and trust: The mediating effects of emotional arousal and self-conscious emotions. *International Journal of Conflict Management*, 23(1), 19–56.

Chen, Y., and Zhang, Y. (2021). Fostering resilience in new venture teams: The role of behavioral and affective integration. *Group & Organization Management*, 46(4), 773–816.

Choi, K., and Cho, B. (2011). Competing hypotheses analyses of the associations between group task conflict and group relationship conflict. *Journal of Organizational Behavior*, 32(8), 1106–1126.

Cosier, R., and Rose, G. (1977). Cognitive conflict and goal conflict effects on task performance. *Organizational Behavior and Human Performance*, 19, 378–391.

Cronin, M. A., and Bezrukova, K. (2019). Conflict management through the lens of system dynamics. *Academy of Management Annals*, 13(2), 770–806.

Cronin, M. A., Bezrukova, K., Weingart, L. R., and Tinsley, C. (2011). Subgroups within a team: The role of cognitive and affective integration. *Journal of Organizational Behavior*, 32, 831–849. doi: 10.1002/job.707

DeChurch, L. A., Mesmer-Magnus, J. R., and Doty, D. (2013). Moving beyond relationship and task conflict: toward a process-state perspective. *Journal of Applied Psychology*, 98(4), 559–578.

De Dreu, C. K. W. (2006). When too little or too much hurts: Evidence for a curvilinear relationship between task conflict and innovation in teams. *Journal of Management*, 32, 83–107.

De Dreu, C. K. W., Beersma, B., Stroebe, K., and Euwema, M. C. (2006). Motivated information processing, strategic choice, and the quality of negotiated agreement. *Journal of Personality and Social Psychology*, 90, 927–943.

De Dreu, C. K. W., and Carnevale, P. J. D. (2003). Motivational bases for information processing and strategic choice in conflict and negotiation. In M. P. Zanna (ed.), *Advances in Experimental Social Psychology* (Vol. 35, pp. 235–291). New York, Academic Press.

De Dreu, C. K. W., Evers, A., Beersma, B., Kluwer, E. S., and Nauta, A. (2001). A theory based measure of conflict management strategies in the workplace. *Journal of Organizational Behavior*, 22, 645–668.

De Dreu, C. K. W., Harinck, F., and Van Vianen, A. E. M. (1999). Conflict and performance in groups and organizations. *International Review of Industrial and Organizational Psychology*, 14, 369–414.

De Dreu, C. K. W., Koole, S., and Steinel, W. (2000). Unfixing the fixed pie: A motivated information-processing account of integrative negotiation. *Journal of Personality and Social Psychology*, 79, 975–987.

De Dreu, C. K., Nijstad, B. A., and Van Knippenberg, D. (2008). Motivated information processing in group judgment and decision making. *Personality and Social Psychology Review*, 12(1), 22–49.

De Dreu, C. K. W., and Van Vianen, E. M. (2001). Managing relationship conflict and the effectiveness of organizational teams, *Journal of Organizational Behavior*, 22, 309–328.

De Dreu, C. K. W., and Weingart, L. R. (2003). Task versus relationship conflict, team performance, and team member satisfaction: A meta-analysis. *Journal of Applied Psychology*, 88, 741–749.

De Dreu, C. K. W., Weingart, L. R. and Kwon, S. (2000). Influence of social motives on integrative negotiations: A meta-analytic review and test of two theories. *Journal of Personality and Social Psychology*, 78, 889–905.

De Grada, E., Kruglanski, A. W., Pierro, A., and Mannetti, L. (1999). Motivated cognition and group interaction: Need for closure affects the contents and processes of collective negotiations. *Journal of Experimental Social Psychology*, 35, 346–365.

De Jong, B. A., and Elfring, T. (2010). How does trust affect the performance of ongoing teams? The mediating role of reflexivity, monitoring, and effort. *Academy of Management Journal*, 53(3), 535–549.

De Wit, F. R., Greer, L. L., and Jehn, K. A. (2012). The paradox of intragroup conflict: A meta-analysis. *Journal of Applied Psychology*, 97(2), 360–390.

Deutsch, M. (2002). Social psychology's contributions to the study of conflict resolution. *Negotiation Journal*, 18(4), 307–320.

Druckman, D. (1994). Determinants of compromising behavior in negotiation. *Journal of Conflict Resolution*, 38, 507–556.

Eaton, J., and Sanders, C. B. (2012). A little help from our friends: Informal third parties and interpersonal conflict. *Personal Relationships*, 19(4), 623–643.

Edmondson, A. C., and Lei, Z. (2014). Psychological safety: The history, renaissance, and future of an interpersonal construct. *Annual Review of Organizational Psychology and Organizational Behavior*, 1(1), 23–43.

Ensley, M. D., and Hmieleski, K. A. (2005). A comparative study of new venture top management team composition, dynamics and performance between university-based and independent start-ups. *Research Policy*, 34, 1091–1105.

Festinger, L. (1950). Informal social communication. *Psychological Review*, 57(5), 271–282.

Garvin, D. A., and Roberto, M. A. (2001). What you don't know about making decisions. *Harvard Business Review*, 79(8), 108–119.

Gelfand, M. J., Leslie, L. M., Keller, K., and de Dreu, C. (2012). Conflict cultures in organizations: How leaders shape conflict cultures and their organizational-level consequences. *Journal of Applied Psychology*, 97(6), 1131–1147.

Gelfand, M. J., Nishii, L. H., Holcombe, K. M., Dyer, N., Ohbuchi, K. I., and Fukuno, M. (2001). Cultural influences on cognitive representations of conflict: Interpretations of conflict episodes in the United States and Japan. *Journal of Applied Psychology*, 86(6), 1059–1074.

Giebels, E., and Janssen, O. (2005). Conflict stress and reduced well-being at work: The buffering effect of third-party help. *European Journal of Work and Organizational Psychology*, 14(2), 137–155.

Greer, L., and Jehn, K. (2007). The pivotal role of emotion in intragroup process conflict. In M. Neale, E., Mannix, and C. Anderson (Eds.), *Research on Managing Groups and Teams*, pp. 21–43. Greenwich, CT: JAI Press.

Greer, L. L., Jehn, K. A., and Mannix, E. A. (2008). Conflict transformation: An exploration of the relationships between task, relationship, and process conflict and the moderating role of resolution potential. *Small Group Research*, 39(3), 278–302.

Greer, L. L., and van Kleef, G. A. (2010). Equality versus differentiation: The effects of power dispersion on group interaction. *Journal of Applied Psychology*, 95(6), 1032–1044.

Haskins, M. E., Liedtka, J., and Rosenblum, J. (1998). Beyond teams: Toward an ethic of collaboration. *Organizational Dynamics*, Spring, 34–50.

Humphrey, S. E., Aime, F., Cushenbery, L., Hill, A. D., and Fairchild, J. (2017). Team conflict dynamics: Implications of a dyadic view of conflict for team performance. *Organizational Behavior and Human Decision Processes*, 142, 58–70.

Janis, I. L. (1982). *Victims of groupthink* (2nd edition). Boston: Houghton-Mifflin.

Jehn, K. (1995). A multimethod examination of the benefits and detriments of intragroup conflict. *Administrative Science Quarterly*, 40, 256–282.

Jehn, K. (1997). A qualitative analysis of conflict types and dimensions in organizational groups. *Administrative Science Quarterly*, 42, 530–557.

Jehn, K. A., and Bezrukova, K. (2010). The faultline activation process and the effects of activated faultlines on coalition formation, conflict, and group outcomes. *Organizational Behavior and Human Decision Processes*, 112(1), 24–42.

Jehn, K. A., Greer, L., Levine, S., and Szulanski, G. (2008). The effects of conflict types, dimensions, and emergent states on group outcomes. *Group Decision and Negotiation*, 17(6), 465–495.

Jehn, K., and Rupert, J. (2008). "Group faultlines and team learning: How to benefit from different perspectives." In V. Sessa and M. London (eds), *Continuous Learning in Organizations: Individual, Group, and Organizational Perspectives* (pp. 119–148). Lawrence Erlbaum Press.

Kimmel, M. J., Pruitt, D. G., Magenau, J. M., Konar-Goldband, E., and Carnevale, P. J. D. (1980). Effects of trust, aspiration, and gender on negotiation tactics. *Journal of Personality and Social Psychology*, 38, 9–23.

Kruglanski, A. W. (1989). The psychology of being "right": The problem of accuracy in social perception and cognition. *Psychological Bulletin*, 106, 395–409.

Lerner, J. S., and Tetlock, P. E. (1999). Accounting for the effects of accountability. *Psychological Bulletin*, 125, 255–275.

Liang, T. P., Liu, C. C., Lin, T. M., and Lin, B. (2007). Effect of team diversity on software project performance. *Industrial Management and Data Systems*, 107, 636–653.

Locke, E. A., Tirnauer, D., Roberson, Q., Goldman, B., Latham, M. E., and Weldon, E. (2001). The importance of the individual in an age of groupism. In. M. E. Turner (ed.), *Groups at Work: Theory and Research* (pp. 501–528). Mahwah, NJ: Lawrence Erlbaum.

Lovelace, K., Shapiro, D. L., and Weingart, L. R. (2001). Maximizing crossfunctional new product teams' innovativeness and constraint adherence: A conflict communications perspective. *Academy of Management Journal*, 44, 779–783.

Maltarich, M. A., Kukenberger, M., Reilly, G., and Mathieu, J. (2018). Conflict in teams: Modeling early and late conflict states and the interactive effects of conflict processes. *Group & Organization Management*, 43(1), 6–37.

Manz, C. C., Barstein, D. T., Hostager, T. J., and Shapiro, G. L. (1989). Leadership and innovation: A longitudinal process view. In A. Van de Ven, H. L. Angle, and M. S. Poole (eds), *Research on the Management of Innovation: The Minnesota Studies* (pp. 613–636). New York: Harper and Row.

Matsuo, M. (2006). Customer orientation, conflict, and innovativeness in Japanese sales departments. *Journal of Business Research*, 59: 242–250.

Messick, D. M., and McClintock, C. G. (1968). Motivational basis of choice in experimental games. *Journal of Experimental Social Psychology*, 4, 1–25.

Mintzberg, H., Dougherty, D., Jorgensen, J., and Westley F. (1996). Some surprising things about collaboration – Knowing how people connect makes it work better. *Organizational Dynamics*, Spring, 60–71.

Murnighan, J., and Conlon, D. (1991). The dynamics of intense work groups: A study of British string quartets. *Administrative Science Quarterly*, 36, 165–186.

Olson, B. J., Parayitam, S., and Bao, Y. (2007). Strategic decision making: The effects of cognitive diversity, conflict, and trust on decision outcomes. *Journal of Management*, 33, 196–222.

O'Neill, T. A., Allen, N. J., and Hastings, S. E. (2013). Examining the "pros" and "cons" of team conflict: A team-level meta-analysis of task, relationship, and process conflict. *Human Performance*, 26(3), 236–260.

Overall, N. C., and McNulty, J. K. (2017). What type of communication during conflict is beneficial for intimate relationships? *Current Opinion in Psychology*, 13, 1–5.

Pai, J., and Bendersky, C. (2020). Team status conflict. *Current opinion in psychology*, 33, 38–41.

Pruitt, D. (1981). *Negotiation Behavior.* New York: Academic Press.

Pruitt, D., and Lewis, S. A. (1975). Development of integrative solutions in bilateral negotiation. *Journal of Personality and Social Psychology*, 31, 621–633.

Pruitt, D. G., and Rubin, J. Z. (1986). *Social Conflict: Escalation, Stalemate, and Settlement.* New York: McGraw-Hill.

Putnam, L. L., and Jones, T. S. (1982). Reciprocity in negotiations: An analysis of bargaining interaction. *Communication Monographs*, 49, 171–191.

Rodríguez-Sánchez, A. M., Hakanen, J., and Salanova, M. (2021). Building efficacy beliefs through team task engagement and past task performance in contemporary teams. *BRQ Business Research Quarterly*, 24(2), 129–142.

Rogers, C., and Farson, R. (1979). Active listening. In D. Kolb, I. Rubin, and J. MacIntyre, *Organizational Psychology* (3rd edition). New Jersey: Prentice Hall.

Römer, M., Rispens, S., Giebels, E., and Euwema, M. C. (2012). A helping hand? The moderating role of leaders' conflict management behavior on the conflict–stress relationship of employees. *Negotiation Journal*, 28(3), 253–277.

Rotter, J. B. (1971). Generalized expectations for interpersonal trust. *American Psychologist*, 26, 443–452.

Rubin, J. (1991). Some wise and mistaken assumptions about conflict and negotiation. *Journal of Social Issues*, 45, 195–209.

Salanova, M., Llorens, S., and Schaufeli, W. B. (2011). "Yes, I can, I feel good, and I just do it!" On gain cycles and spirals of efficacy beliefs, affect, and engagement. *Applied Psychology*, 60(2), 255–285.

Schei, V., Rognes, J. K., and De Dreu, C. K. W. (2008). Are individualistic orientations collectively valuable in group negotiations? *Group Processes and Intergroup Relations*, 11, 371–385.

Simons, T. L., and Peterson, R. S. (2000). Task conflict and relationship conflict in top management teams: The pivotal role of intragroup trust. *Journal of Applied Psychology*, 85, 102–111.

Somech, A., Desivilya, H. S., and Lidogoster, H. (2009). Team conflict management and team effectiveness: The effects of task interdependence and team identification. *Journal of Organizational Behavior: The International Journal of Industrial, Occupational and Organizational Psychology and Behavior*, 30(3), 359–378.

Thatcher, S., and Jehn, K. (1998). A model of group diversity profiles and categorization processes in bicultural organizational teams. In Neale, M. A., Mannix, E. A., and Gruenfeld, D. H. (eds), *Research on Managing Groups and Teams: Vol. 1. Composition* (pp. 1–20). Stamford, CT: JAI Press.

Thiel, C. E., Griffith, J. A., Hardy, J. H., III, Peterson, D. R., and Connelly, S. (2018). Let's look at this another way: How supervisors can help subordinates manage the threat of relationship conflict. *Journal of Leadership & Organizational Studies*, 25(3), 368–380.

Thiel, C. E., Harvey, J., Courtright, S., and Bradley, B. (2017). What doesn't kill you makes you stronger: How teams rebound from early-stage relationship conflict. *Journal of Management*, 45(4), 1623–1659.

Thompson, L. L. (1991). Information exchange in negotiation. *Journal of Experimental Social Psychology*, 27, 161–179.

Thompson, L. L., Mannix, E. A., and Bazerman, M. H. (1988). Group negotiation: Effects of decision rule, agenda, and aspiration. *Journal of Personality and Social Psychology*, 54, 86–95.

Tiedens, L. Z., and Fragale, A. R. (2003). Power moves: Complementarity in dominant and submissive nonverbal behavior. *Journal of Personality and Social Psychology*, 84(3), 558–568.

Todorova, G., Bear, J. B., and Weingart, L. R. (2014). Can conflict be energizing? A study of task conflict, positive emotions, and job satisfaction. *Journal of Applied Psychology*, 99(3), 451–467.

Todorova, G., Goh, K., and Weingart, L. R. (2021). *The Effects of Conflict Type and Conflict Expression Intensity on Conflict Management.* Manuscript submitted for publication.

Tsai, M. H., and Bendersky, C. (2016). The pursuit of information sharing: Expressing task conflicts as debates vs. disagreements increases perceived receptivity to dissenting opinions in groups. *Organization Science*, 27(1), 141–156.

Tyler, T., Degoey, P., and Smith, H. (1996). Understanding why the justice of group procedures matters. *Journal of Personality and Social Psychology*, 70, 913–930.

Tyler, T., and Lind, E. (1992). A relational model of authority in groups. In M. Zanna (ed.), *Advances in Experimental Social Psychology* (Vol. 25, pp. 115–191).

Van de Ven, A. H., and Chu, Y. (1989). A psychometric assessment of the Minnesota Innovation Survey. In A. H. Van de Ven, H. L. Angle, and M. S. Poole (eds), *Research on the Management of Innovation: The Minnesota Studies* (pp. 55–103). New York: Harper and Row.

van den Berg, W., Curseu, P. L., and Meeus, M. T. (2014). Emotion regulation and conflict transformation in multi-team systems. *International Journal of Conflict Management*, 25(2), 171–188.

Van Lange, P. A. M. (1999). The pursuit of joint outcomes and equality in outcomes: An integrative model of social value orientation. *Journal of Personality and Social Psychology*, 2, 337–349.

Von Glinow, M. A, Shapiro, D. L., and Brett, J. M. (2004). Can we talk, and should we? Managing emotional conflict in multicultural teams. *Academy of Management Review*, 29(4), 578–592.

Webster, D., and Kruglanski, A. W. (1994). Individual differences in need for cognitive closure. *Journal of Personality and Social Psychology*, 67, 1049–1062.

Weingart, L. R., Behfar, K. J., Bendersky, C., Todorova, G., and Jehn, K. A. (2015). The directness and oppositional intensity of conflict expression. *Academy of Management Review*, 40(2), 235–262.

Weingart, L. R., Bennett, R. J., and Brett, J. M. (1993). The impact of consideration of issues and motivational orientation on group negotiation process and outcome. *Journal of Applied Psychology*, 78, 504–517.

Weingart, L. R., Cronin, M. A., Houser, C. J. S., Cagan, J., and Vogel, C. (2005). Functional diversity and conflict in cross-functional product development teams: Considering representational gaps and task characteristics. In L. L. Neider and C. A. Schriesheim (eds), *Understanding Teams* (pp. 89–110). Greenwich, CT: IAP.

Weingart, L. R., Hyder, E. B., and Prietula, M. J. (1996). Knowledge matters: The effect of tactical descriptions on negotiation behavior and outcome. *Journal of Personality and Social Psychology*, 70, 1205–1217.

Weingart, L. R., Prietula, M. J., Hyder, E., and Genovese, C. (1999). Knowledge and the sequential processes of negotiation: A Markov chain analysis of response-in-kind. *Journal of Experimental Social Psychology*, 35, 366–393.

Exercises

Personal Assessment of Your Team Conflict Management Style

Using the DUTCH scale (De Dreu, Evers, Beersma, Kluwer, and Nauta, 2001)

1. *Use the following scale to respond to the following items as they describe how you typically approach conflict within a team. Answer in terms of your general tendencies across a broad range of situations.*
   1 = Never
   2 = Once in a while
   3 = Sometimes
   4 = Fairly often
   5 = Very frequently
   6 = Continually

	When I'm involved in a team conflict, I do the following:	Your Response
Y	I give in to other team members' wishes.	
F	I push my own point of view.	
P	I examine issues until I find a solution that really satisfies me and my other team members.	
C	I strive whenever possible toward a fifty-fifty compromise.	
A	I avoid differences of opinion as much as possible.	
F	I search for personal gains.	
P	I examine ideas from different sides to find a mutually optimal solution.	
C	I try to realize a middle-of-the-road solution.	
A	I avoid a confrontation about our differences.	
Y	I concur with the other team members.	
C	I insist we all give in a little.	
F	I do everything to win.	
P	I work out a solution that serves my own and others' interests as much as possible.	
Y	I try to accommodate the other team members.	
A	I avoid a confrontation about our differences.	
C	I emphasize that we have to find a compromise solution.	
Y	I adapt to other team members' goals and interests.	
F	I fight for a good outcome for myself.	
P	I stand up for my own and others' goals and concerns.	
A	I try to make differences loom less severe.	

2. *Average the scores for the questions that have the same letter preceding them (A, C, F, P, Y). For example, if you filled out all 5s for Y, your average score for Y is "5." Each average represents your reliance on a specific conflict management approach.*
3. *Identify your dominant conflict management approach and consider the questions associated with each approach.*

A = Avoiding – you tend to avoid conflicts that occur. *Ask yourself, "Am I avoiding all conflicts (task and relationship)? How is my reliance on avoiding helping or hindering my team's performance?"*

C = Compromise – the higher the score the more likely you are to compromise when faced with a conflict. While meeting in the middle may seem fair, sometimes you can miss opportunities to find creative solutions that are better than average for everyone. *Ask yourself, "When will compromise be the most or least effective way in dealing with my team's conflict?"*

F = Force – People who score high on forcing like to get their way, regardless of others' concerns. While this might be satisfying to you in the short term, it can leave other team members feeling resentful and unwilling to work with you in the future. *Ask yourself, "Under what circumstances do I tend to rely on forcing? What are the typical repercussions that I face? What alternative approaches are usually available to me?"*

P = Problem-solve – Problem-solvers work hard to find solutions that meet the needs of everyone involved in the conflict. They try to satisfy others without losing sight of their own interests. *Ask yourself, "How does problem-solving best promote cooperation within a team? What are the costs of using this approach?"*

Y = Yield – A yielding approach is the opposite of forcing. Yielders give in to the demands of others. This approach may end the conflict, but can leave you feeling taken advantage of. However, yielding can lead to a strategy of reciprocation, that is, "I'll give in now, but you owe me." *Ask yourself, "What are the risks of relying on yielding, especially when you consider that open discussion of alternatives and respect are critical to group success?"*

4. *Break into small groups, ideally groups of people who have worked together before. Share your scores with one another. Discuss whether others see your conflict management approach as determined by this scale. What do they see as your strengths? Weaknesses?*

Video Analysis and Discussion

Please watch the following video(s):

1. Why there's so much conflict at work and what you can do about it: https://www.youtube.com/watch?v=2l-AOBz69KU
2. What productive conflict can offer a workplace: https://www.youtube.com/watch?v=kmNejqbx1M0

Now form small groups to discuss the video(s) and answer the following questions:

1. What are the major points of the video?
2. How can you use information from the video in your career?
3. Based on the video, what advice do you have for leaders in organizations?

Be prepared to present the ideas from your small group discussion with the class as a whole.

Discussion Questions

Gather in groups of three people. Each person needs to come prepared to discuss a conflict situation from their personal work or school experience.

1. Each participant: Come prepared to discuss a conflict situation in which you are currently or were recently involved on a team at work or at school. Describe

who is involved (no names necessary, just their relationship with you), what the conflict is about (describe the nature of the conflict, issues, and concerns), where it occurred (context), when it occurred (how recent, how frequently), and how it unfolded (actions and reactions; how people behave or typically manage the conflict).

2. Discuss the conflict situation in terms of the principles outlined in this chapter. Some possible discussion questions are outlined as follows:
   a) What type of conflict occurred? Task, process, relationship, status, or some combination?
   b) What was the root cause of the conflict? Was it driven by differences in personality, areas of expertise, culture, etc.?
   c) How was the conflict expressed in terms of oppositional intensity and directness? If indirect and/or with high intensity, why? How did this impact the emotionality of the conflict and the information that was gained? How did this influence the team's ability to understand and manage the conflict?
   d) Did the conflict escalate over time? Did it transform from one type to another? At what point did the team begin to address the conflict? What impact did that have on your ability to manage the conflict?
   e) Was everyone in the team equally comfortable in dealing with the conflict? If no, how did you deal with people's differing comfort levels?
   f) What approach did the team use in managing the conflict? Was it an appropriate approach? Were there alternative ways for doing so?
   g) Was the situation ripe for collaboration?
      (i) Was there a focus on teamwork? Did team members feel prepared to manage the conflict that arose? Did team members trust and respect one another? Were the conflict communication norms open?
      (ii) Describe the motives of team members. What were the team members' primary motivations regarding cooperation? Were members epistemically motivated?
   h) Did the conflict help or hinder the team's performance? Why and how?
   i) What role did you play in the conflict? Did you help or hinder its resolution? What were your strengths in handling the situation? What could you do to improve your ability to collaborate through conflict situations?

21

Clarity, Conciseness, and Consistency Are the Keys to Effective Communication

JEAN PHILLIPS

Pennsylvania State University

Communication is a social behavior that constitutes a vital element of our everyday lives, as it enables us to send and receive information and build and maintain relationships. Within the realm of work, organizations can be viewed as a nexus of communications that occur within and outside their boundaries. Communication is the process of exchanging, conveying, or expressing ideas or information to create a shared understanding and feeling. Effective communication does not require agreement between the sender and the receiver, only the transmission and reception by the receiver of information as it was intended by the sender. Effective communication ultimately happens when the sender's message is efficiently received by the intended audience without misunderstanding.

Because it is how trust, respect, and engagement are built and maintained, effective communication is the glue that holds an organization together (Cho, 2020) and that allows individuals, teams, and business units to work interdependently. For example, although deep-level diversity such as the functional diversity of team members can reduce a team's ability to reach a consensus, research findings suggest that staying task-focused and proactively working together to achieve a shared mental model of decision-making help such teams utilize effective communication to overcome this risk (Knight, Pearce, Smith, Olian, Sims, Smith, and Flood, 1999). Organizations with more effective communication are higher performing (Snyder and Morris, 1984) as employees can get their message across faster and with fewer misunderstandings, reducing the chances of mistakes or conflict. The better you personally communicate, the more likely it is that you will be able to get what you need to be successful. Despite its importance, one of the biggest challenges in most relationships, even at work, is communication.

Communicating with clarity, conciseness, and consistency is essential to effectively communicating in the workplace. Unclear messages communicated vaguely or in a lengthy manner are likely to create misunderstandings and result in missed information. Information that is communicated inconsistently is also more likely to lead to conflict, create confusion, and decrease trust (Ayoki and Pekerti, 2008). Taking the time to learn how to be an effective communicator and to avoid common communication errors helps individuals and organizations to be more effective and perform their best. After reviewing the communication process, we will discuss the main types of communication and explore the importance of clarity, conciseness, and consistency in effective communication.

How Communication Happens

Regardless of the message being sent, communication takes place through the process of encoding and decoding. Encoding happens when a message sender's thoughts are converted into a message that is transmitted over a communication channel or media. Decoding is the subsequent process of the receiver turning the communication back into their own thoughts and understandings, which may or may not be the same as those intended by the sender. As illustrated in Figure 21.1, the message sender first encodes an intended message and, then, transmits it over their chosen communication channel or media (e.g. verbally, a text message, a video, a face-to-face meeting, etc.). For example, a CEO might intend to send a supportive message to employees working hard during a busy period. They could encode these thoughts into an email or in-house video (the communication medium or channel) expressing gratitude and support to the employees. The recipients then receive and decode, or interpret, the message into meaning. Noise, including unnecessarily long or vague messages, distraction such as music or sirens, and poor video quality, is anything that disrupts or reduces the clarity of the communication

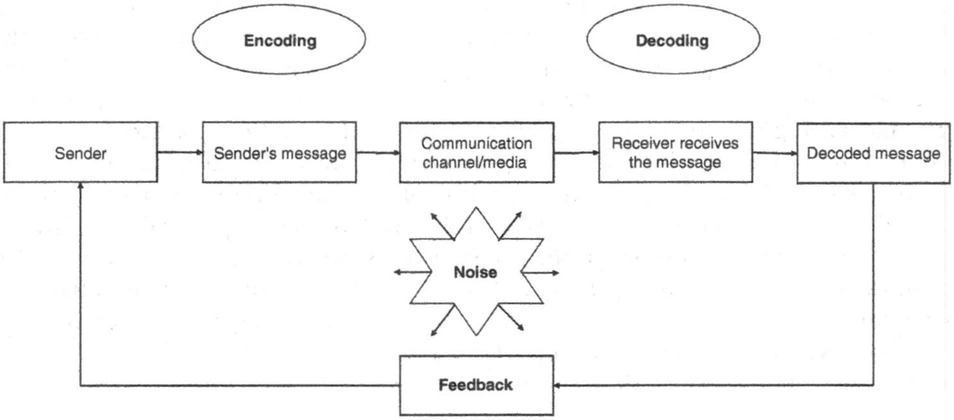

FIGURE 21.1 The communication process

and the nature of the message received. Noise can interfere with the communication process at every step and should be minimized to enhance the accuracy of the decoded message as well as the efficiency of the communication process. Communicating with clarity, conciseness, and consistency helps to reduce noise. Feedback happens when the message receiver communicates any response to the message, verbal or nonverbal, back to the sender, and allows the sender to evaluate how accurately the message has been received. Active listening is an important component of feedback that will be discussed later in the chapter.

Types of Communication

Communication can be verbal, nonverbal, or written. Verbal communication is typically done to inform or persuade, or to express or discuss ideas. Nonverbal communication is an important component of verbal communication (although it can happen without a verbal element) that consists of body language including facial expressions, hand gestures, and eye contact. Albert Mehrabian (1968) found that 7% of meaning is derived from words, 55% comes from our body language, and 38% from our tone of voice. Written communication lacks body language but serves the same purposes as verbal communication.

Given the importance of body language to the receiver's interpretation of a message with or without a verbal component, it is important to understand the nonverbal cues you are sending and to strategically manage them to reinforce your intended message. Consciously sending information via nonverbal behavior has the potential to communicate meaning if the behavior is noticed and depending on how it is interpreted by the receiver, which can be influenced by factors including culture (Bonaccio, O'Reilly, O'Sullivan, and Chiocchio, 2016) and any sort of noise. When we are busy or stressed, it can be harder to do this effectively, but these are often the times when it is most important to ensure that our body language is consistently reinforcing our intended message. Table 21.1 highlights some tips for strategically managing your body language.

Table 21.1 Body language tips

Make regular eye contact (but do not stare)
Lean forward to show interest
Avoid scowling or displaying a negative facial expression, and do use appropriate facial expressions
Occasionally nod to reflect your understanding
Uncross your arms and do not hide or clench your hands
Keep your head up
Do not fidget
Do not check the time
Mimic the sender's body language
Identify and attend to cultural norms including personal space

As interdependent work groups gain experience and skills in working together, their communication is likely to become increasingly nonverbal. Some high-performing teams conduct complex work while hardly saying a word as each member has a shared mental model of the team's work process and can recognize nonverbal cues signaling that other members need help. New team members will not be familiar with the nonverbal information being communicated by established team members, however, requiring the team to take the time to assimilate the new members and adapt to the new person's communication style. Furthermore, the novelty and stress of a new member will require teams to build new communication patterns to adapt to their new dynamics (Harrison, Mohammed, McGrath, Florey, and Vanderstoep, 2003).

Clarity

Clear communication requires an organized message and an avoidance of confusing information or information that could be misinterpreted. Slang and jargon should be avoided unless you are sure it will be correctly understood by the audience. Avoid being vague, and give clear examples where needed. Although always beneficial, communication clarity is essential during goal setting meetings, performance reviews, and succession planning discussions. It is particularly important for complex information to be presented as clearly as possible.

When communicating verbally, nonverbal cues from the listener including head nodding or a furrowed brow can help the speaker identify whether their message is coming across clearly. Occasionally asking for any questions can also help gauge audience comprehension. Taking the time to organize your thoughts before speaking and using reinforcing body language also improves message clarity.

Because we tend to write them quickly, emails are one of the places in which we are most likely to communicate poorly. When writing emails, use the email subject line to convey your main point, draw the reader in, or highlight a deadline. Rather than the subject "Agenda," consider "Agenda for 3 p.m. Thursday meeting to discuss the LDR policy; your input needed by 5 Tuesday." Also try to limit each email to a single topic and state the purpose of the email in the first sentence. Although it can be tempting to send off an email immediately, it is a good idea to read it over and use spellcheck if necessary, to ensure that it is organized, clear, and concise. Also check that misinterpretations are unlikely, and any likely questions are anticipated and addressed in the message.

Conciseness

Conciseness in communication can be conceptualized as a situation where the substance of the message is maximized, while, simultaneously, the time needed to communicate this message is minimized. In general, the aim of concise communication is to "say more with less." Some of the common errors that reduce message conciseness include the lack of a specific focus in the message, digressing to issues/topics that are not the focus of the message (this dilutes the importance of the core message), being unorganized, and communicating unnecessary information (Marques, 2010).

Avoiding information overload is a key to achieving conciseness in our messages. Information overload happens when we feel we have too much information to process and are prevented from making a decision or taking action because of this. One of the best ways to avoid information overload detracting from the receiver's ability to process your message is to ensure that the message you are trying to communicate is well-organized and not too lengthy for the medium you are using or for the audience of your message. This is more than merely avoiding filler words such as "um" or "uh" and requires the sender to avoid extraneous words or information that add length without adding new content. Receivers have limited attention spans, making it in the sender's best interest to focus their attention on the information the sender considers to be most important.

In crafting a message, it is also critical to consider the intended recipient of the message, the message's length, as well as any information that is deemed as necessary and appropriate to effectively communicating the intended message. The characteristics of the recipients (e.g. educational background or fluency in the language used in the communication) and the perceived relevance of the conveyed information are critical as they serve as the basis that will determine the extent to which a message will be perceived as "concise," "unnecessary/unfocused/lengthy," or "lacking information/short." In some situations, it might be worth it to consider communicating the same broad information to different groups via different messages that vary in terms of their length and the depth of information provided. Many large organizations do this with different segments of their intended applicant pool to allow them to highlight the features most important to each group (e.g. interns, new college graduates, experienced hires, and rehires).

Another important aspect of communication conciseness is the way meetings are scheduled and run. It has been estimated that employees attend 55 million meetings a day in the United States, for only modest returns (Rogelberg, 2019). It is, thus, important that before scheduling a meeting, we consider whether the message we want to communicate during that meeting can be communicated more efficiently and concisely through an email, an announcement, or another communication channel/medium. Meetings, however, are often necessary, and it is worth investing in making them more efficient and effective. Clear and concise communication before, during, and after a meeting is key to effective meetings. Table 21.2 summarizes some tips for making meetings more effective.

Consistency

In most cases, we repeatedly communicate a message via various channels/media or multiple times via the same channel/medium. Even our everyday verbal communications are accompanied by planned and unplanned nonverbal communication.

Table 21.2 Running effective meetings

Have a good reason to meet (if email or another technology will suffice, use it instead)
Follow a timed agenda distributed in advance
Limit the meeting time
Ensure everyone has a chance to be heard (this may mean limiting the time of more dominant attendees)
If possible, asking participants to review important materials prior to the meeting gives everyone time to process the information prior to meeting and avoids wasting meeting time while participants read them
Distribute a summary of the meeting after it ends

It is, therefore, important that the messages being communicated be consistent across channels/media or over time. But what does it mean for messages to be consistent? The key principles of message consistency involve ensuring that the core of the message remains the same and that there are no contradictions across messages (Williams and Eosco, 2021).

The concept of integrated marketing communication has been identified as an important element of a product marketing campaign. Integrated marketing communication entails that an organization strategically controls the messages in all communications channels of the company in order to ensure that these messages are consistent (Smith, Berry, and Pulforsd, 1999). By keeping the messages consistent, a company can ensure that consumers have a clear idea about the brand or the product (Holm, 2006). An inconsistently communicated message is unlikely to be interpreted as the sender intended and is likely to lead to confusion and inaction. Inconsistency, for instance, between the verbal and nonverbal components of a message also undermines the ability of the receiver to accurately interpret the message being sent. For example, a verbal message sent by your boss praising your work while they lean back shaking their head with crossed arms and a furrowed brow would not be received as clearly or strongly as the same praise given with a smile, eye contact, and a forward lean.

Communicating important information once and assuming all employees or even a single employee received and understood the message is a mistake. The more important the information, the more important that it be consistently communicated multiple times, often using multiple communication channels. One organization facing an imminent technology change sent employees a single email and assumed everyone was on the same page. No status updates or follow-up information was provided, causing the staff to feel surprised when the technology was implemented. Employees were understandably angry and overwhelmed, which contributed to a decrease in productivity and job satisfaction (Cho, 2020). On the other hand, when Nucor Steel's business slowed during a global recession, its managers relied on regular communication to maintain morale. The CEO doubled the time he spent in the company's plants, and one plant's general manager sent weekly updates to his staff on order volumes (Byrnes, 2009).

The repetition of a consistent message enhances memory (Pang and Elntib, 2021) and is also important for the process of persuasion (Cacioppo and Petty, 1989; Dillard, 2019). Consistently repeating a concise message helps to minimize the effects of noise and increases the chances that the receiver will receive, process, and remember the message being communicated.

Active Listening

Effectively communicating with someone often requires listening as well as communicating. If your communication partner does not feel heard or valued, they are much less likely to respond positively to your message. Letting the other person speak and ask questions, and actively and positively listening while they do without interrupting, is part of an effective communication process. Active listening has often been described as one's ability to accurately perceive both the meaning and the affective components of what someone else communicates (Rogers, 1959) and entails both the attitude of the listener and their technical listening skills (Mineyama, Tsutsumi, Takao, Nishiuchi, and Kawakami, 2007).

According to Bodie (2011), there are three main stages in active listening. First, the listener needs to engage in a process of capturing the information that is being communicated ("sensing") (Gearhart and Bodie, 2011). Second, the listener needs to try to interpret and synthesize the received information ("processing") (Gearhart and Bodie, 2011). Finally, the listener needs to react to this information through verbal or nonverbal cues ("responding") (Gearhart and Bodie, 2011). Even though most of the active listening stages are more esoteric without clear external manifestations, there are some tactics one could follow in order to enhance their active listening and also signal to the speakers that they are actively listening. To actively listen when someone is speaking, be present and devote your time and full attention to them. Check that your body language is conveying positive attention by leaning forward and making eye contact and suspend judgment until the speaker has finished. You can show interest in the speaker's message by nodding, asking for additional information, and inviting additional clarification or elaboration. Table 21.3 highlights some listening behaviors to avoid.

Table 21.3 Listening behaviors to avoid

Interrupting
Criticizing or arguing
Becoming distracted
Responding emotionally
Negative body language (crossing arms, leaning backward, rolling eyes, etc.)
Not making eye contact

Overcoming Communication Barriers

Communication is not simply the message being sent but is an important process that determines the success of employees, teams, and the organization as a whole. However, this communication process can be compromised by many potential barriers that create noise and hinder communication. The sender or receiver's body language, the attitudes and knowledge of the receiver, and cultural differences can all influence how clearly a message is received. If barriers exist in communication, then clarity and understanding of the message do not occur. Table 21.4 describes several common communication barriers.

However, there are ways in which employees and organizations can work to reduce barriers to communication. Training on effective communication strategies can enhance both sender and receiver behaviors to enhance body language as mentioned in Table 21.1 and decrease those issues mentioned in Table 21.3. Furthermore, cross-cultural training could help employees identify and recognize differences in cultural communication patterns and tailor their messages for different individuals. Choosing the most effective medium for the communication of a message is also important. Sometimes a brief text will suffice; other times only a face-to-face meeting is appropriate. The setting and timing of the message also influences how it is received. Some meetings should be private; others timed to avoid holidays or settings that might prompt negative reactions from the receiver.

Changes in organization communication styles might also help to remove barriers. For example, some organizations employ a trickle-down communication style that prevents employees not "in the loop" from receiving the information. These organizations often implement hierarchical structures with large power distance between supervisors and subordinates. This top-down communication style might help in reducing information overload but increases filtering of information from

Table 21.4 Common communication barriers

Barrier	*Description*
Selective perception	The receiver receives a limited amount of the message based on their expectations and beliefs, usually to reinforce preexisting beliefs
Misperception	The receiver does not understand the message in the way the sender intended
Filtering	Information is intentionally withheld by the sender or ignored or distorted by the receiver in a way that influences the message received
Information overload	An abundance of information can make it difficult to process all of it, making clarity and conciseness important in preventing this
Organizational culture or structure	Can influence who is able and allowed to communicate what to whom, and may limit how communications may be sent
Cultural differences	Different national cultures have different norms and ways of expressing information and ideas

lower-level employees, which could cause message distortion. For example, think of the "telephone game" where one person whispers a phrase or thought and then passes it to the next person who passes it to the next, etc. By the end of the game, the last person rarely hears the message the first person intended as meaning was lost from one person to the next. However, a flattened communication structure where information is more widely disseminated decreases distortion as all employees get their information from the same source. This also promotes open communication where employees feel they have a voice and are empowered in their organizations (Kaufman, 2015). The more information is communicated to all employees in a consistent, clear, and concise manner, the more employees will feel engaged to maintain their workplace relationships and empowered to pursue organizational goals.

Case Examples

Effective Communication

Under Bill Gates' leadership, Microsoft was known for having a cutthroat environment in which employees and teams routinely competed against each other. One day, Gates called Satya Nadella, the leader of the Bing search engine project at the time, into a meeting to discuss a possible software acquisition to enhance the company's cloud system Azure. Although Nadella knew that Bing had already incorporated the technology being considered, instead of suggesting that Microsoft fold it into Azure, Nadella sat quietly and said nothing. Nadella believed that higher authorities saw Bing as the loss-making division and self-censored his comment. He later recognized that Microsoft's culture and workplace environment interfered with his taking the appropriate initiative to speak up (James, 2021).

Learning from this experience, one of the things Nadella did when he became CEO of Microsoft is transform the company's meeting culture. He tells employees to skip pointless meetings that waste his time and meets with his top leadership team every Friday for four hours, with one meeting a month lasting eight hours. He feels that it is critical that the senior leadership stays on the same page to avoid devolving into a bunch of silos (Lebowitz, 2015). His three rules for better meetings are (Bariso, 2019):

1. Listen more.
2. Talk less.
3. Be decisive when the time comes.

Questions:

1. How do Nadella's meeting rules enhance communication effectiveness?
2. What other meeting rules do you think would enhance communication effectiveness?
3. In addition to weekly meetings, how else can senior leadership communicate to ensure that team members are all on the same page?

Ineffective Communication

The Deepwater Horizon oil rig explosion in the Gulf of Mexico resulted in eleven worker deaths and the largest oil spill in history. Almost 5 million barrels of oil polluted the gulf, killing millions of animals and damaging ecosystems as well as costing BP, the company that ran the rig, over $42 billion in civil and criminal settlements (The Maritime Executive, 2021).

A Presidential Commission charged with identifying the causes of the disaster identified not only technology failures, but also a failure of management that included major communication failures. BP, its engineering firm Haliburton, and Transocean which owned the rig had failed to clearly share multiple technology issues from the beginning of the drilling operation. On the day of the explosion, although rig technicians' pressure tests indicated that something might be wrong, the results were never communicated to, taken seriously by, or properly interpreted by managers. Additional communication failures complicated the cleanup effort (Hurley Write, 2021).

The President's Report concluded that "better communication within and between BP and its contractors" could have helped to prevent the explosion (National Commission on the BP Deepwater Horizon Oil Spill and Offshore Drilling, 2011). This highlights the need to establish effective communication procedures when different departments or organizations are working together, and the need for technicians, engineers, and scientists as well as public relations and communications employees who need to be able to receive, analyze, and share information effectively.

Questions:

1. At what types of communication should rig technicians be particularly skilled? Why?
2. How can an employer improve communication effectiveness across different departments? Why is doing this important?
3. How can an employer improve the ability of all employees to effectively share information concisely, clearly, and consistently?

Exercise

Rewrite this email to be more concise and to more clearly communicate the intended message.

Title: Meeting

Hi team,

I hope you are all enjoying the wonderful weather we've been seeing this week. I've personally been getting a lot of hiking in after work and hope it continues.

I'm writing to remind you that we will have a full staff meeting next Wednesday from 3-4 in room 323, the long conference room that was recently refurbished. This might be the first time several of you will have a chance to see it. I hope you like it—I think the contractors did a great job.

As always, I'll circulate an agenda for the meeting by noon Tuesday. We have some room left in the meeting if anyone has anything they would like to discuss or remind everyone. Please send me any meeting input by 9 am Tuesday so I have a chance to edit the agenda as needed.

I hope you all have a terrific day!

Sam

Video Analysis and Discussion

Please watch the following video(s):

1. "The Art of Effective Communication" by Marcus Alexander Velazquez (12:07) https://www.youtube.com/watch?v=2Yw6dFQBklA&t=25s&ab_channel=TEDxTalks

Now form small groups to discuss the video(s) and answer the following questions:

1. What is the role of humility in effective communication?
2. What does the speaker mean when he says, "It is what you say?" How can you use this insight to be a more effective communicator?
3. What does the speaker mean when he says, "Your actions will either promote or nullify your words?" How can you ensure that your actions promote your words?
4. What do you think is the most important point made by the video regarding effective communication?

Be prepared to present the ideas from your small group discussion with the class as a whole.

Discussion Questions

1. Provide an example of a miscommunication at work. What could have been done to prevent this from happening?
2. Provide an example of a situation where you felt that "this meeting could have been an email." Why did you feel this way? How could have the same message been communicated more efficiently and concisely?
3. What are some potential consequences of poor communication in the workplace?
4. What are the three components of effective communication? Why is each an important piece of the communication process?

Conclusion

Communication is a vital process of employee, team, and organizational success. Communication allows for the dissemination of knowledge and information to build shared understandings and feelings across communication partners. Effective communication is the use of clarity, conciseness, and consistency when exchanging or expressing ideas or information. Through clarity, information is presented in an organized message that avoids confusing information or information that can be misinterpreted. Conciseness allows for a message to be presented with a specific focus, in an organized manner such that no unnecessary information is presented. Finally, consistency is the continued presentation of the same message no matter the media used to present the message, the channels through which the message travels, or the amount of time that passes between message presentations. The use of clear, concise, and consistent communication ensures that the receiver is able to accurately decode and utilize the information sent in a message.

Effective communication also relies on active listening by the receiver and reductions in barriers to communication. Interruptions, distractions, and negative body language can all impede the success of communication. Furthermore, information overload or poor organizational communication structures might increase message distortion, making it hard for the original message to be decoded by the receiver. As organizations continue to look for ways to reduce the noise that interferes with effective communication, employee morale, satisfaction, and productivity are likely to increase as clear, concise, and consistent messages are conveyed.

References

Ayoki, O. B., and Pekerti, A. A. (2008). The mediating and moderating effects of conflict and communication openness on workplace trust. *International Journal of Conflict Management,* 19(4), 297–318.

Bariso, J. (July 31, 2019). Microsoft's CEO knows how to run a meeting: Here's how he does it, *Inc.* Retrieved from https://www.inc.com/justin-bariso/microsofts-ceo-knows-how-to-run-a-meeting-heres-how-he-does-it.html.

Bodie, G. D. (2011). The Active-Empathic Listening Scale (AELS): Conceptualization and evidence of validity within the interpersonal domain. *Communication Quarterly,* 59, 277–295.

Bonaccio, S., O'Reilly, J., O'Sullivan, S. L., and Chiocchio, F. (2016). Nonverbal behavior and communication in the workplace: A review and an agenda for research. *Journal of Management,* 42(5), 1044–1074.

Byrnes, N. (2009, April 6). A steely resolve. *Businessweek,* 54.

Cacioppo, J. T., and Petty, R. E. (1989). Effects of message repetition on argument processing, recall, and persuasion. *Basic and Applied Social Psychology,* 10(1), 3–12.

Cho, C. (March 25, 2020). Communication: The Glue that holds an organization together. *Forbes*. Retrieved from https://www.forbes.com/sites/forbesnonprofitcouncil/2020/03/25/communication-the-glue-that-holds-an-organization-together/?sh=7484878279c8.

Dillard, J. P. (2019). Currents in the study of persuasion. In M. B. Oliver, A. A. Raney, and J. Bryant (eds), *Media Effects: Advances in Theory and Research* (pp. 115–129), New York: Routledge.

Gearhart, C. G., and Bodie, G. D. (2011). Active-empathic listening as a general social skill: Evidence from bivariate and canonical correlations. *Communication Reports*, 24, 86–98.

Harrison, D. A., Mohammed, S., McGrath, J. E., Florey, A. T., and Vanderstoep, S. W. (2003). Time matters in team performance: Effects of member familiarity, entrainment, and task discontinuity on speed and quality. *Personnel Psychology*, 56, 633–669.

Holm, O. (2006). Integrated marketing communication: from tactics to strategy. *Corporate Communications: An International Journal*, 11(1), 22–33.

James, N. (October 4, 2021). Microsoft CEO Satya Nadella says his 'Moment of Failure' in a meeting with Bill Gates completely changed his leadership style. *Daily Post LA*. Retrieved from https://dailypostla.com/news/finance/banking/microsoft-ceo-satya-nadella-says-his-moment-of-failure-in-a-meeting-with-bill-gates-completely-changed-his-leadership-style/.

Kaufman, B. E. (2015). Theorising determinants of employee voice: An integrative model across disciplines and levels of analysis. *Human Resource Management Journal*, *25*(1), 19–40.

Knight, D., Pearce, C. L., Smith, K. G., Olian, J. D., Sims, H. P., Smith, K. A., and Flood, P. (1999). Top management team diversity, group process, and strategic consensus. *Strategic Management Journal*, 20(5), 445–465.

Lebowitz, S. (October 2, 2015). The CEO of Microsoft has an 8-hour meeting with his leadership team every month. *BusinessInsider.com*. Retrieved from https://www.businessinsider.com/how-microsoft-ceo-satya-nadella-runs-meetings-2015-10?op=1.

Marques, J. F. (2010). Enhancing the quality of organizational communication: A presentation of reflection-based criteria. *Journal of Communication Management*, 14(1), 47–58.

Mehrabian, A. (1968). Communication Without Words. *Psychology Today*, 2(9), 52–55.

Mineyama, S., Tsutsumi, A., Takao, S., Nishiuchi, K., and Kawakami, N. (2007). Supervisors' attitudes and skills for active listening with regard to working conditions and psychological stress reactions among subordinate workers. *Journal of Occupational Health*, 49, 81–87.

National Commission on the BP Deepwater Horizon Oil Spill and Offshore Drilling (2011). Deep water: The gulf oil disaster and the future of offshore drilling. Retrieved from https://cybercemetery.unt.edu/archive/oilspill/20121211005728/http://www.oilspillcommission.gov/sites/default/files/documents/DEEPWATER_ReporttothePresident_FINAL.pdf.

Pang, D. K., and Elntib, S. (2021). Strongly masked content retained in memory made accessible through repetition. *Scientific Reports*, 11(1), 1–10.

Rogelberg, S. G. (2019). Why your meetings stink – and what to do about it. *Harvard Business Review*, 140–143.

Rogers, C. R. (1959). *A Theory of Therapy, Personality, and Interpersonal Relationships: As Developed in the Client Centered Framework.* New York, NY: McGraw-Hill.

Smith, P. R., Berry, C., and Pulford, A. (1999). *Strategic Marketing Communications.* London: Kogan Page.

Snyder, R. A., and Morris, J. H. (1984). Organizational communication and performance. *Journal of Applied Psychology*, 69(3), 461–465.

The Maritime Executive (2021). Deepwater horizon costing BP $42 billion. *The Maritime Executive.* Retrieved from https://maritime-executive.com/article/deepwater-horizon-costing-bp-42-billion.

Williams, C. A., and Eosco, G. M. (2021). Is a consistent message achievable?: Defining "message consistency" for weather enterprise researchers and practitioners. *Bulletin of the American Meteorological Society*, 102(2), E279–E295.

22

Stimulate Creativity by Fueling Passion

COLIN M. FISHER[1] AND TERESA M. AMABILE[2]

[1]UCL School of Management
[2]Harvard Business School

How can organizations support the creativity of their members? Many managers think that tools like rewards and deadlines consistently motivate employees to do their best work. Although external pressures and rewards are motivating for simple, routine tasks, they can undermine interest and enjoyment from the work itself. And, from decades of research on creativity, one of the most important – and surprising insights – is: People will be most creative when they feel motivated primarily by the interest, enjoyment, and challenge of the work itself – and not by external pressures. This "Intrinsic Motivation Principle of Creativity" (Amabile, 1996; Amabile and Pratt, 2016) suggests that the social environment, particularly the presence or absence of external pressures in that environment, can influence creativity by influencing people's passion for their work. Managers can catalyze creativity in their organizations by establishing work environments that support passion for the work.

Intrinsic motivation is the motivation to do work because it is interesting, engaging, or positively challenging. In its highest form, it is called passion and can lead to complete absorption in the work (Csikszentmihalyi, 1990). The elements that make up intrinsic motivation include a sense of *self-determination* in doing the work (rather than a sense of being a pawn of someone else), a feeling that *one's skills are being both fully utilized* and further developed, and *positive feelings about the work*, which may be akin to positive affect or positive emotion (e.g. Deci, Koestner, and Ryan, 1999; Deci and Ryan, 1985; Lepper and Greene, 1978).

Before effects of the work environment on the passion for creativity can be fully understood, it is important to define the basic concepts. Creativity within an organization is the production of novel, appropriate ideas by individuals or small groups.

Those ideas can appear in any organizational activity and are not limited to the domains usually considered to be "creative" (such as R&D, marketing, and strategy formulation). Innovation is the successful implementation of creative ideas by an organization. Notice that ideas cannot be merely new to be considered creative; they must be somehow appropriate to the problem or task at hand. Notice also that it is possible to have many creative contributions – that is, a great deal of creative behavior by individual employees or teams – without having any significant innovation within an organization. This outcome will arise if the new ideas are not communicated or developed effectively within the organization. However, it is not possible to have much innovation in an organization without considerable creativity.

Contrary to popular notions that creativity is the sole province of a few rare geniuses, creativity appears across most levels of human ability. This suggests a continuum of creativity from the simplest "garden variety" ideas for small improvements to the highest levels of creative achievement in any field. Certainly, products at the highest levels of creativity appear to be qualitatively different from products at the lower levels; it seems odd to compare the invention of the microcomputer with an incrementally improved microcomputer processor. However, the underlying processes do appear to be the same. A useful analogy comes from work in dynamic systems, which has shown that the different gaits of a horse on a treadmill (walking, trotting, cantering, and galloping) appear to be qualitatively different activities. Yet these qualitatively different outcomes arise from gradual quantitative increases in the underlying system: the speed of the treadmill and the energy output of the horse. Similarly, it is quite possible that the most astonishing human accomplishments come about by people doing more, and better, work than goes into the more ordinary instances of creativity in everyday life. In fact, people underestimate the value of motivation and effort in creative work – they believe that persistence in creative endeavors is far less important than it actually is (Lucas and Nordgren, 2015). Motivation is, thus, one of the most important, yet misunderstood, determinants of creativity at work.

Contextual Factors: Features of the Work Environment

Several features of the work environment influence intrinsic motivation and creativity. *Challenge,* a sense of having to work hard on personally important, enriched, and meaningful tasks, appears to be crucial. *Autonomy,* a sense of freedom in how to carry out one's work, also plays a significant role. *Work Group Supports* include feelings of mutual support for ideas, constructive feedback on ideas, and shared commitment to the work within a team; they also include a broad *diversity of skills* and backgrounds within the team. Diversity of skills and backgrounds can even mean including individuals lacking "standard" areas of expertise. *Supervisory Encouragement* includes setting clear strategic goals for a project (while allowing the operational autonomy that is important for creativity), encouraging open communication and collaboration within the team, giving useful, positive feedback on ideas, and supporting the work group within the organization. *Organizational Encouragement* is the sense that top management encourages, supports, and recognizes creative work (even when that work might not ultimately lead to a successful product), that there are mechanisms for fairly considering new ideas, and that the entire organization collaborates and cooperates to develop new ideas. *Organizational Impediments* can have negative effects on intrinsic motivation and creativity; these include political problems within an organization, extremely negative criticism of new ideas, and an emphasis on maintaining the status quo.

All of these features have been identified through research within organizations (e.g. Amabile, Schatzel, Moneta, and Kramer, 2004; Amabile and Gryskiewicz, 1987; Amabile and Kramer, 2011; Oldham and Cummings, 1996; Tierney and Farmer, 2002; Zhou, 1998, 2003). One study that used a validated instrument to assess the work environment (Amabile, 1995), and obtained outcome measures from independent expert assessments of creativity, demonstrated that these work environment factors distinguished organizational teams producing highly creative work from those whose work was disappointingly uncreative (Amabile, Conti, Coon, Lazenby, and Herron, 1996).

Note that two of the contextual features that relate to creativity stem from the nature of the work and how it is presented to an individual. A sense of positive challenge arises from the person's perception that the work uses and develops a set of important skills to accomplish an important goal. A sense of freedom arises from the extent to which the person has control over and discretion in carrying out the work. Because these features capture several aspects of the job characteristics model (Hackman and Oldham, 1980), job design must be considered an important part of the context for creativity.

Supervisors and group leaders play a key role in creating a suitable work environment for creativity. For example, recent studies have found *supervisory support* linked with higher creativity (Amabile et al., 2004), but more controlling supervisory behavior linked with lower creativity (Zhou, 2003). Another study found that even dissatisfied employees' creativity can be enhanced through a work environment in which they are supported and encouraged to share their views (Zhou and George, 2001). Creating such an environment can have benefits beyond stimulating creativity; one study found that workers who have appropriate support and autonomy to do challenging, creative work tend to be more satisfied and intend to stay longer with their organizations (Shalley, Gilson, and Blum, 2000).

Supervisor help in creative work is often essential, but difficult to provide. Because creative work is often fast-paced and complex, supervisors need to spend time asking questions to figure out whether their help is needed and what help to give. But, supervisor questions can be perceived as attempts to monitor and evaluate employees (Fisher, Pillemer, and Amabile, 2018) lest they be seen as dreaded "micromanagers" (Fisher, Amabile, and Pillemer, 2021). For supervisors to provide help that is actually seen as helpful, they need to communicate their intention to help and structure the time they spend with creative workers carefully to their needs (Fisher et al., 2018).

Determining Factors

The creative process is generally conceived as composed of five basic stages: task presentation, when people try to understand or articulate the specific problem to be solved; preparation, when they gather potentially relevant information from a number of sources; idea generation, when they try to come up with interesting candidate ideas among which to select; idea validation, when the final idea is worked through and communicated to others; and outcome assessment (Amabile and Pratt, 2016; Fisher, Ananth, and Demir-Caliskan, 2021). These stages may occur iteratively or nonlinearly over time, or in a more immediate and improvisational fashion (Fisher and Amabile, 2009; Fisher and Barrett, 2019; Fisher, Demir-Caliskan, Hua, and Cronin, 2021). *Intrinsic motivation appears to have its strongest influence in the task presentation and idea generation stages.* Both of these stages require particularly flexible thinking and deep involvement in the problem. It appears that intrinsic motivation fosters just this sort of thinking process. One study discovered that people who were more intrinsically motivated toward doing work in a particular domain (verbal activities or problem-solving) produced work that was independently judged as more creative (Ruscio, Whitney, and Amabile, 1998). Moreover, people who were intrinsically motivated were more likely to engage in exploratory, set-breaking behaviors while they were working on the task; that is, they were more likely to take novel, flexible approaches to the activity as they were trying to figure out how to tackle it. And intrinsically motivated people were more likely to concentrate on the activity, becoming deeply involved cognitively in it. Importantly, involvement mediated the effect of intrinsic motivation on creativity; in other words, intrinsic motivation appeared to influence creativity primarily because it influenced the depth of involvement in the task.

Thus, the creative process can be thought of as a maze that the problem-solver has to navigate; getting out of the maze is analogous to finding a satisfactory solution to the problem. Following a familiar, straightforward path for solving problems of that type does indeed lead to an exit. However, such approaches to problems are unlikely to yield creative solutions. In order to discover those more creative solutions – those other ways out of the maze – it is necessary to deviate from the familiar and to take the risk of running into a dead end. If people are *primarily* extrinsically motivated, they are motivated by something outside of the maze – by a reward or a deadline set by someone else, for example. Under these work environment circumstances, they are unlikely to get very involved in the problem itself or do much exploration for a new solution. But if people are primarily intrinsically motivated – if they have a basic interest in the task and if their work environment allows them to retain that intrinsic focus – they enjoy the process of exploring for one of those more creative solutions.

Some research *suggests a connection between positive affect, intrinsic motivation, and creativity* (Baas, de Dreu, and Nijstad, 2008). Experiments demonstrating a negative impact of extrinsic constraint on intrinsic motivation and creativity generally reveal that people not working under extrinsic constraint feel better about the experience and about the work that they have done (e.g. Amabile, 1979; Amabile, Hennessey, and Grossman, 1986). Moreover, in addition to experimental evidence that induced positive affect produces more flexible thinking (e.g. Isen, Daubman, and Nowicki, 1987), there is evidence inside organizations. A recent field study of the daily experiences of workers in seven companies has found that the level of positive mood on a given day predicted creativity that day as well as the next day (taking the next day's mood into account) (Amabile, Barsade, Mueller, and Staw, 2005). This suggests that positive work environments might influence intrinsic motivation in part by influencing how happy people feel about their work (Amabile and Kramer, 2011).

Certainly, the work environment's impact on motivation is not the only determinant of creativity. To stimulate creative productivity, managers should not only engineer supportive work environments (Amabile et al., 2004); they should also *select for employees who demonstrate high levels of each of the individual components of creativity* (see Amabile, 1983, 1996), and they should help to develop those components. The first component is *expertise,* or skill in the domain where the person will be working. This expertise is a function of the person's talent in the domain, as well as formal and informal education and experience. Not surprisingly, research has shown that, all else being equal, people are more creative if they have more education and experience in a field (McDermid, 1965; Scott and Bruce, 1994). The second component is a set of creativity-relevant processes stemming from the person's personality, cognitive style, and working style. In general, *people produce more creative work if they are oriented toward risk-taking and independence, if they know how to take new perspectives on problems and question basic assumptions, if they have a high tolerance for ambiguity, and if they work hard by energetically and persistently pursuing the problems they are trying to solve* (Feist, 1999; MacKinnon, 1965). The third component is *intrinsic motivation.* Although – as discussed above – intrinsic motivation can be influenced positively or negatively by extrinsic constraints in the work environment, people do differ from each other in their baseline levels of intrinsic and extrinsic motivation. Research has shown that there are stable individual differences in people's basic intrinsic motivation toward work (which can be broken down into challenge motivation and enjoyment motivation) and their basic extrinsic motivation toward work (which can be broken down into recognition motivation and compensation motivation) (Amabile, Hill, Hennessey, and Tighe, 1994). These basic intrinsic and extrinsic motivational orientations are more or less orthogonal, however; it is possible for people to be high on both intrinsic and extrinsic motives, high on neither, or high on only one. Recent research supports the importance of individual employees' intrinsic motivation orientation to their creativity at work (Munoz-Doyague, Gonzalez-Alvarez, and Nieto, 2008).

A person's creativity skill (the second creativity component) can interact with features of the work context to influence the level of creative output (Shalley, Zhou, and Oldham, 2004; van Knippenberg and Hirst, 2020). One study demonstrated that technical employees were most likely to produce patent disclosures and receive high ratings on creativity from their supervisors if they not only scored high on a test of individual creative personality, but also if they had both complex jobs and noncontrolling, supportive supervisors (Oldham and Cummings, 1996).

Further, for individuals to aggregate their knowledge and skills to create creative products in a group, *several group processes are necessary.* Workers need to rely on and collaborate with others to be their most creative (Perry-Smith and Mannucci, 2017; Rouse, 2020). To leverage their diverse perspectives, group members need to listen carefully to one another and synthesize competing views (Harvey, 2014; Harvey and Kou, 2013). Recent research has also revealed that teams and individuals rely heavily on feedback in their creative work, such that praise, criticism, and outside ideas can send them back to earlier ideas or spur them on to greater heights (Harrison and Rouse, 2015; Hoever, Zhou, and van Knippenberg, 2017). Creative workers, thus, need to seek out and listen carefully to feedback throughout the creative process.

Exceptions to and Extensions of the Basic Principle

The research evidence overwhelmingly points to the importance of intrinsic motivation for creativity. Yet, there have been recent discoveries that extend this principle and introduce exceptions to it. An important extension is that intrinsic motivation is not the only kind of fuel for the creative fire: a desire to help others (i.e. prosocial motivation) and one's confidence in their own creative abilities are also unique motivational predictors of creative performance (Liu, Jiang, Shalley, Keem, and Zhou, 2016), as are a sense of daily progress and meaning in the work (Amabile and Pratt, 2016; Amabile and Kramer, 2011). These forces interact with one another: Intrinsic motivation leads to creativity most strongly when employees are also prosocially motivated (Grant and Berry, 2011).

The intrinsic motivation principle is based on the idea that extrinsic rewards and pressures eat away at internal passion – that they shift creators' focus away from their sense of interest and challenge in the work. Yet, there are times when extrinsic motivation can actually enhance intrinsic motivation (Cerasoli, Nicklin, and Ford, 2014). This "motivational synergy" (Amabile, 1993) is most likely to occur when people start out highly intrinsically motivated to do their work, and when the extrinsic motivators are limited primarily to the stages of the creative process that involve the preparation to generate ideas or the validation and communication of the final idea. *Synergistic effects are unlikely when people feel that the extrinsic motivator – say, a reward – is being used to control their behavior.* Synergistic effects are likely, however, when people feel that the reward is indirect (i.e. not contingent on their immediate task performance, but is more general), provides positive feedback on their work, confirms their competence and the value of their work, or enables them to do work that they were already interested in doing (Byron and Khazanchi, 2012; Cerasoli et al., 2014).

Other constraints and stressors can sometimes enhance creativity, especially when used in moderation (Acar, Tarakci, and van Knippenberg, 2019; Baer and Oldham, 2006; Cromwell, Amabile, and Harvey, 2018). Approaches that encourage fast experimentation like design thinking or agile management can improve creative performance even when introducing time pressure. Structuring highly uncertain aspects of creative work, such as the brainstorming process, also helps reduce workers' anxiety about the uncontrollable nature of creativity (Byron, Khazanchi, and Nazarian, 2010). But, as the intrinsic motivation principle predicts, these techniques to structure and control creativity are only beneficial when they do not make workers feel evaluated (Byron, Khazanchi, and Nazarian, 2010).

Implementation

Managers can directly affect an employee's intrinsic motivation and creativity by the ways in which they construct assignments, teams, and work environments. The research suggests that it is important *to select people not only on the basis of their skills but also on the basis of their interests.* People should be matched to projects that will effectively use their best skills and tap into their strongest passions. Teams should be formed so that, as long as they have some common language for discussing the problem at hand, the *team members represent a diversity of backgrounds and perspectives. Team leaders and direct supervisors should clearly communicate overall strategic goals for a project, but allow the individuals working on the problem to make decisions about how to accomplish those goals.* Supervisors and peers should be genuinely open to new ideas, but should also give constructively challenging feedback on those ideas. *Top-level managers should clearly communicate their desire for creative ideas throughout the organization,* recognizing such ideas when they occur, and rewarding creative work with additional resources that will enable people to do work that excites them. In general, creativity should be rewarded in ways that convey information about the sort of performance the organization values most highly. Moreover, there should be *mechanisms to foster idea sharing and help* across the organization, as well as mechanisms for containing turf battles and political problems. Finally, *sufficient resources* should be provided for creative projects, and there should be a careful examination of time frames and an avoidance of extremely tight or arbitrary deadlines where possible.

Some specific tools can be useful for fostering creativity in organizations. Techniques for creative thinking, such as the creative problem-solving process, appear to increase the fluency, flexibility, and originality of people's thinking to some extent (e.g. Puccio, Firestien, Coyle, and Masucci, 2006). The paper-and-pencil instrument KEYS: Assessing the Climate for Creativity can diagnose an organization's work environment stimulants and obstacles to creativity (Amabile, 1995; Amabile, Burnside, and Gryskiewicz, 1999). And an "innovation office" within a company can serve as a mechanism for improving the care and attention given to new ideas. However, setting up an innovation office, or hiring consultants to "teach" creativity skills or conduct a work environment assessment, will most likely backfire unless such actions are accompanied by a deep management commitment to understanding and improving the context for creativity for the long term.

Case Examples[1]

Karpenter Versus O'Reilly

As Dwight Walton, the CEO of Karpenter Corporation, looked out across the manicured lawns of his company's sprawling suburban campus, he wondered whether there was a problem in his largest division – Karpenter Indoor Living and Home Maintenance (ILHM). Karpenter was one of the dominant names in power tools and appliances – its products appeared in nearly 80% of American homes – and was among the most highly regarded companies in the world. Much of Karpenter's success came from ILHM, which had created and managed the products that accounted for a healthy portion of the company's revenue. Cross-functional teams within this division were responsible for all aspects of a particular product line (e.g. power tools and food preparation equipment) and were composed of members from R&D, marketing, manufacturing, and finance. Along with maintaining their current product offerings, these teams were responsible for designing and developing many of the new Karpenter products.

Despite Karpenter's long-running success, Walton was concerned that this year's profits looked less certain. Moreover, the stream of creative products from ILHM had slowed considerably, and a few key employees had left in recent months. He began to wonder what was causing these problems; ILHM teams had been successful for many years by leveraging diverse perspectives from across the company and using well the high degree of autonomy they had traditionally had in running their product lines.

Fortuitously, Walton's next meeting was with Heather Shaw – an outside consultant, who had collected data about the daily work experiences of ILHM teams, as well as teams from six other organizations. During his last meeting with Shaw, Walton had asked her to see if there was anything she had found that might help explain the drop in creative productivity. As he cleared away the papers from his prior meeting, he wondered if Shaw could tell him anything useful.

In her presentation, Shaw began by telling Walton that the ILHM teams had the lowest ratings of intrinsic motivation of any teams she had studied, explaining intrinsic motivation and its link to creativity.

"How can that be?" interrupted Walton. "These teams have autonomy, exciting challenges, and support for their work – all the things that they told me in b-school should increase intrinsic motivation."

[1] Karpenter and O'Reilly are pseudonyms for two real companies we studied. Over the course of several months, we collected daily diary entries from teams doing creative work in seven organizations. Names and facts about the companies, teams, projects, and individuals are somewhat disguised to protect confidentiality. The character of Heather Shaw and the vignette presented here are fictional; however, they represent the general findings of our study.

"Yes, those things do help – when they are experienced that way by your employees," Shaw answered. "But, it looks as if your people don't feel that they have a real say in how to do their work and have trouble getting other units and their supervisors to support their ideas and decisions."

Shaw then explained that, despite the teams' nominal autonomy, divisional management often made decisions without consulting or informing the team. Without naming specific individuals or divulging any details about the confidential diary data that the divisional team members had sent her for a period of time, she described the ways in which intrinsic motivation was systematically being stifled. The diaries that Shaw had analyzed contained powerful information about how things had changed since a new ILHM management team had come on board a year earlier. As one team member recounted:

> Once again, Dean [divisional VP of R&D] has struck. Without informing ANYONE on the team, he has the CAD department redesigning one of our products. The team doesn't even know if we want to work on this project at all this year. (Theoretically, we have control of our capital budget and we have much higher priorities, with much greater potential to improve the bottom line, than this project.) . . . So, the team is responsible for the outcome of our business, but someone else is making the decisions that seal our fate. And, not only are they making these decisions, but we have to find out by accident because they don't have the common courtesy to inform us of what they are doing. Just f–king wonderful!!

"You may have told these teams that they have autonomy over decisions about what to work on," Shaw continued. "But, in practice, your people aren't experiencing it that way. Making decisions for a supposedly autonomous team will decrease the team's perceptions of ownership of their work, and, thus, intrinsic motivation. Failing to consult or even inform them only lowers motivation further, by arousing anger and frustration, and leading to perceptions that they are not valued by the organization."

As Walton listened stoically, Shaw began to explain how organizational and supervisory supports for the teams' initiatives were also lacking. She gave several examples of times when a team created a new product but had trouble coordinating with other parts of the organization. Not only were requests for help from central departments, such as manufacturing, not granted, but again, the team was not informed about decisions that affected their products. As described in a team member's diary:

> We have been working very hard to get production running, so we can fill a huge order that has a very tight deadline. Yesterday, production was up and running, and everyone breathed a sigh of relief. But, when we came in this morning, we found out (again by accident, because no one made the effort to tell us) that manufacturing had shut down production and was refusing to start back up until all the packaging arrived. The packaging was due today, and they had an empty warehouse to stage the parts until it got there. But, without asking/threatening/informing anyone on the team, they just did what they damn well pleased. By the way, they definitely knew this was a hot order, but they just shrugged their shoulders and said it wouldn't be their fault if the order didn't ship. Where in the hell are the common goals, communication and sharing, and teamwork that top

management claim they are fostering in this organization? I'm sure not seeing much evidence.

Shaw told Walton that there were several specific instances showing a lack of organizational support for team innovative efforts, and she described the general nature of those instances.

Further, team members within ILHM felt they received mixed messages from leadership – including their team leaders, division leaders, and even top corporate leaders, about innovation priorities:

> Had meetings with Steve (team leader), Allen (finance person on the team), and Beth (product development head for the team), to discuss how to reposition our proposal for a new hand-held mixer. This project has taken over 1 year to develop, mainly because the division's management team (MT) continually asked for more analysis, and R&D was slow in developing a reasonable technology to create a soft grip handle. Finally, the team rallied to present a viable project which the MT approved, only to have the COO say he wants a hard grip handle [instead,] at a $5 lower retail. Steve waffles back and forth. Allen is very helpful in running the financials and giving meaningful discussions on the subject. Beth is contrary on most points - really doesn't seem to care one way or the other. Very frustrating project, getting little support from corporate, MT, or key team members other than myself and Allen. Yet, all agree that the competitive situation is becoming desperate - especially since Boltmann [a key competitor] has just come out with yet another new hand-held mixer. I'm still trying to catch up to their last new mixer - UGH! Result was that Allen and I have prepared yet another proposal to show the MT tomorrow, but I need to get Steve to buy in; not sure which way he will go.

Because of problems coordinating and communicating with the rest of the organization and mixed messages about what to work on, this team ultimately failed to come up with a new product to successfully challenge Boltmann's competitive position.

"The people you need to come up with creative ideas are having trouble coordinating and communicating with other parts of the organization, which leads to trouble even within the teams; this means they devote a lot of energy to this, rather than developing products. Also, they don't feel respected or supported in their work and ideas," Shaw said. "I think you need to address these issues in order to increase the intrinsic motivation that is so essential to creativity."

"So, there are people who don't like their bosses and get frustrated by the reality of working in a big organization," muttered Walton. "You show me a place that doesn't have problems like that . . ."

"Actually," said Shaw, "that's exactly what I'd like to do."

Shaw proceeded to tell Walton about another company she had studied (without divulging its identity) – O'Reilly Coated Materials. O'Reilly was considered an innovative leader in the coated and laminated fabrics industry. Its core products included industrial goods, such as awnings, canopies, tents, and military supplies, and consumer products, such as luggage, toys, and sports equipment. O'Reilly was just coming off another strong fiscal year. The motor behind this impressive performance was O'Reilly Central Research (OCR), which was composed of teams of scientists and technicians responsible for creating the new products and innovations to keep the company healthy.

Protecting the confidentiality of the O'Reilly company, teams, projects, and individuals, Shaw used her analysis of the OCR diaries to tell Walton of specific factors supporting intrinsic motivation and creativity there. In contrast to the reports about feeling disrespected, unsupported, and micromanaged at ILHM, OCR teams reported norms of cooperation and support across the organization. As one OCR team member reported:

> Met with a number of contributors to the project – people in the Research Analyses group [at OCR] who have helped tremendously, although they are not officially team members – to get them to present their contributions at the project review. Meetings went well and I am glad that they will get a chance to show their contribution to the success [of this project].

Supervisory support was also commonly mentioned by the OCR team members. One wrote:

> Our VP/Director of R&D shared what he reported to the CEO, about OCR's very significant contribution to the business of the Corporation this past [fiscal] year. This makes us all feel very good and look forward to an even better year next year.

Another team member wrote:

> The Gate review [project review by upper management, to decide whether to move on to next stage] and the meetings with the Technical Directors of the divisions went very well. They are completely supportive of all aspects of the project and were thrilled by the progress the team has made over the last few months. I could not have asked for anything more!!

"In your ILHM teams, the diary entries I analyzed often focused on the many obstacles and setbacks people had to overcome," Shaw explained. "At this other company, most of the entries described small steps forward in the work, or things in the work environment that enabled people to make those steps forward. Those teams had considerable autonomy, and were always consulted about possible modifications in project priorities." Walton nodded and shifted uncomfortably in his chair. "Your ILHM team members also reported a lot of criticism and negative feedback, almost never reporting praise," she continued. "This was another point of contrast between the companies.

"I think that the work environment here – the factors that are external to the creative work itself – are interfering with your teams' creativity by undermining their intrinsic motivation. It doesn't have to be that way, though. This other company's teams rated their mood, their work environment, and their intrinsic motivation much higher than your teams did. Not surprisingly, their creative productivity was a lot higher, too. The differences can't be explained away by individual personalities or skill levels; our measures of those don't show much difference between the two companies.

"Although I've mentioned that some of the other company's diaries expressed positive emotions, it's really interesting that most of that company's diary entries did not express any emotion at all, but instead talked about the work itself. In contrast, your ILHM teams wrote extensively about their frustrations with the work environment created by superiors and other parts of the organization. Regardless of how that came to be, you don't want these people thinking about their frustrations when you need them to focus on making great new products – you want them thinking about the products."

As their meeting ended, Walton thanked Shaw for her work and saw her out. Despite the report, Walton could not shake the feeling that the comments from his workers were little more than whining at the realities of organizational life. "If my ILHM teams worked harder and smarter," he thought, "they'd get the results we need. On the other hand, maybe there are some things I could change to make it easier for them to focus on the creative work I need them to do . . ."

Epilogue: As in our fictitious vignette, the real Karpenter top management team was shocked to find out how frequently their team members experienced negative emotions, how low their intrinsic motivation was, and the degree to which the team members perceived management as overcontrolling, overly critical of new ideas, indecisive, and generally unsupportive. All of these measures were far more positive at O'Reilly. So were measures of creativity. Coworkers at Karpenter rated each other's creative contributions so low that the averages had almost no overlap with the high coworker ratings at O'Reilly. However, even in the face of this evidence, Karpenter's top management believed the company's work environment to be fundamentally healthy, with a suitable climate for improved creativity.

A year after our study ended, the poor motivation and low creativity exhibited by Karpenter's ILHM employees caught up with the company; profits dropped dramatically. A year later, Karpenter was taken over by a large conglomerate and eventually ceased to exist. O'Reilly, on the other hand, continues as a healthy, profitable firm.

Conclusion

People do their most creative work when they are passionate about what they are doing. Such high levels of intrinsic motivation are influenced both by a person's basic interest in a particular kind of work and by the work environment surrounding the person. Managers can support creative productivity by matching people to projects on the basis of interest as well as skill, by using rewards that recognize competence and support further involvement in the work, and by establishing a work environment across the organization – from the level of top management to the level of work groups – that removes the barriers and enhances the supports to active, collaborative, intrinsic involvement in the work.

In establishing that work environment, managers should strive to first remove micromanagement of creative work and limit excessive time pressure, particularly time pressure when workdays are marked by fragmented demands unrelated to the organization's most important creative work. They should also take steps to calm political problems that play out on the battlefield of creativity, resulting in excessive criticism of new ideas and an emphasis on maintaining the status quo. Managers can enhance supports for intrinsic involvement in the work by giving people tasks that are meaningful to them and that positively challenge their skills. Middle-level managers should form work groups that combine diverse perspectives and talents and, then, facilitate the members of those groups to work collaboratively as they both support and constructively challenge each other's ideas. Low-level managers – immediate supervisors – should set clear overall goals for projects, but give people as much operational autonomy as possible; they should also serve as champions for creative projects in the organization. Top organizational leaders can provide encouragement and support for creative work in a number of ways, including the establishment of well-coordinated mechanisms for developing new ideas and systems for recognizing and rewarding creative efforts. Perhaps most importantly, the passion for creativity can be stimulated by an open flow of ideas across an organization in which people feel safe to give honest, constructive feedback on someone else's brainchild – and to fearlessly share their own.

REFERENCES

Acar, O. A., Tarakci, M., and van Knippenberg, D. (2019). Creativity and innovation under constraints: A cross-disciplinary integrative review. *Journal of Management*, 45(1), 96–121.

Amabile, T. M. (1979). Effects of external evaluation on artistic creativity. *Journal of Personality and Social Psychology*, 37, 221233.

Amabile, T. M. (1983). Social Psychology of creativity: A componential conceptualization. *Journal of Personality and Social Psychology*, 45, 357–377.

Amabile, T. M. (1985). Motivation and creativity: Effects of motivational orientation on creative writers. *Journal of Personality and Social Psychology*, 48, 393399.

Amabile, T. M. (1993). Motivational synergy: Toward new conceptualizations of intrinsic and extrinsic motivation in the workplace. *Human Resource Management Review*, 3, 185–201.

Amabile, T. M. (1995). *KEYS: Assessing the Climate for Creativity*. Greensboro, NC: Center for Creative Leadership.

Amabile, T. M. (1996). *Creativity in Context*. Boulder, CO: Westview Press.

Amabile, T., and Gryskiewicz, S. S. (1987). *Creativity in the R&D Laboratory*. Greensboro, NC: Center for Creative Leadership.

Amabile, T. M., and Kramer, S. J. (2011). *The Progress Principle: Using Small Wins to Ignite Joy, Engagement, and Creativity at Work*. Harvard Business School Press.

Amabile, T. M., and Pratt, M. G. (2016). The dynamic componential model of creativity and innovation in organizations: Making progress, making meaning. *Research in Organizational Behavior*, 36, 157–183.

Amabile, T. M., Barsade, S. G., Mueller, J. S., and Staw, B. M. (2005). Affect and creativity at work. *Administrative Science Quarterly*, 50, 367–403.

Amabile, T. M., Burnside, R., and Gryskiewicz, S. S. (1999). *User's Manual for KEYS: Assessing the Climate for Creativity*. Greensboro, NC: Center for Creative Leadership.

Amabile, T. M., Conti, R., Coon, H., Lazenby, J., and Herron, M. (1996). Assessing the work environment for creativity. *Academy of Management Journal*, 39, 1154–1184.

Amabile, T. M., Hennessey, B. A., and Grossman, B. S. (1986). Social influences on creativity: The effects of contracted for reward. *Journal of Personality and Social Psychology*, 50, 1423.

Amabile, T. M., Hill, K. G., Hennessey, B. A., and Tighe, E. M. (1994). The Work Preference Inventory: Assessing intrinsic and extrinsic motivational orientations. *Journal of Personality and Social Psychology*, 66, 950–967.

Amabile, T. M., Schatzel, E. A., Moneta, G. B., and Kramer, S. J. (2004). Leader behaviors and the work environment for creativity: Perceived leader support. *The Leadership Quarterly*, 15, 5–32.

Baas, M., De Dreu, C. K. W., and Nijstad, B. A. (2008). A meta-analysis of 25 years of mood-creativity research: Hedonic tone, activation, or regulatory focus? *Psychological Bulletin*, 134(6), 779–806.

Baer, M., and Oldham, G. R. (2006). The curvilinear relation between experienced creative time pressure and creativity: Moderating effects of openness to experience and support for creativity. *Journal of Applied Psychology*, 9, 963–970.

Byron, K., and Khazanchi, S. (2012). Rewards and creative performance: A meta-analytic test of theoretically derived hypotheses. *Psychological Bulletin*, 138(4), 809–830.

Byron, K., Khazanchi, S., and Nazarian, D. (2010). The relationship between stressors and creativity: A meta-analysis examining competing theoretical models. *Journal of Applied Psychology*, 95(1), 201–212.

Cerasoli, C. P., Nicklin, J. M., and Ford, M. T. (2014). Intrinsic motivation and extrinsic incentives jointly predict performance: A 40-year meta-analysis. *Psychological Bulletin*, 140(4), 980–1008.

Cromwell, J. R., Amabile, T. M., and Harvey, J.-F. (2018). An integrated model of dynamic problem solving within organizational constraints. In R. Reiter-Palmon, V. L. Kennel, and J. C. Kaufman (eds), *Individual Creativity in the Workplace* (pp. 53–81). Academic Press.

Csikszentmihalyi, M. (1990). *Flow: The Psychology of Optimal Experience*. New York: Harper Perennial.

Deci, E. L., and Ryan, R. M. (1985). *Intrinsic Motivation and Self-Determination in Human Behavior*. New York: Plenum.

Deci, E. L., Koestner, R., and Ryan, R. M. (1999). A meta-analytic review of experiments examining the effects of extrinsic rewards on intrinsic motivation. *Psychological Bulletin*, 125, 627–668.

Feist, G. J. (1999). The influence of personality on artistic and scientific creativity. In R. Sternberg (ed.), *Handbook of Creativity* (pp. 273–296). Cambridge, UK: Cambridge University Press.

Fisher, C. M., and Amabile, T. M. (2009). Creativity, improvisation and organizations. In T. Rickards, M. A. Runco, and S. Moger (eds), *The Routledge Companion to Creativity* (pp. 13–24). London: Routledge.

Fisher, C. M., and Barrett, F. J. (2019). The experience of improvising in organizations: A creative process perspective. *Academy of Management Perspectives*, 33(2), 148–162.

Fisher, C., Amabile, T., and Pillemer, J. (2021). How to help (without micromanaging). *Harvard Business Review*, 99(1), 123–127.

Fisher, C. M., Ananth, P., and Caliskan, O. D. (2021). A winding road: Teresa Amabile and creative process research. In R. Reiter-Palmon, C. M. Fisher, and J. S. Mueller (eds), *Creativity at Work: A Festschrift in Honor of Teresa Amabile* (pp. 35–46). Cham, Switzerland: Palgrave Macmillan.

Fisher, C. M., Demir-Caliskan, O., Hua, M. Y., and Cronin, M. A. (2021). Trying not to try: The paradox of intentionality in jazz improvisation and its implications for organizational scholarship. In R. Bednarek, M. Pina e Cunha, J. Schad, and

W. K. Smith (eds), *Interdisciplinary Dialogues on Organizational Paradox: Investigating Social Structures and Human Expression, Part B* (Vol. 73b, pp. 123–137). Bingley, West Yorkshire, England: Emerald Publishing Limited.

Fisher, C. M., Pillemer, J., and Amabile, T. M. (2018). Deep help in complex project work: Guiding and path-clearing across difficult terrain. *Academy of Management Journal*, 61(4), 1524–1553.

Grant, A. M., and Berry, J. W. (2011). The necessity of others is the mother of invention: Intrinsic and prosocial motivations, perspective taking, and creativity. *Academy of Management Journal*, 54(1), 73–96.

Hackman, J. R., and Oldham, G. R. (1980). *Work Redesign*. Reading, MA: Addison-Wesley.

Harrison, S. H., and Rouse, E. D. (2015). An inductive study of feedback interactions over the course of creative projects. *Academy of Management Journal*, 58(2), 375–404.

Harvey, S. (2014). Creative synthesis: Exploring the process of extraordinary group creativity. *Academy of Management Review*, 39(3), 324–343.

Harvey, S., and Kou, C.-Y. (2013). Collective engagement in creative tasks: The role of evaluation in the creative process in groups. *Administrative Science Quarterly*, 58(3), 346–386.

Hoever, I. J., Zhou, J., and van Knippenberg, D. (2017). Different strokes for different teams: The contingent effects of positive and negative feedback on the creativity of informationally homogeneous and diverse teams. *Academy of Management Journal*, 61(6), 2159–2181.

Isen, A. M., Daubman, K. A., and Nowicki, G. P. (1987). Positive affect facilitates creative problem solving. *Journal of Personality and Social Psychology*, 52, 1122–1131.

Lepper, M., and Greene, D. (1978). Overjustification research and beyond: Toward a means-end analysis of instrinsic and extrinsic motivation. In M. Lepper and D. Greene (eds), *The Hidden Costs of Reward*. New Jersey: Lawrence Erlbaum Associates.

Liu, D., Jiang, K., Shalley, C. E., Keem, S., and Zhou, J. (2016). Motivational mechanisms of employee creativity: A meta-analytic examination and theoretical extension of the creativity literature. *Organizational Behavior and Human Decision Processes*, 137, 236–263.

Lucas, B. J., and Nordgren, L. F. (2015). People underestimate the value of persistence for creative performance. *Journal of Personality and Social Psychology*, 109(2), 232–243.

MacKinnon, D. W. (1965). Personality and the realization of creative potential. *American Psychologist*, 20, 273–281.

McDermid, C. D. (1965). Some correlates of creativity in engineering personnel. *Journal of Applied Psychology*, 49, 14–19.

Munoz-Doyague, M. F., Gonzalez-Alvarez, N., and Nieto, M. (2008). An examination of individual factors and employees' creativity: The case of Spain. *Creativity Research Journal*, 20, 21–33.

Oldham, G. R., and Cummings, A. (1996). Employee creativity: Personal and contextual factors at work. *Academy of Management Journal*, 39, 607–634.

Perry-Smith, J. E., and Mannucci, P. V. (2017). From creativity to innovation: The social network drivers of the four phases of the idea journey. *Academy of Management Review*, 42(1), 53–79.

Puccio, G. J., Firestien, R. L., Coyle, C., and Masucci, C. (2006). A review of the effectiveness of CPS training: A focus on workplace issues. *Creativity and Innovation Management,* 15, 19–33.

Rouse, E. D. (2020). Where you end and I begin: Understanding intimate co-creation. *Academy of Management Review,* 45(1), 181–204.

Ruscio, J., Whitney, D. M., and Amabile, T. M. (1998). Looking inside the fishbowl of creativity: Verbal and behavioral predictors of creative performance. *Creativity Research Journal,* 11, 243–263.

Scott, S. G., and Bruce, R. A. (1994). Determinants of innovative behavior: A path model of individual innovation in the workplace. *Academy of Management Journal,* 37, 580–607.

Shalley, C. E., Gilson, L. L., and Blum, T. C. (2000). Matching creativity requirements and the work environment: Effects on satisfaction and intentions to leave. *Academy of Management Journal,* 43, 215–223.

Shalley, C. E., Zhou, J., and Oldham, G. R. (2004). Effects of personal and contextual characteristics on creativity: Where should we go from here? *Journal of Management,* 30, 933–958.

Tierney, P., and Farmer, S. M. (2002). Creative self-efficacy: Potential antecedents and relationship to creative performance. *Academy of Management Journal,* 45, 1137–1148.

van Knippenberg, D., and Hirst, G. (2020). A motivational lens model of person × situation interactions in employee creativity. *Journal of Applied Psychology,* 105(10), 1129–1144.

Zhou, J. (1998). Feedback valence, feedback style, task autonomy, and achievement orientation: Interactive effects on creative performance. *Journal of Applied Psychology,* 83, 261–276.

Zhou, J. (2003). When the presence of creative coworkers is related to creativity: Role of supervisor close monitoring, developmental feedback, and creative personality. *Journal of Applied Psychology,* 88, 413–422.

Zhou, J., and George, J. M. (2001). When job dissatisfaction leads to creativity: Encouraging the expression of voice. *Academy of Management Journal,* 44, 682–696.

Classroom Exercises

1. "Scribbles"

To illustrate in real time a few "creativity killers" – environmental factors that undermine creativity by lowering intrinsic motivation – you will instruct students to make a creative drawing out of a scribble under tight time pressure, surveillance, constraint, peer competition, and unclear/meaningless goals, with external evaluation looming. This exercise takes 15–30 minutes and is best used at the very beginning of a workshop/class on creativity.

To run this exercise, first tell the class that they are going to take a short test of their individual creativity. Emphasize the word "test" during the instructions, and continue to remind them that their test will be evaluated – judged by their classmates according to a procedure that you will explain after the test. Tell them that this test is used for assessing artistic creativity, but is also a good indicator of their overall levels of creativity. Make sure that all class members have a blank sheet of paper and a pen or pencil. Have students draw a single, large scribble or squiggle on their page and then stop. Then, have students exchange their papers with another person near them and put their names on the new paper (which has someone else's scribble). Tell the class they will have two minutes to make a creative drawing based on this scribble and give it a creative title. Then, give the signal for them to start. As students make their drawings, move throughout the room and look at students' drawings. In reality, give students somewhat less than two minutes (perhaps 90 seconds), and announce how much time is remaining every 30 seconds when there is one minute left. When there are 30 seconds remaining, remind students to give their drawing a creative title. Count down the last 10 seconds aloud. Then say, "Stop! Pencils down!" and have all students pass in their drawings. There is likely to be much nervous laughter among students during the exercise, and it is fine for you to maintain a pleasant demeanor. When drawings are being passed in, begin to make the atmosphere truly light and fun by inviting students to glance at the drawings as they go by.

After you have the drawings, begin by assuring students that their creations will not actually be judged, and that the reason for the exercise was to give everyone the same shared experience of trying to be creative on the same thing at the same point in time. Then, debrief the class on their experience of creating something that was supposed to represent their true creativity, asking them to focus on any factors that made it difficult to be creative. Record their comments on the blackboard in three columns corresponding to the three creativity components. After taking comments for a few minutes (ideally waiting until the major work environment impediments have been mentioned), label these columns "task expertise," "creative thinking skills," and "work environment intrinsic motivation." Emphasize that this task was not really a test of creativity, but a demonstration of what happens to intrinsic motivation and creativity when people are told to "be creative" in a work environment full of extrinsic constraints and extrinsic motivators. The debriefing should include a brief explanation of intrinsic motivation and the other two components of creativity, extrinsic constraints/motivators, and the intrinsic motivation principle of creativity. For an additional element of fun at the end of the class or workshop, spread out the drawings on an empty table for an informal "art show."

2. Your Ideal Work Environment

The purpose of this exercise is to allow students to think about the sort of organizational work environment that they should seek (or create) for their future career moves, if they wish to optimize their own opportunities for creative work. It takes about 30–45 minutes, depending on how much time you allocate for discussion.

In this exercise, students will rate how important various aspects of their work environment are for their own personal creativity. For that reason, the exercise is most appropriate after you have taught them about how various aspects of the work environment can facilitate or impede creativity. Begin the exercise by asking them to reflect for a few moments on their prior work experiences (or school-work experiences, if they have not yet held jobs). They should try to recall, in detail, one or two instances in which they did truly creative work, and think about the work environment surrounding them in those instances. Then, they should recall, in detail, one or two instances in which their creativity was blocked, and think about the work environment surrounding them in those instances.

Next, tell them that they will generalize from these instances (and others like them) to the future work environments that might best support their own creativity. On a sheet of paper (ideally, a form that you have prepared for them in advance), have students privately indicate whether they would like to HAVE or AVOID the following features of the work environment. Then, they should indicate whether each of those features is VERY IMPORTANT to them, SOMEWHAT IMPORTANT to them, or LESS IMPORTANT to them. Remind them that they will likely have to make trade-offs, that it is unrealistic to rate everything as VERY IMPORTANT. This first part of the exercise (remembering specific instances and then completing the form individually) generally takes about 15 minutes.

1. *Freedom* in deciding what work to do or how to do it
2. A sense of *challenge* in your work – working hard on challenging or important projects
3. Sufficient *resources* – including funds, materials, and information – to accomplish the work
4. *Supervisory encouragement* from a good work model who sets goals appropriately, supports the work group, values individual contributions, and shows confidence in the work group
5. *Work Group Supports* from people who are diversely skilled, communicate well, are open to new ideas, constructively challenge each other's work, trust and help each other, and feel committed to the work they are doing
6. *Organizational Encouragement* that promotes the fair, constructive judgment of ideas, rewards and recognizes people for creative work, helps foster an active flow of new ideas, and maintains a shared vision of what the organization is trying to do
7. *Organizational Impediments,* including internal political problems, harsh criticism of new ideas, destructive internal competition, an avoidance of risk, and an overemphasis on the status quo
8. *Workload Pressure,* such as extreme time pressures, unrealistic expectations for productivity, or distractions from creative work

After students have indicated whether they would like to HAVE or AVOID each feature of the work environment, and how important the features are to them, have them brainstorm (in pairs or small groups) ways in which they can find or create their ideal work environments. Have them consider the following questions: What sorts of companies and industries should you look for? What sorts of companies and industries should you avoid? What can you do to proactively create your ideal work environment? If there is time, you may wish to continue with a whole-group discussion in which students share some of the insights they developed through the individual exercise and the small-group discussions. This exercise will help students identify those few key features that deserve most of their attention as they look for jobs or think about establishing their own work environments.

Video Analysis and Discussion

Please watch the following video(s):

1. How to build your creative confidence: https://www.youtube.com/watch?v=16p9YRF0l-g
2. The art of creativity: https://www.youtube.com/watch?v=pL71KhNmnls
3. Creative thinking: https://www.youtube.com/watch?v=bEusrD8g-dM

Now form small groups to discuss the video(s) and answer the following questions:

1. What are the major points of the video?
2. How can you use information from the video in your career?
3. Based on the video, what advice do you have for leaders in organizations?

Be prepared to present the ideas from your small-group discussion with the class as a whole.

23

Manage Stress at Work Through Preventive and Proactive Coping

RALF SCHWARZER AND TABEA REUTER

Freie Universität Berlin

This chapter outlines an approach to coping with stress at work that makes a distinction between four perspectives, namely reactive coping, anticipatory coping, preventive coping, and proactive coping:

- Reactive coping refers to harm or loss experienced in the past.
- Anticipatory coping pertains to inevitable threats in the near future.
- Preventive coping refers to uncertain threats in the distant future.
- Proactive coping involves future challenges that are seen as self-promoting.

This distinction is based on moderators such as the nature of stressors, time-related stress appraisals, coping resources, and on the perceived certainty of critical events or demands (Schwarzer and Knoll, 2009; Schwarzer and Luszczynska, 2008, 2012).

In addition to this approach, numerous ways of coping are presented, and their use at the level of organizations and at the level of individuals is discussed. To begin with, the nature of stress at work will be described.

STRESS AT WORK

The Experience of Stress

The workplace provides numerous sources of stress. The job itself might involve difficult and demanding tasks that tax or exceed the coping resources of the employee. The role of an individual within the organization might be ambiguous or might even be the cause of frequent conflicts. Relationships at work could entail friction and impair functioning or motivation. Career development might be restricted or echo a constant struggle for acknowledgment. The organizational climate might reflect a battleground for competition. Further, it is possible that all of these examples are aggravated by nonwork factors that interact with job stress. Adverse conditions are one of the factors that constitute or set the stage for experiencing stress, such as working shifts, long hours, place of work, work overload, frequent travel, speed of change, and new technology. Often-cited stressors are job insecurity, friction with bosses, subordinates, or colleagues, and role conflict or ambiguity (Cartwright and Cooper, 1997; Quick, Quick, Nelson, and Hurrell, 1997).

Surveys have found a "growing epidemic of stress" (Quick et al., 1997). This does not necessarily indicate that people experience more stress now than they did earlier in their lives, or more stress than earlier generations. Instead, it may signify greater public awareness of the stress phenomenon and the existence of a handy label for a common feeling. Research on the prevalence of stress is difficult because the term is not clearly defined. In the public health literature, and likewise in industrial and organizational psychology, a distinction is sometimes made between "objective stress," also called *stressor*, and "subjective stress," also called *strain* or *distress*. The former is used in research as an independent variable, and the latter as a dependent variable. However, in mainstream psychology, stimulus-based and response-based definitions have become less prevalent. Instead, transactional conceptions are widely accepted, in which stress is understood as a complex process, rather than as a descriptive variable or as a single explanatory concept (Schwarzer and Luszczynska, 2012).

Cognitive-Transactional Theory of Stress

Cognitive-transactional theory defines stress as a particular relationship between the person and the environment that is appraised by the person as taxing or exceeding his or her resources and endangering his or her well-being. Lazarus (1991) conceives stress as an active, unfolding process that is composed of causal antecedents, mediating processes, and effects. *Antecedents* are person variables, such as commitments or beliefs, and environmental variables, such as demands or situational constraints. *Mediating processes* refer to coping and appraisals of demands and resources. Experiencing stress and coping bring about both immediate *effects*, such as affect or physiological changes, and long-term effects concerning psychological well-being, somatic health, and social functioning (see Figure 23.1).

Cognitive appraisals comprise two simultaneous processes, namely primary (demand) appraisals and secondary (resource) appraisals. The terms *primary* and *secondary appraisals* have been often misunderstood as reflecting a temporal order that was not meant by Lazarus (personal communication). Therefore, *demand* and *resource appraisals* are better terms. Appraisal outcomes are divided into the following categories: challenge, threat, and harm/loss. First, *demand appraisal* refers to one's evaluation of a situation or event as a potential hazard. Second, *resource appraisals* refer to one's available coping options for dealing with the demands at hand.

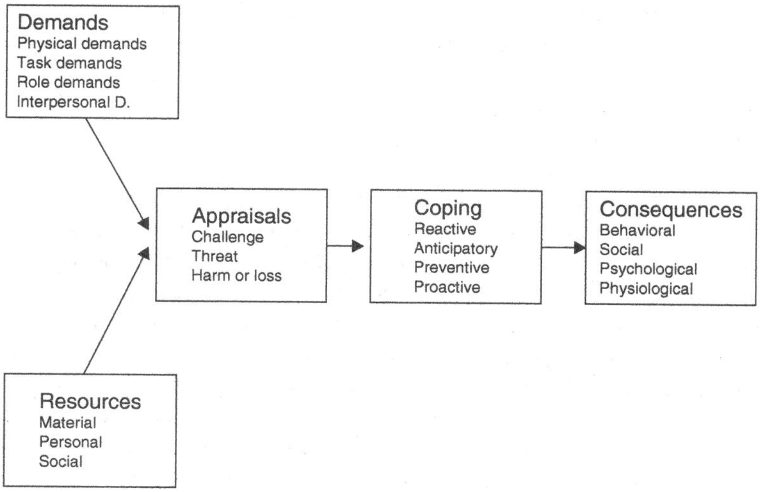

FIGURE 23.1 A process model of stress and coping

The individual evaluates his or her competence, social support, and material or other resources that can help to readapt to the circumstances and to reestablish an equilibrium between the person and the environment. Hobfoll (1989) has expanded stress and coping theory with respect to the conservation of resources as the main human motive in the struggle with stressful encounters.

Three outcome categories occur as a result of demand and resource appraisals: A situation is appraised as challenging when it mobilizes physical and mental activity and involvement. In the evaluation of *challenge*, a person may see an opportunity to prove oneself, anticipating gain, mastery, or personal growth from the venture. The situation is experienced as pleasant, exciting, and interesting, and the person feels ardent and confident in being able to meet the demands. *Threat* occurs when the individual perceives danger, anticipating physical injuries or blows to one's self-esteem. In the experience of *harm/loss*, some damage has already occurred. This can be the injury or loss of valued persons, important objects, self-worth, or social standing (Schwarzer and Luszczynska, 2012).

Assessment of Stress

The main practical problem with transactional theories of stress is that there is no good way of measuring stress as a process. Therefore, all common procedures to assess stress are either stimulus-based, pointing at critical events and demands, or response-based, pointing at symptoms and feelings experienced. Some procedures measure the frequency or intensity of stressors, while others measure individual distress (strain). An example of a *stimulus-based* instrument is Spielberger's (1994) Job Stress Survey. It includes 30 items that describe stressors typically experienced by managerial, professional, and clerical employees. The respondents first rate the severity (intensity) of 30 job stressors (such as excessive paperwork and poorly motivated coworkers). Next, they rate the same list once more on a frequency scale. The two ratings result in scores that can be interpreted as state and trait job stress. Other instruments deal with critical events at the workplace, hassles and uplifts, and the work environment in general.

Response-based measures are available that entail symptoms, emotions, arousal, illness, burnout, and behavioral changes. Job burnout, however, cannot be equated to stress, but has to be seen as a long-term consequence of stress (Klusmann, Kunter, Trautwein, Lüdtke, and Baumert, 2008; Maslach, Schaufeli, and Leiter, 2001; Schaufeli and Bakker, 2004). The Maslach Burnout Inventory is the standard measure in this field (Maslach, Jackson, and Leiter, 1996). Using measures for burnout, symptoms, mental disorder, or illness to tap the concept of "stress" is questionable and misleading because individual changes in these variables occur only at later stages of a stress episode. Thus, stress is confounded with its consequences. Any use of stress inventories involves a particular definition of stress that is not always made transparent and may not even reflect the researchers' theory.

In any case, no matter whether stimulus-based or response-based measures are used, individuals respond to them with their coping resources in mind. The transactional perspective entails the relationship between demands and resources, which is viewed as causing the resulting emotional response.

Coping with Stress at Work

Coping with stress at work can be defined as an effort by a person or an organization to manage and overcome demands and critical events that pose a challenge, threat, harm, or loss to that person and that person's functioning or to the organization as a whole. Coping can occur as a response to an event or in anticipation of upcoming demands, but it can also involve a proactive approach to self-imposed goals and challenges.

Coping with stress is considered as one of the top skills inherent in effective managers. In samples recruited from business, educational, health care, and state government organizations, 402 highly effective managers were identified by peers and superiors. Interviews revealed that coping was second on a list of 10 key skills attributed to managers. The management of time and stress was beneficial to the organization because the leaders were role models for employees. Moreover, the executives themselves benefited from successful coping in terms of performance and health (Whetton and Cameron, 1993). This underscores the importance of coping in the workplace. A host of research conducted during the last three decades has found that poor adjustment to demanding or adverse work environments can lead to illness, in particular to high blood pressure and cardiovascular disease (Kasl, 1996; Marmot, Bosma, Hemingway, Bruner, and Stansfeld, 1997; Siegrist, 1996; Theorell and Karasek, 1996; Weidner, Boughal, Conner, Pieper, and Mendell, 1997).

Consequences of Poor Adjustment to Stress at Work

Stress is inevitable, but the degree of stress can be modified in two ways: by changing the environment and by changing the individual. If coping attempts are unsuccessful, adverse consequences will result. Job performance may decline and job satisfaction fade, burnout symptoms emerge, or accidents happen. Further, social relationships at work may become tense, or mental and physical health could deteriorate, leading to sleep problems and substance abuse, etc. Poor adjustment to demanding or adverse work environments can lead to a number of health conditions, in particular high blood pressure and cardiovascular disease. The study of coping at the workplace has often been reduced to only a few variables, such as demands, control, decision latitude, social support, and opportunities for relaxation and exercise. The literature on occupational health has documented an array of findings where these variables were examined in relation to demand factors and population characteristics. Adverse health outcomes have been demonstrated most often (Kasl, 1996; Marmot et al., 1997; Siegrist, 1996; Theorell and Karasek, 1996; Weidner et al., 1997). Successful individual adjustment to stress at work depends partly on resources and partly on the nature of the stress episode.

In the following section, coping resources are described; then, dimensions and perspectives of coping are examined that help to gain a better understanding of the psychological meaning of coping.

Antecedents of Stress and Coping: Demands and Resources

To characterize *demands* or situational stressors, Lazarus (1991) describes formal properties, such as novelty, event uncertainty, ambiguity, and temporal aspects of stressful conditions. For example, demands that are difficult, ambiguous, unexpected, unprepared, or are very time-consuming under time pressure, are more likely to induce threat than easy tasks that can be prepared for thoroughly and solved at a convenient pace without time constraints. The work environment can be evaluated with respect to the stakes inherent in a given situation. For example, demanding social situations imply interpersonal threat, the danger of physical injury is perceived as physical threat, and anticipated failures endangering self-worth indicate ego threat. Lazarus additionally distinguishes between task-specific stress, including cognitive demands and other formal task properties, and failure-induced stress, including evaluation aspects such as social feedback, valence of goal, possibilities of failure, or actual failure. Large and unfavorable task conditions combined with failure-inducing situational cues are likely to provoke stress.

Personal resources refer to the internal coping options that are available in a particular stressful encounter. Competence and skills have to match the work demands. Individuals who are affluent, healthy, capable, and optimistic are resourceful, and thus, they are less vulnerable toward stress at work. Social competence, empathy, and assertiveness might be necessary to deal with specific interpersonal demands. It is crucial to feel competent to handle a stressful situation. But actual competence is not a sufficient prerequisite. If the individual underestimates his or her potential for action, no adaptive strategies will be developed. Therefore, perceived competence is crucial. This has been labeled "perceived self-efficacy" or "optimistic self-beliefs" by Bandura (see Chapter 6). Perceived self-efficacy or optimism (as a state) are seen as a prerequisite for coping with all kinds of stress, such as job loss, demotion, promotion, or work overload (Schwarzer and Luszczynska, 2007, 2012). Job-specific self-efficacy has been studied (for example, teacher self-efficacy, Schwarzer and Hallum, 2008).

Social resources refer to the external coping options that are available to an individual in a certain stressful encounter. Social integration reflects the individual's embeddedness in a network of social interactions, mutual assistance, attachment, and obligations. Social support reflects the actual or perceived coping assistance in critical situations (see review in Schwarzer and Knoll, 2007). Social support has been defined in various ways, for example, as a resource provided by others, coping assistance, or an exchange of resources "perceived by the provider or the recipient to be intended to enhance the well-being of the recipient" (Shumaker and Brownell, 1984, p. 13). Several types of social support have been investigated, for instance instrumental, for example, assisting with a problem, tangible help such as goods, informational help such as advice, and emotional support such as giving reassurance, among others.

Dimensions of Coping

Many attempts have been made to reduce the universe of possible coping responses to a parsimonious set of coping dimensions. Some researchers have come up with two basic distinctions, that is, instrumental, attentive, vigilant, or confrontative coping, as opposed to avoidant, palliative, and emotional coping (for an overview, see Schwarzer and Schwarzer, 1996). A related approach has been put forward by Lazarus (1991), who *separates problem-focused* from *emotion-focused* coping, or by Locke (2005), who distinguishes between action-focused and emotion-focused coping. Another conceptual distinction has been suggested between *assimilative* and *accommodative* coping, whereby the former aims at modifying the environment and the latter at modifying oneself (Brandtstädter, 1992). This pair has also been coined "*mastery* versus *meaning*" (Taylor, 1983) or "*primary control* versus *secondary control*" (Rothbaum, Weisz, and Snyder, 1982). These coping preferences may occur in a certain time order when, for example, individuals first try to alter the demands that are at stake, and, after failing, turn inwards to reinterpret their plight and find subjective meaning in it.

FOUR COPING PERSPECTIVES IN TERMS OF TIMING AND CERTAINTY

Work demands can be continuous or changing. They can reflect an ongoing harmful encounter, or they can exist in the near or distant future, creating a threat to someone who feels incapable of matching the upcoming demands with the coping resources at hand. Critical events at the workplace may have occurred in the past, leading to layoffs, demotions, or adverse restrictions. In light of the complexity of stressful episodes, coping cannot be reduced to either relaxation or fight-and-flight responses. Coping depends, among other factors, on the time perspective of the demands and the subjective certainty of the events. Reactive coping refers to harm or loss experienced in the past, whereas anticipatory coping pertains to inevitable threats in the near future. Preventive coping refers to uncertain threats in the distant future, whereas proactive coping involves future challenges that are seen as self-promoting (see Figure 23.2).

Reactive coping. Reactive coping can be defined as an effort to deal with a stressful encounter that is ongoing or that has already happened, or with the aim to compensate for or to accept harm or loss. Examples for loss or harm are job loss, failing a job interview, having an accident at work, being criticized by the boss, or having been demoted. All of these events happened in the past with absolute

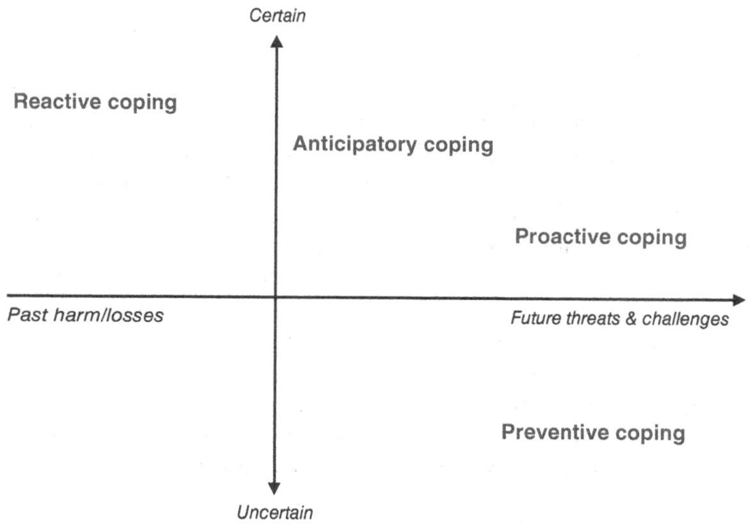

FIGURE 23.2 Four coping perspectives

certainty; thus, the individual who needs to cope has to either compensate for loss or alleviate harm. Another option is to readjust the goals or to search for meaning to reconceptualize one's life (Locke, 2002, 2005). Reactive coping may be problem-focused, emotion-focused, or social-relations-focused. For coping with loss or harm, individuals have to be resilient. Since they aim at compensation or recovery, they need "recovery self-efficacy," a particular optimistic belief in their capability to overcome setbacks (Schwarzer, 2008).

Anticipatory coping. Anticipatory coping can be defined as an effort to deal with imminent threat. In anticipatory coping, individuals face a critical event that is certain to occur in the near future. Examples are speaking in public, a confrontation at a business meeting, a job interview, adapting to a new job, increased workload, promotion, retirement, downsizing, etc. There is a risk that the upcoming event may cause harm or loss later on, and the person has to manage this perceived risk. The situation is appraised as an imminent threat. The function of coping may lie in preparatory actions, for example, practicing speaking to an audience or solving the actual problem at hand through taking actions, such as increasing effort, getting help, or investing other resources. Another function may lie in feeling good in spite of the risk. For example, one could reframe the situation as less threatening, distract oneself or gain reassurance from others. Thus, anticipatory coping can also be understood as the management of known risks, which includes investing one's resources to prevent or combat the stressor. One of the resources is specific "coping self-efficacy." This is the optimistic belief of being able to cope successfully with the particular situation.

Preventive coping. Preventive coping can be defined as an effort to build up general resistance resources that result in less strain in the future (minimizing severity of impact), less severe consequences of stress, should it occur, and less likely onset of stressful events in the first place. In preventive coping, individuals face the risk of a critical event that may or may not occur in the distant future. Examples are job loss, forced retirement, physical impairment, disaster, or poverty. The individual plans for the occurrence of such non-normative life events that are potentially threatening. Again, coping equals risk management, but here one has to manage various unknown risks in the distant future. The outlook creates anxiety sufficient to stimulate a broad range of coping behaviors. Since all kinds of harm or loss could materialize one day, the individual builds up general resistance resources, accumulating wealth, insurance, social bonds, and skills (as in the case of anticipatory coping), "just in case." Skill development is a major coping process that helps to prevent undesirable outcomes. General "coping self-efficacy" is a prerequisite to plan and successfully initiate multifarious preventive actions that help build up resistance against threatening non-normative life events in the distant future.

Proactive coping. Proactive coping can be defined as an effort to build up general resources that facilitate promotion toward challenging goals and personal growth (Locke, 2002, 2005). In proactive coping, people have a vision. They see risks, demands, and opportunities in the far future, but they do not appraise these as threats, harm, or loss. Rather, they perceive difficult situations as challenges.

Coping becomes goal management instead of risk management (Locke and Latham, 2002, 2006). Individuals are not reactive, but proactive in the sense that they initiate a constructive path of action and create opportunities for growth. The proactive individual strives for the improvement of life or work and builds up resources that assure the progress and quality of functioning. Proactively creating better work conditions and higher performance levels is experienced as an opportunity to render life meaningful or to find purpose in life. Instead of strain, the individual experiences productive arousal and vital energy along with perceived self-efficacy.

Preventive coping and proactive coping are partly manifested in the same kinds of overt behaviors as skill development, resource accumulation, and long-term planning. However, the motivation can emanate either from threat appraisal or from challenge appraisal, which makes a difference. Worry levels are high in the former and low in the latter. Proactive individuals are motivated to meet challenges and commit themselves to personal quality standards. Self-regulatory goal management includes an ambitious manner of goal setting and tenacious goal pursuit (Locke and Latham, 2002, 2006; see Chapter 5). Goal pursuit requires "action self-efficacy," an optimistic belief that one is capable of initiating difficult courses of action. The role of beliefs in self-regulatory goal attainment has been spelled out in more detail in the health action process approach (Schwarzer, 2008).

The distinction between these four perspectives on coping is highly useful because it shifts the focus from mere responses to negative events toward a broader range of risk and goal management. The latter includes the active creation of opportunities and the positive experience of challenge, in particular in the work domain. Aspinwall and Taylor (1997) have described a proactive coping theory that is similar, but not identical, to the present one. Schwarzer and Taubert (2002) have made psychometric discriminations between preventive and proactive coping. The Proactive Coping Scale can be downloaded from the web (Greenglass, Schwarzer, and Taubert, 1999).

Ways of Coping

Coping at the Level of Organizations: Designing Healthy Workplaces

When an unexpected event happens, such as a strike or a company takeover, an organization has to cope in a reactive manner. Reducing harm or compensating for loss is required, and the way this is done depends largely on the particular nature of the stress episode. When such events are imminent and certain, anticipatory coping is required. The adequate way of coping is highly idiosyncratic. Preventive coping is called for when no specific events are envisioned, but a more general threat in the distant future comes into view. Such events could be the dangers of economic decline, potential mergers or downsizing, revised governmental employee health regulations, aging workforce, new technology, etc. When visions or challenges and a perceived potential for growth or mastery prevail, proactive coping is initiated.

The latter two perspectives entail about the same set of innovations. In the literature, this is usually discussed as "primary prevention" or "organizational prevention" (Quick et al., 1997), which includes modifying work demands and improving relationships at work.

Physical settings can be redesigned to minimize distressful effects of the physical work environment, such as noise, heat, and crowding. The creation of pleasant and suitable offices or workshops, enriched by cafeterias and fitness centers, can elevate job satisfaction, job safety, and mental health, which indirectly may improve performance and loyalty. *Job redesign* is aimed at changing task demands, for example, by partitioning the workload, job rotation, job enlargement, job enrichment, building teams, opening feedback channels, etc. (c.f. Judge, Chapter 8). *Flexible work schedules* can help to enhance the employee's control and discretion and allow for a better time management and integration of work and nonwork demands (c.f. Balzer, this volume). *Participative management and delegation* expand the amount of autonomy at work by disseminating information, decentralizing decision-making, and involving subordinates in a variety of work arrangements. When a boss promotes trust (see Chapter 17) with the employees, tension and conflict is reduced, and the awareness of partnership may arise. The empowerment approach has a similar focus (see Chapter 14). *Career development* is another method of preventive or proactive coping to improve an estimable portfolio of skills and talents. A set of career paths must be made transparent, and various opportunities for promotion need to be created to motivate employees to set goals for themselves and strive for these goals. This needs to be enriched by an effective feedback and reward system. Self-assessment must be encouraged, and opportunities constantly need to be analyzed (Lawler, 1994).

Organizational prevention is also directed at interpersonal demands placed on individuals at the workplace (Quick et al., 1997). *Role analysis* is aimed at making a person's role within an organization transparent. Clarifying one's role profile in comparison to the profiles of others may help to reduce tension, misperceptions, and conflict. Roles are defined as a set of expectations (by boss, peers, and subordinates) toward a particular position holder. If roles are misperceived, "role stress" will emerge. Thus, role analysis and correction of perceptions constitute a way of preventive coping. *Goal setting* in itself can be regarded as a method of preventive coping in order to avoid miscomprehension about one's responsibilities and expected task performance (Locke, 2005). Negotiating proximal and distal work goals includes an agreement between supervisor and subordinate or team about the conditions under which they should be attained and the criteria that apply for their evaluation (see Chapter 5). *Team building* is a preventive coping method that aims at the establishment of cohesive and effective work groups that perform at a higher level than isolated individuals, partly because they resolve interpersonal conflicts and develop a cohesive spirit (Peterson, Park, and Sweeney, 2008). *Social support* reflects broad-range prevention and intervention at all levels. The term denotes a coping resource as well as an interpersonal coping process, depending on the point in time within a defined stress episode. Social support is generally seen as a buffer against the impact of stress – although, empirically, main effects occur more frequently than statistical interactions (Greenglass, Fiksenbaum, and Eaton, 2006; Schwarzer and Knoll, 2007). As a buffer, social support can be part of reactive coping after the event has struck. As a preventive and proactive coping strategy, social network building equals the institution of a convoy that accompanies and protects the individual throughout the life course when times get rough.

Stress in organizations is related to their culture and leadership, organizational structures, and developments. Proactive leaders have transformed stressed corporations into healthy ones, and restructuring has created relatively stress-free work environments, as has been documented for Southwest Airlines, Chaparral Steel Company, Xerox Corporation, Johnson and Johnson, or, as a negative example, Eastern Airlines (Quick et al., 1997).

Case Examples

Preventive Coping at the Level of Organizations: Improving the Employability of an Aging Workforce

The following example demonstrates how an organization may cope with the demographic changes of its workforce in a preventive as well as a proactive manner. The Deutsche Bahn AG, Germany's national railway company, employs approximately 200,000 personnel, of whom about 30% are 50 years and older. By 2015, this number is expected to double to an estimated 60%. Whereas such a demographic change is often seen as a threat to organizational functioning, the view and strategies taken by the company's human resources department is more differentiated in that it counteracts risks and values opportunities. The risks inherent in an aging work staff are faced by preventive coping strategies and, at the same time, the opportunities seized with proactive measures. Risks of the aging workforce include diminishing health and physical functioning as well as outdated qualifications. The human resources department set up an agenda for maintaining the employability of their workforce. At the organizational level, this refers to the capability to realize potential through sustainable employment. Such preventive coping strategies include comprehensive health promotion strategies, job rotation, job enlargement, job enrichment, and technological advances to minimize physical strain.

The other side of the coin of an increasing percentage of older employees is to value their judgments and competence, along with their sense of responsibility and ability to gauge complex situations. These resources of older employees that are highly correlated with professional experience are coined "demographic return." Comprehending these advantages can be viewed as proactive coping strategies that encompass age-mixed teams, individual tandem solutions, and systematic job selection. In the face of rapidly changing macroeconomic demands, preventive and proactive coping behavior at the organizational level allow organizations to develop their potential for growth.

At the school level, teacher stress and burnout can be prevented and mitigated by making them healthier workplaces. Based on his work in schools in Israel Friedman (1999) suggests tackling the sources of stress by reducing the degree of polarization in the classroom and the number of pupils per class and by changing teachers' work schedules. To treat the symptoms of stress at the school level, he suggests creating a supportive atmosphere, open channels of communication, involve teachers in decision-making, and develop an open and positive organizational climate.

Coping at the Individual Level Within Organizations

At the individual level, Friedman (1999) suggests tackling the sources of stress by training teachers to cope with stressful situations, instruct them about the causes of burnout, and develop and improve their abilities in problem-solving, conflict resolution, and leadership. To treat the symptoms of stress, he suggests in-service training, holidays, support and assistance groups, and workshops.

Some general theoretical comments on individual coping have to be added here, based on the distinction between reactive, anticipatory, preventive, and proactive coping. If a person fails to meet a work goal, is rejected by colleagues, has a conflict with the boss, suffers from repetitive stress injury, or loses a contract or the job itself, *reactive coping* takes place because the demands or events are appraised as ongoing or as prior harm or loss. A range of mental and behavioral coping options are at the individual's disposal, depending on the available resources, preferences, and nature of the stress episode. Relaxation is a commonplace recommendation to alleviate negative emotions or arousal, although it does not contribute much to solve the underlying problem. Cognitive restructuring helps to see the world with different eyes. Instrumental action may solve the problem at hand. As noted earlier, the distinctions have been made between problem-focused and emotion-focused coping (Lazarus, 1991). Social relations coping (Hobfoll, 1989) has been added as a third dimension. Mobilizing support and talking with others are suggestions to cope with adversity. The experience of harm or loss calls for compensatory efforts (mastery) or search for meaning and flexible goal adjustment (Locke, 2002). There is no basic rule or rank order of good and bad coping strategies that apply to harm or loss situations. The individual adapts in an idiosyncratic manner to the situation and evaluates the coping efforts retrospectively as having been more or less successful, which may not correspond with the evaluation of onlookers. If someone fails to adapt, social support needs to be mobilized from outside, and psychological counseling, therapy, traumatic event debriefing, or even medical care may become necessary.

If someone faces a critical event in the near future, such as a public presentation, job interview, medical procedure, or corporate decision about redundancy of jobs – in other words, situations that are appraised as threatening – this stress episode requires *anticipatory coping*. The range of coping options is the same as before. Increased effort to master the situation is adaptive only if the situation is under personal control (interview and presentation), whereas situations under external control (medical procedure and corporate decision) require mainly emotional and cognitive efforts (e.g. relaxation and reappraisal).

An individual who faces increasing work challenges or job volatility in the distant future, such as downsizing, mergers, demotion, promotion, and entrepreneurship, is better off to choose either *preventive coping* strategies (in the case of threat appraisal) or *proactive coping* strategies (in the case of challenge appraisal). The long-term accumulation of general resistance resources includes behavioral, social, and cognitive strategies. Coping with one's work demands, for example, comprises setting priorities, avoiding overload, delegating tasks, acquiring social support, planning, and having good time management (Quick et al., 1997), and, above all, always improving one's skills and developing new ones. Managing one's lifestyle is directed at a healthy balance between work, family, and leisure (Schaer, Bodenmann, and Klink, 2008; see Chapter 26). Workaholics do not maintain such a balance because they are trying to use work to alleviate self-doubt that is not caused by work problems, and they hardly find refuge anywhere. Work stress can spill over into nonwork settings, and vice versa, which places a particular burden on women and dual-career couples (Greenglass, 2002). Protecting life domains from daily hassles is an important aspect of self-regulation. Some companies grant their employees extra time for revitalization and personal growth, for example, by funding sabbaticals. Healthy nutrition and physical exercise are other lifestyle ingredients that bear a protective shield against the experience of stress.

Stress management programs are usually not implemented by corporations as stand-alone programs, but rather as part of more comprehensive *health promotion strategies* that also aim at preventive nutrition, physical exercise, smoking cessation, preventing use of alcohol and drugs, and others. IBM, Control Data Corporation, Illinois Bell, New York Telephone Company, B. F. Goodrich Tire, Citicorp, Johnson and Johnson, and Dupont are among the companies cited frequently that have established high-quality health promotion programs for their employees (see also Quick et al., 1997).

The cognitive way of coping includes stress reappraisal, internal dialogue, constructive self-talk, search for meaning, or optimistic explanatory style, among others. Individuals can develop a more positive view of stressful situations, which may facilitate all kinds of coping. Reinterpreting a threat into a challenge transforms preventive coping into proactive coping. The following case study, inspired by Covey (1989), shall demonstrate how proactive coping behavior may enlarge an individual's range of control at the workplace.

Proactive Coping at the Individual Level Within Organizations: Dealing with an Authoritarian Leader

The president of the organization in which Mr. X is employed is known for his authoritarian leadership style. Even though his executives view the president as being a dynamic and talented person, they feel restricted and alienated by his style of management, which consists of orders and creates an atmosphere of dictatorship. Unlike the other colleagues, who cope with the situation by criticizing and complaining about the conditions, Mr. X tries to compensate for the weak management by trying to enlarge his range of control. When assigned to a task, he acts proactively by anticipating the president's needs. He provides not only requested information on an issue, but also an analysis and recommendations on how to deal with the issue. Eventually, he wins the president's trust. Instead of receiving orders, he is asked for his opinion. This example illustrates how proactively taking the initiative may not only increase one's decision latitude, but also how an obstacle may be turned into a positive experience.

Proactive Coping at the Individual Level Within Organizations: Gain Control by Developing Hardiness

Habitual mindsets that reflect a constructive approach to life are inherent in the concepts of perceived self-efficacy (see Chapter 6), learned optimism (Seligman, 1991), and hardiness (Maddi, 1998). By improving such mindsets, employees can be empowered to take charge of upcoming challenges in the workplace and to gain more control over their lives. In other words, they develop resources as a prerequisite for preventive and proactive coping. The hardiness concept has been applied frequently to prevent and mitigate stress at work. It comprises the attitudes of commitment, control, and challenge. The goal of interventions, for example, as those conducted by the Hardiness Institute, lies in the promotion of these attitudes. Initially, participants respond to the HardiSurvey that assesses these three components and allows one to gauge how much work stress a person experiences. Clients then undergo the 16-hour HardiTraining course, consisting of exercises on how to cope with stress, relax, seek social support, eat right, and work out (Maddi, Kahn, and Maddi, 1998). With a group of 54 managers, hardiness training was compared to relaxation training and to a social support control condition. The first group reported less strain and illness and higher job satisfaction. Thus, hardiness is seen as stimulating effective functioning and protecting wellness under stressful conditions.

Proactive Coping at the Individual Level Within Organizations: Learned Optimism Training

An example of a program at the individual level within organizations is the "learned optimism training" that was conducted at Metropolitan Life Insurance Company (Seligman, 1991; Seligman and Schulman, 1986). Learned optimism is a proxy for a particular explanatory style that can be acquired to improve one's interpretation of stressful events in general or specifically at work. A diagnostic measure, the Attributional Style Questionnaire (ASQ), was developed, which ranks individuals on an optimism/pessimism scale. One prediction of this measure concerns job performance, for example, successfully selling life insurance. Insurance agents with high scores on the ASQ invest more effort and are more persistent in "cold calling" of customers and attain better sales commissions than low scorers. By using this diagnostic instrument to select personnel, Metropolitan Life has saved millions of dollars. Many companies now use such scales in order to identify applicants who possess more than just drive and talent, namely the optimism necessary for success, as well. Based on Seligman's theory and his assessment procedure, a training program has been developed to teach employees cognitive coping with stress. Participants with chronic negative thoughts learn to talk to themselves in a constructive manner. If something goes wrong, pessimists tend to have hopeless thoughts ("I always screw up"; "I'll never get it right"), that is, internal, stable, and global attributions of negative events. They learn to transform these thoughts into external, variable, or specific attributions, such as "Things didn't go well today, but I learned a lot from the experience." Workshop participants learn to listen to their own internal dialogue and to dispute their chronic negative thoughts and come up with a more balanced view of themselves, the world, and the future. The four-day course is administered by Foresight, Inc., at Falls Church, VA. Unlike other courses for sales agents, which teach what to say to clients, this course teaches what to say to oneself when the client says no. Thus, it represents cognitive coping training to reduce stress when facing interpersonal demands. The most typical exercise is to identify adverse events, the corresponding subjective belief, and the most likely subsequent emotions and behaviors. Then, after recognizing one's explanatory style, the participants learn to dispute their thoughts. They are asked to make the revised explanatory style a new habit to supplant their usual automatic pessimistic explanations. In psychotherapy, this is known as cognitive restructuring. This principle has turned out to be a powerful coping strategy that facilitates job performance, job satisfaction, and health.

In sum, the examples have demonstrated the broad scope of coping in organizations and have pointed to the direction in which interventions could go to facilitate more preventive and proactive coping. Coping is a set of mental and physical behaviors, whereas perceived self-efficacy, hardiness, optimism, etc., are social cognitive concepts that may provide the backdrop for improved coping. As such, they can be regarded as moderators of the stress-coping relationship. Those who harbor high levels of resourceful mindsets are better off when it comes to transforming a demanding situation. Emotional or impulsive ways of coping are not compatible with preventive and proactive coping because the latter are based on reason (Locke, 2005).

Conclusion

Coping with stress is a normal and necessary experience in daily life. At the workplace, it gains particular importance because it is related not only to individual career goals, health, and satisfaction, but also to organizational success and social relations. To understand coping, a number of analytical dimensions, perspectives, theoretical models, and approaches have been suggested. In this chapter, a new distinction between reactive, anticipatory, preventive, and proactive coping has been put forward because these coping perspectives have unique value for stress at the workplace, including the positive side of stress. Interventions have to be tailored to these perspectives. Events that are appraised as harm or loss require different coping interventions than those that are appraised as threats or challenges. The current view connects coping theory with action theory and sets the stage for integrative programs at the organizational and individual level. It is in line with the contemporary trend toward a "positive psychology" (Peterson et al., 2008; Seligman, 2008).

References

Aspinwall, L. G., and Taylor, S. E. (1997). A stitch in time: Self-regulation and proactive coping. *Psychological Bulletin,* 121, 417–436.

Brandtstädter, J. (1992). Personal control over development: Implications of self-efficacy. In R. Schwarzer (ed.), *Self Efficacy: Thought Control of Action* (pp. 127–145). Washington, DC: Hemisphere.

Cartwright, S., and Cooper, C. L. (1997). *Managing Workplace Stress.* Thousand Oaks, CA: Sage.

Covey, S. R. (1989). *The 7 Habits of Highly Effective People: Restoring the Character Ethic.* New York: Simon and Schuster.

Friedman, I. A. (1999). Turning over schools into a healthier workplace: Bridging between professional self-efficacy and professional demands. In R. Vandenberghe and A. M. Huberman (eds), *Understanding and Preventing Teacher Burnout* (pp. 166–175). Cambridge, UK: Cambridge University Press.

Greenglass, E. (2002). Proactive coping. In E. Frydenberg (ed.), *Beyond Coping: Meeting Goals, Vision, and Challenges* (pp. 37–62). London: Oxford University Press.

Greenglass, E., Schwarzer, R., and Taubert, S. (1999). *The Proactive Coping Inventory (PCI): A Multidimensional Research Instrument* [On-line publication]. Available at: http://www.ralfschwarzer.de

Greenglass, E., Fiksenbaum, L., and Eaton, J. (2006). The relationship between coping, social support, functional disability and depression in the elderly. *Anxiety, Stress and Coping,* 19(1), 15–31.

Hobfoll, S. E. (1989). Conservation of resources: A new attempt at conceptualizing stress. *American Psychologist,* 44(3), 513–524.

Kasl, S. V. (1996). The influence of the work environment on cardiovascular health: A historical, conceptual, and methodological perspective. *Journal of Occupational Health Psychology,* 1(1), 42–56.

Klusmann, U., Kunter, M., Trautwein, U., Lüdtke, O., and Baumert, J. (2008). Engagement and emotional exhaustion in teachers. Does the school context make a difference? *Applied Psychology: An International Review. Special Issue: Health and Well-Being,* 57, 127–151.

Lawler, E. E. III. (1994). From job-based to competency-based organizations. *Journal of Organizational Behavior,* 15, 3–16.

Lazarus, R. S. (1991). *Emotion and Adaptation.* London: Oxford University Press.

Locke, E. A. (2002). Setting goals for life and happiness. In C. R. Snyder and S. Lopez (eds), *Handbook of Positive Psychology* (pp. 299–312). Oxford, UK: Oxford University Press.

Locke, E. A. (2005). Coping with stress through reason. In A. Antoniou and C. Cooper (eds), *Research Companion to Organizational Health Psychology* (pp. 188–197). Cheltenham, UK: Elgar.

Locke, E. A., and Latham, G. P. (2002). Building a practically useful theory of goal setting and task motivation: A 35-year odyssey. *American Psychologist,* 57, 705–717.

Locke, E. A., and Latham, G. P. (2006). New directions in goal-setting theory. *Current Directions in Psychological Science,* 15, 265–268.

Maddi, S. R., Kahn, S., and Maddi, K. L. (1998). The effectiveness of hardiness training. *Consulting Psychology Journal*, 50, 78–86.

Maddi, S. R. (1998). Creating meaning through making decisions. In Wong, P. T. P., Fry, P. S., et al. (eds), *The Human Quest for Meaning: A Handbook of Psychological Research and Clinical Applications* (pp. 3–26). Mahwah, NJ: Erlbaum.

Marmot, M. G., Bosma, H., Hemingway, H., Brunner, E., and Stansfeld, S. (1997). Contribution of job control and other risk factors to social variations in coronary heart disease incidence. *Lancet*, 350, 235–239.

Maslach, C., Jackson, S. E., and Leiter, M. P. (1996). *Maslach Burnout Inventory manual* (3rd edition). Palo Alto, CA: Consulting psychologists Press.

Maslach, C., Schaufeli, W. B., and Leiter, M. P. (2001). Job burnout. *Annual Review of Psychology*, 52, 397–422.

Peterson, C., Park, N., and Sweeney, P. J. (2008). Group well-being: Morale from a positive psychology perspective. *Applied Psychology: An International Review. Special Issue: Health and Well-Being*, 57, 19–36.

Quick, J. C., Quick, J. D., Nelson, D. L., and Hurrell, J. J., Jr. (1997). *Preventive Stress Management in Organizations.* Washington, DC: APA.

Rothbaum, F., Weisz, J. R., and Snyder, S. (1982). Changing the world and changing the self: A two-process model of perceived control. *Journal of Personality and Social Psychology*, 42, 5–37.

Schaer, M., Bodenmann, G., and Klink, T. (2008). Balancing work and relationship: Couples coping enhancement training (CCET) in the workplace. *Applied Psychology: An International Review. Special Issue: Health and Well-Being*, 57, 71–89.

Schaufeli, W. B., and Bakker, A. B. (2004). Job demands, job resources and their relationship with burnout and engagement: A multi-sample study. *Journal of Organizational Behavior*, 25, 293–315.

Schwarzer, R. (2008). Modeling health behavior change: How to predict and modify the adoption and maintenance of health behaviors. *Applied Psychology*, 57(1), 1–29.

Schwarzer, R., and Hallum, S. (2008). Perceived teacher self-efficacy as a predictor of job stress and burnout: Mediation analyses. *Applied Psychology: An International Review. Special Issue: Health and Well-Being*, 57, 152–171.

Schwarzer, R., and Knoll, N. (2007). Functional roles of social support within the stress and coping process: A theoretical and empirical overview. *International Journal of Psychology*, 42(4), 243–252.

Schwarzer, R., and Knoll, N. (2009). Proactive coping. In S. J. Lopez (ed.), *The Encyclopedia of Positive Psychology* (Vol. II, pp. 781–784). Oxford, England & Malden, MA: Wiley-Blackwell.

Schwarzer, R., and Luszczynska, A. (2007). Self-efficacy. In M. Gerrard and K. D. McCaul (eds), *Health Behavior Constructs: Theory, Measurement, and Research.* National Cancer Institute Website: http://cancercontrol.cancer.gov/constructs

Schwarzer, R., and Luszczynska, A. (2008). Reactive, anticipatory, preventive and proactive coping: A theoretical distinction. *The Prevention Researcher*, 15(4), 22–24.

Schwarzer, R., and Luszczynska, A. (2012). Stressful life events. In I. B. Weiner (Ed.-in-Chief), A. M. Nezu, C. M. Nezu, and P. A. Geller (Vol. eds), *Handbook of Psychology: Vol. 9. Health Psychology* (2nd rev. edition, pp. 29–56). New York: Wiley.

Schwarzer, R., and Schwarzer, C. (1996). A critical survey of coping instruments. In M. Zeidner and N. S. Endler (eds), *Handbook of Coping: Theory, Research and Applications* (pp. 107–132). New York: Wiley.

Schwarzer, R., and Taubert, S. (2002). Tenacious goal pursuits and striving toward personal growth: Proactive coping. In E. Frydenberg (ed.), *Beyond Coping: Meeting Goals, Visions and Challenges* (pp. 19–35). London: Oxford University Press.

Seligman, M. E. P. (2008). Positive health. *Applied Psychology: An International Review. Special Issue: Health and Well-Being*, 57, 3–18.

Seligman, M. E. P. (1991). *Learned Optimism.* New York: Knopf.

Seligman, M. E. P., and Schulman, P. (1986). Explanatory style as a predictor of productivity and quitting among life insurance sales agents. *Journal of Personality and Social Psychology*, 50(4), 832–838.

Shumaker, S. A., and Brownell, A. (1984). Toward a theory of social support: Closing conceptual gaps. *Journal of Social Issues*, 40, 11–36.

Siegrist, J. (1996). Adverse health effects of high-effort/low-reward conditions. *Journal of Occupational Health Psychology*, 1, 27–41.

Spielberger, C. D. (1994). *Professional Manual for the Job Stress Survey (JSS).* Odessa, FL: Psychological Assessment Resources.

Taylor, S. E. (1983). Adjustment to threatening events: A theory of cognitive adaptation. *American Psychologist*, 38, 1161–1173.

Theorell, T., and Karasek, R. (1996). Current issues relating to psychosocial job strain and cardiovascular disease research. *Journal of Occupational Health Psychology*, 1(1), 9–26.

Weidner, G., Boughal, T., Connor, S. L., Pieper, C., and Mendell, N. R. (1997). Relationship of job strain to standard coronary risk factors and psychological characteristics in women and men of the Family Heart study. *Health Psychology*, 16(3), 239–247.

Whetton, D. A., and Cameron, K. S. (1993). *Developing Management Skills: Managing Stress.* New York: HarperCollins.

Exercises

1. Coping Behaviors

In your classroom or work group, you may share each other's experience with proactive coping behaviors and, thus, provide and find role models for future situations. In the following, you find the proactive coping subscale of the Proactive Coping Inventory by Greenglass, Schwarzer, and Taubert (1999). The statements deal with reactions you may have to various situations. Indicate how true each of these statements is depending on how you feel about the situation. Do this by responding to one of the four statements "not at all true," "barely true," "somewhat true," or "completely true."

1. "I am a 'take charge' person."
2. "I try to let things work out on their own." (-)
3. "After attaining a goal, I look for another, more challenging one."

4. "I like challenges and beating the odds."
5. "I visualize my dreams and try to achieve them."
6. "Despite numerous setbacks, I usually succeed in getting what I want."
7. "I try to pinpoint what I need to succeed."
8. "I always try to find a way to work around obstacles; nothing really stops me."
9. "I often see myself failing so I don't get my hopes up too high." (-)
10. "When I apply for a position, I imagine myself filling it."
11. "I turn obstacles into positive experiences."
12. "If someone tells me I can't do something, you can be sure I will do it."
13. "When I experience a problem, I take the initiative in resolving it."
14. "When I have a problem, I usually see myself in a no-win situation." (-)

Complete the assignments and then, in small groups of four to five individuals, compare your own answers with those of your colleagues. Choose a statement on which you responded "completely true" (statements marked with a (-) demand reverse coding) as a positive example for proactive coping and one statement as a negative example ("not at all" or "completely true" for (-) statements) and share your experience by illustrating a situation in which you responded in the way it is described in the statements.

2. Personal Coping Experiences

Identify a situation you encountered in the past where you behaved in a reactive manner (e.g. reacting toward criticism, working on a project with a colleague who is permanently late). Review the situation in the context of your range of control and potential alternate pathways. How could you have responded? Take several moments and create the experience vividly in your mind. Share your experience with your classmates/colleagues and discuss further ways of coping with challenging situations.

Video Analysis and Discussion

Please watch the following video(s):

1. How to make stress your friend: https://www.youtube.com/watch?v=RcGyVTAoXEU
2. The cost of workplace stress: https://www.youtube.com/watch?v=QE8kNh52EeU

Now form small groups to discuss the video(s) and answer the following questions:

1. What are the major points of the video?
2. How can you use information from the video in your career?
3. Based on the video, what advice do you have for leaders in organizations?

Be prepared to present the ideas from your small group discussion with the class as a whole.

Discussion Questions

1. Imagine that the revenue of your company is declining and there is a danger of downsizing within the next couple of years and you may be one of those who become unemployed. How much stress do you feel? What are your coping resources? How do you cope?
2. Your boss is nerve racking. Yesterday, he has criticized your performance again. How much stress do you feel? What are your coping resources? How do you cope?

24

Conflict Resolution Through Negotiation and Mediation

KEVIN TASA AND ENA CHADHA

Schulich School of Business, York University

A manager is by default a negotiator and mediator. They mediate task, process, and relationship conflict; establish rules and goals; and negotiate resources – the latter being one of the more intractable sources of conflict. Conflict is inevitable in all organizations and often is rooted in several predictable catalysts, such as ambiguous lines of authority, conflicting goals, high levels of interdependence, and scarce resources. These structural factors generate a perfect storm of conditions for conflict in the workplace and, whether it is in North America or South Asia, it is estimated that managers spend about 40% of their time managing conflict (Desikan, 2018; Ilgaz, 2014).

What exactly is meant by the term *conflict*? Conflict may be defined as a "sharp disagreement or opposition, as of interests, ideas, etc." and includes "the perceived divergence of interest, or a belief that the parties' current aspirations cannot be achieved simultaneously" (Pruitt and Rubin, 1986). Conflict frequently occurs across many aspects of the manager's job; for example, in interactions with their own superiors, dealings with peers or associates, and supervision of employees. Therefore, managers face and must attempt to resolve conflict on a daily basis. Various studies establish that effective conflict management is positively correlated with higher employee performance and job satisfaction, whereas the costs of conflict mismanagement are evidenced in poor employee morale, absenteeism, loss of productivity, and potentially even litigation (e.g. Elangovan, 1995; Karambayya, Brett, and Lytle, 1992; Porath, 2016).

This chapter focuses on the manager's role as conflict resolver and is based on the meta principle that negotiation and mediation processes, when deployed appropriately, enhance manager effectiveness in resolving many of the conflicts that arise at work. With that in mind, we present empirically derived negotiation and mediation strategies that managers can utilize to proactively deal with conflict, mitigate the likelihood that conflict will arise, and support the productivity and health of their organization.

The Sources of Conflict and Effectiveness Criteria

People who are inexperienced in dealing with conflict commonly assume that disputes are caused by traits or attributes of the specific parties involved in the strife. For example, if two employees are unable to work together effectively, this is often attributed to "personality clashes" or different working styles. This tendency to diagnose conflict as stemming from individual characteristics is an indicator of the fundamental attribution error, which is the tendency to overemphasize internal causes of others' behavior and discount or ignore external or situational factors. While it is certainly true that some employees generate greater conflict than others, it is also more likely true that certain conditions within organizations increase the likelihood of conflict.

Managers who are attuned to the structural sources of conflict are better able to envision a wider range of solutions and are better equipped to find alternatives that satisfy the interests of all involved parties. Four key structural sources of conflict in organizations that managers should be aware of include (i) goal incompatibility, (ii) interdependence, (iii) ambiguous rules, and (iv) scarce resources. *Goal incompatibility* occurs when the goals of one person or unit intrude on, or impede, the goals of another. A classic example would be the tension between a production department, which strives for consistently high quality, and the sales department, which strives for speed of delivery. *Interdependence* refers to the fact that employees or units must rely on each other to perform a task and, in doing so, share things like materials, information, or expertise. Conflict can arise when an employee or team believes the other person or team they depend on is not providing necessary data or supplies or adequately fulfilling their part of the performance process. *Ambiguous rules* also breed significant conflict. This is because uncertainty or lack of transparency increases the potential for one party to be perceived as acting inappropriately, perhaps by using tactics that are perceived as political. *Resource scarcity* stems from the reality that budgets and assets are rarely unlimited, and conflict can arise over who should, or should not, be given resources.

These four structural conditions of organizational conflict are not mutually exclusive and are often compounding. A manager who is aware of the effects of the four organizational sources of conflict will be less likely to jump to the conclusion that a particular problem is being caused by the incalcitrant personal traits of the parties involved. There are benefits of a manager first identifying the structural roots of the workplace conflict, as opposed to focusing on the employees' characteristics. This approach allows the manager to detect and tackle systemic issues that underlie the pressure points that are causative of the friction. This also helps the manager proactively address problems that, if left to fester, can become further entrenched and complex.

After examining the conflict to ascertain the structural sources, it is also important to consider the factors that determine whether a particular conflict resolution method is effective. In many cases, managers can either use their managerial authority to impose a solution, delegate the disputants to resolve the issue among themselves, evaluate the problem, and determine the outcome premised on past precedent, rules, or other form of rights. In certain conflictual circumstances, it may be incumbent upon the manager to mediate a solution between the parties in order to preserve relationships and foster viable and sustainable results. When assessing whether to trigger a unilateral, delegated, precedent-based or mediated method of dispute resolution, Ury, Brett, and Goldberg (1988) proposed a framework that focuses on four helpful elements to consider when deciding whether to opt for a certain conflict resolution approach: (i) various transaction expenses, including those that are economic, psychological, and time based; (ii) parties' satisfaction with the fairness of the outcomes and of the resolution process in general; (iii) the effect of the resolution on the parties' relationship, particularly on their ability to work together on a day-to-day basis; and finally, (iv) the likelihood of conflict recurrence, either between the two parties or between one of them and another party. Ury et al. (1988, p. 15) concluded that: "in general reconciling interests is less costly than determining whose rights are more clearly supported by the contract or precedent, which in turn is less costly than determining who is more powerful," a process likely to result in a protracted battle of wills. The notion that conflicts are best resolved by tapping into the interests of the respective parties is what gives rise to the use of negotiation and mediation as essential tools for managers in dealing with workplace problems.

Negotiation as a Managerial Tool for Reconciling Interests

The word *interests* has a very important meaning in the domain of negotiation and conflict. Specifically, *interests* refer to primary needs, imperatives, wants, or desires. In negotiation, people often state their position, saying things like "I want this much," but hide their *interests,* which is the motivating dynamic that actually lies at the core or beneath what they need, want, or would settle for. For example, someone in a job offer negotiation might state that they would only accept the job if the salary is at least at a certain level. However, it is also possible that the quantum of the salary the person is willing to accept is flexible when other job features, such as start date, location, and job title, are taken into account. Thus, the person's interests, i.e. convenience and prestige, are best captured in terms of a whole package as opposed to a particular single issue, i.e. remuneration.

An essential step for resolving conflict, and one of the most important things a manager can do to problem-solve a dispute, is to try to glean the underlying interests of each of the parties. Potential solutions come into sharper focus when the underlying desires and motivating needs of the parties are shared. Information about the triggering interests of disputants is something that expert mediators deftly ascertain in helping parties negotiate a mutually satisfactory solution. An effective manager must learn how to uncover and negotiate interests as a viable tool of dispute resolution. When a manager helps disputing parties self-identify their respective interests in an effort to resolve their differences and reach an agreement, the manager is usually supporting the parties through negotiation and mediation.

Before describing the strategies used to discover and negotiate interests, it is necessary to understand the distinction between *distributive* and *integrative* negotiations. Negotiations can be distributive or integrative in nature depending on the interconnection of parties' goals, the context of the negotiation, and the scope of the relationship. When the parties' interests are strictly competing, their goals are separate and discrete, and relationship temporary, this often gives rise to a *distributive* deal. The aim of a distributive negotiation, known as a zero-sum negotiation, is to succeed in claiming the most value. In distributive situations, the parties apply win-lose tactics and dominating strategies to overcome the competition to secure the largest gain of the fixed resource that they are fighting over. Distributive bargaining is premised on the fact that for one party to gain, the other party must give something up. Distributive negotiations are characteristically focused on the singular issue of value or profit, for example, negotiating the price of a used bike at a garage sale, and the connection between the parties is usually transitory.

In an *integrative* negotiation, the parties' interests can converge, and their objectives are associated such that one parties' attainment of their goals can help their counterpart to satisfy their interests. This integrative exchange is often called a win-win or, in other words, a mutual-gain situation where the successful servicing of the interests and goals of both parties creates expanded value. The 55-year relationship between Elton John, a highly talented musician, and Bernie Taupin, a brilliant lyricist, is the real-life example of an integrative arrangement. John's piano skills may be mesmerizing and Taupin's poetry may be heartfelt, but when merged they are a musical powerhouse team of over 30 successful albums. Similarly, an integrative negotiation seeks to develop symbiotic solutions that benefit all parties.

The individualism of a distributive deal and the interdependence of an integrative negotiation are important distinctions and impact the negotiation strategies that should be applied. A manager may opt for a distributive approach if the situation is fleeting and little other than price is at stake. A manager should opt for an integrative negotiation where a continuing or long-term, rather than temporary, relationship exists, where the interests and aspirations of the parties intersect, and where there are multiple issues at stake. If these elements are present, there is a better prospect of creating more optimal solutions that engender greater and lasting value than the short-term focus of a distributive deal. Unfortunately, inexperienced managers tend to resolve conflict with a distributive mentality because of the allure of a big win and fast solution and lack knowledge about how to facilitate integrative dispute resolution. Next, we provide a number of principles about the nature of integrative negotiation and also generate several recommendations for enhancing a manager's negotiation effectiveness.

Negotiation Principles and Recommendations

Negotiation refers to decision-making situations in which two or more interdependent parties attempt to reach agreement (Lewicki, Saunders, Barry, and Tasa, 2020). Any time we must work with others to determine a future course of action, we negotiate, and despite the frequency with which we negotiate, many people have limited knowledge about the strategies, techniques, and behaviors that correspond with successful outcomes. Our presentation of negotiation principles distinguishes between two phases: the preparation phase and the negotiation phase (Jang, Elfenbein, and Bottom, 2018).

Phase 1: Preparation Prudent negotiators understand that preparation is essential to avoid reactive decision-making and to facilitate productive discussions between parties. Although most people would agree that preparation is useful, most have no idea what it is they should do to prepare. Regardless of the type of negotiation situation, all negotiators should consider their goals, the best alternative to a negotiated agreement (BATNA), and their limits.

Prepare and Set Goals. One of the most important questions to ask yourself is what it is you hope to accomplish in the negotiation. Focus broadly on your underlying interests and do not just focus on quantitative indicators, such as the final price for the purchase of a new commodity. Ask yourself about your overall interests, what is motivating you, and the reasons underlying the positions you might take. For example, earlier we mentioned that salary might not be the only thing that matters when you are starting a new job. A more comprehensive look at the situation might reveal that you want to work in a place that allows you to use skills you recently acquired, to work on interesting tasks, or to live close to family. This type of introspective analysis draws out your interests and values and ultimately determines what you really care about. By identifying these interests and assessing the issues in advance, you minimize the likelihood that you will narrowly focus on just one issue in the negotiation. Preparation will help you pivot and better evaluate your choices.

Know Your BATNA. Next, ask yourself if you do not secure your ideal outcome in this negotiation, what is the best outcome you might achieve through some other means, such as negotiating with someone else, seeking a different option or continuing with the status quo. This comparison is called the BATNA and focuses on what is your next top preferred outcome if you are unable to achieve the current deal. BATNA reflects your power in the negotiation because it represents the estimated cost of walking away from the relationship. If others are willing to negotiate with you for the product or service you need, then you have a high BATNA and considerable power in the negotiation because it would not cost you much to walk away. Classic advice for people buying a new home is to "fall in love with two houses, not just one." Seriously considering a second house means you are less likely to overpay for the one that is your most preferred option.

Know Your Limits. Finally, ask yourself whether you can identify a specific point or threshold beyond which you are indifferent to a negotiated outcome. This point, sometimes called a resistance point or "bottom line," helps you decide whether or not you should call off a negotiation. If you are a seller, your resistance point is the least you will accept in exchange for what you are selling. If you are the buyer, your resistance point is the most you are willing to pay for an item. The reason you should think about this in advance is that too many people, especially those who do not even consider their limits, shift the way they view their bottom line in the face of a competitive offer from a counterpart. It is best to avoid this unless the evidence you receive clearly indicates that your limits may be unreasonable.

Phase 2: Integrative Negotiation If the aim of integrative negotiation is to create agreements that make all parties better off, then it is best to avoid the competitive behaviors associated with distributive bargaining. This is especially true in conflictual situations because competitive tactics often engender resistance, withholding of information, and in some cases, can prompt retaliation or aggression. What, then, are the strategies that work when integrative outcomes are possible?

Gather Information. It is always prudent to assume you have imperfect information in a negotiation or conflict situation. As a result, skilled negotiators focus more on listening than telling. Skilled negotiators also ask many more questions. This means that we should present our position or claim only after spending more time listening closely to the other party and asking for details. It is particularly important to look beyond the opponent's stated justifications to the unstated or in other words the underlying motivation for their stance or claim. As mentioned earlier, people often state their position with little appreciation of their own primary interests. Probing questions (such as asking "why is X important to you" or "what do you need to help X problem") and listening carefully for clues of underlying interests can reveal better solutions for both parties. Gleaning insight about the other party's interest can help you reframe the issues and facilitate more creative problem-solving.

Discover Priorities Through Multi-issue Offers. People often prefer to negotiate unique issues one at a time; for example, they might say to a counterpart, "Let's negotiate issue X, before moving on to issue Y." This is usually a mistake. The reason this is a mistake is that it presumes both sides have opposite and symmetrical priorities on each issue, which is rarely the case. It is far more likely that both sides will view the issues differently, with each having different priorities. For example, a job candidate might approach a negotiation with a potential employer by ranking salary highest, then location assignment, and finally start date. If the employer needs to fill a particular position immediately, they will likely rank start date higher than the candidate. Value is created if both sides agree to have the job candidate start at an early date (satisfying the employer) while also agreeing to a slightly higher salary (satisfying the candidate). The key lesson here is to always be prepared to exchange low-priority issues for high-priority issues.

One way to figure out the relative importance of the issues to each party is to make multi-issue offers rather than discussing one issue at a time. You might offer a client a specific price, delivery date, and guarantee period, for example. The other party's counteroffer to multiple items signals which items are more and which are less important to them. Your subsequent concessions similarly signal how important each issue is to your group. Negotiating a global package of proposals allows you to trade low/high-priority items and enables you to get a sense of your counterpart's priorities.

Build the Relationship. The positive link between trust and satisfaction with negotiation outcomes has been clearly established, and this gives rise to an important question: How do you build trust in negotiations? One approach is to share information that might expose you to a slight degree of perceived vulnerability. When useful information is shared by one party, the other party usually feels a sense of obligation to reciprocate and, therefore, also shares useful information.

Signaling that we are trustworthy also helps strengthen the relationship. We can do this by demonstrating that we are reliable and will keep our promises as well as by identifying shared goals and values. Trustworthiness also increases by developing a shared understanding of the negotiation process, including its norms and expectations about speed and timing. Finally, relationship building hinges on our ability to show concern for the other side's priorities, issues, and circumstances. This includes managing the emotions you display to the other party, particularly avoiding an image of superiority, aggressiveness, or insensitivity.

In summary, the negotiation skills and techniques that facilitate integrative negotiations focus on the development of a sound understanding of a counterpart's interests, the creation of value by exchanging low-priority for high-priority issues, and showing concern for all the parties involved. While these strategies help with the creation of successful negotiated agreements, they also serve as useful behaviors when parties are in conflict.

The Manager as Mediator

Managers routinely become involved in workplace disagreements where they are supervising disputing employees or part of a team debating an issue. Consequently, a manager must be able to act as an intermediary to assist all levels of the organization to respond and resolve internal complaints quickly and effectively. How do successful managers handle such conflictual situations? Building on the negotiation skills and techniques noted earlier, experienced managers serve as mediators enabling conflict resolution discussions and, sometimes, as mediator-arbitrators with final say over the outcome of the parties' negotiated proposal (Karambayya and Brett, 1989).

Mediation is a process of discussions or meetings conducted by a third party who acts as a facilitator to encourage cooperative dialogue to assist individuals achieve resolution of their concerns or issues (Moore, 2014). Mediation allows the individuals in a conflict an opportunity to create solutions that best fit their circumstances. The role of the manager-mediator is to facilitate constructive communication in a structured meeting or series of meetings in the workplace to foster the likelihood of a joint agreement between the disputing parties. Managers are encouraged to use integrative negotiation strategies to facilitate mediations because integrative strategies improve disclosure of interests, aspirations, and priorities, exchange of information, trade-offs, and concessions and brainstorming of ideas, all of which promotes constructive resolution of conflicts.

Managers who mediate a dispute control the process and articulate ground rules to create optimal conditions where employees or peers can safely discuss their differences, disclose their interests, share their goals, engage in creative problem-solving, and achieve a communal resolution. Since mediated solutions are collaboratively agreed upon, these arrangements are often more effective and durable and minimize the risk of conflict resurfacing because parties have participated in crafting the mutually satisfactory resolution.

Key Components of Mediation

There are certain key characteristics for a mediation to be successful. First, each party to the mediated discussions must be willing to work together to participate in the process and to pursue solution-oriented negotiations. While mediation is typically voluntary, certain jurisdictions and business sectors have instituted binding mediations. As such, some organizations have mandated as part of their organizational core values and culture that employees should first attempt mediation in good faith before proceeding with formal grievance mechanisms. If both parties do not agree to participate in a mediated process in good faith, then mediation is unlikely to be effective or efficient and, therefore, an alternative mode of conflict determination must be explored. Thus, before commencing mediation, managers must confirm that the parties are participating in the process in good faith and are willing to come together to discuss the problem.

Second, formal mediation is often a confidential process. Confidentiality is considered a central principle of mediation because it helps foster candid and constructive dialogue. As such, before commencing the mediation process, the manager should ensure that all participants understand and accept to what degree the process will be or will not be confidential and that all parties are aware that they must comply with this level of confidentiality. For example, if the mediation is strictly confidential, then all statements made, along with any information disclosed as part of the process, are only for the purposes of the mediation and cannot be referenced, repeated, or used in any future matters or complaints. Alternatively, the manager may decide that all work-related information shared during the mediation is to be reported to the organization after the completion of the mediation and only personal matters that are not relevant to the workplace problem will be held in confidence. Prior to the commencement of the mediation, the manager must establish the confidentiality parameters and ensure that parties understand whether the information they reveal will be subject to disclosure.

Third, in addition to being willing to speak and/or meet to discuss their issues, all participants must agree to adhere to cooperative and respectful conduct during the mediation process. Agreeing to participate in good faith means that the parties agree to speak politely, genuinely attempt to see their counterpart's perspective, exchange information honestly, and engage in collaborative problem-solving with the sincere goal to pursue a mutually satisfactory outcome in everyone's interests. Managers must set ground rules that establish a positive and respectful tone to the mediation and require courteous dialogue and behavior from all parties aimed at generating ideas to help solve the dilemma.

Finally, aligned with the concept of integrative negotiations, the mediation process is intended to be a creative, interest-based method for constructive and positive problem-solving. The structure of the mediation meeting and how discussions will unfold depends on the issue at hand, the interests of the parties, and the resources and facilities of the organization. While there are no prescribed rules to how the mediations should be structured, managers should first attempt to collect the parties' perspectives, interests, and information about the conflictual situation to help identify each party's needs and goals. At the outset, the manager may give the parties the option to meet in the same room for the introduction of ground rules and to exchange their preliminary views. Alternatively, the manager may decide that it is best to hold separate introductory meetings with each party to allow them a private opportunity to describe their respective perspectives with the manager alone. Private discussions can often help the parties open up about their interests and feelings that they may not be able to express in the presence of the counterpart. To achieve a mutually beneficial solution, an important aspect of this information gathering also includes the manager diplomatically helping each party recognize their underlying interests and acknowledge their interests, responsibilities, or past conduct may be impacting the situation.

Essentially, the manager-mediator serves as the conduit for communicating information between the parties about their interests and goals to encourage discussions to bring forth additional facts, ideas, interests, and proposals from which the parties can create solutions to the issues in dispute. In addition to facilitating open, courteous discussions between the parties, the manager may help generate creative ideas to address the issues, recommend appropriate options, and speak to the organization's standards or best practices, to guide the parties to cooperative results that meet their needs and the organization's goals. The manager may provide some insight or reality check on the reasonableness of the parties' positions and the feasibility of proposed outcomes consistent with the organization's rules and policies. Included at the end of this chapter is a tip sheet of questions to help manager-mediators prepare and implement a mediation meeting.

Key Qualities of a Mediator

To serve as an effective mediator, a manager must demonstrate three important attributes that are essential for fostering integrative negotiations: (i) an aptitude for active listening, (ii) sensitivity to issues of fairness, and (iii) ingenuity and transformative thinking. Active listening in mediation means listening for the parties' individual and overlapping interests and signs of structural sources of conflict. Fairness in mediation is delivered not just in controlling the process to ensure that the parties are treated equitably, but it also means being attuned to power differentials. Finally, a successful mediator promotes an integrative mindset in the parties so that they can come together in the future to solve their problems. Experienced mediators bolster collaboration and conflict resolution by role modeling all three qualities throughout the mediation process.

Active listening means to completely, with concentration and intention, tune into the speaker. It requires the mediator to silence their inner subvocalization and listen without judgment and interruption. Active listening is essential for creating a trusting relationship with the parties because it assists the mediator to better understand the parties' viewpoints. To gain insight into the underlying motivations of each of the parties, the mediator must listen carefully as the party communicates their position to hear for cues of needs and interests that may remain unspoken or unclear. A mediator needs to be able to address the emotions and needs of the parties at stake in a negotiation before tackling substantive issues, and this can only be done by first actively listening to each party's perspective (Fisher and Shapiro, 2005).

Through active listening, a mediator can glean the causal interests and imperatives that lie beneath the party's presentation of their side of the situation to assist the other party to better understand their counterpart's outlook. Active listening is especially key to integrative negotiations because it helps the mediator identify the structural triggers to the conflict, i.e. goal incompatibility, interdependence, ambiguous rules, and scarce resources. As discussed in the introductory section of this chapter, systemic sources of conflict are often overlooked or masked by the common misapprehension that the conflict is a personality clash. Active listening is the mediator's most important skill to help the parties shift from a dysfunctional personalization of the problem to finding common ground that fosters constructive and cooperative problem-solving.

Parties' satisfaction with the mediation process and outcome is heavily dependent on their impressions of fairness and objectivity. To trust the mediation process, parties must believe that the mediator is treating them in a fair manner and is not favoring one side over the other. In workplace mediations, a manager-mediator is rarely a neutral entity. As such, a manager-mediator must be very careful to appear and act fairly or else a perceived inequity may undermine the process. To be effective, the mediator must ensure that both their role and their process is perceived as even-handed. Time spent carefully explaining the mediator's role and the process to the parties and how the mediator will take turns listening to each side and openly sharing information is never wasted time because it protects against concerns of bias and supports better understanding of how the manager will serve the needs and interests of all participants. Managers should be clear that, although they will be fair, balanced, and try to remain objective, their role is to try to diagnose the source of the conflict and help the parties reach agreement, and so they are not a totally disinterested party, but rather are attempting to address the conflict because they have an interest in it being resolved appropriately. In social justice sectors, an important element of promoting fairness in the mediation is helping mitigate any extreme power disparity between the parties. For example, this may mean that the lower power party be permitted to have a support person present or be provided with extra time or that the mediator takes a more active role in asking questions to secure information that may impact the fairness of the outcome.

The ability to engage in creative problem-solving is a vital trait of a successful mediator. Because parties come to the process with a firm idea of their version of the events, parties rarely attend a mediation with an open mind, and this frequently means mediations start with parties entrenched in their viewpoints. Mediators help parties break through impasses by showing them different ways to look at the situation, exploring potential integrative options arising out of their intersecting interests and the prospect of strengthening their relationship. Mediators help parties envision viable solutions often by objectively evaluating the pros and cons of various ideas and formulating solutions by packaging proposals. Building on their respective interests and needs collected through the first stages of active listening, the mediator works with the parties to generate ideas and options to reframe the conflict into an opportunity to constructively collaborate. This requires imagination, improvision, and insight to know when to push a party to think "outside the box." Along with crafting a picture of possible resolutions, another important role of an effective mediator is helping the party appreciate that, what they have fixated on as their answer to the problem, lacks objective standards, is unrealistic from the counterpart's perspective, or is elusive at this time.

CASE EXAMPLE

Conflict at TelComm: An Exercise Stressing the Different Negotiation and Mediation Approaches to Handling Conflict

Introduction. The following text presents two unique viewpoints of a conflict situation between two managers who each work for the same organization. The Customer Service Manager worked with the Education Content Manager to design an in-house training program for the Customer Service staff and things have gone wrong. Conflict has escalated with respect to issues such as the content of the program, payment of fees, and timing of program delivery. Each person's perspective on the facts of the case and their role in the conflict is explained in their unique role information.

This case can be used in several ways. First, the case could be used as a two-party role-play exercise. Each party could be given one set of role information, and the two parties could be asked to simulate how they would try to resolve the conflict. Using the case this way would be a suitable method for practicing the negotiation skills discussed in the chapter.

Second, the case could be used as a three-party role-play in which the third party attempts to mediate the situation. Each manager in the case reports to the VP of Operations, and a third person could be asked to assume this role with limited information. For example, the VP of Operations could be told that a dispute has arisen between the two managers over a training program, the two parties do not seem to be able to resolve it themselves, and that the VP should attempt to mediate the situation. The VP could also be provided with the tip sheet at the end of this chapter and asked to practice managing the meeting accordingly.

Finally, the case could also serve as the basis for a discussion about the various approaches managers can use to negotiate and mediate conflictual situations. Questions that might serve as the basis for a case discussion are the following:

1. If you were one of the managers in the case, how would you prepare for your meeting with the other manager?
2. If you were one of the managers in the case, what type of a negotiation approach would you take? What specific strategies or tactics would you anticipate using?
3. If you were the VP of Operations, how would you mediate this dispute?
4. Instead of being the VP of Operations, how would you mediate this dispute if you were a peer at the same managerial level as the two protagonists?

Role Information for "Customer Service Manager" You work at TelComm, a large nation-wide mobile and wireless telecommunications company, and were hired five years ago. Last year you were promoted to be Manager of TelComm's Customer Service (CS). Your department of 30 CS representatives handles all types of customer contact, including sales, and routes calls for technical assistance. After your arrival to this position, you conducted a full review of the CS unit and concluded the CS team needed immediate improvement in the areas of sales and relationship management. You specifically observed that the entire CS team could benefit by increasing their aptitude for direct and cross-sales and promoting customer relationship management skills. You approached TelComm's Corporate Communication department and were pleased to learn that the Education Content Manager (EC Manager) was responsible for overseeing in-house training materials and specialized in the creation of web-based professional development courses. These courses allow employees to access educational programs via the Internet on their own time.

After deliberating between a costlier well-known training agency, you decided to issue an internal training requisition. You asked the EC Manager to implement an eight-hour online training course in sales and customer relationship management skills for all department staff. You explained that your team also needed to develop skills to increase sales and to be able to manage customers' expectations through the sales process. One of the key performance indicators of your department are cross-sales. These are sales that your team achieves by offering extra mobile services to TelComm's customers calling for assistance (e.g. long-term contracts, data to download, download speed, calls to different countries, etc.). The CS team needs sales training to improve on this task because sales are important for the company's overall revenue and your department's position in the organization.

For the past two quarters, your team has been a low performer on sales. You clearly want to change this pattern. Therefore, you need the team to improve fast. Your next review period is in two months, and you told the EC Manager that the training was urgent. Consequently, the online course needed to be launched within a month's time. Two weeks ago, the EC Manager notified you that the course was up and running, and you then notified your staff that you expected them to begin their training immediately. Although you had expected that the training course would improve productivity, your staff find the orientation tutorials too time consuming and boring. They want to more quickly get into the interesting stuff like the training exercises. They also complain that the course interface is nonintuitive, clumsy, and that the server is often down. As a result, interest has lapsed among staff who had started the course and others who heard about the technical difficulties are reluctant to spend time on the course. Considering how urgent this training program is and how much CS had agreed to pay, this is outrageous!

The EC Manager stated that a consultant specializing in relationship management was necessary to help custom-design the course. The EC Manager recommended a consultant from their professional network and indicated that, with the consultant's guidance, the EC Manager's web-training expertise and your input, the three of you could have the training online within one month. In return, you agreed to pay $10,000 for the consultant's fees. Since this amount was beyond what you had readily available in the CS budget, you felt you were going out on a limb with this arrangement. However, you needed rapid staff improvement and were optimistic top management would agree to a one-time budget infusion once the training program was successfully launched based on positive employee feedback.

Although you attempted to remain abreast of the curriculum content and module design, you found the EC Manager was often unavailable to discuss things in person. You became concerned the EC Manager and consultant were focusing primarily on relationship management and overlooking the fact that sales techniques are important for the company's overall revenue and your department's position in the organization. As such, you were forced to leave multiple voice mail messages explaining your needs and reiterating your concerns that the training needed to focus on promoting both sales and customer relations. You recall that you expressly left a voice mail message instructing the EC Manager to ensure the training included a sales techniques survey that provided individualized feedback to each team member about how they intuitively addressed sales. You hoped that with this personalized insight, the staff would increase sales.

Things got heated on Monday when you called the EC Manager. They started by ordering you to transfer payment of the consultant's fee, and you were shocked by the authoritarian tone. You told the EC Manager that before you would pay the fee the bugs in the system had to be fixed, as due to log-in and interfacing problems staff were saying the course was "a waste of time." When you tried to focus the conversation on specific problems with the course content, the EC Manager insisted that everything was fine. Regarding your complaints about the problematic interface, it seemed as if the EC Manager was accusing your staff of being technologically inept and lazy. Before the call ended, the EC Manager angrily accused you of shirking your obligation to pay the consultant's fee. Very upset, you told the EC Manager that they had completely ignored the need for sales training and unnecessarily focused on the consultant's ideas. You stated that until staff received personalized feedback and the system was fixed, *only* then would you talk about the money. The conversation ended on a very angry note with the phone being slammed down, but you cannot remember who hung up on whom.

You considered taking the matter to the VP of Operations, who you and the EC Manager both report to, but are concerned that it would reflect poorly on your management ability. Also, you have not transferred payment for the consultant, even though the EC Manager sent you a strongly worded email request saying that payment is due in 15 days. Tomorrow is the progress meeting that was originally scheduled when the online course was launched for the purpose of reviewing the team's feedback. You received a calendar reminder from the EC Manager to check if the meeting is proceeding and you agreed to attend the meeting. As you prepare for the meeting, your thoughts on several important matters are as follows:

- Course Content: Most importantly, you think the EC Manager could easily modify the course content to add more information on sales techniques while keeping the eight-hour module structure. This could be accomplished by reducing the amount of introductory tutorial, deleting one full relationship management module, and adding a personalized sales technique survey for the team members to help identify their individual deficiencies.

- Timing: You are really concerned about timing because your staff needs the proper training to improve. Your next review meeting is in two months and you need to show some results. Therefore, you must insist that changes are made quickly.
- Payment of Fees: You are adamant you will not pay the consultant's fee as the product delivered is neither complete nor functioning properly.

Role Information for "Education Content Manager" You joined TelComm, a large nation-wide mobile wireless telecommunications company, three years ago in the Corporate Communications department. When you started, your duties included developing instructional material for customers and designing training packages for employees. Your skills in producing high-quality educational content were recognized when 16 months ago you were promoted to the position of EC Manager. You are responsible for overseeing the creation of in-house training materials, curriculum, and occasionally training other in-house trainers. You have also gained expertise as a designer of web-based courses in which the training content is all online. Employees access professional development courses via the Internet on their own time and study at their own convenience. Last year, you successfully launched an online workplace safety course for all new hires with glowing compliments.

About three months ago, the Manager of TelComm's Customer Service (CS) asked you to design an eight-hour online course regarding sales and customer relationship management skills for the 30 employees that constitute the CS team. The CS Manager also alluded to the need for training to help with customer relations. You have been interested in relationship management skills for a long time, and you think they are fundamental for practice at almost any level of the organization. When you heard about this opportunity, you thought finally the time had come to develop this training. You hope this relationship management training can be extended to other job positions in your organization and become mandatory internal training. During the planning phase, you were not sure the CS Manager had a clear idea of what the center's needs were regarding sales and customer relationship management. Therefore, to fully understand the skills needed by the CS team, you did a two-day job shadowing of a CS team and designed a course specially tailored to the center's needs, with emphasis on relationship management.

The ambitious timeline requested by the CS Manager presented a challenge in terms of curriculum design. You reached out to a well-known consultant who specializes in relationship management and asked whether she would assist. When you presented this option, the CS Manager agreed to pay the $10,000 fee for consultation services out of the CS budget. At that point, you believed the CS Manager was committed to the project, trusted you and the consultant with the content, and agreed to reimburse the costs for the consultation services.

Most of the conversations with the CS Manager were about the timing in which the course would be available. You were aware of the time pressure, and you went without sleep for most of that month to launch the online course by the due date. A few weeks ago (right on schedule!), you notified the CS Manager that the course was up and running. Considering the enormous amount of work achieved, and your satisfaction with a job well done, you felt you were finally getting ahead of the game. As it turned out, your troubles were only beginning.

Although your initial contacts with the CS Manager over curriculum, technical aspects, scheduling, and the consultant's fees were conducted amicably, you feel this deteriorated in the weeks that followed. While you usually encourage 'in-house clients' to keep in close contact throughout the development process, the CS Manager was extreme in this regard. It felt as though you were receiving voice mail messages from the Manager on a daily basis, in order to give (and repeat!) overly detailed input for customizing the course to the department's needs. You began to get the feeling the Manager did not trust your expertise and was micromanaging the project, including expressing opinions about things that are your area of expertise, for example, layout design, modules, content, one-on-one online exercises, etc. During the first week after the launch, while monitoring the online course through your course management interface, you noticed that very few staff had begun the course. Most of those who had started ignored the tutorials you had laboriously designed for explaining how best to interface with the course, choosing to "save time" by jumping straight into the training exercises. As a result, they were experiencing difficulties with everything from logging in to using the interactive modules and interfacing with the content. This caused many of them to stop trying after a couple of efforts. You sent the CS Manager an email, suggesting that the staff needed a bit of managerial pressure to get them to first study the tutorials, apply themselves, and follow directions, but you received no reply.

On Monday, when you telephoned the CS Manager to request payment for the consultant and to advise the Manager to remind staff to not jump ahead of the tutorials, you found yourself facing a wave of complaints and accusations. The CS Manager alleged that you never answered your phone, the staff cannot access the course, and those that could log on found the content hard to work with. The CS Manager did not listen to your points regarding staff ignoring the tutorials, and how best to interface, choosing instead to blame everything on you and using that as an excuse to deny payment of the consultant's fees. The Manager also accused you and the consultant of failing to deliver a personalized survey concerning how each team member intuitively addressed sales. You rebutted that, while the idea had been floated by the consultant, the Manager never formally agreed to this additional component and, given the tight timeline, no survey was instituted. The CS Manager responded that the course was mostly a waste of time and accused you of ignoring the need for training in sales techniques and unnecessarily focusing on relationship management. Your efforts to explain the specific problems you had identified and attempts to enlist the Manager's support were ignored, as were your requests for payment. "Fix the course and then we'll talk about the money," the Manager kept on saying. The conversation ended on a very angry note with the phone being slammed down, but you cannot remember who hung up on whom.

You considered taking the matter to the VP of Operations, who you and the CS Manager both report to, but are concerned that it would reflect poorly on your management ability. Payment for the consultant fee remains outstanding, despite the fact that you sent the Manager a strongly worded email request. Tomorrow is the progress meeting that was originally scheduled when the online course was launched. The purpose of the meeting was for you and the CS Manager to meet and discuss the staff feedback. You emailed a calendar invite to the Manager to check if the meeting was proceeding and received confirmation that the Manager is attending the meeting. As you prepare for the meeting, your thoughts on several important matters are as follows:

- Course Content: Most importantly, you believe in the value of the course content and see no reason to change it. You put a lot of time and effort into the design, including two days of job shadowing, and agree with the consultant that the content is sound. Plus, you have now moved on to other important tasks that were deferred while working on this course.
- Payment of Fees: The payment deadline for the consultant is in 15 days and you are adamant the CS Manager must pay on time. Your good reputation with the consultant is at risk with further delay. Paying the fee from your own budget is not feasible because it goes against company policy.
- Timing: From the beginning, the CS Manager has repeatedly put pressure on you to work quickly. You are getting fed up with those urgent demands for change, and now that things have soured you feel that your own heavy workload needs to be recognized.

Conclusion

The meta principle that guided this chapter is that negotiation and mediation processes, when deployed appropriately, enhance a manager's effectiveness in resolving conflicts at work. Many of the behaviors and strategies that lead to successful negotiation outcomes also lead to successful mediation outcomes. The following is a summary of several principles that help create the conditions for conflict resolution at work:

1. *Uncover Interests.* Employees in the midst of conflict are usually suspicious or nervous about sharing their underlying interests, and sometimes they are so focused on the problem that they have not given any thought to what they really want. A successful manager-mediator creates a safe environment where parties feel more comfortable discussing and sharing their true wants and needs.
2. *Use Negotiation Skills.* Successful negotiators and mediators share a number of common behaviors. They actively listen, they ask many questions, they look for intersecting interests and goals, and they appreciate that creative solutions can emerge when priorities are discovered. Importantly, they focus on trust-building behaviors.
3. *Manager-Mediators Control the Process.* Mediated agreements are most likely to succeed when the conflicting parties perceive that their interests have been understood and they contributed to the solution. Therefore, a manager who shapes and shepherds the process with transparency, rather than imposes a solution, will be viewed by the parties as highly collaborative and fair. We recommend following the tip sheet at the end of this chapter when you need to mediate a conflict between disputing parties.

References

Desikan, A. (April 28, 2018). "Managers spend about 40% of time resolving employees conflict at work." *The Times of India.*

Elangovan, A. R. (1995). Managerial third-party dispute intervention: A prescriptive model of strategy selection. *Academy of Management Review,* 20(4), 800–830.

Fisher, R., and Shapiro, D. (2005). *Beyond Reason: Using Emotions As You Negotiate.* Penguin: New York.

Ilgaz, Z. (May 15, 2014). Conflict resolution: When should leaders step in? *Forbes.* https://www.forbes.com/sites/85broads/2014/05/15/conflict-resolution-when-should-leaders-step-in/?sh=63e0246a3357;

Jang, D., Elfenbein, H. A., and Bottom, W. P. (2018). More than a phase: Form and features of a general theory of negotiation. *Academy of Management Annals,* 12(1), 318–356.

Karambayya, R., and Brett, J. M. (1989). Managers handling disputes. *Academy of Management Journal,* 32, 689–704.

Karambayya, R., Brett, J. M., and Lytle, A. (1992). Effects of formal authority and experience on third party roles, outcomes and perceptions of fairness. *Academy of Management Journal,* 35, 426–438.

Lewicki, R. J., Saunders, D. M., Barry, B., and Tasa, K. (2020). *Essentials of Negotiation* (4th Canadian edition). McGraw Hill: Toronto.

Moore, C. (2014). *The Mediation Process: Practical Strategies for Resolving Conflict* (4th edition). San Francisco: Jossey-Bass.

Porath, C. (2016). *Mastering Civility: A Manifesto for the Workplace.* Grand Central Publishing: New York.

Pruitt, D. G., and Rubin, J. Z. (1986). *Social Conflict: Escalation, Stalemate, and Settlement.* McGraw-Hill Book Company: New York.

Ury, W. L., Brett, J. M., and Goldberg, S. J. (1988). *Getting Disputes Resolved.* San Francisco: Josey Bass.

Exercise

Video Analysis and Discussion

Please watch the following video(s):

1. Why there's so much conflict at work and what you can do to fix it: https://www.youtube.com/watch?v=2l-AOBz69KU&t=50s
2. Conflict Resolution Pranks: https://www.youtube.com/watch?v=lqLv4AT1_ps

Now form small groups to discuss the video(s) and answer the following questions:

1. What are the major points of the video?
2. How can you use information from the video in your career?
3. Based on the video, what advice do you have for leaders in organizations?

Be prepared to present the ideas from your small group discussion with the class as a whole.

Tip Sheet for Mediation Preparation and Implementation

If you are convening a meeting to deal with workplace friction, here are some important points to consider that can help reduce the risk of further conflict. Most importantly, advance preparation can help you foster a constructive atmosphere during the meeting and provide a better chance of generating consensus and resolution.

Considerations Prior to Convening the Meeting:

1. Where/when should you meet?
2. Who should be present? Should it be a joint or individual meeting(s) of the parties or a hybrid of some individual and some joint sessions?
3. What should parties be notified about in advance about the situation? What can you do in advance to enhance the parties' level of commitment to the process?
4. How will the parties participate in the process? Should parties be asked to prepare a brief summary of their position?
5. What issues will be dealt with in the meeting (can issues be narrowed to smaller neutral problems)?
6. Do you have a sense of the problem from the perspective of each of the parties? What are the differences in how the parties see the problem?
7. What are each parties' interests (procedural, substantive, emotional, etc.)?
8. What interests do the parties have in common, in conflict, and that are independent of each other?
9. Do you have a sense of the potential options that may satisfy the parties' various interests?
10. What are barriers that have stalled the parties from solving the problem on their own? How can you address those barriers?
11. Should you set an explicit agenda?
12. Have you planned how to engage the parties in a discussion about the issues?
13. Do you anticipate that emotions will be a concern? If so, what steps can you take to reduce the risk of emotional volatility?
14. Do any of the potential (viable) options require third-party participation or approval, e.g. senior management? Should the third party be alerted in advance?
15. What are the parameters with respect to confidentiality? Have you considered whether you are able/unable to keep the content of discussions confidential?

Commencing the Meeting:

1. Maintain control of the session and set the tone by establishing ground rules of honesty, respect, and no interruptions.

2. Ensure that parties understand to what extent (if any) discussions are private and their obligation to abide by this degree of confidentiality after the meeting.
3. Make sure parties are comfortable (water, tissue, paper and pens, and washroom access).
4. Ensure your body language and expressions convey impartiality and openness.
5. Show appreciation for parties' willingness to meet to discuss the issues.
6. Remind everyone that engagement is mutual, and they are responsible for ensuring that the other party also feels included, heard, and respected.
7. Explain the purpose of the meeting, how the meeting will proceed and duration.
8. Explain if final decision rests with you or the individual parties or third party.

During the Meeting:

1. Ask each party (either together or separately) to concisely describe their perspective.
2. Actively listen for clues about underlying interests and be observant of nonverbal cues.
3. Summarize what was said in neutral terms with a focus on problem-solving, i.e. frame the issue as a question that parties must work together to solve.
4. Watch for signs of understanding and emphasize your understanding to reinforce their understanding.
5. Acknowledge interests and recognize emotion, but do not press for emotions.
6. Generate options, secure small concessions, and look for interim agreements to build upon.

If Encountering Problems During the Meeting:

1. If parties are arguing or ignoring each other's concerns, ask for their complete attention and summarize the issues in neutral terms or meet with them separately to present the issues in a neutral manner.
2. Seek parties' acknowledgment of your summary of the issues and ask parties to keep discussion to those issues.
3. If one party dominates the conversation, redirect to the other party by saying: "Please hold on – I want to hear XX's reaction to what you have said and then we will get back to you."
4. Reframe and ask questions that help everyone to better understand the situation.
5. Withhold judgment but consider whether or not you need to impose a solution.
6. Take necessary breaks to deal with emotions or disruptive comments.
7. Consider caucusing with each party separately.
8. Tell parties that the meeting will need to be reconvened until everyone can maintain a respectful tone.

Conclusion

1. If parties have reached a consensus, congratulate the parties for their cooperation.
2. Explicitly confirm the terms and conditions of their agreement to ensure that there is full understanding and consent of the arrangements.
3. Ensure that the parties fully understand what is expected of them and what needs to be done to satisfy those expectations.
4. Ensure any follow up action that is required to implement the resolution is also explicitly stated and understood and responsibility for those follow up steps is identified.
5. Explain the consequences of any failure to abide by the terms of the mediated agreement.
6. If parties do not achieve an agreement, discuss next steps for alternate conflict resolution determination in accordance with the organization's policies.

25

Achieve Entrepreneurial Growth Through Swiftness and Experimentation[1]

JAUME VILLANUEVA,[2] HARRY J. SAPIENZA,[3] AND J. ROBERT BAUM[4]

[2] Rutgers Business School, Newark & New Brunswick, Rutgers University
[3] University of Minnesota
[4] University of Maryland

Entrepreneurs must manage much greater uncertainty in decision-making than do leaders of established businesses, and they must do so with fewer resources and while facing better-endowed competitors. Uncertainty is extreme for entrepreneurs because they typically introduce new-to-the-market products and processes, new channels of distribution, and even completely novel business models. Little market information is available to resolve uncertainty, and the products or processes they wish to introduce may be untested. However, the reward for being first to serve a market niche or for being the first to establish a presence in a new market territory can be astounding. For example, Brian Chesky and Joe Gebbia (Airbnb), Sergey Brin and Larry Page (Google), Steve Jobs (Apple), Oprah Winfrey (Harpo Productions), and Michael Dell (Dell) all acted effectively to overcome resource shortages, failed products, skeptics, and production challenges. They did it, in part, through the rapid introduction of new products, services, and business models. However, quick action alone is not sufficient to ensure ongoing success. Indeed, an emerging trend in entrepreneurial practices has been to emphasize the critical importance for "high-aspiration" entrepreneurs to take rapid and inexpensive actions that generate feedback on their ideas from the marketplace about what will and will not

[1]This chapter is a thorough update of "Gain Entrepreneurship Success Through Swiftness and Experimentation" by J. Robert Baum. Nevertheless, some materials from that chapter are reproduced here.

work. These actions (or "experiments") then provide guidance to resolve some of the unknowns they face. In short, two interrelated principles for achieving high growth are to launch the venture with a combination of *swiftness* and *experimentation*.

The idea that entrepreneurs must both act quickly and conduct "experiments" to test their hypotheses (i.e. their "best guesses") about their products, services, or business models has become widespread "received knowledge" in practitioner and scholarly circles (Baum and Bird, 2010; Bocken and Snihur, 2020; Leatherbee and Katila, 2020; Shepherd and Gruber, 2020). Savvy entrepreneurs are increasingly depicted by scholars and practitioners alike as actors engaged in quasi-scientific experimentation (Felin, Gambardella, Stern, and Zenger, 2019). Indeed, a highly popular approach to starting new ventures – i.e. the "lean startup" approach (Blank, 2013; Reis, 2011) – depends heavily on the principles of swiftness and experimentation. The "lean startup" method is based on the belief that the venture landscape is far too complex and uncertain to be either fully known beforehand or to be fully anticipated solely through analysis. Therefore, entrepreneurs are urged to engage the market quickly and scientifically, i.e. to be empirical and "get out of the building" as soon as possible to test and validate their ideas. In other words, rather than engage in lengthy *a priori* planning and analysis, entrepreneurs should quickly test their ideas in the real world with real people. Then, they should adapt (i.e. "pivot") their products, services, or business models in accordance with what they have learned. In short, the "lean startup" method is based on validated learning through empirical experimentation. The goal is to fashion the product, service, or business model to the actual conditions in the market to avoid significant investing of time and effort (Blank, 2013).

The founding story of Google is an illustrative example of swiftness in the experimentation process. In 1996, founders Sergy Brin and Larry Page found themselves short of the computing capacity needed to fully test their latest search engine. Instead of waiting to acquire enough money to purchase a large server, they quickly moved through an eight-iteration experiment and found a way to link multiple borrowed servers together to create a network of inexpensive PCs. This pattern of swiftness through rapid experimentation was repeated as they acquired a terabyte of storage space and built their own computers in their dorm room, negotiated for only five minutes with their first $100 000 investor, and improved features related to posting such as post removal and threading for more than 500 million messages.

Google's founders were skilled programmers with good ideas, but good ideas are necessary but not sufficient to build a highly successful new business. Over time, successful entrepreneurs modify their initial visions, plans, and products to fit their new understanding of the market. In this chapter, we prescribe swiftness and experimentation as the best way to adapt to unknown or shifting market demands; swiftness and experimentation involve intense initial market monitoring, rapid variation, fast reintroduction, and quick follow-up monitoring. Swift entrepreneurial action means moving from step to step, with little or no delay between steps, during problem-solving and opportunity-taking; it involves fast-paced thinking and action. The results of these actions become meaningful when entrepreneurs mindfully observe and compare outcomes with expectations. For high-potential entrepreneurs to reach that potential, they must both act quickly and learn from their actions.

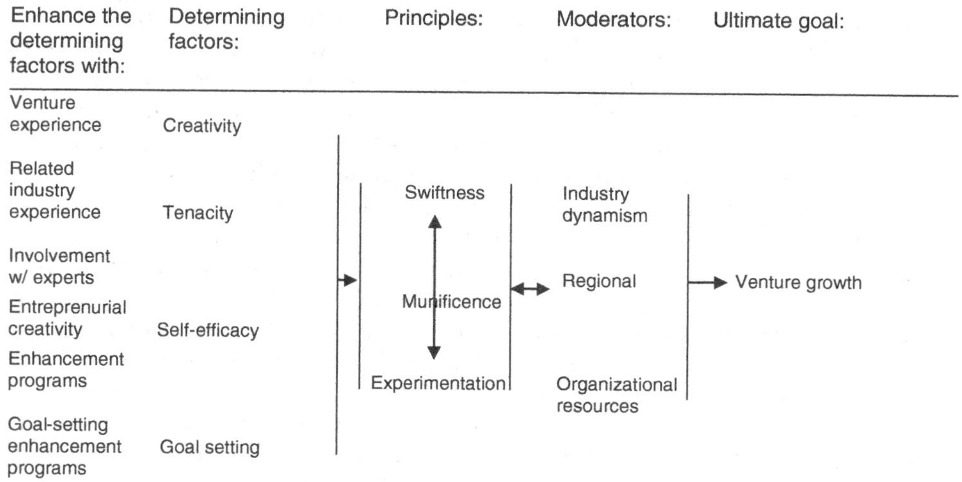

FIGURE 25.1 Gain entrepreneurship success through swiftness and experimentation

Swift, mindful actors can reach conclusions and achieve accomplishments surprisingly quickly. A virtuous cycle of rapid action and learning may evolve (see Figure 25.1).

Our underlying premise is that swiftness and experimentation are key to successful entrepreneurship. Figure 25.1 provides an overview of our model. We argue that "(personal) determining factors" (creativity, tenacity, efficacy, and goal setting) are enhanced by (i) having or gaining startup and industry experience, (ii) involving experts, and (iii) attending creativity and goal-setting programs. We further argue that additional "moderating factors" (industry dynamism, regional munificence, and organizational resources) can change the propensity to act swiftly and to experiment and can change the extent to which swiftness and experimentation will lead to successful outcomes. Thus, these factors influence both entrepreneurs' propensity to act quickly and experiment and influence the outcomes of such actions.

We begin with a brief discussion of what scholars mean when they refer to "entrepreneur" and "entrepreneurship." We then discuss the unique and important context that surrounds entrepreneurial behavior. The context helps us understand the types of factors that enable and motivate entrepreneurs to enact successful behaviors. In short, we describe swiftness and experimentation, and we explore factors that increase thinking and acting speed and inspire an effective and continual search for improved products, processes, and business models.

Entrepreneurs and Entrepreneurship

Hundreds of conceptions of "entrepreneurs" exist. These include "successful small businesspersons," "retired founders," "failed founders," and "(innovative or risk-taking) managers." To avoid confusion about what *we* mean by entrepreneur and to avoid a discussion about "who is an entrepreneur," we focus on early-stage entrepreneurs who intend to make a *significant* difference in people's lives – i.e. entrepreneurs with big dreams and high potential, often referred to as "high-growth entrepreneurs." No studies that included the solitary self-employed or small business managers were used to derive our principles. The high-growth entrepreneurs we evoke in this chapter are people involved in a process of discovery, evaluation, and exploitation of opportunities that will introduce significant new products, services, processes, ways of organizing, business models, or markets.

We define the entrepreneurship process as the process through which these new products, services, and models are developed. The entrepreneurship process typically begins with exploration for ideas and proceeds through opportunity evaluation and recognition all the way to startup. Startup is followed by emergence (revenues and employees) and, finally, early-stage growth. The process is often nonlinear and iterative. Although the principles described in this chapter apply in virtually all venture stages, they are particularly important in the early stages of the opportunity exploration, evaluation, validation, and new venture creation; however, they are also useful for the startup, emergence, and growth stages. Furthermore, the conclusions that are drawn herein about behaviors that impact venture success may also apply to ambitious managers in other contexts.

The Entrepreneurial Context

Entrepreneurs face situations of extreme risk and uncertainty. They typically operate in contexts where information is scant, hard to interpret, or fast-changing. They may introduce new products to established markets with powerful incumbents, which often provokes severe resistance, or they may create new markets where none previously existed. In either case, they are likely to face aggressive competitive challenges from powerful parties, and unless intellectual property is protected, competitive advantages may be fleeting. Better-endowed competitors will be on the continual lookout to copy successful actions and to discover viable substitutes.

Very few entrepreneurs have sufficient financial resources to implement their ideas. They seldom have the necessary resources to acquire complete facilities, equipment, or professional talent, and few can withstand significant startup losses on their own. The financing challenge is heightened in high-growth-oriented new ventures because of the investment demands that high growth involves. In fact, very few entrepreneurs manage to gain adequate access to external resources at all, given that the resource-access tools at their disposal are fairly limited (Rawhouser, Villanueva, and Newbert, 2017). The few entrepreneurs who manage to obtain significant external financing are frequently forced to accept capital from financiers who negotiate from aggressive and powerful positions and who minimize their own risk by setting high goals for the entrepreneurs and offering just-in-time cash. Thus, entrepreneurs who manage high-potential startups with outside financing confront a threatening array of demands for high performance, and they experience a continual and stressful sense of urgency as they try to survive (Smith and Smith, 2000).

In summary, high-aspiration entrepreneurs operate in the midst of high uncertainty, urgency, surprise, complexity, personal risk, and resource scarcity (Baum, Frese, Baron, and Katz, 2006; Smith and Smith, 2000). High-speed, continual improvements are required to thwart erosion of competitive advantages (Baum et al., 2006; Eisenhardt, 1989). High uncertainty increases the *value* and the *danger* of fast decision-making and fast action. Possessing few resources, such entrepreneurs must engage in rapid, low-cost experiments with vigilant monitoring and continual adaptation to gain and maintain competitive advantages. Entrepreneurship is not a career for the fainthearted.

Swiftness – Principle 1

High-aspiration entrepreneurs have little to gain from hesitating to act. They face new or immature markets with scant existing information, so the only way to get market information is through entry. The acceptance or rejection of ideas tried in rapid, inexpensive "experiments" is full of important information. It enables a quick, directed search for the right products, services, markets, and organization forms; this information, we argue, affords the opportunity to stay ahead of competitors.

Thus, the principle offered is expressed in two simple rhetorical questions: "When you start something new, why wait for certainty when certainty does not exist? and, why *not* act quickly to uncover potential markets?" It is not surprising that experienced entrepreneurs advise, "Just start, move quickly, and watch the unfolding action for answers and opportunities" (Jones, 1993, p. 110). This principle also underlies the philosophy of the "lean startup" method (Blank, 2013), which has gained so much acceptance in recent years. The "lean startup" methodology advises entrepreneurs to "get out of the building" to test their unformed and, perhaps, premature ideas in the actual marketplace, rather than trying to make sense of an uncertain and fast-changing reality through *a priori* analysis.

Early action can generate information, dynamic learning, and knowledge ahead of rivals. Unexpected opportunities sometimes emerge but only if action is started. Swiftness increases the number of trials that can be attempted within time and resource constraints; it provides more information and provides it sooner. It allows entrepreneurs to act with greater confidence and decisiveness. Also, given that variance is correlated with time, the more the entrepreneur waits to act, the more risk (changing conditions) he/she will be exposed to.

Swiftness has been touted as an organizational competency in studies of product development projects (Eisenhardt and Tabrizi, 1995), global competition (Stalk and Hout, 1990), and successful competitive actions (Ferrier, Smith, and Grimm, 1999). Swift decisions, precursors to swift actions, have been found to relate positively with firm performance in new industries (Eisenhardt, 1989) and in new ventures in mature industries (Baum and Wally, 2003).

In many ways, *swiftness* is a relative term that may be thought of in several distinct ways. Our discussion so far has implied that being "swift" means taking action as soon as possible, either to provide more opportunities to get feedback from the market or to beat competitors to a desired market niche. While more well-endowed businesses can perhaps wait to see how these risky actions turn out, new high-growth ventures may have little choice but to gamble that their experiments pan out. Of course, all actions (and inactions) involve risk, and there is a fine line between efficacious speed and undue haste.

The burgeoning literature on "born global" ventures has focused on two other aspects of speed in entrepreneurial action. Autio, Sapienza, and Almeida (2000) found that the earlier in their life cycle that new ventures entered international markets, the more rapidly they would grow both domestically and internationally. In this conception, swiftness in action refers to how quickly a new venture begins international activities. Autio et al. (2000) predicted more rapid growth for such precocious "early internationalizers" because they have fewer routines to unlearn and fewer interorganizational obligations constraining them. Furthermore, acting early establishes a culture of confidence and aggressiveness that serves the venture well as challenges arise. Oviatt and McDougall (2005) deepened this discussion by asking not just "how soon in its life cycle does a venture cross borders?" but also "how broadly and how quickly do ventures expand international operations?" That is, they focused attention on the manner in which new ventures internationalize, how rapidly they do so, and with what consequences.

By and large, subsequent research has supported the idea that the truly big winners in the new venture internationalization race are those who move first, who move quickly, and who continue to take rapid action. In other words, speed is essential to explosive growth, but it is not sufficient. Sapienza, Autio, George, and Zahra (2006) argued that early, rapid action might threaten the survival prospects of very-early-stage ventures but would increase the chances for extreme high growth for those that survived these rapid forays into untested waters. This argument reinforces the need for high-potential ventures to combine rapid action with learning from experimentation. The potential created by rapid action is only realized when entrepreneurs learn from the market feedback and shape their subsequent (rapid) actions in accordance with what they have learned. Empirical evidence indicates that, in fact, the pace of internationalization is positively affected by what entrepreneurs believe they have learned in their early forays into new foreign markets (Casillas, Barbero, and Sapienza, 2015).

EXPERIMENTATION – PRINCIPLE 2

"Experimentation" involves repeatedly conducting trials or tests to discover something that is not known. It involves *continual searches for betterment with repeated goal-driven revision* (Thomke, 2003). Particularly in the new venture context, experimentation examines actions toward goals that will involve new (or better) products, services, processes, business models, or organizations. Experimentation implies having a conceptual model (or a series of hypotheses) rather than proceeding simply with "trial and error," which reflects a more random set of variables for each trial. Both experimentation and trial and error suggest repeated cycles of action with monitoring and revision or reformulation.

Experimentation is useful for high-growth entrepreneurs because it reveals information about potential markets where no established markets exist or uncovers information that cannot be accessed outside the market. Experimentation reveals customer reactions to disruptive products, services, and business models (Bhide, 2000, p. 60), and it may enable recovery from poor past decisions or missed opportunities. Experimentation exposes competitors' "barriers to entry" and guides the rapid changes that are required (Smith and Smith, 2000); it may also reveal opportunities to build new products or offer new services. In short, quick and inexpensive experimentation is probably the best way for entrepreneurs to gather insight into fast-moving and previously unexplored markets.

Research about entrepreneurs indicates that successful entrepreneurs are comfortable enacting changes to cope with hard-to-fathom processes, products, or markets (Baum and Bird, 2010). Miner, Bassof, and Moorman (2001) and Hmieleski and Corbett (2006) found that entrepreneurial behaviors related to experimentation (improvisation and trial and error) are used by entrepreneurs to deal successfully with their changing urgent situations. Similarly, Eisenhardt (1989) noted successful entrepreneurs tended to engage in the significant use of "trial actions." These findings illustrate the value of experimentation for new venture growth. More recent studies support the notion that experimentation is critical to the entrepreneurial process. For example, McGrath (2010) found that entrepreneurs engage in significant experimentation and learning to uncover new business models, and Andries, Debackere, and Van Looy (2013) found that engaging in simultaneous experimentation facilitates the long-term survival of new ventures.

Experimentation is one of the key components of the "lean startup" method. The "learn startup" method is based on "validated learning," by which entrepreneurs empirically test their hypotheses in the real world, especially "guesses" related to the market and potential customers (Shepherd and Gruber, 2020). Some suggest that the lean startup methodology is not well suited to meaningful experimentation because it limits the scope of what entrepreneurs can learn to what is readily observable (Felin et al., 2019). However, most have found that the "lean startup" methodology is the best approach to identifying and sorting through opportunities quickly and cheaply (Bocken and Snihur, 2020). The popularity of the "lean startup" framework in entrepreneurship circles attests to its resonance with entrepreneurs as a key principle and tool.

DETERMINING FACTORS

There are several important factors that inspire and enable swiftness and experimentation. We focus on creativity, tenacity, self-efficacy, and goal setting as primary predictors because each has been consistently identified as important across entrepreneurship studies.

Creativity

Creativity is intellectual inventiveness. It is the ability both to generate high-quality, novel ideas that meet the needs of a task or context and to implement them in novel ways. Those who have high creativity challenge the status quo and seek alternative ways to solve problems and gain advantage from opportunities. Creativity is a "stereotypical" trait of high-growth entrepreneurs, the movers and shakers behind creative destruction (Schumpeter, 1934). Those entrepreneurs who possess low levels of creativity must look elsewhere for innovations by partnering with an inventor or developer through licensing or joint venturing. Of course, some entrepreneurs simply copy the basic ideas of others and express their creativity through innovative execution.

High-growth entrepreneurs are more likely to succeed in commercializing their products and to service their customers when they engage their creativity to generate imaginative options. Those who are creative can conduct multiple market experiments because they can envision multiple novel paths to get their products to market and multiple outcomes from each path. Similarly, high creativity speeds the conception of variant paths, which may speed market trials. Thus, creativity enables entrepreneurs to minimize delays in their search for options.

Sometimes, option generation is urgent. When surprise barriers to success emerge in environments laden with risk and uncertainty, high-creativity entrepreneurs are able to quickly see novel solutions. For example, in his early years, Sam Walton (founder of Walmart) was surprised at the ability of competitors to retain their customers – even though they charged more for their goods than he charged. In a flash of creativity, he conceived, designed, selected, and began work on his first store within a few days of his insight: it was to be located in a small community where existing competition was weak, and it was to be very large with broad and deep stocks of general merchandise and with costs so low that customers would travel a great distance to shop there (Huey and Walton, 1992). When Walton enacted this vision, he turned the competitive environment upside down.

Although option generation is the stage we have focused on here, creativity is also present during other stages of the startup process including idea generation, opportunity recognition, and market entry stages. Entrepreneurs who can quickly envision a whole set of market options and outcomes have a competitive advantage at all stages, but it is especially important in those stages where the range of potential options is extremely wide and uncertain.

Tenacity

Tenacity, or perseverance, is a trait that involves sustaining goal-directed action and energy in the face of severe obstacles. Tenacious people do not give up when things go wrong. Tenacity has been identified consistently as an essential entrepreneurial trait because the business startup process invariably involves formidable barriers. Grit, conceptualized as perseverance toward long-term goals (Duckworth, Peterson, Matthews, and Kelly, 2007), is a related concept that has received recent attention in the popular literature as a factor for entrepreneurial success. Some conceive grit as a malleable, domain-specific behavior rather than a general and enduring personality trait (Mueller, Wolfe, and Syed, 2017). Whether conceived as a trait or as a situation-specific behavior, grit or tenacity has often been identified as something that sets the successful entrepreneur apart from others: successful entrepreneurs do not give up when things go wrong (Gartner, Gatewood, and Shaver, 1991).

Tenacity is important for high-growth entrepreneurs because they must be able to conduct rapid, frequent experiments. They must persist with their search for options and solutions and continue market monitoring after they institute trials, even when results are disappointing or confusing. Monitoring must persist following the revision of products and services. The examples of tenacity, perseverance, and grit among successful entrepreneurs are numerous. Mary Kay Ash staggered through the death of two husbands, the failure of her first beauty show, and a disastrous sales decline before making her beauty products company a huge international success. It took Bill Gates and Microsoft seven years to develop a viable Windows operating system. Sam Walton failed with a drug chain, a home improvement center, two Hypermarts, and several disastrous store openings, before he made it big with Walmart's magnet stores.

Where does a successful entrepreneur draw the line between *productive* tenacity and foolish persistence or adamant stubbornness (Locke, 2000)? Sometimes it is hard to know until after the fact, especially in the case of an entirely new product. However, one common type of foolish persistence is to stick to a strategy that worked in the past in the face of mounting evidence that the competitive environment has changed. Another common error is to persist when it is clear that the new product or service is not being accepted by the market. If the product or service is totally new, the entrepreneur should decide beforehand the amount of resources that he is willing to bet to keep the project going (Locke and Baum, 2007). The longer the "runway," the higher the stakes; thus, it is often best to quit early. A key idea offered by the lean startup methodology is that if you are going to fail, you are far better off failing as "quickly and cheaply" as possible. How long should entrepreneurs keep experimenting? When is it time to "pivot" to a different iteration of the product, or to change the type of experiment? These are difficult questions and do not have straightforward answers (Shepherd and Gruber, 2020). To twist an old Emersonian phrase, *a foolish persistence is the hobgoblin of little entrepreneurial growth.*

In summary, tenacity is important for experimentation and venture success because entrepreneurs who hold to their goals and who hate to give up increase their chances of finding the solution for a market need when they persist in experimenting for more information. Baum et al. (2001) found that tenacity was the most powerful trait predictor of new venture growth. At the same time, doggedly determined entrepreneurs would be well advised to estimate beforehand the amount of resources they would be willing to commit to the new venture development – and to stick to this guideline if necessary.

Entrepreneurial Self-Efficacy

Creative and tenacity are most effective when entrepreneurs believe strongly in themselves and, therefore, execute actions mindfully and at the first opportunity. Such a belief in self is often termed *self-efficacy* – the belief or degree of confidence that one has in her or his ability to successfully perform a task (see Chapter 6). Bandura (1997) points to the central role of self-efficacy in causing high performance through its impact on motivation; Stajkovic and Luthans (1998) explained that self-efficacy enhances focus, direction, persistence, and intensity of action. These claims are supported by an early meta-analysis (Judge and Bono, 2001). And subsequent empirical research has deepened our understanding of the positive role of such confidence in entrepreneurial performance.

Without self-efficacy, actions are delayed or even avoided. We hold that high self-efficacy enhances entrepreneurs' experimentation and swiftness because both depend on their having the confidence that they can move quickly and successfully. Confidence motivates quick action and aids belief in the meaning of the outcomes of experimentation. Entrepreneurial success rarely comes to the faint of heart.

Entrepreneurship researchers have produced quantitative evidence that *general* self-efficacy (i.e. belief in one's general capacities) predicts both new venture creation (Markman, Balkin, and Baron, 2003) and venture growth (Baum and Locke, 2004; Chandler and Jansen, 1992). *Entrepreneurial* self-confidence was studied by Chen, Green, and Crick (1998). The authors defined entrepreneurial self-efficacy (ESE) as "the strength of a person's belief that he or she is capable of successfully performing the various roles and tasks of entrepreneurship"; measure of ESE consisted of five factors – innovativeness, risk-taking, marketing, management, and financial control. They found that entrepreneurs generally have higher levels of ESE than managers in other contexts.

Subsequent research has shown how self-efficacy affects behavior and performance in a variety of circumstances. Consistent with the model developed in this chapter, Baum and Bird (2010) found self-efficacy to be positively related to both more "experimentation" and greater "swiftness" in taking action. Generally speaking, self-efficacy has been shown to be positively related to propensity to start ventures and to succeed once started (e.g. Khedhaouria, Gurau, and Torres, 2015).

Nuances to these findings are offered in several studies. For example, Hmieleski and Corbett (2008) found that improvisation actions enhance venture growth when self-efficacy is high but actually reduce growth when self-efficacy is low. Hmieleski and Baron (2008) found that in highly dynamic environments, those entrepreneurs high in self-efficacy did best when their confidence was tempered by *moderate* levels of optimism; those that were high in self-efficacy but who also had *very* high levels of optimism did worse. Self-efficacy and confidence are likely to affect how high-growth entrepreneurs set their goals, and, as we discuss in the next section, appropriate goal setting is an important element in entrepreneurs' arsenal.

Goal Setting

Goal-setting theory is a theory of motivation (Locke and Latham, 2002). It proposes that specific, difficult goals lead consistently to higher performance than vague and/or easy goals. Goal setting works most effectively when people are *committed* to their goals and have *feedback* regarding their progress in relation to their goals (see Chapter 5). Thus, self-efficacy affects how high entrepreneurs set their goals and how committed to them they may be, and experimentation provides the feedback needed to make the goal-setting process effective.

No theory of motivation has deeper or broader empirical support at the individual, group, and unit level than does goal-setting theory (Landy and Becker, 1987; Locke and Latham, 1990, 2002). Entrepreneurship theorists cite goals as an important positive factor in venture growth (Covin and Slevin, 1997) and new venture survival (Carsrud and Krueger, 1995). Baum and Locke (2004) found that goals had a direct positive effect on firm growth over six years. Similarly, in a study of entrepreneurial firms in the printing business, Tracy, Locke, and Renard (1999) found significant positive relationships between financial, growth, and innovation goals of entrepreneurs.

We posit that appropriate goal setting is an enhancer of entrepreneurs' swiftness and experimentation because goals motivate and direct action. They require entrepreneurs to employ suitable task strategies or to search for greater information or more suitable strategies when lacking the knowledge they need. The types of goals chosen influence what resources are gathered and how they are allocated (Dunkelberg, Moore, Scott, and Stull, 2013). Swiftness and experimentation prompted by specific goals are extremely useful in the entrepreneurial context because of the uncertainty endemic to new markets and untested products. Without action and feedback, new ventures are unlikely to choose a path that allows them to grow and succeed.

Hechavarria, Renko, and Matthews (2012) posit that the very act of setting and revising goals makes startup and growth more likely. They imply that a learning process occurs that makes practice more effective with repetition. Locke and Latham's theory (2002) states that goals should be as high as possible but still be attainable. This view is consistent with the lean startup perspective that emphasizes the need to "stretch" and to act quickly. Learning what is "high but attainable" is a sometimes overlooked but crucial aspect of the theory. Baron, Mueller, and Wolfe (2016) noted that entrepreneurs tend to be very high in self-confidence, a generally beneficial attribute. Consistent with goal-setting theory, however, they found that setting goals too high can be counterproductive: in their study, higher goals were generally associated with better performance, but beyond a certain level, higher and higher goals were negatively related to performance outcomes. They speculated that frustration and demotivation may have contributed to these results.

Goal setting is especially useful in smaller, newer ventures because CEOs of small firms have relatively direct control over the actions that lead to goal accomplishment. In larger, more established firms, layers of management and delegation separate actors from decision-makers. Furthermore, strategies in large organizations are more complex than those in smaller companies and, thus, more prone to error. Complex strategies are also less easily and less rapidly changed when problems occur. In summary, evidence and strong theory suggest that entrepreneurial goal setting provides a potent competitive advantage in newer ventures compared with its effects in larger, more established companies, because it directly inspires the entrepreneur's swiftness and experimentation.

MODERATING FACTORS

Many organizational characteristics (e.g. structure and size) and external conditions (e.g. industry, economic conditions, and zeitgeist) impact the levels of swiftness and experimentation entrepreneurs choose as well as the outcomes of these choices (Baum, Locke, and Smith, 2001; Rauch and Frese, 2000). Because of their empirically demonstrated importance (Baum and Wally, 2003; Covin and Slevin, 1997), we focus on two external factors – industry dynamism and regional munificence – and one internal factor – organizational resources.

Industry Dynamism

Dynamism (i.e. instability or turbulence) refers to the level of environmental *unpredictability*; it is manifested in the variance in the rate of market and industry change and the level of uncertainty about forces beyond the control or even influence of individual businesses. Although there is some disagreement about whether industry dynamism favors entrepreneurial ventures or larger, more established firms, we hold that dynamism creates relative competitive advantages for entrepreneurs because new ventures are typically nimbler (more responsive and more able to change direction) than big companies. Dynamic markets especially disrupt large cumbersome companies when product revision is required – and product revision is almost always a characteristic of dynamic industries. Theories of organizational change suggest that decisions to change occur most readily when the organization is aware of the need to change, is willing to change, and has the perceived capacity to change (Penrose, 1959). Change is not easy for large established firms that have many resources, processes, personnel, and relationships devoted to the status quo (Tsang and Zahra, 2008). In many cases, larger firms will decide to sacrifice flexibility in order to sustain efficiency (Eisenhardt, Furr, and Bingham 2010).

The foregoing suggests that entrepreneurs will be more inclined to experiment with new directions and to do so more quickly than will leaders in larger ventures. Thus, we expect that entrepreneurial ventures will be more apt to "pivot" (or change direction) when new issues arise and may be more likely to perceive a *need* for change, given that their scant resources make them sensitive to even small disruptions in the environment. Even if such ventures are short on resources to enact change (a topic handled later in this section), they may be more convinced that they *must* change in order to survive. Thus, the propensities to act swiftly and to experiment (which are outcomes of creativity, tenacity, self-efficacy, and goal-setting practices) are much more likely to be induced when the environment is dynamic than when it is predictable.

Empirical evidence regarding the performance effects of speed and experimentation in extremely dynamic environments is scant. Some have suggested that swiftness is not necessarily better in dynamic markets. Yet, Eisenhardt (1989) found that fast decision-makers were also more comprehensive and more successful than were those reaching decisions more slowly. At the same time, some unsuccessful entrepreneurs lurch quickly from one bad idea to another. Our core point here is that industry dynamism is more likely to induce entrepreneurial firms to act quickly (if not rashly). The creative, highly motivated, confident, and tenacious entrepreneurs need to develop a compensating discipline to temper their enthusiasm (Baron et al., 2016), especially when tempted by volatile industry dynamics. Decisions should be the result of thought, not change for the sake of change.

Regional Munificence

Regional munificence refers to the local environment's abundance of support for organizational growth. In established industries, munificence is manifested in high industry sales growth (Dess and Beard, 1984). Munificent environments provide a reserve against competitive and environmental threats through the availability of sufficient financing, intellectual support from institutions, and developed human resource markets. Both new ventures and larger competitors benefit from environmental munificence. But how do these affect the propensity for speed and experimentation?

Change logic suggests that munificent environments may have countervailing effects on the likelihood of quick action and experimentation. The "need" for change will be arguably reduced, as most decision-makers will be inclined to avoid "fixing" what is not broken. Yet the capacity for effective change may be significantly enhanced when the tide of available resources and opportunities is rising. Nevertheless, munificent environments diminish the *need* for experimentation. Indeed, we expect that, all else equal, ventures will be less inclined to make rapid changes or to experiment when the environment is resource rich and venture friendly.

We suspect, too, however, that some ambitious and adventurous entrepreneurs with high mixtures of creativity and self-confidence will view a munificent environment as a great opportunity for unprecedented growth and success and may, therefore, increase decision speed and experimentation. One other point worth noting is that while we have spoken about regional munificence as a generalized source of resources, in fact, each environment may be especially rich in certain types of resources and not others. When a savvy entrepreneur perceives that the resource abundance particularly matches or *complements* the resources her or his venture possesses, that entrepreneur would be wise to take quick and decisive action to see how she or he may leverage the opportunity. In summary, we expect that munificence will tend to dampen speed and experimentation, though some entrepreneurs will be inspired to react in exactly the opposite manner to pursue previously unexplored opportunities. Such behavior appears to us to be especially valuable when the abundant resources complement their own existing capacities (Debrulle, Steffens, De Bock, De Winne, and Maes, 2020).

Organizational Resources

Organizational resources (i.e. the resources available to or under the control of the new venture) typically increase the chances for survival and growth when they are in abundant supply (Baum and Bird, 2010; Smith and Smith, 2000; Stevenson, 1985) but may have countervailing effects on how quickly entrepreneurs act and how much they engage in experimentation.

Organization theory asserts that all new firms must obtain some external resources in order to survive and grow (Villanueva, Van de Ven, and Sapienza, 2012). Those ventures that start with few internal resources will be especially motivated to act quickly to access the external market before their own limited resources are depleted. Market access, through relationships, reputation, and the like, is itself an organizational resource that many will fail to adequately develop (Rawhouser et al., 2017). Nevertheless, resource-poor entrepreneurs have little choice but to act quickly and to try as many different approaches as they can in order to survive. In short, the lack of organizational resources certainly spurs action and experimentation.

On the other hand, some high-potential ventures are started with relatively abundant financing, reputational advantages, and other internal resources that can sustain the venture for long periods. Because well-endowed ventures are not forced to take risky leaps, they may be less inclined to act right away and may be less inclined to experiment. If the entrepreneurs are "satisficers," they will only do what is needed to reach the next step. Indeed, we expect this will be the common response to having an abundance of resources. On the other hand, some will seek to maximize their opportunities and go "all in" to reach a big payoff. Indeed, the venture's abundance of resources does not diminish the value of testing the uncertain environment to learn what may and may not work. So, speed and experimentation still appears to be the best path even for resource-rich, high-aspiration ventures.

Resource-rich ventures, thus, may experience less desperation in deciding whether to engage in experimentation. At the same time, abundant resources may induce entrepreneurs to conceive of the many options that can be created from their resources. Brinckmann, Villanueva, Grichnik, and Singh (2019) argue that strategic flexibility can be achieved when entrepreneurs use their resources to test several markets, products, services, or business models. Indeed, some will be tempted to make a quick, big bet and gain first-mover advantage. The payoff can be great. However, haste can also be deadly. For example, after raising over $1 billion, Jeff Katzenberg (former head of Paramount and Disney and co-founder of DreamWorks) placed a large bet on Quibi (a short-form video venture). Quibi closed down barely six months after launch. The speed was there, but Katzenberg appeared to eschew the experimentation and learning part of the equation when he failed to test his business model.

In summary, as in the case of regional munificence, we expect that organizational resources will tend to curb the felt need to act extremely quickly and may generally dampen experimentation. However, some entrepreneurs will be (and should be) induced to seek to leverage abundant resources to maximize opportunities.

IMPROVING YOUR ENTREPRENEURIAL SKILL SET

High levels of creativity, tenacity, ESE, and goal setting enable and motivate swiftness and experimentation, which, in turn, yield high venture growth. But, how can an entrepreneur – or wannabe entrepreneur – gain in creativity, tenacity, self-efficacy, and goal setting? We explore the possibilities and offer suggestions. Our treatment here of learning opportunities points to the importance of venture and industry experience, as well as the value of building relationships with expert models. We also suggest that creativity-building and goal-setting educational programs may enhance entrepreneurs' creativity and ability to set effective goals.

Improving Your Creativity

Creativity is sometimes seen as an innate trait – a human characteristic that is inherent and stable. However, evidence suggests that in reality, creativity can be enhanced with training (Runco, Plucker, and Lim, 2001). For example, group exercises, involving analogies, brainstorming, cross-fertilization, devil's advocacy, lateral thinking, and vertical thinking, have shown to improve creativity. We believe that aspiring entrepreneurs may be well served to engage in creativity-boosting group programs because they offer for a means for improving personal creativity. In particular, a focus on the creative process and practices (such as divergent thinking) (Mumford, Supinski, Baughman, Constanza, and Threlfall, 1997) or on thought processes such as formulating analogies and paradoxes (Ward, 2004) improve creativity in high uncertainty settings and in the entrepreneurial setting in particular.

In addition to practices aimed at building "general" creativity skills and processes, domain-specific skills and knowledge also enhance creativity (Amabile and Pillemer, 2012). Relevant domain experience can enhance creative processes at both the group and individual levels. Combining general and specific practices may be especially useful. For example, Angel Johnson Organics (AJO), an early marketer of organic foods, was unsuccessful in placing products in established supermarkets. However, a creative AJO marketing manager who had formerly worked for Honest Tea noticed the success that Honest Tea had in health-oriented institutions such as gymnasiums and hospital facilities. After a brainstorming session with her sales, marketing, and operations staff, she developed a refrigerated display cabinet that enabled the successful introduction of her organic fruit and vegetable products to health-oriented institutions. Success led to a joint venture with Honest Tea and subsequent placement of AJO *and* Honest Tea products in established supermarkets. Thus, we prescribe both creativity-enhancing programs and access to industry or domain experience to develop creative thinking processes and practices that aid in fast action and insightful experimentation.

Improving Your Tenacity

Tenacity is also typically thought of as a trait, a predisposition. However, tenacity can be increased, or improved, regardless of the innate level that one possesses. After all, perseverance is clearly reflected in a behavior, and, grit, which is a related construct, is a malleable trait that is highly influenced by motivation (Mueller et al., 2017). Although tenacity (or perseverant behavior) can be hard to influence through formal training, it can nevertheless be ingrained through reinforcement, practice, and imitation.

Tenacity should be promoted as a cultural norm within the top managers of an entrepreneurial venture. It can be embedded in the venture's mission statements, its slogans, and its "mantras." Creative entrepreneurial leaders may put in place annual or monthly recognition or awards for the most tenacious and perseverant individuals. These may take the form of simple recognition or praise (e.g. posted photos of the "Bulldog-of-the-Month/Year") or of publicly announced cash bonuses and the like. Explicit "tenacity goals" and rewards influence both intrinsic and extrinsic motivation to act tenaciously (Locke and Latham, 1990; Mueller et al., 2017). Tenacity as a personal characteristic may be explicitly included in annual reviews and/or used as a hiring criterion. Additionally, films or documentaries (e.g. *Remember the Titans* or *Hoosiers*) may be watched at organizational retreats to illustrate the dimensions of and the benefits of tenacity. The modeling of tenacious behavior may be among the best ways to embed, spread, or reinforce this critical trait.

Improving Your Entrepreneurial Self-Efficacy

Self-efficacy can be thought of as one's (confident) belief in her/his ability to successfully tackle or master the challenges of the task at hand. Because of the enormous challenges inherent in the severely uncertain and uncontrollable forces in an entrepreneurial setting, high levels of confidence may be rare. Yet, it is critical for the entrepreneur to develop confidence in their abilities and choices so that he/she does not get "frozen" into inaction by fears and self-doubt. But where does this confidence come from and how might it be bolstered?

Often, ESE is developed from childhood experiences in which one undertakes independent projects (e.g. running a paper route, building a computer, and selling it), masters difficulties, and succeeds. Confidence may also stem from one's awareness of one's own cognitive abilities and mental structures; as well as from *prior* venture experience, including experience of new venture processes that have been used, revised, and reused. Indeed, multiple entrepreneurship researchers have found that "habitual" or repeat entrepreneurs are more likely to start new ventures or to grow their new ventures than are those who lack prior new venture experience (Davidsson and Honig, 2002). Pre-venture sources of knowledge (or learning) in the entrepreneur is labeled "congenital learning" by Huber (1991) and provides a quick and relatively effortless source of knowledge for goal setting and experimentation. Entrepreneurs' most valuable experiences are related to time spent starting a new company or with others who start new companies. The new venture situation is dominated by newness; however, not everything is totally new. Some decision processes, resource aggregation activities, customer fulfillment conditions, and market characteristics appear and reappear. Prior experience of and knowledge of these situations can provide needed bolstering to the entrepreneur's self-efficacy.

The second important type of experience for developing ESE is current industry experience. Herron and Robinson (1993) posit that industry knowledge and related industry networks are important assets in specifying what new resources are needed, finding those resources, selecting partners, and structuring flexible resource contracts; they conclude that a significant proportion of new venture performance variance is attributable to the entrepreneur's technical industry experience. Financiers also point to specific career experience as highly important for predicting entrepreneurs' job performance. Huber (1991) labels such learning "experiential learning." It is perhaps the most useful and compelling source of self-efficacy but is also time-consuming and costly to obtain.

Other learning methods (e.g. vicarious learning, searching, and "grafting" – i.e. hiring-on outsiders) are also useful to increase entrepreneurs' confidence in their venture's decisions and their willingness to act quickly and to "experiment" with innovative ideas. An additional benefit to bolstering one's self-efficacy is that extremely high levels of belief in one's own capacities is also likely to bolster that individual's tenacity in undertaking and following through on actions. As mentioned in the prior section, this tenacity in the face of success and failure may be critical to the survival and growth of the venture.

The one trap that the entrepreneur must guard against is becoming *overconfident* because of past successes, for these can lead to overestimating what one can achieve and to taking rash actions (Villanueva and Sapienza, 2021). Entrepreneurs who have experienced extreme past successes must guard against the tendency to see themselves as invincible and to dismiss feedback from experiments that may suggest that what they are doing is not working. *Overconfidence* can cause leaders to take self-aggrandizing, rash decisions, and fall victims to prideful hubris (Villanueva and Sapienza, 2021; Hayward, Shepherd, and Griffin, 2006). In other words, a greater and greater level of self-efficacy may have downsides if not tempered. There are times that an entrepreneur must engage in a level of "unlearning" when circumstances have changed from those prevailing at the time of her/his prior successes.

Improving Your Goal Setting

Chapter 5 explains how personal and employee performance can be improved through goal setting. Goal setting motivates entrepreneurial behavior; thus, when done appropriately, it enhances the pace of action and experimentation in new ventures and improves performance. Those who aspire to venture success may productively devote their time, money, and other resources to improving their expertise with appropriate personal and organizational goal setting.

In the very earliest stages of a new venture, goals are likely to be highly personal. The solitary entrepreneur who maintains a timeline with goals will have an important tool for personal motivation and for attraction of financial and human resources. A formal written timeline should include benchmarks such as time to complete prototype, obtain patent or copyright, sell first unit, employ needed personnel, attain a high annual revenue rate, reach cash break-even, etc. As the venture team is formed, the goals/timeline should be formalized, communicated, and updated to elicit and include team members' views about indicators of success and the *appropriate* levels of these indicators. Frequent adjustment and practice in these processes will improve the knowledge and skill of all.

It is also important to develop compensation schemes that motivate team members on the basis of the established performance goals, particularly goals that they can directly influence. Compensation may include cash awards, stock options, and noncash rewards. Incentive practices are addressed in Chapter 7. In particular, goal-based pay for performance, including the entrepreneur's own compensation, is important. As the organization develops, the range of goals should be expanded to include product improvement (pace of innovation and level of product and market experimentation), product quality, and market penetration. Similarly, the range of goal-based rewards should be expanded to include public recognition and increased noncash benefits, and regular team/employee sessions should address employee knowledge about goals and associated rewards.

Wanna-be entrepreneurs gain knowledge about goal setting through relevant venture and industry experience. *Management by Objective* (MBO) seminars are based in goal theory, and they offer guidance about the types of goals and rewards that are most effective. We recommend exposure to these programs and emphasize that specific and highly challenging but attainable goals are effective for personal and venture success across all levels of the new venture and through all stages of new venture creation.

Early MBO programs often failed because managers set their own (inappropriately conceived) goals. The problem was that because they were judged only on goal achievement, they set easy goals that ensured personal "success" while their firms often failed. To avoid this problem, goals below the CEO level must be assigned and "stretch" goals should be encouraged with the proviso that falling short on a goal will not be punished – so long as the manager has made a sincere and creative effort. For example, at GE, Jack Welch set minimum goals that were mandatory and also stretch goals that were meant to encourage extraordinary innovation but did not have to be met on a regular basis.

EXCEPTIONS

Swiftness is usually better than slow action because more work is accomplished, more value is added, and learning opportunities appear in advance of competitor's learning. However, even high-growth entrepreneurs have periods when urgency is not great – when sufficient time and resources are available for a thorough and comprehensive information search and analysis, and swiftness is not as critical. So, it may be all right to reflect rather than act, but entrepreneurs need to realize that down time can be used (i) to gain advance learning about how to find the needed explicit information, or (ii) to find the best way to conduct the evaluation of new ideas. Sometimes, entrepreneurs will not have time to experiment and wait for feedback. In these instances, they *must* just act and react as best and quickly as they are able.

CASE EXAMPLES

1. AIRBNB

In 2007, a couple of years after graduation, Brian Chesky and Joe Gebbia, two friends and alumni from the prestigious Rhode Island School of Design, were living together in San Francisco. Sparked by Gebbia, Chesky had just moved there from Los Angeles with the vague intention of starting some kind of business together, like everyone else in the Bay Area seemed to be doing at the time. That same year, thanks to a design conference that was taking place in San Francisco, the two friends learned that lodging in the Bay Area was not only expensive but also that it was scarce during periods of high demand, whenever conferences or other large events took place. Realizing that they had space available in their apartment, they acquired some air mattresses to put in it and quickly created a simple website, which they asked the conference organizers to promote and link to. They ended up hosting three guests that week, and so, humbly, Airbnb ("air bed and breakfast"), the now behemoth home rental marketplace, was born.

Airbnb is an online marketplace for lodging, primarily for vacation rentals (and currently also tourism activities), where guests book their stays and pay the hosts through the Airbnb platform. The company does not own the rental properties and gets paid through commissions. Since its founding in 2007, Airbnb grew to dominate the vacation rental market, outstripping the volume and the value of the largest and better-known hotel chains. Airbnb went public in 2020 with a market valuation of $47 billion.

The $47 billion company that came to dominate the vacation rental market, however, was not born as the Airbnb we know today. The founders started out with the idea of renting air mattresses in extra rooms during periods of high demand for lodging in cities due to conferences or special events, when hotel room prices are very high or even perhaps unavailable. The process by which Airbnb became the company we know today is characterized by both the swiftness in which the founders operated from day 1, as well as for the experimentation they engaged in, adapting their idea to the needs of the market as they tried out different alternatives.

Clearly, they wasted no time jumping onto the opportunity that first time, during the design conference in San Francisco. They did not sit around for weeks drafting an elaborate business plan and systematically implementing it months later. They created a website on the spot, contacted the organizers, and bought a few air mattresses. That swiftness allowed them to test whether the idea was good, what parts of it worked and what parts of it needed to change (e.g. they discovered that a payment system had to be incorporated into the platform).

The Airbnb founders engaged in frequent experimentation from the early days, as a matter of common practice. For example, while trying to repeat the successes of the design conference at the South by Southwest festival in Austin and the Democratic National Convention in Denver, they realized that their event-based business model was not a viable option. The problem with that model was that for every event, the process had to be replicated from scratch. They had to convince each event organizer to link to their site, generate awareness in both hosts and guests, etc. Essentially, it almost meant starting the business anew every single time, without the benefits of scale. They subsequently switched to the vacation home rental market, with a sustainable business model that allowed them to create a permanent and scalable platform. From early on, they also experimented with the design and the visuals of the listings, providing hosts in strategic locations with professional photography services, even helping them out with the language, to see what worked and what did not. Airbnb's safety reputation, a critical piece in a platform in which people share their homes with strangers, was also an innovation that grew out of experimentation in the early days. At first, it was nothing more than a reputation system based on customer ratings. As the platform grew, and new problems and new situations arose, the founders tested different approaches, incrementally leading to the more sophisticated system in place today, which includes customer hotlines in multiple languages, identity-verification and background checks, and monetary coverage for potential damage.

This case also illustrates the roles that creativity, tenacity, and self-efficacy can play in facilitating quick action and experimentation. An anecdote about the early days of the company is revelatory. During the disappointing attempt at making the event-based platform work (specifically, at the Democratic National Convention in Denver in 2008), the founders created two brands of breakfast cereals (the "Obama O's" and the "Captain McCain"). The idea was born of their need to generate some extra cash flow to deal with their burgeoning debt problems that threatened to bury their nascent venture. The novelty and originality of the initiative was validated by the instant success of the initiative: at $40 per box, they sold about $35 000 worth of cereal in a very short period of time! The proceedings allowed them to survive and keep afloat a few more months. The creativity (perhaps not unexpected in design graduates), grit, determination, and chutzpah involved in such initiatives were signatory of their *modus operandi* and marked the explosive growth and success that continues today.

2. *Fluent Systems*[2]

Chad Sorenson and Jaume Villanueva met while attending the MBA program at the University of Wisconsin–Madison in 2001. They joined the Weinert Applied Ventures program for their last academic year (2001–2002), since they were both interested in entrepreneurship and had in mind starting a business. They took the opportunity that the framework of the program presented and joined forces to develop a new venture project based on a new technological solution to improve the process of applying fertilizer (anhydrous ammonia) in corn crops.

The problem they set out to solve was that, while applying fertilizer (a liquid gas stored in pressurized tanks, which are in effect metallic cylinders on wheels being pulled by an implement about 12 meters behind the tractor), farmers had no way

[2]For a more complete depiction of this case please see: Villanueva, J., and Urriolagoitia, L. (2018) Fluent Systems. *The Case Centre. ESADE Entrepreneurship Institute.* Reference no. 818-0047-1.

of knowing how much liquid was left in the tank, or indeed if there was any liquid left in the tank. This problem resulted in inefficiencies. The farmer had to either step out of the tractor to climb on the tank to check the liquid level by reading a gauge sitting on top of the tank at regular intervals or just keep applying fertilizer without knowing whether any fertilizer was being applied at all. Leaving the field unfertilized obviously results in lower yields and loss of productivity. Sorenson, a mechanical engineer by training, had spent some time developing a solution to this problem, the existence of which he learned from his cousin, a farmer in Iowa. He had developed a prototype for a device that was able to read the fluid level in the tank and transmit it to the tractor cabin via a wireless device. He joined forces with Villanueva to make this project a business venture, and they both founded Fluent Systems in 2002.

While developing this new venture project, Sorenson and Villanueva focused on honing and perfecting their business plan. In fact, still in school, they successfully entered several business plan competitions across the nation, winning the International Business Plan Competition at the University of Nebraska, which yielded a $10 000 cash prize and an entry into the "super bowl" of business plan competitions, i.e. the Moot Corp Business Plan competition at the University of Texas (first prize: $100 000). They made it to the semifinals of this competition; they were also selected to win the "best presentation" award. This early success drew the attention of investors and allowed them to raise enough capital to launch Fluent Systems after graduation.

For the first few months, they set out to fully develop the product with the help of a professional product development firm. Soon after, they contracted out the manufacturing of the first batch of units from a local manufacturer. By the spring of 2003, one and a half years after founding the company and after having spent a considerable amount of resources developing and manufacturing the product, they were finally ready to go to market. Unfortunately, the immediate results were not what they had expected: they were able to sell only 150 units in that first spring fertilizer application season. Their response was to quickly ramp up marketing and sales activities for the fall season. However, they soon discovered that customers were not ready to buy their product and that the investors' excitement and buzz surrounding their venture did not translate into actual sales. What had happened?

They were forced to conclude that their product's value proposition was not sufficiently compelling for their target customers. In lean startup terms, they did not manage to achieve product-market fit, and they had acted without sufficiently testing the ideas on the ground. Their product was perceived as overengineered, excessively complex, and simply too expensive to solve what in effect was a simple problem. Sorenson and Villanueva learned this too late because they had focused on developing a solid and attractive business plan, rather than on ensuring that their value proposition was attractive and compelling to their intended customers. They had focused on satisfying investors, so that they could get the financial resources they needed to pay for product development and manufacturing capability. *They* believed the product was compelling and, therefore, devoted themselves fully to developing it, with the help of the engineers at the product development company. The engineering took over, and they focused on developing a sophisticated solution that took too much time and financial resources. They tried out no alternative versions and spent little time testing their idea with potential customers. If they had tested and experimented with their product and their value proposition, they would have realized, before investing all their cash in the wrong product, that they needed to take a different route.

Furthermore, by waiting so long to launch the first iteration of their product, they missed on the developments of the anhydrous ammonia market. The market had begun to shift by 2003. Regulation and licensing burdens had increased due to environmental pressure, and pressures surrounding anhydrous ammonia in some states due its use in the manufacturing of illicit drugs. Oddly, while they acted very rapidly in starting the business, they took too long to get the product to market. Their actions failed to have the backing of sensible experimentation, and the delays caused by focusing on fund raising and product and manufacturing developments ultimately caused them to burn away their stock of financial resources.

In early 2004, Sorenson and Villanueva were able to sell the company and recuperate some of their investment, thanks to the valuable intellectual property that was generated in the invention of the product. What would have happened if they had experimented with a prototype, tested it, and gone quicker to market with it? What product would have they ended up developing? Could it have been a success? We will never know.

Conclusion

This chapter proposes swiftness and experimentation as entrepreneurial behaviors that contribute to new venture success. Entrepreneurship occurs in the midst of uncertainty, risk, and competitive barriers that accompany new market entry with new products, processes, and business models. Swiftness and experimentation are invaluable responses because they produce quick market feedback where little information exists. Information can guide revision of market offerings, value propositions, and business model choices, any of which may make the difference for new ventures' chances of growing and succeeding.

Research in the field of management and entrepreneurship shows that creativity, tenacity, self-efficacy, and goal setting are among the factors that enable swiftness and experimentation. The factors that contribute to the focal entrepreneurial behaviors, presented here as principles of entrepreneurship, are enhanced with industry and venture experience, as well as learning from expert models and creativity and goal-setting enhancement programs.

References

Amabile, T. M., and Pillemer, J. (2012). Perspectives on the social psychology of creativity. *The Journal of Creative Behavior*, 46(1), 3–15.

Andries, P., Debackere, K., and Van Looy, B. (2013). Simultaneous experimentation as a learning strategy: Business model development under uncertainty. *Strategic Entrepreneurship Journal*, 7(4), 288–310.

Autio, E., Sapienza, H., and Almeida, J. (2000). Effects of age at entry, knowledge intensity, and imitability on international growth. *Academy of Management Journal*, 43(5), 909–924.

Bandura, A. (1997). *Self-Efficacy: The Exercise of Control.* New York: Freeman.

Baron, M. T., Mueller, B. A., and Wolfe, M. T. (2016). Self-efficacy and entrepreneurs' adoption of unattainable goals: the restraining effects of self-control, *Journal of Business Venturing*, 31(1), 55–71.

Baum, J. R., and Bird, B. J. (2010). The successful intelligence of high-growth entrepreneurs: Links to new venture growth. *Organization Science*, 21(2), 397–412.

Baum, J. R., and Locke, E. A. (2004). The relationship of entrepreneurial traits, skill, and motivation to subsequent venture growth. *Journal of Applied Psychology*, 89(4), 587–598.

Baum, J. R., and Wally, S. (2003). Strategic decision-making speed and firm performance. *Strategic Management Journal*, 24, 1107–1129.

Baum, J. R., Locke, E. A., and Smith, K. G. (2001). A multidimensional model of venture growth. *Academy of Management Journal*, 44(2), 292–303.

Baum, J. R., Frese, M., Baron, R., and Katz, J. A. (2007). Entrepreneurship as an area of psychology: An introduction. In J. R. Baum, M. Frese, and R. Baron (eds), *The Psychology of Entrepreneurship* (pp. 1–18). New York: Erlbaum.

Bhide, A. V. (2000). *The Origin and Evolution of New Businesses.* New York: Oxford University Press.

Blank, S. (2013). Why the lean start-up changes everything. *Harvard Business Review*, 91(5), 63–72.

Bocken, N., and Snihur, Y. (2020). Lean Startup and the business model: Experimenting for novelty and impact. *Long Range Planning*, 53(4), 101953.

Brinckmann, J., Villanueva, J., Grichnik, D., and Singh, L. (2019). Sources of strategic flexibility in new ventures: an analysis of the role of resource leveraging practices. *Strategic Entrepreneurship Journal*, 13(2), 154–178.

Carsrud, A. L., and Krueger, N. F., Jr. (1995). Entrepreneurship and social psychology: Behavioral technology for the new venture initiation process. In J. A. Katz and R. H. Brockhaus, Sr. (eds), *Advances in Entrepreneurship, Firm Emergence, and Growth* (pp. 73–96). Greenwich, CT, JAI Press.

Casillas, J., Barbero, J., and Sapienza H. (2015). Knowledge acquisition, learning, and the initial pace of internationalization. *International Business Review Journal*, 24(1), 102–114.

Chandler, G. N., and Jansen, E. (1992). The founder's self-assessed competence and venture performance. *Journal of Business Venturing*, 7, 223–236.

Chen, C. C., Greene, P. G., and Crick, A. (1998). Does entrepreneurial self-efficacy distinguish entrepreneurs from managers? *Journal of Business Venturing*, 13, 395–316.

Covin, J. G., and Slevin, D. P. (1997). High growth transitions: Theoretical perspectives and suggested directions. In D. L. Sexton and R. W. Smilor, (eds), *Entrepreneurship 2000* (pp. 99–126). Chicago: Upstart.

Davidsson, P., and Honig, B. (2002). The role of social and human capital among nascent entrepreneurs. *Journal of Business Venturing*, 18, 301–331.

Debrulle, J., Steffens, P., De Bock, K. W., De Winne, S., and Maes, J. (2020). Configurations of business founder resources, strategy, and environment determining new venture performance. *Journal of Small Business Management*, DOI: 10.1080/00472778.2020.1831807

Dess, G. D., and Beard, D. W. (1984). Dimensions of organizational task environments. *Administrative Science Quarterly*, 30, 52–73.

Duckworth, A. L., Peterson, C., Matthews, M. D., and Kelly, D. R. (2007). Grit: perseverance and passion for long-term goals. *Journal of personality and social psychology*, 92(6), 1087.

Dunkelberg, W., Moore C., Scott, J., and Stull, W. (2013). Do entrepreneurial goals matter? Resource allocation in new owner-managed firms. *Journal of Business Venturing*, 28, 225–240.

Eisenhardt, K. M. (1989). Making fast strategic decisions in high velocity environments. *Academy of Management Journal*, 32, 543–576.

Eisenhardt, K. M., Furr, N. R., and Bingham, C. B. (2010). CROSSROADS – Microfoundations of performance: Balancing efficiency and flexibility in dynamic environments. *Organization Science*, 21(6), 1125–1179.

Eisenhardt, K. M., and Tabrizi, B. N. (1995). Accelerating adaptive processes: Product innovation in the global computer industry. *Administrative Science Quarterly*, 40(1), 84–110.

Felin, T., Gambardella, A., Stern, S., and Zenger, T. (2019). Lean startup and the business model: Experimentation revisited. *Long Range Planning* (Open Access).

Ferrier, W. J., Smith, K. G., and Grimm, C. M. (1999). The role of competitive action in market share erosion and industry dethronement: A study of industry leaders and challengers. *Academy of Management Journal*, 42(4), 372–388.

Gartner, W. B., Gatewood, E., and Shaver, K. G. (1991). Reasons for starting a business: Not-so-simple answers to simple questions. In G. E. Hills and R. W. Lafarge (eds), *Research at the Marketing / Entrepreneurship Interface* (pp. 90–101). Chicago, IL: Office of Entrepreneurial Studies, University of Illinois at Chicago.

Hayward, M. L., Shepherd, D. A., and Griffin, D. (2006). A hubris theory of entrepreneurship. *Management Science*, 52(2), 160–172.

Herron, L. A., and Robinson, R. B., Jr. (1993). A structural model of the effects of entrepreneurial characteristics on venture performance. *Journal of Business Venturing*, 8, 281–294.

Hmieleski, K. M., and Baron, R. A. (2008). When does entrepreneurial self-efficacy enhance versus reduce firm performance? *Strategic Entrepreneurship Journal*, 2, 57–72.

Hmieleski, K. M., and Corbett, A. C. (2008). The contrasting interaction effects of improvisational behavior with entrepreneurial self-efficacy on new venture performance and entrepreneur work satisfaction. *Journal of Business Venturing*, 23, 482–496.

Hmieleski, K. M., and Corbett, A. C. (2006). Proclivity for improvisation as a predictor of entrepreneurial intentions. *Journal of Small Business Management*, 41(1), 45–63.

Huber, G. P. (1991). Organizational learning: an examination of the contributing processes and the literatures. *Organization Science*, 2, 88–115.

Huey, J., and Walton, S. (1992). *Sam Walton: Made in America – My Story*. Garden City, New York: Doubleday.

Jones, J. W. (1993). *High Speed Management: Time-Based Strategies for Managers and Organizations*. San Francisco: Jossey Bass.

Judge, T. A., and Bono, J. E. (2001). The relationship of core self-evaluations traits – self-esteem, generalized self-efficacy, locus of control, and emotional stability – with job satisfaction and job performance: A meta-analysis. *Journal of Applied Psychology*, 86(1), 80–92.

Khedhaouria, A., Gurau, C., and Torres O. (2015). Creativity, self-efficacy and small firm performance: The mediating role of entrepreneurial orientation. *Small Business Economics*, (44), 485–504.

Landy, F. J., and Becker, W. S. (1987). Motivation theory reconsidered. In L. L. Cummings and B. M. Staw (eds), *Research in Organizational Behavior* (Vol. 9, pp. 1–38). Greenwich, CT: JAI Press.

Leatherbee, M., and Katila, R. (2020). The lean startup method: Early-stage teams and hypothesis-based probing of business ideas. *Strategic Entrepreneurship Journal*, 14(4), 570–593.

Locke, E. A. (2000). *The Prime Movers: Traits of the Great Wealth Creators*. New York: AMACOM.

Locke, E. A., and Baum, J. R. (2007). Entrepreneurial motivation. In J. R. Baum, M. Frese, and R. Baron (eds), *The Psychology of Entrepreneurship* (pp. 93–112), New York: Erlbaum.

Locke, E. A., and Latham, G. P. (1990). *A Theory of Goal Setting and Task Performance*. Englewood Cliffs, NJ: Prentice Hall.

Locke, E. A., and Latham, G. P. (2002). Building a practically useful theory of goal setting and task motivation: A 35-year odyssey. *American Psychologist*, 57, 705–717.

Markman, G. D., Balkin, D. B., and Baron, R. A. (2002). Inventors and new venture formation: The effects of general self-efficacy and regretful thinking. *Entrepreneurship Theory and Practice* (pp. 149–165). Winter.

McGrath, R. G. (2010). Business models: A discovery driven approach. *Long Range Planning*, 43(2–3), 247–261.

Miner, A. S., Bassof, P., and Moorman, C. (2001). Organizational improvisation and learning: A field study. *Administrative Science Quarterly*, 46(2), 304–337.

Mueller, B. A., Wolfe, M. T., and Syed, I. (2017). Passion and grit: An exploration of the pathways leading to venture success. *Journal of Business Venturing*, 32(3), 260–279.

Mumford, M., Supinski, E. P., Baughman, W. A., Constanza, D. P., and Threlfall, K. V. (1997). Process-based measures of creative problem-solving skills: Overall Prediction. *Creativity Research Journal*, 10(6), 73–85.

Oviatt, B., and McDougall, P. (2005). Defining international entrepreneurship and modeling the speed of internationalization. *Entrepreneurship Theory and Practice*, 30, 537–553.

Penrose, E. (1959). *The Theory of the Growth of the Firm*. Oxford: Oxford University Press.

Rauch, A., and Frese, M. (2000). Psychological approaches to entrepreneurial success: A general model and an overview of findings. In C. L. Cooper and I. T. Robertson (eds), *International Review of Industrial and Organizational Psychology* (Vol. 15, pp. 101–142). New York: John Wiley and Sons, Ltd.

Rawhouser, H., Villanueva, J., and Newbert, S. L. (2017). Strategies and tools for entrepreneurial resource access: A cross-disciplinary review and typology. *International Journal of Management Reviews*, 19(4), 473–491.

Reis, E. (2011). *The Lean Startup* (Vol. 27). New York: Crown Business.

Runco, M. A., Plucker, J. A., and Lim, W. (2000). Development and psychometric integrity of a measure of ideation behavior. *Creativity Research Journal*, 13, 391–398.

Sapienza, H., Autio, E., George, G., and Zahra, S. (2006). A capabilities perspective on the effects of new venture internationalization on survival and growth. *Academy of Management Review*, 31, 914–933.

Schumpeter, J. A. (1934). *The Theory of Economic Development*. Cambridge, MA: Harvard University Press.

Shepherd, D. A. (1999). Venture capitalists' assessment of new venture survival. *Management Science*, 45(5), 621–632.

Shepherd, D. A., and Gruber, M. (2020). The lean startup framework: Closing the academic–practitioner divide. *Entrepreneurship Theory and Practice*, 1042258719899415

Smith, K. S., and Smith, R. L. (2000). *Entrepreneurial Finance*. New York: Wiley.

Stajkovic, A. D., and Luthans, F. (1998). Self-efficacy and work related performance: A meta analysis. *Psychology Bulletin*, 124, 240–261.

Stalk, G., and Hout, T. M. (1990). *Competing Against Time: How Time-Based Competition is Reshaping Global Markets*. New York: Free Press.

Stevenson, H. H. (1985). A new paradigm for entrepreneurial management. In J. J. Kao and H. H. Stevenson (eds), *Entrepreneurship: What It Is and How to Teach It*. Boston: Harvard Business School Press.

Thomke, S. H. (2003). *Experimentation Matters*. Boston: Harvard Business School Press.

Tracy, K., Locke, E. A., and Renard, M. (1999). Conscious goal setting vs. subconscious motives: Longitudinal and concurrent effects on the performance of entrepreneurial firms. *Paper presented at the Academy of Management Conference.*

Tsang, E., and Zahra, S. (2008). Organizational unlearning. *Human Relations*, 61(10), 1435–1462.

Villanueva, J., and Sapienza, H. J. (2021). The mask of the red death: Leadership, hubris, and the Covid-19 crisis. *BRQ Business Research Quarterly*, 24(3), 258–265.

Villanueva, J., Van de Ven, A. H., and Sapienza, H. J. (2012). Resource mobilization in entrepreneurial firms. *Journal of Business Venturing*, 27(1), 19–30.

Ward, T. B. (2004). Cognition, creativity, and entrepreneurship. *Journal of Business Venturing*, 19(2), 173–188.

Exercises

1. Adaptation and Change Through Experimentation

In most successful ventures, the products, services, processes, value propositions, or business models that ultimately find market acceptance, growth, and profitability are some variations of the original market entry versions. Choose an example of a startup company that you are familiar with (conduct research online about different startups in your areas of interest if nothing comes to mind) and write a short history (two paragraphs) of the original product, service, business model, or value proposition the company initially started with and of some key changes that occurred over time. Identify the period from market entry to today and make sure to address the following questions:

1. Can you point to an instance in which there is a clear example of experimentation?
2. How long did it take from initial market entry until the version of product, service, or business model that made the company succeed or reach explosive growth?

2. Business Venture Idea

Divide into small groups. Come up with an idea for a new business venture and assume that you have $1 million in financing available to implement the idea. As a group, through discussion and consensus building, address the following questions and present them to the rest of the cohort:

1. How easily do you think your idea could be copied? How long do you believe it would take for someone else to copy your idea?
2. Given the above time-frame considerations and the resources at your disposal, how could you best and most swiftly test your value proposition, product, service, or business model? Think of what you would design, product or prototype, and how you would make it available to your potential customers or other stakeholders.
3. What would be the parts/areas of your value proposition, product, service, or business model that you would be most interested to test or learn more about? In other words, what are the key insights you would be looking for? How would you design and experiment to learn more about them?

Video Analysis and Discussion

Please watch the following video(s):

1. The power of an entrepreneurial mindset: https://www.youtube.com/watch?v=Ihs4VFZWwn4
2. How I became an entrepreneur at 66: https://www.youtube.com/watch?v=Ogce5D2XMZ0

Now form small groups to discuss the video(s) and answer the following questions:

1. What are the major points of the video?
2. How can you use information from the video in your career?
3. Based on the video, what advice do you have for leaders in organizations?

Be prepared to present the ideas from your small group discussion with the class as a whole.

Discussion Questions

1. How would you encourage experimentation in your work group?
2. Are there any "ground rules" you would suggest when it comes to experimentation at work?
3. How would you reward experimentation at work?
4. What specific actions would you take when experimentation "fails" at work?

26

Achieve Work-Family Balance Through Individual and Organizational Strategies

MALISSA A. CLARK[1], KATELYN N. SANDERS[1], AND BORIS B. BALTES[2]

[1] University of Georgia
[2] Wayne State University

As the average workweek is steadily increasing in the United States along with the number of dual-earner households, many workers today find themselves struggling to balance their work and family lives. Indeed, a recent poll by the Equal Opportunities Commission found that nearly three out of five adults believe it is harder now for working parents to balance work and family life than 30 years ago. Because of concerns such as this, both organizations and researchers have become increasingly focused on a better understanding of what helps employees to balance their work and family lives. To date, most of the focus has been on how organizational initiatives (e.g. flextime) can help individuals manage these two goals, but recent research has begun to realize the importance of individual-level strategies in achieving this balance. The guiding principle of this chapter is that both individual and organizational strategies are necessary if employees are to achieve work–family balance. In the present chapter, we present a definition of work–family balance, explain how work–family conflict and enrichment episodes contribute to balance perceptions, and outline several individual and organizational strategies that can help one to achieve balance.

WORK–FAMILY BALANCE

Work–family balance (also called work–nonwork balance) can be defined as "employees' evaluation of the favorability of their combination of work and nonwork roles, arising from the degree to which their affective experiences and their perceived involvement and effectiveness in work and nonwork roles are commensurate with the value they attach to these roles" (Casper, Vaziri, Wayne, DeHauw, and

Greenhaus, 2018, p. 197). There are several important features of this definition. First, work–family balance is an attitude – a person's subjective evaluation. Second, employees' perceptions of balance involve a blend of how satisfied, involved, and effective they believe they are in each role. Finally, balance does not require equality across different roles – perceptions of balance are commensurate with the value placed on each role. If an individual is satisfied and effective in their own highly valued roles, they will experience feelings of balance. This also means work–family balance will look different for all individuals as each person has different values surrounding their work and their nonwork experiences. In order to experience balance, employees do not need to experience equal involvement and effectiveness in every role. For example, an employee who highly values their career and has less value placed on their nonwork life will find balance when more time is spent at work, and they feel as though they are being effective in their role at work, compared to time spent at home.

Although the term *work–life balance* has long been a part of popular discussion, scholarly research on the topic has been relatively limited until recently. Early research on work–family balance was plagued with conceptual ambiguities and unclear measurement. However, there have recently been some important studies that have significantly advanced our ability to measure and understand work–family balance. In one of these studies, researchers Wayne, Vaziri, and Casper (2021) created a new measure of work–family balance that includes assessments of three specific dimensions of balance (affective, involvement, and effectiveness balance) as well as an assessment of global balance. The different balance dimensions involve the perception that one experiences sufficiently pleasant positive emotions (affective balance), feels effective (effectiveness balance), and is involved (involvement balance) in work and nonwork roles commensurate with the value attached to those roles. Global balance is the overall combination, fit, balance, harmony, or integration of one's work and nonwork roles. Curious about your perceptions of balance? We have included this new self-assessment at the end of the chapter.

What Factors Influence Balance Perceptions?

An individual's perception of work–family balance can change over time and even from day to day, based on what events and experiences are going on in someone's life. Two key factors influencing perceptions of balance are *work–family conflict* and *work–family enrichment.* Work–family conflict is defined as "a form of inter-role conflict in which the role pressures from the work and family domains are mutually incompatible in some respect" (Greenhaus and Beutell, 1985, p. 77). Individuals may feel conflict because their work life is interfering with their family life, termed "work interfering with family conflict," or they may feel conflict because their family life is interfering with their work life, termed "family interfering with work conflict" (Frone, Russell, and Cooper, 1997). Work–family conflict can occur when time spent on tasks in one role interferes with or inhibits the completion of responsibilities in the other role (e.g. a late-night work assignment prevents an employee from attending their child's soccer game), or when pressures and stress from one role spill over to the other role (e.g. stress from caring for a sick relative hinder role performance at work).

Work–family enrichment, on the other hand, is when individuals experience benefits and gains from engaging in multiple roles. Work–family enrichment can be defined as "the extent to which experiences in one role improve the quality of life in the other role" (Greenhaus and Powell, 2006, p. 73). Like conflict, work–family enrichment is bidirectional (i.e. work can positively affect family, and vice versa). When individuals experience work–family enrichment, they are gaining various resources (e.g. affect, psychological, social capital, and material resources) in one role that are then used to improve performance in another role. Some examples of enrichment include applying a skill learned in a work training (empathic listening) to improve communication with spouse or children at home, or positive affect experienced at home spilling over to enhance performance at work.

When individuals reflect on their own level of work–family balance, they mentally take a "snapshot" of their recent experiences of conflict and enrichment between their different life roles (work, family, and other important roles that are valued). Experiences of work–family conflict and enrichment feed directly into perceptions of balance (Maertz and Boyar, 2011; Wayne, Butts, Casper, and Allen, 2017). For example, individuals may consider recent instances where experiences of conflict or enrichment affected their emotions, feelings of effectiveness, or degree of involvement in their valued roles. Based on this, we argue that both individual and organizational strategies can facilitate work–family balance by reducing experiences of conflict, enhancing increased experiences of enrichment, or by directly impacting perceptions of balance.

Individual Strategies

Individuals may engage in a variety of strategies to maintain a healthy balance between work and family. Here, we outline several different types of individual strategies people can use to reduce work–family conflict, increase work–family enrichment, and attain goals in both work and family domains. The first set of strategies (i.e. selection, optimization, and compensation (SOC) strategies) involves the use and allocation of resources when individuals are faced with work and family challenges. The second set of strategies (boundary management) focuses on how individuals manage the boundaries between work and personal life, and the third set of strategies (action-regulation strategies) is based on how individuals jointly pursue work and family goals.

The Selection, Optimization, and Compensation Model

SOC was originally developed as a lifespan model to explain successful adaptation to the loss of resources due to aging through adjustments in the use and allocation of resources (Baltes and Baltes, 1990; Baltes, 1997). It is based on the underlying assumption that limited internal and external resources (e.g. mental capacity, time, and social support) require people to make choices regarding the allocation of those resources. These limitations of resources necessitate the use of several processes: selection, optimization, and compensation.

Selection involves *choosing goals* and is based on the idea that individuals have a limited amount of resources, so selection is needed to focus on a subset of possible goals. Elective selection involves choosing from among positive options. Loss-based selection occurs when an individual is pressured to change or abandon certain goals (or change one's goal hierarchy) by the loss of some internal or external resource. Optimization and compensation pertain to the means for attaining the chosen goals. Optimization refers to the acquisition of and refinement in the use of resources to achieve selected goals. General categories of optimization include persistence, practice, learning of new skills, modeling of successful others, as well as the scheduling of time. Finally, compensation occurs when lost resources (or those anticipated to be lost, for example time) are replaced by new ones in order to sustain progress toward one's existing goals. The use of external aids (e.g. the Internet) or help from others (e.g. childcare) are examples of compensatory behaviors.

The theory of SOC hypothesizes (and research supports) that, when faced with the limitation of resources (e.g. time and energy), those who use SOC strategies are more likely to maximize gains and minimize losses, it is plausible to assume that individuals who use SOC behaviors will be more successful at dealing with the competing roles of work and family. For example, after the birth of a child, an individual could engage in loss-based selection and choose to focus on a more limited number of work goals (e.g. no longer focus on organizational networking) and/or family goals (only focus on the immediate and not extended family) given that their resources have become more limited. Further, an individual could engage in optimization and decide what individual skills (e.g. organizational and technological) could be acquired or improved to help ensure successful goal completion. For example, if an employee has decided that successfully leading/managing her workgroup is a goal she will pursue, then she can decide to take a leadership training program to enhance her skills. By enhancing her skills, she should more efficiently achieve the same level of productivity allowing more time for family commitments. Finally, individuals can engage in compensation by maintaining their prior productivity (even though they may have to work less because of family commitments) through the use of delegation. They could attempt to give more responsibility to subordinates to decrease their actual workload but maintain overall productivity.

Research has now demonstrated that the use of these SOC strategies is related to lower amounts of job and family stressors and thereby lower amounts of work–family conflict (WFC). For example, Baltes and Heydens-Gahir (2003) show that employees who reported using SOC strategies at work and/or at home also reported lower amounts of job and family stressors, and subsequently work–family conflict. Additional research appears to indicate that, given one's selected goals, the strategy of optimization seems to be the most effective in reducing work and family stressors. Of course, the exact way individuals choose to engage in SOC strategies is open to much variability.

While the use of the SOC model as a framework has demonstrated that at a broad (or general) level, the reported use of SOC strategies is related to lower work–family conflict, the use of SOC strategies has not, to our knowledge, been examined in relation to work–family enrichment or work–family balance. However, it is plausible that resources utilized or acquired through the use of SOC strategies could enhance performance in work and family domains and positively impact perceptions of work–family balance. For example, individuals could engage in optimization to learn mindfulness skills, which have been shown to increase work–family enrichment and balance perceptions (Allen and Paddock, 2015).

Boundary Management Styles

Boundary management is the process by which individuals manage the relationship between the multiple roles (i.e. work and family) in our lives, ranging from integration to segmentation. The integration of work and family lives would be answering a family call while at work, whereas segmentation behaviors would consist of someone not taking any work calls or emails after hours. However, as technology has advanced over the years, the permeability of boundaries between work and home has increased. This increase in permeability has required that individuals learn to identify their preferences of integration or segmentation and increase their strategies for managing the boundaries between work and home. Similar to the work–family conflict, boundary management is a bidirectional concept; therefore, some individuals may blur the lines at work (i.e. allowing family to integrate into the work place), but not allow work to permeate into the home (i.e. segmentation).

Research has shown that managing the boundaries between work and home has implications for workplace outcomes (i.e. productivity, satisfaction, and commitment; Rothbard and Ollier-Malaterre, 2016). In addition, research has begun to understand specific implications between boundary integration and work–family conflict (Allen, Cho, and Meier, 2014). Specifically, research has found that the integration of family at work is associated with increased family-to-work conflict (Bulger, Matthews, and Hoffman, 2007). When there is more permeability of work at home, individuals experience more work–family conflict. Too much integration has also been associated with decreased productivity at work, decreased work commitment, and increased turnover (Kossek, Lautsch, and Eaton, 2006).

In order to better balance work and family, research has shown that personal preference has a large impact on the effectiveness of integration and segmentation and the relationship between work–family balance (Dumas, 2004; Hecht and Cluley, 2014). If an individual highly identifies with multiple roles, then segmentation and less permeable boundaries may be more beneficial in reducing work–family conflict and increasing engagement. Conversely, if someone identifies with one role (i.e. family) more than another (i.e. work), then the integration of boundaries can be more beneficial (Rothbard et al., 2016).

Action-Regulation Strategies

In a recently published article, Hirschi, Shockley, and Zacher (2019) outlined an action-regulation model that explains how individuals can jointly attain work and family goals, thus fostering work–family balance. The four strategies outlined in their model include (i) allocating resources, (ii) changing resources and barriers, (iii) sequencing goals, and (iv) revising goals. The first two strategies can be considered goal engagement strategies in which individuals strive to achieve goals directly through allocating and utilizing resources or indirectly by changing resources and/or barriers. The second two strategies can be considered goal disengagement strategies in which individuals strategically disengage from certain goals, revise goals, or abandon goals in their current form.

Allocating Resources to Work and Family Goals

To achieve balance, individuals can activate and allocate existing resources that simultaneously facilitate the goal of attaining goals in multiple domains – called boundary-spanning resources. For example, if individuals can find ways to increase their earning potential at work, this facilitates the goal of being successful at work and also facilitates the goal of providing for one's family. Positive emotions in one domain can facilitate goals in that originating domain, but through the process of spillover, it can facilitate goals in the other domain. This is the simplest form of goal engagement and is often the first strategy employed by individuals.

Changing Resources and Barriers Pertaining to Work and Family Goals

When existing resources are not sufficient to jointly attain work and family goals, individuals can take actions to *create additional resources* (i.e. increase boundary-spanning resources) and *reduce barriers* (i.e. reduce boundary-spanning barriers). For example, if individuals are experiencing emotional exhaustion because of an abusive supervisor, an individual can attempt to reduce this barrier by confronting their supervisor or requesting a transfer. Or, individuals can try to create additional resources by encouraging their spouse to take on more household responsibilities, which can facilitate the goal of having more time and energy to be a good parent and productive employee. The SOC strategies of optimization and compensation are both strategies involving changing or acquiring new resources – hiring outside help can also increase additional time and energy resources; learning new communication skills can facilitate goals at work (getting a promotion) and at home (increasing ability to troubleshoot problems with one's spouse).

Sequencing Work and Family Goals

A third option is to sequence work and family goals by prioritizing some goals over others. This strategy allows individuals to focus on one goal at a time. This strategy is similar to the selection strategy of SOC, with a few minor differences. In this action-regulation model, Hirschi and colleagues (2019) emphasize that this sequencing strategy will be most effective in increasing work–family balance when individuals prioritize a goal in one domain that promotes goal attachment in the other life domain in the long run. For example, individuals may pause their pursuit of one goal (seeking promotion at work) in order to focus attention and energy toward attaining another important goal (e.g. caring for an aging parent).

Revising Existing Work and Family Goals and Selecting New Goals

A final strategy in Hirschi et al.'s (2019) action-regulation model is revising or abandoning goals, and this strategy is typically implemented when they are unable to attain existing goals in both life domains with any of the prior three strategies. Individuals can still attain some sense of work–family balance if they are able to revise or abandon unattainable goals. For example, individuals may have originally sought to rise to district manager but may now revise their goal to be a more realistic goal of rising to store manager. Abandoning goals can be difficult for individuals to cope with, so individuals will be most successful if they are able to fully reengage in the pursuit of their new goal.

Moderators of Individual Strategies

The effectiveness of these strategies can be affected by several other factors. Individual differences may affect the type of strategy utilized and also the effectiveness of this strategy. For example, having a promotion versus prevention focus could play an important role in what strategies an individual chooses to attempt as well as how effective certain strategies are. Life stage is another important factor to consider. Qualitative research studies have shown both dual-career men and women use certain coping strategies more during stages of their life cycles, which included more stressful situations (i.e. young children at home). Similarly, Becker and Moen (1999) found that many dual-earner couples engaged in what they called scaling back strategies (i.e. reducing and restructuring a couple's commitment to paid work) at certain times in their lives.

Another possible moderator would be job type. For example, some research suggests that the use of SOC strategies is affected quite a bit by job type/level. A manager may have much more flexibility when it comes to prioritizing his/her workload (i.e. elective selection) than a clerical employee has. Thus, even if a clerical worker would choose to engage in elective selection, they do not have the autonomy to do so. Job type may also moderate the relationship between boundary management style and work–family balance. Some jobs (i.e. surgeon) may not allow for an individual to integrate their family into their work, even if that is their preference. Finally, socioeconomic level could act as a moderator with respect to the ability to apply some strategies, such as compensation. For instance, families of higher socioeconomic status (SES) would be able to engage in compensatory behaviors such as the use of daycare and/or household help, privileges that are not possible for lower SES individuals.

Organizational Strategies

Organizational initiatives intended to help employees balance their work and family lives continue to increase in popularity. For example, in the Families and Work Institute's 2020 Effective Workplace Index report, a central component of being an effective workplace involved improving *employee perceptions of work–life fit* – a concept that closely resembles the concept of work–family balance. According to this report, organizations must not only offer formal work–family organizational policies, but they also must have a culture of flexibility that supports access to and use of these policies. Formal organizational initiatives include implementing flexible work hours (flextime), allowing telecommuting, compressed workweeks, offering on-site childcare, and implementing part-time schedules and job sharing. Research has shown that these initiatives can reduce employees' work–family conflict and increase their family satisfaction. For example, in their Executive Summary Series, the Boston College Center for Work and Family found multiple benefits for both the employee (e.g. improvements in employee health and well-being, work–life effectiveness, employee satisfaction, engagement, and commitment) as well as the organization (e.g. improvements in employee productivity, reduced costs, improvement in employee attraction and retention, etc.). We believe that with careful implementation and a supportive organizational culture, organizational initiatives have the potential to increase employees' work–family balance. We will first discuss formal organizational policies, followed by a discussion of the importance of family-friendly culture.

Formal Organizational Policies

Flextime. To date, the most widely used organizational initiative to help workers balance their work and family lives is flextime, or flexible workweeks. Flextime involves setting a band of time where all employees are required to be in the office (typically from 9 or 10 a.m. until 2 or 3 p.m.), but employees have the discretion as to exactly what time they will arrive and leave work outside that band of time. An obvious benefit of a flexible workweek is that employees can start or end their day earlier or later, depending on their other nonwork obligations and needs at that time. Thus, if employees have an outside obligation in the afternoon on a particular day (e.g. doctor's appointment and child's sporting event), they can simply arrive at work earlier in the morning, which allows them to leave earlier in the afternoon. According to a Families and Work Institute national study, 68% of companies allow at least some employees to periodically change starting and quitting times (although only 34% of companies allowed employees to do this on a daily basis), and the percentage of companies offering flextime has increased from 1998 to 2005. This national study also found that flextime was offered more frequently in smaller companies (50–99 employees) than larger companies (1000+ employees). Also, according to a large-scale study of over 30 000 government employees, approximately 41% of employees surveyed utilize flextime (Saltzstein, Ting, and Saltzstein, 2001).

Overall, research has shown that flextime is associated with many individual as well as organizational benefits. Several studies have found that flextime is associated with positive attitudinal outcomes. For example, flextime has been associated with greater employee loyalty to the organization and greater employee job satisfaction (Baltes, Briggs, Huff, Wright, and Neuman, 1999). Additionally, employees who have greater control over their work hours have also reported reduced work–family conflict. In addition to these attitudinal outcomes, research has linked flextime to various organizational outcomes, such as increased productivity and reduced turnover.

There is some evidence that all forms of flextime are not created equal, however. For example, researchers have found that some flexible schedules offered by organizations allow for very little flexibility, and that the number of hours in which an employee actually works may increase with a flexible schedule. In fact, one study of Canadian employees found that the percentage of employees working 50+ hours doubled or sometimes tripled in the presence of flexible work arrangements (Comfort, Johnson, and Wallace, 2003). In a Boston College Center for Work and Family's 2000 study, researchers made a distinction between traditional flextime and daily flextime. Whereas traditional flextime involves employees choosing their start and end times, which must include certain core hours, daily flextime is a working schedule in which employees are allowed to vary their work hours on a daily basis. The researchers at the Center for Work and Family found that employees using daily flextime were more satisfied with their jobs, lives, and more productive than employees using traditional flextime.

Compressed work weeks. Compressed workweeks are used in a broad range of industries, including manufacturing, health care, food service, government, the airline industry, and law enforcement (Harrington and Hall, 2007). With a compressed workweek, the workweek is shortened to fewer than five days by having employees work longer hours on the days they do work. There are many different variations of a compressed workweek, but the most typical is to have full-time employees (i.e. 40-hour workweek) work four 10-hour days per week instead of five eight-hour days per week. According to the Families and Work Institute's study, 39% of companies allow at least some employees to work a compressed workweek schedule, and the number of companies offering compressed workweeks has increased since 1998.

As with many of the family-friendly policies we discuss, there are pros and cons to implementing a compressed workweek in an organization. Among the benefits are that compressed workweeks have been shown to decrease work–family conflict, stress, and fatigue, as well as increase satisfaction and positive attitudes about the effect of work schedules on one's family and social life. In addition to these attitudinal benefits, compressed workweeks have been shown to reduce employee absenteeism and increase productivity.

Compressed workweeks can be problematic for some employees, however; specifically, for those employees who have time-specific responsibilities (e.g. picking up a child from school). Indeed, Saltzstein et al. (2001) found that mothers with an unemployed spouse (who can presumably help with childcare or eldercare obligations) experienced significantly more satisfaction with their work–family balance as a result of a compressed workweek, whereas unmarried mothers experienced significantly *less* satisfaction with work–family balance. This finding illustrates that compressed workweeks may only benefit employees when they have someone to assist in their time-specific responsibilities. In the case of childcare, most daycare facilities close at 6 p.m., which can make it difficult for employees who do not have outside assistance to find childcare on the days they work extended hours.

Telecommuting. Telecommuting is generally defined as working from home or off-site for all or part of the workweek, made possible by advances in telecommunication and information technology. According to the 2005 Families and Work study of employers, 31% of companies allowed some of its employees to work from home or off-site on a regular basis. However, telecommuting is not suitable for all jobs, or all people. Telecommuting is most often used in jobs that rely heavily on phones, the Internet/computers, and other technology devices, where face-to-face time with other employees or customers is not as essential, and where constant supervision is not necessary. Further, researchers have identified several personality traits and skills that differentiate employees suitable for telecommuting from those who would struggle with such a work arrangement. Examples include self-motivation, time management and organizational skills, trustworthiness, comfort with solitude, strong communication skills, independence, and confidence.

Like flextime and compressed work weeks, there are pros and cons to telecommuting. From an employee's perspective, telecommuting can have many advantages, including the cost savings on gas, reduced time spent commuting to work, greater autonomy, and greater flexibility of the work schedule. From an organization's perspective, telecommuting can increase employee productivity, lower employee absenteeism, and reduce overhead costs. Research has shown telecommuting to have a positive impact on employees, in that telecommuting has been linked to greater work–family balance than traditional occupations, more perceived control over one's work and family roles, higher performance ratings, and reduced depression rates.

Conversely, telecommuting can pose challenges to employees and organizations alike. Employees may feel isolated from their coworkers or have difficulty separating their work and family roles, while organizations may have difficulty monitoring employees as well as fostering team synergy. Indeed, research has linked telecommuting to increased work–family conflict, increased spillover from work to family, and higher depression rates. Kossek et al. (2006) point out that telecommuting may lead to increased work–family conflict because the border between the work and family domains is more permeable if one is working at home. To resolve this, some employees have developed routines to help solidify the role boundaries between work and family, such as putting on work clothes, reading the business section of the newspaper, or saying goodbye to the family before stepping into the home office.

On-site childcare. Another recent trend within organizations is to provide a daycare facility on-site. Providing an on-site childcare facility has the potential to increase work–family balance for employees with children, presumably because employees do not have to travel to drop off and pick up their children, and they can visit their children at various times in the workday (e.g. during their lunch hour), thus helping parents to feel close to their children even while at work. Although a recent study found that the usage of employer-provided childcare is relatively low, those using such services have reported more positive attitudes toward managing their work and family responsibilities and were less likely to experience problems with daycare. On-site childcare has also been found to result in positive organizational outcomes, such as increased organizational loyalty, and reduced absenteeism and turnover. A potential unintended outcome for on-site childcare is that there may be a backlash, or "frustration effect," from workers who are not able to take advantage of such a policy, either because they do not have children, are on the waitlist, or cannot afford such services.

Part-time and job sharing. Another type of organizational policy aimed at helping employees balance their work and family involves reducing the total number of hours employees work per week. This can be accomplished through either reducing the number of hours an employee works from full-time to part-time or by dividing up the responsibility of one full-time position among two employees (i.e. job sharing). Many organizations currently use these policies, with 53% allowing employees to switch from full-time to part-time and 46% allowing employees to share jobs (Bond, Galinsky, Kim, and Brownfield, 2005). Research has shown that employees who reduced their hours to part-time experienced greater life satisfaction, increased work–family balance, felt less stressed, and reported better relationships with their children.

However, part-time work may not be a feasible alternative for certain occupations (e.g. lawyer and doctor), thus limiting its usefulness. Job sharing is also only suitable for some positions, mostly ones that require long workweeks (greater than 40 hours/week) or jobs that cannot be easily reduced to part-time positions. If the employees sharing a particular position are able to coordinate and work well together, job sharing can be a great option for employees. For example, if one employee has an unexpected family situation, he/she can work out an arrangement with his/her job-sharing partner to cover this time lost. Understandably, there are some potential disadvantages that come with sharing a job with another person, particularly if one of the partners is not carrying his/her share of the workload, or there are communication breakdowns. Additionally, sometimes the job performance of each individual employee is not easily distinguished, which can be problematic if individuals make unequal contributions.

Informal Organizational Supports

It has been consistently shown that formal organizational work–family policies to help employees balance their work and family lives will not be successful if the employees perceive that the organization is not fully supportive of the use of such policies. For example, if the organization offers on-site childcare, but charges so much for these services that only the top executives in the company can afford such a service, then it will not be effective in helping most of the organization's employees manage their work and family (a point we discuss later in one of our case studies). Second, employees will not take advantage of such policies if they perceive negative ramifications may come from utilizing such a policy. For example, if an organization offers telecommuting but employees believe that if they take advantage of such a policy their manager will think negatively of their work ethic, which may subsequently impact their potential for promotions or pay raises, then they will not take advantage of such a policy. In other words, offering family-friendly policies may not be sufficient; rather, it is the *perception* that the organization is family supportive that mediates the relationship between the family-friendly policies available and positive outcomes. The cumulative findings from this research indicate that formal family-friendly policies will have a greater impact on facilitating work–family balance in organizations with a family-friendly culture than those with a culture that does not support its policies. Indeed, Thompson, Beauvais, and Lyness (1999) found that a supportive work–family culture was related to employees' use of work–family benefits, and both the availability of such policies and a supportive work culture predicted lower work–family conflict.

Another important factor in improving employees' work–family balance is support from one's supervisor and coworkers. First, supervisors and others at work can help to reduce employees' work–family conflict by providing different types of support, including emotional support (e.g. comforting an upset coworker) and instrumental support (e.g. assistance with a task). Supervisors can help to increase employees' work–family enrichment by providing opportunities skill growth, personal development, and learning opportunities – in other words, providing opportunities for employees to gain new resources. Finally, supervisors can directly impact employees' perceptions of work–life balance through *family-supportive supervisor behaviors.* Family-supportive supervisors "empathize with employees' attempts to balance work and nonwork, while also actively facilitating employees' ability to manage work and nonwork demands" (Cain and Stevens, 2018). Studies linked family-supportive supervisory behaviors to a wide variety of positive outcomes in addition to increased employee work–family balance, perceptions of control over work and family, and job satisfaction, as well as improved sleep quality, physical, and psychological health.

In sum, while formal organizational initiatives can be successful at increasing work–family balance, they will be most effective when the organizational culture is supportive of its employees' work–life balance. Support for employees can help reduce levels of conflict and increase levels of enrichment, and family-supportive supervisory behaviors have been found to improve employees' work–life balance as well as a wide variety of positive outcomes.

Moderators of Organizational Strategies

Similar to the individual strategies, there are several factors that can enhance or mitigate the effectiveness of formal and informal organizational strategies. Formal organizational policies and family-supportive supervisory behaviors will be more effective when the organizational culture is also family-friendly. Different organizational policies (e.g. flextime and telecommuting) may be more effective with some types of jobs than others. Additionally, organizational policies aimed at reducing their employees' work–family balance are not one-size-fits-all solutions. Thus, the effectiveness of each organizational strategy may also depend on the individual employees' personal characteristics, life stage, segmentation preferences, etc. Thus, the effectiveness of organizational strategies can be moderated by employees' use of individual strategies, and vice versa.

Case Examples

1. First Tennessee Bank

First Tennessee Bank has earned top ratings when it comes to being a family-friendly company by both *Business Week* and *Working Mother*. First Tennessee offers a wide variety of family-friendly programs, including flextime, telecommuting, on-site childcare or vouchers, job sharing, prime-time schedules (reduced hours with benefits), and adoption benefits. In addition, First Tennessee was one of the only companies surveyed by *Business Week* that have actually measured the effect of work–family strategies on profits. However, perhaps even more impressive is that family-friendliness is ingrained in both culture and business strategy. Realizing that family issues do affect business results, executives have integrated issues pertaining to balancing work and family into job design, work processes, and organizational structures. Company executives have made strides to show workers that the company is serious in their endeavors to help employees balance their work and family lives. To ensure that the work–family policies are working smoothly and that employees are satisfied with them, First Tennessee has created the First Power Council, which is comprised of high-level executives and currently chaired by the HR manager. The First Power Council meets quarterly to go over employee satisfaction surveys and to discuss any matters (work–family related and otherwise) of concern to the employees. John Daniel, HR manager at First Tennessee, views the work–family benefits offered to employees as a win-win: "I often get more productivity from the people we offer work–family benefits to than the average person because they are so appreciative of the flexibility the program allows. In sum, offering work–family benefits is a great way to attract and retain the right people."

First Tennessee Bank provides a great example of how a supportive culture can enhance the effectiveness of family-friendly policies. Regardless of how many benefits are offered to employees, if only a select few are able/allowed to use them, or if the company culture still does not support the use of such policies on a regular basis, then employees will not feel the benefits of such programs.

2. XYZ Company

The top management at XYZ Company (a fictional but representative company) has recently implemented several work–family policies in response to employee satisfaction surveys that indicated many employees were concerned about balancing their work and families. After consideration of which policies would work best for their particular company, executives decided to offer flextime and part-time work to employees. Despite their good intentions and initial excitement for these work–family programs, recent events at the company suggest that the top management did not follow through to ensure that these work–family policies were being properly implemented.

Since the implementation of the two work–family policies, several employees have filed complaints that they have been denied the opportunity to use them. Several employees were denied flextime because their supervisor reportedly stated that their particular job within the company required that they be there during normal operating hours to deal with clients. Other supervisors reportedly denied part-time work because, in their opinion, it was an "all or nothing" position – either the employee commits to full-time work, or they will find someone who will commit to full-time. Some complaints were filed because managers did offer flextime or part-time work, but only when the employees agreed to a lesser pay or a lower-level position. Upon the investigation of these instances, top management discovered that some supervisors were strongly opposed to such policies because they feared this would decrease the productivity of their work group.

According to recent focus groups held with XYZ employees, once employees learned of these grievances regarding the flextime and part-time work options offered to employees, employees began to fear that taking advantage of such policies would in fact limit their ability to move up within the organization. These fears were not entirely unwarranted, as there have been at least two documented instances of an employee being demoted or transferred to a less desirable position within two months of requesting either the flextime or part-time work option from his/her supervisor. Although the supervisors in these two instances deny such a link, the focus group discussions revealed that many employees believe otherwise.

In sum, although XYZ Company had intended to help employees balance their work and family by offering flexible benefits, these policies are not having the intended consequences. First, because top management have not clearly conveyed to company supervisors that these work–family policies should be encouraged, and every attempt should be made to accommodate employees who wish to take advantage of them, some supervisors have been reluctant to grant these flexible arrangements to their subordinates for fear that they would decrease their work group productivity. Thus, in many ways, these work–family policies failed in their attempt to help employees balance their work and family, because either the employees have been denied such benefits or the employees were reluctant to ask for such an arrangement for fear of demotion or other work-related consequences. Most importantly, at XYZ Company, the implementation of the work–family policies has actually caused more damage than benefit. Specifically, since the flextime and part-time work policies have been implemented, recent employee satisfaction surveys have shown a decrease in job satisfaction and organizational commitment. Moreover, turnover has increased from 20–28% since flextime and part-time work were first offered to employees. Thus, not only have these work–family policies failed to help improve employees' work–family balance, they have actually *lowered* (based on the employee surveys mentioned earlier) employee satisfaction and commitment to the organization. Company XYZ is a prime example of just how important it is that all company employees, as well as the company culture, are supportive of such policies.

The bottom line is this: if you are going to offer work–family policies to employees, you have got to do it right.

Conclusion

A goal of this chapter was to clarify the concept of work–family balance and outline actionable steps individuals and organizations can take to enhance it. To foster work–family balance, individuals can take an active role in decreasing instances of work–family conflict and increasing instances of work–family enrichment, as well as utilizing strategies to manage the boundaries between work and home and to simultaneously attain work and family goals. Moreover, organizations can reduce instances of conflict through formal processes (e.g. implementation of one or more family-friendly policies) or informally (through fostering an organizational culture supportive of its employees' desire to balance work and family or by improving supervisors' use of family-supportive supervisory behaviors).

References

Allen, T. D., Cho, E., and Meier, L. L. (2014). Work–family boundary dynamics. *Annual Review of Organizational Psychology and Organizational Behavior*, 1, 99–121.

Allen, T. D., and Paddock, E. L. (2015). How being mindful impacts individuals' work-family balance, conflict, and enrichment: A review of existing evidence, mechanisms and future directions. In J. Reb and P. W. B. Atkins (eds), *Mindfulness in Organizations: Foundations, Research, and Applications* (pp. 213–238). Cambridge, England: Cambridge University Press.

Baltes, P. B. (1997). On the incomplete architecture of human ontogeny: Selection, optimization, and compensation as foundation of developmental theory. *American Psychologist*, 52(4), 366–380.

Baltes, P. B., and Baltes, M. M. (eds) (1990). *Successful Aging: Perspectives from the Behavioral Sciences.* Cambridge, MA, US: Cambridge University Press.

Baltes, B. B., Briggs, T. E., Huff, J. W., Wright, J. A., and Neuman, G. A. (1999). Flexible and compressed workweek schedules: A meta-analysis of their effects on work-related criteria. *Journal of Applied Psychology*, 84, 496–513.

Baltes, B. B., and Heydens-Gahir, H. A. (2003). Reduction of work-family conflict through the use of selection, optimization, and compensation behaviors. *Journal of Applied Psychology*, 88, 1005–1018.

Becker, P. E., and Moen, P. (1999). Scaling back: Dual earner couples' work-family strategies. *Journal of Marriage and the Family*, 61, 995–1007.

Bond, J. T., Galinsky, E., Kim, S. S., and Brownfield, E. (2005). *National Study of Employers.* New York: Families and Work Institute, 6.

Bulger, C. A., Matthews, R. A., and Hoffman, M. E. (2007). Work and personal life boundary management: Boundary strength, work/personal life balance, and the segmentation-integration continuum. *Journal of Occupational Health Psychology,* 12, 365–375.

Cain, T. L., and Stevens, S. C. (2018). Family-supportive supervisory behaviors: A review and recommendations for research and practice. *Journal of Organizational Behavior,* 39, 869–888.

Casper, W. J., Vaziri, H., Wayne, J. H., DeHauw, S., and Greenhaus, J. (2018). The jingle-jangle of work–nonwork balance: A comprehensive and meta-analytic review of its meaning and measurement. *Journal of Applied Psychology,* 103, 182–214.

Comfort, D., Johnson, K., and Wallace, D. (2003). *Part-Time Work and Family-Friendly Practices in Canadian Workplaces.* Victoria, BC, Canada: Micromedia, ProQuest.

Dumas, T. L. (2004). When to draw the line: Effects of identity and boundary management strategies on interrole conflict. Annual National Academy of Management Meeting, New Orleans, LA.

Frone, M. R., Russell, M., and Cooper, M. L. (1997). Relation of work-family conflict to health outcomes: A four-year longitudinal study of employed parents. *Journal of Occupational and Organizational Psychology,* 70, 325–335.

Greenhaus, J. H., and Beutell, N. J. (1985). Sources of conflict between work and family roles. *Academy of Management Review,* 10, 76–88.

Greenhaus, J. H., and Powell, G. N. (2006). When work and family are allies: A theory of work-family enrichment. *Academy of Management Review,* 31, 72–92.

Harrington, B., and Hall, D. T. (2007). *Career Management & Work-life Integration: Using Self-Assessment to Navigate Contemporary Careers.* Thousand Oaks, CA: Sage.

Hecht, T. D., and Cluley, H. (2014). *A Daily Study of Work-Nonwork Boundary Permeability and Affect with a Self-Concept Lens.* New York, NY: Work and Family Researchers Network.

Hirschi, A., Shockley, K. M., and Zacher, H. (2019). Achieving work-family balance: An action regulation model. *Academy of Management Review,* 44(1), 150–171.

Kossek, E. E., Lautsch, B. A., and Eaton, S. C. (2006). Telecommuting, control, and boundary management. Correlates of policy use and practice, job control, and work-family effectiveness. *Journal of Vocational Behavior,* 68, 347–367.

Maertz, C. P., and Boyar, S. L. (2011). Work-family conflict, enrichment, and balance under "levels" and "episodes" approaches. *Journal of Management,* 37(1), 68–98.

Rothbard, N. P., and Ollier-Malaterre, A. (2016). Boundary Management. In T. D. Allen and L. T. Eby (eds), *The Oxford Handbook of Work and Family.* Oxford, England: Oxford University Press.

Saltzstein, A. L., Ting, Y., and Saltzstein, G. H. (2001). Work-family balance and job satisfaction: The impact of family-friendly policies on attitudes of federal government employees. *Public Administration Review,* 61, 452–467.

Thompson, C., Beauvais, L. L., and Lyness, K. S. (1999). When work-family benefits are not enough: The influence of work-family culture on benefit utilization, organizational attachment, and work-family conflict. *Journal of Vocational Behavior,* 54, 392–415.

Wayne, J. H., Butts, M. M., Casper, W. J., and Allen, A. D. (2017). In search of balance: A conceptual and empirical integration of multiple meanings of work-family balance. *Personnel Psychology,* 70, 167–210.

Wayne, J. H., Vaziri, H., and Casper, W. J. (2021). Work-nonwork balance: Development and validation of a global and multidimensional measure. *Journal of Vocational Behavior,* 127, 103565.

Exercises

1. What Is Your Level of Work–Family Balance?

The following are several items from a measure of work–life balance that was developed by Wayne, Vaziri, and Casper (2021) to assess perceptions of balance across multiple life roles. *Work roles* are those roles and activities that you pursue as part of your paid employment including the responsibilities that are part of your job. Examples include job-related tasks and duties, and anything that is part of your occupational or organizational roles. *Nonwork roles* are roles and activities that you pursue outside of paid employment, including family-related roles and activities and other activities you engage in due to personal interest or for people outside your family. Examples include family relationships and responsibilities, working on a hobby, spending time with friends, volunteering, religious activities, and exercising. **Thinking about the past month, rate your agreement with each statement about how you combine your work and nonwork roles. When responding to items, consider the work and nonwork roles that matter most to you.** Rate your agreement with each item using a five-point Likert scale:

1) Strongly Disagree, 2) Disagree, 3) Neither Agree nor Disagree, 4) Agree, 5) Strongly Agree.

Overall Balance:

1. There is harmony in how I blend my work and nonwork roles.
2. Overall, my work and nonwork roles are integrated.
3. Overall, my work and nonwork roles fit together.

Involvement Balance:

4. I am able to devote enough attention to important work and nonwork activities.
5. I am able to be adequately involved in the work and nonwork roles that matter most to me.
6. The time I spend in work and activities outside of work reflects my life priorities.

Effectiveness Balance:

7. I perform well in the life roles that I really value.
8. I am able to effectively handle important work and nonwork responsibilities.
9. I am successful in work and nonwork roles that matter to me.

Affective Balance:

10. I am happy in the work and nonwork roles that are most important to me.
11. I feel satisfied in the work and nonwork roles that are most important to me.
12. I am content with how things are going in the life roles that are my top priorities.

Calculate your overall balance score and your separate involvement, effectiveness, and affective balance scores. In small groups of four to five individuals, compare your responses to those of your peers. What nonwork roles did you factor into your perceptions of work–life balance? Which dimension of balance did you score the highest and lowest? Were there any specific episodes of work–family conflict or work–family enrichment that affected your responses to the items? Meet in groups of two to discuss your results and be prepared to discuss your conclusions with the class as a whole.

2. Small Group Discussion

In small groups of three to four, discuss the following questions:

1. As you have worked to improve your own work–life balance, which individual strategies have you personally found to be the most effective? Most challenging?
2. Have you personally found value in your organization's formal work–family policies (e.g. flextime and telecommuting)? Does your organization show support for their employees' work–family balance in other ways, aside from formal policies?
3. Has the COVID-19 pandemic impacted the values you attach to work and nonwork roles? If so, in what ways? How has this changed your individual approach to work–family balance? Has the pandemic changed your organizations' support of employees' work–family balance?

Video Analysis and Discussion

Please watch the following videos

1. Nigel Marsh: How to make work–life balance work
2. Anne-Marie Slaughter: Can We All "Have It All"?

Now form small groups to discuss the video(s) and answer the following questions:

1. What are the major points of the video?
2. How can you use information from the video in your career?
3. Based on the video, what advice do you have for leaders in organizations?

Be prepared to present the ideas from your small group discussion with the class as a whole.

Discussion Questions

1. Why does work–family balance matter?
2. Do you see any trends in work–family balance? Do you expect this to continue?
3. What advice do you have for colleagues regarding work–family balance?
4. What would you advise employers regarding work–family balance?

27

Use Advanced Information Technology to Transform Organizations

Dongyeob Kim[1], Maryam Alavi[2], and Youngjin Yoo[3], Ph.D.

[1, 3] The Weatherhead School of Management, Case Western Reserve University
[2] The Scheller College of Business, Georgia Institute of Technology

Dramatic and rapid developments in information technology (IT) have brought fundamental changes to the competitive landscape, and to the ways companies operate and compete. Whether digital-native or traditional, companies can no longer rest on the successes of yesteryear. Instead, they must constantly be on the lookout for emerging IT developments that could render their core offerings, business models, and strategies outmoded overnight. Companies that once dominated their markets have seen their key products quickly become obsolete due to these disruptive technologies. In this chapter, we summarize some of the key technologies and trends that underpin these fundamental changes. We also discuss five different ways companies can use IT as a catalyst for organizational transformation in the digital age.

Traditionally, organizations have used technologies that come from three broad categories: production technology, information technology, and communication technology. Production technology refers to the machines that have powered production systems since the Industrial Revolution. These technologies convert natural resources into products and market offerings. In his historical review of the rise of large-scale vertically integrated conglomerates in the early twentieth century, Chandler (1990) notes the critical role machines played in shaping industrial architecture and bolstering the mass production systems that dominated the last century.

Ever since organizations started using large mainframe digital computers for back-office automation in the 1950s, the development of IT has created new opportunities for organizational change. As microprocessors became smaller, faster, and cheaper, organizations started to use smaller and more powerful computers including workstations, personal computers, and portable computers in their operations. The impact of the use of IT in organizations is well documented by

Zuboff (1988), Castells (2003) and other information systems scholars (Hitt and Brynjolfsson, 1996; King, Grover, and Hufnagel, 1989).

When IT was first introduced, computers were, by and large, separate from communication technologies. At that time, communication technologies largely relied on analog signals. They were distinguished by their content, relying on dedicated communication networks such as radio, telephone, and later, digital data. As communication technologies started leveraging efficient digital signals, it was only natural that information and communications technologies began to converge. The convergence of these technologies accelerated in the 1990s with the introduction of the Internet and the World Wide Web. The convergence process then exploded with the introduction of smartphones and Web 2.0, which ushered the world into the age of user-created digital content.

Over the last 25 years, the convergence of information and communication technologies has fundamentally reshaped organizations. We saw the emergence of collaborative networked organizations that could outsource much of their operations globally. Organizations began to collect unprecedented amounts of data. This shift enabled them to optimize operations and exercise tight and efficient coordination across a globally distributed network of supply chain and distribution channels. Leveraging powerful analytics tools, organizations became agile in sensing and responding to changes in the market. Using the Internet and, lately, smartphones, organizations started directly engaging with clients and customers, opening possibilities of new business models.

Today, we are at another major turning point as digital technologies are beginning to converge with production technologies. The convergence of digital and physical technology started with the proliferation of smartphones and wearable technologies. This change has allowed organizations to sense and shape what happens in the physical environment in a way that was not previously possible (Baskerville, Myers, and Yoo, 2020; Yoo, 2010). Emerging technologies like the Internet of Things (IoT), social media, artificial intelligence (AI), blockchain, and 5G are accelerating the convergence of physical and digital technologies. Just as the convergence of information and communication technologies fundamentally reshaped organizations, we expect that the convergence of digital and physical technologies will lead to additional profound changes in organizations and industries. In this chapter, we summarize key technological trends that will further influence the way organizations operate.

Emerging Technologies

Social Media

Social media platforms (e.g. Facebook, Instagram, WeChat, and YouTube) are the key IT developments currently driving the convergence of physical and digital worlds. Before the early 2000s, mobile phones, emails, and fax machines were the only means of connecting people digitally. Today, there are approximately 4 billion social media users worldwide with an average of 16.5 new users every second. Combined with smartphones, which most users use to access these platforms, social media has begun to penetrate our everyday lives. Also, the data exhaust generated by the vast number of daily online activities is iteratively analyzed by algorithms that seamlessly curate and influence our interactions and consumption behaviors (Aral, 2020). The use of social media has transformed and disrupted politics, marketing, financial services, journalism, and countless other industries.

Internet of Things

Another important development in technology is the IoT. Everyday physical objects are increasingly becoming "smart" as they are embedded with sensors and software (Yoo, Henfridsson, and Lyytinen, 2010). Digital components enable these devices to collect, analyze, and exchange data among themselves. Examples of IoT solutions range from small items, like home appliances, intelligent hairbrushes, and medical sensors, to connected vehicles and smart farming applications. By connecting the physical and digital worlds, the IoT equips organizations with better insight into their operations and environments and, thus, enables firms to continually improve products, services, and value propositions.

Artificial Intelligence and Big Data

Advancements in AI have attracted enormous attention across various organizational and industry settings. AI differs fundamentally from other IT in three facets, namely their autonomy, ability to learn, and inscrutability (Berente, Gu, Recker, and Santhanam, 2021). The success of many current AI applications is owed largely to recent developments in deep learning, a form of machine learning (ML) that uses multiple layers of simulated interconnected neurons. The large volume of data generated as a by-product of automation, social media activities, and IoT devices is fed into ML systems for training purposes. This process recursively enhances the performance and accuracy of ML applications. From substituting mundane manual work to solving more complex problems that seemingly require human cognition and creativity, AI is projected to augment or automate most tasks currently performed by humans.

5G Networks

The development in 5G wireless technology offers a significant increase in the speed and reliability of communication. By utilizing a greater bandwidth, 5G has the capacity to carry an increased number of simultaneous connections between devices and people. Connection density of up to 1 million devices per square kilometer will result in the exponential growth of the IoT ecosystem at a lower cost. This connectivity is particularly important as it reduces latency to provide virtually zero lag time in communication between IoT devices controlled autonomously by AI. This capability will allow for highly responsive solutions like autonomous vehicles and telesurgery.

3D Printing

3D printing, or additive manufacturing, enables the layer-by-layer production of physical items of different materials from the same machine, reducing the steps and cost of production assembly. 3D printing has the potential to replace traditional factory production lines. The ability to handle complex geometric configurations and increasingly diverse sets of materials gives 3D printing the potential to transform manufacturing flexibility by enabling mass customization. 3D printing can radically reduce production costs, lowering barriers to entry into manufacturing sectors that once required substantial capital investments and centralized manufacturing facilities. The radically lowered barriers to entry democratize the innovation process. This technology also enables collaboration and distributed manufacturing as each production team can easily transmit the "tangible" copy of their part.

Blockchain

Known mostly for providing the backbone for cryptocurrencies such as Bitcoin, blockchain is a distributed ledger technology that provides a way for digitally recording and sharing information. Each data entry is validated by the network and encapsulated in a block, which is then connected to a chain of encrypted events. Blockchain promises to enhance trust, security, immutability, transparency, and the speed of transactions. By eliminating a central third-party authority, individuals and organizations can further reduce the time lapse and cost of trading. Beyond its more obvious uses for finance and cryptocurrency, blockchain technology is being developed to maintain data integrity in other areas such as supply chain management and personal data handling in health care.

Three Broad Themes of Information Technologies

Taken together, individual developments in IT have given rise to three broad themes that affect the future of organizations. These include the emergence of global digital infrastructure, layered modular architecture, and generativity.

First, the extensive penetration of digital technologies into various aspects of our physical, social, economic, legal, and professional lives was fundamentally enabled by the emergence of global digital infrastructures. These are defined as "shared, unbounded, heterogeneous, open, and evolving sociotechnical systems comprising an installed base of diverse information technology capabilities and their user, operations, and design communities" (Tilson, Lyytinen, and Sørensen, 2010, p. 748). Constituted by the ubiquitous penetration of broadband networks, the Internet, and wireless and mobile technologies, the scope and scale of digital infrastructures extend well beyond the confines of a single organization. As such, digital infrastructures serve as the basic technological structures necessary for any contemporary organizations to function (Tilson et al., 2010).

Second, within the traditional modular architecture of physical products, the components of a product follow a single functional design hierarchy and assume a fixed product boundary and function (Baldwin and Clark, 2000; Clark, 1985). Digital technologies, however, are uniquely differentiated from other forms of technology by their reprogrammability, data homogenization, and self-referential nature (Yoo et al., 2010). The integration of these three properties into physical products led to the emergence of a new product architecture referred to as *layered modular architecture* (Yoo et al., 2010). With layered modular architecture, previously tightly coupled hardware, software, content, and network are now decoupled, allowing organizations to pursue new combinations of heterogeneous components across different layers and product boundaries. Such novel recombination across layers and product boundaries allows organizations to create disruptive innovations.

Finally, generativity refers to "a technology's overall capacity to produce unprompted change driven by large, varied, and uncoordinated audiences" (Zittrain, 2006, p. 1980). Digital technology exhibits a *procrastinated binding of form and function,* which refers to the ability to add new capabilities after the design and production of a tool or a product (Yoo, Boland Jr, Lyytinen, and Majchrzak, 2012). As innovative activities have become pervasive with the ubiquity of computing resources (von Hippel, 2005), this creates almost unlimited possibilities for recombination by heterogeneous actors even after a product's initial conception and production. Such generative potential is further amplified with the current opportunities for integrating the unprecedented volume of data generated as the by-product of everyday online activities (Yoo et al., 2012). The explosive growth of smartphone ecosystems that resulted in the creation of millions of apps (almost all of which are created by small independent developers) is a prime example of the power of generativity.

Five Ways It Can Change Organizations

We see five major ways that IT can change organizations: *(i) by increasing large-scale efficiencies, (ii) improving decision-making and communication, (iii) blurring organizational boundaries, (iv) changing industry structures, and (v) designing digitally enabled products and services.* These categories are not mutually exclusive, and a particular firm can bring about a variety of changes simultaneously through the effective use of different types of IT capabilities.

Increasing the Speed and Efficiency of Operations

The use of IT for transaction processing systems and enterprise resource planning (ERP) systems has greatly enhanced the operational efficiency and the speed of organizational processes. The development of technologies such as service-oriented architecture and data warehouses previously enabled the development of enterprise-wide integration across different business functions. For example, an ERP system is a tightly integrated set of software modules designed to handle the most common types of business processes, such as general ledger accounting, accounts payable and receivable, inventory management, order management, and some HR functions, among others. At the heart of an ERP system is a single common database that collects and feeds data into all the software modules that comprise the system. When an information item is changed in one of the software modules, related information is automatically updated in all other modules. By integrating information, streamlining data flow, and updating information across an entire business in a real-time mode, ERP systems can lead to dramatic speed and productivity gains in business operations.

The continued development of IT to automate structured, repetitive, and high-volume processes can further accelerate this trend. For instance, robotic process automation (RPA) technologies can increase productivity through innovations such as software bots that perform rote and repetitive cognitive tasks. In turn, human workers are free to attend to higher-value tasks that require human cognition and expertise. This is exemplified by UPS, the leading global package delivery and logistics company. The company has a fleet of over 119 000 delivery vehicles worldwide and delivered an estimated 7.5 billion packages in the US in 2020. The complex operations of UPS are coordinated through an integrated platform of data, algorithms, software, and other forms of digital technologies, including installing wireless communication equipment in their delivery trucks. Process automation at UPS has led to an estimated $3 billion in savings per year. Further advancement in the integration of RPA and AI capabilities promises to streamline more complex processes. For example, new recruiting software can analyze a candidate's voice tone and facial expressions in prerecorded video interviews.

Whereas these enhancements have previously been limited to intraorganizational processes, the recent emergence of blockchain technology offers efficiency gains even for processes in interorganizational contexts (Jensen, Hedman, and Henningsson, 2019). The global container shipping industry, for example, has long faced efficiency problems due to the unpredictability that is inherent in the global supply chain. Various regulations require the use of many unstandardized paper-based documents that must be updated by each party in the supply chain. While individual organizations operate their own proprietary IT systems, they do not typically share their systems with other companies. TradeLens, a joint venture of IBM and Maersk (the world's largest container shipping company), uses blockchain technology to provide secure and permission-based access to digital information for all participants in the global logistics processes, including shippers, cargo owners, freight forwarders, ocean carriers, intermodal operators, customs and government authorities, financial service providers, and others. Using open application programming interfaces that ensure the encrypted, verifiable, and secure exchange of information, TradeLens provides real-time information sharing with all participants. By providing a secure, real-time information sharing platform on a global scale, TradeLens can increase the volume of container-based global trade by 15%.

In summary, IT offers organizations substantial gains in operational efficiency. Installing advanced process automation technologies can lead to significant cost savings in operations. Future growth in this area will see machines that can increasingly automate and augment a wider range of complex tasks.

Enhancing Decision-Making and Communication

Decision-making and communication constitute two core organizational processes. Due to globalization and increased volatility in business and competitive environments, complex and challenging demands are increasingly being placed on organizational communication and decision-making processes.

In response to globalization, large firms have dispersed their operations throughout the world, increasing the need for effective and efficient ways to communicate across time and distance. For the past three decades, scholars have been studying virtual teams and online communities as viable ways of organizing and coordinating group work (Faraj, Jarvenpaa, and Majchrzak, 2011; Faraj, von Krogh, Monteiro, and Lakhani, 2016; Jarvenpaa and Majchrzak, 2010; Lipnack and Stamps, 2008). A virtual team is defined as a group of dispersed members that collaborate via computer-mediated communication to accomplish common goals. Online communities are new forms of informal organizations that consist of "open collectives of dispersed individuals with members who are not necessarily known or identifiable and who share common interests" (Faraj et al., 2011, p. 1224). Faced with global competition and an increased need to draw on more diverse pools of talent, organizations are employing virtual teams to tap into the creative potential of online communities.

The trend toward virtual work environments grew exponentially in response to the COVID-19 pandemic, which required a large portion of the global labor force to transition quickly to remote work. This trend is likely to persist as a dominant way of working. A survey of employees at companies revealed that 64% of workers would, if given the choice, prefer to work from home permanently over receiving an annual raise of $30 000 (Kelly, 2021). The sudden transition to a fully virtual environment had a few benefits over colocated work. Employees reported an improved ability to manage work–life balance and increased productivity due to no longer being required to commute. Conversely, the elimination of spontaneous face-to-face conversations makes collaborative work more challenging, with interactive and creative activities becoming more difficult to coordinate (Whillans, Perlow, and Turek, 2021). Another key challenge that stems from the work-from-home environment is the blurring of work–life boundaries. By sharing workspaces with individuals external to their work domain (e.g. family), other commitments may take precedence over work. Also, remote work environments can engender trust issues toward team members who are not available online (Chamakiotis, Panteli, and Davison, 2021). These challenges signal that organization leaders should reconfigure and embed new co-ordination practices to promote sustainable technology-mediated virtual work.

IT not only helps organizations improve their own internal decision-making and coordination processes, but also helps push the locus of decision-making toward the organization's edge. AI plays an important role in this configuration. Analytics provided by machine-learning-based tools are distinct from those of conventional decision-support tools in several ways. First, the labor-intensive activities of data acquisition, curation, and analysis can be automated. Manual input is essentially only required at the outset of the process when setting parameters to initiate the algorithmic problem-solving loop (Seidel, Berente, Lindberg, Lyytinen, Martinez, and Nickerson, 2020). Second, AI can process large volumes of data from multiple formats and sources. For example, digital trace data from social media platforms, transactions, and equipment and machinery sensors can be combined to generate a more comprehensive understanding of customers and support decision-making (Lehrer, Wieneke, vom Brocke, Jung, and Seidel, 2018). By harnessing the power of algorithms that can digest large volumes of unstructured data sets, firms can predict in real time how an individual user is likely to behave (Newell and Marabelli, 2015). This in turn enables organizations to provide accurately targeted offerings to their customers. Finally, prediction capabilities are not static, but are continuously evolving and changing with additional data due to their propensity to learn. The iteration of problem-solving loops never ceases and constantly modifies recommendations and decisions based on previous feedback at virtually zero additional cost (Verganti, Vendraminelli, and Iansiti, 2020). For example, Netflix offers highly personalized recommendations based on an individual member's past viewing history. Instead of using the same thumbnail image for each movie, Netflix's AI-based recommendation engine presents personalized thumbnail images to each user by capturing a scene from a movie that appeals to a user's preferred genres or actors. This tool helps users discover new content that they are likely to find interesting (Chandrashekar, Amat, Basilico, and Jebara, 2017). This tool is also an example of the dynamic ways that organizations assist their customers in making personalized decisions while still keeping the customer in their digital value loop (Baskerville et al., 2020).

In summary, IT can play a transformational role in organizations through its impact on the key organizational processes of decision-making and communication. Future developments in this area will depend not only on technological advances but also on our understanding of and openness toward IT applications and the resulting organizational and cultural changes.

Softening/Extending Boundaries of Organizations

In the past, organizations had clearly defined boundaries. With the speed, scope, and ubiquity of IT, however, an organization's boundaries are becoming increasingly soft and malleable. A platform refers to a "building block, providing an essential function to a technological system – which acts as a foundation upon which other firms can develop complementary products, technologies or services" (Gawer, 2009, p. 2). Companies like Apple, Google, Amazon, and Facebook all built powerful platforms. Platforms create indirect network effects by connecting users and suppliers of complementary products (Parker and Van Alstyne, 2005) and are monetized by charging advertising or transaction fees to complementors (Gawer, 2020; Teece, 2018).

Firms may adopt closed or open forms of platform based on their business models. In a closed platform model, firms choose to collaborate only with partners that are integral to their product or service (Smedlund, 2012). In an open platform model, a firm's offerings become jointly created by complementors who are not bound by long-term contracts. For example, Uber creates value by working with independent drivers. Airbnb creates value by working with independent property owners. By joining these large existing platforms, complementors, who are often individuals or small businesses, can lower their own barriers to entry into the market (Cusumano and Gawer, 2002). As a result, these platforms can enjoy economies of scale and of scope.

Organizations can also use IT to actively reach out to user communities and harness the power of crowd-based open innovations (Lakhani and Panetta, 2007; von Hippel, 2005). For example, organizations can build complex software products by leveraging the use of independent outside developers and sourcing software engineering skills globally (Lakhani and von Hippel, 2003). Consider the examples of Linux and Apache, two of the most popular and important software systems that are used to power most websites on the Internet. Tens of thousands of volunteer programmers from around the world worked together to build these systems with minimum hierarchical control (O'Reilly, 1999; von Hippel and von Krogh, 2003). Similarly, upon the launch of its iOS operating system, Apple loosened restrictions on access to its software to outside developers, which resulted in the proliferation of over 2 million applications on its App store (Eaton, Elaluf-Calderwood, Sørensen, and Yoo, 2015). The success of open forms of digital innovation is not limited to software. Organizations like NASA, General Electric, and Proctor and Gamble have turned to online innovation platforms and communities to discover new ideas and solutions (Chesbrough, Vanhaverbeke, and West, 2006; Lifshitz-Assaf, 2018).

In summary, the proliferation and prevalence of IT is making organizational boundaries much more permeable. By taking advantage of platform-based business models, organizations invert their production and innovation processes by working with an array of complementors. Organizations can further move production and innovation activities to the external collaborators by adopting open innovation platforms.

Changing Traditional Industry Structures

In addition to its impact on organizational boundaries, IT can further enable profound changes in the competitive landscape by making product and industry boundaries more porous. With interfirm relationships being at the core of business ecosystems, emerging technologies are reshaping the way firms operate and collaborate within a given industry. For example, previously, firms in the architecture, engineering, and construction (AEC) industry formed collaborative relationships among each other through the use of building information management (BIM) systems (Boland Jr, Lyytinen, and Yoo, 2007). Such collaborations were based on information and knowledge sharing via BIM platforms. With the use of BIM systems, contractors use a central repository of data and models that contain layers of information that are contributed by different parties involved in the project. In traditional building projects, inconsistencies in design are often discovered at the construction site, causing delays and budget problems. With BIM systems, conflicts in design are usually detected during the design stage and negotiated much earlier in the process, saving time and money. By using a centralized BIM platform, communications that used to be sequential and time-consuming have become more dynamic, timely, and reciprocal. AEC firms that use these technologies have become more competitive with their improved efficiency along with the ability to build more complex and challenging projects (Berente, Srinivasan, Lyytinen, and Yoo, 2008). Today, the transformation of the AEC industry is further accelerated by using "digital twins." Digital twins are digital models of a building or structure that leverage data from the BIM system, sensor networks, and building automation systems to create a seamlessly connected and constantly evolving version of its physical counterpart. These tools enable real-time collaboration throughout the entire life cycle of a project and enhance the ability to predict and solve issues in a timely fashion. Virtual and augmented reality (VR/AR) technologies give users the ability to go beyond videoconferencing and be immersed in a shared virtual design space to share perspectives and knowledge. While digital twins are 3D models visualized on 2D screens, combining them with VR/AR technologies allows participants to gain a clearer understanding of a structure's inner dynamics and therefore aids in decision-making.

IT is not only changing the structure of existing industries, but also fundamentally reshaping the boundaries of industries. While organizations were traditionally assumed to be affiliated within clearly definable industrial segments (Porter, 1980), the convergent nature of digital technology assembles previously disconnected product components and knowledge resources from heterogeneous industries or professions, such that the term *industry* itself has become rather amorphous (Yoo et al., 2010; Yoo et al., 2012). This shift has facilitated the entry of new, nontraditional, digitally enabled "disruptors" that break away from established ways of conducting business. For example, AirbnB, a start-up with no physical property, entered into the highly competitive hospitality industry with traditional hotel chains including Marriott, Hyatt, and Hilton.

Digital disruptors are finding new ways to offer enhanced value propositions by catering to the fundamental needs of customers in ways that traditional firms cannot. For example, banks and financial services industries are being disrupted by fintech companies. These software-enabled companies offer fast, easy, and low-cost or free services to customers, including payments (e.g. PayPal), securities trading and micro investment (e.g. Robinhood), and personal loans (e.g. LendingClub). In this way, fintech companies are steadily disintermediating traditional banks from customers by presenting a broader and low-cost range of service offerings and driving financial inclusion. These implications are not limited to the realm of digital services but extend to industries that are largely based on physical goods. In the mobility industry, the traditional rivals – Ford Motor Company, GM, and Fiat-Chrysler – are now also competing with technology companies including Google and Tesla, among others. These new entrants are upending the automobile industry by integrating digital capabilities directly into vehicles, which incumbent firms have found extremely challenging (Henfridsson and Yoo, 2014).

The emergence of large digital platform ecosystems that span multiple traditional industries is exasperating incumbent firms that have typically focused on one or few selected vertical industries (Adner, 2006, 2017; Autio and Thomas, 2014; Furr and Shipilov, 2018). Ecosystems, as used here, are the "collaborative arrangements through which firms combine their individual offerings into a coherent, customer-facing solution" (Adner, 2006, p. 2). Large digital-native platform players like Apple, Google, and Amazon often rely on their superior digital assets to move laterally across multiple vertical boundaries. For example, Google relies on its AI algorithm and vast amount of user data to offer value in media, advertising, mobility, health care, consumer electronics, retail, and a host of other industries.

In summary, IT is changing the way firms collaborate inside existing industry boundaries, while also radically altering the way firms in different industries compete and collaborate with one another. IT lowers entry barriers, enabling new entrants to disrupt the status quo. In order to ensure viability in this new competitive environment, incumbent firms must extend their partnerships beyond traditional industry boundaries, and either build or join existing ecosystems. To this end, the facilitation of interfirm collaboration can take advantage of emerging technologies that promise to deliver elevated ways of knowledge sharing and project management.

Developing Digitally Enabled Products/Services Firms can increase the value of their offerings by embedding products with digital capabilities (Baskerville et al., 2020; Yoo et al., 2010). This leads to "servitization," in which the distinction between products and services is obscured (Barrett and Davidson, 2008). For example, online training tutorials make software and hardware products easier to adopt and use, and digital capabilities can enable operation via voice command and the remote diagnosis of equipment problems. Peloton, a popular indoor stationary bicycle with a tablet computer, provides an interesting example. Peloton's value proposition not only includes a high-quality physical product, but also a Netflix-like subscription service that delivers high-quality online fitness classes, expert instructors, and an effective personalization engine. It also offers an online community of millions of users who share their experiences through an online platform. In Peloton's case, the physical product, subscription service, and online community do not exist in isolation. Rather, it is the tight coupling across these individual elements that collectively creates a pleasant and valuable user experience.

Furthermore, with its programmability and standard interfaces, IT allows for seemingly unlimited opportunities to recombine existing digital assets to create new offerings (Arthur, 2009; Yoo et al., 2010). These new products allow firms to reimagine user experiences in novel ways. By combining ridesharing and online commerce, many traditional restaurants were able to quickly adapt and offer food delivery service during the COVID-19 pandemic. Online video streaming services like Netflix and Disney+ are now offering newly released films, often on the same date as the film's theatrical release. Online trading services like Robinhood and AmeriTrade combine smartphone apps, online communities, analytics, and high-frequency trading to offer free stock trades, fundamentally altering the way users experience financial investments.

Furthermore, these new offerings are often paired with novel business models. For example, instead of charging a customer for each transaction, a firm can generate alternate revenue through new business models based on advertisement or subscription (Osterwalder and Pigneur, 2010). Firms can also use digital connectivity to continually enhance physical products long after the product was sold. For example, Tesla offered new features such as autonomous driving and a "summon" function that allows drivers to "fetch" the vehicle autonomously from its parking spot (Verganti et al., 2020). Sensors embedded in vehicles collect data on user driving patterns so that companies can continue to offer new services that were not foreseen when the vehicle originally entered the market.

Finally, the very nature of the offering can be simply digital instructions. These digital instructions can be used later to create value by mobilizing physical and intangible resources. Consider COVID-19 vaccines based on messenger RNA (mRNA). Traditionally, vaccines are comprised of key proteins (antigens) extracted from weakened or killed pathogens, or their parts. Vaccine manufacturers traditionally produce fully manufactured product (vaccine) into individual vials for deployment. In contrast, with mRNA, the process is entirely different. Moderna, one of the leading digital biopharmaceutical firms, notes that "mRNA is the software of life – so the very essence of our medicines is digital." With its four possible nucleotides of C, T, G, and A, mRNA acts as a four-bit digital code. Using synthetic mRNA, a vaccine manufacturer encodes digital instructions to produce protein antigens in human bodies. Therefore, an mRNA-based vaccine only carries a set of digital instructions to make our bodies function as an antigen biofactory. Unlike its traditional counterpart, an mRNA-based vaccine is not a final product. Rather, it is a digital instruction to "print" the final product in the body of humans. We see a similar phenomenon with the use of 3D printing and powerful edge computing capabilities. Instead of delivering a final physical product, a firm can simply sell digital instructions to a customer who can then 3D print the product locally. As a result, the digital offering remains incomplete until it is "printed" into a physical form by users. Such procrastinated binding of digital offerings can have profound implications for the ways firms create value (Yoo et al., 2012; Zhang, Yoo, Lyytinen, and Lindberg, Forthcoming).

In summary, IT no longer merely plays a supporting role for a firm's core offerings. Increasingly, digital technology is the core business offering. IT opens up new ways to deliver value to users and consumers through enhanced functions, novel experiences, new business models, and by enabling the continued evolution of a product's features. In the near future, firms may simply sell digital instructions as their core offerings.

Potential Risks of Large-Scale IT Applications

Due to the ubiquitous presence of IT and its enormous impact on the contemporary economy, it is easy to imagine that the pace of IT development and adoption will accelerate. New IT will continue to emerge, and entrepreneurs and large established firms alike will continue to leverage these new technologies to deliver value and stay ahead of the competition. The continuing and accelerating push for new IT applications is shaped by an assumption that technology is inherently a force for good. However, both research and practice have shown that there are risks and unintended negative consequences associated with a large-scale pervasive IT application in contemporary society. We discuss three such risks: algorithmic bias, misinformation and fake news, and cybersecurity threats.

First, growing reliance on algorithmic decision-making can introduce unintended biases into the decision-making process or exacerbate existing ones. Algorithms are trained by prespecified data sets. However, training data sets are often mired with existing biases (Kellogg, Valentine, and Christin, 2020). As a result, the use of AI tools trained with biased data sets reinforces existing biases and discrimination. A notable example is Amazon's recruiting engine algorithm that showed bias against female candidates, after having been trained with résumé data that reflected the dominant pattern of male employees in the tech industry. Also, companies such as Revlon have started using facial analysis software on Instagram photos to gain insights into users' lipstick preferences. However, such models are often trained with data sets that do not include people of color (Olson, 2020). Similarly, many of the AI models used to diagnose and treat cancers are being developed at leading academic hospitals, which use their own sample patient data. However, patients of color are disproportionately underrepresented at many of those leading academic hospitals, as they cannot afford health care services at such hospitals. As a result, the relevance of these AI-based tools for cancer diagnosis and treatment may be of limited use for patients of color. The opaque nature of these advanced algorithms exacerbates the algorithmic bias (Burrell, 2016; Faraj, Pachidi, and Sayegh, 2018). Due to the multilayered and complex ways in which ML models transform input data into output, the exact inner logic of these tools is often unexplainable and remains as a black box. Despite growing efforts to build ethical and explainable AI tools, algorithmic bias, and discrimination remain risks for organizations that increasingly rely on such tools in their decision-making.

Second, as individuals increasingly rely on social media platforms for various informational needs, society faces the risk of misinformation and fake news. In traditional information platforms, information is typically centrally created, curated, and distributed by a responsible few. If misinformation is produced – intentionally or unintentionally – the source of misinformation can be quickly identified, and its distribution can be minimized or even reversed. In contrast, the creation, distribution, and consumption of information is, by design, highly distributed in social media platforms. The original source of misinformation is often anonymous and can be difficult to identify. Furthermore, in social media platforms, information is distributed to individual users through highly effective personalization engines, and each user is individually targeted with hyperpersonalized messages. As a result, there is no one general pattern of information dissemination on social media platforms. Although social media platforms are proven to be extremely effective with their highly personalized messages (whether news or advertisements), they can be used as weapons of mass misinformation when used to deliberately distribute misinformation. A recent study revealed that fake news stories on Twitter were able to spread significantly more broadly and rapidly than valid news (Vosoughi, Roy, and Aral, 2018). Leveraging the power of personalization algorithms, social media platforms can deliver fake news to unsuspecting users who then in turn share it with others. The vicious cycle of the creation, distribution, and amplification of misinformation on social media platforms has led to major disruptions in the political, financial, and health systems (Aral, 2020). For example, 73% of all COVID-19 antivaccine misinformation on Facebook was found to have originated from a dozen individuals with a combined 59 million followers across multiple platforms (Salam, 2021). The risk of misinformation is a dark side of the democratization of information. When paired with valid information, digital infrastructure is a highly effective tool in creating and disseminating information. However, intentionally or unintentionally, the same tool can easily disseminate misinformation.

Finally, as organizations increasingly rely on large volumes of data and digital infrastructures, cybersecurity has emerged as another key risk. In order to offer personalized services, many organizations collect personal information from their customers. Hackers target sensitive personal information such as social security numbers, email addresses, passwords, bank accounts, and even health information, which can then be traded in the black market. For example, in 2018, a breach in Marriott International's reservation system exposed the private details of up to 339 million customer records, which included passport numbers, credit card details, and other sensitive personal information (Tidy, 2020). The incident incurred an expense of $28 million for the chain. Moreover, in 2020, Marriott faced a fine of $23.8 million by the UK's Information Commissioner's Office for violating European Union General Data Protection Regulation (GDPR) due to the inadequacy of their IT infrastructure (Hodge, 2020). Another security failing on Marriott's part was that, although the credit details were in encrypted form, the encryption keys were locked up in the same server as the data, which were taken by the hackers in the breach (Telford and Timberg, 2018). Data breaches can be further used in subsequent acts of cybercrime such as ransomware attacks. For example, in April 2021, Colonial Pipeline, one of the largest pipeline networks in the United States, suffered a ransomware attack by a small group of hackers. Only its billing system was compromised, but Colonial had to shut down its entire pipeline system for the next few days to prevent further unauthorized access to its network, disrupting a large portion of the country's fuel supply (Duffy, 2021). Hackers also stole 100 gigabytes of Colonial's data and threatened to leak them if the company did not meet their demands. As a result, Colonial paid the hackers a $4.4 million ransom one day after the attack (Turton and Mehrotra, 2021). The Colonial example illustrates that due to the growing convergence between IT and operational technology systems, even a relatively unsophisticated ransomware can paralyze an entire network, just by attacking an organization's IT systems (Isenberg, Kristensen, Mysore, and Weinstein, 2021).

In summary, to realize the creative potential of IT, the impact of advanced IT should be considered along with its potential risks. Failure to do so may lead to negative outcomes both at the organizational and societal levels.

CASE EXAMPLE

Digital Transformation of the Mobility Industry

At the turn of the twentieth century, the mobility industry was transformed by the invention of the automobile. Now, more than 100 years later, the mobility industry is facing yet another paradigm shift as society is rushing toward the second great inflection point (Dhawan, Hensley, Padhi, and Tschiesner, 2019; Heineke, Padhi, Pinner, and Tschiesner, 2019). This forthcoming paradigm will be characterized by the global convergence of breakthroughs in diverse digital technologies and will reconfigure how automobiles are conceptualized. The four core trends that are shaping the future of mobility are represented by the acronym CASE: connected, autonomous, shared, and electrified (Heineke, Holland-Letz, Kässer, Kloss, and Müller, 2020). These disruptive trends are increasing the complexity of the competitive landscape for traditional car manufacturers, with tech giants and digital-native startups now investing heavily in mobility innovations (Gao, Kaas, Mohr, and Wee, 2016). For example, China has seen large companies, like smartphone maker Xiaomi and telecom equipment manufacturer Huawei, expand into the electric vehicle market. It has also seen the emergence of three unicorn manufacturers: XPeng, Li Auto, and NIO.

Traditionally, automobile manufacturers were assemblers of physical components. They needed to have strong industrial design and engineering capabilities (Choi, 2015). They were also required to manage a large supply chain of thousands of physical parts and operate the manufacturing plants where those parts were assembled into vehicles. They also managed distribution channels through national dealership networks. Also, all major auto manufacturers had their own sales divisions.

Modern vehicles are not just assemblages of physical parts: they contain integrated software systems and digital sensors connected to the digital infrastructure. Software capabilities, connectivity, and digital user experiences are increasingly becoming key differentiators for the automobile industry (Henfridsson, Mathiassen, and Svahn, 2014; Henfridsson and Yoo, 2014). As a result, the concept of a car is now rapidly becoming a key part of the software-defined ecosystem of mobility service platforms. Excellence in fuel efficiency, style, and safety are no longer sufficient conditions for competitiveness and have become the prerequisite "ticket to entry" (Hau, 2019). While the mobility sector has largely been siloed in the past, the typical next-generation vehicle has a software architecture that integrates infotainment modules, telematics, advanced driver-assistance systems, and third-party applications (Henfridsson et al., 2014). As such, car manufacturers must engage multiple players across industries in developing new capabilities (Fletcher, Mahindroo, Santhanam, and Tschiesner, 2020). Connectivity not only exists within the vehicle, but also enables the vehicle to interact seamlessly with its environment. In route optimization, a vehicle's embedded sensors instantaneously collect and exchange large amounts of data with the surrounding infrastructure (e.g. street signs and traffic) and other connected vehicles. For example, BMW's integration of Deutsche Telekom's SmartHome app into its vehicles enables drivers to monitor and control the temperature, lighting, and alarm systems of their homes while on the road. Whereas manufacturers have previously competed against one another, interconnectedness is now altering the basis of competition. Customer value is becoming increasingly contingent on the aggregate experience provided by the entire network of services providers, and not just the manufactured vehicle itself.

The mobility industry is also facing a major change in consumer preferences. The COVID-19 pandemic led to a structural shift centered on remote work. The resulting reduction in the number of commuters may translate to a decline in privately owned vehicles (Heineke, Kampshoff, Möller, and Wu, 2020). Complementing the traditional business model of vehicle sales, the industry has seen the creation of new business models such as on-demand vehicle subscription services. These models cater to the changing preferences and mobility behaviors of consumers. Vehicle subscriptions cover expenses including car insurance and registration fees, giving consumers the flexibility to switch between different cars. In addition to incumbent automakers (e.g. Nissan and Volvo), new app-based startups have emerged (e.g. Fair and Flexdrive) that are built entirely around the subscription-based model. Ridesharing services such as Uber and Lyft have also gained traction in recent years, but their relatively high price remains inaccessible for many consumers to enjoy on a regular basis. As driver pay currently takes up a big portion of the cost, autonomous vehicles are expected to make ridesharing more affordable (Dhawan et al., 2019). Google's Waymo already launched their driverless robo-taxi service in 2018, and Lyft prepares to do so by the end of 2021 in partnership with Ford and Argo AI (Subin, 2021).

The process of designing cars has also evolved. Manufacturers like GM are using advanced AI-based design software from Autodesk to generate hundreds of car design alternatives based on the parameters set by human users. Once the AI design tool generates alternatives, human automobile designers determine the best option. Moreover, by pairing AI-based design with 3D printing, GM uses rapid prototyping to gain feedback from users, fundamentally transforming the design process. GM also uses advanced 3D simulation tools to conduct expensive crash testing virtually, cutting down the time and cost (Leonardi, 2012).

Automakers also use advanced IT for the operation and maintenance of their assembly lines. At Ford's transmission plant, robotic arms have been added in the assembly lines. These robotic arms learn from previous attempts which motions most efficiently assemble the pieces for torque converters (Knight, 2021). To prevent unexpected equipment failures at assembly lines, the volumes of data from assembly line sensors are used for anomaly detection and maintenance planning. The development of the underlying AI algorithms used in production are increasingly being sourced externally. BMW, for example, shares its digital image tagging algorithms on GitHub where software developers around the world change and improve the source code.

During the first half of the last century, the dominant organizational structure of the industrial age – vertically integrated, hierarchical, and multidivisional – emerged as big automakers like General Motors, Ford, and Chrysler were trying to deal with organizational challenges. The underlying issues arose from the complexity of managing large assembly lines with a spiraling array of suppliers and distributors (Chandler, 1990; Clark and Fujimoto, 1991). A class of professional managers emerged as these large hierarchical firms had to manage a large number of employees (Chandler, 1977). In the second half of the last century, as large auto manufacturers adopted information and communication technologies, we saw the emergence of sophisticated automated manufacturing facilities, as well as the complex global supply chain and the outsourcing of many of the functions of these firms (Morton, 1990).

We are indeed experiencing major shifts in the automobile industry. Digital technology is redefining the mobility industry, evolving the very definition of car, from design to manufacturing. The way automakers structure their internal division of labor and their IT units has started shifting (King and Lyytinen, 2004; Lee and Berente, 2012). As digital platforms like Google and Apple are playing increasingly important roles in the industry, traditional original equipment manufacturer (OEM) automakers are losing ground (Jacobides, MacDuffie, and Tae, 2016). In the era of CASE mobility services, leaders of organizations in the auto industry will face a new set of complex challenges. Some are old problems that require new solutions. Some are entirely new issues that we have never seen before.

Conclusion

Advanced and emerging IT can serve as a strategic catalyst for organizational change. IT can dramatically improve operational efficiencies across an organization and alter communication and decision-making processes. Departing from traditional industry structures, IT can soften and extend organizational boundaries and enable new and enhanced offerings. To realize these key benefits, however, the potential risks of large-scale and advanced IT applications need to be recognized and effectively managed. Failure to address these risks may lead to negative and unintended consequences.

Furthermore, the tremendous potential for digital transformation is only fully realized when existing organizational processes, incentives, and culture are also changed accordingly. This all-around transformation requires strong organizational commitment and a clear vision and strategy.

References

Adner, R. (2006). Match your innovation strategy to your innovation ecosystem. *Harvard Business Review,* 84(4), 98–107.

Adner, R. (2017). Ecosystem as structure: An actionable construct for strategy. *Journal of Management,* 43(1), 39–58.

Aral, S. (2020). *The Hype Machine: How Social Media Disrupts Our Elections, Our Economy, and Our Health – and How We Must Adapt.* Currency.

Arthur, W. B. (2009). *The Nature of Technology: What It Is and How It Evolves.* New York, NY: Simon and Schuster.

Autio, E., and Thomas, L. (2014). *Innovation Ecosystems: Implications for innovation Management.* Oxford: Oxford University Press.

Baldwin, C., and Clark, K. (2000). *Design Rules: The Power of Modularity* (Vol. 1). Cambridge, MA: MIT Press.

Barrett, M., and Davidson, E. (2008). Exploring the diversity of service worlds in the service economy. In *Information Technology in the Service Economy: Challenges and Possibilities for the 21st Century* (pp. 1–10). New York, NY: Springer.

Baskerville, R. L., Myers, M. D., and Yoo, Y. (2020). Digital first: The ontological reversal and new challenges for Information Systems research. *MIS Quarterly,* 44(2), 509–523.

Berente, N., Gu, B., Recker, J., and Santhanam, R. (2021). Managing Artificial Intelligence. *MIS Quarterly,* 45(3), 1433–1450.

Berente, N., Srinivasan, N., Lyytinen, K., and Yoo, Y. (2008). Design principles for IT in doubly distributed design networks. Paper presented at the Twenty Ninth International Conference on Information Systems (ICIS), Paris.

Boland, R. J., Jr, Lyytinen, K., and Yoo, Y. (2007). Wakes of innovation in project networks: The case of digital 3-D representations in architecture, engineering, and construction. *Organization Science,* 18(4), 631–647.

Burrell, J. (2016). How the machine 'thinks': Understanding opacity in machine learning algorithms. *Big Data & Society,* 3(1), 2053951715622512.

Castells, M. (2003). *The Internet Galaxy: Reflections on the Internet, Business and Society.* New York: Oxford University Press.

Chamakiotis, P., Panteli, N., and Davison, R. M. (2021). Reimagining e-leadership for reconfigured virtual teams due to Covid-19. *International Journal of Information Management,* 60, 102381.

Chandler, A. D. (1977). *The Visible Hand: The Managerial Revolution in American Business.* Cambridge, MA: Harvard University Press.

Chandler, A. D. (1990). *Scale and Scope: The Dynamics of Industrial Capitalism.* Cambridge, MA: Harvard University Press.

Chandrashekar, A., Amat, F., Basilico, J., and Jebara, T. (2017). Artwork personalization at Netflix. Retrieved from https://netflixtechblog.com/artwork-personalization-c589f074ad76

Chesbrough, H., Vanhaverbeke, W., and West, J. (2006). *Open Innovation: Researching a New Paradigm.* Oxford, UK: Oxford University Press

Choi, E. (2015). Hyundai's dynamics of styling-driven capability development: a historical analysis of the 1970s–1990s. *International Journal of Automotive Technology and Management,* 15(3), 292–310.

Clark, K. B. (1985). The interaction of design hierarchies and market concepts in technological evolution. *Research Policy,* 14(5), 235–251.

Clark, K. B., and Fujimoto, T. (1991). *Product Development Performance: Strategy, Organization, and Management in the World Auto Industry.* Boston: HBS Press.

Cusumano, M. A., and Gawer, A. (2002). The elements of platform leadership. *MIT Sloan Management Review,* 43(3), 51.

Dhawan, R., Hensley, R., Padhi, A., and Tschiesner, A. (2019). Mobility's second great inflection point. *McKinsey Quarterly.*

Duffy, C. (2021, May 16). Colonial Pipeline attack: A 'wake up call' about the threat of ransomware. *CNN Business.* Retrieved from https://www.cnn.com/2021/05/16/tech/colonial-ransomware-darkside-what-to-know/index.html

Eaton, B., Elaluf-Calderwood, S., Sørensen, C., and Yoo, Y. (2015). Distributed tuning of boundary resources. *MIS Quarterly,* 39(1), 217–244.

Faraj, S., Jarvenpaa, S. L., and Majchrzak, A. (2011). Knowledge collaboration in online communities. *Organization Science,* 22(5), 1224–1239.

Faraj, S., Pachidi, S., and Sayegh, K. (2018). Working and organizing in the age of the learning algorithm. *Information and Organization,* 28(1), 62–70.

Faraj, S., von Krogh, G., Monteiro, E., and Lakhani, K. R. (2016). Special section introduction – Online community as space for knowledge flows. *Information Systems Research,* 27(4), 668–684.

Fletcher, R., Mahindroo, A., Santhanam, N., and Tschiesner, A. (2020). The case for an end-to-end automotive-software platform. *McKinsey & Company.*

Furr, N., and Shipilov, A. (2018). Building the right ecosystem for innovation. *MIT Sloan Management Review,* 59(4), 59–64.

Gao, P., Kaas, H.-W., Mohr, D., and Wee, D. (2016, January 1). Disruptive trends that will transform the auto industry. *McKinsey & Company.*

Gawer, A. (2009). Platform dynamics and strategies: from products to services. In *Platforms, Markets and Innovation.* Cheltenham, UK: Edward Elgar Publishing.

Gawer, A. (2020). Digital platforms' boundaries: The interplay of firm scope, platform sides, and digital interfaces. *Long Range Planning,* 102045.

Hau, T.-T. (2019). Ford's evolving sense of self: An interview with Hau Thai-Tang. *McKinsey Quarterly.*

Heineke, K., Holland-Letz, D., Kässer, M., Kloss, B., and Müller, T. (2020). ACES 2019 survey: Can established auto manufacturers meet customer expectations for ACES. *McKinsey Center for Future Mobility.*

Heineke, K., Kampshoff, P., Möller, T., and Wu, T. (2020). From no mobility to future mobility: where COVID-19 has accelerated change. *McKinsey Center for Future Mobility.*

Heineke, K., Padhi, A., Pinner, D., and Tschiesner, A. (2019). Reimagining mobility: A CEO's guide. *McKinsey Quarterly.*

Henfridsson, O., Mathiassen, L., and Svahn, F. (2014). Managing technological change in the digital age: The role of architectural frames. *Journal of Information Technology,* 29(1), 27–43.

Henfridsson, O., and Yoo, Y. (2014). The liminality of trajectory shifts in institutional entrepreneurship. *Organization Science,* 25(3), 932–950.

Hitt, L. M., and Brynjolfsson, E. (1996). Productivity, business profitability, and consumer surplus: Three different measures of information technology value. *MIS Quarterly,* 20, 121–142.

Hodge, N. (2020, October 30). In second drastic reduction, ICO fines Marriott $23.8M. *Compliance Week.* Retrieved from https://www.complianceweek.com/regulatory-enforcement/in-second-drastic-reduction-ico-fines-marriott-238m/29674.article

Isenberg, R., Kristensen, I., Mysore, M., and Weinstein, D. (2021). Building cyber resilience in national critical infrastructure. *McKinsey & Company*. Retrieved from https://www.mckinsey.com/business-functions/risk-and-resilience/our-insights/building-cyber-resilience-in-national-critical-infrastructure

Jacobides, M. G., MacDuffie, J. P., and Tae, C. J. (2016). Agency, structure, and the dominance of OEMs: Change and stability in the automotive sector. *Strategic Management Journal,* 37(9), 1942–1967.

Jarvenpaa, S. L., and Majchrzak, A. (2010). Research commentary – Vigilant interaction in knowledge collaboration: Challenges of online user participation under ambivalence. *Information Systems Research,* 21(4), 773–784.

Jensen, T., Hedman, J., and Henningsson, S. (2019). How TradeLens delivers business value with blockchain technology. *MIS Quarterly Executive,* 18(4).

Kellogg, K. C., Valentine, M. A., and Christin, A. (2020). Algorithms at work: The new contested terrain of control. *Academy of Management Annals,* 14(1), 366–410.

Kelly, J. (2021, May 21). Survey asks employees at top U.S. companies if they'd give up $30,000 to work from home: The answers may surprise you. *Forbes.* Retrieved from https://www.forbes.com/sites/jackkelly/2021/05/21/survey-asks-employees-at-top-us-companies-if-theyd-give-up-30000-to-work-from-home-the-answers-may-surprise-you/

King, J. L., and Lyytinen, K. (2004). Automotive informatics: Information technology and enterprise transformation in the automobile industry. In W. Dutton, B. Kahin, R. O'Callaghan, and A. Wyckoff (eds), *Transforming Enterprise: The Economic and Social Implications of Information Technology* (pp. 283–312). Cambridge, MA: MIT Press.

King, W. R., Grover, V., and Hufnagel, E. H. (1989). Using information and information technology for sustainable competitive advantage: Some empirical evidence. *Information & Management,* 17(2), 87–93.

Knight, W. (2021, April 28). Ford's ever-smarter robots are speeding up the assembly line. *Wired.* Retrieved from https://www.wired.com/story/fords-smarter-robots-speeding-assembly-line/

Lakhani, K. R., and Panetta, J. A. (2007). The principles of distributed innovation. *Innovations: Technology, Governance, Globalization Summer,* 2(3).

Lakhani, K. R., and von Hippel, E. (2003). How open source software works: "free" user-to-user assistance. *Research Policy,* 32(6), 923–943.

Lee, J., and Berente, N. (2012). Digital innovation and the division of innovative labor: Digital controls in the automotive industry. *Organization Science,* 23(5), 1428–1447.

Lehrer, C., Wieneke, A., vom Brocke, J., Jung, R., and Seidel, S. (2018). How big data analytics enables service innovation: materiality, affordance, and the individualization of service. *Journal of Management Information Systems,* 35(2), 424–460.

Leonardi, P. M. (2012). *Car Crashes Without Cars: Lessons about Simulation Technology and Organizational Change from Automotive Design.* Cambridge, MA: MIT Press.

Lifshitz-Assaf, H. (2018). Dismantling knowledge boundaries at NASA: The critical role of professional identity in open innovation. *Administrative Science Quarterly,* 63(4), 746–782.

Lipnack, J., and Stamps, J. (2008). *Virtual Teams: People Working Across Boundaries with Technology.* Hoboken, NJ: John Wiley & Sons.

Morton, M. S. (1990). *Corporation of the 1990s: Information Technology and Organizational Transformation.* Oxford, England: Oxford University Press, Inc.

Newell, S., and Marabelli, M. (2015). Strategic opportunities (and challenges) of algorithmic decision-making: A call for action on the long-term societal effects of 'datification'. *The Journal of Strategic Information Systems,* 24(1), 3–14.

O'Reilly, T. (1999). Lessons from open-source software development. *Communications of the ACM,* 42(4), 32–37.

Olson, P. (2020, August 14). The quiet growth of race-detection software sparks concerns over bias. *Wall Street Journal.* Retrieved from https://www.wsj.com/articles/the-quiet-growth-of-race-detection-software-sparks-concerns-over-bias-11597378154

Osterwalder, A., and Pigneur, Y. (2010). *Business Model Generation: A Handbook for Visionaries, Game Changers, and Challengers.* Hoboken, NJ: John Wiley & Sons.

Parker, G. G., and Van Alstyne, M. W. (2005). Two-sided network effects: A theory of information product design. *Management Science,* 51(10), 1494–1504.

Porter, M. E. (1980). *Competitive Strategy: Techniques for Analyzing Industries and Competitors.* New York: The Free Press.

Salam, E. (2021, July 17). Majority of Covid misinformation came from 12 people, report finds. *The Guardian.* Retrieved from https://www.theguardian.com/world/2021/jul/17/covid-misinformation-conspiracy-theories-ccdh-report

Seidel, S., Berente, N., Lindberg, A., Lyytinen, K., Martinez, B., and Nickerson, J. V. (2020). Artificial intelligence and video game creation: A framework for the new logic of autonomous design. *Journal of Digital Social Research,* 2(3), 126–157–126–157.

Smedlund, A. (2012). Value cocreation in service platform business models. *Service Science,* 4(1), 79–88.

Subin, S. (2021, July 21). Ford and Argo AI to launch self-driving cars with Lyft by the end of the year. *CNBC.* Retrieved from https://www.cnbc.com/2021/07/21/ford-and-argo-ai-to-launch-self-driving-cars-with-lyft-by-end-of-year.html

Teece, D. J. (2018). Profiting from innovation in the digital economy: Enabling technologies, standards, and licensing models in the wireless world. *Research Policy,* 47(8), 1367–1387.

Telford, T., and Timberg, C. (2018, November 30). Marriott disclose massive data breach affecting up to 500 million guests. *The Washington Post.* Retrieved from https://www.washingtonpost.com/business/2018/11/30/marriott-discloses-massive-data-breach-impacting-million-guests/

Tidy, J. (2020, October 30). Marriott Hotels fined £18.4m for data breach that hit millions. *BBC.* Retrieved from https://www.bbc.com/news/technology-54748843

Tilson, D., Lyytinen, K., and Sørensen, C. (2010). Research commentary – Digital infrastructures: The missing IS research agenda. *Information Systems Research,* 21(4), 748–759.

Turton, W., and Mehrotra, K. (2021, June 4). Hackers breached Colonial Pipeline using compromised password. *Bloomberg.* Retrieved from https://www.bloomberg.com/news/articles/2021-06-04/hackers-breached-colonial-pipeline-using-compromised-password

Verganti, R., Vendraminelli, L., and Iansiti, M. (2020). Innovation and design in the age of Artificial Intelligence. *Journal of Product Innovation Management,* 37(3), 212–227.
von Hippel, E. (2005). *Democratizing Innovation.* Cambridge, MA: MIT Press.
von Hippel, E., and von Krogh, G. (2003). Open source software and the "private-collective" innovation model: Issues for organization science. *Organization Science,* 14(2), 209–223.
Vosoughi, S., Roy, D., and Aral, S. (2018). The spread of true and false news online. *Science,* 359(6380), 1146–1151.
Whillans, A., Perlow, L., and Turek, A. (2021). Experimenting during the shift to virtual team work: Learnings from how teams adapted their activities during the COVID-19 pandemic. *Information and Organization,* 31(1), 100343.
Yoo, Y. (2010). Computing in everyday life: A call for research on experiential computing. *MIS Quarterly,* 213–231.
Yoo, Y., Boland, R. J., Jr., Lyytinen, K., and Majchrzak, A. (2012). Organizing for innovation in the digitized world. *Organization Science,* 23(5), 1398–1408.
Yoo, Y., Henfridsson, O., and Lyytinen, K. (2010). Research commentary – the new organizing logic of digital innovation: An agenda for information systems research. *Information Systems Research,* 21(4), 724–735.
Zhang, Z., Yoo, Y., Lyytinen, K., and Lindberg, A. (Forthcoming). The unknowability of autonomous tools and the liminal experience of their use. *Information Systems Research.*
Zittrain, J. (2006). The generative Internet. *Harvard Law Review,* 119(7), 1974–2040.
Zuboff, S. (1988). *In the Age of the Smart Machine: The Future of Work and Power* (Vol. 186). New York: Basic books.

Exercises

1. For each option below, provide and discuss an example of IT-catalyzed organizational change in which IT:
   a. increases efficiency and speed of operations;
   b. enhances the effectiveness of decision-making and communication;
   c. changes the industry's structure by lowering barriers for new entrants into the industry.
2. Identify and discuss the benefits of a digitally enhanced product/service that you may use as a consumer/customer.

Video Analysis and Discussion

Please watch the following video(s):

1. Technology – Its impact on your world of work: https://www.youtube.com/watch?v=oQQbPhfsASI
2. Information technology, the first 1,500 years: https://www.youtube.com/watch?v=V1qHNrQQHZI

Now form small groups to discuss the video(s) and answer the following questions:

1. What are the major points of the video?
2. How can you use information from the video in your career?
3. Based on the video, what advice do you have for leaders in organizations?

Be prepared to present the ideas from your small group discussion with the class as a whole.

Discussion Questions

1. What specific approaches might an organization take to mitigate the risks of IT applications described in this chapter? Are there additional risks that you can identify?
2. Discuss specific managerial and operational issues that must be addressed to successfully implement the organizational changes discussed in this chapter.

28

Make Management Practice Fit National Cultures and the Global Culture

MIRIAM EREZ

Technion – Israel Institute of Technology

This chapter focuses on the interface between cultures that takes place in the global work context. This change in focus is driven by the changes in the work environment, as more and more people around the world work for multinational and global organizations that cross geographical zones and cultural borders.

Organizational behavior (OB) principles should take into consideration the context in which they are implemented and the work context that may be shifting from local to global. This global context is characterized by economic interdependence across countries, a free flow of capital, and goods, knowledge, and labor moving across national and geographical borders (Erez and Shokef, 2008; Govindarajan and Gupta, 2001). It is not very difficult to understand why Thomas Friedman used the metaphor *World Is Flat* as the title of his book, in which he reviewed the factors that are flattening the global business environment, including historical, technological, and communication issues (Friedman, 2005).

Yet, is the world really flat, and are managers developing identical or nearly identical principles for managing organizations and people around the world? The answer, as reported both by practitioners and researchers, is "no." Cross-cultural differences in values, norms, and accepted modes of behaviors still exist, and they differ across cultures.

The next question is, therefore, how do managers cope with the paradox of operating in the globally flat business world and, at the same time, also manage culturally diverse employees working in culturally diverse subsidiaries and business units? The aim of this chapter is to answer this question by providing some principles to serve as guidelines for managers in navigating between the macrolevel of the global, flat culture and the uneven level of diverse national cultures lying underneath.

From Local to Global Work Contexts

For many years, the dominant theories of OB were mostly Western/American, generated and validated on Western samples of managers and employees, working in Western organizations.

In the late 1980s, the fierce competition between Japan and the USA called attention to cultural issues. During this period, articles in business papers reflected fear of Japan, attempting to understand how Japan was growing, why it was dangerous, and what could be done about the supposed threat to Western hegemony (Smith, 1990). Over the years, an increasing number of American managers found themselves negotiating with the Japanese, marketing their products in Japan, offering services to foreign customers, and managing operations outside their home countries. As a result, the popularity of guidebooks on how to do business with the Japanese and other foreign countries grew. The demand for such books testified to the fact that managers recognized their lack of knowledge and competence in managing across cultural borders.

By the late 1990s, the competition between companies situated in different cultures turned from conflict to cooperation in the form of international mergers and acquisitions, joint ventures, and business alliances. A wedding ceremony becomes a common metaphor for international mergers, with a question mark overhanging these unions: will they last, or unravel?

Cooperation rather than competition requires a better understanding of one's international partner. One needs merely to know one's competitor but does not necessarily need to understand him or her. In fact, the need for understanding cross-cultural differences and similarities is becoming increasingly crucial for effective international partnerships and their managers.

However, recognizing and accepting cultural diversity is necessary, but not sufficient for operating across cultural borders. What is needed is a shared meaning system that enables players in the global work context to communicate and understand each other, so there is a basis for collaboration and coordination (Gelfand, Erez, and Aycan, 2007). This shared meaning system reflects the emergence of a global work culture. The global work culture has emerged as the most macrolevel of culture which subsumes the national, organizational, group, and individual levels of cultural values nested within each other, portraying a multilevel model of culture (Erez and Gati, 2004), as shown in Model 1, Figure 28.1.

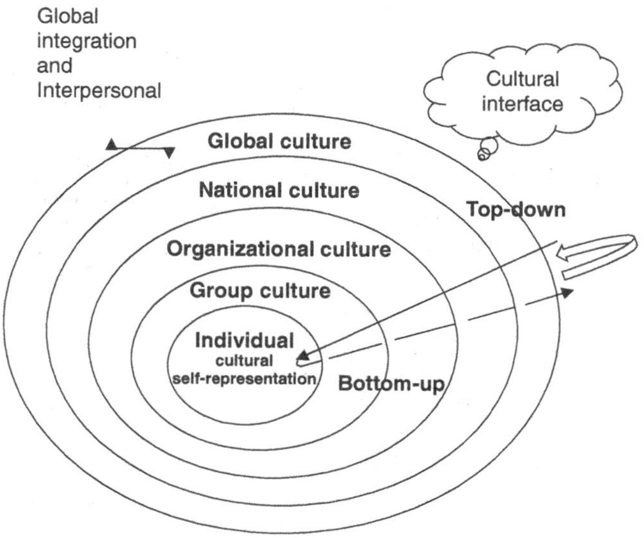

FIGURE 28.1 A multilevel model of culture
Source: Based on Erez and Gati (2004)

The Global Work Culture

Social scientists drew attention to the dissemination of three sociocultural values around the world: *rationalization, professionalization, and actorhood* (Drori, Jang, and Meyer, 2006). Rationalization pertains to systemization, standardization, and routinization of actions. Rationalization facilitates comparability across cultures, as evident by the global rating systems of economic, educational, and government institutions. Comparability enhances global competition across all institutional domains. Organizations compete for their relative ranking: Business companies, as well as national educational systems, universities, business schools, legal systems, etc., make every effort to be ranked at the top of their respective world list. Furthermore, rationalization enforces universal criteria for professionalism, pertaining to universal knowledge, and expertise that are necessary for becoming a certified professional and a member of local professional organizations, recognized by international professional organizations. Finally, globalization also diffuses the value of actorhood, which champions the proactive individual, with the capacity and motivation for taking a proactive stand and control over him/herself. This value has been globally disseminated by educating for democracy around the world. Such global values provide the infrastructure for the development of a global organizational culture, common to all organizations operating in the global work context.

Values are instrumental for adaptation to and/or changing of one's environment. The global work environment is known to be geographically dispersed and culturally diverse, highly competitive, dynamic, and uncertain. Paradoxically, while

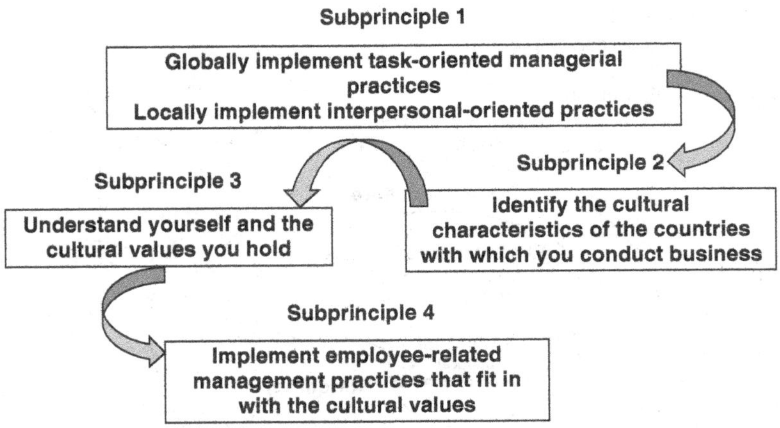

FIGURE 28.2 The four principles of global management

this global environment emerges beyond national cultures, it also consists of diverse cultures representing the multiple subsidiaries and business units of the global organization. Unlike managers operating in local organizations, nested within one culture, managers of global organizations operate in a complex environment, where they need to safeguard the global integration of the companies' operations; on the other hand, alongside this global integration, they must maintain local responsiveness to their diverse subsidiaries and business units, nested within diverse local cultures. The global context determines the principles that should guide managers operating in the global work context. The following is a set of subprinciples for the global manager, as summarized in Figure 28.2.

As evident, the core principle relates to the interplay between global integration and local responsiveness (Kostova and Roth, 2002).

The First Subprinciple: Globally Implement Task-Oriented Managerial Practices and Locally Implement Interpersonal-Oriented Practices

Research has demonstrated that managers should differentiate between two groups of values and practices: those pertaining to the execution of tasks and operations, and those pertaining to interpersonal relationships with employees, peers, superiors, and customers (Berson, Erez, and Adler, 2004; Erez and Shokef, 2008).

Task-oriented practices enable managers to cope with the highly competitive global work environment, where the competition is on market share, customers, new products, and prices. To cope with such demands, managers of multinational and global organizations should uniformly share the values of competitive performance orientation and customer orientation. They should agree on the importance of their task-related managerial roles of planning and coordination, and initiating changes and innovation, wherever on the globe they manage business units.

On the other hand, interpersonal practices pertain to the relationship between managers and subordinates, peers, superiors, and customers. These relationships should be tuned to the diverse local cultural values and norms. Therefore, interpersonal practices should be loosely implemented, respecting the diverse local cultural values. To maintain the fit between interpersonal-related management practices and local cultures, managers need to identify the variations in cultural values.

The Second Subprinciple: Identify the Cultural Characteristics of the Countries with Which You Conduct Business

Managers and employees in different cultures bring to their workplace their cultures' behavior codes and norms. These norms and cultural values shape organizational processes and managerial practices. Therefore, different managerial practices, in particular the relational ones, are implemented in different parts of the world within the same global organization. For example, in individualistic cultures, such as that of the USA, the selection procedure of new employees is based on his or her personal records. In collectivistic cultures, such as that of Mexico, recommendations by family members, who already work for the company, serve as an important criterion for selecting new employees. In the USA, promotion to higher managerial levels is based on personal achievements, as they appear in an employee's performance appraisal records. However, in collectivistic and hierarchical cultures such as Japan, seniority plays a major role in promotion decisions. Payment based on results constitutes a greater part of Americans' compensation packages compared to those in Europe. In European countries, flat salaries are more common than in the USA. The compensation package of American managers includes a large portion of stock options, whereas this is less common for local European and Far Eastern managers. Explicit feedback on performance is highly valued in Western countries, whereas in the Far East, implicit feedback is the norm, and explicit feedback is not acceptable. Explicit feedback if negative violates the important value of face saving; if positive, it violates the important value of collectivism and the sense of being part of the group rather than being unique and different than others.

There are so many different codes of behavior and variations of management practices that relate to employees and interpersonal relationships that they cannot all be described in the "how to" books. Managers, therefore, should recognize the key cultural values that determine which practices will be positively evaluated by employees, enhancing their sense of self-worth and well-being, and consequently motivate them to stretch their goals (see Chapter 5) and improve their performance (Erez and Earley, 1993). Managerial approaches that are at odds with prevailing cultural values are unlikely to be effective. Since cultures differ in the values they endorse, people from these cultures often interpret the same managerial practices quite differently than a manager coming in from the "outside" would expect. Identifying the core cultural values will enable managers to fit their management practices to cultural context.

Culture can be defined as a shared meaning (value) system (Schwartz, 1992; Shweder and LeVine, 1984). In metaphorical terms, culture is the software of the mind (Hofstede, 1991). Culture shapes the core values and norms of its members. These values are transmitted from one generation to another through social learning processes of modeling and observation, as well as through the effects of individual actions (Bandura, 1986). Homogenous societies form tight cultures, and their norms and values are closely shared by most members of the society. Societies consisting of subgroups with dissimilar norms and values form loose cultures (Gelfand, Nishii, and Raver, 2006; Triandis, 1989).

Cultures differ in their content components. The two values that depict most of the variance among cultures are: collectivism versus individualism, and power distance.

Individualism-collectivism signifies the level of interrelatedness among members of one culture (Hofstede, 1991; Brewer and Chen, 2007). Collectivism means preferring to work in teams, subordinating personal goals to group goals, being concerned about the group integrity, and having an intense emotional attachment to the in-group. In contrast, individualism emphasizes personal autonomy and independence, adherence to personal goals, and less concern and emotional attachment to the in-groups (Triandis, Bontempo, Vilareal, Masaaki, and Lucca, 1988). The United States, Australia, and England are highly individualistic cultures, whereas South America, Pakistan, Korea, Japan, and Taiwan are highly collectivistic.

Power distance reflects the level of equality in society. High power distance means low equality in society and a clear power structure in organizations. Employees in such cultures know their place in the organizational hierarchy, and there are clear status symbols that differentiate between employees of different organizational levels. On the other hand, in low power distance cultures, employees feel free to disagree with their superiors and to express their ideas openly. Malaysia, Philippines, Arab countries, India, and far eastern countries are known for their high level of power distance. In contrast, Israel, Scandinavia, and New Zealand are known for their low levels of power distance. A group of more than 80 researchers, headed by Robert House from the Wharton School, joined together to conduct the *Globe Study* in 60 different countries (House, Hanges, Javidan, Dorfman, and Gupta, 2004). This study assessed differences and similarities in cultural and organizational values, as well as in preferences for leadership characteristics. Table 28.1 depicts the cultural values of collectivism and power distance in a sample of eight countries that includes the USA, England, West Germany, East Germany, Russia, Finland, Japan, and Israel.

The results demonstrate that in this sample, Japan is the country with the highest level of power distance, and Israel is the most egalitarian country. Similarly, the USA is the most individualistic culture, and Japan and Russia have the most collectivistic cultures.

Three additional values that help differentiate cultures are uncertainty avoidance, masculinity/femininity, and future time orientation.

Table 28.1 Differences in cultural values across selected countries

	Collectivism		*Power Distance*		*Uncertainty Avoidance*	
England	4.08	(C)*	5.15	(B)	4.65	(B)
USA	4.25	(C)	4.88	(B)	4.15	(B)
Israel	4.7	(B)	4.73	(C)	4.01	(C)
Germany (W)	4.02	(C)	5.25	(B)	5.22	(A)
Germany (E)	4.52	(B)	5.54	(A)	5.16	(A)
Russia	5.63	(A)	5.52	(A)	2.88	(D)
Finland	4.07	(C)	4.89	(B)	5.02	(A)
China	5.8	(A)	5.04	(B)	4.94	(A)
Japan	4.63	(C)	5.11	(B)	4.07	(C)

Source: Based on House et al. (2004).

Uncertainty avoidance reflects the extent to which members of society feel threatened by uncertain or unknown situations. High levels of uncertainty lead to anxiety. Organizations that seek to avoid uncertainty have formal rules and regulations, clear task definitions, and low tolerance for deviation from their rules and norms. In opposition, organizations with a high tolerance for uncertainty are less formal, more flexible, and allow for higher levels of heterogeneity in norms and behavior. Cultures with high levels of uncertainty avoidance are Switzerland, Sweden, and Singapore; cultures with low levels of uncertainty avoidance are Greece, Venezuela, and Russia.

Masculine versus feminine cultures – the former pertains to societies in which social gender roles are clearly defined (i.e. men are supposed to be assertive, tough, and focused on material success, whereas women are supposed to be more modest, tender, and concerned with the quality of life). Femininity pertains to societies in which social gender roles overlap (i.e. both men and women are concerned with the quality of life; Hofstede, 1991). Japan is classified as the most masculine country, followed by Austria, Venezuela, and Italy. The most feminine cultures are Sweden, Norway, the Netherlands, and Denmark.

Future time orientation reflects the extent to which the culture focuses on long-term planning and outcomes and on the delay of gratification. The Dragon countries, including Japan, Hong Kong, and Korea, are high on this scale.

Employees internalize the respective cultural values and use them to evaluate the meaning of different managerial and motivational approaches as either opportunities or threats. For example, differential reward systems would be positively viewed by employees in individualistic cultures, and team-based incentives would be appreciated by employees in collectivistic cultures.

People in different cultures internalize the prevalent cultural values of their society. Therefore, they differ in the meaning they ascribe to a particular managerial approach. To further understand what motivates employees in other cultures, and how they interpret the meaning of various managerial practices, managers should first develop self-awareness and understanding of their own motives and values (see Chapter 4).

The Third Subprinciple: Understand Yourself and the Cultural Values You Hold

The self is shaped by the choices one makes and by the shared understanding within a particular culture of what it means to be human (Cushman, 1990; Markus and Kitayama, 1991). People develop self-knowledge through introspection (see Chapter 2), direct experience, and evaluations provided by significant others.

People strive to have positive self-perceptions and to experience self-worth and well-being. They do their utmost to fulfill the motives of enhancement, efficacy, and consistency. Self-enhancement is the experience of a positive cognitive and affective state of self-worth and well-being; self-efficacy (see Chapter 6) is the conviction that one is competent and efficacious in relation to specific tasks; self-consistency is the desire to sense and experience coherence and continuity.

People monitor and evaluate the extent to which their behavior leads to the fulfillment of the three motives and the degree to which the work setting offers opportunities for such behaviors (Bandura, 1986; Markus and Warf, 1987).

The self and self-motives are shaped by one's choices and one's cultural values, and they set the standards and criteria for self-evaluation. These criteria vary across individuals and cultures and, consequently, result in different self-conceptions. Individualistic cultures support the *independent self,* who attends to personal criteria and standards for evaluating the meaning of certain management practices as enhancing or inhibiting opportunities for self-worth and well-being (Markus and Kitayama, 1991; Triandis, 1989). On the other hand, collectivistic cultures support the *interdependent self,* who internalizes the criteria and standards advocated by one's reference groups. One common measure of the independent and interdependent selves is the Twenty Statement Test, which asks a person to write 20 statements starting with the words "I am . . ." People with a strong independent self-use individual characteristics, such as: "I am smart" or "I am tall", more frequently than those who rank high on the interdependent self-scale. The latter use attributes that reflect their relationships with others, such as: "I am a father," "I am a member of the ABC organization," etc.

Managerial and motivational practices that satisfy self-motives of the independent self would be different from those satisfying the interdependent self. For example, self-enhancement driven by the independent self motivates individuals toward personal accomplishment. The independent self positively evaluates managerial practices that provide opportunities for individual success. People driven by the interdependent self, on the other hand, experience enhancement when they contribute to the group's success because their self definition is in terms of their relationship to others. This does not mean that independent people cannot work in groups, but it would be out of self-interest rather than duty. Similarly, self-efficacy is salient for people with a strong independent self, whereas collective efficacy, or the perceptions of the group as competent, is important for the interdependent self. Finally, self-consistency of the independent self is interpreted in reference to the individual's personal history. Conversely, the interdependent self evaluates the level of collective consistency in line with the collective history of the group to which one belongs.

The self constitutes the link between the macrolevel of culture and managerial practices and the microlevel of employee behavior. Employees use their cultural values as criteria for evaluating the potential contribution of various management practices to the fulfillment of their self-derived motives (Erez and Earley, 1993).

Managers who are aware of their own cultural values and motives are more amenable to developing an understanding of other people's values and motives. Once they identify the cultural characteristics of people from other cultures, they can more easily follow how employees in foreign cultures would react to various managerial approaches.

However, employees working in the global work context belong not only to their local national culture, but also to their global organizational culture. The social identity theory (Tajfel, 1981) proposes that individuals develop a sense of belongingness to the group that is meaningful to them. Extrapolating, we can say that individuals working in the global work context develop a dual identity – a local identity, which reflects their sense of belongingness to their local cultures, and a global identity, reflecting their sense of belongingness to their global work culture. People may hold multiple identities, and they apply the relevant identity to the context. When they communicate with others in the global work context, their global identity and sense of belongingness to the global organization becomes dominant, regardless of their location and national culture. On the other hand, when they relate to others in their local organizational unit, their local identity becomes dominant, and they expect to be treated according to the norms of their local culture. Thus, successful managers working in the global work context should be able to recognize the dominant facet of the other person's self-identity, whether it is the global or the local self-identity and relate to the dominant facet accordingly.

The Fourth Subprinciple: Implement Employee-Related Management Practices That Fit in with the Cultural Values

Managerial practices represent certain ideological or philosophical frameworks. For example, individual-based differential reward systems and flat salary or team-based reward systems reflect different values. The former represents cultural values of individualism and the importance of personal achievement, whereas flat salary or team-based rewards represent cultural values of collectivism, where productivity is often measured on the team level and compensation is based on team performance. Top-down communication systems represent high power distance cultures, whereas two-way communication systems represent low power distance cultures.

Formal rules and regulations and extensive written documentation represent high uncertainty avoidance, whereas flexibility, risk-taking, and low levels of formality represent low uncertainty avoidance. Long-term investment in R&D represents future time orientation, whereas short-term goals and balance sheets reported every quarter represent a short-term orientation. Finally, the high percentage of women in socially oriented professions rather than in engineering and sciences and their low representation at the top managerial levels represent masculine rather than feminine cultures.

Very often, consultants and practitioners serve as agents of certain managerial techniques. They advise management how to implement these techniques, following success achieved in other places, while overlooking the cultural and ideological meaning of such techniques. For example, the CEO of one steel company in Israel, who came to the company after many years of military service, was known for his authoritarian leadership style. He visited the steel industry in Japan and was very impressed with the participative management approach and the quality control circles he saw. Upon his return to Israel, he called in all his senior managers, told them about his visit, and instructed them that "from now on, you are going to implement participative management in the organization." Obviously, his style of dictating to his subordinates was not a good model for participative management.

The three principles – understanding the cultural values, knowing your motives and values, and understanding the values reflected by various managerial approaches – should serve managers when selecting and implementing managerial practices. These principles enable the fit between people-oriented management practices and local cultural values.

Matching Management Practices to Cultural Variations

Management practices represent the way things are done in the organization: The way managers delegate authority, allocate rewards, make decisions, and design jobs.

Figure 28.3 depicts the differences in management practices between collectivistic versus individualistic cultures, in combination with high versus low power distance.

The following section elaborates on the implementation of goals and feedback, reward allocation, participation in decision-making and empowerment, and quality improvement systems in different cultures.

Power distance	Collectivism	Individualism
High	**Top-Down – Group:** Assigned group goals group feedback Face saving – error prevention Team-based bonus – high differential	**Top-Down – Individual:** Assigned individuals goals individual feedback Be successful – promotion Individual-based bonus – high differential
Low	**Lateral – Group:** Participative group goal setting Team reflexivity – feedback Face saving/harmony – error prevention Team-based bonus – low differential	**Lateral – Individual:** Empowering personal goal setting 360-degree personal feedback Risk-taking/uniqueness – promotion toward new opportunities and new records Individual-based bonus – low differential

FIGURE 28.3 Fit interpersonal management practices with local cultures

Goals and Feedback

One major responsibility of managers is to set goals and motivate their employees to achieve them. There are different ways to set goals – either by assigning them or by involving employees in making the decision about them – and different ways to realize them. In some cases, employees can be empowered to set their own work goals. Employees in Western cultures are more intrinsically motivated when they are involved in setting the goals rather than when goals are externally set for them. Empowerment is considered to be a strong motivational approach in Western cultures. This is not the case in India and the Far East. In these high power distance cultures, employees expect their boss to set goals for them, and they are highly motivated to accomplish externally set goals. In fact, managers who empower their employees to set goals are considered to be weak, and they often lose the respect of their subordinates.

Employees in Asian countries where there is high collectivism and high power distance are often more strongly motivated to avoid errors and failures than they are motivated to win and be the first one. This may be because of the fear of authority should they fail, and because of fear of failing the group to which a person belongs, as his/her personal failure is attributed to the entire group. Therefore, employees in the Far East are likely to set moderate rather than difficult goals, to reduce the risk of failure.

The motivations to avoid failure and to save face have implications for what is deemed the acceptable form of feedback. Feedback is considered to be a strong motivational factor in Western cultures, in particular when it is provided at the individual level. Yet, in countries such as Japan, feedback takes a different form. Explicit individual feedback threatens the individual's status in the team. It violates the important value of face saving, causing a person to feel shame. For this reason, implicit and impersonal feedback, oriented to the collective rather than to the individual, is considered to be the norm. Consequently, Western managers operating in the Far East should recognize such cultural differences and adjust their feedback to their employees to the local culture.

Reward Allocation

A key issue is how to allocate rewards in order to enhance motivation. If you are an American manager, you most likely implement the principle of equity. Indeed, in most individualistic cultures, the rule of individual merit serves as the criterion for reward allocation. Employees receive rewards based on their individual contribution to goal attainment. Implementing rewards for performance requires the setting of criteria and standards for performance and an appraisal system for evaluating employees according to these criteria.

Payment-by-results dominates individualistic cultures such as the USA, England, and Australia. In collectivistic cultures, payment-by-results may violate group harmony. Furthermore, it threatens the organizational hierarchy, as the most effective employee may not necessarily be the most senior and respected one. In that case, seniority plays an important role in the reward structure. Furthermore, when the work design is for teams, as is often the case, the reward differential is team based.

Managers in different cultures value different work components when evaluating their employees. Western managers evaluate employees mostly on the basis of performance effectiveness. Yet, Chinese managers put less emphasis on work performance as a criterion for rewards when compared with American managers. Rather, they consider the quality of interpersonal relationships to be more important for work than Americans (Zhou and Martocchio, 2001).

Rewarding for performance is less acceptable in collectivistic cultures and mainly when it is public. Chinese managers use the rule of equality more often than Americans mainly with respect to in-group members. However, for out-group allocation, equality is used when the allocation is public, to maintain face saving, while in-group favoritism often takes place when allocation is done privately. Similarly, Koreans, as opposed to Americans, perceive allocators who use equality rather than the merit rule more favorably. Swedish people use equality more frequently than Americans. The Swedish educational system discourages competition, in favor of cooperation and teamwork.

In addition, the Swedish view the idea of need more positively than do Americans. The need rule is most highly preferred in India and in other collectivistic cultures, particularly when needs become visible (Murphy-Berman, Berman, Singh, Pachauri, and Kumar, 1984).

The findings mentioned earlier lead to the conclusion that the application of an inappropriate distribution rule may engender feelings of injustice, mitigating employee motivation. Therefore, knowledge about cross-cultural differences with regard to preferences of allocation rules is vital for managers who operate outside their home country.

Teamwork and Multicultural, Virtual Teams

Teams have different meanings in individualistic versus collectivistic cultures. Metaphors of teams in Puerto Rico and the Philippines, two collectivistic countries, are often in relational terms such as family and community. On the other hand, Americans use metaphors involving sport teams, reflecting an instrumental approach to teams as the means of accomplishing certain outcomes (Gibson and Zellmer-Bruhn, 2001).

Teamwork and tasks of high interdependence among team members prevail in collectivistic cultures. Yet, individualists prefer to be personally responsible for their job and to get personal recognition for their performance outcomes. Individualists are intrinsically motivated when empowered by their managers and when given the autonomy to craft their jobs to fit their personal resources. In contrast, collectivists are empowered when participating in the team decision-making process and when their team voice is being heard. Work autonomy, whether at the individual or the team level, is not acceptable in high power distance cultures. Yet, in low power distance cultures, such as that of Israel, employees react negatively to goals that are assigned to them, as compared to employees who were allowed to participate in goal setting (Erez and Earley, 1987). Social loafing as observed by group performance loss is more prevalent among individualists who do not share responsibility and prefer to take a free ride, mainly when their individual contribution to the team cannot be identified. In contrast, social loafing was not observed in group-oriented cultures, such as China and Israel, providing the team members had a specific goal to achieve (Earley, 1989; Erez and Somech, 1996). In individualistic cultures, social loafing disappears when team members' contribution can be identified and when they are held personally accountable and responsible for the group outcomes (Weldon and Gargano, 1988).

Recent developments in communication technology have supported a relatively new form of virtual multicultural teams (see Chapters 21 and 27). Such teams collaborate on joint projects while their members are located in different geographical zones and cultural environments.

Managing multicultural, virtual teams requires first and foremost the creation of a shared understanding among the team members. This is done by cultivating the global work values to be shared by all team members and by creating a team identity that strengthens the sense of belongingness to and identification with the team.

Case Examples

1. Personal Dilemma in an International Acquisition

David A. is the CEO of Diamob, a young Israeli startup in the medical instrument industry that develops high-resolution ultrasound diagnostics equipment on mobile computers. Diamob has just been acquired by a large US-based multinational company – Medica. Right after the acquisition, there were rumors that Medica was going to transfer the new technology to other existing departments, closing Diamob Israel. The small group of 40 engineers and scientists was in a state of high ambiguity, and each one of them had to decide what to do next. There were two options: to leave the company and search for another job or to stay as a group and negotiate with Medica to let Diamob grow to a self-sustained profit unit.

David A., Diamob CEO, knew that he could easily get a job in another company. Yet, if he quits, it will probably lead to the end of Diamob. David was a personal friend of most of the other engineers in Diamob. Many of them served together in the Israeli Defense Forces and have remained friends since then. David was proud to see that in the first month after the acquisition, the group stayed together and no one left in search of a new job even though their job security was at risk.

David gathered together the unit managers to discuss their future strategy. After long hours of discussions, they developed a business plan that justifies their continuous growth as a sustainable profit unit. David had to go meet with Jeff S. – Medica CEO – and present to him the new Diamob business plan.

The meeting took place in a hotel airport on the East Coast. David's voice represented the voice of all his 40 engineers, and he was very determined to succeed in getting Jeff to support the new business plan. Jeff listened to David and said: "Listen David, you are a very small group. We acquired Diamob because of your technology innovation and your initiative to develop the new product. We plan to recruit a small number of key experts from Diamob to Medica by offering them a high salary and then close Diamob, letting all other members go. You are the first one we want to hire. Your salary will be equal to the top executives in Medica, with a nice package of bonuses and stock options. You and the few people we hire will have to move to the USA. Israel has a very small market and there is no reason for us to keep the site here."

David reflected upon what he just heard. From a personal point of view, he has an opportunity to grow, to open up his horizon and scope, and to get promoted in a large MNC. His salary and compensation package are going to be much higher than the present one. He will be able to easily support his family without any financial worries. On the other hand, this means that he will be separated from his colleagues, they will be losing their jobs, and their dream to develop the small startup company into a large profit organization will not be materialized.

What is going to be David's reply? To answer this question, please take into consideration the cultural values of Israel, as summarized in Table 28.1.

What do you think would be David's reply if he were an American, working in the USA and getting an offer from a European MNC?

Please take into consideration the tension between global integration and local responsiveness and elaborate how this tension is going to influence David's decision.

2. Cultural Differences Between Employees and Their Manager

Red Algea is a Japanese company located in Eilat, a tourist town on the Red Sea, the south point of Israel. The location, the water, and the temperature are most suitable for growing Red Algea, which is considered to be a very healthy food supplement consisting of high percentages of beta-carotene.

The company grows the Red Algea in Eilat, produces it as a food supplement pill in Japan, and sells it in the global market. The patent for Red Algea was written by life science researchers at the Weizmann Science Institute in Israel. The climate and type of soil in Eilat are considered by scientists to be most suitable for this purpose. The founder of the company and the top management team are all Japanese, but the chief scientist and the employees are all Israelis. The profit gain on the raw material grown in Israel is not that high. Most of the profit is being made on the food supplement pills. The Israeli inventor who has the technological patent is interested in making a joint venture with the Japanese company and to produce the pill in Israel. However, the Japanese headquarters strongly objects to it. In their view, Israeli employees do not strictly follow the rules; they like to improvise, and they do not pay enough attention to detail. They are good in idea generation and innovation, but not in careful, error-free implementation.

Mr. Takashi was appointed the Israel site manager. He oversees the process of growing the Red Algea in a special outdoor farm. The process is highly automatic, and for this reason, the number of employees is relatively small, about 35, including Dan, the chief scientist. Mr. Takashi learned the production process with the help of Dan. He carefully read all the existing literature on growing Red Algea, including the patent of the Weizmann Institute. He then developed a set of procedures that should be carefully followed by the employees, to ensure the high quality of the Red Algea.

Mr. Takashi wanted to implement Japanese management procedures. He expected all employees to appear on time, early in the day, to get together for the morning meeting to get updated about special problems and to align expectations. However, he has difficulties controlling the Israeli employees. First, they do not arrive at the same time in the morning. For this reason, he cannot properly hold the morning meeting. Second, they hardly follow the rules that he set for them. Some of them take a break during working hours to complete some family duties they have outside the workplace. Then, they stay late on their own, to compensate for the time taken, rather than working in close coordination with all other employees. Furthermore, employees are careless with respect to documenting their activities, as he requested. He often worries that the lack of standardization and documentation will result in a big disaster – the Red Algea will not grow to the quality and size needed. It often gets to critical points when he does not know how to cope with unexpected situations. These are exactly the moments when the Israeli employees become very alert, full of energy, and resourcefulness, and they manage to improvise, rather than going by the book and to resolve the problem.

Mr. Takashi keeps saying to his Israeli employees: "Please, do what you are required to do, please follow the rules very accurately. If you do this, you will not have to improvise. I gave you specific guidelines. Simply follow them. Why argue with me all the time that there is a better way to do things. If I gave your instructions, you need to follow them without any arguments."

Mr. Takashi felt that he did not properly manage the site and he did not want to fail. Therefore, he asked his board to send him back to Japan. The Red Algea site in Israel remained without a CEO.

Please answer the following questions:

1. *Should the company replace the Japanese manager with a local manager?*
2. *What are the main differences between the Japanese and the Israeli culture?*
3. *Do you see these cultural differences as an advantage or a disadvantage to the company?*
4. *How can managers turn a potential disadvantage of cultural diversity into an advantage?*
5. *Think of culturally diverse teams. How can you bring people from diverse cultural backgrounds to work, communicate, and collaborate with each other effectively?*

Conclusion

Global managers in the third millennium operate across cultural borders and geographical zones. They need to cope with the complexity of the global work environment, which consists of both the macrolevel of the global culture and the level of diverse national cultures nested underneath it. The core principle is, therefore, one of maintaining a global integration of one unified organization, but, in parallel, understanding the cultural values and norms of the diverse workforce and relating to employees in each cultural setting according to their codes of behavior.

Global integration should take place with respect to the task-oriented managerial roles and values. These values should be homogeneously adopted across all subsidiaries and business units to allow communication and coordination of all organizational activities toward organizational goal accomplishment.

Nonetheless, local responsiveness should be implemented, mainly with respect to interpersonal relationships. Sensitivity to others begins with self-knowledge. Managers who learn about their own motives and cultural values recognize how such values shape the motives for coming to work, the desire to achieve goals, identification with the organization, and adaptation to the changing requirements. Managers who are aware of the meaning of their own self-worth and well-being values can be sensitive to others' values, and they are aware of the meaning of respecting these values for a person's sense of self-worth and well-being. Recognizing the diverse cultural environment should guide managers in selecting and implementing management practices that best fit the cultural values of employees in the business units they manage. While there are potentially many different practices that managers can implement, cultural values, once acknowledged, should serve as criteria for selecting and implementing the most effective management practices.

References

Bandura, A. (1986). *Social Foundations of Thoughts and Action: A Social Cognitive Theory.* Englewood Cliffs, NJ: Prentice-Hall.

Berson, Y., Erez, M., and Adler, S. (2004). Reflections of organizational identity and national culture on managerial roles in a multinational corporation. *Academy of Management Best Paper Proceedings,* Q1–Q6.

Brewer, M. B., and Chen, Y. (2007). Where (who) are collectives in collectivism? Toward conceptual clarification of individualism and collectivism. *Annual Review of Psychology,* 114(1), 133–151.

Cushman, P. (1990). Why the self is empty? Towards a historically situated psychology. *American Psychologist,* 45, 599–611.

Drori, G. S., Jang, Y. S., and Meyer, J. W. (2006). Sources of rationalized governance: Cross-National Longitudinal Analyses, 1985-2002. *Administrative Science Quarterly,* 51, 205–229.

Earley, P. C. (1989). Social loafing and collectivism: A comparison of United States and the People's Republic of China. *Administrative Science Quarterly*, 34, 565–581.

Erez, M., and Earley, P. C. (1987). Comparative analysis of goal-setting strategies across cultures. *Journal of Applied Psychology*, 72, 658–665.

Erez, M., and Earley, P. C. (1993). *Culture, Self-Identity, and Work.* NY: Oxford University Press.

Erez, M., and Gati, E. (2004). A dynamic, multi-level model of culture: From the micro-level of the individual to the macro-level of a global culture. *Applied Psychology: An International Review*, 53, 583–598.

Erez, M., and Shokef, E. (2008). The culture of global organizations. In P. Smith, M. Peterson, and D. Thomas (eds), *The Handbook of Cross-Cultural Management Research* (pp. 285–300). Thousand Oaks, CA: Sage Publications, Inc.

Erez, M., and Somech, A. (1996). Group Performance Loss: The rule of the exception. *Academy of Management Journal*, 39, 1513–1537.

Friedman, L. T. (2005). *The World is Flat: A Brief History of the Twenty-First Century.* New York: Farrar, Straus and Giroux

Gelfand, M., Erez, M., and Aycan, Z. (2007). Cross-cultural organizational behavior. *Annual Review of Psychology*, 58, 479–514.

Gelfand, M. J., Nishii, L. H., and Raver, J. L. (2006). On the nature and importance of cultural tightness-looseness. *Journal of Applied Psychology*, 91(6), 1225–1244.

Gibson, C. B., and Zellmer-Bruhn, M. E. (2001). Metaphors and meaning: An intercultural analysis of the concept of teamwork. *Administrative Science Quarterly*, 46(2), 274–306.

Govindarajan, V., and Gupta, A. K. (2001). *The Quest for Global Dominance.* San Francisco, CA: Jossey-Bass.

Hofstede, G. (1991) *Cultures and Organizations: Software of the Mind.* New York: McGraw-Hill.

House, R., Hanges, P. J., Javidan, M., Dorfman, P. W., and Gupta, V. (2004). *Culture, Leadership, and Organizations: The GLOBE Study of 62 Societies.* Thousand Oaks, CA: Sage.

Kostova, T., and Roth, K. (2002). Adoption of organizational practice by subsidiaries of multinational corporations: Institutional and relational effects. *Academy of Management Journal*, 45, 215–233.

Markus, H. R., and Kitayama, S. (1991). Culture and the self: Implications for cognition, emotion, and motivation. *Psychological Review*, 98, 224–253.

Markus, H. R., and Wurf, E. (1987). The dynamic self- concept: A social psychological perspective. *Annual Review of Psychology*, 38, 299–337.

Murphy-Berman, V., Bernan, J., Singh, P., Pachuri, A., and Kumar, P. (1984). Factors affecting allocation to needy and meritorious recipients: A cross-cultural comparison. *Journal of Personality and Social Psychology*, 46, 1267–1272.

Schwartz, S. H. (1992). Universals in the content and structure of values: Theoretical advances and empirical tests in 20 countries. In M. Zanna (ed.), *Advances in Experimental Social Psychology* (Vol. 25, pp. 1–65). Orlando, FL: Academic Press.

Shweder, R., and LeVine, R. (1984). *Culture Theory.* NY: Cambridge University Press.

Smith, L. (1990). Fear and loathing of Japan. *Fortune*, No.26, February, pp. 50–60.

Tajfel, H. (1981). *Human Groups and Social Categories: Studies in Social Psychology*. Cambridge: Cambridge University Press.

Triandis, H. C. (1989). The self and social behavior differing cultural contexts. *Psychological Review,* 96, 506–520.

Triandis, H. C., Bontempo, R., Vilareal, M. J., Masaaki, A., and Lucca, N. (1988). Individualism and collectivism: Cross-cultural perspectives on self-ingroup relationships. *Journal of Personality and Social Psychology,* 54, 328–338.

Weldon, E., and Gargano, G. M. (1988). Cognitive loafing: The effects of accountability and shared responsibility on cognitive effort. *Personality and Social Psychology Bulletin,* 14, 159–171.

Zhou, J., and Martocchio, J. J. (2001). Chinese and American managers' compensation award decisions: A comparative policy-capturing study. *Personnel Psychology,* 54(1), 115–145.

Exercises

1. The Multicultural Team (MCT) Project – Bonus Allocation

You are the global HR Manager in a big multinational company that provides services of programming. The company received a big project from a new global Chinese customer. The estimated time for accomplishing the project was one year.

A MCT from a few subsidiaries was nominated to complete the mission. The virtual MCT consisted of five employees who worked on this project, which was estimated to bring revenues of about $2 000 000. However, the customer needed to have the project completed within nine months due to some changes in the market.

You talked with the team and promised them a bonus if they meet the new deadline. The team members stayed long hours and put a lot of effort into it. As a result of the extra time and effort, the team was able to make it on time.

You have $100 000 to allocate as a bonus to the five group members.

You have the following information about the five employees:

Person A: American nationality. He was the team leader. Put a lot of effort and extra time to accomplish the project. He is very young (26 years old), single, individualist, and promising manager.

Person B: German nationality. Did his best to get the project done within nine months and stayed extra hours at work, despite the fact that he is a single parent with two young children.

Person C: Mexican nationality. She is an excellent team member, very helpful to the other members. She badly needs more money to cover extra medical expenses for her parents.

Person D:	Chinese nationality. He is a very influential person in his community. His social network helped the company to get this project. He spends a great deal of time socializing with employees of the customer Chinese company during the project.
Person E:	Indian nationality. She is a specialist. She had the specialized knowledge necessary to do the work. Her contribution was crucial to the project and accounted for about 30% of the total time saving.

Please distribute $100 000 among the five team members.

Please indicate the percentage allocated to each member, the amount of money allocated to each member, and why. Please specify the reasons for your decision.

Person	*%*	*Amount*	*Why*
A			
B			
C			
D			
E			
Total			

2. Getting to Know the Host Culture

Practice target: Develop awareness of cultural differences and identify the underlying cultural values of observed behaviors.

Instructions:

1. Four volunteers leave the classroom for a few minutes.
2. The remaining students receive the instructions below:

   When your friends return to class, you will act as employees from a foreign country. When you answer their questions, you must follow these rules:

   A. You refer to "We" and not to "I." You do not respond to very personal questions concerning your personal opinion, feelings etc. You look at your classmates, trying to get their agreement to what you say. *(Individualism–Collectivism)*

   B. You answer only when they use your family name, or another gesture of respect (e.g. Mr., Dr.). You also respond with gestures of respect. *(Power distance)*

   C. When a woman is being asked, the man sitting next to her will reply instead. *(Masculinity–Femininity)*

D. Your answer should not be factual or evidence based. Rather, you should respond in vague and ambiguous terms. (For example, "it will be all right"; "people say . . ."; "we'll give it a try"; etc.) *(Uncertainty avoidance)*

E. You avoid conflicts and disagreements. *(Harmony)*

3. Please call back the volunteers and say: "Your multinational organization sent you as expatriates to work on a project which runs in a foreign country. This is your first day on the new site. You want to establish relationships with the local employees. Employees in your host country have different cultural values and rules than the one you have. Your objective is to discover these rules. You can ask your foreign employees any question you like."
4. Let the class play the game for 15 minutes.
5. *Discussion* – At the end of the exercise, you ask your class to interpret the rules in terms of Hofstede's cultural dimensions (1980, 2001). Identify differences between the host country and the expatriates. Ask the class to reflect upon the process of discovering the rules of behaviors and their underlying values. In addition, ask the participants to say how they felt about each other, what frustrated them, whether they were able to relate to each other and whether they believe they could successfully work together.

Video Analysis and Discussion

Please watch the following video:

1. How cultural differences affect business: https://www.youtube.com/watch?v=zQvqDv4vbEg

Now form small groups to discuss the video and answer the following questions:

1. What are the major points of the video?
2. How can you use information from the video in your career?
3. Based on the video, what advice do you have for leaders in organizations?

Be prepared to present the ideas from your small group discussion with the class as a whole.

Discussion Questions

1. What is culture?
2. What are the basics of culture?
3. Why does culture matter?
4. What advice would you have for a person moving to a different country?
5. What advice do you have for managers regarding organizational and societal culture?

29

Strategy and Structure for Effectiveness

JOHN JOSEPH[1] AND METIN SENGUL[2,*]

[1] The Paul Merage School of Business, University of California
[2] Carroll School of Management, Boston College

A fundamental aspect of strategy work concerns how a firm's organization affects how strategic choices are implemented and hence how it should be designed. A long tradition of research has examined this question, focusing initially on the relationship between strategy and overall organizational structure. Starting with Alfred Chandler's (1962) eponymous book *Strategy and Structure*, early research focused on the efficiency of various structures (Child, 1972; Donaldson, 1976; Miles and Snow, 1978; Williamson, 1975). Building on this early research, following studies have examined a variety of antecedents and outcomes associated with alternative ways of organizing (Burton and Obel, 1984; Joseph and Gaba, 2020; Puranam, 2018). These advances in research have come together in the contemporary field of organization design: the study of design choices and how they influence the decisions, behavior, and performance of an organization, its constituent units, and members (Joseph and Sengul, 2022). Design choices reflect the formal and informal structures, systems, and processes of the organization and include a variety of design levers and mechanisms.

Organization design research is united in common observation that managers face two design problems: (i) how to best divide the organization into subunits and (ii) how to best coordinate those subunits in support of the firm's overall mission (Burton, Obel, and Håkonsson, 2020; Joseph and Wilson, 2018; Puranam, 2018). This distinction was established by Nobel laurate Herbert Simon (1947) who emphasized the division of labor and its impact on individual attention and the mechanisms for aggregating individual decisions to organizational levels. Generalizing Simon's observations, subsequent work argued that firms must balance "differentiation" and "integration" in response to the demands of the external

*Both authors contributed equally to this chapter.

environment (Burton, Obel, and Håkonsson, 2020; Lawrence and Lorsch, 1967; see also Mintzberg, 1979). In this context, differentiation refers to the segmentation of the organization into subunits and integration refers to the quality of collaboration among units. Ultimately, an effective organization design brings "about a coherence between the goals or purposes for which the organization exists, the patterns of division of labor, and inter unit coordination and the people who will do the work" (Galbraith, 1973, p. 2).

Importantly, a firm's organization should be closely associated with the strategic choices that executives and managers make (Ocasio and Joseph, 2005). Strategic choice refers to decisions concerning a firm's strategy in support of creating value for customers and/or capturing some of the value created. Given the powerful influence that a firm's organization has on its ability to create and capture value, firms design their internal organization in line with their overall strategy. In turn, the existing design of a firm's organization partially determines its subsequent strategic choices and the outcomes of those choices by rendering some strategic choices more feasible or effective than others and by influencing what managers perceive as possible.

In what follows, we elaborate the link between organization design and strategic choice. First, we highlight the principles that guide the study of organization design from the perspective of strategic management. We then review the key design levers that managers have at their disposal and consider the mechanisms through which the recursive relationship between organization design and strategic choice is articulated. Finally, we consider the dynamics of organization design, and how organizations evolve structurally.

Principles of Organization Design

There are three overarching principles that guide organization design choices. The first principle is that *there is no one ideal design for all organizations.* This idea was established by contingency theorists, who held that "the most effective organizational structure would vary with the situation of the organization" (Donaldson, 2001, p. xi; Lawrence and Lorsch, 1967; Thompson, 1967). The basic premise of contingency theory is that external context and internal organization must fit together if the firm is to perform well. This implies that firms' internal organization is likely to differ markedly across firms that face different environments (think about Apple versus IKEA); across firms that face different instances of similar environments (General Electric versus Siemens); and within firms over time as their external environments change (General Motors in the 1950s versus today).

Contingency theory focuses on the nature of information processing within the firm and the fit between a firm's internal organization and its external environment. Information processing is defined as the gathering, interpreting, and synthesis of information. It is about who talks to whom about what, and who makes which decisions based upon what information (Marshak and Radner, 1972). The key premise of the information processing view is to create a design that matches the organization's demand for information with its information processing capacity

(Galbraith, 1974; Tushman and Nadler, 1978). By implication, a firm facing high information processing requirements (e.g. due to high interdependence across its units or high turbulence and uncertainty in its industry) may need to increase information processing capacity through coordination mechanisms (e.g. cross-functional teams) to match its heightened information processing needs. Although subjected to a variety of critiques (e.g. Child, 1972) and updates (e.g. Burton, Obel, and Håkonsson, 2020), contingency theory "remains, arguably, the most influential theory of organizations to this day" (Thompson, 2003, p. xxi).

A second principle is that *organizational design is multifaceted*. This second principle reflects the idea that there are a variety of lenses through which to understand the problem of organization design, and that while they are broadly related, each lens utilizes a different set of theories to understand the relationship between organization design and strategic choice. In other words, organization design includes a variety of levers, and each design lever influences firm strategy through multiple mechanisms: through its influence on the way managers configure components of the firm, the way managers interpret their environment, the way managers control the activities of those below them, and the way managers can facilitate coordination (Joseph and Sengul, 2022). These mechanisms articulate the unit of analysis (e.g. individuals, teams, and units) and the structure that they are placed in (e.g. centralized and decentralized), as well as describe the causal mechanism relating structure to strategy.

Consider, for example, the provision of incentives to outlet managers in a Polish bank (Obloj and Sengul, 2012). In addition to their fixed wage, managers were compensated for number of "primary" loans sold to first-time customers with the bank and for number of "secondary" loans sold to returning customer (at a piece-rate rate only 10% of that for primary loans). Such a compensation plan not only motivates managers to sell more loans but also sets the decision premises of managers by putting much greater emphasis on primary loans (unlike the preceding compensation plan which did not differentiate between primary and secondary loans). Similarly, all R&D efforts of Google take place in one division, renamed as "Google AI" in 2018 (Forbes, 2018), which both increases the likelihood of collaboration between R&D projects and sets the decision premises of R&D managers and employees by making it clear which type of R&D the company values most.

A third principle is that *strategy and organizational design are interdependent*: strategy affects organization design, which in turn shapes subsequent strategic choices. Strategic choices will not lead to intended results without an organizational design that would allow those choices to be implemented effectively. By implication, a firm's organization design evolves as its strategic objectives and competitive context evolves. Chandler (1962) makes this point forcefully in his aforementioned book and showed that the twentieth century American industrial enterprises – such as DuPont and General Motors – adopted multidivisional structures as they expanded their size and scope. Cisco's change of its organization from a customer-centric one to a technology-centric one in 2001 (Gulati and Puranam, 2009) and Microsoft's shift from multidivisional structure to a functional one in 2013 (Wingfield, 2013) are reflections of the same principle.

At the same time, a firm's current organization design determines, to a large extent, what the firm managers can or cannot do effectively in the short or medium term. Some strategic choices may not be feasible or too costly given a firm's current organization design. For example, the presence of competing teams that challenge one another in different markets allowed the household appliance company Haier to aggressively pursue market share (Campbell, Meyer, Li, and Stack, 2015) but would likely impede the firm's ability to pursue other strategic choices that rely on effective intrafirm collaboration. That is why, as a part of his competitor analysis framework, Michael Porter (1980, pp. 47–74) noted that understanding rivals' future goals involved understanding several features of its organization design: What is the rival's organizational structure? Who is responsible for key decisions? What systems of control and incentives systems are used? And so on. By understanding the organization design of rivals, a firm can better anticipate what the rival can and cannot do effectively in terms of its strategy.

Furthermore, the design may constrain what managers perceive as possible in the first place. That is, the goals and roles of organizational members are largely shaped by their position in the organization, and by extension, the organizational structure. These goals and roles with which individuals identify constitute what Simon (1947) called "decision premises" and therefore serve as the basis for any type of decision-making and may be especially important for decisions about strategy. Decision premises will ultimately shape what problems and opportunities decision-makers attend to and how they are perceived, and therefore shape the initiatives that they pursue. Over time this consistency in attention focus will yield a coherent strategic agenda for the firm, which affects how it designs its organization, which, once in place, affects what the firm can and cannot do effectively.

When combined, these three principles suggest that the relationship between organization design and strategy is a complex one. In order to articulate this relationship, it is necessary to understand the various levers of organization design, how they impact strategy, and the mechanisms through which this occurs.

Levers of Organization Design

Organization design includes both formal and informal levers of the organization. Formal organization refers to features planned and managed by formal authority, such as unit groupings, decision rights, incentives, and reporting relationships; and informal organization refers to emergent patterns of social interactions, such as social networks and organizational culture (Gulati and Puranam, 2009). These are occasionally referred to as "hardware" and "software," respectively, of organization in practice (e.g. Sharer, 2019).

The first key design lever of formal organization is *divisionalization* or *grouping*: division of a firm's activities into distinct units, with each responsible for a specific set of activities. Firms group activities that are highly interdependent or that are exposed to the same environmental contingencies into the same unit because it allows for more effective and efficient coordination among those activities (Thompson, 1967; Tushman and Nadler, 1978; Sengul and Yu, 2022). Thus, these groups create simplified decision-making environments for managers (Joseph and Gaba, 2020). Consequently, coordination across separate units is relatively more difficult, especially in complex organizations, and divisionalization decisions often involve a cost-benefit calculus across design options.

Divisionalization can take several different forms. Most common forms are functional, multidivisional, and matrix structures (see Figure 29.1). In a *functional structure* (also known as functional or unitary form), each unit has a particular functional specialization. A classic example is Apple, which is organized around functions such

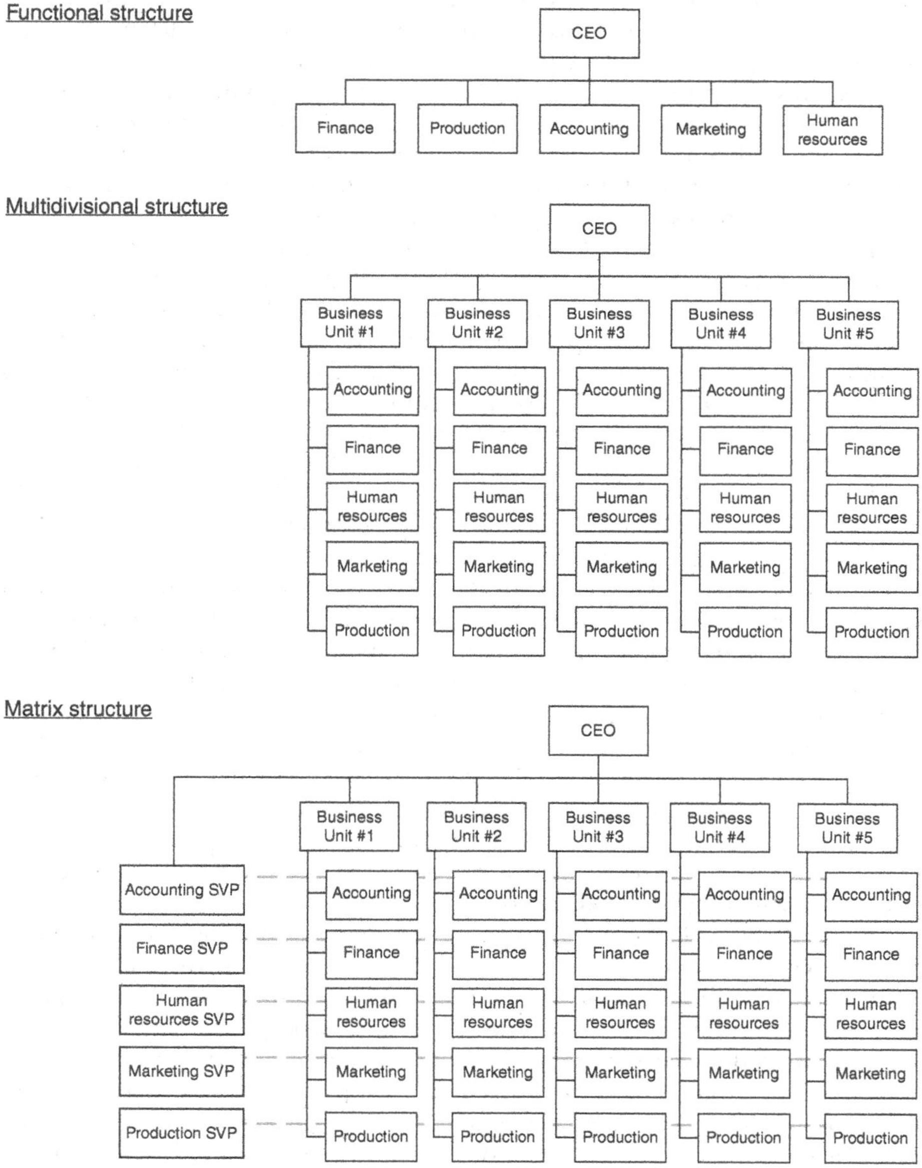

FIGURE 29.1 Common forms of divisionalization: functional, multidivisional, and matrix structures

as engineering, marketing, sales, and retail. Such a structure allows for the development of expertise in each functional domain. Decision-making is usually centralized at the corporate office, which makes communication efficient and avoids the duplication of activities. Also, since a functional structure avoids overly parochial behavior concerning products or technologies, they are more likely to demonstrate a unified corporate culture. Functional structures have drawbacks in that because decision-making is usually centralized at the corporate office, the headquarters can suffer from information overload. Also, functional structures require a high level of interactions between functions to bring products and services to market, which makes them "tightly coupled." For example, R&D, manufacturing, and marketing functions must work together in order to develop and commercialize a new product. However, this makes responding to external shocks (such as entry of a new competitor) more difficult, since to adapt they usually have to change multiple activities across multiple functions at the same time. In addition, no single unit has responsibility for profit and loss; this usually resides with the corporate office or CEO.

In a *multidivisional structure* (also known as multidivisional or M-form), each unit focuses on a particular set of products, customer segments, or geographic regions and is responsible for the entire value chain of functional activities associated with it. For example, Siemens, a large German conglomerate, is divided into three major business units: a digital industries division that sells automation equipment and software to industrial customers, a smart infrastructure division that sells technologies for smart buildings and smart power grids, and a mobility division that makes trains, railway-signaling systems, and other vehicles for commercial transportation. Each business unit controls its own research, manufacturing, marketing, and sales/distribution. The biggest advantage of an M-form structure is that each division is responsible for its own profitability and is rewarded based on the performance of its own products or services. The modular structure of the M-form makes it easier to add businesses, which facilitates diversification and growth. It also ensures that if there is an external shock to one unit, there are fewer perturbations to other units, which makes it easier to adapt to shocks and to divest poorly performing units. The downside of the M-form is that there is a great deal of duplication since each unit has its own R&D, manufacturing, marketing, sales, etc. This redundancy can increase overall costs. Also, the focus on profitability within the units increases parochial behavior, and thus, managers are prone to distorting information in their favor and to making decisions that benefit their own unit, often at the expense of other units. Internal competition between units can prevent them from coordinating and creates challenges in creating a unified corporate culture.

Whether units within an M-form structure are grouped by product markets, customer segments, or geographic regions depends on what types of interactions would be most beneficial. Danaher, like Siemens and other industrial conglomerates, is organized around units grouped by product markets to benefit from close interactions in product development and commercialization among similar products. Suitcase maker Tumi is organized around units grouped by customer segments, such as premium customers or young adults, to cater their different needs. Consulting firms, like law, accounting, and other professional service firms, are often organized around independent geographic offices to offer a full range of services to local clients efficiently.

A third type of divisionalization is the *matrix structure* that includes elements of both the functional and the multidivisional structures. Matrix structures are typically organized by both functional area *and* at the same time, by product, customer, or geographic category. They are characterized by a dual-reporting structure: organizational members typically report to a functional head (such as a chief marketing officer), but also report to a general manager of a business unit. Such a design can increase the amount, quality, and speed of information flow among units that have distinct task environments and reduces the cost of information transfer and coordination (Ford and Randolph, 1992; Galbraith, 1977). But it often suffers from complexity as members must balance the demands of two bosses, which creates ambiguity in the authority structure and may produce conflicts inside the organization because subordinates may receive contradictory directives (Davis and Lawrence, 1977; Simon, 1947). Hence, matrix structures operate effectively only with the presence of leaders who are comfortable sharing power and managing complex communication networks, incentive and control systems that facilitate contributions to overall firm performance, and a culture that welcomes differences of opinion and that allows for constructive debate.

There are other organizational structures beyond these. One worth highlighting is *self-managed organizations*, like Morning Star, Valve, and Zappos. For example, Valve, a gaming company, has completely eliminated the grouping of units and formal hierarchy and radically decentralized authority to each individual (Puranam and Håkonsson, 2015). Communication and interactions among individuals and entities are based largely on shared interest and expertise. An advantage of this structure is that people get to pick which projects they work on, and lateral information flow between peers is abundant. However, at the same time, people may not be efficiently allocated to the right tasks (and those that align with their expertise); the division of labor may not be optimized, and people may not choose task best aligned with company needs. Another problem is that activities of one unit may conflict with other units since there is no corporate function allocating tasks and therefore limited vertical information flow up to a manager (Lee and Edmondson, 2017; Puranam, 2018).

A second important design lever is *hierarchy*. Whereas divisionalization is about the horizontal segmentation of organization structure into units, hierarchy is about the vertical coordination across layers of organization. Most organizations have hierarchical structures where the subdivided units (and their tasks) are grouped at a higher level, and these, in turn, are grouped at an even higher level. Entry-level members report to a superior who report to his/her own superior and so on until the apex of the organization. US equipment manufacturers, for example, have two to seven layers of corporate hierarchy (Zhou, 2013). The number of hierarchical levels, as well as the number of units and overall organizational complexity, typically increases with firm size. Large firms, like Walmart, have tall hierarchies with several layers. Hierarchy is often accompanied by a vertical division of labor between a corporate office or headquarters and operating units, with individuals at higher levels having greater authority and power and less operational responsibility than individuals at lower levels.

Hierarchical structures are not without potential drawbacks (Poppo, 1995). Unless managed well, they may stifle initiative and innovation at lower levels as decision premises tend to flow top down leaving organizational members at lower levels of the hierarchy with little discretion. Collaboration and coordination with other parts of the organization and with the top management also tend to be limited because organizational members are structured to interact with those that are hierarchically adjacent (i.e. their immediate superordinate, peers, and subordinates). Furthermore, as the chain of command has to be followed, organizations with tall hierarchies are typically slow in reacting to environmental and competitive changes because in such structures, vertical information transfer is slow and can cause delays in decision-making.

Despite these potential drawbacks, hierarchies are a defining characteristic of all but the smallest organizations because they are very effective in directing information flow and assigning authority and responsibility. In a hierarchical organization, lines of authority and communication are well defined and known to everyone, making it easier to implement strategic and operational decisions. There is limited scope for confusion regarding who is in charge of a given decision as organizational members, from bottom to the top, have to own their responsibilities and are accountable for their own activities. In flatter hierarchies, limited number of hierarchical layers results in large spans of control (i.e. high number of employees under a manager), which weakens control properties of the organization. That is why flatter organizations imply a higher degree of autonomy to organizational members and are more likely to be adopted in companies that benefit from it (e.g. creative organizations like Valve).

A third design lever is *delegation* of decision-making across levels of the hierarchy. Delegation determines at what level in the organization final decisions concerning firm activities are made. In theory, firms may centralize all decisions at the corporate office or, at the other extreme, delegate all decision-making to units and give them full autonomy. However, firms are seldom, if ever, entirely centralized or decentralized. There is a complex set of decisions to be made in organizations, and they are distributed across levels of the hierarchy. For example, it is common in multidivisional firms to delegate operational decisions to business units, who possess market specific knowledge and information, but to limit their decision rights regarding financial policies and large investments.

Delegation entails the selection of managers or agents to whom the decision(s) will be delegated, their decisions rights concerning the delegated decisions, and provision of incentives. In addition to knowledge and expertise, individuals' underlying preferences, such as willingness to take risks and tolerance for ambiguity, affect who will be assigned to a position because such characteristics affect their behavioral patterns (Hambrick and Mason, 1984). For example, units pursuing growth are more likely to be run by managers with greater willingness to take risk (Gupta and Govindarajan, 1984). Which decisions will be delegated to an organizational member and how much latitude she will have for those decisions is a function of her ability and appropriateness for a given role in the organization.

A related category are *goals and incentives*. Goal setting and incentives play a crucial role by communicating what is expected of individual organizational members and by aligning their compensation (i.e. own benefits) with organizational objectives (Prendergast, 1999). Organizational goals communicate what the organization stands for and thereby affect actions and choices of organizational members by directing attention and effort to relevant activities. Monetary incentives (such as pay for performance) and nonmonetary incentives (such as awards and promotions) direct organizational members to make choices that are aligned with organizational goals as they seek to increase their own private benefits. Consider, for example, compensating customer services agents on their customer satisfaction surveys or compensating the manager of a unit on market share. Planning and control systems provide the necessary support by allowing the top management to keep track of delegated decision-making and its consequences, so that they identify areas of concern and address them as needed. These efforts, and organization design in general, are complicated due to the fact that most organizations simultaneously follow multiple goals. For example, manufacturing firms often aim to decrease costs and increase margins and revenues and dual-purpose companies pursue financial and social goals simultaneously (Battilana et al., 2019; Gaba and Greve, 2019; Obloj and Sengul, 2020).

A fifth category of design levers of formal organization is *lateral linking mechanisms* that cut across lines of authority and connect units directly (Galbraith, 1974; Joseph and Ocasio, 2012; Tushman and Nadler, 1978). Lateral linking mechanisms include dual-reporting relationships that characterize matrix structures and project-based organizations, and communication channels such as committees, liaisons, or cross-functional teams. Such mechanisms allow for interactions and rich information flow between otherwise disconnected or only indirectly connected parts of the organization. They cross levels and functions in the organization and are themselves linked, as information flows through these channels and as individuals participate in a variety of channels. Rules, programs, and standard operating procedures also serve as coordination mechanisms between interdependent parties since they can simply follow preprogrammed behavior without having to communicate directly with one another.

Informal organization encompasses the various patterns of social interactions that constitute a firm's organization culture, including shared beliefs, language, and activities (i.e. organizational code) and social networks. Organizational culture, and informal organization more generally, affects how an organization creates and captures value in two ways (Di Stefano, Gambardella, and Verona, 2012; Rindova and Martins, 2018).

First, culture can reduce monitoring costs. Culture complements formal control systems, which are based on incentives and monitoring, on the basis of the organizational members' attachment to the firm. Individuals will naturally align their goals and behaviors to the firm if they value belonging to the culture of organization. Second, culture fosters cooperation in that it aligns individuals toward a common set of goals. A cooperative culture changes individual preferences and expectations regarding cooperation from others. These mutually reinforcing values and norms may help firms to find solutions to agency problems that would be more difficult to achieve through bargaining and negotiation.

Organizational culture can be a source of sustained competitive advantage when it is specific to the firm (and not just common to the country and/or the industry). Because culture is complex and embedded in the organization's structures and processes, it is difficult for other firms to imitate. However, this complexity also makes it challenging for managers to alter the culture in order to improve firm performance. Informal organization, unlike formal organization, cannot be directly managed. In fact, when the firm must adapt to a changing environment, a culture that was once a source of competitive advantage can be a barrier to change and end up impairing performance.

In all, there are many levers of organization design. Similar firms in the same industry may differ in form, extent of hierarchy, and degree of centralization and delegation. Since many diversified firms have important interactions along multiple dimensions, there often is no clear-cut structure or prescription for specific levers that is appropriate. Adopting a functional structure, for example, may lead to problems adapting to environmental change, but a multidivisional structure may lead to duplication, perhaps with multiple sales forces calling on the same customer. Organizations with tall hierarchies are often bureaucratic with many layers of approvals but self-managed organizations often do not have an efficient division of labor since people can pick which projects they want to work on. Hence, each design choice has both benefits and costs.

Organization Design and Strategy

The impact of organization design on strategic choice is reflected in the firm's capacity to create and capture value (Sengul, 2018). Organization design contributes to the firm's ability to create value through its impact on decisions concerning the development, allocation, and utilization of organizational resources and capabilities (e.g. Burton and Obel, 1984; Galbraith, 1977; Mintzberg, 1979; Roberts, 2006), which can be a source of sustainable competitive advantage. In particular, design choices may shape information processing capacity and the attention focus of decision-makers, which allow firms to recognize and adapt to environmental change and pursue new strategies (Nadler and Tushman, 1997; Ocasio and Joseph, 2005; Joseph and Ocasio, 2012). For example, in the pursuit of a seamless mobility strategy in the early 2000s, Apple's integrated functional structure allowed it to galvanize the entire organization and coordinate in support of developing a few key integrated products like iTunes and the iPhone. In contrast, Motorola's multidivisional structure led the core business units to continue to pursue their own strategic agendas with little focus on seamless mobility and to continue their focus on distinct customer bases, technologies, value propositions, and business models.

Organization design contributes the firms' ability to capture value as well in that it helps firms to contain diversion of value associated with agency problems and organizational inefficiencies (e.g. Holmstrom and Milgrom, 1994; Obloj and Sengul, 2012; Puranam, Singh, and Chaudhuri, 2009). From the perspective of the top management, such "loss prevention" can take many forms, including monitoring the performance of the units, checking on the use of the resources allocated, and, when necessary, redefining what each unit is responsible for so as to continue to use effectively the firm's organizational capabilities (Chandler, 1991, p. 33). Many levers of organization design are primarily aimed at corralling diversion of value and thereby increasing the share of the created value captured by the firm.

Also, organization design has an influence on firms' ability to capture value through its effect on competitive behavior and rivalry. Organizational choices can make a firm more or less competitively aggressive and thereby, acting as organizational commitments, can affect strategic choices of rivals (e.g. Fershtman and Judd, 1987; Vickers, 1985; Vroom, 2006; see Sengul, Gimeno, and Dial, 2012 for a review). Consider, for example, compensating a unit manager solely on an increase in sales and market share (instead of profits). This manager is likely to be very competitively aggressive because she will focus on increasing the top line revenue, without much consideration for how much it will cost to do so. In turn, this is likely to have an impact on rival behavior. For example, rivals may also shift activities to gain market share. As a result, the unit's organizational choices affect its value capture without necessarily affecting its value creation. Conversely, intense rivalry affects organizational design of a firm as well. As firms need to be more efficient in highly competitive environments, firms operating in such environments are more likely to adopt organizational choices, such as leaner structures, to increase their efficiency (e.g. Cunat and Guadalupe, 2009; Guadalupe and Wulf, 2010).

The Four Lenses of Organization Design and Their Impact on Strategy

There are four major ways that organizational design choices affect how strategy is enacted in a firm (and vice versa): through configuration, through control, through channelization, and through coordination. Each approach offers managers a different view of the organization, considers a different set of problems and central questions, and prescribes a different roadmap and set of levers for enabling strategic choice in support of improving value creation and/or capture.

Configuration: A configurational approach to organization design views the organization as a set of features or contingencies such as goals, tasks, structure, people, and processes (Burton and Obel, 2004; Burton, Obel, and Håkonsson, 2020). The relationships between these features can be represented as a series of interconnected design rules, which capture "what should be," as well as feasibility of "what might be" and desirability for the organization (Burton and Obel, 2018).

The configurational approach is concerned with the fit among these contingencies and specifically between the firm's strategy and organization design choices. Internal fit occurs when there is a coherent configuration of design choices within the firm, and external fit occurs when the configuration is appropriate given the environmental conditions facing the firm (Siggelkow, 2001). Internal fit is present when the various levers of the design demonstrate complementarities – that is, they are reinforcing whereby the presence of one benefits from the presence and alignment of another. For example, Apple's emphasis on a differentiation strategy with an emphasis on product leadership was supported by a functional structure that emphasized cooperation and the design of integrated products, highly skilled software and hardware engineers, and routines, which emphasized the development of great products (Ocasio and Joseph, 2018). This high degree of fit allowed Apple to introduce products, such as the iPhone, and create an ecosystem to support it.

In parallel, external fit is present when the internal configuration aligns with the degree of complexity and dynamism in the environment – in particular, with its information processing demands. In other words, external fit is present if the internal configuration of a firm is sufficient to deal with the information processing demands of its external environment. For example, multinational firms that operate in many countries are likely to have a structure that reflects its geographic diversification and delegation of key decisions to managers located in those geographies to enhance responsiveness to local customer demands.

Designs that achieve fit result in better performance, whereas misfits result in lower performance (Burton and Obel, 2018; Donaldson and Joffe, 2014). Achieving fit involves simultaneous choices with respect to multiple formal and informal design levers, including reporting relationships, divisionalization, incentives, and so on. This makes organization design a challenging task because it is necessary to create alignment across a multitude of different and disparate levers of design. It is also an essential task because if the different levers undermine one another, the design is unlikely to yield the intended results. This would be the case, for example, if the firm creates a structure that fosters collaboration within and across teams and compensates them solely on their individual performance.

Thus, according to the configuration approach, managers must identify the source of the misfit when the configuration is "off" and redesign the organization to regain fit. This usually means managers must actively adjust one or more internal contingencies required to bring it in alignment with the external environment. Hence, we have a cycle whereby managers are continuously adjusting strategy and structure as a function of changes in competition, technologies, regulation, or trends (Donaldson, 1999; McKinley and Mone, 2003). An example of a misfit occurred at Toyota when its strategy of growth, lean production systems, and its internal design became misaligned (Camuffo and Wilhelm, 2016). Between 1990 and 2000, Toyota became an established leader in the automotive industry known for its emphasis on quality. To do so, Toyota developed a tight fit among design components including decentralized decision-making, an emphasis on collaboration, focus on eliminating defects in manufacturing, collaboration with suppliers, and training to support all this. However, Toyota's size and geographic dispersion increased dramatically between 2000 and 2007; keeping up with growth proved challenging. Turnover increased in many of its manufacturing facilities and made it hard to maintain a high quality of training and close collaboration. This created misfit between design components and its approach to quality and led to a series of internal design changes to return Toyota to improve its fit.

Control: A control approach to organization design views the organization as a collection of individuals, each with their own preferences, skills, goals, and aspirations. Organizational members with different backgrounds (e.g. engineering versus accounting) may approach a problem with a different set of assumptions (Hambrick and Mason, 1984). For example, a manager with a higher propensity to take risk may pursue a project that others would not, or an "empire building" CEO may grow the size of a firm beyond what is optional for the firm (Jensen, 1986).

The control approach is concerned with how design choices mitigate agency costs associated with delegation of decision-making to organizational members. "Agency costs" arise when self-interested subordinates act opportunistically and take self-serving decisions (Fama, 1980; Jensen and Meckling, 1976). For example, a salesperson may push a low-margin product over a high-margin one to the customers, to the detriment of firm profitability, if his bonus pay is higher for the former or it is easier (i.e. takes less effort) to sell the former at the same amount of pay. It is also possible that organizational members may not be effective in creating value for the organization even when they are not acting opportunistically. This may be due to their low or mismatching skills, insufficient decision support systems, or ineffective organizational coordination mechanisms.

Thus, according to the control approach, managers must utilize design choices to mitigate costs associated with delegated decision-making and to direct disparate organizational members toward achieving organizational goals and aspirations. This entails maintaining control over delegated decision-making and creating alignment between organizational goals and actions and choices of organizational members (Gibbons, 2005). Control mechanisms and systems, which are often under the purview of those higher in the hierarchy, are meant to ensure that individuals, groups, and units act so as to achieve organizations' goals. A key distinction is between output controls (which focuses on results, such as return on investment (ROI) or sales growth) and behavioral controls (which focuses on actions that ultimately lead to results, such as investment decisions) (Ouchi and Maguire, 1975). Output controls are more likely to be used for self-contained units (i.e. not highly interdependent with the rest of the firm) that operate in mature, stable industries because output metrics are more likely to be a valid measure of underlying effort. In contrast, behavioral controls are more likely to be used by interdependent units that operate in a rapidly changing industry that the headquarters is familiar with and pursue interests that are not easily measurable, such as learning. There are additional types of control, such as input controls, which focus on the selection and preparation of employees before they perform tasks, such as hiring and training. Firms also use design levers, such as selective constraints on managerial autonomy, to control organizational members' ability to take specific actions, such as engaging in competitively aggressive behavior (e.g. Corts, 2001; Sengul and Gimeno, 2013).

Control mechanisms and systems are accompanied by incentive systems. The objective of every incentive system is to create a link between employees' compensation and organizational objectives. An effective system leads organizational members to make choices that positively contribute to the objectives of the organization as they seek to optimize their own individual benefits. Hence, not surprisingly, changes in organizational goals are followed by accompanying changes in incentives, or at least should be. For example, the history of Jack Welch's tenure as the CEO of General

Electric shows that the introduction of every major change into corporate practices of the company (e.g. benchmarking, six-sigma efforts, and service aspects of manufacturing) was followed by the inclusion of or greater emphasis on them in compensation packages of organizational members (Bartlett and Wozny, 2005).

Channelization: The channelization approach to organization design views the organization as a pattern of communication and relations, which provide the mental models and decision premises that are used in decision-making. Mental models are representations of reality held in the mind of an individual or collectively within a group or unit. The representation is used to focus attention, categorize external stimuli, make inferences, address problems, find solutions, and guide decisions (Csaszar and Levinthal, 2016; Holland, Holyoak, Nisbett, and Thagard, 1986; Simon, 1947).

The channelization approach is concerned with how design choices constrain individual mental models and decision-making. From this vantage point, the structure creates a simplified view of the external environment, which aids members, who have limited attention, in their decision-making. Because a unit focuses its attention first and foremost on the environment in which it operates, decision-makers in that unit respond directly to the problems and solutions associated with its immediate environment (March and Simon, 1958). Hence, this approach generally – though not entirely – concerns itself with the position of managers within an organizational hierarchy.

Problems may arise when the mental models fail to change with the external environment. In such cases, organization design becomes a source of "cognitive inertia," which occurs when mental models do not change along with the environment and eventually become an impediment to value creation (Csaszar, 2013; Keum and See, 2017; Reitzig and Maciejovsky, 2015). The canonical example of this phenomenon is corporate executives at Polaroid in the 1960s, 1970s, and 1980s. Polaroid's executives had developed a mental model based on the firm's historic success with photographic film – the razor/blade model – which emphasized the low pricing of cameras in order to stimulate sales of film. Since the corporate office was separate from daily operations, they did not immediately recognize the changing external environment and shift away from analog photography occurring in the 1990s. Because digital photography did not require film and so went against their mental model, corporate executives delayed the launch of a standalone digital camera product (Tripsas and Gavetti, 2000). As a result, Polaroid missed the shift to digital imaging from analog.

Thus, according to the channelization approach, managers must design their organization to allocate cognitive resources to both existing businesses and new opportunities. That is, managers should direct attention via design choices in such a way as to promote the identification and pursuit of new opportunities as well (Gavetti, 2005; Joseph and Wilson, 2018; Shepherd, McMullen, and Ocasio, 2017). This proactive cognitive search facilitates the processes that reorganize existing mental models. For example, executives may create separate divisions to pursue new opportunities or may use integration mechanisms, such as communication channels, liaisons, or committee meetings, which allow for the interaction of the corporate office and units (Joseph and Ocasio, 2012; Stan and Puranam, 2017). Such interactions have the potential to disrupt existing mental models and direct corporate and unit attention to changes in the external environment so as to prompt swift strategic changes. Therefore, the balance between useful existing models and the development of new ones is the key to high performance.

For example, in the late 1990s, many newspaper executives viewed the Internet as a threat to their existing business model and, therefore, did not want to invest resources in digital publishing. However, some firms created a new unit focused on the pursuit of digital publishing and were, therefore, more successful with their digital publishing strategy (Gilbert, 2006). The new unit pursued the Internet as an opportunity, rather than viewing it as a threat, and thus allowed the firm to pursue digital publishing, while maintaining their activities in the traditional publishing business. The new unit was also autonomous and hence (i) protected from being stifled by older, larger, and hence more powerful units within the organization, and (ii) could develop its own perception of opportunities and threats in the environment, apart from other units and the corporate office. The corporate office – through its old and new units – could thus maintain a balanced view of the Internet as both an opportunity and a threat.

Coordination: The coordination approach to organization design views the organization as a system of interacting agents (Puranam, 2018; Siggelkow and Levinthal, 2003). These agents can be individuals, groups, or units, and they often face interdependencies and, therefore, must consider each other in making decisions. For example, a marketing unit must consider input from R&D since the value that the firm offers to its customer rely to a large extent on the firm's technologies, and the R&D unit must consider input from marketing since understanding customer demands is essential to direct R&D efforts effectively.

The coordination approach is concerned with the interactions within and between units in support of a better performance, given the presence of interdependencies between individuals, groups, and units. Thus, the main mechanism is the feedback resulting from each organizational member's decisions and actions, where the feedback contains information not only about that person's or unit's choice but also about the choices of others in the organization (Denrell, Fang, and Levinthal, 2004). The relevant decisions may include choices concerning activities, policies, strategies, tasks, resources, products, or technologies. They manifest as connected decisions between downstream and upstream functional departments (e.g. R&D and marketing), business units that collaborate on new initiatives (e.g. a new technology), components of the value chain which are adjacent (e.g. research and engineering), or highly integrated product development activities such as those at Apple (see Sorenson, 2003; Sosa, Eppinger, and Rowles, 2004; Stan and Puranam, 2017). Given the complexity of such interdependencies, it is generally not possible for a manager to be aware of – much less to comprehend – all these interactions.

Thus, according to the coordination approach, managers must design organizations that enable organizational members to adapt collectively to their interdependencies (i.e. to coordinate). Organization designers may use a hierarchical structure to increase the awareness of a centralized decision-maker of the interdependencies between units (Baumann, 2015; Puranam, Raveendran, and Knudsen, 2012). High levels of centralized coordination at the top of the organization is beneficial in that it provides basic checks on quality, timing, and resource requirements as well as serves as a mechanism to improve goal alignment and to ensure coordinative requirements of projects are met. Furthermore, optimal choices for a task or business may have adverse consequences (e.g. cannibalization of the sales, competitive escalations in other businesses) for the company as a whole (Sengul and Gimeno, 2013). Such externalities are difficult to observe and act on within an organizational hierarchy, with the exception of top management who has access to information and has authority and responsibility for the well-being of the entire organization.

Alternatively, designers may increase the direct communication between units to make coordination easier. Extensive communication among actors who are interdependent allows for a reciprocal predictability of their actions. In these cases, the units can make mutual adjustments to help ensure that their coordinated efforts create value and avoid changes that may positively affect one unit, but be detrimental to another (Knudsen and Srikanth, 2014). For example, such communication allows two different units to launch new products sequentially so as not to divert internal resources and attention from each other.

Firms may also make direct coordination less necessary by maintaining a modular structure that delegates decision-making to the units and limiting the interdependencies between units (Baldwin and Clark, 2000; Ethiraj and Levinthal, 2004). For example, at a PC manufacturer, different parts of a computer may be designed by separate, specialized groups working independently of one another. The modules can then be connected and function seamlessly if they conform to a predetermined set of design rules. To coordinate activities, firms also rely on common ground – knowledge that is shared and known to be shared (Bechky, 2003; Srikanth and Puranam, 2011) – enacted through, for example, standardized procedures or interfaces.

Evolution of Organization Design and Strategy

As we noted at the beginning, firms design their organization in line with their overall strategy, and the existing design of a firm's organization partially determines its subsequent strategic choices and the outcomes of those choices. If a firm's organization does not fit to its strategy, it cannot effectively compete. Thus, strategy and structure follow each other and coevolve.

This relationship between organization design and strategy is especially visible in the context of reorganization or restructuring that occurs following a merger or acquisition – a process known as post-merger integration (PMI) – since it makes the subject of design explicitly actionable. PMI is the process, following closing of the deal, of adding, redeploying, or divesting resources, products, or entire businesses in order to achieve the expected combination benefits or "synergies" (Bodner and Capron, 2018). PMI efforts are targeted at creating value given the combination of the acquiring firm and target unit or units. Here, managers must wrestle with questions concerning whether a new unit should remain a standalone unit or integrated into the acquiring organization and whether individuals from the target should be geographically colocated. Other design considerations include whether the processes and incentives of the target should be dropped in favor of the acquirer's and whether this entire process should occur immediately or over a long period of time (Karim, 2006; Karim and Mitchell, 2000).

Many firms reorganize to respond to competitive, technological, or customer changes and to better align the organization with its external environment, echoing the dictum of the contingency theory. In other words, organizational design must change along with an organization's objective and evolution of external forces. Consider, for example, Microsoft's 2018 reorganization that de-emphasized the company's flagship operating software and created two major engineering groups, Cloud and AI Platforms group and Experiences and Devices group, to reflect the changing technological environment.

Firms may also make changes to their organization to improve organizational effectiveness and to reduce costs. For example, restructuring often involves increasing the average span of control, which is the number of direct reports for a manager (on average) within the organization. Even though the optimal span may differ within organizations (whereby a call center may have a very large span of control, but a business development department is likely to have a rather narrow one), experts we interviewed typically recommend a span of about seven to eight. As organizations age, however, they often become very hierarchical with many layers and managers in such "out-of-shape" organizations typically have few direct reports and a too narrow span of control. Having an optimal span of control has a variety of benefits including better decision-making, enhanced accountability, faster communication, better morale, and more favorable cost structure in support of both value creation and capture.

Additionally, firms make changes to the design of their organizations due to the close tie between organizational design and performance measurement. Over time, performance measures lose their effectiveness and capacity to discriminate good from bad performance. For example, variance in the number of defects across different automobiles has declined over time, making this measure of reliability less useful in distinguishing high- and low-quality automobiles. This occurs, in part, because in general people will make improvements on what is measured and, in some cases, improve what is measured without improving the underlying improvement that is sought. As a result, performance measurement and incentive systems have to be renewed (Meyer and Gupta, 1994; Obloj and Sengul, 2012). In fact, there is considerable evidence that organizations change their incentive systems every one to two years. To avoid such a trap, firms may also benefit from temporal changes to their structures or goals (Ethiraj and Levinthal, 2009; O'Reilly and Tushman, 2013; Siggelkow and Rivkin, 2009).

Organizations also may reorganize in response to growth. Growth is an important organizational outcome that may come in many forms, including growth in sales, the firm's scope, number of employees, partnerships, and the organization's administrative structure (Aggarwal and Wu, 2015; Chandler, 1990; Joseph and Wilson, 2018). Simple designs are easier to manage but are insufficient to achieve the strategic objectives of large and complex organizations. Many firms in the 1950s transitioned from a functional structure to a multidivisional structure in order to better handle the coordination required from increasing geographical and product-related diversification. Firms such as General Motors and General Electric created strategic business units, which focused on particular brands (for the former) and different industries (for the latter). It is also true that while very young firms typically rely on self-managed organizations or functional structures, they typically transition to other forms. In older organizations, decision-making is commonly decentralized more than in the early years of a firm's life, and the transition to multidivisional structures creates high-powered incentives to motivate managers to focus on profitability (Greiner, 1998).

Of course, not all organizations have the same path to growth. Consider, for example, diversified multinationals, which are likely to adopt a form of global matrix organization eventually (Stopford and Wells, 1972). To grow from a single-product, single-country company to a more complex organization, they typically start with an international sales division. Their subsequent paths tend to differ depending on their growth trajectory. Firms that initially grow their foreign sales in one or a few products (i.e. have limited product variety) create geographic area divisions, whereas firms that initially grow their foreign product variety create worldwide product divisions. Complex designs come with a bundle of challenges but are inevitable in those organizations.

Case Examples

Organization Design in Practice: Apple Versus Motorola in Mobile Devices

In the late 1990s, both Motorola and Apple pursued similar strategies of seamless integration of voice, data, and Internet access. For Apple, early iteration of the strategy concerned making the firms' suite of products Internet-accessible. Apple referred to it as their Internet strategy as reported in their 10Ks during the period: "Apple's Internet strategy is focused on delivering seamless integration with and access to the Internet throughout the Company's product lines."

In 2001, Apple unveiled its digital hub strategy which put the PC at the center: "The Company believes that personal computing is entering a new era in which the personal computer will function for both professionals and consumers as the digital hub for advanced new digital devices such as digital music players, personal digital assistants, digital still and movie cameras, CD and DVD players, and other electronic devices." Linking the digital hub strategy with the idea of mobility came later and was concomitant with entry into the mobile phone market. Concerned with the possibility that cell phones with the ability to download music would overtake its iPods, Apple entered into a joint venture with Motorola to develop a phone, the ROKR, introduced in 2005. The joint product was not successful, but Apple proceeded on its own to develop what later became the iPhone, introduced in 2007.

At the time, Apple featured a *functional organizational structure* whereby the heads of various functional subunits (engineering, design, and marketing) all reported to Steve Jobs, the company's CEO. In other words, the company was centralized with the CEO making many of the final decisions concerning products. Centralization allowed for the integration of the various activities needed to bring seamless integration and seamless mobility to fruition. The functional units held a common vision of the strategy and were able to coordinate activities effectively in support of that strategy. The units were able to bring each of the different product lines together and link the various hardware and software together in a powerful ecosystem.

During the same period, Motorola, which had a *multidivisional structure*, focused on the infrastructure side of Internet access – providing wireless and broadband access to enable seamless connectivity. By 2000, this had also translated to a "hub" strategy with emphasis on the home as the hub: "The home of the future could have multiple TVs, phones and personal computers doing high-speed Internet access simultaneously – all connected to home hubs from Motorola that provide the interfaces to broadband cable systems."

Motorola further reinforced its home hub strategy with a series of acquisitions strengthening its strategic position. In particular, they acquired General Instrument Corporation, a major US manufacturer of digital cable set-tops and created a Connected Home business unit. The Mobile Devices business unit was a separate existing business unit based in Libertyville, IL, with little integration with the Connected Home unit, which was based in Horsham, PA. Communication and interactions between the units were limited.

Motorola's home hub strategy, which emphasized the infrastructure underlying integration, gave way to their seamless mobility strategy in 2004, with the intention of emphasizing the customer experience side of integrated products (i.e. between the home, the car, and the phone). However, Motorola decentralized decision-making to the individual business units with only limited involvement of the corporate office and the CEO, and as a result, the firm had two competing strategies and business models in effect. The Connected Home business unit sold set-top boxes (DVRs) to cable companies such as Time Warner. The unit's value proposition was building technology to order and to ensure conditional access to content (e.g. limiting HBO access to subscribers only). The Mobile Devices business unit sold cellular phones to the telecom operators. The unit's value proposition was to enable the operators, who did not make much money on the phones, to increase their revenue through services. The Mobile Device managers were, therefore, concerned that the carriers would object to mobile phones that connected through the home's set-top boxes and modems and not via the operator's network.

Because the two units had different views on what seamless mobility meant and did not believe it would necessarily increase performance in their own unit, they did not have much incentive to pursue it. Compounding the problem was the different cultures that existed in each of the business units (in part because Connected Home was an acquisition and never fully integrated into the firm). As a result, Motorola never realized the seamless mobility strategy.

The divergent tales of Apple and Motorola with respect to their seamless mobility strategies illustrate the importance of aligning strategy and organization design to shape organizational behavior. Motorola's decentralized decision-making and multidivisional structure with divisions that held different interpretations of seamless mobility and views of the technology did not work together and could not deliver on the strategy. However, Apple's centralized hierarchical authority coupled with its functional structure allowed it to pursue the kind of integration between products and services, hardware, and software that was needed to truly create seamless mobility. More generally, the strategy and structure must fit together. A strategy that involves interdependent units and requires high levels of interactions between units, as it was the case for seamless mobility, must employ an organization design that can achieve high levels of coordination. The organization must integrate through communication between units and a shared understanding (common mental model) of the goal and what it takes to reach the goal.

Conclusion

In this chapter, we offered three overarching principles of organization design: (i) there is no one ideal organizational design; (ii) organizational design is multifaceted; and (iii) strategy and organization design are interdependent. These three principles, in conjunction with the specific levers and lenses of organization design, help us understand the relationship between design and strategic choice and when a firm's organization design will enable it to create and capture value. Ultimately, value creation and capture depend on the organization design to: (i) create internal and external fit and identify and fix misfits; (ii) mitigate costs associated with delegated decision-making and direct organizational members toward achieving collective organizational goals; (iii) create simplified mental models to aid decision-making as well as the adaptation of those models as the environment changes; and (iv) manage interdependencies to enable coordination. In all, organization design is important for managers to understand because it is only through the right design choices can they properly influence the decisions, behavior, and performance of organization, its constituent units, and members so as to ensure ongoing success.

References

Aggarwal, V. A., and Wu, B. (2015). Organizational constraints to adaptation: Intrafirm asymmetry in the locus of coordination. *Organization Science*, 26(1), 218–238.

Baldwin, C. Y., and Clark, K. B. (2000). *Design Rules* (Vol. I). Cambridge, MA: MIT Press.

Bartlett, C. A., and Wozny, M. (2005). *GE's Two-Decade Transformation: Jack Welch's Leadership.* Harvard Business School Case, 9-399-150.

Battilana, J., Pache, A.-C., Sengul, M., and Kimsey, M. (2019). The dual-purpose playbook. *Harvard Business Review,* 97(2), 124–133.

Baumann, O. (2015). Models of complex adaptive systems in strategy and organization research. *Mind & Society,* 14(2), 169–183.

Bechky, B. A. (2003). Sharing meaning across occupational communities: The transformation of understanding on a production floor. *Organization Science,* 14(3), 312–330.

Bodner, J., and Capron, L. (2018). Post-merger integration. *Journal of Organization Design,* 7(1), 1–20.

Burton, R. M., and Obel, B. (1984). *Designing Efficient Organizations: Modelling and Experimentation.* Amsterdam: North-Holland.

Burton, R. M., and Obel, B. (2004). *Strategic Organizational Diagnosis and Design: The Dynamics of Fit* (3rd edition). New York, NY: Springer.

Burton, R. M., and Obel, B. (2018). The science of organizational design: Fit between structure and coordination. *Journal of Organization Design,* 7(1), 1–13.

Burton, R. M., Obel, B., and Håkonsson, D. D. (2020). *Organizational Design.* Cambridge, England: Cambridge University Press.

Campbell, D., Meyer, M., Li, S. X., and Stack, K. (2015). *Haier: Zero Distance to Customers (A).* Harvard Business School Case, 9-115-006.

Camuffo, A., and Wilhelm, M. (2016). Complementarities and organizational (Mis) fit: A retrospective analysis of the Toyota recall crisis. *Journal of Organization Design,* 5(1), 1–13.

Chandler, A. D. (1962). *Strategy and Structure: Chapters in the History of American Industrial Enterprises.* Cambridge, MA: MIT Press.

Chandler, A. D. (1990). *Strategy and Structure: Chapters in the History of the Industrial Enterprise.* Cambridge, MA: MIT press.

Chandler, A. D. Jr. (1991). The functions of the HQ unit in the multibusiness firm. *Strategic Management Journal,* 12(S2), 31–50.

Child, J. (1972). Organizational structure, environment and performance: The role of strategic choice. *Sociology,* 6(1), 1–22.

Corts, K. S. (2001). The strategic effects of vertical market structure: Common agency and divisionalization in the US motion picture industry. *Journal of Economics & Management Strategy,* 10(4), 509–528.

Csaszar, F. A. (2013). An efficient frontier in organization design: Organizational structure as a determinant of exploration and exploitation. *Organization Science,* 24(4), 1083–1101.

Csaszar, F. A., and Levinthal, D. A. (2016). Mental representation and the discovery of new strategies. *Strategic Management Journal,* 37(10), 2031–2049.

Cunat, V., and Guadalupe, M. (2009). Globalization and the provision of incentives inside the firm: The effect of foreign competition. *Journal of Labor Economics,* 27, 179–212.

Davis, S., and Lawrence, P. R. (1977). *Matrix.* Reading, MA: Addison Wesley.

Denrell, J., Fang, C., and Levinthal, D. A. (2004). From T-mazes to labyrinths: Learning from model-based feedback. *Management Science,* 50(10), 1366–1378.

Di Stefano, G., Gambardella, A., and Verona, G. (2012). Technology push and demand pull perspectives in innovation studies: Current findings and future research directions. *Research Policy*, 41(8), 1283–1295.

Donaldson, L. (1976). Woodward, technology, organizational structure and performance – A critique of the universal generalization. *Journal of Management Studies*, 13(3), 255–273.

Donaldson, L. (1999). *Performance-Driven Organizational Change.* Thousand Oaks, CA: Sage.

Donaldson, L. (2001). *The Contingency Theory of Organizations.* Thousand Oaks, CA: Sage.

Donaldson, L., and Joffe, G. (2014). Fit-the key to organizational design. *Journal of Organization Design*, 3(3), 38–45.

Ethiraj, S. K., and Levinthal, D. (2004). Modularity and innovation in complex systems. *Management Science*, 50(2), 159–173.

Ethiraj, S. K., and Levinthal, D. (2009). Hoping for A to Z while rewarding only A: Complex organizations and multiple goals. *Organization Science*, 20(1), 4–21.

Fama, E. F. (1980). Agency problems and the theory of the firm. *Journal of Political Economy*, 88(2), 288–307.

Fershtman, C., and Judd, K. L. (1987). Equilibrium incentives in oligopoly. *American Economic Review*, 77, 927–940.

Ford, R. C., and Randolph, W. A. (1992). Cross-functional structures: A review and integration of matrix organization and project management. *Journal of Management*, 18(2), 267–294.

Gaba, V., and Greve, H. R. (2019). Safe or profitable? The pursuit of conflicting goals. *Organization Science*, 30(4), 647–667.

Galbraith, J. R. (1973). *Designing Complex Organizations.* Boston, MA: Addison-Wesley.

Galbraith, J. R. (1974). Organization design: An information processing view. *Interfaces*, 4(3), 28–36.

Galbraith, J. R. (1977). *Organization Design.* Boston, MA: Addison Wesley.

Gavetti, G. (2005). Cognition and hierarchy: Rethinking the microfoundations of capabilities' development. *Organization Science*, 16(6), 599–617.

Gibbons, R. (2005). Incentives between firms (and within). *Management Science*, 51(1), 2–17.

Gilbert, C. G. (2006). Change in the presence of residual fit: Can competing frames coexist? *Organization Science*, 17(1), 150–167.

Greiner, L. E. (1998). Evolution and revolution as organizations grow. *Harvard Business Review*, 76(3), 55–64.

Guadalupe, M., and Wulf, J. (2010). The flattening firm and product market competition: The effect of trade liberalization on corporate hierarchies. *American Economic Journal: Applied Economics*, 2(4), 105–127.

Gulati, R., and Puranam, P. (2009). Renewal through reorganization: The value of inconsistencies between formal and informal organization. *Organization Science*, 20(2), 422–440.

Gupta, A. K., and Govindarajan, V. (1984). Business unit strategy, managerial characteristics, and business unit effectiveness at strategy implementation. *Academy of Management Journal*, 27(1), 25–41.

Hambrick, D. C., and Mason, P. A. (1984). Upper echelons: The organization as a reflection of its top managers. *Academy of Management Review*, 9(2), 193–206.
Holland, J. H., Holyoak, K. J., Nisbett, R. E., and Thagard, P. R. (1986). *Induction: Processes of Inference, Learning, and Discovery*. Cambridge, MA: MIT press.
Holmstrom, B., and Milgrom, P. (1994). The firm as an incentive system. *American Economic Review*, 972–991.
Jensen, M. C. (1986). Agency costs of free cash flow, corporate finance, and takeovers. *The American Economic Review*, 76(2), 323–329.
Jensen, M. C., and Meckling, W. H. (1976). Theory of the firm: Managerial behavior, agency costs and ownership structure. *Journal of Financial Economics*, 3(4), 305–360.
Joseph, J., and Gaba, V. (2020). Organizational structure, information processing, and decision-making: A retrospective and road map for research. *Academy of Management Annals*, 14(1), 267–302.
Joseph, J., and Ocasio, W. (2012). Architecture, attention, and adaptation in the multibusiness firm: General Electric from 1951 to 2001. *Strategic Management Journal*, 33(6), 633–660.
Joseph, J., and Sengul, M. (2022). The foundations and future of organization design research.
Joseph, J., and Wilson, A. J. (2018). The growth of the firm: An attention-based view. *Strategic Management Journal*, 39(6), 1779–1800.
Karim, S. (2006). Modularity in organizational structure: The reconfiguration of internally developed and acquired business units. *Strategic Management Journal*, 27(9), 799–823.
Karim, S., and Mitchell, W. (2000). Path-dependent and path-breaking change: Reconfiguring business resources following acquisitions in the US medical sector, 1978–1995. *Strategic Management Journal*, 21(10–11), 1061–1081.
Keum, D. D., and See, K. E. (2017). The influence of hierarchy on idea generation and selection in the innovation process. *Organization Science*, 28(4), 653–669.
Knudsen, T., and Srikanth, K. (2014). Coordinated exploration: Organizing joint search by multiple specialists to overcome mutual confusion and joint myopia. *Administrative Science Quarterly*, 59(3), 409–441.
Lawrence, P. R., and Lorsch, J. W. (1967). *Organization and the Environment*. Boston, MA: Harvard Business School Press.
Lee, M. Y., and Edmondson, A. C. (2017). Self-managing organizations: Exploring the limits of less-hierarchical organizing. *Research in Organizational Behavior*, 37, 35–58.
March, J. G., and Simon, H. A. (1958). *Organizations*. New York: Wiley.
Marshak, J., and Radner, R. (1972). *Economic Theory of Teams*. New Haven, CT: Yale University Press.
McKinley, W., and Mone, M. A. (2003). Micro and macro perspectives in organization theory: A tale of incommensurability. In C. Knudsen and H. Tsoukas (eds), *The Oxford Handbook of Organization Theory: Meta-Theoretical Perspectives* (pp. 345–372). Oxford, England: Oxford University Press.
Meyer, M. W., and Gupta, V. (1994). The performance paradox. *Research in Organizational Behavior*, 16, 309–309.

Miles, R. E., and Snow, C. C. (1978). *Organizational Strategy, Structure, and Process.* New York: McGraw-Hill.

Mintzberg, H. (1979). *The Structure of Organizations: A Synthesis of the Research.* Hoboken, NJ: Prentice-Hall.

O'Reilly, C. A., III, and Tushman, M. L. (2013). Organizational ambidexterity: Past, present, and future. *Academy of Management Perspectives*, 27(4), 324–338.

Obloj, T., and Sengul, M. (2012). Incentive life-cycles: Learning and the division of value in firms. *Administrative Science Quarterly*, 57(2), 305–347.

Obloj, T., and Sengul, M. (2020). What do multiple objectives really mean for performance? Empirical evidence from the French manufacturing sector. *Strategic Management Journal*, 41(13), 2518–2547.

Ocasio, W., and Joseph, J. (2005). An attention-based theory of strategy formulation: Linking micro-and macroperspectives in strategy processes. *Advances in Strategic Management*, 22, 39–61.

Ocasio, W., and Joseph, J. (2018). The attention-based view of great strategies. *Strategy Science*, 3(1), 289–294.

Ouchi, W. G., and Maguire, M. A. (1975). Organizational control: Two functions. *Administrative Science Quarterly*, 20, 559–569.

Poppo, L. (1995). Influence activities and strategic coordination: Two distinctions of internal and external markets. *Management Science*, 41(12), 1845–1859.

Porter, M. E. (1980). *Competitive Strategy: Techniques for Analyzing Industries and Companies.* New York: Free Press.

Prendergast, C. (1999). The provision of incentives in firms. *Journal of Economic Literature*, 37(1), 7–63.

Puranam, P. (2018). *The Microstructure of Organizations.* Oxford, England: Oxford University Press.

Puranam, P., and Håkonsson, D. D. (2015). Valve's way. *Journal of Organization Design*, 4(2), 2–4.

Puranam, P., Raveendran, M., and Knudsen, T. (2012). Organization design: The epistemic interdependence perspective. *Academy of Management Review*, 37(3), 419–440.

Puranam, P., Singh, H., and Chaudhuri, S. (2009). Integrating acquired capabilities: When structural integration is (un)necessary. *Organization Science*, 20(2), 313–328.

Reitzig, M., and Maciejovsky, B. (2015). Corporate hierarchy and vertical information flow inside the firm – A behavioral view. *Strategic Management Journal*, 36(13), 1979–1999.

Rindova, V. P., and Martins, L. L. (2018). From values to value: Value rationality and the creation of great strategies. *Strategy Science*, 3(1), 323–334.

Roberts, J. (2006). *The Modern Firm.* Oxford, UK: Oxford University Press.

Sengul, M. (2018). Organization design and competitive strategy: An application to the case of divisionalization. *Advances in Strategic Management*, 40, 207–228.

Sengul, M., and Gimeno, J. (2013). Constrained delegation: Limiting subsidiaries' decision rights and resources in firms that compete across multiple industries. *Administrative Science Quarterly*, 58(3), 420–471.

Sengul, M., Gimeno, J., and Dial, J. (2012). Strategic delegation: A review, theoretical integration, and research agenda. *Journal of Management*, 38(1), 375–414.

Sengul, M., and Yu, T. (2022). A socio-cognitive explanation of organizational groupings in multidivisional firms. *Working paper*.

Sharer, K. (2019). Headquarters as hardware and software. *Journal of Organization Design*, 8(1), 1–3.

Shepherd, D. A., McMullen, J. S., and Ocasio, W. (2017). Is that an opportunity? An attention model of top managers' opportunity beliefs for strategic action. *Strategic Management Journal*, 38(3), 626–644.

Siggelkow, N. (2001). Change in the presence of fit: The rise, the fall, and the renaissance of Liz Claiborne. *Academy of Management Journal*, 44(4), 838–857.

Siggelkow, N., and Levinthal, D. A. (2003). Temporarily divide to conquer: Centralized, decentralized, and reintegrated organizational approaches to exploration and adaptation. *Organization Science*, 14(6), 650–669.

Siggelkow, N., and Rivkin, J. W. (2009). Hiding the evidence of valid theories: How coupled search processes obscure performance differences among organizations. *Administrative Science Quarterly*, 54(4), 602–634.

Simon, H. A. (1947). *Administrative Behavior*. New York: Macmillan.

Sorenson, O. (2003). Interdependence and adaptability: Organizational learning and the long–term effect of integration. *Management Science*, 49(4), 446–463.

Sosa, M. E., Eppinger, S. D., and Rowles, C. M. (2004). The misalignment of product architecture and organizational structure in complex product development. *Management Science*, 50(12), 1674–1689.

Srikanth, K., and Puranam, P. (2011). Integrating distributed work: Comparing task design, communication, and tacit coordination mechanisms. *Strategic Management Journal*, 32(8), 849–875.

Stan, M., and Puranam, P. (2017). Organizational adaptation to interdependence shifts: The role of integrator structures. *Strategic Management Journal*, 38(5), 1041–1061.

Stopford, J. M., and Wells, L. T. Jr. (1972). *Managing the Multinational Enterprise: Organization of the Firm and Ownership of the Subsidiary*. New York: Basic Books.

Thompson, G. (2003). *Between Hierarchies and Markets: The Logic and Limits of Network Forms of Organization*. Oxford, England: Oxford University Press.

Thompson, J. D. (1967). *Organizations in Action*. New York: McGraw–Hill.

Tripsas, M., and Gavetti, G. (2000). Capabilities, cognition, and inertia: Evidence from digital imaging. *Strategic Management Journal*, 21(10–11), 1147–1161.

Tushman, M. L., and Nadler, D. A. (1978). Information processing as an integrating concept in organizational design. *Academy of Management Review*, 3(3), 613–624.

Vickers, J. (1985). Delegation and the theory of the firm. *Economic Journal*, 95, 138–147.

Vroom, G. (2006). Organizational design and the intensity of rivalry. *Management Science*, 52(11), 1689–1702.

Williamson, O. E. (1975). *Markets and Hierarchies: Analysis and Antitrust Implications*. New York: The Free Press.

Wingfield, N. (2013). Microsoft overhauls, the Apple way. *New York Times*, July 11. https://www.nytimes.com/2013/07/12/technology/microsoft-revamps-structure-and-management.html

Zhou, Y. M. (2013). Designing for complexity: Using divisions and hierarchy to manage complex tasks. *Organization Science*, 24(2), 339–355.

Exercise

You are the new CEO of Apple. Your first project is to create an electric Apple Car, the iA100. This will require bringing together Apple's key functional areas (design, hardware engineering, software, services, machine learning/AI, marketing, sales, and retail). What are features of Apple's organization design that you need to ensure are in place to develop and successfully market the new car?

Video Analysis and Discussion

Please watch the following video(s):

- **Configuration:** Designing organizations: Fits and misfits, by professors Richard Burton and Borge Obel: https://www.youtube.com/watch?v=slHiknWtt5U
- **Control:** Designing incentive systems: How behavioral economics can improve incentives, by Professor David Asch: https://www.youtube.com/watch?v=LQ5zfJXXLD4&
- **Channelization:** Designing cultures and organizational architectures, by professor William Ocasio: https://vimeo.com/140343600
- **Coordination:** Designing remote collaboration, by professor Phanish Puranam: https://www.youtube.com/watch?v=qNt_wPSLk-g

Now form small groups to discuss the video(s) and answer the following questions:

1. What are the major points of the video?
2. How can you use information from the video in your career?
3. Based on the video, what advice do you have for leaders in organizations?

Be prepared to present the ideas from your small group discussion with the class as a whole.

Discussion Questions

- What was Apple's organizational structure? Please describe.
- Along what dimensions did Motorola's organizational structure differ from Apple's?
- Identify three features of Motorola's organizational design that explains its failure in creating seamless mobility. Identify three features of Apple's organizational design that allowed it to succeed in creating seamless mobility.
- How might you have advised Motorola to improve its organization design to support the seamless mobility strategy?

Index